The Family Life Cycle:
A Framework for Family
Therapy

Edited by

ELIZABETH A. CARTER, A.C.S.W.
Director, Family Institute of Westchester

MONICA MC GOLDRICK, A.C.S.W.
Director of Family Training,
C.M.D.N.J.–Rutgers Medical School and
Community Mental Health Center
Faculty, Family Institute of Westchester

GARDNER PRESS, INC., NEW YORK

GARDNER PRESS, INC.
19 Union Square West
New York 10003

Library of Congress Cataloging in Publication Data
Main entry under title:

The Family life cycle.

   1. Family—United States—Addresses, essays, lectures.
2. Family psychotherapy—United States—Addresses,
essays, lectures.   I. Carter, Elizabeth A. II. Mc Goldrick,
Monica   III. Orfanidis, Monica Mc Goldrick
    IV. Family Institute of Westchester.
    V. Title: Life Cycle.
HQ536.F375   301.42'0973   79-17131
ISBN 0-89876-028-3

Printed in the United States of America

The editors dedicate this book
to Sam, Bennett, and Timmy Carter,
to Sophocles Orfanidis,
and to all the other members of our families.

Contents

CONTRIBUTORS

NORMAN J. ACKERMAN, M.D.,
Assistant Clinical Professor of Psychiatry,
Albert Einstein College of Medicine;

EDWARD W. BEAL, M.D.,
Clinical Assistant Professor,
Georgetown University School of Medicine,
Washington, D.C.;
Private Practice of Psychiatry,
Bethesda, Maryland

JACK O. BRADT, M.D.,
Director, Groome Center,
Washington, D.C.;
Clinical Assistant Professor,
Department of Psychiatry,
Georgetown University Hospital,
Washington, D.C.

ELIZABETH A. CARTER, A.C.S.W.,
Director, Family Institute of Westchester,
White Plains, New York

FERNANDO COLÓN, PH.D.,
Family Therapist and Consultant, Catholic Social Services,
Ann Arbor, Michigan

ELAINE DANNEFER, A.C.S.W.,
Family Therapist and Consultant in Private Practice,
Rochester, New York

CELIA J. FALICOV, PH.D.,
Director, Family Systems Program,
Institute for Juvenile Research,
Illinois Department of Mental Health, Chicago;
Faculty, San Diego Family Institute

EDWIN H. FRIEDMAN, M.A.,
Consultant, Family Therapy,
Saint Elizabeth's Hospital, Washington, D.C.

NORA REINER GLUCK, A.C.S.W.,
Faculty, Family Institute of Westchester,
White Plains, New York;
Assistant Clinical Professor of Social Work in Psychiatry,
Yale University School of Medicine;
Family Therapist,
Dana Psychiatric Clinic,
Yale–New Haven Hospital

FREDDA HERZ, R.N., PH.D.,
Assistant Professor and Coordinator,
Graduate Program in Primary Care Nursing:
Child and Adolescent Mental Health,
Herbert H. Lehman College,
New York;
Faculty, Family Institute of Westchester,
White Plains, New York

LYNN HOFFMAN, A.C.S.W.,
Senior Faculty,
Ackerman Institute for Family Therapy,
New York

BETTY M. KARRER, M.A.,
Director, Bilingual Early School Home Intervention Program,
Institute for Juvenile Research,
Illinois Department of Mental Health,
Chicago

PAULINA MC CULLOUGH, A.C.S.W.,
Assistant Clinical Professor of Psychiatry (Social Work),
University of Pittsburgh

MONICA MC GOLDRICK, A.C.S.W.,
Adjunct Assistant Professor, Psychiatry Department
Director of Family Training,
College of Medicine and Dentistry of New Jersey–Rutgers Medical School
and Community Mental Health Center;
Faculty, Family Institute of Westchester,
White Plains, New York

PATRICIA H. MEYER, A.C.S.W.,
Clinical Instructor,
Department of Psychiatry,
Georgetown Family Center,
Georgetown Medical School
Washington, D.C.

KATHRYN MILEA,
Free lance journalist specializing in marriage and the family;
Public Information Specialist,
College of Medicine and Dentistry of New Jersey–Rutgers Medical School

ROBERT M. SIMON, M.D.,
Director of Clinical Training,
Ackerman Institute for Family Therapy,
New York

KENNETH G. TERKELSEN, M.D.,
Associate Director,
Family Institute of Westchester,
White Plains, New York;
Assistant Clinical Professor of Psychiatry,
College of Physicians and Surgeons,
Columbia University

FROMA WALSH, PH.D.,
Research Staff, Center for Family Studies,
The Family Institute of Chicago;
Assistant Professor,
Department of Psychiatry and Behavioral Sciences,
Northwestern University Medical School

Acknowledgments

Our primary acknowledgment goes to the "family" of family therapists. We ourselves are "third generation" family therapists, and as we worked on this book we became more deeply aware of what we owe to the "grandparents" who founded our family and established our traditions: Murray Bowen and Jay Haley particularly; and to the "parents" who taught, supervised, and sponsored us as we joined the family: Phil Guerin, Tom Fogarty, and Don Bloch, among others. Many of our "siblings" produced the chapters that make up the book, and one of them, Eloise Julius, is responsible for first drawing the attention of our faculty at the Family Institute of Westchester to this important, but often neglected, study of the family life cycle. Finally, we owe a special debt to our "children," the family therapy trainees who carry on our work by using and improving on our ideas. It was a "fourth generation" family therapist, Lannie McRill, of Mt. Clemens, Michigan, who urged us to write this book after participating in a seminar on the family life cycle led by one of us.

We owe an immense debt of gratitude to Myra Wayton of Rutgers Mental Health Center, without whose moral support and endless efforts on the manuscript this book would never have appeared: and to Lillian Fine, Joan Craig, Helen McGoldrick, and M. Duncan Stanton, who went out of their way to help our work along when we needed them. Our special thanks go to our publisher, Gardner Spungin, who never hassled us about deadline delays.

We are very grateful to Dr. Paul Glick at the Bureau of the Census for his work in this area, which has been our bible, and for his availability and patience during many phone calls to check statistical data and trends of change in the family life cycle.

Acknowledgments

Foreword

To my knowledge, Betty Carter, Monica Mc Goldrick, and their collaborators, are the first to present a life cycle format for thinking about the family in a carefully structured way. They have done rather well at defining a life cycle format and there are some unique advantages in this way of thinking. They are aware of the difficulty in going beyond the nuclear family toward defining a multigenerational life cycle for the family.

It is not easy for people to shift from thinking about the individual to thinking about the family as an emotional unit. What emerges is thinking about the family as a collection of individuals. The difference in this is subtle and powerful. The more the family therapist can *see* the family as a unit, and *think* of the family as a unit, the more helpful the therapy. The family life cycle format may be a practical and effective way to help people move toward seeing the family as a unit rather than as a collection of individuals.

The editors wonder if some notion of the life cycle is not implicit in the thinking of most family theorists and family therapists. I agree. I think that life cycle thinking is second nature in all people. The human has always been aware of the sequential stages of life from birth to death. This has been recorded in history, religion, cultural rituals, novels, drama, and art, since earliest time. There were special emphases on life cycle thinking during the first half of the twentieth century with the proliferation of psychological and sociological literature. Psychoanalysis specified the stages of psychosexual development that began with birth and ended with the genital stage. A partial arrest at any stage was thought to cast a shadow into the future. The population has been well informed about the *norms* of physical and emotional development. Gesell became an authority on the normal stages of child development. Spock became a popular interpreter of child behavior for the public. As the percentage of older people increases, it may soon be time for a popular book on understanding the life and behavior of older people.

All of these developments are based on the model of the life cycle of the individual. It is a big step to move from life cycle thinking about the individual to life cycle thinking about the family. I believe the dilemma is similar to that of some of the early family researchers and therapists as they attempted to shift from individual to family systems theory. I am personally familiar with the principles involved in that, and I shall use personal experiences to illustrate the conceptual problem.

Individual theory focuses on intrapsychic forces within the person with only indirect reference to relationships. Individual therapy is directed at the hypothesized pathology in the patient. I think the individual orientation is much deeper than a theory learned in professional school. Most societies have an indoctrination that views symptoms as arising from some abnormality in the person with the symptoms. Family research in the 1950s, however, brought relationships into focus for the first time; and resulted in observations never previously recorded in the literature. These relationship patterns had always been there, and I wondered how it was possible to see this new world of facts, previously hidden from view. I, and most of the other early researchers, had *been thinking toward the family* for years before the formal research started.

I think the new view depended on several factors, most important of which was the gradual change in the thinking of the researchers. The research settings provided a level of objectivity that would not otherwise have been possible. Most of the research was on families with schizophrenia in which the relationship patterns were most intense. The observations probably would not have been possible in people with less severe problems. After it was possible to see the relationship patterns in families with schizophrenia, it was easy to see the exact patterns in families with less severe problems, and even those in *normal* families. From the new theoretical orientation that regarded the family as an emotional unit and the symptom in the patient as a product of the total family problem, it was an easy and logical step to devise a therapeutic approach to the family unit that became family therapy.

The family field erupted in 1957. It began at a national meeting for family researchers when the notion of family psychotherapy was casually mentioned. Some investigators had been working privately toward family therapy for several years. It was as though family therapy suddenly became legitimate. The notion of *therapy* attracted new therapists in such numbers that they dominated the family field. However, these new therapists had not had the advantage of several years of *thinking toward the family,* nor the opportunity to *see* the family as a unit. The focus on research and theory was lost in the rush to develop family therapy. Therapists used their previous training in individual theory to develop numerous therapeutic methods and dozens of different therapy techniques. Most used methods from group therapy, which is based on individual theory. The number of therapists multiplied and they began training numerous new people. Family therapy became a conglomerate of approaches that treated the family as a collection of individuals. I have referred to the period as an *unstructured state of chaos;* I expected that experience would help the therapists *see* the family as a unit, and that this would lead to research and new theory. This did not occur. The *doing* orientation of the therapist is different from the *theoretical* orientation of the researcher or theorist. After the family therapists spun out into their own orbit in 1957, the number of therapists multiplied many times, and a high percentage are still in that orbit without a solid theoretical base from which to operate.

However, an interesting development began in the late 1960s. There has always been a small group of researchers and theorists who have worked to develop new concepts. Gradually the more experienced therapists began to incorporate bits and pieces of these concepts into their therapy. Very slowly the field began moving toward a family systems orientation. In 1980, after twenty-three years, there is a bit more order to the field, but the vast majority of clinicians still view family therapy as a technique grafted onto individual theory.

For those theoretically aware, the gulf between individual and family systems theory is deep and wide. How does one go about communicating this to family therapists who still think in terms of the individual and who have no way of knowing there is another way to think about the human phenomenon? In the 1950s even I noticed I could lose my family orientation for several days after carefully listening to psychoanalytic presentations. I considered this to be my own emotional rigidity. For several years I attended frequent psychoanalytic meetings in an attempt to develop more flexibility and the ability to shift more quickly from one theoretical orientation to the other. My colleagues did not know what I was trying to do and I had no way to explain it so they could understand. They had no way to understand this different way of thinking about the human phenomenon. My ability to shift easily was slowly acquired over a period of ten years or more. I now have the ability to maintain the two orientations side by side without losing self in either direction.

Some twenty years ago, I was sure I had a fairly clear understanding of systems theory. A year or two later there would come new knowledge and awareness that made my previous orientation seem primitive. This same process still continues for me, perhaps at a slower pace than before, but it is alive and present. This makes me wonder how far one can go at learning and mastering systems concepts in a lifetime. A family systems view of the world is completely different from conventional theory. This is not communicable to people unless they can begin to see for themselves and be motivated to learn more. The systems field is so broad, with so many ramifications, that further exploration is limited only by the conceptual power of the observer. I suspect the best systems knowledge currently available is still far short of what it will be a generation or two into the future.

In the past ten years the use of family systems terminology has become popular. There are people who announce themselves as using family systems theory and family systems therapy who have grasped no more than one or two systems ideas. From my position they have not yet scratched the surface. From their position they understand perfectly. How does one go about conceptualizing this gap? People don't know what they do not know about a subject if they have no frame of reference for knowing what it is they do not know. Yet, the field of family therapy is moving very slowly toward a systems orientation. The study of the family is an ideal situation in which to study systems concepts.

I wish the field could move more rapidly, but systems thinking also encourages understanding the slowness of change. It requires about three generations for a majority of people to hear and accept a new discovery, a new idea, or a belief that threatens a firmly held view of the world. Each generation hears and accepts a little more until the third generation accepts it as established fact. The time may be less for certain scientific discoveries or impersonal concepts, but I am not sure it can be less when people have the option of retaining the old belief or accepting the new. I do not believe the time is any less, even during a period of rapid social change when scientific discoveries are accepted quickly. The best example is Darwin's theory of evolution. It was about seventy-five years (three generations) before a majority of people could accept the theory of evolution. The shift from thinking about the human as an individual to thinking about him as a part of a family may not be as important as the theory of evolution, but the family systems idea does threaten some basic human notions about individuality. Family systems theory does not change anything—it merely provides a different way to think about the human condition.

I believe family systems theory, or some version of systems theory, will eventually replace our conventional individual "psychodynamic" theory of human adaption. Systems theory has the breadth and flexibility to conceptualize the interplay of numerous forces with the family. It can explain the human phenomenon all the way from functioning within an individual to functioning in society. It has the flexibility to comprehend the flow of forces between neurophysiology, psychopharmacology, and emotionality. It is not that one theory is more accurate or better. Each theory is a different way of looking at the same thing. Each person is an individual, but each is also part of the emotional amalgam of the family and society. With individual theory, the therapist has a narrower view and is more inclined to become involved in a polarized struggle between two opposing forces.

XVI

Mental health professions have moved toward closing the conceptual gap between individual and family systems theory. The pattern is similar to the acceptance of new beliefs in a family. There is complementary and rejecting activity on both sides of the issue. The higher the level of emotion in the family systems advocate, the more likely is the rejection of the advocate and his or her idea. The establishment is less reactive and there is a better chance it might hear a point or two in a calm presentation. On the side of the advocates have been those with clearly defined systems concepts, those who are moving toward systems concepts, and those who view family as a therapeutic technique. The teaching institutions have not been able to really hear systems concepts. The average institution is more accepting of family therapy than an approach that implies a different theory. By the early 1960s institutions were including some courses in family therapy, but family therapists could not influence the core curriculum. By the 1970s some family systems concepts were sufficiently well known that they were introduced in some professional schools as examples of isolated "schools of thought." There were some exceptions to this general pattern that involved special people in special administrative positions. However, if a chair or head of department moved too rapidly toward a family orientation, there was often resistance from higher administrative offices.

The acceptance of a new idea by society is pretty much determined by its acceptance in the important teaching institutions. After almost twenty-five years, the core curriculum in professional schools is still oriented around conventional individual theory, and a great majority of the graduates still practice conventional therapy. Though the number of family therapists has increased tremendously, they are still in a minority among all mental health professionals. One of the most interesting changes has come from individually oriented faculty members in teaching institutions. Very slowly they have incorporated bits and pieces of family systems theory into individual theory as if it had been there all the time.

At the present time, we have come perhaps one-third of the way in bridging the gap between individual and family systems theory. This is difficult to estimate because this kind of change goes in spurts and stops. We are currently in a period of rapid social change, and I have wondered if social change can influence the time required for the acceptance of a new idea. Yet, since emotion plays a critical role in the ability to hear new ideas, I am inclined to believe that a change to systems thinking will require three generations. My guess is that in another generation, systems ideas will have pretty much replaced the more cumbersome psychodynamic concepts. Then will come the period of individual versus systems debates that will continue until it is no longer necessary to teach individual theory before introducing the student to systems concepts.

The review of the evolution of family systems theory is a prelude to some ideas about the family life cycle format presented in this volume. Through the years I have used life cycle thinking in everything that has to do with family. However, I have never consistently used the life cycle format as a way of communicating theory, either in my clinical work or in teaching. The reason is that my thinking automatically goes to theory, and I have chosen other concepts as more consistent for theory.

I believe the life cycle format may provide one of the most practical and effective ways to help people toward a quicker understanding of the family as a unit. Communication is easier if the teaching is done around two areas of knowledge that are well known. For instance, much of my teaching involves comparisons between one *known* area, individual theory, and an *unknown* area, family systems theory. The concepts of individual theory have been known for centuries. It is second nature for the human to think of a symptom in a person as related to a pathology in that person. It is not automatic for people to think of a symptom in one family member as related to emotional events in the larger family unit. The use of theoretical concepts provides an advantage for me, but it may impose a conceptual dilemma for another. The use of family life cycle thinking involves comparison between two *known* areas of knowledge. The life cycle of the individual has been basic human knowledge since people began thinking. Knowledge about the family life cycle is also well known in human history. Everyone knows the main stages in a nuclear family life cycle from marriage, to reproduction, to the rearing of children as they grow up and move away, to grandchildren, to old age and death. The family life cycle format may provide a quicker and more practical avenue to family systems concepts than one that uses more complex concepts. If people can grasp the family systems idea more quickly through a life cycle format, we need to know about it. I am glad Betty Carter, Monica McGoldrick, and their group have elected to pursue the family life cycle idea in a disciplined way.

It is fortunate that the family movement has gifted people approaching family systems ideas from a number of different angles. Systems concepts ramify in all directions. Wherever a systems idea makes contact with the more static concepts of individual theory, there is an explanatory point to be made. Some people can suddenly hear a systems point after they have missed a dozen more obvious ones. There is always the process of people hearing a systems idea and suddenly having it dissolve when they are back in contact with more conventional thinking. I think the best way of communicating family systems ideas is through the orientation and the self of the teacher. A teacher who has not mastered the concepts for self will be less effective in communicating these ideas to others. A good teacher will find his or her own ways for communicating the concepts and dealing with the communication blocks. There are no right or wrong ways for accomplishing the mission. A right way is one that works and a wrong way is one that does not work. As the family movement matures, more and more people are presenting family systems ideas in all kinds of different ways. Family therapists and students of family systems theory have the responsibility to familiarize themselves with the different ideas and approaches to the central systems theme. The family literature welcomes this volume on the family life cycle as yet another look at family systems theory.

Murray Bowen, M.D.
CLINICAL PROFESSOR AND DIRECTOR
DEPARTMENT OF PSYCHIATRY
GEORGETOWN FAMILY CENTER
GEORGETOWN UNIVERSITY MEDICAL CENTER

Preface

This book is about the predictable developmental stages of American middle-class families in the second half of the twentieth century. It is written by and for family therapists in an attempt to sensitize those of us who work with troubled families to the specific issues facing families as they move through the family life cycle. It is our purpose to explicate as fully as we can the very complex processes of normal family development on which our work is based and to reduce the tendency of therapists, focused as we are on problems, to rely on narrow definitions of pathology.

After our overview of the family life cycle and its clinical relevance, we have included chapters that give an integrated theory of the family life cycle by Kenneth Terkelsen, and an explication by Lynn Hoffman of change theory used by therapists to intervene in a stuck or derailed family system. Hoffman discusses, in particular, the concept and use of "second order change" or change that changes the system itself—the goal of family therapy.

Chapters 4 through 9 by Meyer, McGoldrick, Bradt, Ackerman, McCullough, and Walsh describe each stage of the middle-class American family life cycle and give clinical illustrations of typical family problems at each transition.

In Part 3, we have addressed special issues that have a profound effect on the life cycle and on family therapy. The first three chapters, written by Herz, Beal, and McGoldrick and Carter, deal with transitions that cause serious dislocation of the family life cycle: death, divorce, and remarriage. We have come to see these processes as so complex that they can most fruitfully be viewed as additional emotional transitions in the family life cycle for those families in which they occur. We have attempted to outline the emotional process that must be negotiated in order for these families to restabilize and proceed along their more complex family life course.

We have included a special chapter on women in families by Gluck, Dannefer, and Milea because we felt that their changing role in the family and its impact on the family life cycle required particular attention. The final chapter in this section, by Robert M. Simon, addresses the potential "triggers" for family therapists that may interfere in our work with families because of lack of perspective on our own family life cycle issues.

In Part 4, Fernando Colón describes the ways in which the family life cycle of multiproblem poor families differs from the middle-class norm, and Falicov and Karrer deal with the crucial issue of cultural variations, with particular exploration of the effects of immigration and acculturation on the Mexican-American family. We did not address the issues of "alternate life-style" families, e.g., homosexual marriage, living together arrangements, communes, and the like, since their numbers are so small (less than 1% of the population) and although widely publicized, to date there has been little serious research about them. This might be a fruitful area for future study.

Our concluding chapter, by Ed Friedman, on family life cycle rituals, offers suggestions to help families use their resources and energies creatively as they move through major developmental milestones. Perhaps our greatest hope for this chapter and for the book as a whole, is that it will suggest wider applications on a preventive basis to facilitate the movement of families through the normal process of living.

Monica Mc Goldrick and Elizabeth A. Carter

A genogram is a map that provides a graphic picture of family structure and emotional process over time. It was developed by Murray Bowen, M.D., as part of his family systems theory, and it has become a standard form among clinicians for describing families. Our version of the genogram is used in case examples throughout this book. Bowen uses other symbols to denote other details. Also, to provide more space for dates and notations about each family member, he uses a different way of connecting the spouses rather than the line between the spouses, □—○ used by the authors in this book. The following is a key to some important points in the genogram.

A complete genogram should include:

1. Names and ages of all family members.
2. Exact dates of birth, marriage, separation, divorce, death, and other significant life events.
3. Notations with dates, about occupation, places of residence, illness, and changes in life course, on the genogram itself.
4. Information on three or more generations.

Key to Important symbols:

Male: □   Female: ○   Death ⊠ or ⊗

Marriage: Husband on left, wife on right

Children: Listed in birth order beginning on the left with the oldest:

Example: First child (daughter):   Second child (son):

Common Variations:

Living together or common-law relationship

Marital separation:

Divorce:

Miscarriage or abortion:

Twin children:

Adoptions or foster children:

Part 1

Conceptual Overview

1
The Family Life Cycle and Family Therapy: An Overview

Elizabeth A. Carter, A.C.S.W.

Family Institute of Westchester

Monica McGoldrick, A.C.S.W.

C.M.D.N.J.–Rutgers Medical School and
Community Mental Health Center
Family Institute of Westchester

All the world's a stage
And all the men and women merely players.
They have their exits and their entrances,
And one man in his time plays many parts.
William Shakespeare, As You Like It, II, ii

From Erik Erikson to Daniel Levinson, there has been a growing interest in the life cycle of the adult. This interest indicates a more optimistic attitude toward human psychological growth than previous views. It suggests that adults may continue to develop throughout their lives and are not doomed to the effects of what happened to them from birth to six years of age, the so-called "formative years." This is not to say, of course, that the early years aren't formative, but they are not as final in determining the rest of our lives as we have been led to believe. Adult development still has quite a way to go to catch up with child development as a scientifically explored

3

field, but it is certainly on the move. The immense popularity of Gail Sheehy's *Passages: Predictable Crises of Adult Life* indicates that the general public shares this growing interest in the life cycle of adults.

But what of family development? Is it simply the concurrent development at different phases of several children and adults who happen to be related? Or is the family itself a basic unit of development? Is the whole family involved in each member's development merely in the sense that each influences and reacts to the other's individual phase of life, or can the family itself be said to go through a life cycle that is the major context and determinant of the development of individual family members?

This book presents the view that the family is more than the sum of its parts. It is itself a basic unit of emotional development, the phases and course of which can be identified and predicted. It is our view that this perspective is crucial to understanding the emotional problems that people develop as they struggle together through this basic process.

A number of trends have converged in bringing family therapists to focus on family developmental processes: psychologists pursuing the concept of adult developmental psychology, sociologists conceptualizing family developmental processes, and currently family therapists bringing innovative ideas of change to clinical intervention with families as they traverse the life cycle.

Daniel Levinson and Roger Gould were among the first in the field of psychology to study the course of adult development (Levinson, 1978; Gould, 1972, 1978). Their work, in fact, formed the basis of Sheehy's book *Passages*. Levinson, whose excellent book, *The Seasons of a Man's Life* (1978) is based on a ten-year study of the life course of forty American men, states that the thinking of his research team about adult development grows out of an intellectual tradition formed by Freud, Jung, and Erikson, and includes Rank, Adler, Reich, and other socially oriented psychologists. Levinson has done much to expand the purview of psychology to include the complexities of adult development.

Gould made a major contribution in his study that attempted to define the phases of adult life (1972). Although working from an individual rather than a family viewpoint, Gould underscored the importance of time-related interpersonal changes in adult life: "Why, in our conceptualizations, do we seem to assume that time no longer functions systematically after 21 years of age and to rely henceforth on thematic and adventitious factors to anchor our understanding of change? After all, both interpersonal and biological changes continue through life. In fact, interpersonal changes are even more dramatic in the period after 21 than before 21" (Gould, 1972).

Bernice Neugarten, who has been doing studies of adult developmental patterns for many years, emphasizes the idea that in charting the course of the life cycle we must consider the interweaving of historical time and biological time in the context of a third dimension, that of socially defined time:

> Every society is age graded, and every society has a system of social expectations regarding age appropriate behavior. The individual passes through a socially regulated cycle from birth to death as inexorably as he passes through the biological cycle: a succession of socially delineated age-statuses, each with its recognized rights, duties and obligations. There exists a socially prescribed timetable for the ordering of major life events: a time in the life-span when men and women are expected to marry, a time to raise children, a time to retire ... Men and women are aware not only of the social clocks that operate in various areas of their lives, but also of their own timing ... with regard to major life events. From this perspective, time is at least a three-dimensional phenomenon in charting the course of the life cycle, with historical time, life time (or chronological age) and social time all intricately intertwined" (Neugarten, 1976).

As Neugarten mentions, all the various turning points in life, the end of formal schooling, marriage, parenthood, occupational achievement, and the like, are "punctuation marks along the life cycle." They call forth changes in self-concept and sense of identity. They mark the incorporation of new social and emotional roles and accordingly they are precipitants of new adaptations (Neugarten, 1976).

Neugarten notes many changes in the timing of the family life cycle over the past several decades. The general historical trend has been toward a quickening of events through most of the life cycle, followed by a much longer post-childrearing period than has ever been the case before. As a result, children have more surviving grandparents than in past eras, although they may be geographically more distant. The quickened pace means that not only do different generations grow up in different historical eras, but they go through the life cycle at different ages and are influenced by differing social expectations as time moves along. Neugarten points out that life cycle events are much more likely to be traumatic if they occur off-time than in the expected course of life. The major stresses of life, she notes, are those "caused by events which upset the sequence and rhythm of the life cycle, as when the death of a parent comes in childhood rather than in middle age; when marriage does not come at its desired or appropriate time; when the birth of a child is too early or too late; when occupational achievement is delayed; when the empty nest, grandparenthood, retirement, major illness or widowhood occur off-time. In this sense, then, psychology of the life cycle is not a psychology of crisis behavior so much as it is a psychology of timing" (Neugarten, 1976).

Two cautions in using a life cycle perspective are worth mentioning. Christopher Lasch has pointed out in his book, *The Culture of Narcissism* (1978), that a rigid application of the psychology of the "normal" life cycle to adult life may have a detrimental effect. It is important not to promote anxious self-scrutiny that creates the fear that any deviation from the norm is pathological. Lasch also warns that viewing adult life solely in terms of individual developmental stages can create a sense of historical discontinuity. He argues against any view that devalues the guiding role of parenthood and renders meaningless the relationships between generations by overemphasizing the uniqueness of the "brave new world" faced by each new generation.

Our book is an attempt to view the life cycle in terms of the meaningfulness of intergenerational connectedness in the family. We believe this to be one of our greatest human resources. We do not mean to oversimplify or encourage stereotyping by prompting classifications of "normality" that constrict our view of human life. On the contrary, our hope is that by superimposing the family life cycle framework on the natural phenomenon of lives through time, we are adding to the depth with which clinicians can view family problems and family strengths.

Hadley and others have looked at symptom onset and found it correlated with family developmental crises of addition and loss of family members (Hadley et al., 1974). Walsh and Orfanidis found a specific death in the third generation correlated with the birth of the identified patient in schizophrenic families (Walsh, 1978; Orfanidis, 1977). Much more research needs to be done on the impact of family developmental shifts on dysfunction throughout the three-generational system as a unit.

The first steps toward a family view of the life cycle were taken in the field of sociology when Reuben Hill and Evelyn Duvall worked together on the preparation of background papers for the National Conference on Family Life in May, 1948. Although still conceptualizing "family" primarily as a collection of individual life cycles, this committee underscored their interdependence. Hill and Duvall observed that each member of the younger, middle, and older generations in the family has his or her own developmental tasks, and the successful achievement of one person's tasks is dependent on and contributes to the successful achievement by other family members of their appropriate tasks. The final step—that the family as a whole has developmental tasks—evolved during a workshop on marriage and family research led by Duvall in 1950. She broke the family life cycle into eight stages, and subsequently outlined the developmental tasks at each stage. Duvall's landmark work, first published in 1957, is now in its fifth edition and is still considered the basic text in the field (Duvall, 1977). Although there are many variations on Duvall's eight stages, all of them address the nodal events related to the comings and goings of family members: marriage, the birth and raising of the children, the departure of children from the household, retirement, and death. The most complex of these breakdowns is that proposed by Rodgers (1960), who expanded his schema to twenty-four separate stages to account for the progress of several children through the nodal events of the life cycle. Hill emphasized three-generational aspects of the life cycle, describing parents of married children as forming a "lineage bridge" between the older and younger generations of the family. His view is that at each stage of the family life cycle there is a distinctive role complex for family members with each other. Obviously, the many ways family members of one generation rely on another within the "generation spiral" (Duvall, p. 153) in a mutual interdependence are part of the richness of the family context as generations move through the life cycle.

At the same time that sociologists were beginning in the early 1950s to define the family as a developmental unit, the founders of what was to become known as family therapy were similarly experimenting with psychiatric treatment of the family as a unit (Bowen, Ackerman, Jackson, Satir, and others). As these early family clinicians and researchers struggled to understand and to change disturbed and dysfunctional families, they obviously could not proceed far without confronting the question of the "normal" model of family development to which they were trying to restore their treatment families.

In fact, Hill (1970) has commented that any researcher or clinician who seeks to generalize about families without taking into account variations resulting from the stage of development, will encounter tremendous variance for which they will not be able to account.

However, explicit reference to the family life cycle as a useful framework for clinicians did not appear in the family therapy literature until the 1970s. Implicitly, it has long been a basic assumption of most family therapy approaches. For instance, one has only to hear Murray Bowen conduct an evaluation interview to realize that before he intervenes with a family, he obtains a complete picture of the family's life cycle. In the space of the first hour, Bowen, who does not explicitly talk or write about the family life cycle, has obtained the names and ages of all members of a family over three generations, the dates of birth, marriage, illness, and death, as well as separations, dislocations, geographical moves, and circumstances of contact within the family over its life cycle. If the family's adult children have not left home, or a grandfather has just retired and moved to Florida, or the wife's parents have recently divorced, Bowen will have that information within the first session, regardless of the family's presenting problem.

Satir also, as early as 1964, outlined taking a Family Life Chronology as a central part of the initial interview.

Nathan Epstein and his colleagues (1978) in defining the basic assumptions of the model they have been developing over many years state that the primary function of the family is to support the development of its members; and that in carrying this out, all families must deal with basic tasks (provision of food, shelter, and the like), developmental tasks related to individual growth and to the stages of the family life cycle, and hazardous tasks such as illness, death, moving, and loss of income.

Perhaps the family life cycle was not particularly focused on earlier because it seemed to fall in the area of premises that "everyone knows." After all, "everyone knows" that most people in our culture marry in their twenties, have a couple of children who go off to school at age six, throw the household into turmoil in their teens, and then move out on their own at eighteen or twenty-one, leaving their parents to deal with each other, their own aging parents, retirement, and eventually death. The problem with basic things that "everyone knows" is that they tend to fade into the background and may be hard to focus on when needed. Perhaps our examination of the family life cycle in the 1970s is a result of the changing role of women, which received great impetus in the late 1960s, and is radically altering the family life cycle patterns that have applied through history until the present generation. Then too, the upheavals in the 1960s, when so many middle-class young people suddenly dropped out of the usual family developmental pattern, challenged these basic assumptions as well.

In any case, direct references to the family life cycle and its clinical implications first appeared in the family therapy literature in 1973 in a book by Jay Haley and in an article by Michael Solomon published the same year. Haley's book, *Uncommon Therapy,* is a presentation of the brilliant and intriguing therapeutic strategies of Milton Erickson, organized conceptually around the stages of the family life cycle. Haley describes the family life cycle in six stages and states his belief that family stress is highest at the transition points from one stage to the next. Symptoms are most likely to appear in a family member when there is an interruption or dislocation in the unfolding family life cycle and are a signal that the family is "stuck," having difficulty moving through the transition to its next phase. Therapeutic efforts need to be directed toward remobilizing the family life cycle, so that normal developmental progress can continue.

Solomon's article, "A Developmental, Conceptual Premise for Family Therapy," condenses Duvall's eight-stage life cycle schema into five stages and suggests that since these developmental stages and the tasks at each stage apply to all families, they can be used as a diagnostic base from which a treatment plan can be developed.

In 1974, Minuchin, in his book, *Families and Family Therapy,* described the family developmental cycle as a key component of any schema based on viewing the family as a system. "With this orientation," he states, "many more families who enter therapy would be seen as average families in transitional situations, suffering the pains of accommodating to new circumstances." Minuchin traces the features of the early stages of the life cycle and includes transcripts of several developmental interviews with "normal" families that highlight typical difficulties and transitions at their particular stage.

Recently, a number of family therapists have been moving along the lines set out by the Haley-Erickson formulation that looks at problems as derailments from the family life cycle, and therapy as getting the family back on the track. They have built on the concepts of change put forth by Watzlawick et al., (1974), viewing life cycle transitions as requiring "second order change" or systemic change (Hughes et al., 1978: Weeks & Wright, 1979). Difficulties within a stage are viewed as alterable by "first order change" or a rebalancing of the family within its present organization. Second order change, on the contrary, is discontinuous. It requires a quantum leap that changes the system itself. Lynn Hoffman develops this idea in Chapter 3. The strategic techniques employed for helping families transform themselves in this way are primarily paradoxical, as in the work of Watzlawick (1974), Haley (1973), Palazzoli (1978), Hoffman (Chapter 3), and Papp (1980).

The sociological literature on the family life cycle tends to convey the idea that a developmental event (such as the birth of a child, or a marriage) automatically moves a family from one stage to the next. Family therapists are faced with those families in which the shifts are not automatic because the emotional pattern does not promote the move to the next stage.

TRANSGENERATIONAL AND LIFE CYCLE STRESSES

Throughout this book, when we refer to "family" we are referring to the entire family emotional system of at least three generations. This, we are convinced, is the operative emotional field at any given moment. We do not restrict the meaning or influence of family to the members of a particular household or a given nuclear family branch of the system. Thus, although our presentation recognizes the dominant American pattern of a separately domiciled nuclear family, this nuclear family is viewed as itself an emotional subsystem, reacting to both past and present relationships within the larger three-generational system.

As illustrated in Figure 1.1, we view the flow of anxiety in a family as being both "vertical" and "horizontal." The vertical flow in a system includes patterns of relating and functioning that are transmitted down the generations in a family primarily through the mechanism of emotional triangling (Bowen, 1978). It includes all the family attitudes, taboos, expectations, labels, and loaded issues with which we grow up. One could say that these aspects of our lives are like the hand we are dealt: they are a given. What we do with them is the issue for us.

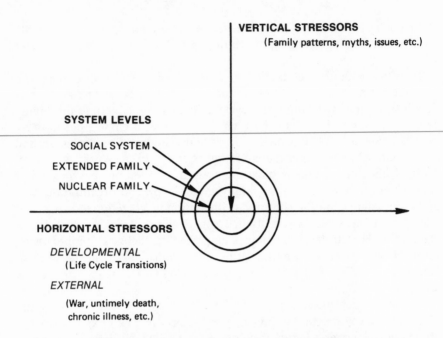

Figure 1.1 Horizontal and Vertical Stressors.

The horizontal flow in the system includes the anxiety produced by the stresses on the family as it moves forward through time, coping with the changes and transitions of the family life cycle. It includes both the predictable developmental stresses, and those unpredictable events, "the slings and arrows of outrageous fortune" that may disrupt the life cycle process (untimely death, birth of a defective child, chronic illness, war, etc. Given enough stress on the horizontal axis, any family will appear extremely dysfunctional, and even a small horizontal stress on a family in which the vertical axis is full of intense stress will create great disruption in the system (Bowen, 1978).

While we generally share Haley's concept that symptoms reflect family life cycle derailment, and therapy aims for change that reestablishes the developmental momentum of the system, his formulation does not address the enormous impact of the vertical stresses passing down the generations in the family. In our view, the degree of anxiety engendered by the stress on the vertical and horizontal axes at the points where they converge is the key determinant of how well the family will manage its transitions through life. It becomes imperative, therefore, for the family therapist to assess not only the dimensions of the current life cycle stress, but also its connections to family themes, triangles, and labels coming down in the family over historical time (Carter, 1978). Although all normative change is to some degree stressful, we have observed as clinicians that when the horizontal (norma-tive) stress intersects with a vertical (transgenerational) stress, there is a quantum leap in the anxiety engendered. If, to give a global example, one's parents were basically pleased to be parents and handled the job without too much anxiety, the birth of the first child will produce just the normal stress of a system expanding its boundaries from two to three members. If, on the other hand, parenting was a *cause célèbre* of some kind in the family of origin of one or both spouses, and has not been dealt with, the birth of a baby will produce heightened anxiety for the couple in making the transi-tion to parenthood. The greater the anxiety generated in the family at any transition point, the more difficult or dysfunctional the transition will be.

In addition to the stress "inherited" from past generations, and that expe-rienced while moving through the family life cycle, there is, of course, the stress of living in *this* place at *this* time. Without going into the details of the impact on family relationships of women's liberation, the increasing divorce rate, the sexual revolution, pollution, and the energy shortage, suffice it to say that one cannot ignore this context and its impact on families moving through the life cycle at this point in history. Personal attitudes on particu-lar issues aside, one must recognize the strain that the vastly accelerated rate of change puts on families today, whether the changes themselves are for better or worse.

We decided to embark on this book out of a growing sense of the clinical need for an explicit model of family development. Families come for ther-apy at a certain moment when things have gone wrong for them. Usually this means that they have lost a sense of their motion through time: some-thing that is "supposed to happen" is not happening or vice versa; a young adult has not left home, or a marriage is breaking up, or a child is failing in school. Therapy that focuses only on the symptoms, or on the family's inter-actions at the time of the crisis, may miss the most important aspects of where they are trying to go in relation to where they have been.

We felt there was a need for a book that would take a closer look at the family life cycle and consider the interlocking tasks, problems, and relation-ships of the three-generational family system as it moves through time and as issues and stresses move down from one generation to the next. Our hy-pothesis is that there are emotional tasks to be fulfilled by the family system at each phase of its life cycle, requiring a change in status of family mem-bers, and that there is a complex emotional process involved in making the transition from phase to phase.

We have offered as a general paradigm the modern American middle-class family life cycle, although we realize that cultures and socio-economic groups differ enormously in their breakdown of the life cycle stages and definitions of the tasks at each stage. Family life cycle patterns vary consid-erably among different cultural groups even several generations after immigration (Gelfand & Kutzik, 1980; Lieberman, 1974). We have tried to allude to some of the profound variations in life cycle patterns by offering special chapters on socio-economic (Colón, Chapter 16) and cultural (Falicov & Karrer, Chapter 15) variations, but we are well aware of the over-simplification required in presenting this generalized paradigm.

It is easy, with the help of Erickson, Levinson, and others, to focus on the individual as (s)he moves through the life cycle. Considering the couple (the two-person system) has also been facilitated by recent studies of marriage over the life cycle (Gould, 1972; Campbell, 1975; Harry, 1976; Schram, 1979). The most carefully elaborated three-person or family model, Duvall's, focuses primarily on childrearing as the organizing element of family life. We would like to go beyond this model, to consider the motion of the entire three- or four-generational system as it moves through time. Our relationships with our parents, siblings and other family members go through stages as we move along the life cycle, just as parent-child and spouse relationships do. It is extremely difficult, however, to think of the family as a whole because of the complexity involved.

As a system moving along through time, the family has basically different properties from all other systems. Unlike all other organizations, families incorporate new members only by birth, adoption, or marriage, and members can leave only by death, if then (see Terkelsen, Chapter 2). No other system is subject to these constraints. A business organization can fire members it views as dysfunctional, or conversely, individual members can resign if the structure and values of the organization are not to their liking. The pressures of membership with no exit available can, in the extreme situation, lead the family down the road to psychosis. (Cecchin, 1979). In non-family systems, roles are filled by different individuals at different times. In the main, though, the functions of the system are carried out in a stable fashion (or else the system self-destructs) by the replacement of those who leave for any reason. While there are also roles and functions in family systems, the main value is in the relationships, which are irreplaceable. For example, a stepmother may take over the role and functions of a mother, but will never completely replace her.

Family life cycle passages are concerned with shifting membership over time, and the changing status of family members in relation to each other. Dysfunctional families characteristically confuse shifts in status, exits, and functions. This occurs particularly through a process whereby the family pretends to have more power over the membership or status of family members than it actually has. Parents may pretend that their children are not growing up and leaving, or that their own parents are not dying when they are. Or a mother may pretend that her son is not really married (i.e., that his status in relation to her has not changed), by ignoring her daughter-in-law, and seeking an exclusive relationship with her son.

One of the most complex aspects of the status of family members is the confusion that occurs over whether one can choose membership and function in a family or not. Many people act as though they can choose in this matter, when in fact there is very little choice. Children, for example, have no choice about being born into a system; nor do parents have a choice, once children are born, as to the existence of the responsibilities of parenthood, even if they neglect these responsibilities. In fact, no family relationships except marriage are entered into by choice. Even in the case of marriage, the freedom to marry whomever one wishes is a rather recent option, and the decision to marry is probably much less freely made than we usually recognize at the time (see McGoldrick, Chapter 5). While we can choose not to continue a marriage relationship, the fact of having been married is acknowledged in the present with the designation, "ex-spouse," now applied to that person. *Whom* we are related to in the complex web of family ties over all the generations is unalterable by us. Obviously, family members frequently act as if this were not so—they cut each other off because of conflicts or because they claim to have "nothing in common." But when family members act as though family relationships were optional, they do so to the detriment of their own sense of identity, and of the richness of their emotional and social context.

THE STAGES OF THE FAMILY LIFE CYCLE

This book is about the predictable developmental stages of American middle-class families in the last quarter of the twentieth century. In the first section, this overview is followed by chapters offering a thoughtful consideration of a theory of the family life cycle and a discussion of the process of change required of families at each transition.

In outlining the stages of the family life cycle, we have departed from the traditional sociological depiction of the family life cycle as commencing at courtship or marriage and ending with the death of one spouse. Rather, considering family to be the operative emotional unit from the cradle to the grave, we see a new family life cycle beginning at the stage of the "Unattached Young Adult," whose adequate or inadequate completion of the primary task of *coming to terms with his or her family of origin* will most profoundly influence whom, when and how he or she marries and all succeeding stages of the new family life cycle. Adequate completion of this task would require that the young adult separate from the family of origin without cutting off or fleeing reactively to a substitute emotional refuge.

Seen in this way, the Unattached Young Adult phase is a cornerstone. It is a time to formulate personal life goals and to become a "self" before joining with another to form a new family subsystem. The more adequately the young adult can differentiate himself or herself from the emotional program of the family of origin at this phase, the fewer vertical stresses will follow him or her through the new family's life cycle. This is the chance to sort out emotionally what one will take from the family of origin and what one will change for oneself. Of great significance is the fact that, until this generation, this crucial phase has historically never been considered necessary for women, who were traditionally handed directly from their fathers to their husbands. Obviously, this tradition has had profound impact on the functioning of women in families, as does the current attempt to change it.

Marriage, in this view, should signify that significant progress has been made in the task of becoming emotionally independent of the family of origin, *not* that the task is about to begin, or is automatically accomplished by the fact of the marriage. If the young adult has not adequately differentiated from his or her family of origin at the preceding stage, then a spouse is likely to be chosen to please or to spite the family. This reaction to the emotional process in the family of origin will interfere with the attempts of the newly married couple to become a separate, but connected subsystem, and will continue to interfere with succeeding phases of their life cycle.

We have chosen to include as one long phase "The Family with Young Children," where others have tended to break this into several different phases. Although it does, obviously, have subphases within it, it has not seemed to us that the change from infant to toddler, or from five-year-old to "school child," requires the level of change of the system itself, as do the birth of a child at one end of the phase, and the emergence into adolescence at the other.

Chapter 7 depicts our view that "adolescence" is something that happens to a family, not just to an individual child. The family boundaries, having remained fairly stable around the nuclear and extended family for twelve or thirteen years, are suddenly required to develop the elasticity necessary to alternately let adolescents go, shelter their retreats, and encompass the barrage of people and ideas they bring into the family from the outside. Their pushing and pulling in family relationships goes through the system with a domino effect.

The phase of "Launching Children and Moving On" is now the longest phase of the family life cycle because families have fewer children and a longer life expectancy. It also requires the greatest flexibility. This phase not only requires a total renegotiation of the marriage, but also involves dealing with the greatest number of exits (dying parents and departing children) and entries (in-laws and grandchildren) of all family life cycle phases. Neugarten (1976) has pointed out that during this period people have a tendency to describe themselves in terms of their relationships and their work, rather than by their age. This probably relates to two factors. The first is that the shifts in relationships at this stage are more significant and bring more change than the attainment of a particular chronological age. Secondly, without the task of childrearing, people's status in relation to their work and social context takes on added meaning.

The issues for families with older members in our youth-oriented, geographically mobile society are explicated in Chapter 9. The biologist, Alexander Comfort (1978), forsees mounting protest in the future as increasingly healthy and longer lived older people object to their compulsory exclusion from meaningful work and relegation to a play-space, or to marginal subsistence. Comfort's article describes the two approaches of gerontologists toward aging: one, the improvement of medical treatment and elimination of disease; and the other; a search for the biological "clock" that times the human lifespan in hopes of finding ways to slow the aging process itself. The social, political and psychological impact of the latter would be profound. As for the prevailing view of older age, Comfort observes that the technologically advanced societies espouse a self-fulfilling expectation of decline and dependency without providing the compensations of status, respect and authority available in simpler societies.

One result of older people's acceptance of second-class status is the fact that the older generation is the least likely to appear in the office of the family therapist. Their treatment requires special approaches by clinicians if they and their families are to be helped.

In Part 3, we have presented chapters on untimely death, divorce, single-parent and remarried families as special issues which interrupt the developmental course of the family life cycle. We have come to see these processes as so complex that they can most usefully be viewed as additional stages in the family life cycle for those families in which they occur. We have attempted to outline the emotional process that must be negotiated in order for these families to restabilize and proceed along their more complex life course. The chapter, "Women in Families," outlines what amounts to a radical reshaping of the form of the traditional life cycle by women. By developing their own personal life goals, marrying later, having fewer children, and working, divorcing, and remarrying in unprecedented numbers, women are changing American families dramatically. The last chapter in this section points up the special concerns of family therapists as our own personal family life cycle issues interface with those of treatment families.

Part 4 of the book describes the ways in which the family life cycle of the multiproblem poor differs from the middle-class norm and outlines the influence of cultural variations, with particular exploration of the effects of immigration and acculturation on the Mexican-American family.

The book's final chapter, on family life cycle rituals, may provide suggestions to help families use their varied resources and energies creatively as they move through the major developmental milestones. Perhaps our greatest hope for the entire framework presented in this book is that it will suggest wider application on a preventative basis to facilitate the movement of families through the normal developmental process of living.

We would like to emphasize that, while transitions in the family life cycle are described as relating to the presence of children, since that is the statistical norm, we do not mean to imply that those who do not follow the pattern of marriage and childrearing are stunted in their development. Although the vast majority of families are involved with raising children, we consider that most of the phases of the life cycle would hold also for family members who do not marry and do not have children. An unmarried man who does not go through the child-oriented phases of the life cycle must still relate to his family and social network on the issues other families go through. He still lives within the context of those who went before him, those who go along with him, and those who will come after him.

In certain respects, those not following the norms do, of course, have special difficulties in shifting their status within their families. This is often related to family expectations. For example, an unmarried daughter may be expected to remain at home and over the years to become the caretaker of her parents. She may have special problems in defining her identity in relation to the family, given their expectation of her unmarried status.

Table 1.1 is an outline of the stages of the family life cycle in a schema which emphasizes the major points at which family members enter and exit from the family system, upsetting the family homeostasis. Column two delineates the emotional process of the transitions from stage to stage. This is a variation on the idea suggested by Barnhill and Longo (1979). Our outline of this process highlights the view that the central underlying process to be negotiated is the expansion, contraction, and realignment of the relationship system to support the entry, exit, and development of family members in a functional way.

Once the key principles of the transition process have been acknowledged, the family can move on (column three) to the various relationship shifts involved in entering and proceeding developmentally through the next stage of the family life cycle.

We think there is clinical value in the distinctions made in columns two and three. If one thinks of column two as the "attitudes" which enable family members to make the transition, then it is clear that clinical work directed at column three will not succeed if the family is stuck in column two. We have wondered if the powerful effects of some of the paradoxical techniques used by strategic family therapists are related to the fact that they zero in on the futile resistance in the family to the principles outlined in column two.

We have extended our schema to include the additional phases required for families going through divorce (Table 1.2) and remarriage (Table 1.3).

THE STAGES OF THE FAMILY LIFE CYCLE

Family Life Cycle Stage	Emotional Process of Transition: Key Principles	Second Order Changes in Family Status Required to Proceed Developmentally	
1. Between Families: The Unattached Young Adult	Accepting parent offspring separation	a.	Differentiation of self in relation to family of origin
		b.	Development of intimate peer relationships
		c.	Establishment of self in work
2. The Joining of Families Through Marriage: The Newly Married Couple	Commitment to new system	a.	Formation of marital system
		b.	Realignment of relationships with extended families and friends to include spouse
3. The Family With Young Children	Accepting new members into the system	a.	Adjusting marital system to make space for child(ren)
		b.	Taking on parenting roles
		c.	Realignment of relationships with extended family to include parenting and grandparenting roles
4. The Family With Adolescents	Increasing flexibility of family boundaries to include children's independence	a.	Shifting of parent-child relationships to permit adolescent to move in and out of system
		b.	Refocus on mid-life marital and career issues
		c.	Beginning shift toward concerns for older generation
5. Launching Children and Moving On	Accepting a multitude of exits from and entries into the family system	a.	Renegotiation of marital system as a dyad
		b.	Development of adult to adult relationships between grown children and their parents
		c.	Realignment of relationships to include in-laws and grandchildren
		d.	Dealing with disabilities and death of parents (grandparents)
6. The Family in Later Life	Accepting the shifting of generational roles	a.	Maintaining own and/or couple functioning and interests in face of physiological decline; exploration of new familial and social role options
		b.	Support for a more central role for middle generation
		c.	Making room in the system for the wisdom and experience of the elderly; supporting the older generation without overfunctioning for them
		d.	Dealing with loss of spouse, siblings and other peers and preparation for own death. Life review and integration.

Table 1.1

The family life cycle is a powerful paradigm which has been greatly overlooked as a therapeutic framework. We hope that this book will inspire therapists to consider their clinical families in the larger time frame of the family life cycle, and to see their problems as being a part of the ebb and flow of change in the multigenerational family system. Hopefully, in the future more clinical attention will be focused on the process of family devel-

DISLOCATIONS OF THE FAMILY LIFE CYCLE REQUIRING ADDITIONAL STEPS TO
RESTABILIZE AND PROCEED DEVELOPMENTALLY

Phase	Emotional Process of Transition Prerequisite Attitude	Developmental Issues
DIVORCE		
1. The decision to divorce	Acceptance of inability to resolve marital tensions sufficiently to continue relationship	Acceptance of one's own part in the failure of the marriage
2. Planning the break up of the system	Supporting viable arrangements for all parts of the system	a. Working cooperatively on problems of custody, visitation, finances b. Dealing with extended family about the divorce
3. Separation	A) Willingness to continue cooperative coparental relationship B) Work on resolution of attachment to spouse	a. Mourning loss of intact family b. Restructuring marital and parent-child relationships; adaptation to living apart c. Realignment of relationships with extended family; staying connected with spouse's extended family
4. The Divorce	More work on emotional divorce: Overcoming hurt, anger, guilt, etc.	a. Mourning loss of intact family: giving up fantasies of reunion b. Retrieval of hopes, dreams, expectations from the marriage c. Staying connected with extended families
POST–DIVORCE FAMILY		
A. Single-Parent Family	Willingness to maintain parental contact with ex-spouse and support contact of children with ex-spouse and his family	a. Making flexible visitation arrangements with ex-spouse and his family b. Rebuilding own social network
B. Single-Parent (Noncustodial)	Willingness to maintain parental contact with ex-spouse and support custodial parent's relationship with children	a. Finding ways to continue effective parenting relationship with children b. Rebuilding own social network

Table 1.2

opment and change, especially those changes that add flexibility and depth
to the family context. This is all the more important because of the increasing strain that is being placed on families as a result of the erosion of wider
social structures which previously supported the family as it moved along
its course.

REMARRIED FAMILY FORMATION: A DEVELOPMENTAL OUTLINE *

ps	Prerequisite Attitude	Developmental Issues
Entering the new Relationship	Recovery from loss of first marriage (adequate "emotional divorce")	Recommitment to marriage and to forming a family with readiness to deal with the complexity and ambiguity
Conceptualizing and planning new marriage and family	Accepting one's own fears and those of new spouse and children about remarriage and forming a stepfamily Accepting need for time and patience for adjustment to complexity and ambiguity of: 1. Multiple new roles 2. Boundaries: space, time, membership and authority. 3. Affective Issues: guilt, loyalty conflicts, desire for mutuality, unresolvable past hurts	a. Work on openness in the new relationships to avoid pseudomutuality. b. Plan for maintenance of cooperative co—parental relationships with ex—spouses. c. Plan to help children deal with fears, loyalty conflicts and membership in two systems. d. Realignment of relationships with extended family to include new spouse and children. e. Plan maintenance of connections for children with extended family of ex—spouses(s).
Remarriage and Reconsitution of Family	Final resolution of attachment to previous spouse and ideal of "intact'" family; Acceptance of a different model of family with permeable boundaries	a. Restructuring family boundaries to allow for inclusion of new spouse—stepparent. b. Realignment of relationships throughout subsystems to permit interweaving of several systems. c. Making room for relationships of all children with biological (non—custodial) parents, grandparents, and other extended family. d. Sharing memories and histories to enhance stepfamily integration.

Variation on a developmental schema presented by Ransom *et al.* (1979)

Table 1.3

REFERENCES

Barnhill, L. & D. Longo, "Fixation and Regression in the Family Life Cycle," *Family Process,* 17/4, December 1978.

Bowen, M., *Family Therapy in Clinical Practice,* New York: Jason Aronson, 1978.

Campbell, A., "The American Way of Mating," *Psychology Today,* May 1975.

Carter, E. A., "Transgenerational Scripts and Nuclear Family Stress: Theory and Clinical Implications," *Georgetown Family Symposia:* Vol. III (1975–76), Ruth Riley Sagar, ed., Washington D.C.: Georgetown University, 1978.

Cecchin, G., Personal Communication, July 1979.

Comfort, A., "A Biologist Laments and Exhorts," in *Aging Into the 21st Century,* L. Jarvik, ed., New York: Gardner Press, 1978.

Duvall, E., *Marriage and Family Development,* 5th Edition, Philadelphia: Lippincott, 1977.

Epstein, N., D. Bishop, & S. Levin, "The McMaster Model of Family Functioning," *Journal of Marriage and Family Counseling,* 4/4, October 1978.

Gelfand, D., and A. Kutzik, *Ethnicity and Aging,* New York: Springer, 1980.

Gould, R., "The Phases of Adult Life: A Study in Developmental Psychology," *American Journal of Psychiatry,* 129/5, November 1972.

———, *Transformations: Growth and Change in Adult Life,* New York: Simon & Schuster, 1978.

Hadley, T. et al, "The Relationship Between Family Developmental Crises and the Appearance of Symptoms in a Family Member," *Family Process,* 13/2, 1974.

Haley, J., *Uncommon Therapy: The Psychiatric Techniques of Milton H. Erickson,* New York: Norton, 1973.

Harry, J., "Evolving Sources of Happiness for Men Over the Life Cycle: A Structural Analysis," *Journal of Marriage and the Family,* 38/2, May 1976.

Hill, R., "Methodological Issues in Family Development Research," *Family Process,* 3:186–204, 1964.

———, *Family Development in Three Generations,* Cambridge: Schenkman, 1970.

Hughes, S. F., M. Berger, & L. Wright, "The Family Life Cycle and Clinical Intervention," *Journal of Marriage and Family Counseling,* 4/4, October 1978.

Jarvik, L., ed., *Aging Into the 21st Century,* New York: Gardner Press, 1978.

Lasch, C., *The Culture of Narcissism: American Life in an Age of Diminishing Expectations,* New York: Norton, 1978.

Lieberman, M., "Adaptational Patterns in Middle Aged and Elderly: The Role of Ethnicity," paper presented at the Gerontological Society Conference, Portland Oregon, October 1974.

Levinson, D., *The Seasons of a Man's Life,* New York: Knopf, 1978.

Minuchin, S., *Families and Family Therapy,* Cambridge: Harvard University Press, 1974.

Neugarten, B., "Adaptation and the Life Cycle," *The Counseling Psychologist,* 6/1, 1976.

Orfanidis, M., "Some Data on Death and Cancer in Schizophrenic Families," presentation, Georgetown Pre-Symposium Meeting, Washington, D.C., 1977.

Palazzoli, M. S., L. Boscolo, G. Cecchin, & C. Prata, *Paradox and Counterparadox,* New York: Jason Aronson, 1978.

Papp, P., "The Greek Chorus and Other Techniques of Family Therapy," *Family Process,* 19/1, 1980.

Rodgers, R., "Proposed Modifications of Duvall's Family Life Cycle Stages," Paper presented at the American Sociological Association Meeting, New York, August 1960.

Satir, V., *Conjoint Family Therapy,* Palo Alto: Science & Behavior Books, 1964.

Schram, R. W., "Marital Satisfaction Over the Family Life Cycle: A Critique and Proposal," *Journal of Marriage and the Family,* 41/1, February 1979.

Sheehy, G., *Passages: Predictable Crises of Adult Life,* New York: Dutton, 1976.

Solomon, M., "A Developmental, Conceptual Premise for Family Therapy," *Family Process,* 12:179–88, 1973.

Walsh, F., "Concurrent Grandparent Death and the Birth of a Schizophrenic Offspring: An Intriguing Finding," *Family Process,* 17/4, December 1978.

Watzlawick, P., J. H. Weakland, & R. Fisch, *Change: Principles of Problem Formulation and Problem Resolution,* New York: Norton, 1974.

Weeks, G. R. & L. Wright, "Dialectics of the Family Life Cycle," *American Journal of Family Therapy,* 7/1, Spring 1979.

2
TOWARD A THEORY OF
THE FAMILY LIFE CYCLE

Kenneth G. Terkelsen, M.D.

Family Institute of Westchester

College of Physicians and Surgeons, Columbia University

For some years now, I have wondered how the concept of *therapeutic change* (25) might be linked to the concepts of *adult development* (8, 9, 14) and the *family life cycle* (7, 10, 12). Although these lines of thinking have developed independently in the literature, I became aware of a possible theoretical unity while reading Watzlawick et al. (25) and Haley (10) together in 1974. In fact, the parallels were so striking that it seemed that a unifying statement might be written within short order. In the same year, I began talking about the combined ideas with all my students, and inserted the notion of their compatibility into every conceivable theoretical discussion with my colleagues at the Family Studies Section, the Lincoln Community Mental Health Center, the Center for Family Learning, and most recently in faculty meetings at the Family Institute of Westchester.

As these discussions proceeded, other concepts seemed to attach themselves naturally. There was the somewhat suspect (possibly teleological) but somehow essential idea that a system has *purpose*. There were numerous allusions to patterning of behavior, i.e., *family structure*. And we all wanted these abstract concepts to lead us on toward our more clinical notions of *family dysfunction* and *family therapy*. I became increasingly convinced that all these could be brought together. But I also came to see that the task of clear theoretical linkage would prove more difficult than I had initially thought. After three years of talk, the path seemed longer than it had at the outset. And still no one had published the seemingly self-evident unifying statement.

When Betty Carter and Monica McGoldrick advanced their plan, in late 1977, for a book dealing with clinical aspects of the family life cycle, I shared with them my sense that they simply must include a discussion of these concepts in the book. They graciously responded by inviting (and challenging) me to write the theoretical chapter. I felt that I could not possibly write such a thing. Not yet. The ideas needed further care and feeding. But considering that this was to be a book about development, I soon came to the view that its contents should be regarded as in development. So, what has come together here is in the nature of a preliminary statement.

Each component idea derives from earlier work (8, 10, 11, 14, 19, 24, 25, 27). What I am offering the reader is the present status of my efforts to bring this material in under one roof. I believe the resultant paradigm[1] contributes to the theory of family therapy in several ways. For instance, the idea that a *family system operates purposefully* leads naturally to the proposition that *family therapy operates purposefully*. This in turn points to a clinical principle: effectiveness is served when the family therapist functions directionally (and hence directively), ever mindful of the goal-oriented nature of normal family processes. Additionally, the paradigm highlights the unity between the concepts of *family structure* and *therapeutic change*: what is changed in therapy is family structure. From this unity emerges a general framework for viewing the processes involved in the family life cycle (linking family structure and normative development), in symptom formation (linking family structure, developmental disruption, and dysfunction), and in symptom resolution (linking family structure, normative development, disrupted development, and treatment planning).

If I were reading this book, I might ask, "Why a book on the family life cycle? Family therapists can apply the plethora of literature on the individual life cycle to their work with families." But the collective experience of those teaching family therapy in many centers suggests otherwise, at least for the beginner. Students find that jumping from individual thinking to family thinking is difficult. Often our students' efforts to absorb the individual life cycle literature seems to slow acquisition of a family-oriented general framework.

Why does this happen? The problem stems from the fact that individual and family studies extract different *levels*[2] of data from the human condition. So it is unwise for us to assume that concepts derived from study at the one level will apply directly at the other. If we have assumed that individual-level concepts can serve as building blocks for family-level concepts, then we have asked too much of our students, requiring that they simultaneously acquire the concepts and accomplish the translation into the next higher level of organization. Since every living system possesses attributes that are not contained in any of its separate parts, the task is formidable indeed. Teachers of family therapy have repeatedly said that it makes better sense to begin with the broad strokes of the family in its normative and dysfunctional aspects, and then to proceed to more elemental paths, including readings on the individual life cycle. But we have always said this without having a text to give to our students that would support this line of inquiry.

My objectives in presenting this material are twofold. First, I want to communicate to the reader this system of ideas, which represents a paradigm for understanding family therapy done with a developmental emphasis. I expect that the student will be able to rapidly incorporate the developmental frame of reference into his or her own general framework of family therapy. Second, I expect that the paradigm will ease the task of acquiring material from the individual life cycle literature, by supporting the integration of those ideas with family-level developmental concepts.

A word about style. The paradigm is composed of statements that are axiomatic in the sense that they are not directly testable. It is preempirical. Although no defense is offered for this state of affairs, I call it to the reader's attention because, for the sake of exposition, the material is presented in very affirmative language. This mode of presentation might of itself seem to suggest that the material has been tested and verified to the point of representing true principles. Now, I have confidence in the utility of the paradigm by reason of its enabling influence on my own clinical work and its acceptability among my students during the past four years. But in no way do I mean to imply that it represents established scientific fact. I refer to each major proposition as a "Consideration" to underscore this point. I ask that the reader keep in mind the tentative nature of the paradigm, even when the language would seem to indicate that the author thinks otherwise.

DEFINITIONS

A *family* is a small social system made up of individuals related to each other by reason of strong reciprocal affections and loyalties, and compromising a permanent household (or cluster of households) that persists over years and decades. Members enter through birth, adoption, or marriage, and leave only by death.[3]

For our purposes, family also refers to any subdivision of this kind of social unit, which itself possesses these same attributes of affection, loyalty and durability of membership. So a married couple without children, a couple with several young children, three-generation units, units with a single parent and several children, and units evolved by remarriage from parts of previously existing units, are all families within our meaning of the word. Such terms as "couple," "nuclear family," "single-parent family," and "extended family" specify attributes of membership, but the units so designated are neither more nor less "families" by reason of such labeling.

Family therapy is any form of verbal-interactional treatment in which the therapist intends to alter one or more of the family unit's organizational properties, and in which the therapist conceives of such alteration as the central therapeutic action.

This definition is broad enough to include therapeutic work directed at changes in communication patterns, family structure, level of self-differentiation within the family, and more. However, family therapy so defined is fundamentally of a different order from all other forms of treatment. Family therapy is a therapy of social units. Unlike virtually all other forms of clinical intervention, which are directed at some aspect of individual functioning, family therapy changes the functioning of a whole family of individuals. To be sure, family-level changes impact on all members, leading to changes in personality structure. But these are indirect and secondary effects. Family therapy is first and foremost a therapy of transactions rather than of experiences.

Two disclaimers are required at this point. First, in speaking of family therapy, I do not intend to convey the impression that there is a unitary view of what it is or how it is done. Just as the past ten years has witnessed the appearance of life cycle literature, so also the field of family therapy has seen, in the same period, a very wide diversification of its theoretical base. There are now several distinct forms of family therapy, and it seems unlikely that any one of them will be shown to have greater overall validity than the others. The present work is to be regarded not as another kind of family therapy, but as a general frame of reference that can be applied whenever therapeutic attention is brought to the family, and in conjunction with a host of special techniques.

Second, family therapy is rarely practiced in pure form. In addition to focusing on the unit as an organization, most family therapists also focus on psychobiological, intrapsychic, and social network phenomena as they manifest themselves in members of the family. Circumscribed, individually-oriented interventions are regularly performed as a part of a broader plan to change the family. For our purposes here, when I speak of family therapy I am referring only to that aspect of the whole therapeutic effort that addresses the family as an organizational whole.

FIRST CONSIDERATION: PURPOSE

The purpose of the family is to provide a context that supports need attainment for all its individual members.

Purpose as an Attribute of Social Systems

Let us look briefly at purpose as a general attribute of all social systems.[4] The purpose of any social system is to evoke between its members a shared reality, a reality consisting of actions, experience, and intentions, and creating a product of some kind. That is to say, participation induces members to interact in a complementary manner, such that the system produces something of shared value.

Look, for example, at the school. The purpose of a school is to evoke between its members—teachers, students, administrators—an ambience that we might call a "learning context." Within the learning context one observes instructional interactions. The product of these interactions is increased competence in students.

I distinguish between purpose and motive. Motive is an attribute of individuals, whereas purpose is a property of social systems.[5] Motives orient a person's present time action toward the fulfillment of needs. Motives can be discovered by inquiring what the person wants to do, get, or accomplish, or alternatively it can be inferred from his or her behavior. Thus persons experiencing hunger are motivated by that experience to eat. They can tell us they are moved by hunger should we ask, and we can infer "moved by hunger" from their foraging and eating behavior.

In contrast, purpose orients a system of individuals interacting to fulfill multiple needs simultaneously. Since it is not a property of an individual, we cannot discover it simply from what individuals say about self, about each other, or even about the entire system. Nor can observation of one member, even over a prolonged period of time, or of all members for a short period of time, reveal purpose. Purpose can be inferred only after direct and extended observation of the whole system. Thus a child experiences hunger and communicates about that experience. Mother brings food and the child eats. The child is moved by hunger, mother by her distress at the child's distress. Each might describe the motives of self and other, and yet be unable to state the purpose of the social system of which they are members. Both are too close to the situation to notice that it is their membership in the family unit that brings them into proximity over time, thereby evoking powerful bonds of attachment between them. Neither comprehends that the unit is so constructed as to evoke in each motives complementary to those in the other, and then to permit interactions of need fulfillment between them. Finally, neither may be aware in any real sense that this arrangement and the affectional bonds, motives and interactions that emerge from it, all serve to promote the survival and development of both mother and child. A social system is purposeful regardless of the consciousness, intentionality, or motives of its members.

The Purpose of the Family

What of the family? What is its purpose? What does it produce? These are, of course, very large questions that no one has been able to satisfactorily answer in full. Notwithstanding the complexity of the issues, three observations coming from clinical experience with families point toward an answer. First, virtually all family units promote member-to-member interactions that are suffused with attachment behavior in its various forms. In healthy families, the ambience is nurturant, and the relationships are filled with love, caring, affection, and loyalty. In dysfunctional families, the relationships take on qualities like hate, guilt and retribution; the ambience is disjunctive. But in both healthy and dysfunctional families, the attachments are intense and their vicissitudes pervade the whole life of the family. Second, these interactions continue over whole lifetimes. Third, the outcome of these interactions is physical survival and personal development for all members. We can conclude, in a preliminary fashion, that the purpose of the family is to evoke between members sequences of affectional interaction sustained over lifetimes, thereby producing survival and development for all members.

I wish to emphasize that the family is oriented to need attainment in all its members. Clinical experience points to an emphasis on the entire membership of the family unit. There is never a time when any member's needs are completely met. Every person, regardless of age or role, continues to require that some primary needs be addressed in present time. The life cycle work of the past decade, delineating distinctive stages within adulthood, points to the inadequacy of previous models, which largely treated adulthood as a level-function, no-growth, and hence no-need phase of life.

Generally family therapists are aware of this fact. I think exposure to families on a day-to-day basis in clinical practice engenders a consciousness of the importance of attending to the needs of every family member. Often it is the family members who are oblivious to this fact. Parents in particular often require considerable consciousness raising in therapy before they are able to take their own needs as seriously as they do their children's needs.

I have asserted that the family unit is oriented around needs and their fulfillment. But all social systems fulfill needs, and many are organized to meet the needs of members. What, then, distinguishes the family from those other social systems? What is unique about the needs addressed within the family? I believe there are two properties that taken together, are completely unique to the family, and that distinguish it from all other types of organization.

First, membership in a particular family unit, once conferred through birth, adoption, or marriage, is virtually permanent, ending only at death. There are some other types of organization that grant permanent membership, but for most organizations, membership rules dictate routine means of termination. Two basic forms of termination can be recognized: diminished value of individual to organization, and diminished value of organization to individual. Regarding the first, organizations oriented to a task value instrumental capabilities. Members are regularly expelled either because of decreased ability to function for the organization, or because of a change in the instrumental priorities of the organization. As for the second, the needs of every person change and evolve over time. Individuals regularly drop their membership in an organization when the organization ceases to address present needs.

In contrast, family membership is not subject to expiration. In the life of the family, there is nothing like being fired or laid off. Family members do not quit or drop their membership. In clinical practice, of course, one often sees families in which a member is pemanently cut off from the rest of the family, and there is an occasional family that has disowned or banished a member, or in which someone has disappeared. But these are extreme actions indicating serious trouble. Disregarding the extremes, there is no routine form of termination of family membership other than death. (In fact, even death does not fully terminate membership: one's place in the family is actively sustained in the reveries and conversations of the surviving members).

The second property distinguishing the family from other social systems is that the relationships are principally affectional in nature. Like all other organizations, families place a high value on competence in instrumental role performance. But unlike all others, the family places a still higher value on attachment, caring, and personal loyalty. I believe clinical experience shows us again and again that the family that reverses these priorities is in trouble. I also think that task-oriented organizations that permit loyalty to come before competence are similarly in trouble.

So families are unique in permanence of membership and in the primacy of affectional relationships over task performance. What, then, are the needs that are addressed uniquely in the family unit? There are two fundamental orders of such needs:

(a) *Needs Pertinent to Survival.* The family unit is uniquely committed to the physical security of all members, hence to such needs as food and shelter.

(b) *Needs Pertinent to Development.* Additionally, the family is committed to the cognitive, emotional, and spiritual development of its members, and hence is committed to creating and sustaining the sense of being valued, the sense of being cared about, the sense of being accepted "as is," and the sense of permanence of affectional ties.[6] The family unit is, in this sense, a primary context for need-attainment. For the sake of clarity I will refer to these needs as *primary needs*, and say that the purpose of the family is primary need-attainment.

Corollary: The condition under which a family unit is able to address the developmental needs of its members is that survival needs are being adequately met.

We follow Maslow (16) in postulating a hierarchy of needs within the family. At any given moment, a family unit will address developmental needs of members only if survival needs are being actively and sufficiently met. A family in which even one member is experiencing a threat (or a presumed threat) to personal security automatically orients itself, as an organization, to handle that threat. That is, the unit's purpose shifts at that moment to survival, and it operates in a *homeostatic* mode. When no such threat or presumed threat exists, the family unit orients itself around the developmental requirements of members; its purpose shifts to growth, and it operates in a *heterogenetic*[7] mode. We will return to this hypothesis in interpreting dysfunctional behavior and the family's response to therapeutic intervention, especially the pheonomenon of resistance. It is sufficient for now to point out that actual physical survival is a condition of family therapy. Clinical experience generally indicates that no therapy can proceed when physical survival is immediately and substantively at issue. All verbal/psychological treatments, and family therapy is no exception, assume that the family unit is attending well enough to the security needs of its members. Certainly there are many families that come to clinical attention while survival is at issue, but the order of priorities intrinsic to the family demands that the clinician address such issues first, through the delivery of concrete services. Meaningful attention to developmental issues begins when the family unit is able to do a good enough job of meeting the survival/security needs of its membership.

SECOND CONSIDERATION: STRUCTURE

The structure of a family at a given point in its history corresponds to the combined and interacting primary needs of its members at that moment.

Patterned and Variable Sequences

Let us begin by clarifying the terms *element of structure* and *main structure* as they will be used in this chapter. The basic unit of family structure is a *patterned sequence of behaviors*, observable in the interaction between two or more members (11). A sequence of behaviors is patterned when there is an observable consistency, in the behaviors and in their temporal relationship to each other, from one instance of its enactment to another. Each patterned sequence of behaviors is an *element of structure*, or simply an *element*. The whole vast array of elements taken together comprise the family's *main strucure*. In speaking of the whole array over time, I will refer to ongoing main structure, or simply *ongoing structure*, to emphasize its enduring qualities. Thus, the family unit's ongoing (main) structure is made up, at a given moment in time, of a set of elements (of structure).

I wish to emphasize here that the concept of structure does not subsume all behaviors of family members. There are two important exclusions. First, family structure does not include those member behaviors that occur outside of the sphere of operation of the family and in relation to nonmembers. Thus, an interaction between a child and a teacher is not an element of family structure because it includes only one family member. (If the interaction is patterned, then it comprises an element of school structure). An interaction between a child, parent, and teacher, however, is an element of family structure (and of school structure), provided that it is patterned.

Second, family structure does not include single, one-of-a-kind interactions. For all the events that are patterned there are many more that are variable. They are first-and-only enactments. Variable sequences are not a part of family structure.

The distinction between patterned and variable sequences is very important. The current interest in family structure, and the general sensitivity of clinicians to observing patterns in interactions, is obscuring the fact that variable sequences are in the majority. Readers who are in doubt about this need only consider for a moment that interactional patterning is difficult for the untrained observer to detect. The difficulty exists precisely because a patterned sequence is like a needle in a haystack. It is mixed in with a large number of variable sequences.

Several examples of elements of structure may help to clarify these concepts. Phenomena that represent elements of structure include mutual greeting sequences, complaining-consoling sequences, reporting-praising and reporting-critiquing sequences, conflict-clarifying and conflict-resolving sequences, and many more. (A careful description of all elements comprising a single family unit's main structure at a given moment would take up several large volumes.)

All of this is a fairly widely accepted way of defining "structure" of social units, including families. What I wish to underscore here is the notion that, in the family, *structure evolves in the service of need-attainment*. I believe this is a neglected aspect in ideas commonly held by family therapists about the source of family structure. It is beyond the scope of this chapter to detail the other theories of the source of structure. Briefly, there are three types of theory:

(a) the "transgenerational," hypothesis (4): present time family structure is a function of that in the previous generation or generations;
(b) the "unit of socialization" hypothesis (21): family structure conforms to that of the wider society;
(c) the "vicissitudes of membership" hypothesis (23): structure arises from the particulars of age, sex, birth order, household composition, and so on.

But none of them permits easy linkage to concepts of development and change. How the linkage of structure to need attainment does accomplish this end will become apparent in the sections to follow.

Additive and Interactive Sequences

Family unit structure reflects both *additive* and *interactive* need-attainment sequences, but there is a premium placed on interactive sequences. Theoretically it is possible to devise a family unit in which each element of structure fulfills only one need of one member. The whole structure of the family would then be composed of a huge number of elements. And the amount of time needed to perform all elements one at a time, in linear fashion, would far exceed the total waking time available to the family. In short, although additive organization of family structure is possible, it is very impractical, and accounts for only a fraction of the total repertoire of structure.

In the real world of real families, interactive organization of structure prevails. Hence, each element fulfills several needs of several members in a simultaneous and reciprocal fashion. Imagine for a moment what takes place when a family of five sits down for dinner. Think about each member, and note that each one is fulfilling the basic survival need (intake of food), and several developmental needs such as acquiring information about the world; getting nurturance in the form of being listened to, or in the form of receiving reassurance for the day's frustrations; practice in socialization skills such as proper manners, taking turns with others, conflict resolution, influencing other members as a group; and giving nurturance to others by consoling their hurts, applauding their successes, and so on. Within the space of an hour, each member will have experienced satisfaction of several developmentally relevant primary needs. Furthermore, at many moments during the event, several members will have experienced need-attainment simultaneously. Simultaneity is an essential feature of interactive organization, and a constant feature of family unit structure.

A second aspect of interactive organization is reciprocity, i.e., the mutual reciprocal satisfaction of needs of two family members by and with each other. Reciprocal need fulfillment is manifest in parent-child, husband-wife, and sibling-sibling elements. For instance, in the example above, notice that while one member receives nurturance in the form of attention, consolation, or praise, another or several others are affirmed in their abilities to attend, console, or praise another. These latter members are attaining satisfaction of the universal need to experience oneself as caring for and about another person.

Simultaneous, mutual, and reciprocal need-attainment sequences are pragmatically the most important elements of family structure inasmuch as they permit frequent, repetitive, and extensive fulfillment of a wide range of primary needs in relatively short time spans. Family units that develop such elements are characterized as cohesive, and generate for their members a sense of resource sufficiency. Families that fail to do so are characterized as fragmented and typically generate among their members a sense of resource scarcity.

Homeostasis

We have thus far been emphasizing those aspects of structure that serve development. What about survival functions? Surely these aspects of the family's purpose shape family structure, and profoundly. Indeed, survival is the underlying generating principle for those aspects of family structure referred to as homeostasis. There are two reasons why these important aspects of structure will not be treated in detail here. First, the concept of homeostasis has received ample attention in recent years. Second, it is our contention that within the context of clinical work with families, the developmental aspects of the family's structure must take priority over its homeostatic elements. Clinicians must, of course, become familiar with and acquire an abiding respect for the power of homeostatic mechanisms. These mechanisms operate to protect the family unit from threats (real or apparent) to its survival. But I believe family therapy achieves its fullest potential when the therapist subordinates his or her interest in homeostasis to the more inclusive objective of rekindling developmental processes. By placing development ahead of homeostasis, the therapist counteracts the defect that is at the heart of family dysfunction, namely that development has become subordinated to homeostasis. We will return to this in discussing the theoretical basis for the concepts of dysfunction and treatment.

THIRD CONSIDERATION: SUFFICIENCY

A family is sufficient or good enough to the extent that it is matching specific elements of structure to specific needs.

Corollary: Matching of structure to need is an absolute condition of human development.

I want to discuss the corollary first. There is a general property of all living things that is salient to our discussion. I learned about it while raising plants and hamsters as a small boy. The idea is this: if you give a living thing what it needs, it grows itself up. That is, *under conditions of need-attainment,* growing up is something that the organism does for itself. The heart of the matter is that *need-attainment is the mainspring of development.* And despite our complexity, we human beings share this property with the rest of the living world. The implication for our notion of sufficiency is simply this: the task of the family is to create a resource, in the form of interpersonal enactments, that matches or meets a need. When the family performs this task, each member "grows itself up."

How can something so fundamental as the notion of need-attainment have received such short shrift among family therapists? Why is it not already and more broadly accepted in the theory of family therapy? I believe the answer lies in the fact that it is often impossible to observe a need in its nascent, unsatisfied form. This is partly due to the operations of the mind. As nature abhors a vacuum, the mind will not tolerate the sustained awareness of an unmet need. The need is quickly deleted, transformed, or filled in imagination. The result is that to the outside observer there may be no obvious indications of the need.

The answer also lies in the operations of the family. In a family functioning at sufficiency, members cue to actual evidence of need, as manifested in the behavior of other members. Through daily contact, family members become exquisitely sensitive to each other, and in time respond automatically, almost without recognizing what, in the actual behavior of the others, has triggered an enactment. This is especially true of needs addressed by structure. With frequent repetition, family members unwittingly train themselves to respond to the very earliest cues of need. In consequence, it is often difficult to actually capture or witness "structuralized" needs. They are met before ever becoming very obvious. If family members are responding subliminally to subtle cues, then it follows that an outside observer will very often be unable to pick out the triggering behavior at all. And having failed to observe the behavior, the observer does not posit the existence of a need.

The Good-Enough Family

The concept of the good-enough family is a direct extension of Winnicot's concept of the good-enough environment (27). I intend, however, a broader focus, highlighting the impact of persons other than mother, on the developmental welfare of each family member. Recent contributions to the study of father-child interactions, highlighting the importance of father even in very early childhood, are pertinent in this regard. Additionally, we include such concepts as good-enough grandparent, good-enough sibling, and good-enough aunt/uncle in our concept of the good-enough family. These are largely unexplored concepts at present. The reader is referred to Chapter 8 of this book for a discussion of grandparenting, and to Bank and Kahn (2) on brotherhood and sisterhood.

The good-enough child. The concept of the good-enough child is probably underappreciated and deserves separate emphasis. *The good-enough child is a child who is able to engage with parenting figures in a mutual and reciprocal fashion, learning behavioral sequences that simultaneously promote attainment of its own and its parenting figure's developmental needs.* Banham (1) asserted that the ability to nurture others begins in infancy. Bowlby (5) has detailed exquisitely the contributions of the child to the developing parent-child interactions. Tracing attachment behaviors from their emergence in earliest infancy, he emphasizes the importance of the child's role, describing the mother-child relationship as a partnership.

But such child-to-parent contributions are hardly limited to the child's infancy. They continue throughout the life of the parent. I will discuss these phenomena as they affect one particular developmental juncture, namely middle-aged parents vis-á-vis their young adult children. The reader is referred to his or her clinical work and own family experience for additional examples.

My own clinical experience bears out Bowen's (4) proposition that the young adult who maintains contact with the family of origin is better equipped for continuing development than is the young adult who breaks off such contact. Under conditions of continuing contact, the young person and the parents each maintain an awareness of one's own and the other's continuing needs, while learning to accept—and insist upon—diminishing involvement of each in the other's ongoing life projects. In consequence, the young person acquires the capacity to create his or her own life structures, expecting less direct structuring from the parent, while continuing to benefit from parental acknowledgement of autonomy and, in most cases, from parental counsel.[8] The parent in turn learns to take pleasure in the grown child's continuing development even though the need for present time parental input is decreasing. But additionally, both parent and grown child learn to see and acknowledge *in the parent* those pursuits that are keyed not to the offspring, but to the parent, e.g., new careers, mature avocations. Thus, in the *post-childrearing epoch*, through continuing substantive contact, both parent and offspring come to view self and other as able to take care of oneself, to take pleasure in autonomous (instead of mutual/reciprocal) accomplishments, and finally to affirm without guilt the development of new ties, new affections, and new loyalties. While not supplanting prior bonds, the new ties attain primacy over those to members of the family of origin.

In contrast, families in which such parent-offspring contact is not maintained are prone to a continuation of expectations of complete mutuality/reciprocity and enduring loyalty. These expectations, and the accompanying intolerance of divergence between what parent expects of grown child and what grown child is becoming, is a prime source of relational dysfunction for the young adult. However, it is also a source of trouble for the parents: when deprived of the opportunity to wean from complete to very partial reciprocity, and when not afforded the experience of adult relationships with grown children, the middle-aged adult continues to focus inappropriately on his or her role expectations as a parent, in a manner that stifles not only the child's, but also his or her own continuing development. The good-enough child will, by way of his or her autonomous, nonmutual reciprocal activities, press the middle-aged other to wean from active parenthood and enter the post–childrearing epoch.[9]

What of extra-familial resources? Certainly no family can meet, within itself, all primary developmental needs of all its members. So in what sense do the resources within the family determine its sufficiency? A need-attainment sequence begins with *recognition* and *validation* of a primary need by the family. Only when a need has been recognized and validated can a sequence come to life, leading to *fulfillment*. In the good-enough family the processes of recognition and validation emerge within the family, directly from the membership, and without external initiative. In contrast, fulfillment operations usually require an active interdependence between the family unit and its network.

So far I have been talking as if being "good-enough" were a global attribute of the family, as if a particular family unit were either good enough or not good enough. In point of fact sufficiency is a determination made over and over, on each of the thousands of need-attainment sequences that make up the family's structure. Each family clearly has its strengths (those needs that it readily recognizes, validates, and fulfills) and its weaknesses. In this sense all families are both good enough and not good enough. Furthermore, sufficiency is an evanescent property, dependent on the vicissitudes of life. So a family can be good enough in a particular area of function at one time in its life cycle, and not good enough in the same area at another time.

FOURTH CONSIDERATION: CHANGE

The appearance of a novel primary need in one member sets in motion a new need-attainment sequence, causes temporary destabilization of existing elements, and eventuates in a new ongoing structure in which the existing elements have undergone modification.

When one member attains a new level of individual maturation, alterations in family unit structure follow. These alterations are much more extensive than is generally realized. In point of fact, even very small, incremental developments can produce surprisingly widespread perturbations in family structure. Trace what happens when a child in an imaginary family of five learns to dress herself:

> The elements of structure attached to the old need (mother dresses child, and simultaneously engages in reciprocal nurturing by giving attention, physical contact, verbal repartee) drop away. Child and parent seek out new behavioral sequences that allow the child to dress herself, and create an alternative format for reciprocal nurturing. For example: child enters kitchen, announces, "Mommy, I dress myself!" Mother praises her, helps her into a chair, brings her food, and straightens her dress.

However, these alterations also trigger *trials of new behavior in other family members,* as adaptations to the new element of structure. Inevitably, conflict emerges between elements of structure that were previously well-integrated, but are now dyssynchronous. For example:

Instead of dressing her child, mother now goes directly to the kitchen, and has more time to attend to her husband and two boys. Husband gets fed faster, but now finds himself criticized for reading at breakfast. The boys have more time for verbal repartee with mother, but simultaneously have acquired an increase in maternal supervision of their play. Father, in turn, may object to mother's supervision, initiating a discordant interaction between husband and wife. And so on.

A series of such sequences unfolds as the family searches either by trial and error, or out of awareness, for a new structure through which the novel element is integrated into ongoing structure in such a way as to permit fulfillment of the new need, "girl experiences mastery of self-dressing," with a minimum of disruption to the fulfillment of ongoing needs of other members. The new structure is comprised of ongoing structure, plus the novel element, minus several (old) elements. But it also contains several (new) elements arising in adaptation. Notice that in order to accommodate a new need, the family is forced to make adjustments in its mode of operation in areas of functioning that are contiguous to the area in which the new need has emerged. The whole family, and not just one member, is touched by each development.

Processes of Change

What are the steps involved in integrating new elements into family structure under normal conditions? Based on clinical experience with families, I believe there are three phases in this process:

1. *Insertion.* A new need becomes manifest in need-signaling behaviors. The new need is *recognized* and *validated* by other family members, and behavioral sequences permitting its fulfillment are activated.
2. *Destabilization.* Perturbations occur as the new behavioral sequences are appended to ongoing structure, meshing with some preexisting elements, but clashing with others. The behavior of the family is momentarily more variable and more conflictual. Some needs go unmet. Experiences of frustration become more frequent. Uncertainty and anxiety appear.
3. *Resolution.* A compromise structure gradually takes shape. Trial sequences consisting of merged elements of new and of preexisting struc-

ture arise one after another, each an attempt at integration, and some more effective than others. One of these sequences is finally accepted as a permanent element of ongoing structure. Trial sequences fall away. Satisfaction and behavioral predictability increase. Uncertainty and anxiety abate.

These processes overlap so that, for any given insertion, interactions embodying destabilization and resolution are, for some period of time, taking place simultaneously.

Deletion. At the same time that this chain of events is unfolding, a parallel process occurs, through which now obsolete need-attainment sequences are removed from ongoing structure. This occurs because, generally, the newly emerging sequences negate, obviate, or preempt some elements previously salient to attainment of the relevant need. I wish to highlight the process of deletion because it makes two substantial contributions to the process of developmentally induced change.

First, it accounts for a major portion of the variability in family behavior during moments of change. Second, it is the source of the dominant affects associated with change. If inserting new elements evokes frustration, uncertainty, and anxiety, it is all the more true that deleting preempted elements, no matter how obsolete, gives rise to the experience of loss in its various forms—hurt, sadness, irritability, anger, etc. I am reminded of Steinbeck's observation, "Progress always looks like destruction." In work with families, it has become apparent that the experience of loss is a regular concomitant of therapeutically induced change.

This is not a new observation, of course, but it bears repeating here. Clinicians who work with families must cultivate a readiness to witness previously functional members becoming transiently symptomatic in response to recovery in the index patient. This phenomenon is extremely common, and occurs because recovery requires deletion of elements of structure that are highly valued by the newly symptomatic member. Families are usually surprised by these developments, and will often invoke homeostatic operations as means of "treating" the new symptoms. By approaching these symptoms as derivatives of the experience of loss, induced by therapeutic change, the therapist can minimize the risk that the family's thrust toward recovery will be halted unwittingly by homeostatic responses.

Attributes Required for Integration into Ongoing Structure

Every developmental step by a family member disrupts family structure. What are the limits on disruption, and the principles by which particular putative elements are selected over others, for inclusion into ongoing structure? Clinical experience suggests that there are three attributes that a putative element must possess if a family is to select and integrate it into ongoing structure:

1. *Goodness of fit.* The final new state of ongoing structure must permit good-enough need-attainment by all members. When a new element is introduced, perturbations within trial behavioral sequences continue until all members are again experiencing sufficient need-attainment to permit them to get on with their major life business.
2. *Maximal reciprocity.* The elements chosen for integration into ongoing structure are those that, taken with preexisting elements, permit the greatest number of fully reciprocal need-attainment sequences.
3. *Survival value.* No new behavioral sequence will be allowed that threatens the survival of any member or of the unit as a whole. Similarly, no element will be allowed which is *perceived* by members as threatening survival.

Each of these attributes is a criterion by which a family unit implicitly passes on the acceptability of any new or proposed element of structure. Putative elements must meet these criteria, much as applicants must meet admissions before being incorporated into an organization.

The Tempo of Change

Family units place a premium on rapid integration of new elements of structure. Once an element emerges that permits fulfillment of the new primary need, and that also meets the criteria detailed above, the family is very likely to absorb that element quickly and move on to other business, rather than continuing the search, looking for a better element. This preference for rapid integration serves two purposes. First, it prepares the family for subsequent developments. The work of structural change typically draws the family's attention to selected elements of structure, rendering the family temporarily insensitive to other incipient developments. Completion of that change permits the family's attention to move on to these other elements. Second, it minimizes the risk that the family will experience development as harmful. As I have pointed out earlier, virtually every development is somewhat disruptive of structure, and hence somewhat stress-inducing. But persistent structural perturbation is frankly dangerous. It sets up a state of turmoil within the family unit, leading eventually to sustained physiological arousal, with its concomitant increase in risk of physical illness, and sustained interpersonal conflict, with its associated risk of family unit disruption.

Orders of development.

Although every development disrupts family structure, it is readily apparent that some developments disrupt more than others. I believe all possible developments can be reliably divided into two basic categories: *First-order developments involve increments of mastery and adaptation,* a need to do something new (e.g., "Mommy, I dress myself!"). Several elements fall away (e.g., interactions revolving around the child's need to be dressed), as others take their place (e.g., those stemming from the child's need to dress herself), but the family's main structure is retained.

Since the change is an addition to existing states of self and family, members experience no substantive alteration in identity or self-concept. That is, there is no change in the prevailing consensual reality. And consequently, affects predominating in first-order developments are pride and satisfaction. Additionally, members note a generalized but transitory increase in frustration.

Second-order developments involve transformations of status and meaning, a need to be something new. The change is less in the performance than in the status of the performer, less in what is done and more in the meaning of the doings. In order to meet such needs, very basic attributes of the family unit must change. A member leaves or enters the family. Loyalties are realigned. Affections deepen or fade. Roles are reassigned. Ultimately the family's prior system of meaning gives way under the advance of a new shared reality. With the new system of meaning comes affirmation of a new status for the index member.

In the course of these changes, the family's main structure is substantially altered. But instead of deletions and additions in single elements, a whole new ensemble of behavioral sequences emerges. The new ensemble is a new *segment of structure,* with sequences supporting the index member's change of status.

The index member experiences a sense of discontinuity, of being a changed person in a changed family. Other members will share in the sense of strangeness, losing their sense of the predictability of events, and feeling that their usual sense of purposefulness is challenged.

Metamorphosis evokes powerful affects. As with first-order developments, there is a generalized increase in frustration. But in addition, affects such as sadness, despair, confusion, anxiety, panic, a sense of betrayal, rage, boredom, anomie, and loneliness are regularly in evidence. These affects derive from the experiences of emptiness, uncertainty, and aimlessness, all of which are in the ascendancy during second-order developments.

Let us clarify the contrast further. A first-order development requires additions to and deletions from structure, while the family's consensual reality is preserved. A second-order development calls for extensive revisions in consensual reality, with substantial secondary elaborations in structure.

Further, there are differences in time sense. Second-order developments occur infrequently, and the family experiences itself, in this regard, as stable. In contrast, first-order developments occur very frequently, and the family experiences itself, in this regard, as constantly in flux. Each perception is accurate: at the level of first-order phenomena, the family is continuously evolving, while at the level of second-order phenomena, it is episodically reformed.

Finally, how do the two orders of development relate to each other? Successful first-order developments may pave the way for later second-order developments. Each increment of competence takes a member toward the transition from child to adult status. Similarly, failed first-order developments may set the stage for failures in second-order development. These in turn give rise to symptoms.

In demarcating two orders of development, I have drawn heavily on the notions of first-order and second-order change presented by Watzlawick, Weakland, and Fisch (25), and on the notion of adult developmental epochs described by Levinson (14). And deliberately so. Merging them in the concept of orders of development will permit us to speak, in a single technical language, about the whole gamut of phenomena including incremental development, transformational development, symptom formation, and therapy.

FIFTH CONSIDERATION: THE FAMILY LIFE CYCLE

Second-order developments trigger periodic, all-encompassing transformations of meaning and structure that, taken with the periods of stability between them, make up the superstructure of the family's life cycle.

The family life cycle corresponds in its broad, overall shape to that of the individual life cycle. Specifically it is made up of a series of epochs, each epoch consisting of a "plateau" period and a "transistion" period. The plateaus are extended periods of relative structural stability. Such changes as do occur are limited to changes evoked by first-order developments. These are the times of change by accretion. In contrast, transitional periods are characterized by structural unpredictability. The dominant theme is change by transformation, and it occurs in response to second-order developments.

Each epoch is named for the principal second-order development that evokes the transformation. There is some question whether this form of designation represents the process accurately. However, it has become very common in the field, and I follow it here. There are two types of transformations ushering in developmental epochs in families:

1. *Normative events* are events with a distinctive second-order quality. They occur regularly in the vast majority of family units, arising directly from the procreative and childrearing functions. These include:

   a. marriage
   b. birth of child
   c. child enters school
   d. child enters adolescence
   e. child launched into adulthood
   f. birth of grandchild
   g. retirement
   h. senescence

2. *Paranormative events* are events that modify the normative momentum of the family unit. Each of these events occurs frequently but not universally. They are mediated by conflict, illness, extrinsic circumstances, or combinations of these, and include:

   a. miscarriage
   b. marital separation and divorce
   c. illness, disability, and death
   d. relocations of household
   e. changes in socioeconomic status
   f. extrinsic catastrophe with massive dislocation of the family unit

Among both normative and paranormative events, *the most pronounced effects occur with first events.* Subsequent events of the same type (e.g., second births, second household moves) are less likely to trigger major transformations of structure, and less likely to herald the advance of a new system of meaning. The family's response to subsequent events occurs along paradigmatic lines laid down by events in the life of the trailblazer member.

There are exceptions, of course. For instance, many families respond with special intensity to an event that, although a repeat in kind, is first-for-sex, or is a last event. In addition, there are certain events that have special meaning in each family unit. An example of such idiosyncratic meaning is the "Second Birth Syndrome," in which father becomes dysfunctional at the time of the birth of his second child. For some men it is the second child which signals definitive entry into manhood. Another example is the phenomenon that Berman has termed the "N-minus-one Syndrome" (3), in which a woman will have one less child than her mother had, to avoid identification with her mother. This woman will push her family to enter the next developmental epoch after the "N-minus-one" birth.

The work of Levinson (14) and Gould (9) has yielded a fresh and conceptually powerful emphasis on the idea that development of the self is a continuous and enduring process—which never stops being a major force—shaping and reshaping personality from birth to death. In applying this approach to family therapy two notions have arisen, one cross-sectional and the other longitudinal. Each serves as a bridge between concepts of adult development on the one hand, and of family systems theory on the other.

Developmental Interaction (DI) Effects

The cross-sectional notion is that *the developmental particulars of each family member are shaped by, and in turn shape, the particulars of each other member's development.* Each member's growth is a stimulus in present time for growth in each other member.

The DI effect constitutes a different order of influence from the simple present time behavioral interaction. From its inception, the theory of family therapy has detailed the impact of one member's behavior on another. But the impact of one member's *growth* (i.e., change in behavior) upon another member and upon family structure has received very little attention.

The impact of this notion on clinical work is still being assessed, but two spinoffs are already apparent. First, the concept presses the therapist to view all members of the family in nonpathological terms. Second-order developments are regarded as triggering emotional turmoil in healthy families, so it follows that families in therapy are playing out a largely normative process when their members respond adversely to therapeutically induced change. The therapist working within a developmental framework will view such responses as typical consequences of change, and not simply as the results of pathology.

Second, the concept provides an explanation for the common clinical observation that two members of a family initiate second-order developments more or less simultaneously. I have frequently observed middle-aged parents creating structures for the postparental epoch at the same time that a previously dysfunctional adult child is recovering. It is often impossible to determine from clinical observation which change came first. It seems increasingly plausible to me that DI effects are linked to one another in positive feedback loops, in the manner of Maruyama (15), Wender (26) and Hoffman (13). That is to say, growth in one member activates a developmental move in another, which in turn influences the first member, augmenting the initial change, and so on.

Multigenerational Transmission (MT) Effects

The longitudinal notion is that *the multigenerational history of a family unit is made up of an endless chain of influence linking the developmental experience of each generation to that of its immediate and distant ancestors.* Each member's life cycle unfolds in a context made up of all past life cycles, embodied in the family's present time structure. By making a kind of cognitive map of current enactments, each growing member internalizes this heritage, storing a behavioral program that will unfold in subsequent enactments over an ensuing lifetime. Interlocking sets of enactments and internalizations form the chain of influence, through which the member is deeply influenced by former lives.

Our knowledge of the ways in which MT effects operate at the level of the family is in a very primitive state. It is intuitively obvious that past lives exert their influence indirectly, inasmuch as the attitudes and behaviors of the dead are carried forward only in the internalizations and enactments of the living. And elements of structure can conceivably be stored and transmitted in the same manner. But we have not gone beyond these self-evident preliminaries to a detailed study of intermediate mechanisms. There is, of course, a major technical problem confronting us here, namely, that although the end of the chain is observable in present time enactments, earlier enactments are not subject to direct observation.

Notwithstanding this difficulty, the family consulting room provides beginnings for the study of mechanisms. Indirect evidence is obtained by focused historical inquiry: the therapist directs the family to seek past experiences that relate to a specific present time problem. The generic form of the inquiry is, "How do you suppose 'X' came to possess the 'Y' trait?" The recollections obtained permit the therapist to make inferences regarding the actual interpersonal context in which the problematic trait crystallized, and thereafter to model the relevant chain of enactments and internalizations in some detail.

For example, Israel Zwerling has created a unique documentary of MT effects and of the interviewing process which elicits the evidence, in a videotaped interview known only as "Solid Gold." In the interview,

An eighteen-year-old boy experiencing difficulty with school comes into therapy with his parents, complaining about his father's demands that he complete college. The parents regard the son as having a problem, and father does not initially regard his own expectations as disruptive (though son is clearly in pain). The interview turns on a crucial interchange between Dr. Z. and father, during which father's intense "college-bound" expectations for his son are suddenly cast in historical perspective. Father reveals that he was a college dropout, that his own father had been deeply disappointed by his decision to leave college, and that his father had himself failed to finish high school. None of these facts were known to son prior to the inquiry. It had never occurred to father to link them with his present time attitudes toward his son's education. And it had not occurred to the son to suppose that father's attitude had such real-life antecedents.

We come from this inquiry with evidence in the form of father's recollections of his relationship with his own father. We draw the inference that unfulfilled expectations are crucial intermediates of MT effects. The product of interactions between father and son is that son experiences himself as incomplete. When son turns father, he presses his son, cueing to his own sense of incompleteness rather than to the son's developmental needs. The product of these interactions is that son experiences himself as incomplete, and so on, into subsequent generations.

Clinical Implications of the Paradigm

We are finally in a position to examine the clinical implications of the family life cycle paradigm. In these concluding remarks I will address two questions. First, what can the paradigm contribute to a general theory of symptom formation? Second, what are the implications of the paradigm for the conduct of family therapy?

At this juncture I wish to underscore my earlier assertion that the paradigm delineates principles that encompass longitudinal phenomena only. So in these remarks, I will address only those aspects of symptom formation and family therapy that are outgrowths of and complications in longitudinal processes. In discussing *dysfunction,* my aim is to reveal what developmental processes have gone awry when symptoms appear, and not why a particular symptom appears rather than some other. And in discussing *therapy,* I will be concerned less with specifics of technique, and more with the implications of the developmental viewpoint for treatment planning.

SIXTH CONSIDERATION: SYMPTOM FORMATION

Symptoms appear in a member of a family when a second-order development is not met by an appropriate and sufficient transformation of ongoing structure.

Symptom and Dysfunction

Very often in discussions of symptom formation in families, no clear distinction is made between *intrapersonal* and *interpersonal* disturbances, and in consequence it is usually impossible to determine the organizational level which is under discussion. For our purposes here, we will use the following definitions:

1. A *symptom* is an undesirable and persisting (or persistently recurring) internal state. A symptom is an unwanted experience.
2. A *dysfunctional behavior* is a behavior that disrupts the ongoing structure of the particular family system in which it occurs. Dysfunctional behavior is behavior that interferes with reciprocal need attainment.
3. A *dysfunctional transaction* is a sequence of behaviors containing two or more dysfunctional behaviors.

As defined here, a symptom is experienced inside the symptomatic member, and is not directly observable by others. We infer its presence from the self-reports and the behavior of the symptomatic member.[10] Dysfunctional behaviors and dysfunctional transactions are observable as events between members.

The relationship between symptom and dysfunction is in the nature of a feedback loop. We can trace this relationship in the following description of the general case.

> A family member in a dysphoric state (let us call him the index member) cannot remain reciprocally related to other members. His behavior is keyed to relief of his own dysphoria, and not to their needs. As important needs of these others (the target members) go unmet, they too begin to experience dysphoria. As they seek to dissipate their own distress, they diminish their efforts to maintain reciprocity with the index member. Thus, symptom evokes dysfunction (in index member) evokes symptom evokes dysfunction (in target members), and so on. The net result is a chain of dysfunctional behaviors, i.e., a dysfunctional transaction.

This process seldom remains confined to transactions between index and target members. It spills secondarily into contiguous elements of structure, affecting target member behavior in relation to still other family members. With disruption of these elements, the impact of the index member's symptom is felt by more and more members, and in transactions increasingly remote from the initial site of dysfunction. The original disruption is repeated in kind, and dysfunction spreads to include even quite peripheral members.[11] When unchecked, these loops and their secondary elaborations grievously disrupt the family's capacity to sustain adequate sequences of need attainment among any of its members. The family becomes dysfunctional for all its members. It ceases to be a good-enough family. Developmental disruption ensues.

It will now be apparent how dysfunction and structure are related. When repeated often, dysfunctional transactions become elements of structure with the very same status as sequences of behavior emerging from more purely developmental sources. The same process of integration absorbs the dysfunctional transaction into the family's ongoing structure. The reader is encouraged to review the discussion of processes of change above, noting how the stages of Insertion, Destabilization, and Resolution apply to both normative and dysfunctional transactions.

Conditions of Symptom Formation

What is the source of this disruptive process in the family? What activates symptom formation? I believe that a careful examination of the conditions under which a symptom emerges will usually reveal that the family is failing to address a developmentally relevant need. Such a failure is a necessary condition of symptom formation. I believe that this is so even if the immediate precipitant was the onset of physical illness or extrinsic adversity. These events disrupt need-attainment sequences, and thereby disrupt normative development.[12] To my knowledge, Haley (10) was the first to link symptom formation and disruption of the family life cycle.

However, we might ask whether there is any difference, in the risk of symptom formation, between first-order and second-order developments. Does the family's failure to respond to a push for altered status carry the same pathogenic force as its failure to respond to an increment of mastery? I think not. A failure to address a first-order development, that is, a *first-order dysfunction,* can retard movement toward skill acquisition. But the affected member is often oblivious to the family's failure to respond. Sensing a deficit state, he or she shifts to another arena of action, in which the family does respond adequately. Even when the family's deficit leads to significant disappointment, the outcome is ultimately the same. Now, these processes may shape the course taken along developmental paths, and determine the specific profile of possibilities actualized in each member. However, no first-order dysfunction is significant enough in and of itself to produce the pervasive need frustration that drives true symptom formation. There is always some alternate path along which the member can move, some way to bridge the deficit, and hence to maintain developmental momentum. Since the impact of first-order dysfunction can, in this way, be circumscribed, the affective quality of first-order dysfunction is never more than moderate, transitory unrest.

In contrast, *second-order dysfunction* involves a deficit in aspects of development that, by their very nature, cannot be circumvented. Consider the difference in impact between denying a child access to a particular friend and denying access to all friends, or between ignoring a child's skill at the piano and ignoring all of the child's capabilities. These latter deficits block the emergence of extrafamilial attachments and the sense of basic competence, each of which is a crucial condition of separation/individuation. And while the deficits involved in first-order dysfunction can be bridged, those involved in second-order dysfunction cannot: it is impossible to be without friends and simultaneously develop significant extrafamilial attachments. There is no way to develop confidence in one's own capabilities while all one's efforts are viewed as manifestations of incompetence. There is no escape from the impact of second-order dysfunctions, no way around, and hence no way to sustain developmental momentum. As the forward thrust of development comes to a halt, self-respect on the part of the target member plummets, and significant psychic pain and suffering take up residence. Since there can be no attainment of the needs in question, the pain persists, evoking dysfunctional behavior in the index member. If this behavior persists, it eventually leads to the elaboration of dysfunctional transactions, which enter as elements into the ongoing structure of the family.

What of disturbance at the first order of development? Does the primacy of second-order developmental arrests in symptom formation mean that we can regard arrests at the first order as innocuous? Of course not. In addition to shaping the particular trajectories that family members follow as they develop, first-order deficits heavily influence the course that symptoms take once established. For example, among the best predictors of recovery following acute psychosis are premorbid personality and premorbid social adjustment, which roughly translate as the sum of social and cognitive skills that the individual possessed at the time symptoms emerged. The absence of good socialization skills—which is in part the result of first-order failures of development—does not by itself evoke psychotic symptoms, but may operate to decrease the likelihood of recovery after a psychotic episode.

SEVENTH CONSIDERATION: THERAPY

The goal of therapeutic intervention with a dysfunctional family is to restore its capacity to adequately support need-attainment in its members.

We have come full circle now. We began by establishing that the purpose of the family is to support the attainment of needs, especially developmental needs, in its members. We traced the connections between structure and development. And we advanced the notion that dysfunction is preceded by developmental arrest at the second order. Now we can begin to speak about treatment planning in these same terms.

Developmental Theory and the Medical Model

The notion that treatment might be oriented to the removal of barriers to the normative developmental process is unfortunately not commonly held in the field. I believe this is due in some measure to an overuse of the medical model. Because of its explanatory and predictive power, the orientation to disease has greatly influenced the approach to psychological problems. But it cannot serve as the sole basis of treatment planning. Key aspects of the clinical situation, emerging from nondisease processes, are not accounted for by the medical model. Normative phenomena are really of a different order from actual tissue damage and deranged function of physical systems.

Developmental theory has only begun to influence the thinking of clinicians in adult and family practice. Except for the work of Erikson (8) and Levinson (14), there has been very little work done toward the end of creating a comprehensive theoretical base for these nonpathological processes as they apply to clinical phenomena in adults. This is so despite the fact that developmental phenomena play such a large part in the theoretical base of child psychiatry.

All of this does not, of course, mean that we must now rid ourselves of the medical model as many contemporary spokesmen of the family view have advocated. The evidence for the contribution of actual tissue damage and deranged function of physical systems to many symptoms is compelling. The medical model has earned its place among paradigms precisely because it is useful in explaining behavior and in directing treatments. I believe the more productive position is to regard the medical model as representing one paradigm among paradigms that when taken together might provide the basis for a comprehensive theory of symptom formation.

Developmental Theory in Family Therapy

The developmental view advances the notion that therapy restores to the family the capacity to address the ongoing primary needs of its members. But how realistic is this goal in practice? How frequently do clinicians see families that are really restored to sufficiency? I think these questions must be asked for each family.

Let us imagine a spectrum of sufficiency ranging from good-enough families on one end through families with increasing degrees of insufficiency on the other. At a given point in time, a family might be placed on the spectrum by evaluating the extent to which it succeeds or fails in addressing needs of members. When we look at families in treatment, we will find a wide variation in the extent of movement, during treatment, along the spectrum. Some families move so far that, at some point in time, no further therapeutic attention is necessary. They continue on in life, doing a good-enough job at meeting needs of members. Other families appear to require some continuing therapeutic support system to maintain sufficiency. Finally, there is an occasional family that is so severely inadequate that no amount of therapy will restore it to sufficiency, even with a more or less permanent external support system.

To give order to the relation between sufficiency and therapy, I propose that we conceive of three levels of goal-attainment in developmentally oriented family therapy:

1. *Restoration.* Through the work of family therapy, the family recaptures its capacity to adequately promote need attainment in all its members. In this type of work we say that the family has fully recovered when there is consensus between family and therapist that the family is satisfying the criterion of sufficiency.

2. *Supplementation.* The family does not and is not expected to attain sufficiency in and of itself. The plan for treatment deliberately includes the creation of some more or less permanent attachment between the family and some external helping system. The external system (commonly a therapeutic reference group such as a multiple family group or a paratherapeutic group such as Alcoholics Anonymous, Overeaters Anonymous, Alanon) subserves functions that are crucial to the ongoing sufficiency of the family, and in this sense the family is only sufficient while it maintains semiautonomous status.

3. *Replacement.* A family viewed in terms of replacement is one for which too much is missing. Recalling the notion of the good-enough child, as well as those of the good-enough parent, good-enough sibling, etc., I suggest that some families find themselves in such deficient psychosocial networks, and/or have members with such severe psychobiological vulnerability, that they cannot operate at sufficiency even with extensive supplementation. These are not just fragmented families: they are extremely fragmented families. Typical replacement processes eventuate in one or more members of the family living in foster homes, in group living situations (halfway houses, communal apartments), or in institutions.

The notion of *levels of attainability* frees us to think of restoring developmental momentum as an overriding goal of family therapy. The goal of treatment becomes movement toward the highest attainable degree of sufficiency.

There is an apparent departure here from ideas about treatment goals advanced by theorists of the several schools of family therapy. I believe the contradiction is only apparent. Take for example the idea advanced by Minuchin (20), that realignment of the relational field within the family leads to symptom resolution, and that "the goal of family therapy is to re-structure the family." The paradigm advanced here is in fundamental agreement with Minuchin's conception regarding treatment goals, except that it requires the addition of the qualifying phrase, "in order to return to the family its capacity to support growth." Similarly, the goal of treatment espoused by Bowen (4), namely "the differentiation of a self," is not in con-flict with the paradigm, requiring the same qualifier to be linked fully with a developmental framework.

ACKNOWLEDGMENT

The author wishes to thank C. Christian Beels, Joel S. Feiner, and Ken-neth Porter for their valuable criticisms of the first draft.

NOTES

[1]In this chapter I use "the paradigm" to refer to the entire system of ideas. The paradigm offered is a system in that each component idea points to the others, and has been found to be necessary for the conceptual unity of the whole.

[2]See James Miller's application of general systems theory for an excellent discus-sion of the important concept of levels (18).

[3]See below for a discussion of the issue of membership and death.

[4]See J. Miller (19) for a discussion of the scientific validity of the concept of pur-pose and its differentiation from teleological explanation.

[5]I anticipate a possible objection here. Although the concept of motivation has a rich history in the study of the individual, it has quite legitimately had no place in the social sciences. Coming largely from a social science background, theoretical family therapy has taken the one-sided position that the concept is not necessary (to give an adequate account of transactional phenomena), and therefore might well be avoided. Scheff (22) quotes Max Weber regarding the value (for science) of deliber-ately one-sided constructions. But although such an approach serves science, it does not serve therapy. Faced with the complexity of the typical patient encounter, ther-apists are well advised to keep at their disposal a wide range of clinical concepts, and not just those favored by scientists looking at one facet of that complexity. So I include the concept of motivation, not on the grounds that it is necessary, but be-cause it is useful.

[6]The work of Cassel (6) points to the relevance of such experiences as being val-ued, cared about, and accepted to the prevention of physical illness. It is a small step to the importance of these experiences in promoting growth.

[7]Menninger et al. (17) spoke of *homeostasis* and *heterostasis,* but I think the latter term misses the point by not implying growth in the concept of differentiation.

[8]Cf. D. Levinson (14) on mentorship, which appears, as a natural process, to be an extension of such adult offspring-to-parent interactions.

[9]This line of reasoning suggests another corolary: it is *optimal* to have both a good-enough parent and a good-enough child, but it is *sufficient* to have one or the other in order for the family to successfully enter the post–childrearing epoch. I don't think there is any real evidence for this point of view. Yet it is compatible with two observations: exceptional children who, despite seemingly overwhelming circumstances, grow up into outstanding adults, and exceptional families that take very impaired children and turn them into productive citizens.

[10]*Symptomatic behavior* is the term most commonly used in the family therapy literature. With the definitions above in mind, we will regard symptomatic behavior as the behavior of one who is experiencing a symptom. However, from the point of view of the family, the crucial feature of behavior is not that it communicates distress, but that it is not congruent with ongoing need-attainment sequences. Hence the emphasis on the *dysfunctional* aspect of such behavior in the argument above.

[11]Enter family systems theory: the pathways along which these loops of symptom and dysfunction spread into the structure of the family are highly specific, governed by aspects of family structure and individual functioning, the principal mechanism of propagation being *triangulation*. But now we are moving well beyond the scope of this work. The reader is referred to Bowen (4) for a full explication of the concepts of family systems theory.

[12]It is now clear that for most behavioral phenomena, genetics and actual tissue damage create physical vulnerabilities that make important contributions to the form that symptoms take. However, the timing of symptom appearance is much more heavily influenced by the vicissitudes of development. There is a growing realization in our field that these two generic types of factors must be studied together, and that when they are studied together they show strong interactions. For a wide variety of clinical syndromes, each will cause a symptom to appear only in the presence of the other. And as neither is sufficient, we must conclude that each is a necessary condition of symptom formation.

REFERENCES

1. Banham, K. M., "The Development of Affectionate Behavior in Infancy," *Journal of Genetic Psychology* 76:283–89 (1950), also in Haimowitz, M.L. and Haimowitz, N. R. (eds.) *Human Development: Selected Readings* (New York: Crowell, 1960), pp. 206–212.
2. Bank, S., & Kahn, M. D., "Sisterhood-Brotherhood Is Powerful: Sibling Subsystems and Family Therapy," *Family Process* 14:311–37.
3. Berman, E. M., "Adult Developmental Stages and Marital Interaction," *Audio-Digest (Psychiatry)* 7:1 (1/16/78).
4. Bowen, M., Family Therapy in Clinical Practice (New York: Jason Aronson, 1978)
5. Bowlby, J., *Attachment and Loss,* Volume I: *Attachment,* (New York: Basic Books, 1969), especially Chapter 13.

6. Cassel, J. C., "Psychiatric Epidemiology," in Caplan, G. (ed.) *American Handbook of Psychiatry*: *Vol. II* (New York: Basic Books, 1973).
7. Duvall, E. M., *Family Development* (Philadelphia: Lippincott, 1962).
8. Erikson, E., *Identity and the Life Cycle* (New York: International Universities Press, 1959).
9. Gould, R. L., *Transformations: Growth and Change in Adult Life* (New York: Simon & Schuster, 1978).
10. Haley, J., *Uncommon Therapy: The Psychiatric Techniques of Milton H. Erickson, M.D.,* (New York: Norton, 1973), p. 42.
11. Haley, J., *Problem Solving Therapy* (San Francisco: Jossey-Bass, 1976), p. 105.
12. Hill, R., "The Developmental Approach to the Family Field of Study," in Christensen, H. T. (ed.) *Handbook of Marriage and the Family* (Chicago: Rand McNally, 1964), pp. 171-211.
13. Hoffman, L., "Deviation-Amplifying Processes in Natural Groups," in Haley, J. (ed.) *Changing Families* (New York: Grune & Stratton, 1971), pp. 285-311
14. Levinson, D. J. et al., *The Seasons of a Man's Life* (New York: Knopf, 1978).
15. Maruyama, M.' "The Second Cybernetics: Deviation-Amplifying Mutual Causal Processes," in Buckley, W. (ed.) *Modern Systems Research for the Behavioral Scientist* (Chicago: Aldine, 1968), pp. 304-312.
16. Maslow, A.H., *Motivation and Personality* (New York: Harper & Row, 1970).
17. Menninger, K., Mayman, M., & Pruyser, P., *The Vital Balance: The Life Process in Mental Health and Illness* (New York: Viking, 1963), pp. 83-86.
18. Miller, J., "Living Systems: Basic Concepts," in Gray, W., Duhl, F. J., & Rizzo, N. D., *General Systems Theory and Psychiatry* (Boston: Little, Brown & Co., 1969), pp. 88-108.
19. Miller, J., "Living Systems: Basic Concepts," in Gray, W., Duhl, F. J., & Rizzo, N. D., *General Systems Theory and Psychiatry* (Boston: Little, Brown & Co., 1969), pp. 123-25.
20. Minuchin, S., *Families and Family Therapy* (Cambridge: Harvard University Press, 1974).
21. Parsons, T., & Bales, R. F., *Family, Socialization and Interaction Process* (New York: Free Press, 1955).
22. Scheff, T. J., *Being Mentally Ill: A Sociological Theory* (Chicago: Aldine-Atherton, 1966), pp. 25-27.
23. Toman, W., *Family Constellation,* 2d ed. (New York: Springer, 1969).
24. von Bertalanffy, L., "General Systems Theory and Psychiatry—An Overview," in Gray, W., Duhl, F. J., & Rizzo, N. D., *General Systems Theory and Psychiatry* (Boston: Little, Brown & Co., 1969), pp. 33-46.
25. Watzlawick, P., Weakland, J. H., & Fisch, R., *Change: Principles of Problem Formation and Problem Resolution* (New York: Norton, 1974).
26. Wender, P., "Vicious and Virtuous Circles: The Role of Deviation Amplifying Feedback in the Origin and Perpetuation of Behavior," *Psychiatry* 31:309-324 (1968).
27. Winnicott, D. W., "Aggression in Relation to Emotional Development [1950-5]," in *Through Paediatrics to Psychoanalysis* (New York: Basic Books, 1975), pp. 213-14.

3
The Family Life Cycle and Discontinuous Change

Lynn Hoffman, A.C.S.W.
Ackerman Institute for Family Therapy

EVOLUTIONARY FEEDBACK

A recent paper by Dell and Goolishian examines the concept of "evolutionary feedback," a term developed by the physicist Prigogine, to describe a "basic, non-equilibrium ordering principle that governs the forming and unfolding of systems at all levels" (1). One can turn to Bateson's latest book, *Mind and Nature*, and find a similar description in Bateson's comparison between epigenesis and evolution:

> In contrast with epigenesis and tautology, which constitute the worlds of replication, there is the whole realm of creativity, art, learning and evolution, in which the ongoing processes of change *feed on the random*. The essence of epigenesis is predictable repetition; the essence of learning and evolution is exploration and change. (2)

Prigogine's concept of "order through fluctuation," as described by Dell, emphasizes not stability and homeostasis but the idea of discontinuous change:

> At any point in time, the system functions in a particular way with fluctuations around that point. This particular way of functioning has a range of stabil-

53

ity within which fluctuations are damped down and the system remains more or less unchanged. Should a fluctuation become amplified, however, it may exceed the existing range of stability and lead the entire system into a new dynamic range of functioning. An autocatalytic step or surge into positive feedback is needed to obtain such instability. (3)

Dell points out the tendency of systems thinkers in the field of family therapy to deny the epistemological revolution, of which the family movement is part, by using the language of linear causality in place of the very different language of circular causality espoused by Bateson. Dell particularly objects to the vulgar use of the idea of homeostasis. Family theorists have fallen prey to the mistaken notion that a family is like a homeostatic machine with a governor. Thus it is said that a "family needs a symptom," or a "symptom serves a homeostatic function in the family." To use this kind of language is to assume a dualism between one part of the system and another part. It is more correct to say that all parts are engaged in whatever ordering of constancy or change is in question, in an equal and coordinate fashion. To speak otherwise is to engage in what Bateson calls "chopping the ecology," or what Dell describes as a kind of "fuzzy systems animism."

What must be kept in mind is the continuous recursiveness of all circuits in complex systems. It is not valid to say that the parents are "using" the child's problems to keep them together. One could just as well say that the child is using the parents' overprotectiveness to keep him or her safely close to home. Or that without the child's problem, there would be no link between mother and father's mother. Or that a valued older child keeps being drawn back home because of it. Or that the problem child is the primary comforter of mother, and so forth. Dell uses analogies to biology and other sciences: "DNA is not a governor of biological systems; biological functions are regulated by the total system of DNA and cytoplasm" (4).

The most important point made by Dell is that one cannot use a cybernetic analogy based on a mechanical model of closed system feedback. Rather, one must realize that there is a different cybernetics of living systems which cannot be explained by the negative feedback view. This point is dramatized by the step-wise, sudden leaps to new integrations characteristic of such systems, which are not only unpredictable, but irreversible. The conceptual emphasis is on self-organizing processes that reach toward new evolutionary stages rather than on processes that tend toward equilibrium.

What makes this argument so crucial is that families that come in with distress in one or more members seem to be having difficulty with evolving; they are or seem *nonevolved*—"stuck" in an outmoded stage. Perhaps it is this stuckness that made the early version of the homeostatic model so convincing to therapists working with troubled families. In such families there is too much emphasis on maintaining equilibrium. For this reason, the task of therapy should be to make available to a group that is becoming more and more like a homeostatically controlled piece of machinery, the power inherent in all living systems: the ability to transcend the stuckness and move to a different stage.

Certainly, putting an evolutionary framework around our cybernetic analogy is in itself an evolutionary step forward in family theory and theory of change. For one thing, it fits the process we are trying to describe far better than the static model of error-activated feedback mechanisms does. For another, it affords a far more satisfying rationale for the success of some of the so-called "paradoxical" approaches to therapy, which produce rapid shifts in families or individuals. These shifts can take place with incredible suddenness, and indeed seem to be self-generated. To go further into this subject, let us turn to the ideas of another physicist who has written about discontinuous change, John Platt.

HIERARCHICAL GROWTH

One property that families share with other complex systems is that they do not change in a smooth, unbroken line but in discontinuous leaps. Platt, in an imaginative paper, speaks of a process physics where the emphasis is not on static structure but on what he calls a "flow hierarchy": forms that maintain a steady state even though matter, energy, and information are continually flowing through them (5). A bit of thought will convince the reader that families, too, are like waterfalls or cascades, where the many-tiered pattern of the generations persists as an overall structure, even though individuals pass through it as they are born, grow old, and die.

Platt argues that many natural systems are of this type, and that change, in such systems, occurs in a startling and sudden way. He cites falling in love, acts of creation, conversions, evolutionary leaps, reformations, or revolutions as examples, and says that when a system is conflicted or dysfunctional, this may not necessarily portend disaster but indicate that pressure toward a new and more complex integration is mounting.

Platt makes a useful distinction between three kinds of change that depend on the way the entity in question is organized. If it is externally designed, like a watch, then a change will have to be made by an outside agent, like the watchmaker who takes the watch apart and reassembles it. If it is internally designed, like a plant that contains a genetic blueprint, then only mutations of the gene pattern can produce a change.

Among living systems that follow a self-maintaining design, a great number present a third model for change. In such entities, change takes the form of a transformation, a sudden appearance of more functionally organized patterns that did not exist before. Platt calls this type of change "time emergence." One might think of a kaleidoscope, which keeps the same geometric pattern as the tube turned until all at once a small particle shifts in response to gravity and the whole pattern changes to an entirely new one. The most interesting feature of a kaleidoscope is that one can never go back.

This is consonant with the way systems, which have what Ashby calls "bimodal feedback mechanisms" or "homeostats," operate (6). They will remain stable as long as the environment around them does not change, or as long as internal elements within do not change; but if this happens, the system will either break down or respond by shifting to a new "setting" that will meet the demands of the new field. The change in the setting creates a discontinuity because the range of behaviors, the "grammar" for allowable activities, has changed. Thus, a set of completely different patterns, options, and possibilities emerges. It is usually organized more complexly than the previous one. But it, too, is rule governed and will not change again until new pressures from the field enforce a new leap.

The natural history of a leap or transformation is usually as follows. First, the patterns that have kept the system in a steady state relative to its environment begin to work badly. New conditions arise for which these patterns were not designed. Ad hoc solutions are tried and sometimes work, but usually have to be abandoned. Irritation grows over small but persisting difficulties. The accumulation of dissonance eventually forces the entire system over an edge, into a state of crisis, as the homeostatic tendency brings on ever-intensifying corrective sweeps that get out of control. The end point of what cybernetic engineers call a "runaway" is either that the system breaks down, creates a new way to monitor the same homeostasis, or else may spontaneously take a leap to an integration that will deal better with the changed field.

Families are notable examples of entities that change through leaps. The individuals making up a family are growing (at least partially) according to an internal biological design, but the larger groupings within the family, the subsystems and the generations, must endure major shifts in relation to each other. The task of the family is to produce and train new sets of humans to be independent, form new families, and repeat the process, as the old sets lose power, decline, and die. Family life is a multigenerational continual changing of the guard. And although this process is at times a smooth one, like the transitions of political parties in a democracy, it is more often fraught with danger and disruption. It is common knowledge now that most psychiatric symptoms (and many medical ones) cluster around these stress periods. One must assume from this evidence that most families do not leap to new integrations with ease, and that the "transformations" referred to by Platt are by no means self-assured. This brings us to an accumulation of research by sociologists and clinicians studying the family life cycle.

EXPECTABLE LIFE STAGE CRISES

The family life cycle was discovered by a circuitous route. Of major importance was the work of Erik Erikson, whose depiction of individual life stages, and the interplay between these stages and the shaping processes of social institutions, challenged the narrow focus of intrapsychic theories of development (7). At the same time, clinicians studying the responses of individuals to stress began to question the notion that there were some individuals who had better coping patterns or better "ego strengths" than others. One of the first pioneers in this area, Eric Lindemann, noticed that the difference between a normal and an abnormal grief reaction had to do with the overall makeup of the family network of the bereaved one, not with his or her coping mechanisms as shown by previous attempts to handle stress. Lindemann notes in his classic study of survivors and relatives of victims of the Coconut Grove fire that:

> Not infrequently the person who died represented a key person in a social system; his death was followed by disintegration of this social system and by a profound alteration of the living and social conditions for the bereaved (8).

The intensity of a grief reaction did not have to be tied in with a previous neurotic history, but with the type of loss for the person involved.

Not only a loss, it then appeared, but also the acquisition of new family members can trigger off an upset. A now classic study by Holmes and Rahe, who compiled a "Social Readjustment Rating Scale," indicated that there was no correlation between the negative perception of an event and the degree of stress that was attached to it (9). Out of a list of forty-three life stress events, rated by 394 subjects in terms of intensity and length of time necessary to accommodate to them, ten out of the top fourteen involved gaining or losing a family member. It is fascinating to realize that events with presumably positive meanings, like "marital reconciliation," ranked higher on the scale than ones with negative connotations, like "difficulties with sex."

The stress researchers began to realize that they were dealing with normal, expectable life stage crises that had to do with bodies entering and leaving the family system. Soon two terms were coined: crisis of accession (when somebody joined the family), and crisis of dismemberment (when somebody left or died). One could add to this list various shades of departures, or effects due to major shifts in roles: a child going to kindergarten might in some families produce a crisis, as would the retirement of the head of the household in others.

At the same time, pioneering family sociologists like Reuben Hill were studying the relationship between family life stages and their impact on individuals in the family (10). It is interesting that no consensus has ever been reached as to the number of stages; some researchers have listed up to twenty-four, and others have limited themselves to seven or eight. Generally, courtship, marriage, advent of young children, adolescence, leaving of the children, readjustment of the couple, and growing old and facing death are the major categories. Studies linking these periods to the production of symptoms of all kinds have justified a growing interest. Accompanying this interest has been a gradual realization that a symptom may not be a disturbance pertaining to an individual member, but a sign that a family is having trouble negotiating a transition.

In support of this idea, Haley has stated that pathological behaviors tend to surface at points in the family life cycle when the process of disengagement of one generation from another is prevented or held up (11). For instance, members of a family in which a child is mediating a parental conflict may seem to resist this person's departure, or even to block it. A symptom seems to be a compromise between staying and leaving; the child becomes incapacitated to a greater or lesser degree and never really leaves home, or may leave but may find it hard to negotiate the new molecule of marriage and may fall back, or else a child of the new marriage may have to serve as mediator in turn. One can often see the truth of the Biblical statement: "The fathers have eaten sour grapes and the teeth of the children are on edge." One frail, psychotic child can sometimes appear to be holding an entire kin network on his shoulders, like the key person in a family high-wire act, displaying incredible strength and impeccable sense of balance.

What we may now justifiably ask, is the mechanism that somehow prevents people in a family from making the leap to a new integration? The answer is suggested by the concept of another kind of shift, which occurs when a homeostatically regulated system is about to exceed its parameters or break. For this we shall have to turn to Ashby and his idea of step-mechanisms.

THE CONCEPT OF STEP-MECHANISMS

In *Design for a Brain*, Ashby describes four types of movement as an entity or a material passes from one state to another (12). A "full-function" moves in a progressive fashion without a finite interval of constancy between states, like a barometer. A "step-function" has intervals of constancy separated by discontinuous jumps, like a set of stairs. A "part-function" is like a step-function except that from one state to another the line is progressive, rather than instantaneous. A "null-function" indicates simply an absence of movement or change.

Here we will only be concerned with the step-function. Ashby comments on the fact that many step-functions occur in the natural world. He includes as examples the tendency of an elastic band to break when the proportion of pull versus length reaches a certain point; or a fuse to blow when the circuit is loaded beyond a certain number of amperes; or the sudden change that takes place when strong acid is added to an alkaline solution.

Looking at more complex entities, like machines, Ashby notices that some of their variables may exhibit a sudden shift in character whenever they reach a certain value that he calls a "critical state." In fact, he says, it is common for systems to show step-function changes whenever their variables are driven too far from some usual value. He goes on to speculate that it would be useful for a system to have at least one such element. A clear example is the wiring of a house for electricity. If there is no circuit breaker, the whole system will break down and have to be replaced. But the device of the circuit breaker means that only a fuse will blow, and when that is replaced (assuming that the overload has been corrected), the system will still be functioning. Ashby calls this type of arrangement a *step-mechanism.*

One difficulty with Ashby's ideas is that he is not really concerned with living systems at the group level and above. He is attempting to devise a cybernetic model that would account for the evolution and structure of the brain, and most of his examples are drawn from the worlds of biology, chemistry, and physics. One has to pull his ideas out of context to make them apply to social systems. However, without some notion similar to the step-mechanism, the sudden shifts in behavior one often sees in families with symptomatic members could never be explained.

Let us take the psychosomatic child whose symptom deflects parental conflict. In the case of a family, one of many essential variables is the relationship between members of the executive dyad, who are usually the parents. There are probably homeostatic arrangements regulating dimensions like closeness/distance, or balance of power, that limit the behaviors allowed in this dyad. Let us hypothesize that one of these sets of limits is constantly being overpassed. With a symmetrical couple, a slight advantage accruing to one party may provoke an escalation that, if not blocked, may end in violence or divorce. With a complementary couple, too much inequality may produce depression in the "low" spouse and concomitant anxiety in the "high" one. Whatever the nature of the plateau (and it is usually not a pure example of either model depicted above), there will be a "critical state" that represents some value beyond which the system may not go and remain intact.

At this point, different things can happen. A couple may have techniques for handling this threat, like a cooling-off period for an angry symmetrical couple, or a "good fight" for a distant complementary one. Another way would be for one of the spouses to develop a severe or chronic symptom, which again will prevent a split, though at a cost. However, it often happens that a third party, like a child, becomes drawn into the conflict. Once this happens, the child's discomfort grows while parental tensions lessen. Perhaps some minimal cue indicating parental conflict will trigger off anxiety in the child, who reacts with irritating behavior. At this point, one of the parents may start to attack him, while the other moves in to his defense. Caught in the tightening spiral, the child may start to respond with a physical symptom; he may show signs of an asthmatic attack and start to wheeze. This will cause the parents to stop their covert struggle and unite. A very real issue joins the couple, since the child's physical well-being is at stake. Their getting together, especially if it is accompanied by supportive behavior, allows the child's anxiety to diminish, even though the momentum of his physiological condition carries its own dangers.

In this example, one could say that warning signals are at work whenever a feedback chain reaches a critical state in a set of relationships. These signals prevent events from taking place that might endanger the system. For instance, the child's symptom is a warning signal that diverts the parents from having a fight.

But what if the child's discomfort proceeds to a level that is unacceptable, and a positive feedback chain develops that cannot be countered by the usual warning signals? Here we move up to the next level of homeostatic control, where the interface is not between the child and his parents, but between the family and the wider society. Ashby calls attention to the fact that:

> A common, though despised, property of every machine is that it may "break." In general, when a machine "breaks" the representative point has met some critical state, and the corresponding step-function has changed the value .... As is well known, almost any machine or physical system will break if its variables are driven far enough from their usual value (13).

It is possible that what is known in psychiatry as a "nervous breakdown" is similar in function to what Ashby is talking about. In a family, the individual's "breakdown" operates as a step-mechanism signaling the failure of the family's homeostatic mechanisms and necessitating the intervention of the larger system, the community. Here is where helpers in various guises come in, and an attempt is made to repair the broken element, the person.

However, to go back to the image of the electric circuit, as long as it continues to be overloaded, it will not do any good to fix or replace the fuse. Sometimes the problem is temporary; the overload has been due to a sudden plugging in of an extra appliance (a mother-in-law visiting, for instance), and once that is taken away, the system will return to normal. But often the change is permanent. Somebody has died, or there is a shift in family circumstances that is irreversible, or a maturation level has been reached by a family member that is built into the growth of every human being. Then the family must make a shift in its own behavioral responses to meet the new demands. Otherwise the person's symptomatic behavior may continue, or another problematic behavior may replace it. What we are dealing with, in a family with a troubled member, is a situation where the transformation needed to effect a leap to the next stage might threaten the family, through impairing some important member, or a subsystem.

Symptomatic displays could thus be thought of negatively as aborted transformations or positively as negotiations around the possibility of change. Antonio Gramsci, in *Prison Notebooks*, says: "The crisis consists precisely in the fact that the old is dying and the new cannot be born; in this interregnum a great variety of morbid symptoms appear" (14). A symptomatic redundancy is an arrangement which usually springs up to handle this interregnum between the old and the new. It represents a compromise between pressures for and against change. The symptom is only the most visible aspect of a connected flow of behaviors and acts as a primary irritant that both monitors the options for change, lest too rapid movement imperil someone in the family, but also keeps the necessity for change constantly alive. You then have a turmoil of behaviors that spiral rather than cycle around the possibility of a leap. Sometimes the leap is taken simply because of some accidental shift brought about by the spiral, which is always moving forward in time. Even if a very narrow, bunched-up spiral appears that chronically circles around some central point, it is still always shifting and is never without some potential for change.

The next question to consider is how to help the family to make a leap up, rather than to continue in this chronic spiral, and achieve a transformation to a new stage that will obviate the presence of symptoms or distress.

PARADOXICAL INJUNCTIONS AND THE "SWEAT-BOX"

Platt, as we saw, was stressing the positive—even extraordinary—capacity of living systems to achieve transformations that go beyond what could previously have been predicted or achieved, thus not only "saving the day" but pointing the way toward a new one. Ashby is looking at a different kind of shift, perhaps equally extraordinary, the ability of one element of a system to "break" if too much pressure for change has been introduced. In a family or other group, the shift to a symptomatic configuration saves the day, but it emphatically does *not* point the way to a new one. This may be seen as a nonevolution or failed leap, as it not only keeps the family from making a new integration, but seems to happen at the expense of one family member, who has often sentimentally been thought of as the "scapegoat" (a punctuation that is more apparent than real).

The question for therapy, when cast in this new light, then becomes: How does one interfere with a mechanism that ensures family stability (morphostasis) and instead help the family achieve a transformation that will represent a more complex integration (morphogenesis)? Here a discussion of what Rabkin has called "saltology" (from the Latin *saltus*, "to leap"), and which might more prosaically be called "leap theory," is in order. Also important in this connection is some extremely good thinking Rabkin has done in relating transformations or leaps to the appearance of that communicational oddity, the "paradoxical injunction."

Rabkin has presented a refreshing examination of the original double bind concept in a paper called "A Critique of the Clinical Use of the Double Bind" (15). This paper reclassifies most of the examples used by clinician-researchers to illustrate double binds, to wit: masked hostility, sarcasm, strategic deceit, or ordinary "damned-if-you-do, damned-if-you-don't" dilemmas.

A case can be made for equating one of these dilemmas, the paradoxical injunction, with the double bind. A paradoxical injunction is described as a statement that intrinsically contradicts itself unless teased apart into a "report" level and a "how this report is meant" level, the second level inclusive of the first. This is also how the researchers in Palo Alto thought of the double bind. The double bind, as we have seen, was associated with manifestations of irrational behavior such as schizophrenia.

However, the paradoxical injunction is a form of communication that all parents and all children (all superiors and all subordinates, for that matter) have become involved with at some time in their lives. But in few cases do these people literally go crazy. Of course, they often get upset. This, Rabkin argues, is because the paradoxical injunction is the best our poor language can do to suggest that a systems change is required.

Rabkin takes an example already used by clinicians to equate a paradoxical injunction with a double bind. The parent says to the child, at a point when the child is about to pass into the grey area of adolescence: "I insist you go to school because you enjoy the beauties of learning." (The Bateson group in Palo Alto used a similar example, a *New Yorker* cartoon where an employer is telling a baffled-looking employee: "But Jones, I don't want you to agree with me because I say so, but because you see it my way.") Rabkin then quotes Koestler on the process of creation: Before a creative leap can occur, says Koestler, all previous pathways must be blocked. It is only from the accumulated intensity of the stress that the pressure to take the leap will occur.

Seen in this light, the paradoxical injunction appears the communicational form most likely to create sufficient pressure for change. The paradoxical injunction of parent to adolescent child says, in effect, "I want you to be independent, but I want you to want that independently of my wanting that." What might be called, for want of a better term, a "simple bind" is set up. The receiver is directed to remain simultaneously in a symmetrical and a complementary relationship with the communicant. This being impossible, a leap must be taken to what Rabkin calls an "achievement," his word for the transformation or new integration spoken of by Platt.

The impossible situations set up by the Zen Master for the student are now understandable in this light. The whole point is for the student to become "equal" to the Master, but this cannot be done by an order from the Master, or from within the Master-student relationship at all. The student must somehow get the idea "on his own" that this is the course he must take. In line with this thinking, one should reserve the term "paradoxical injunction" or "simple bind" for the confusing directive that often appears as a harbinger of a leap into a new stage, and the term "double bind" for the very different message sequences that block this leap or imply unthinkable consequences should it occur.

The introduction of this concept of the *simple bind* solves many issues that have perplexed researchers and clinicians for years. For one thing, there is no longer the vexing question: If paradoxical communication is operating in art, fantasy, play, and most creative activity, how do we distinguish between that form of paradoxical communication which is associated with schizophrenic communication and that which is associated with the complex achievements of the artist or the prophet? For another, we have a way to explain the idea of the therapeutic double bind or counterparadox, which has been likened to homeopathic medicine: The cure resembles the disease. A therapeutic double bind might be rephrased as a reinstatement of the conditions of a simple bind, although this time within a different context: the relationship between the therapist and the client or family. The bind is reimposed, the period of confusion is gone through, the family or client takes the requisite leap, and the new integration is then rewarded, rather than invalidated or dismissed.

An example of this process is described by Bateson in an essay on "learning to learn" (16). Bateson had become interested in porpoises who had been trained to show "operant conditioning" to the public by exhibiting special behaviors, hearing a whistle, and then receiving fish. The porpoises possessed a considerable repertoire of these behaviors. Bateson realized that these animals, since they did not produce the same behavior every time, must have "learned to learn" how to produce a piece of conspicuous behavior. He asked to watch the process by which a porpoise was taught to do this, and in fact created an experimental situation in which to conduct his observations. First, the trainer rewarded the porpoise for a piece of conspicuous behavior, such as raising its head. The animal repeated this action several times, each time being rewarded with a fish. However, the next time the porpoise came in, no fish. The trainer waited for the animal to produce accidently another behavior—perhaps an annoyed tail flap—and then rewarded that. Each behavior was rewarded three times in the session in which it occurred, but not in the next. Rewards were only given when the porpoise again produced a piece of unusual behavior. This process was evidently so disturbing to both man and beast that the trainer kept breaking the rules to reinforce the creature at times that were not appropriate. The porpoise, in turn, began to act more and more agitated as attempts to gain a previously reinforced reward would prove futile, and began to exhibit behaviors that, in a human, would be called "psychotic."

Before the fifteenth session, however, a remarkable event took place. The porpoise rushed about the tank, acting intensely excited. When she came on for her performance, she put on an elaborate display of eight behaviors, three of which had never been noticed in this species before. Bateson makes the point that the disruption of habitual patterns of stimulus and response can be intensely upsetting to a creature if this disruption constantly puts the creature in the wrong in the context of an important relationship. He adds, however, that if the disruption and pain do not cause the animal to break down, the experience may produce a creative leap, a fact noted also by Wynne in an essay, "On the Anguish and Creative Passions of Not Escaping the Double Bind" (17).

This example reinforces the notion that a prerequisite for creative leaps in complex systems is a period of confusion accompanied by self-contradictory messages, inconsistencies, and above all, paradoxical injunctions: I command you to be independent; I want you to spontaneously love me; I order you to be the dominant one. These messages, with their threatening implications that the relationship between the communicants may be endangered if the change does not take place, can be called the "sweat-box." The "sweat-box," in mild or severe form, often seems to be necessary before morphogenetic or rule-setting change can take place, in a person, in a family, or in larger systems.

However, if and when a move in an appropriate direction is taken, there must be immediate confirmation and reward. The essence of the double bind is to disconfirm a leap once taken, to indicate that change is not desired, or to disqualify the whole event. In other words, the double bind is a simple bind that is continually imposed, and then continually lifted; pressure to change followed by injunctions not to change; a yes do, no don't kind of thing, which produces the disruption and pain that Bateson argued were untenable for humans and other creatures. Rabkin, carrying this idea further, argues that a paradoxical injunction that brings about a systems change followed by a paradoxical injunction to undo that systems change might well result in intense disorganization in the recipient of such messages.

Take the example of a mother caught in a struggle with an adolescent son. She wishes him to display more adult ("symmetrical") behavior. But if she enjoins him to do so, she is defining him as a child (a "complementary" relationship). There is no way out of this difficulty, as every exasperated parent, and resentful teenager knows, except for some shift whereby both find that they are relating more pleasantly and more as peers than as parent and child, at least in the area the struggle was about. This shift can take place suddenly, or a long back-and-forth battle may be required. But the necessary condition is that the shift in the setting governing their relationship happens "spontaneously," since for the mother to enforce it, or for the child to seize it, would merely reaffirm their previous situation.

If the parent giving the original paradoxical messages responds positively to an integration of the relationship at a more equal level, then this is a successful resolution of the dilemma. There has been no double bind, or at least no harmful one. But if at the moment the child and mother do reach that desired state, one of them, or someone else in the family, signals that this would be bad, or would be inadmissible by family rules, then you have the preconditions for a double bind. And then you have the appearance of symptoms embedded in cycles in which the pressure for change builds up, followed by injunctions against change, in endless sequence like a stuck record: the famous "game without end."

The way a simple bind might either become resolved or else turn into a symptom can be illustrated by the following hypothetical case.

Peter, thirteen, begins to sleep late in the morning and be late for school. His mother becomes tired of pushing him to get up and finally says, "Why do I always have to kick you out of bed to go to school? Act like a grown-up. You ought to want to go to school for the sake of your own future. Your father used to get up at six and run a paper route before he even got to school—in zero degree weather," etc., etc.

This is a bind (simple variety) because if the boy "acts like a grown-up" he is demonstrating a symmetrical relationship, but at the same time, if he does go to school, it is in response to his mother's demand, and his relationship to her is thereby defined as complementary. What he does do is to become even more reluctant to go to school. His mother oscillates between washing her hands of him and going after him, a process that only escalates the tension between them. The school calls, saying that the boy is beginning to cut whole days, putting on even more pressure. Father, who usually can sleep later than his son and hates to get up early, is constantly awakened by the morning fusses. Although he prefers to stay out of his wife's dealings with his son, he begins to protest. "Lay off the boy," he says to his wife. "You're only making things worse." He compares her to his father, who made his own adolescent years miserable by insisting that he get up and take the paper route. He says that he can sympathize with the boy. This statement brings out the latent split within most parenting dyads, the split between a permissive stance and an authoritarian stance. The mother, intensifying her position, says, "It's about time you stopped babying the boy." Father says, "It's about time you stopped nagging him." They end up shouting and get into a state of unresolved anger with each other. Peter draws the covers up over his head and succeeds again in not going to school.

This is the normal type of confusion a family faces when children become adolescent. It is usually resolved if the parents can overcome their differences and establish a united front. Perhaps adolescent rebellion serves not only to establish beginning independence for a child, but offers an issue that the parents, who by a natural process will one day be child-free again, can use to test out the nature and strength of the bond between them. It seems not to matter which way the parents go; the situation is solved if the parents can say: "It's your own life, mess it up and take the consequences," or "Get to school, and no more nonsense." Somehow, from this microtest of whether the parents are together enough to survive their son's eventual departure, he gets enough confirmation to really begin to leave, and the school issue drops away. The boy may find that an attractive female schoolmate waits at the same busstop. Suddenly it is no longer, "Why don't you get up and go to school?" but "Why aren't you ever at home any more?"

Here is the alternative scenario that might establish a symptom.

The boy does get up and go to school. He finds the aforesaid female, and he also regains his interest in studying (an unlikely story, but this remains a hypothetical case). However, father begins to feel more and more depressed. His work is not going well, and his ulcer begins to act up. It seems that this is the last child at home and the one who was closest to his father, all the more in that he has a rather domineering wife and chooses to remain distant from her rather than fight anything out openly. He has experienced a small feeling of elation when the boy defied his mother over not going to school in a way that was never possible for the father while growing up. The boy is very important to him. The mother, too, is strangely caught up in the fight she has with her son. It is as though he is able to stand up to her in a way that her husband never can, and although she is angry, she gains a kind of satisfaction from his assertiveness. With her husband, there is only shadowboxing; with her son, someone is really there.

At the same time, perhaps both are unconsciously aware that the boy's growing up means the emergence of many difficult issues between them, and the father's ulcer seems to signal that he will probably turn his feelings about these issues inward, rather than hazard an open conflict with his wife. A sense of ominous possibilities fills the air. The father eats little at night and complains about his ulcer. When he does, mother seems annoyed rather than sympathetic and says, "I'm sick of your always going on about your ulcer and never going to the doctor about it. I always have to push you to make an appointment. Why can't you take responsibility for your own problems, instead of making the whole family miserable?" The father becomes moody and quiet, and the son feels his own stomach tighten. He says, "I don't want any more supper," and starts to leave the table. Mother says, "You sit right there till we're all finished." The father says, "Let him go, for God's sake, do you have to run everybody's life like you run mine?" The evening ends with the boy in his room, depressed, father watching TV in silence, and mother furiously washing the dishes.

The next day, the boy complains that he has an attack of nausea and cannot go to school; in fact, he throws up. The parents fight about whether or not he should be made to go to school. In the end, he stays home. This is the beginning of a fine school phobia. Two months later, having tried everything and on the advice of the school, the parents start looking for a psychotherapist.

What the psychotherapist decides falls outside the lines of this story. But a contextual reading of the situation would be to perceive that the boy's appropriate behavior in going to school was not rewarded. Instead, intimations of catastrophe (parental discord, father's illness) erupted. The polarization of views, permissiveness versus punitive action, increased, with the boy's symptom now at the center, maintaining these parental behaviors and being maintained by them in a self-perpetuating loop. The bind most evidently cannot be resolved by a creative leap, such as the boy's falling in love (an involuntary act that could be seen as an appropriate response to a simple bind: "He" did not decide to go back to school; "falling in love" is what decided it). In fact, the hints of catastrophe redouble when the boy mentions that he has met a wonderful girl. The leap that should be made is invalidated by the *context*, not by any one villain: it is messages from the people who make up his context that covertly frame his eventual departure as a betrayal, a harmful thing, possibly even a murder. One can even see the school phobia turning into something more serious: The boy hears "voices" telling him that he is the son of God and is destined to save the world, and that his mission requires that he stay in his room and write a long book that describes his new understanding of the meaning of the universe.

To summarize, a theory of discontinuous change suggests that there will be no way to avoid the period of stress and disruption that is the prelude to what we have called a transformation. A common feature of these periods is the type of message known as the paradoxical injunction, or, using different terminology, a simple bind. The double bind only results when this simple bind is negated or denied, so that the necessary pressure for the transformation or leap cannot take place. In such a case, one might expect a symptom to arise that both expresses the family's need for change, and the prohibition against it. Since family structures are under most pressure to change at natural transition points, it is no surprise that most symptoms occur at these times. The knowledgeable clinician or student of family life will know that these behaviors are expectable concomitants of family change. He or she will seek to disrupt the homeostatic sequence that forms about a symptom, so that pressure for change will be allowed to build and a transformation will hopefully take place that makes the presence of a symptom unnecessary.

REFERENCES

1. Dell, P. and Goolishian H., "Order Through Fluctuation: An Evolutionary Epistemology For Human Systems," Paper presented at the Annual Scientific Meeting of the A.K. Rice Institute, Houston, Texas, March 1979.
2. Bateson, G., *Mind and Nature*, New York: Dutton, 1978, 47–8.
3. Dell and Goolishian, *op. cit.*, p. 10.
4. *Ibid.*, p. 13.
5. Platt, J., "Hierarchical Growth," *Bulletin of Atomic Scientists*, November, 1970.
6. Ashby, W. R., *Design for a Brain*, London: Chapman and Hall, Science Paperbacks, 1960.
7. Erikson, E., *Childhood and Society*, New York: Norton, 1963.
8. Lindemann, Eric, "Symptomatology and Management of Acute Grief, in Parad, H. J., and Caplan, G. (eds.), *Crisis Intervention: Selected Readings*, New York: Family Service Association of America, 1969, 18.
9. Holmes, T. H., and Rahe, R. H., "The Social Readjustment Rating Scale," *Journal of Psychosomatic Research*. 2, 213–18, 1967.
10. Hill, R. L., and Hansen, D. A., "The Identification of Conceptual Frameworks Utilized in Family Study," *Marriage and Family Living*. 22, 299–311, 1960.
11. Haley, J., "The Family Life Cycle," in *Uncommon Therapy: The Psychiatric Techniques of Milton Erickson, M. D.,* New York: Norton, 1973.
12. Ashby, *op. cit.*, pp. 87–89.
13. *Ibid.*, pp. 92–93.
14. Gramsci, Antonio, *Prison Notebooks*.
15. Rabkin, R., "A Critique of the Clinical Use of the Double Bind," in Sluzki, C. E., and Ransom, D. C. (eds.), *Double Bind: The Foundation of the Communicational Approach to the Family*, New York: Grune and Stratton, 1976.
16. Bateson, G., *Steps to an Ecology of Mind*, New York: Ballantine Books, 1972, 277.
17. Wynne, L., "On the Anguish and Creative Passions of Not Escaping the Double Bind," in Sluzki, C. and Ransom, D. (eds.), *Double Bind: The Communicational Approach to the Family*, New York: Grune and Stratton, 1976.

Part 2

Stages of
The Family Life Cycle

4

Between Families:
The Unattached Young Adult

Patricia H. Meyer, A.C.S.W.

Georgetown Family Center, Georgetown Medical School

INTRODUCTION

To evaluate a person at any period in his life without the broader perspective of his or her entire life cycle, is to view that person outside of context. This broader view provides for a kaleidoscope of human existence from birth to death—life phases through which everyone will pass—and gives the observer the means to compare, evaluate, and contrast one individual with another. At the same time, defining the physiological and emotional tasks that must be mastered in each phase provides a framework for understanding what developmental accomplishments are necessary for an individual to reach personal satisfaction even through the twilight of life.

During each life cycle phase, two separate processes are occurring. First, a person is building a foundation of self-knowledge with which to understand himself. At the same time, he or she is developing a foundation of knowledge about who (s)he is in relation to all other people with whom (s)he interacts.

The young adult has probably just completed one of the stormiest phases in the entire life cycle, for in adolescence it has been the task of the teenager to sufficiently sever emotional ties with parents in order to develop a separate emotional identity. This separate identity allows the adolescent to proceed toward becoming fully responsible for his or her life, launching a career, and being able to relate fully in an intimate way with a nonfamily member. While these will be the tasks addressed in this chapter, they will be discussed in light of the tasks that follow in the middle years as well.

In this chapter, young adult will include any unattached person between the ages of eighteen and thirty. Adults who are married and divorced by the

71

late twenties are included because there are a rising number of them in modern society and because the issues and tasks faced by such briefly married persons are consistent with, albeit more complicated than, those of never-married young adults.

The Young Adult in the 1970s

Before the specific tasks and associated problems of the young adult years can be examined, it seems necessary to discuss briefly the potential impact of the environment of the 1970s on the young adult struggling with the tasks that have long been associated with this particular phase of the life cycle.

While the social trends to be discussed represent different phenomena, they share the common characteristic of differing from the traditional pattern in which most young adults had previously been reared. In earlier times, children were routinely expected, conceived, and raised. Women rarely seriously engaged in a career. Working, if it occurred for women, was the result of financial necessity. However, primarily due to the resurgence of the women's movement in the late 1960s, the picture of an adult no longer necessarily includes a spouse or children and may include instead multiple marriages, postponement of marriage, living alone unmarried or divorced, or living in a one-to-one unit that is without marital bond.

The postponement of marriage. According to Glick (1976), during the past fifteen years more and more women under thirty years of age have been postponing marriage. Since 1970, the proportion of women who were still single at ages twenty to twenty-four has increased from 28% to 43%. Several factors may account for this change. First, during the Vietnam War large numbers of young men postponed marriage because of active military service or as a result of entering college to avoid being drafted. At the same time, growing numbers of young women were pursuing their own education, embarking on a career and experiencing financial and personal independence. A "marriage squeeze" was occurring because the number of women reaching the usual age of first marriage (eighteen to twenty-four) was 5% to 10% higher than the number of men who were at the usual age of first marriage (twenty to twenty-six). The effect of the post-World War II baby boom on the job market was an increase in competition for work in every type of employment. This pessimistic occupational picture created uncertainty for many about their ability to establish a home and provide for a family. Hence, some young adults have postponed commitment to this responsibility (Glick & Norton, 1976).

The large number of young adults divorcing in their twenties. Currently, the usual age when young adult women divorce is between twenty and twenty-four years of age. For young adult men, the usual age is between twenty-five and twenty-nine (Glick, 1976). The impact of the large number of divorces occurring in the early twenties can be seen in several shifts in society. Young adults have delayed their entrance into a first marriage, but have at the same time shortened the intervals between marriage, divorce, remarriage, and redivorce. Hence, for those who do marry, divorce, and remarry, the process has been compressed into a briefer span of years.

The large number of young adults living alone. During the years between 1970 and 1976, the rate of living alone among men rose faster than the rate of living alone among women. This is so because of the increase in the divorce rate of couples with children and the frequency with which custody is awarded to the mother. Hence, fathers often establish a household of one. Although 43% of all those who live alone are elderly persons, the number of young adults who choose to live alone is steadily increasing, particularly among well-educated young adults (Glick & Norton, 1976).

The large number of young adults living with an unrelated adult of the opposite sex. In 1977, 957,000 adults shared living quarters with an unrelated adult of the opposite sex. Four of five of the unmarried couples maintained households with only the one other person. A smaller number of couples, 204,000, had one or more children in the home as well. In general, data reveal that more nonmarital living-together situations now consist of a young man sharing living arrangements with a young woman than was true fifteen years ago, when large numbers of unmarried households included elderly and middle-aged women with a young man as tenant (Glick & Norton, 1976). The question that arises, of course, is whether these shifts represent progress and greater flexibility in society, or whether they indicate serious family and social problems. While a long-term evaluation of these trends must necessarily be suspended, it certainly seems clear that there are significant difficulties inherent in such widespread radical change. The usual generation gap is wider than ever, and young people traveling new pathways must do so without the support and guidance of the past.

MAJOR TASKS TO BE MASTERED BY THE YOUNG ADULT

In *The Person* (1968), Theodore Lidz discusses two principal developmental tasks encountered by the young adult, involving the most important decisions a person will make in a lifetime: occupational and marital choice.

According to Lidz (1968), occupational choice represents the selection of a way of life. It can also be viewed to some degree as a reflection of a person's overall emotional development, indicated by the type of occupation selected and the manner in which the decision is made. On one end of a spectrum of occupational choice would be people who, because of multiple personal problems, cannot seriously engage in an occupation; on the other end of the spectrum would be people who have had clear occupational direction from an early age and have followed that direction to completion. Between these extremes lie various approaches to work. There are those who cannot seem to hold a job because of lack of industry or embroilment in personality problems with supervisors. Others hold steady jobs but fail to perform well enough for satisfactory promotions. While some perform satisfactorily but work without direction or future goals, others work well but limit the effort they are willing to devote to work.

Excepting special circumstances such as physical handicap or social and economic discrimination or disadvantage, the interaction of family factors and the individual's personal drive, dedication, and discipline seem to determine occupational choice and achievement. The degree of emotional maturity a young adult has developed in the process of establishing his identity and separating from his family will most strongly determine whether he will pursue occupational choice on the basis of self-defined interest, or parental expectations. Those who fall in the latter category may simply comply with parental expectations regarding occupation, or reactively choose an occupation opposed by their parents. Other family factors that strongly influence the young adult's approach to work are the family attitudes regarding specific occupations, money, status; and their values concerning occupational effort, achievement, and satisfaction.

In the second major task of young adulthood, marital choice, the strongest factor at play will again be the degree of solid personal identity achieved in the process of separation from the family of origin. This sense of self, coupled with other family influences, will inform the young adult's conduct of intimate relationships. If (s)he has established a strong identity, (s)he will be able to relate fully to another while maintaining his or her own interests and pursuits. If (s)he has left his or her family still emotionally dependent and poorly defined, (s)he will tend either to withhold him or herself emotionally and not engage in intimate relationships with peers, or to fling him or herself into intense relationships, which, while they last, supercede his/her own personal pursuits. The marital choice of a dependent young adult is very likely to conform to, or be the opposite of, parents' wishes.

In the conduct of intimate relationships, the spectrum goes from those who maintain a marital relationship with one person for life, to those unable to engage in an intimate relationship at all. In between are those who marry and divorce; those who can maintain an intimate relationship as long as there is no marital commitment; and those unable to maintain an intimate relationship beyond a few years, months, or weeks.

In addition to the obvious impact of the parents' marriage on the young adult (s)he will also be influenced by such factors as the type of relationships (s)he has had with each parent, and by his/her experiences in the sibling subsystem.

THE FAMILY LIFE CYCLE:
GENERATIONAL INTERCONNECTEDNESS

A consistent theme of the family life cycle concept is the inter-connectedness that can be seen between generations. Such inter-connectedness can be divided into three separate categories: emotional, financial, and functional. At certain points in a family's life cycle, there may be generational connectedness in all three categories, while at other periods connectedness may include only one or two of the categories.

Emotional Interconnectedness

Of the three categories, emotional connectedness can be observed to be the most powerful force in a family and it is clearly the one which is continually in operation—albeit appearing inactive in some relationships. Emotional interconnectedness has to do with the impact of a parent generation upon its child generation. With a majority of individuals, a life course is grounded in a likeness or opposition to the life course of parents. In other words, an individual follows the behavioral patterns that he or she has experienced or establishes behavioral patterns opposite to those experienced in growing up. With this notion, a life course can be viewed as a reflection of an individual's emotional connection and reactivity to parents. For one young woman, becoming a university professor in a prestigious university was a major life goal that was connected to her sense of well-being and identity. She was the eldest child in her family and had taken on her father's high value of academia. She found it extremely difficult to separate her own view of the importance of such a position from that of her father. In an opposite situation, a woman raised in a family that valued occupations associated with substantial incomes and the materials that can be obtained from them, found herself attracted to and marrying a college graduate who selected a nonprofessional occupation for his life work. In this case, the selection of such a mate demonstrated that she had become independent of her family and its money "hangup." These individuals were unaware of the family's impact on their own life choices, yet the family theme had represented a major force in the decision making of their lives. Family influence can be seen in many other types of life decisions, as well as in choices about where to settle, life-style, political attitudes, and raising children, to name a few.

This is not to say that every life decision necessarily is connected to one's family of origin. Rather, life decisions that are emotional in nature may predictably evoke the emotional themes that a family of origin has had about the issue. The more intensely a family experienced an issue, the more likely it is to influence children's views.

Financial Interconnectedness

Parent generations provide financial support for children. Once children become late adolescents, variations will occur in the continuation of generational financial support. In some families, older adolescents split off from the parent generation, ending financial support and at times also active emotional or functional connectedness as well. In other families, parents continue financial support for several years while the young adult attempts to form a life direction or continues his/her education. In some families, the financial bond never really ends. Parents may actually finance the young adult's business, home, or life-style, or simply cover such items as insurance, hospitalizations, taxes, and other special expenses. At times parents may re-support their adult child over many years at crisis points such as when bankruptcy or divorce occurs.

The resolution of financial connectedness of the parent and child generations at this period may be reactivated later when the aging of the parent generation may increase the financial bonding between the generations, now flowing in the opposite direction, as illness and physical care requires finances that the aged parent may not have. The death of parents may also reactivate financial issues, as wills, which supposedly transfer money, are often noted instead for transferring emotional issues down the generations.

Financial connectedness between the generations may end abruptly as a child reaches late adolescence, may continue with the young adult in an undefined way, may be tied to the pursuance of specific educational or business attainments, or may never end at all.

In the evaluation of a family's financial connectedness, one criterion can be to determine whether financial connectedness of adult children to their parents appears based in reality (for example, pursuing professional education often precludes time to earn an income), or represents the inability or failure of the young adults to become stable income creators for themselves.

Functional Interconnectedness

In evaluating such generational connectedness, what is important is whether or not one generation is consistently dependent, or functions as if dependent, upon the other generation in order to get by. As with the other two categories, functional interconnectedness is the responsibility of the parent generation during the childhood years for health care, extracurricular activity participation, and the like. As with financial connectedness, once children reach late adolescence, functional connectedness may end, never to reactivate. But functional connectedness may occur at various specific occasions in the family life cycle, as for instance when grandmothers lend assistance in cooking and child care when a new baby is born.

The change in generational interconnectedness that occurs as a member of the child generation moves into young adulthood can be particularly confusing to parent and young adult alike. The degree to which young adults have mastered the tasks of adolescence in the formation of their own identities will determine how dramatic changes in family relationships will be at this point. This adjustment will be influenced as well by the response of the parent generation to the changes in their offspring and the personal impact that such change has on each parent.

With young adults who have achieved little solid identity, remaining instead dependent on parents either covertly (as in a rebelliousness that is paraded as independence) or more overtly (by compliance with parental direction which precluded the formation of a separate self), the transition into young adulthood can be tumultuous indeed. Society has established an expectation that young adults who have achieved majority age be fully responsible for themselves in society, from obeying the laws to paying their bills and the like. Yet individuals who have not mastered the development of a solid identity may well not have the emotional ability to establish and maintain a job or relationship as is required in the formation of a marital dyad. Hence, in some instances, society expects one type of functioning from its young citizens, and parents observe quite another. One of the factors which contributes to the incomplete development of young adults in the first place is the parents' overattachment and overfunctioning. Frequently, the very process that created the problem is repeated as the parents attempt to "cushion" the irresponsibility of their adult children. Such a cushion might include supporting young adults financially, purchasing for them the items they have not worked to earn, or bailing them out of crises which they have created—with a creditor, a landlord, a spouse, or others.

Individuals who fall into the category of dependent functioning tend to respond in one of two general ways. One group exhibits smooth relations with the parent generation. Individuals go out in society only to cycle home each time the latest venture ends in failure. The other group appears to respond directly to the felt dependency and to rage at the parents upon whom they are so dependent. Such individuals may experience a kind of hatred for their parents, though they cannot exist without them.

It is with young adults who have partially formed an independent existence that the greatest confusion may occur. A parent knows, in general, what to expect from either a highly dependent or highly independent young adult. With a young adult who has partially established independence, parents cannot necessarily predict which part of his or her functioning will be operative at one point or another.

When a young adult has become relatively independent, the relationship between the generations can be expected to be less chaotic or confusing. Such an individual will be busy taking responsibility for his/her own development emotionally, functionally, and financially, leaving the parents little room to question whether their assistance is required. In such families, parents are not personally threatened by having a child separate into an independent adult. If one generation or the other becomes anxious and attempts to reestablish greater dependency on the other, little regression will usually occur because the responding generation will protect and maintain the developed separation.

Family relationships and family constellation are factors in how well young adults handle the transition to adulthood. Both Murray Bowen and Walter Toman have studied and written in depth about the nuclear family. Bowen (1978) emphasized the unique emotional relationship that every child has with his or her mother and father and the varying levels of emotional attachment of parent to child. Toman (1976) emphasizes the impact of specific birth order positions and the impact of each on a family member's relationships with brothers and sisters as well as with parents.

Every child is born into an emotional position within the family that is predetermined by multiple factors bearing little connection to the new infant who has gained ownership of them. The factors governing a child's potential specialness to the family include, for example, stressful events occurring in the family at the time of the birth, the basic levels of emotional maturity of each parent, and the manner in which the marital couple handle their emotional relationship to maintain equilibrium. The interrelationship of such factors, as well as nodal events throughout the family life cycle, determines to what degree a particular child will be able to achieve emotional independence from his parents during young adulthood.

In addition to the impact of the general level of functioning of a family unit on an emerging young adult, the age of the parents and the traumatic events that may be occurring in their lives at this time are important as well.

Whatever the relationship with a child generation, functional interconnectedness will be reactivated at the time when an aged parent generation can no longer do for themselves.

Life Cycle Events in the Parent Generation

Parents with an emerging young adult may range in age from the mid- to late-thirties to mid- to late- sixties. Whatever the exact age, the middle-age years include multiple transitions and adjustments to which family members must respond. Many of these transitions involve losses and are of a negative nature.

Many couples maintain marital equilibrium through parenting. Finding marital tensions threatening or difficult to face, a couple may discover that relating to each other through parenting stabilizes the marriage. The process can occur in several ways. A spouse experiencing emotional dissatisfaction in the marriage may seek to find greater satisfaction in a parent/child relationship, automatically taking some built-in pressure off the marital relationship. For many couples, such an arrangement can work successfully until children begin to separate from the family unit. When separation of children does occur, the early unresolved marital tensions are reactivated. For some couples, this reoccurrence can threaten marital survival. The young adult struggling to achieve independence from parents who have maintained their equilibrium through an emotional focus on parenting may have great difficulty with this task. The young adult's very achievement of successful development may directly threaten the marital future of the parents. At times young adults give in to parental reactions and never do emerge into independent adult functioning.

In other families, parents who havs achieved significant satisfaction through the parenting process may encounter yet another problem. If the parents have gained an enhanced sense of self by "doing for" their children over the years, as opposed to "relating to" children who have learned to do for themselves, the task required when their children move to young adulthood can be very anxiety producing. Such parents may experience confusion and uncertainty in establishing a way to relate to a child who no longer seeks or needs their assistance. Moves of the young adult toward emotional independence can be mistakenly taken personally rather than as a positive achievement of the emerging adult member. Parental anxiety may then negatively affect the separation of their young adult child.

Should the young adult be the youngest of the children, his or her successful entrance into adulthood would signal an end to parenting. This "empty nest" phenomenon, while related to the preceding two factors, has its own special intensity and bears mention as a separate factor.

Retirement in the parent generation may be yet another factor influencing a family around the time of a family member's emergence into adulthood. Whether retirement represents a planned change or an unplanned one as a result of physical illness or a lessening of job competence, the termination usually involves confusion, uncertainty, and fear about what the transition may mean to the quality and meaning of life. For a parent whose own sense of worth and well-being have been interwoven over the years with job achievements and job status, the end of a career can be very threatening. At just this point, the young adult's attempts to establish a career may be quite threatening to the parent, which in turn may increase the level of anxiety with which the young adult approaches this developmental task.

Physiological deterioration or illness in one parent or both can be expected to create substantial anxiety throughout the family. Should the physical problem be in one parent, the other parent's anxiety may result in enhanced attachment and need for the continued participation of the young adult as a part of the family unit. The young adult struggling to build a solid, separate identity in these circumstances will encounter multiple emotional obstacles, which may limit the achievement of independence from the family.

The final factor has to do with parents who encountered traumas in their own childhood. Such traumas might include early death of parents or other significant losses, parental alcoholism, child abuse, or intense negative experiences with one or both parents. The impact of negative growing-up experiences can cause some individuals to attempt to compensate—to "right the wrong"—with their own children. Such a parent seeks to assure that his or her children will not experience what the parent has experienced, and in this effort frequently will go to the opposite extreme. If as a child, (s)he knew poverty, the theme of compensation might be to provide his or her own children with everything wished for. The emergence of a young adult in a family with a parental compensation theme may create reactivation of parental anxiety as no plan of the young adult's will seem sufficient to provide the sought after emotional security. The requirements for achieving responsible independence in such a family may be nearly unreachable.

While each of the parental factors discussed represent different life situations, there are certain similarities. Each situation represents a transition in the parent generation which could be expected to raise the level of family anxiety. The impact of such anxiety would include possible guilt in the emerging young adult for the efforts to become independent from the family unit that is now in stress, a reaction of wanting to do for the parent generation as a result of the heightened family anxiety, a loss of clarity about oneself resulting from the heightened emotion, and so on. The task of developing solid independence from one's family is substantial enough when it does not occur in concert with life stress and trauma in the parent generation. When the attempt does occur simultaneously with high parental anxiety, efforts to emerge into adulthood may be hampered or limited entirely.

Life Cycle Events in the Grandparent Generation

Stressful occurrences to grandparents may not directly affect an emerging adult. However, anxiety that builds in the parent generation regarding grandparents will indeed be transmitted to the third generation.

If grandparents already have died, the sense of loss in the departure of an adult child from the family unit may be exacerbated. It is as if the emotional significance of children is increased as a function of the absence of parents. Hence, greater emotional attachment by parents increases the task for the emerging adult.

Parental anxiety can be expected to be heightened in families where a grandparent is dying. The forthcoming death will stimulate anxiety in parents and the push for togetherness as well. Hence, efforts toward independence by the young adult may be thwarted or resisted in such circumstances.

If the grandparents are still alive and functioning but are in failing health, family anxiety may be quite high. Such deterioration may necessitate a reactivation of generational interconnectedness of an emotional, functional, or financial nature. Transactions of this kind between parents and grandparents may stimulate confusion, resentment, and other forms of anxiety that will make the task of defining and separating more difficult for the young adult.

The most significant determinant of the degree to which any of these circumstances will impinge on the youngest generation will be the emotional maturity of parents as reflected in their own accomplishment of their family life cycle tasks. Thus, the more mature the parents, the higher the stress can go before they will respond with high anxiety. It would seem, then, that the success of the young adult's efforts to develop independence will relate directly to the success of his or her parents in achieving independence from *their* parent generation. Hence, what appears to be a developmental achievement in an individual can be seen in fact as an achievement interwoven with those achievements of earlier generations.

A CLINICAL FOCUS ON THE YOUNG ADULT

I would like to outline six principles I follow in working with clients at this phase of the family life cycle, describe five phases of clinical work, and give a clinical example as illustration.

Clinical Principles

While there are multiple clinical principles that are the basis for my work with clients, six have been chosen for discussion here.

1. The objective of "solid" change. From the initial phone conversation until the final session, a major focus will be on the objective facts about the life and presenting problem of a client. Such an approach comes from the belief that factual understanding of life's realities may be the bridge to change.

To focus on the feeling state of the client—bringing forth the active emotion interwoven with the presenting problem—may bring some relief for the client. However, doing so may also tend to increase the client's emotional reactivity, which will ultimately limit his or her capacity to change. That a client is uncomfortable and anxious at the start of therapy or coaching and will remain so for a good while is accepted as a given, as is the belief that resolution of life problems comes not from shifts that bring emotional relief but from objective clarity on which to base decisions for solid change.

There are basic differences between shifts in functioning and solid change. A functional shift is usually based on reaction to a perceived functional pattern and as such is often the opposite of the original pattern. Such would be the case with a parent who went from an overpermissive stance with a child to an overauthoritarian stance. The clue would be the extreme fluctuation from one end of a spectrum to another. Functional shifts can occur simply as the result of lowered or increased anxiety rather than as a result of a solid change in a person's overall emotional state. Change can be measured by observing whether under increased levels of anxiety the person can maintain the new capacity to define and hold to a course of behavior. Solid change has to do with a new clarity of personal belief—an ability to observe, define oneself, and act accordingly—grounded entirely within the person, neither based upon nor influenced by any important relationship. It provides individuals with the capacity to maintain a defined course, while being in ongoing contact with others, in spite of their emotional reactivity and in spite of high levels of anxiety about doing so. People experiencing a functional shift may find themselves wishing to explain or defend their new behavior to important others. Those achieving change can proceed on course without relationship support from others. The final difference to be discussed is the technique orientation often associated with a functional shift. A technique orientation has a short time frame and a specific result in mind, and focuses on success and failure. Solid change has to do with individuals acting in accordance with their own principles, which are followed regardless of whether they "work" in altering behavior in another.

2. *Generational neutrality*. The generational entanglement associated with a floundering young adult contains a repertoire of traps into which a therapist or coach can fall. The client can be expected to have an emotionally charged stance in regard to parents that combines, for instance, guilt for not functioning better, blame of parents for the client's dilemma, and anger at parents for not presenting a solution to the problem. Such feelings create an environment in therapy in which the young adult can be expected to react should the coach appear to side with either generation, and can govern how successful coaching may be. An indication by the therapist that the parent generation has created the young adult's dilemma can create a

comfortable sense of alliance with the therapist, but may well limit any movement in the client toward an objective view of the emotional system in which client and parents have grown up, as well as any significant focus on the ways in which the client has contributed to the current situation.

If, on the other hand, the therapist appears to blame the client and to dismiss the contribution of the parents to current situations, the client may feel defensive or misunderstood, and terminate coaching. Hence, the objective is to maintain absolute neutrality, neither blaming nor siding with either generation, and being able to acknowledge the client's emotional discomfort, while focusing on an objective view of the broader picture.

3. *Neutrality in the outcome.* Monitoring one's clinical practice for the tendency to become caught in wishing for one outcome or another for a client can last the lifetime. Such a tendency can occur with any client around any problem, be it a decision for divorce, for marriage or remarriage, for adoption of a child, etc. With a floundering young adult client, this common problem may be exacerbated by the emotional issues that are part and parcel of the phase. The young adult may remain entangled in struggles with authority and the paradox of needing and wanting parental approval while needing and wanting to demonstrate independence from parental approval.

What is important is to be aware of this potential snag and to be able to work freely with the client without communicating that the coach will be affected one way or another by the client's ultimate outcome—launching into adulthood or remaining entangled in unresolved adolescent themes. Only then can the coach be sure that the client has not accepted a challenge to change in order to gain the approval of the coach, which would certainly limit the degree of change achieved.

4. *A context for the parent generation.* One of the strongest themes in floundering young adults is the belief that the current situation has been created as a result of defects and failures in the parents. Such a view is understandable in an individual who is aware that somehow he or she has not been able to successfully move to adulthood as have peers and siblings. Rather than feel guilty about this, the young adult may have a tendency to place blame on the parent generation.

The force of angry blame can be a strong obstacle to progress in the young adult. Hence, it becomes important to assist a client in evaluating the behaviors of the parent generation in terms of the context in which they occurred. In other words, what were the life experiences of parents that influenced their patterns of behavior? This involves an effort to replace blame with new awareness of the degree of emotional maturity with which each parent entered adulthood, marriage, and parenthood. Based on a belief that individuals function as they do because they lack emotional ability to function better (although they may "intellectually" know how to function better), the communication becomes one of "your parents have made mistakes in raising you, but they did the best that they knew how to do." When a struggling young adult can begin to think in these terms, he or she will discover a new capacity to think about personal and family functioning and to observe the emotional system. There is now a chance that solid change may occur.

5. *The interrelationship between functional momentum and anxiety.* Two factors at play in human functioning are momentum and anxiety. The interplay of these two forces governs whether an individual functions on a high level, becomes bogged down in reacting more and thinking less, or becomes emotionally paralyzed by emotion.

Functional momentum is here defined as the amount of productivity that a person demonstrates on a regular basis—the capacity to accomplish. It has to do with such factors as personal discipline and motivation to reach goals and objectives, coupled with a person's level of anxiety.

Functional momentum has properties that are similar though opposite to negative momentum, in which each new emotional event breeds additional anxiety, and negative momentum.

Anxiety is defined as pressure in an individual that is triggered by an occurrence in the environment. It is a force present in all individuals to some degree as a result of life stresses (being audited by the I.R.S., illness in the family, moves or job changes, and the like).

The quality and quantity of both functional momentum and anxiety will vary somewhat over time. However, with observation of an individual's functioning, it is possible to see general patterns. The strength of each factor has to do with the emotional solidness of the individual. The greater the solidness, the greater the probability that the individual will have defined principles and goals upon which a life course has been based, thus lessening the impact of the anxiety.

When an individual becomes bogged down, certain characteristics can be expected regardless of his or her normal level of functional momentum. There will be an inability to observe interactions and feelings accurately. Decision making will be based on an emotional, reactive foundation. Finally, attempts of the individual to take and sustain a defined position in the family will likely fail as a result of either the emotionality of the plan or the reactive anxiety present in its execution. The initial work with a client who is clearly bogged down or emotionally paralyzed would be to focus first on raising the functional momentum of the individual. Once such momentum has become stronger than the anxiety, coaching can shift to the client's evaluation of the system, a focus on the client's own functioning, and the long-term effort of defining a responsible position for the client in the family.

6. *The basis of coaching.* Whether coaching a couple regarding a decision to separate, a family regarding placement for an aged parent, or a young

adult regarding whether or not to seek an abortion, the focus is on evaluating the process through which the client is moving.

Thought-based coaching can assist the client to maintain a balance in viewing all sides of a problem, and thus broadening alternatives. It is a process that focuses on the broad picture, the "here and now," and the far distant future as well, providing a full context in which an evaluation of all available alternatives can be placed. Such a process is very different from therapy that focuses on what choice should be made. The goal is to assist the client in developing his decision making process and not to attempt to influence the direction of a decision.

Phases of Coaching

Coaching can be described in five separate phases:

1. *Focusing on patterns.* The client is moved from a concern with content and personal feeling states to a focus on the patterns of self-functioning and family themes.

2. *Accounting for defined patterns.* The client's patterns are now placed in the multigenerational context of the family. During this phase, clients can expect to become less blaming of themselves and less angry at their parents.

3. *Looking toward the future.* The client is asked how he or she will handle these problems in five, ten, or fifteen years. Such questions frequently uncover a fantasy or myth on which current behavior is based. Clients' sense of personal responsibility for their own lives is frequently awakened during this phase.

4. *Defining what needs to be changed.* This concerns defining the ways in which the client participates in establishing, responding to, and maintaining the dysfunctional family patterns in which he or she is involved. This phase ends with completion of a plan for changing him or herself by changing his/her part in identified patterns.

5. *Coaching a client through the defined strategy.* In this phase, the client will work actively on the plan, taking full responsibility for the task. Coaching sessions will not be frequent, but may occur over a long period of time.

The Process of Change From a Clinical Perspective

The process of change has been divided into three general sections, the characteristics of which will be discussed separately, followed by a clinical illustration.

1. The observation phase. This first general stage in the process of change involves the discovery of patterns of behavior in the individual and the extended family as well. What is important in the phase as it pertains to discussion here is its passive nature, which will affect the client.

The client may well experience frustration in this early work as a result of the new insights and facts uncovered without the benefit of a new capacity to act differently. The result can be a temporary depression fraught with frustration. One client described the phase as a period when she could no longer "play her games with people," but at the same time did not know any other way to relate. Another client described the frustration of becoming painfully aware of an overreactivity to her mother while lacking the self-knowledge required to reduce it.

If clients were encouraged to begin to act and respond differently without first understanding the intricate patterns that sustain the current situation, the presenting problems could become worse or take on new complexities.

2. The problem-focused phase. The second general stage of the process of change can begin once the individual has identified the central dysfunctional patterns in his/her family and the role (s)he has played in them. The second phase is one of action and the focus is on the resolution of specific problems—those identified as the presenting complaints as well as those uncovered during the observation process.

3. Enhancement of personal functioning. Individuals whose life course is no longer limited by personal symptoms are in the third stage of change. For them, the focus shifts to enhancing personal functioning and establishing personal responsibility for their lives. Focus broadens to include evaluation of areas that have never been considered "problems." Life events that were once considered crises may now be viewed as opportunities for development.

A Clinical Example

The following is a description of a clinical case in each of the five phases of coaching. In each phase, predefined goals of the coach will be described, followed by a summary of the accomplishments of the individual. Specific questions that would be used in each category will be included. A genogram of the family is illustrated in Figure 4.1.

Twenty-four-year-old Carol, the middle of three children, entered coaching immediately following her return to her parental home after the traumatic breakup of a two-year intense fusion with a live-in boyfriend. Carol presented herself as a frantic, physically shaking young woman, and described being phobic in any crowded situation—be it a grocery aisle or a museum. Her general state at the first session was such that I was prompted to ask how she had managed to avoid hospitalization.

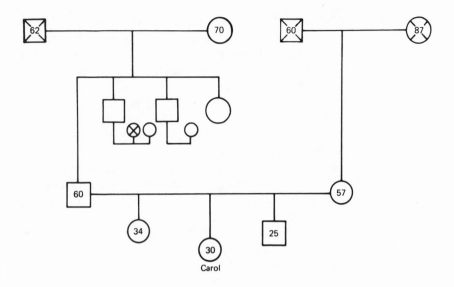

The Unattached Young Adult

Figure 4.1 Genogram

At the time of graduation from college, she had obtained a waitressing position in order to support her art work until she began to experience blackouts from anxiety. As a result, Carol had moved from the area to get away from it all and in the process had become deeply involved with a young man who was experiencing much the same difficulty with launching himself into adulthood.

Carol's father was the eldest of four children. His childhood was described as "morbid"—parents separating and his mother deserting the children on more than one occasion. Her father had left home at sixteen years of age in order to work. He never really returned. Instead, he went on to achieve success as a businessman. In personal areas he did not fare quite so well, with frequent health problems, a conflictual marriage, and two of three children showing problems.

Carol's mother was an only child whose father died when she was twenty-five. She left home at twenty-three to marry. Carol's mother had remained deeply connected to her own mother, although often without comfort. Life for Carol's mother following marriage had centered on her children and was complicated by tensions within the marriage.

Carol's relationship with her parents had been one of emotional distance beginning in adolescence and intensifying with each passing year. She had adapted to this void by living in a dream world which was "outside the family."

Focusing on patterns. The major goal in this phase is to shift the client from a personal, emotional focus on the current situation to a wider focus encompassing the entire emotional system out of which he or she has developed. This can be achieved when an individual gains objectivity about the personal dilemma. Multiple factors influence the development of objectivity. One major factor is the establishment of curiosity in the individual that lessens the hold of fixed, emotional assumptions about life occurrences: *what* actually occurred, *how* such situations came to be, *who* has been instrumental through overfunctioning or underfunctioning in the system, and *when* events occurred in relation to each other.

Questions used in this initial phase fall into two categories: those focusing on extended family history, or the genogram data, and those tracing the symptom history of the individual as it exists in the context of the nuclear and extended family. To avoid creating resistance in the individual to such questions, it is continually necessary to increase knowledge of the facts about extended family and the symptom history as each influences the person. The basic data used to complete a genogram are common knowledge. Therefore, the questions listed below relate to inquiry about symptoms and patterns. Sample questions are as follows:

1. What is the nature of the problem that brings you in?
2. When did the problem begin to appear?
3. Could you have predicted that you would encounter such a problem?
4. Could your mother or father have done so?
5. What has it been like for you to experience a pattern of...?
6. Have you responded better or worse than you would have predicted?
7. What factors have prevented you from overcoming the symptom?
8. What have been your parents' views of the problem?
9. Has this symptom pattern been similar to patterns found in the extended family?
10. What has been the impact of the maternal (and then paternal) side of the family on your characteristics?

For Carol, such questions were a counterforce to her frequent exclamations of "I feel terrible" (i.e., so anxious), and "It's all so hopeless," for they led her to broaden her awareness beyond her emotional discomfort. Each separate "problem" began to be seen as part of a process that had been evolving over a series of years. For Carol, the focus began to shift away from a "quick solution" to a desire to know how her circumstances came to be. The grip of blaming assumptions had begun to lessen.

Accounting for defined patterns. The major goal of this phase is to place a current, specific emotional dilemma into a multigenerational context where patterns were initially created and sustained.

This is a phase of seeking any replication (or opposite pattern) of the individual's dysfunctional patterns by tracking the patterns through the extended family. The following questions address a young adult who has sought therapy as a result of an inability to make decisions:

1. What is it like to be unable to formulate and carry through a decision?

2. Can you clarify the factors that have created such a pattern?

3. How would you describe the impact of such a pattern on your life course to date?

4. Can you account for your inability to formulate decisions in light of your siblings' decisiveness? How would you account for your difference from others?

5. How does your mother function when faced with a decision?

6. If your mother is decisive, how can your indecisiveness be accounted for?

7. Is her pattern of being decisive similar to or different from her mother's?

8. When your parents are simultaneously confronted with a decision, what is the pattern that emerges?

9. What impact has this pattern had on you?

This type of questioning had an "eye opening" impact on Carol. She began to see similar as well as opposite patterns and ways of functioning in each of her parents. The result was that Carol no longer viewed her poor functioning as a "virus" with which she alone had been infected. Rather, a sense of connectedness to her family began to develop, which resulted in reduced self-blame and a very new observation of her parents. Relieved to discover that the poor functioning was perhaps explainable, Carol began to see the possiblity for change. Her paralyzing anxiety overtly lessened.

Looking toward the future. The purpose of this phase is to expose any fantasy in the person that the problem is current but will disappear automatically in time. Questions placing the dilemma of today into the distant future might include:

1. If your ways of functioning remain unchanged, history suggests that current dysfunctional characteristics will be present in the future as well. What will it be like to have difficulty establishing and maintaining an intimate relationship when you are forty years old?

2. Will this pattern be more or less difficult for you to experience when you are ten years older?

3. What new life factors may be active in fifteen years that will have an impact upon the dysfunctional pattern (i.e., children leaving home)?

For Carol this process of thought was useful. A look into the future led her to realize that unless she could increase her emotional stability she would not only be unable to function freely in crowds of people or maintain an intimate relationship in which she was not "done in," she could not expect to return to a successfully evolving career as an artist. Looking to the future was a strong motivator.

Defining what parts of one's functioning to change. If the individual has completed the previously discussed phases, he will have a foundation of knowledge for deciding what parts of him- or herself need to be changed and what it will take to establish a position of responsible functioning in his/her nuclear and extended family. The major goal of this phase is to assist the individual to: define priorities in his or her efforts; anticipate the work it will take to accomplish them; predict reactions of important others; and think through a plan for dealing with their reactivity. Questions may follow the themes listed below:

1. What do you want to change?
2. What will it take to accomplish each part?
3. What reactions can you expect from important others to such actions?
4. What will it be like for you to experience potential disapproval?
5. What is your plan for maintaining your planned course once disapproval is experienced?

After months of thought about her dysfunctional characteristics and attempts to account for each in her multigenerational family system, Carol found the task of developing a plan of action relatively simple to complete.

Coaching the individual through the defined strategy. After the client has observed, evaluated, and formulated a plan of action, therapy becomes a process of coaching the client to stay on the identified course of action. Questions might include:

1. What has occurred in your efforts to change yourself?
2. What made it possible to succeed in the effort?
3. What will be the next step?
4. What obstacles can you anticipate?
5. How do you plan to counteract the obstacles?

Or:

1. It sounds as if you have bogged down a bit in your effort. If that is so, can you account for this problem?
2. What kept you from succeeding?
3. What factors complicated the effort?
4. Had you predicted the factors? If not, can you account for the failure to do so?
5. What will it take to succeed in the next effort?

Carol's initial efforts were directed at increasing her responsibility in her parents' home, contributing both money and work. Efforts then began to shift to establishing person-to-person relationships with parents and siblings. Long-term efforts would focus on building relationships with a "disliked grandmother" and other casually known relatives, establishing a residence of her own, and developing her career. Carol has achieved the ability to function on a more stable, productive level in the midst of now minimal anxiety. Completion of her goals will necessitate continued work. Sessions now occur on a regular although infrequent basis.

REFERENCES

Bowen, Murray, *Family Therapy in Clinical Practice*, New York: Jason Aronson, 1978.

Glick, Paul C. & Arthur J. Norton, "Number, Timing, and Duration of Marriages and Divorces in the U.S.," in *Current Population Reports*, Series P-20, No. 297, Bureau of the Census, Oct. 1976.

Lidz, Theodore, *The Person*, New York: Basic Books, 1968.

Toman, Walter, *Family Constellation*, 3rd Edition, New York: Springer, 1976.

5

The Joining of Families Through Marriage: The New Couple

Monica McGoldrick, A.C.S.W.
C.M.D.N.J.–Rutgers Medical School and
Community Mental Health Center
Family Institute of Westchester

INTRODUCTION

Becoming a couple is one of the most complex and difficult transitions of the family life cycle. However, along with the transition to parenthood, which it has long symbolized, it is seen as the easiest and most joyous. The positive and romanticized view of this transition may add to its difficulty, since everyone from the couple to the family and friends wants to see only the happiness of the shift. The problems entailed may thus be pushed underground, only to intensify and surface later on.

Weddings, more than any other rite of passage, are viewed as the solution to problems, such as loneliness or extended family difficulties. The event is seen as terminating a process, though it does not; "And they lived happily ever after" is the myth. Families will often say, "At last they're settled," as though the wedding resolved something rather than coming in the middle of a complex process of changing family status.

This chapter will outline the issues in becoming a new family and discuss clinical interventions for those who have trouble negotiating this phase. The meaning of marriage in our time is profoundly different from its meaning throughout previous history, when it was tightly embedded in the economic and social fabric of society. The changing role of women and the increasing social mobility of our culture, along with the dramatic effects of widely available contraceptives, are forcing us to redefine marriage.

Marriage requires that a couple renegotiate together a myriad of personal issues they have previously defined for themselves or that were de-

93

fined by their parents, including everyday decisions like when and how to eat, sleep, talk, have sex, fight, and relieve tension. They must decide about vacations, and how to use space, time, and money. Then there are the familial decisions about which traditions and rituals to retain from each family of origin and which ones the partners will develop for themselves. These and thousands of similar decisions can no longer be determined solely on an individual basis. They must be worked out compatibly so the two can fit together. The couple will also find themselves having to renegotiate their relationships with their parents, siblings, friends, and other relatives in view of the new marriage. It places no small stress on a family to open itself to an outsider who is now an official member of its inner circle. Frequently no new member may have been added for many years. This challenge can affect a family's style profoundly. The tendency of its members to polarize and see villains and victims under the stress of change can be very high. In fact, Haley has commented that what distinguishes man from all other animals is the fact of having in-laws. All other animals mature, separate, and mate on their own. Only man carries his whole family into the bargain. Haley goes so far as to remark that perhaps man has developed such a large brain in order to be able to cope with the complexity of his kinship system (Haley, 1973).

In the animal kingdom, mating involves only the two partners. For mankind it is the joining of two enormously complex systems. The joke that there are six in the marital bed is really an understatement. In fact, it is possible that if couples could fully appreciate the emotional complexity of negotiating marriage right at the start, they might not dare to undertake the proposition.

Nowadays couples are marrying later and delaying conception of children longer than ever before. The average age at first marriage in 1975 was 21.3 for women and 23.8 for men, which was one year later for both sexes than the marriage age a decade ago (Glick, 1977). Only about 7% of women never marry, although this rate has been on the rise. For the past two decades the annual marriage rate has declined almost continuously. Postponing marriage has been especially common among women in their early twenties. Probably related to this is college enrollment of women in their twenties, which doubled between 1960 and 1972 (Glick, 1975). The proportion of women still single between the ages twenty and twenty-four has gone up by half since 1960, from 28% to 43% (Glick & Norton, 1977).

Another trend has been the tremendous increase in recent years in the number of unmarried couples living together. Although statistics are hard to get on this, it appears they represent at least 4% of all couples. Between 1970 and 1977, the number almost doubled from one to two million couples (Glick & Norton, 1977). In all likelihood this forecasts considerable change in the patterns of couple formation in the future. The widespread use of contraceptives and the changing role of women, especially in the past few years, has influenced these changes strongly. In fact, one researcher has estimated that if the present trends continue, the entire family life cycle will look drastically different within the next century, because less than half of adult life will be organized around raising children, where throughout human history most families were involved in raising children during their whole active adult lives (Calhoun, 1978).

Childbearing patterns are also changing greatly. There has been a remarkable decline in recent years in the number of couples who remain childless—only about 4–6% (Glick, 1977). This decrease results primarily from advances in medicine that have greatly decreased involuntary infertility. However, this is being offset by the increasing number of couples who are choosing not to have children; the number of young women saying they do not plan to have children is going up (Blake, 1979). In addition, couples are waiting much longer than they had previously before having children. For couples who marry before pregnancy, 42% have their first child within three years of marriage (Bureau of Census, 1979),[1] but an increasing number of couples (more than 15%), are now waiting more than five years before having children—an increase from 9% twenty-five years ago (Bureau of the Census, 1979).

Thus there is an increasing trend toward delaying both marriage and pregnancy. In spite of this trend, there is still, for most couples, a relatively short interval between marriage and the birth of the first child. This means that there is only a short time in which the couple must adjust to this phase of their life cycle with its accompanying stresses before moving on. The overwhelming majority of the population marries and moves on to the childrearing phase before age thirty.

There seems to be a timing to this phase, with those who fall outside it often having more difficulty. Women who marry before the age of twenty (38% of women) are twice as likely to divorce as those who marry in their twenties. Those who marry after thirty (6% of women) are half again as likely to divorce as those who marry in their twenties (Glick & Norton, 1977). Thus it appears that in our culture there is a time for coupling and, while it may be better to marry later than sooner, those who fall too far out of the normative range on either end are more likely to have trouble making the transition. Such people are often responding to family stresses that make the process of coupling more difficult to achieve. Those who marry early may be running away from their families of origin, but are unable to

---

[1]In fact one-third of all first births in the early 1970s were premaritally conceived (Glick & Norton, 1977). Of these, an increasing proportion (9%) are children born before their mothers marry, and the other 23% are born within the first nine months of marriage (Bureau of the Census, 1979).

take the needed step toward independent development first. They leave home by fusing with a mate in an attempt to gain strength from one another. Those who marry late are frequently responding to some negative image of coupling they saw at home, and/or they have been enmeshed in their family of origin and have had trouble leaving home and forming outside relationships. Of course, an additional factor in this is, at least for women, the conflict between marriage and career. It should be noted also that the step toward independent development was never considered necessary for women until the present generation. The profound implications of this are obvious.

What is amazing, considering the long range implications of the decision to marry, is that so many couples seem to spend so little time thinking out the decision. One family therapist has commented that many Americans seem to spend more time deciding which car to buy than selecting the spouse they expect to keep for life (Alymer, 1977). It seems, as a number of family therapists have observed, that the timing of most marriage decisions is influenced by extended family events, such as the illness or death of a parent, or events with siblings, and that most couples are unaware of the correlation of these events and the process which underlies their decision to marry (Friedman, 1977; Alymer, 1977).

FUSION AND CLOSENESS

The basic dilemma in coupling is the confusion of closeness with fusion. Fogarty has clarified the problem in the following way:

> The forces of togetherness spring from the natural human desire for closeness. Carried to extremes, they lead to a search for completeness. Carried beyond the possible, such forces lead to fusion, a uniting of two people, and resultant distance. They try to defy the natural incompleteness of people and systems, as if one can become complete by fusing into a united twosome. (Fogarty, 1976, p. 39).

There is a vast difference between forming an intimate relationship with another separate person and using a couple relationship to try to complete one's self and improve one's self-esteem. The natural human desire to share one's experience often leads to this confusion between seeking closeness and seeking fusion in coupling. Poets have long talked about the difference. Rilke writes:

> Love is at first not anything that means merging, giving over, and uniting with another (for what would a union be of something unclarified and unfinished, still subordinate?); it is a high inducement to the individual to ripen, to become

something in himself, to become world, to become world for himself for another's sake, it is a great exacting claim on him. (Rilke, 1954, p. 54)

Bowen Systems Theory elucidates this process in human relationships (Bowen, 1978). This model views the tendency to seek fusion as related to the incomplete differentiation from one's family of origin. In other words, couples who seek to complete themselves in each other have failed to resolve their relationships with their parents, which alone would free them to build a new relationship based on each person's freedom to be himself or herself and to appreciate the other as he or she is. The process whereby people who have not resolved family relationships seek to enhance their self-esteem in marriage is based on denying their "differentness" from their spouse, and can result in severe distortions in communication to maintain the myth of agreement (Satir, 1967).

Couples during courtship are usually most aware of the romantic aspects of their relationship. Marriage shifts the relationship from a private coupling to a formal joining of two families. Issues that the partners have not resolved with their own families will tend to be factors in marital choice and are very likely to interfere with establishing a workable marital balance.

It may be that much of the intensity of romantic love is determined by one's family values. From this perspective, Romeo and Juliet might have felt such intensity in their attraction to each other precisely because their family situation prohibited it. Such obstacles may lead to an idealization of the forbidden person. They, and many other romantic heroes, from Tristan and Isolde on down, were conveniently spared a more complete view of their relationship by their tragic deaths, thus preserving the romance and obscuring the more pedestrian view of the underlying family dramas that probably fostered their attraction.

In everyday life, the outcome of such love affairs is often not so romantic, as the following case material illustrates.

Nancy met her husband, Tom, during her last year of high school. Nancy's parents had been very unhappily married and had invested all their energies in their children's success. Nancy planned to go to college and her younger brother was expected to go even further academically. A month after her high school graduation, Nancy's lawyer father had a severe stroke and became an invalid. Her mother, who had never responded well to stress, became even more critical of her husband now that he was so dependent. Nancy began college, but within three months she decided to drop out and marry Tom, who had begun working for an insurance company after finishing high school the previous year. He was an only child from a lower-middle-class family. For him, not only was Nancy very attractive, but her family represented a step-up socially. She was an intense, dynamic, and attractive woman. Her intensity appealed to him perhaps because his own family life had been marred by his father's inability to work following a war disability, and his mother's added disappointment in being able to have only one child. Tom hoped to escape the lonely and rather depressed atmosphere of his family home by marrying Nancy. He had always felt responsible for his parents' well-being but powerless to make them happy. He was delighted when Nancy left college and suddenly began pushing to marry him. He had been threatened by her college pursuits anyway. For Nancy, he represented the only way she knew to get away from her family's expectations. He at least would not push her to achieve. He liked and accepted her as she was. He had a steady income and this would mean she would not have to worry about her inability to concentrate on her studies or her fear of failure. She would become his wife; they would raise a family and her worries would be over.

Both found the other attractive and saw their relationship as making them feel better than they ever remembered feeling before. Tom's parents were not generally disapproving, but suggested strongly that they wait, since they were both so young. Nancy's family disapproved of her marrying someone without a college education and thought she should finish school herself. In private moments, Nancy wondered if she might find someone more intelligent and with more promise, but her parents' disapproval pushed her to defend her choice and to reject their "snobbism." Prior to marriage Nancy and Tom had little chance to be alone together. What time they did have was filled with wedding arrangements and discussion of the families' pressures on them. Almost immediately after the wedding, Nancy felt restless. Things with her family had quieted down after the marriage—they had no more reason to protest. Nancy quickly became bored and began to pressure Tom to get a better job. Tom felt guilty now about having "abandoned" his parents, something he hadn't let surface during courtship. To improve things financially and to deal with his feelings about his parents, he suggested buying a two-family house that his parents had been considering. They could share expenses and it would make a good investment. Nancy agreed because it meant they would have much nicer living quarters. Almost immediately she began to feel pressure from Tom's parents to socialize with them and to have children for them. Having married to escape her own parents, she now felt saddled with two others, with the added burden of not knowing them well. Suddenly Tom's personality irritated her. Where initially she had liked him for his easygoing style and his acceptance of her, she now saw him as lacking ambition. She was embarrassed to have him spend time with her friends because of his manners and lack of education, so she began avoiding her friends, which left her even more isolated. She tried pressuring him to fulfill her dreams and satisfy all her relationship needs. He felt increasingly inadequate and unable to respond to her pressure. Sexually, she felt he was clumsy and insensitive and began to turn him away. His sense of inadequacy led him to retreat further and he took to going out in the evening with his friends, with whom he felt accepted and not on trial.

Nancy's resistance to parental expectations had now been transferred into the marriage. Tom's hopes for moving beyond his parents disappointing lives had now been transformed into pressure from Nancy for him to succeed, and he resented it. Neither Nancy nor Tom had worked out for themselves individually what they wanted. Each had turned to the other to fulfill unmet needs and now each was disappointed.

What began to happen between Nancy and Tom is what happens to many couples when the hope that the partner will solve one's problems proves false. Under stress, there is a tendency to personalize the stress and seek to blame someone for what goes wrong. At times people blame themselves, at times their spouse. Given enough stress, there is a great tendency for couples to define their problems solely within the relationship. They may blame the spouse ("He let me down; he doesn't love me") or themselves ("I'm no good; I'd be able to satisfy her if I were"). Once this personalizing process comes into play, it is very difficult to keep the relationship open. Nancy began to lay the blame for her disappointments in life on Tom and he saw himself as responsible for her unhappiness.

A major factor influencing the tightening of couple relationships over time is the increasing interdependency of the couple and their tendency to interpret more and more facets of their lives within the marriage. For example, during courtship, if one partner becomes depressed, the other is not likely to take it too personally, assuming, "There are many reasons to get depressed in life; this may well have nothing to do with me." Such an assumption of not being responsible for the other's feelings permits a supportive and empathic response to the other. After several years of marriage, however, this partner has a much greater tendency to view the other's emotions as a reflection of his or her input and to feel responsible for the other's depression. After five years of marriage the partner may think, "It must mean I'm not a good wife, or I would have made him happy by now." Once each starts taking responsibility for the other's feelings, there is a tendency for more and more areas in the relationship to become tension-filled. Couples then develop a pattern of triangulation in order to avoid areas that arouse tension between them. Over time they will avoid more and more areas. For example, if a wife thinks her husband is depressed because of her, she may feel inadequate, guilty, and resentful. She may then decide to avoid dealing with him because she doesn't want to be blamed, or she may become very protective of him and not say anything upsetting for fear of making him feel worse. In either case, the more her reactions are a response to his, the less flexibility there will be in the relationship and the more the couple's communication will become constricted in the areas that are emotionally charged.

The period when couples are courting is probably the least likely time, of all phases of the family life cycle, to seek therapy. This is not because coupling is so easy, but rather because of the romanticization of the attraction between them. The partners will have a strong tendency to idealize each other and to avoid looking at the enormous and long-range difficulties of establishing an intimate relationship. While the first years of marriage are the time of greatest overall marital satisfaction, they are also the time of the highest rate of divorce. This is probably because the degree of disillusionment and mutual disappointment will match the degree of idealization of the relationship during courtship, as in the case of Nancy and Tom. During courtship, the pull toward the relationship is likely to prevent openness to potential difficulties (Friedman, 1977), so they do not show up until further down the road. On one hand, there is the tendency toward pseudomutuality during courtship, and on the other, as Bowen has observed, this can be the time of greatest openness in the relationship because years of interdependency have not yet tightened things:

> Most spouses can have the closest and most open relationships in their adult lives during courtship. The fusion of the two pseudoselves into a common self occurs at the time they commit themselves to each other permanently, whether it be the time of engagement, the wedding itself, or the time they establish their first home together. It is common for living together relationships to be harmonious, and for fusion symptoms to develop when they finally get married. It is as if the fusion does not develop as long as they still have an option to terminate the relationship. (Bowen, 1978, p. 377).

Haley has also commented on the paradoxical effect of marriage on couple relationships:

> When a man and woman decide their association should be solemnized and legalized with a marriage ceremony, they pose themselves a problem which will continue through the marriage: now that they are married, are they staying together because they wish or because they must? (Haley, 1963, pp. 192–3).

While marriage frequently tightens a relationship, the fusion often starts developing during courtship, when couples say they like everything about each other, share all free time together, and so on.

People often seem to meet their spouse or decide to marry shortly after the retirement, illness, or even untimely death of a parent, or after other traumatic family loss. The sense of loss or aloneness often appears to be a strong contributing factor in the desire to build a close relationship. Often, it can blind a person to the aspects of a prospective spouse that do not fit the idealized picture that the other will complete them and make their life worthwhile. This desire for completion is likely to lead to difficulty accepting the spouse's differentness, which will necessarily show itself in the course of the relationship. As one woman put it, "My husband and I have always been afraid of the stranger in each other. We kept wanting to believe that the other thought the same as we thought they were thinking, which could never be. We just couldn't appreciate that here was a new and different person, with his own thoughts and feelings, who would make life more interesting."

The failure to appreciate or allow for the differentness in the other person comes from never really having become emotionally independent of one's parents. This leaves a person in the position of trying to build self-esteem in the marriage. It leads to a relationship built on what Satir has called a "survival pact" (1967), wherein the partners make an implicit bargain to live for each other (which, by the way, fits with our "romantic ideals"). Neither partner dares to communicate his inner fears to the other: "I must never let her know that I am really nothing or I will lose her, and I will never tell her that at times she is boring and talks too much." Each partner puts the other in charge of his or her self-esteem: "I am worthwhile because you love me." This leaves them ever after vulnerable to the converse possibility: "If you do not love me, I am not worthwhile." A corollary which intensifies the difficulty is "If you are different from me or disagree with me, you do not love me and therefore I am not worthwhile." Thus couples can become bound in a web of evasiveness and ambiguity, because neither can dare to be straight with the other, for fear of things turning out—as they did in the families of origin—unhappily. Messages between them may become more and more covert the more they define their own worth on the basis of the relationship. It can lead to the content of communication becoming totally obscured by the need of each partner to validate his sense of himself through mutuality with the spouse. It may end with the absurdity of couples spending their time doing things neither wants to do because each thinks the other wants it that way.

While many couples seem to make it to couplehood with the help of romance, pseudomutuality, or the resistance of their parents to the idea, some couples, perhaps an increasing number, get stuck in the process of becoming a pair.

> Mary and David applied for counseling over the question of whether to marry after living together for eight years. Mary saw David's refusal to marry as a rejection. David saw Mary's push to marry as reflecting other insecurities, since they were happy in their life together. He saw marriage as tying them into unpleasant obligations such as his parents had shared. He also feared becoming the caretaker for her should she inherit the disabling genetic disease from which her mother suffered. Mary was preoccupied with David's refusal to marry her, saying she would leave him unless he changed his mind, though she admitted they were compatible in most things and she was very happy with their life together. She obsessed over the possibility of his leaving her.

In such situations, family patterns contribute to the inability of each to successfully negotiate the transition to couplehood. In such instances, the concept of "marriage" has taken on a meaning far beyond the fact of two people sharing their lives with each other. It is not uncommon for two people who have been living happily together to find that things change when they do get married because they have now added to the situation the burdensome definitions of "husband" and "wife." These words often bring with them conceptions of heavy responsibility *for* (rather than *to*) one another, which living together did not impose. There may also be the burden of having definitely passed beyond youth into "serious" adulthood.

> Another unmarried couple who had lived together for four years, Ann and Peter, both in their early thirties, applied for therapy because of an unsatisfying sex life. The couple had never discussed marriage. Peter said he was just too unprepared and Ann that she feared learning that he did not want to marry her. She heard his silence as a statement of his basic indifference to her. For Peter, marriage meant loss of spontaneity, such as he saw in his parents. His father had left college to marry his mother when she became pregnant. Both his parents had seen this as a serious mistake they had never moved beyond, because it had left them both stifled in their ambitions and with the burden of a family to support. Peter felt that somehow he had to resolve all his insecurities and become completely self-sufficient before marrying. Ann had begun to worry about having children, fearing that if Peter did not marry her she would have to start a new relationship soon or she would be too old. This had affected their sexual relationship, which had become increasingly tension-filled.

This couple represents one type of misperception about marriage, seeing it as such an enormous task that one can never be prepared. Many couples have the opposite misperception, that marriage will fulfill them regardless of their work on all other aspects of their lives. Family attitudes and myths about marriage filter down from generation to generation making such transitions, proportionately smoother or more difficult.

PATTERNS WITH EXTENDED FAMILY

Couples deal with their families in several different ways. Many find marriage the only way to separate from their families of origin. They tend to be enmeshed with their families, and this pattern continues even after the marriage. Patterns of guilt, intrusiveness, and unclear boundaries are typical of such systems. Other couples cut off their families emotionally even before marriage. In these situations, the partners may not even invite their parents to the wedding. Parents are seen as withholding and rejecting and the couple decides to do without them. Another pattern involves continued contact with parents but with ongoing conflicts. In such families, there is usually involvement of the extended family in the marriage plans but often with fights, hurt feelings, and "scenes" around the time of the wedding. This pattern is perhaps the most helpful for future resolution of the issues. The conflicts indicate that at least the family is dealing with the struggle of separating and is not forcing it underground as in enmeshed or cutoff families. The ideal situation, and one very rarely found, is the one in which the partners have become independent of their families before marriage and at the same time maintain close, caring ties. In such instances the wedding would serve for all the family as a sharing and celebration of the new couple's shift in status.

Arlene and Howard are a clear example of difficulties of enmeshment. They married when both were nineteen. They had met and dated perfunctorily in high school. Arlene's father worked eighteen hours a day and her mother devoted herself exclusively to her son and daughter. Arlene feared her mother's loneliness if she should leave her and remained at home, while her brother was able to leave through academic achievement. After high school, Arlene got a job selling in a department store. She considered moving away to work or study but could not see how to do it. She felt her parents, and especially her mother, would see it as a rejection if she moved into an apartment and stayed in the same city, and she feared moving further away on her own. Following a pregnancy "scare" during which she and Howard decided they would have to marry, she concluded this was the best thing to do anyway and a few months later they were married. Her family paid for the wedding and exerted primary control over the guest list, which bothered Howard. However, he felt he was not financially in a position to complain. His family was rather poor and could not contribute to the costs, and he had no extra money himself. Following the wedding, the couple moved to their own apartment but Arlene and her mother were in daily phone contact and the couple visited her parents most weekends. Howard began using the excuse of work to avoid these family gatherings. Arlene's mother was centrally involved in decorating their apartment, offering to pay for items the couple could not afford on their own. Howard resisted these presents since they left him feeling indebted and guilty, but Arlene said rejecting gifts only hurt her parents and the couple kept taking them. It was not until many years later, when their own children began to break away, that Arlene and Howard recognized the need to find new ways to cope with this enmeshment. Intervention at the time of the marriage might have helped this couple establish the necessary boundaries to avoid these later complications.

The second pattern of dealing with parents involves cutting off the relationships in an attempt to gain independence.

Jack and Mary were married in a civil ceremony with two friends as witnesses. They were "not into marriage" and only got married for convenience. Jack had won a scholarship to college at eighteen and worked nights to pay his extra expenses. He had decided to do it all on his own because he hated his alcoholic father's abuse. At first he kept up contact with his mother but when she refused his urgings to leave her husband, Jack decided she deserved what she got and he kept up only perfunctory and sporadic contact. He met Mary in college and afterwards they began living together. She had had a stormy adolescence during which her parents disapproved of her boyfriends, her politics, and her use of pot. She disapproved of what she called her parents' hypocrisy since they drank rather heavily. After many stormy fights, she began to avoid going home. Jack discouraged her family contact. He said it only upset her and that her parents were never going to change. After she told her parents she and Jack were going to live together, the relationship became even more strained. They disapproved, and she disapproved of their disapproval. Jack was just as happy to have her cut off her relationship with her parents since in his view parents just meant trouble and they could make it on their own. The couple drew in on each other in a "two against the world" stance that remained balanced until the couple could no longer maintain their fusion in face of their children's challenges. Many spouses develop restrictive couple patterns like Jack and Mary that work until later developmental stages destabilize them.

The third common pattern of relationships with extended family involves some contact, some closeness, some conflict, and some generally avoided issues. In such families, the time of coupling is an excellent opportunity to reopen closed relationships, for example, inviting to the wedding relatives with whom parents are out of touch. It is a good chance to detoxify emotional issues, reviewing marital and family ties over several generations as part of the redefining of the system. However, the underlying tensions often surface reactively at the time of transition, in emotional scenes or arguments around wedding plans, only to go underground again as family members try to act happy and friendly so as not to create "unpleasantness." The attempt to smooth things over in itself often increases the likelihood of outbursts because tensions will necessarily be high. The fact that all change creates disruption and uncertainty in the system needs to be dealt with in the family if the developmental processes are to move along. For example, it may be easier for the family to move on if they are in touch with their sense of loss at the time of the wedding, and if they are a bit confused and uneasy about how to manage the new relationships.

Whatever the patterns of difficulty with extended family—conflict, enmeshment, distance, or cutoff—the lack of resolution of these relationships is the major problem in negotiating this phase of the family life cycle. The more the triangles in the extended family are dealt with by an emotional cutoff of the relationship, the more the spouse comes to represent not just who he or she is, but also mother, father, brother, and sister. This input of intensity will surely overload the circuits in time. If a husband's relationship with his wife is his only meaningful relationship, he will be so sensitive to her every reaction, and especially to any hint of rejection, that he will overreact to signs of differentness by pulling her to agree with him or blaming her for not accepting him. The intensity will probably make the relationship untenable eventually. Our culture's social mobility and overfocus on the nuclear family to the neglect of the larger systems contributes to this tendency to place more emotional demand on a marriage than it can bear. Once a spouse becomes overly involved in the other's response, both become bound up in a web of fusion and unable to function for themselves.

Paul and Lucy, two graduate students, applied for marital therapy after a marriage of two years because they were both concerned about the tension between them. They thought they were not enjoying their relationship as much as other couples, in spite of their best efforts. Among other things, Paul said he tried to take Lucy out to dinner as often as possible, a struggle, he said, because they had so little money. Lucy said she never enjoyed it, that she could sense his discomfort and did not like spending money that way herself, but went along since it seemed to mean a lot to Paul. Paul got annoyed and said she always seemed to want to go and he was doing it to please her. She said she only acted happy because it seemed to mean so much to him. It turned out that Paul's mother, who had died of cancer the year Paul and Lucy married, had always seen his father as stingy. She frequently complained about her husband for not taking her out. Paul did not want to appear like his father. Lucy was trying to be accommodating to Paul because she did not want to end up with a divorce as her parents had done. The couple was well on its way to a life-style that neither of them wanted, out of fear of disappointing each other.

Therapy for this couple involved reducing their focus on the marriage and placing their relationship in the broader context of their extended families. This therapeutic approach, the hallmark of Bowen Systems Therapy, appears to have great merit for the many couples who become myopic and see their partner as the source of all pain and joy in their lives.

Some couples transfer parental struggles to the spouse directly. One such young couple's marriage foundered when the husband John's possessiveness led to his striking his wife for starting an affair. The wife, Roberta, had played the role of "bad girl" and rebel in her family of origin. Her incestuous affair with a first cousin at age seventeen had led to a thunderous response by her parents. She met John while still involved with her cousin, and married him the following spring. Within a few months, the cycle of John's possessive intrusiveness and Roberta's rebellious acting out had developed full swing.

A related coupling problem occurs when people choose partners to handle their families for them. A man may choose a wife totally unacceptable to his parents and then let her fight his battles with his parents while he becomes the "innocent bystander." The price everyone pays in such situations is the failure to achieve any real intimacy, since issues can never be resolved when other members are brought in to handle one's relationships.

When family members have served a central function in their parents' lives or in the preservation of their parents' marital balance, they may not feel the parents have granted "permission" for them to marry successfully. Stanton (1980) has gone so far as to suggest that this is the reason for 80% of marital failures. This is very much in line with the view presented here, that most marital problems derive from unresolved extended family problems, and not from the specific marital conflicts on which the spouses may focus.

While it is less common in our time that a parent dies before the children marry, when this does occur, the power of death-bed instructions regarding marriage (Stanton, 1980), and of other unresolved parental directives about marriage, are crucial in evaluating a couple's functioning and expectations of themselves and each other in marriage.

Among the problematic triangles for the couple, the one between husband, wife, and mother-in-law is probably the most renowned. In-laws are easy scapegoats for family tensions. It is always much easier to hate your daughter-in-law for keeping your son from showing his love, than to admit your son doesn't respond as much as you wish he would. It is easier for a daughter-in-law to hate her mother-in-law for her intrusiveness, than to confront her husband directly for not defining a strong enough marital boundary to keep his mother from interfering. In-law relationships are a natural arena for displacing tensions in the couple or in the family of origin of each spouse. The converse of this is the pattern of a spouse who has cut off his own family and seeks to adopt his spouse's family as his own, forming a warm, enmeshed fusion with his in-laws, based on defining his own family as cold, rejecting, uninteresting, etc.

Siblings may also displace their problems in dealing with each other on the intrusion of a new spouse. Predictable triangles are especially likely between a husband and his wife's brothers or between the wife of an only brother and his sisters. The sisters may often see their brother's wife as having "no taste," infusing the brother with poor values, etc. What is missed by the system in such instances is that the brother probably chose his wife intentionally as a protection from his sisters, perhaps to set limits he never dared to set alone, or to allow him to distance without the guilt of doing it directly. Now he has an excuse: "I'd love to come over, but my wife isn't feeling well," or "We can't come this week, we have to visit my wife's sister." Often the brother will get his wife to take over dealing with his family altogether, which usually succeeds only in escalating the tension. Of course, a person may also use the extended family to distance from his spouse without taking responsibility for it, under the guise of family duty: "I'd love to spend all day with you, honey, but I have to visit my parents."

Good clues about a new couple can be gotten from the marital relationships of the parents, the couple's primary models for what marriage is about. The other basic model for spouses is their relationships with their siblings, their earliest and closest peers. Research indicates that couples who marry mates from complementary sibling positions enjoy the greatest marital stability (Toman, 1976). In other words, the older brother of a younger sister will tend to get along best with a younger sister of an older brother. They will tend not to have power conflicts, since he will be comfortable as the leader and she as the follower. In addition, they have both had close contact with the opposite sex in their homes growing up, so they will tend to be comfortable in this as well. Couples who marry spouses not from complementary sibling positions will have added adjustments in marriage. An extreme case would be the oldest brother of many brothers who marries the oldest sister of many sisters. Both would expect to be the leader and would probably have difficulty understanding why the other did not take orders well, since they are used to having their orders taken at home. In addition, they will be less comfortable with the opposite sex, since they grew up in strongly single-sexed environments (Toman, 1976).

The most difficult thing about sibling position differences is that we are not generally aware how many of our assumptions about life are based on them. In fact, a great number of our basic life expectations come from implicit assumptions we formed in our families. We rarely realize how much we have to learn about differentness when we join with someone else, as in the following example.

> A young couple applied for therapy after two years of marriage for vague complaints that the relationship was not working out. Both spouses were the youngest in rather large sibling systems. Their complaints focused on the vague feeling that their needs were not being met in the relationship and the other one never seemed to be doing his or her share. It was pointed out that since each had been considered the "baby" in the family of origin, they were probably both waiting for the other to be responsible, as youngests grow up expecting and knowing that a good, appreciative parent or older sibling can always be relied on to take care of everything. The couple laughed and said that it was true that they had both been the little prince and princess of their families. They had to do considerable work negotiating the taking of responsibility. This was a new task for both of them, and one they had not known they needed to learn.

The kind of dilemma this couple presented is typical of many marital problems that are not really marital problems. They are problems that get focused in the marriage, but really derive from the couple's finding in the marriage a different situation than they were used to in their families of origin. Again, the biggest problem is that these differences in experience are so difficult to recognize. So often, if one's expectations are not met, the assumption is that the spouse is at fault for not responding "right." One often hears the complaints, "If you loved me, you would know how I feel," and "If you loved me, you wouldn't always challenge my plans" (especially common for oldest married to another oldest), as if "love" included mindreading.

Another arena of patterns that become problematic in a marriage under stress is that of cultural or family style differences. This may be more of a problem in our country, where people from so many diverse cultural backgrounds marry and find themselves in conflict because each starts out with such different basic assumptions.

A young couple applied for therapy after a year of marriage because the wife said she was convinced her husband did not love her and that he had changed after they got married. The wife was the fifth of seven children from a Brooklyn family of Italian extraction. She had met her husband in college and was extremely attracted to his quiet, stable strength and strong life ambitions. He was from a midwestern Protestant family, where, as an only child, he was strongly encouraged by his parents to work hard and have a morally upright life. He had found her vivacious and charming and had also been attracted to her family because of their open affection and because, in contrast to his own "uptight" parents, they always seemed to have a good time. Under stress, the couple found that the very qualities that had attracted them became the problem. The husband became for the wife, "an unfeeling stone." She complained: "He doesn't care about my feelings at all and ignores me completely." For the husband, the wife's vivaciousness now became "hysteria" and he found her "nagging, emotional outbursts, and screaming" unbearable. As we discussed in therapy their very different family styles of coping with stress, their opposing assumptions became obvious. In the husband's family the rule was that you should keep your problems to yourself and think them out; with enough effort and thought, most problems could be worked out. The wife's family dealt with stress by getting together and ventilating. The family related intensely at all times, but especially when family members were upset. These styles had been turned inward in the marriage and were tightening things even more. The more the wife felt isolated and needed contact, the louder she sought attention and the more the husband withdrew to get some space and to maintain his balance. The more he withdrew, the more frustrated and alone the wife felt. Both partners had turned their differences, initially labeled as the source of attraction, into the problem, and had begun to see the other's behavior as a sure sign of not caring. Neither had been able to see that their family styles were just different. They were compounding the difficulty by moving further into their own pattern and each blaming the other for his or her response. Once the family patterns could be clarified in the context of the extended family and ethnic backgrounds, the spouses were able to temper their responses and to see their differences as neutral rather than as signs of psychopathology or rejection.

ISSUES IN MARITAL ADJUSTMENT

Generally speaking, it is possible to predict that marital adjustment will be more difficult if any of the following are true:

1. The couple meets or marries shortly after a significant loss.
2. The wish to distance from one's family of origin is a factor in the marriage.
3. The family backgrounds of each spouse are significantly different (religion, education, social class, ethnicity, the age of the partners and the like).

4. The couple has incompatible sibling constellations.

5. The couple resides either extremely close to or at a great distance from either family of origin.

6. The couple is dependent on either extended family financially, physically, or emotionally.

7. The couple marries before age twenty or after age thirty.

8. The couple marries after an acquaintanceship of less than six months or more than three years of engagement.

9. The wedding occurs without family or friends present.

10. The wife becomes pregnant before or within the first year of marriage (Christensen, 1963; Bacon, 1974).

11. Either spouse has a poor relationship with his or her siblings or parents.

12. Either spouse considers his or her childhood or adolescence as an unhappy time.

13. Marital patterns in either extended family were unstable.

Most of these factors have already been given support by sociological data on divorce (Burchinal, 1965; Goodrich, 1968; Ryder, 1970; Bumpass, 1972; Becker, 1977; Mott, 1979).

A number of other factors probably add to the difficulty of adjusting to marriage in our time. Changing family patterns as a result of the changing role of women, the frequent marriage of partners from widely different cultural backgrounds, and the increasing physical distances between family members are placing a much greater burden on couples to define their relationship for themselves than was true in traditional and precedent-bound family structures (Rausch, 1963). While any two family systems are always different and have conflicting patterns and expectations, in our present culture couples are less bound by family traditions and are freer than ever before to develop male-female relationships unlike those they experienced in their families of origin. Couples are required to think out for themselves many things that in the past could have been taken for granted. This applies also to the enormous gap that often exists in our culture between parents and children in education and social status. While it is much better for marital stability for children to be more successful than their parents (Glick, 1977), any large gap is obviously a strain, since both parent and child will have to adjust to large differences in experience.

The economics of our culture have meant that a fair percentage of children are able to leave their families and support themselves financially much earlier than was previously possible. Economic independence may increase the tendency to distance from the extended family. At the other extreme, the requirements of our lengthy educational process for many professions may also complicate the adjustment to this phase of the life cycle by setting up the problem of prolonged dependence on parents. For example, couples who are trying to define themselves as separate from their families, but who are still being supported by them, are in a difficult and ambiguous position. It is impossible to become emotionally independent while still relying on one's parents financially, so many couples struggle to develop couple boundaries in relation to their parents but are basically unable to maintain them.

A special word should be said about the impact of the changing role of women on marriage and the family life cycle (see also Chapter 13, "Women in Families"). It appears that the rise in women's status is positively correlated with marital instability (Pearson, 1979), and with the marital dissatisfaction of their husbands (Burke, 1976). When women used to fall automatically into the adaptive role in marriage, the likelihood of divorce was much lower. The adaptive spouse was not prepared to function independently either economically or emotionally. In fact, it appears very difficult for two spouses to be equally successful and achieving. There is evidence that either spouse's accomplishments may correlate negatively with the same degree of achievement in the other (Ferber, 1979). Thus, achieving marital adjustment in our time, when we are moving toward the equality of the sexes (educationally and occupationally) may be extraordinarily difficult.

THE WEDDING

One of the best indicators of the family process at the time of couple formation, and one of the best places for preventive intervention, is the wedding itself. As family events, weddings are the only major ceremonies organized by the family itself, and they are the family ceremonials that involve the most planning (Barker, 1978). The organization of the wedding, who makes which arrangements, who gets invited, who comes, who pays, how much emotional energy goes into the preparations, who gets upset and over which issues, are all highly reflective of family process. It seems generally that those who marry in unconventional ways, in civil ceremonies, or without family or friends present, have their reasons. Most often the issues in such situations are family disapproval, premarital pregnancy, an impulsive decision to marry, a previous divorce, or the inability or unwillingness of the parents to meet the costs of the wedding (Barker, 1978). From a clinical point of view, the emotional charge of such situations, when it leads to downplaying the marriage as a family event, may well indicate that the family will remain stuck and will have difficulty with future stages of the family life cycle. Weddings are meant to be transition rituals that facilitate family process. As such they are extremely important for marking the change in status of family members and the shifting in family organization.

The opposite problem ensues when the family overfocuses on the wedding itself, at times spending way beyond their means, focusing all their energy on the event, and losing sight of the marriage as a process of joining two families.

More than any other ritual, the ceremony of the wedding is often substituted for the process of joining. Families and couples will assume that once the wedding has occurred, everyone should feel close and connected. Nowadays, with the changing mores, this focus on the wedding may be less intense, but there is still a large overlay of myth associated with marital bliss, which gets displaced onto wedding celebrations in a way that may be counterproductive.

Surprisingly, few couples ever seek premarital counseling in spite of the obvious difficulties in negotiating this transition (Friedman, 1977), and in spite of the fact that preventive intervention in relation to the extended families might be a great deal easier at this time than later in the life cycle. The most that can be said is that it is extremely useful when working with any member of a family around the time of a wedding to encourage him or her to facilitate the resolution of family relationships through this nodal event. One can only encourage all participants to make maximum use of the event to deal with the underlying family process. For example, it is often fruitful to convey to the couple that in-law struggles are predictable and need not be taken too personally. It is important for couples to recognize that the heightened parental tension probably relates to their sense of loss regarding the marriage. When families argue about wedding arrangements, the issues under dispute are only coverups of the underlying and much more important system issues as in the following example.

A couple about to marry was very upset because of the wife's mother's preoccupation with invitations and seating arrangements. The wife's previous marriage, which had been annulled, had never been dealt with openly by the family. Initially, the daughter got caught up in anger at her mother for not accepting her new marriage. The mother was embarrassed to invite her family since they had come to the first wedding and would now know for certain that it had not worked out. The mother hoped that with a small wedding "no one would notice," and over time the issue of the annulled marriage would be totally forgotten. She hoped her relatives would think that the new husband was the same one the daughter had married at the first wedding. The daughter was incensed at what she perceived as her mother's rejection of her and her new husband. Once she was able to begin talking to her mother about this, emphasizing how hard this second marriage must be for her mother, the tension diminished considerably. The daughter was able to give up her indignation and move toward her mother with some compassion for her mother's fear of her family's reactions. The daughter's move released the tension binding the system.

Since family members so often view others as capable of "ruining" the event, a useful rule of thumb is for each person to take his or her own responsibility for having a good time at the wedding. It is also useful for the couple to recognize that marriage is a family event and not just for the two of them. Looked at from this perspective, parents' feelings about the service need to be taken into consideration in whatever meaningful ways are possible. An interesting example is the young woman mentioned above who was having conflict with her mother about the undiscussed annulment. She had always been allied with her father. For the wedding, she asked both parents to walk her down the aisle and give her away, since she said they had both helped to bring her to the point of marriage. The mother was extremely touched by the invitation, and this small gesture allowed the young woman to make a significant family statement to her parents about their meaning in her life. Probably the more responsibility the couple can take for arranging a wedding that reflects their shifting position in their families and the joining of the two systems, the more auspicious for their future relationship.

An ideal to work toward in planning a wedding would be that achieved by Joan and Jim Marcus. They were one of the unusual couples who sought coaching to help them through the premarital period. They were aware of budding conflicts between them and wanted to resolve them before they got worse. Jim's parents had divorced when he was five. His father had remarried briefly when he was eight and again when he was sixteen. He had grown up in his father's custody with several housekeepers involved between his father's marriages. Jim had distanced from his alcoholic mother and from both stepmothers for many years, but was able to reverse the process of cutoff in his planning for the wedding. He called each of them to invite them specially to his wedding, discussing with each their importance in his life and how much it would mean to him to have them present at his wedding celebration. The next problem was Joan's parents, who were planning an elaborate celebration and wanted everything to go according to the book. This would have made Jim's less affluent family very uncomfortable. Initially, Joan became quite reactive to her mother's fancy plans and to her making decisions without discussion. At the suggestion of her therapist, she spent a whole day with her mother, discussing her own feelings about marriage and approaching her mother as a resource on how to handle things. She discovered for the first time that her mother had been married in a small civil wedding because her parents had little money and disapproved of her wedding. They had married during the Korean war, just before her father went overseas. Joan learned how much her mother had yearned for a "proper wedding." She realized that her mother's wishes to do everything in a fancy way had grown out of her own unrealized dreams and were an attempt to give Joan something she had missed. With this realization, Joan could share her own wish for a simple celebration, and especially her anxiety about Jim's family's discomfort, which she had not mentioned before. She asked her mother for advice on how to handle the situation. She told her how uncomfortable she was about the divorces in Jim's family and her fears that her own relatives would disapprove of him, especially if all his mothering figures attended the wedding. Suddenly her mother's attitude changed from dictating how things had to be done to a helpful and much more casual attitude. A week later, Joan's mother got Jim alone and told him that if there was any way she could facilitate things with his mother, stepmothers, or other guests she would be happy to do so.

Another young couple, Ted and Andrea, perhaps the only couple I have seen who sought premarital counseling specifically to work on extended family issues, were able to field stormy emotional reactions in the family so well that they probably prevented years of simmering conflicts that had hampered both extended families over several generations. When they sought help, they said they planned to marry with only a few friends present unless they could bring their families around to accepting them as they were. Andrea's parents had eloped after their parents refused to agree to the marriage because of "religious differences." Ted's paternal grandfather had had a heart attack and died three days after Ted's father married. Weddings thus became dreaded events for both extended families. The couple began their work by contacting extended family members personally to invite them to their marriage, raising their concerns in the conversations. For example, the husband called his father's mother who was eighty-five and whom his parents had assured him would never be able to come. He told her his parents were sure she couldn't make it, but that it meant a great deal to him to have her there since he feared his father might have a heart attack and he needed her support. The parents had been acting to protect the grandmother "for her own good." She not only made her own arrangements to have a cousin fly with her, but she arranged to stay with her son, the groom's father, during the week after the wedding. At the wedding, both bride and groom made poetic toasts to their families in which they ticked off the charged issues, with humor and sensitivity, and made a special point of spending time with family members.

THE EARLY YEARS OF MARRIAGE AND DECIDING
ABOUT PARENTHOOD

Generally speaking, the first years of marriage are seen by couples, especially wives, as the happiest time in the family life cycle (Campbell, 1975). Although the transition to parenthood may not be as much of a trauma or crisis as it was thought to be a few years ago (LeMasters, 1957; Hobbs, 1976), it is still a tremendous shift for the couple, and one they are often unprepared to make (Rossi, 1968). While couples have the period of courtship to prepare for marriage, there is virtually no direct preparatory experience for having a baby. It appears that men view marriage with much greater ambivalence than women do (Campbell, 1975), and increasingly women view having children with much greater ambivalence than men do. Having at least a year to adjust to marriage before pregnancy is an important factor in marital stability. Joint planning for pregnancy, of course, also makes a considerable difference in this.

Although in our time the decision to have children is increasingly separated from the decision to marry, the agreement to have children together is an underlying assumption in almost all marriages. Nowadays an increasing, but still small, number of couples are choosing to remain childless. For the rest, the fantasy of becoming a threesome is a factor in becoming a twosome. The question of when and how is an increasingly complex part of coupling negotiations. This is particularly so because the changing role of women has redefined many former axioms about childcare. Fears about the spouse's lack of participation in childrearing is an issue especially for women, and some couples seek therapy when they get stuck on these issues.

The choice is, of course, hardest for women with successful careers, but is increasingly difficult to resist as the biological clock moves on. Men need not be as concerned, obviously, but for women the question persists as they move through their childbearing years. Even childless career women are likely to struggle with the urge to have children, and therefore work may have a somewhat different meaning for them, especially during their thirties.

Some couples find the level of responsibility required in having a child a great burden. They are able to handle the responsibility of living with another adult, realizing they are not responsible for the other's survival, or even for being emotionally available more than a certain amount of the time. There is a qualitatively different level of commitment to parenthood than to marriage. As everyone knows, marriage vows can be broken. Parenthood is forever. Often, of course, the decision to have children is taken as carelessly as the decision to marry, and with disastrous results. For both of these life cycle shifts, the simplicity of doing it belies the extreme complexity of the experiences involved over time. It is unfortunately possible to misunderstand the enormous lifelong commitment to relationships and invisible loyalties in the simplicity of the moment of marriage or conception.

As with the overlay of preconceptions about "husbandhood" and "wifehood" which may intensify the process of marriage by adding a complex layer of "shoulds," adding the roles father and mother to the couple brings in a whole other geometrically more complex layer. In a certain sense one could say that except for a very small minority of couples, the fantasy of becoming a triangle is a part of their relationship from the beginning. It would be difficult to say how much of a role such fantasies play in the relationship between the couple before they have a child.

According to Campbell (1975), couples and especially women, report the greatest marital satisfaction just after marriage and before they have children. Women report less stress after marriage than before, but men report more stress after then before. When there are in-law conflicts, as often happens, the relationships do not tend to soften until the in-laws become grandparents, at which point there is often a mellowing of the relationships. This again may reflect a greater commitment to blood ties than marital ties.

Couples who do not have children, for whatever reason, are sometimes thought not to proceed through the family life cycle, although, of course, this is not so. All aspects of the family life cycle, apart from direct child-rearing, obviously apply to them. They must go through the process of re-negotiating relationships with their parents, siblings, and friends through each successive life cycle stage. Virtually none of us is so cut off from our families and friends that the process of our lives does not proceed with theirs. We share with close friends and siblings their struggles with child-rearing and continue to redefine our lives as we move along. Older childless couples may feel a lack of family continuity because they do not have children or grandchildren, but the focus on these issues as the cause of distress often appears more related to other family issues, such as parental problems or difficulty with intimacy, than to the lack of children in itself. Of course, the death of a spouse may be much more difficult when one has no children or grandchildren to turn to for support. Childless older couples may tend to be more cut off from significant ties with younger people than are those with direct family ties. At times such people intentionally cultivate relationships with other families and such relationships may be deeply enriching for all. The difficulty is that nonfamily ties are easier to break when problems arise, as they surely do over a lifetime of relating. It may be difficult to preserve contact through periods of physical distance and when immediate mutual interests are not apparent.

The widespread use of contraceptives has greatly changed the life cycle for women. Previously, marriage was the major change in their lives with motherhood assumed as part of the process. Nowadays, the major change for women often occurs not at marriage but with their first pregnancy, which may be several years later. The changing sexual mores have also greatly altered the meaning of marriage, which used to offer the only legitimate occasion for women to have sex. It is possible that greater sexual freedom could mean fewer impulsive marriages, since marriage and sex are not as closely linked as before.

The shift in the meaning of marriage for our culture, however, points in the direction of increasing marital instability. Our society tends to assess marriage by two norms: happiness and stability. Our reverence for emotional satisfaction is a relatively recent development. During the nineteenth century, mate selection was guided instead by rationality that stressed good health, strong character, and similarity of religion (Abernathy, 1976). The earlier standards were based on a pressing need of spouses for each other as working partners in agricultural or home-centered enterprises. In our more industrialized society, there is no longer a need for marital partners to have specialized and complementary roles. The stabilizing pressure of maintaining the structure to insure survival is no longer necessary. Marriage bonds are coming to rest on personal and emotional attachment. As Abernathy notes, "This fragile bond of conjugal emotion is invoked and supported through the romanticization of the mass media, the cosmetic industry, marriage counseling, and psychotherapy directed toward improved communication and interpersonal relationships" (1976, p. 35).

In previous eras, marriages were contracted by families for economic and social stability and advantage. Nowadays, families often meet for the first time at the wedding and play no role whatsoever in mate selection. Naturally then, when marriages near dissolution, families can bring little pressure to bear, since they have little vested interest in the alliance beyond a personal wish for family stability, and particularly a concern for the grandchildren.

With childrearing now occupying only one-half of the family life cycle, and couples now living generally for many years alone together after their children are grown, the grounds for remaining together must be different from all earlier times when marriage formed the basic structure for social and economic stability, and was focused primarily on providing the foundation for rearing children.

The increasing education and career orientation of women is also changing the face of marriage. More and more women are taking higher career goals more seriously. Naturally, career oriented women have greater ambivalence about having children, since it puts a tremendous burden on them in particular. Dual career families are becoming an increasingly frequent phenomenon, although our social structure is not particularly supportive of such arrangements. Couples are having to forge their way without much precedent in their family backgrounds that would provide them with models. Naturally, these shifts are causing much marital stress for couples. Indications are that working wives are more satisfied and more effective in their pursuits than are nonworking wives (Burke, 1976). And not surprisingly, the opposite is true for husbands: husbands of nonworking wives express more satisfaction than those whose wives work (Burke, 1976). This fits with clinical experience that husbands of working wives do not have a role precedent for the relationship they must work out with their spouses.

Historically, the wife's role in a marriage was to adapt to her mate's needs and direction. A good marriage would have been equated with fusion of the wife into the husband's personality, career, and network. In our time, when women are becoming people with their own work and friendship systems, as well as their own family systems, fitting into a smoothly running marriage is increasingly difficult. Adjusting a marriage within the demands of two careers is enormously more difficult than moving around to accommodate the needs of one. In addition, when both spouses' needs and interests are taken into account equally, all manner of negotiations about married life become extremely complex.

Friendships, for example, become a knotty problem. In earlier times, a wife was expected to socialize with the wives of her husband's friends. Now that both partners are free to make friend decisions, working out "couple friendships" is much more difficult. An added problem seems to be the myth that if the couple really loved each other, they would be attracted to the same friends and this area would not be problematic. Difficulties in negotiating friendships can often lead to the couple having minimal social contacts as a couple, since they may see their different preferences as a sign that something is wrong with their relationship. Normalizing the difficulties here is an important factor in helping such couples. If each partner is going to think and evaluate for him-or herself, they will not be able to share every friend or every activity. The problem here becomes that of finding a balance between shared activities and friendships and those each pursues independently. Each partner will need a degree of independent activity to feel fulfilled. However, beyond a certain point of separateness, the question will arise (now more so since marriage is no longer tied to economic or social networks particularly) about how the couple can direct enough of their emotional energy into the marriage to keep it viable.

CLINICAL IMPLICATIONS

If couples seek therapy at this phase of the life cycle, it is more often for difficulty tolerating closeness; sexual problems; problems negotiating their differences, particularly male-female issues; or over the question of whether or not to have children (more common for couples where the wife is over thirty). Although we hypothesize that failure to work out relationships with extended family is the main reason for marital failure, it appears that couples are very unlikely to present with this as the overt problem.

Therapy at this phase will be directed primarily toward helping partners relate realistically to each other and to their families of origin. The major pitfalls for couples are perhaps:

1. The "Utopia Syndrome" (Lederer and Jackson, 1968; Watzlawick, 1974): the mythical expectation that love, sex, and marriage mean a perfect fit forever, including mind-reading, sharing friends, philosophies, values, and expectations in life.

2. Boundary problems with extended family: (a) too-closed boundaries

(cut off or distancing from family), so that too much energy is left concentrated in the too-small space of the marital relationship; and (b) Too-open boundaries (enmeshment with extended family), so that the family interferes with the development of sufficient marital boundaries for intimacy.

3. "Triangling" to stabilize a marital relationship by overfocusing on children, overinvesting in work, alcohol, affairs, or negative attention to relatives (e.g., mother-in-law), and the like.

Couples do not usually seek professional help even when problems arise at this transition, although intervention at this time could prevent later problems which arise either when unresolvable marital problems have been transmitted to the children or after the children leave, when the couple must again face the issues they did not resolve earlier.

The requirements of this phase of the family life cycle are changing drastically in our time and leaving couples and families with little precedent for the processes they must go through, particularly in terms of male-female relationships based on equal options for each. With childrearing taking up less of the life cycle, many new opportunities open up. As the meaning of marriage changes, we are left to deal with great risks to the stability of the family system.

REFERENCES

Abernathy, Virginia, "American Marriage in Cross Cultural Perspective," in *Contemporary Marriage,* eds. H. Grunebaum & J. Christ, Boston: Little, Brown, 1976.

Alymer, Robert C., "Emotional Issues in Divorce," *The Family* 4/1, 1977.

Axelson, L., "The Marital Adjustment and Marital Role Definitions of Husbands of Working and Non-Working Wives," *Marriage and Family Living* 25:189–95, 1963.

Bacon, L., "Early Motherhood, Accelerated Role Transition and Social Pathologies," *Social Forces* 52:333–41, March 1974.

Barker, D. L., "A Proper Wedding," in *The Couple,* ed. M. Corbin, New York: Penguin, 1978.

Becker, G. et al., "Economics of Marital Instability," *Journal of Political Economy* 85:1141–87, December 1977.

Blake, J., "Is Zero Preferred? American Attitudes Toward Childlessness in the 1970's," *Journal of Marriage and the Family* 41/2, May 1979.

Bowen, M., *Family Therapy in Clinical Practice,* New York: Jason Aronson, 1978.

Bumpass, L., & J. Sweet, "Differentials in Marital Instability, 1970," *American Sociological Review* 37:754–66, December 1972.

Burchinal, L.G., "Trends and Prospects for Young Marriages in the United States," *Journal of Marriage and the Family* 27/2, May 1965.

Burke, R.J., & T. Weir, "The Relationship of Wives' Employment Status to Husband, Wife and Pair Satisfaction," *Journal of Marriage and the Family* 38/2, May 1976.

————, "Satisfaction with Various Aspects of Marriage over the Life Cycle: A Random Middle Class Sample," *Journal of Marriage and the Family* 32:29, 1970.

Calhoun, J., "The Human Family." Conference, Georgetown Family Center, Washington, D.C., September 1978.

Campbell, Angus, "The American Way of Mating, Marriage Si, Children Only Maybe," *Psychology Today* 8/12:37-43, May 1975.

Christensen, H.T., "The Timing of First Pregnancy as a Factor in Divorce: A Cross-Cultural Analysis," *Eugenics Quarterly* 10:119-30, September 1963.

Ferber, M., & J. Huber, "Husbands, Wives and Careers," *Journal of Marriage and the Family* 41/2, May 1979.

Fogarty, Thomas, "On Emptiness and Closeness, Part II," *The Family* 3/2, 1976.

Friedman, E.H., "Engagement and Disengagement: Family Therapy with Couples During Courtship," *Georgetown Family Symposia*, Vol I, eds., F Andres & P. Lorio, 1977.

v   Glick, Paul C., "A Demographer Looks at American Families, *Journal of Marriage and the Family* 37/1, February 1975.

————, "Updating the Life Cycle of the Family," *Journal of Marriage and the Family* 39/1 February 1977.

————, & A.J. Norton, "Marrying, Divorcing and Living Together in the U.S. Today," in *Population Bulletin* 32/5 (Pop. Ref. Bureau, Inc. Wash. D.C.) 1977.

Goodrich, W. et al., "Patterns of Newlywed Marriage," *Journal of Marriage and the Family* 30/3, August 1968.

Haley, Jay, "Marriage Therapy," *Archives of General Psychiatry* 8:213-34, March 1963.

————, *Uncommon Therapy: The Psychiatric Techniques of Milton H. Erickson, M.D.,* New York: Norton, 1973.

Hobbs, D.F., & S.P. Cole, "Transition to Parenthood: A Decade Replication," *Journal of Marriage and the Family* 38/723-31, November 1976.

Lederer, W.J., & D.D. Jackson, *The Mirages of Marriage,* New York: Norton, 1968.

LeMasters, E.E., "Parenthood as Crisis," *Marriage and Family Living* 19/4:352-5, November 1957.

Mott, F.J. & S.F. Moore, "The Causes of Marital Disruption Among Young American Women: An Interdisciplinary Perspective," *Journal of Marriage and the Family* 41/2, May 1979.

Pearson, W. & L. Hendrix, "Divorce and the Status of Women," *Journal of Marriage and the Family* 41/2, May 1979.

Rausch, H.L. et al., "Adaptation to the First Years of Marriage," *Psychiatry,* 26/4:368-80, November 1963.

Rilke, R.M., *Letters to a Young Poet,* revised edition, translated by M.D. Hester, New York: Norton, 1954.

Rossi, A.A., "Transition to Parenthood," *Journal of Marriage and the Family,* 30/1:26-39, February 1968.

Ryder, Robert, "Dimensions of Early Marriage," *Family Process,* 9/1, 1970.

Satir, V., *Conjoint Family Therapy,* revised edition, Palo Alto: Science and Behavior Books, 1967.

Stanton, M.D., "Marital Therapy from a Structural/Strategic Viewpoint," in *Marriage is a Family Affair: A Textbook of Marriage and Marital Therapy*, ed. G.P. Sholevar, Jamaica, New York: SP Medical and Scientific Books, in press.

Toman, W., *Family Constellation: Its Effect on Personality and Social Behavior,* 3rd edition, New York: Springer, 1976.

U.S. Bureau of the Census, *Current Population Survey*, June 1978.

Watzlawick, P., J. Weakland, and D. Fisch, *Change,* New York: Norton, 1974.

6

The Family With Young Children

Jack O. Bradt, M.D.

Groome Center, Washington, D.C.

Department of Psychiatry, Georgetown University Hospital

INTRODUCTION

If actions speak louder than words, Americans like marriage. Based on projections of present statistics, it is estimated that contemporary newborns will have a greater number of marriages than their number of children. This chapter concerns that increasingly uncommon "simple" family: The couple married only once, who become parents of at least two biologic children, with whom they live in one household. I will review family life before the children reach adolescence.

THEORETICAL CONCEPTS

I will outline briefly the conceptual framework on which my perceptions of the family system are based to prevent us from groping like the proverbial blindmen at the elephant of the family.

1. A viable human system is a complex or whole of interdependent persons, who (in relating) assure that the whole of the system has primacy over its individual members.

2. No system, including the family system, is independent of other human systems.

3. There is no self without others, no self without a system, and no system without selves.

4. A person's self is realized through his or her multiple relationships in two spheres that I call the dumbbell of modern life (see Figure 6.1). The domestic sphere includes friends and family. The nondomestic sphere is largely defined by one's work and public life. Dialectic process exists between the two spheres. I represent the domestic sphere by another image: the jack (see Figure 6.2). Like the child's toy, domestic reality is organized on a vertical axis and two horizontal axes. Specifically, the metaphor represents the grandparent-parent-child vertical relationship axis (on which the jack is balanced) intersected by two horizontal axes—one's siblings and friends before marriage (a dialectic), and the dialectic between one's spouse and friends after marriage. The jack is always resting on a vertical and two other poles.

5. Nodal events are the usual happenings of family life that create instability in membership and/or function in the family system, events that bring up the possibility of loss or gain of membership and challenge the integrity and growth of the family unit. A nodal event can affect the balancing implied in the images of a dumbbell or a jack.

6. To be a contributing member of any system, a person is called upon to be one of many (peers), and also to complement with others in some kind of hierarchy (nonpeers) whose functions lock together with one's own in a dominant and adaptive interdependency.

7. A person's readiness to form peer or complementary relationships is largely determined by the place he or she has had in the family structure (e.g., only children have no family experience of peers and identical twins

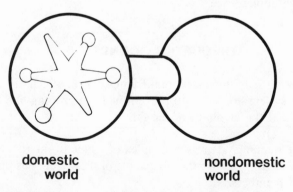

domestic
world

nondomestic
world

Figure 6.1 The Dumbbell of Modern Life

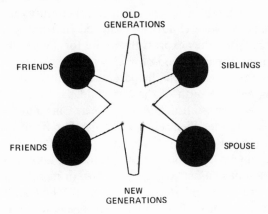

Figure 6.2 The Domestic Jack

have the ultimate peer experience). On the jack (Figure 6.2), peer relationships are represented on the horizontal, complementary to the vertical axis.

8. Within this system, a dialectic process operates between poles of relationship and between vertical and horizontal axes. Dysfunction is related to a predominance of one pole or axis of a potentially bipolar, multiaxed relationship complex.

9. Dialectic potential is manifested as tension that can result in either disconnection between poles (unipolar fixation) or resolution in which bipolar tension creates synthesis. Resolution of tension between the axes creates self. Resolution of tension (rather than disconnection) between spheres creates integrity.

The reflections on family life that follow are formulated within the perspective of these concepts.

MARRIAGE AND PARENTHOOD

> I'm tired of relationships with no more commitment than four hours, two days, or a weekend, but I can't imagine making a seventeen-year commitment to raising a child or being that long responsible for someone else.

Parenthood and marriage have been tied inseparably together by tradition and practice for many generations. But today's divorce statistics make marriage seem to be negotiable, not a permanent commitment. Becoming a parent is seen as a more prolonged commitment, and less negotiable than marriage. The view that childhood is long (and so therefore is parenthood) is affirmed by the prolonging of childhood by married and single young adults who see their own childhoods lasting as long as they don't become parents.

I hear few people these days saying that it is their duty to society to have children, or that they love children, or indeed that life would be empty without children. Often they express the desire for the personal experience or accomplishment of parenthood or a wish to pass on the family name or be acknowledged as "a grownup" by parenthood. In any case, the time between marrying and the birth of the first child has been dramatically increasing with each new statistical survey. Increasing numbers of *couples* without children consider themselves a family. The Family Impact Seminar, a privately funded group in Washington, D.C., attempting to assess the impact of government legislation on the American families, took a broad working definition of *family*: "any group of two or more persons with a legal or biological relationship" (Ooms, 1977, p. 1). John Calhoun, renowned for his multigenerational studies of rats, gives a generic definition of family as "an assembly of adults." Children exist to "become educated and adult members of the family." He predicts that in one hundred years, two-thirds of the population will have nothing to do with the rearing of children (Calhoun, 1978).

Creating a two-parent family with biologic children living together in one household is not happening as quickly or with the same lack of self-consciousness as it used to. Some people would see this as a manifestation of human enlightenment: alternative life-styles unencumbered with the convention of responsibility for children. Some might ascribe this to the "pill" triumphing over biology. Field surveys indicate that in some nations as many as one-fifth of the children were "mistakes" who presumably would not have been born if parents had better contraceptive technology (Rockefeller Illustrative, 1978).

Increasingly, young adults seem to be asking, "Why choose to become a parent?" We may wonder why this attitude is developing and what it has to do with the family experience these young adults had themselves. Are they uncomfortable about the burdens in their parents' lives, and avoiding a family situation that cultural anthropologists describe as possibly the most unsupported family structure to emerge in social evolution?

Does narcissism arise out of a threat to survival?

There is today new ethic, the quest for *self*—to think it mature to be more devoted to oneself than to any collective unit like one's family, church, community, neighborhood, or nation. Coexistent with the fad "Search for Self" is the "Urge to Merge," to find a nondeviant consensus, a reflection of self through association with others who see, feel, hear, touch, and smell the same. Increasing numbers of young marrieds see being a parent as a disturbance in the quest for self, an unwelcome sacrifice. They see marriage without children as offering greater closeness, pleasure, and equality in their relationship, and fear that children will reduce the time they have to themselves, and for each other. "Two's company, three's a crowd," seems to be the attitude.

SPACE FOR CHILDREN

The environment into which children are born can be one in which there is no space for them, there is space for them, or there is a vacuum they are brought in to fill. Many factors determine which context will be present in a family at the time of birth. All available family space may already be taken up with other activities or relationships. Or there may be little space because there are few available family members.

Space for parenting (space for children) is difficult for contemporary parents to make. From the time of the industrial revolution to the present, the sexes have been unevenly distributed between the spheres of home and work, with men predominant in the nondomestic sphere and women in the domestic sphere. Presently, women are approaching 50% of the labor force. They work out of necessity and as a natural outcome of the cultural values of success, achievement, and financial reward. As the work force becomes more evenly populated by men and women, there has been no comparable shift of men to the domestic sphere, no revaluing of domestic life, and a devaluing of child rearing. Urie Bronfenbrenner asks, "Who cares for America's children? ... Who cares?" (1977). We are a nation of single-parent families—those who actually have only one and those who functionally lack a parent, usually father. Are we in danger of becoming a nation of "no parent families" or of childless couples?

This disproportionate shift in the direction of the nondomestic sphere leaves children often in a relatively adultless relationship context, particularly since the *increased mobility* of career oriented parents occurs during the child-bearing years. Moving away usually encourages "permanent" psychological distance from the extended family as well. An added effect of this situation is that children are tending to give greater allegiance to their peer group than to parents, teachers, the church, or the state. In fact, today the question becomes pertinent, are children raising each other? Is the society becoming age-stratified? In effect, the outcome is that adults have less space in their lives for children. Our materialistic society encourages the competitive pursuit of money over other values. Good is determined more by what is consumed, enjoyed, or displayed as products of success, achievement, and the pursuit of pleasure. Parenting in its more fundamental and necessary dimensions requires more sacrifice, cooperation over competitive values, and conservation of invested energy to produce an ongoing chain of life.

At the other extreme are parents overinvested in the domestic sphere. Children may be used to fill an emptiness in the lives of the parents, often resulting from the loss of their own parents or nonparticipation in the nondomestic sphere of life by choice or by failure. Clinically this may emerge as the child-focused family in which a child becomes a replacement for the unrealized achievement or place in the world or loss of relationship with a family member who is dead or out of contact (cut off).

Conception and birth can activate fantasies of one's own childhood and the idealized fantasy of making up in the present for the imagined deprivations of the past. As one parent put it, "I determined when our first child was born that I would not be overly affectionate. My mother smothered me. Her love caused me so much pain, I held back on affection because I did not want my son to be tied so tightly."

Overcloseness in parent-child relationships is often the outcome of filling the vacuum created by a relationship loss with another. It tends to involve generational blurring, and overloading of the parent-child relationship. As Gorney has noted, "High intensity interpersonal bonding may be a prerequisite for various human behaviors, one of which is aggression" (1968, p. 146). Interpersonal intensity derives from two factors, 1) Urgency: emotional conditioning prevalent within our culture and 2) Exclusivity: the degree to which drives are focused upon one or very few persons. Conditioned to intense relationships, one is made vulnerable to loss.

Although strength of character is a possible adult outcome of adversity or an unfavorable environment in childhood, in general the yield of a generation of children is greater when the social soil that surrounds the family is more nourishing. In a technical, mechanical, material age, it is important to remember that people, like plants, are living organisms in need of basic tending, care, nourishment, protection, and cultivation in order to thrive.

THE IDEAL: INTIMACY

Somewhere in the midrange of the spectrum between distance (when a family has no space for the child) and overcloseness (when the family uses the child to fill a vacuum) is the favorable space of intimacy. *Intimacy* involves a caring relationship without pretense, and revelation without risk of loss or gain from one or the other. It is giving and receiving, an exchange that enhances because it facilitates the awareness of selves, of their differences and sameness. It is discriminant, encouraging elaboration of facets of each person. It creates and sustains belonging, while appreciating each individual's uniqueness. Intimacy encourages continuity. It is the sustaining energy of the human tide moving through time. It allows us to belong with those who came before and those who come after.

It follows that two parents must sustain the intimacy of their marriage relationship to avoid developing a vacuum or lack of space, both unfavorable environments for the flourishing of children (see Figure 6.3).

As Bronfenbrenner has noted, "The psychological development of the child is brought about through his continuing involvement in progressively

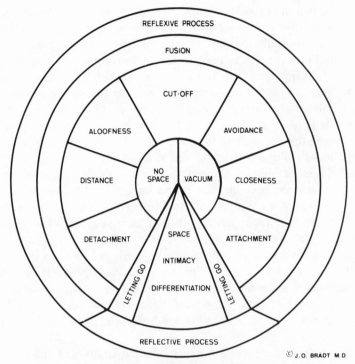

Figure 6.3 Closeness-Distance Intimacy Schema

more complex patterns of reciprocal activity with persons with whom the child develops a strong and enduring emotional attachment" (1977, p. 11). He believes that bonding involves the development of an "irrational emotional attachment" that requires many interactions with the same person. These days, children who have this experience with one adult, let alone two, are fortunate.

NEW PARENTHOOD

Becoming a parent can influence sexual attitudes and practice. Pregnancy has certain requirements of the female body that distort the erotic form, fantasy, and sexual practices that some men and women consider essential to sexual fulfillment. Breastfeeding, back in vogue, restores breasts to their teleologic function, but may interfere with the breast symbol that characterized the preparental sexual relationship. Occasionally a husband reports that his attitude toward his wife changed from a sexual playmate to a mother—a sort of incest taboo. (This is best treated by more contact with one's real mother.) Women are more competent than men in accepting the waxing and waning of anatomy and physiology but are especially sensitive to their visual appeal during and after pregnancy. Sexual interest and appetite varies accordingly. Sex as a cause of disfiguration (pregnancy) may lower sexual interest. Sex as reassurance of desirability may encourage sexual interest. Males are often clumsy in their sensitivity to their mate's concern, as well as being a bit (or a lot) awed by the biologic power of the female. Husbandly humorousness is often the outcome, but for most women this is not a laughing matter. Humours, and hormones more than humor, bathe the postpartum female psyche. Humoring the female hormonal vagaries of childbirth, if continued as a relationship style, can result in a family balance of "humor the old lady" and "don't upset your mother," which dismisses the accountability (and importance) of the wife.

The presence of a child in the home (especially an ambulatory or older child) deprives parents of privacy, even in their bedroom. There is a threat of too little time and too many levels of concern occupying the minds of both husband and wife for intimacy to be easily achieved in sexual experience. Wives place sex without intimacy in the category of wifely duties. ("If he doesn't get it at home, he'll get it out on the streets.") Husbands, self-righteously occupied with being good, hard-working husbands and fathers, interpret their wives' disinterest as a rebuff, nonappreciation for all their hard work.

Most people prefer privacy when relating sexually and children require boundary realignment in the family. Closed doors help children keep sex on the back burner and other growth-facilitating curiosities more active, and help parents put children on a "back burner" at least occasionally. Some parents put locks on doors that once were open, some give up what requires privacy.

During a recent visit to a public library I noticed a book display entitled, "How to Parent." Among the many books on the shelves of the display were five with "mother" in their title, three on exceptional children (handicapped, hyperactive, and disabled), a transactional analysis guidebook on how to talk with your children, and no books with the word "father" in their title. The American myth of parenthood, if current literature is reflective of continuing trends of society, is still that parenthood equals motherhood. Happily there are some fathers who are discovering the pleasure and challenge of becoming a participant father-parent, actively involved in the domestic sphere, a peer with his wife and a full parent to their children. Unfortunately, there may be fewer males who find fatherhood *in marriage* rather than *through divorce*.

For generations, the birth of a child has signaled a shifting away of would-be fathers toward work. The typical notion of the good father has been, "He's a responsible father; he's always worked hard and provided for his wife and children." The traditional shift of the husband away from the home and fatherhood has been determined not only by society but also by the process of pregnancy, which literally puts distance between mother and father by the omnipresence of the baby between them, even in the privacy of the marriage bed. Mothers-to-be cannot leave their uterine cargo until nine months have past. The literature suggests that even then mothers more than fathers are supposed to be with the young. It may be that most of this literature is written by men who have overinvested in the nondomestic sphere and therefore view the domestic sphere as not their domain.

As one rethinks human relationships in multigeneratinal systemic terms, the idea of the primacy of the mother may have come to be enshrined only because fathers and extended family have not stayed around to participate as coparents (or as grandfathers, godfathers, uncles, and the like). When the nuclear family is isolated and the economic system is set up so that fathers work outside the home, the result will be that mother and baby are together and are therefore more likely to bond and create, as Mahler (1952) describes it, "an omnipotent system, a dual entity within one common boundary," which in past years was interpreted as *Momism.*

The library display also illustrated the concerns of parents about the possibility of their child being "special," i.e., handicapped. Some people consider this kind of concern during pregnancy to be self-fulfilling prophecy. Others see it as a part of the bonding process that is essential to the development of an "irrational attachment." It may be either, neither, or both. It is, as the presence of the books suggests, a common concern for new parents. I am still impressed by the reported consequences of abortion among contemporary young people. Abortion influences expectations and the meanings of later pregnancies.

Having survived conception, nine months of pregnancy, and all the wives' tales regarding delivery and the postpartum period, new parents, in spite of their late nights and new responsibilities, might be relieved to read: "During the first 8 months, the baby's general progress in development is assured by nature. In terms of having to make choices, it is probably the easiest of all times for parents: *If they* [italics mine] provide the baby with a normal amount of love, attention and physical care, nature will pretty much take care of the rest" (White, 1975).

Realizing that a normal amount of care will ensure the healthy development of their child may be more helpful to parents than learning that during this period their child passes through a phase of "normal autism" and "normal symbiosis" (Mahler, 1952). During the first two years of life, all children appear to have a special need to establish a strong attachment to one or more older humans (White, 1975). Attachment requires repeated contact to achieve more than a facade of relationship. Spitz's (1945) studies make us mindful of the importance of consistency of these persons (in recent generations, mother alone). The limitation of studies of early child development is in the cultural assumption that only mothers are essential, discounting both the direct relationship possibilities of fathers and their presence or absence as intimate partners in parenting and marriage. Though the need for repeated contact is necessary for bonding, a study of two-year-old middle-class children from intact families indicates that they hear their fathers' voices in the same room no more than 37.7 seconds a day (Rebelsky, 1971).

For couples whose bond was more fusion than intimacy, the arrival of a child brings the nuclear family triangle into play (Bowen, 1966), challenging the stability of the parents' relationship with the close position threatened by the baby. The baby's presence and behavior may draw one parent close, leaving the other distant. Commonly the triangle shifts so that the father is in the distant position and mother and child become close. A vacuum may also have been created by the parents' previous experience of pregnancy. For some distant couples, the baby represents a desired closeness of each to the other through the baby. The involvement of the infant in the closeness-distance process of the parental triangle may be good enough to sustain the infant's growth and development, but developmental achievements of the child can become "nodal events" that threaten the stable triangular family patterns.

In families organized to avoid difference or conflict, even early developmental milestones of infancy may cause problems, particularly the defiant "No!" of the terrible twos. Parents who need to avoid conflict look to the other for approval. They are ready to capitualate in the face of the other's opinion. Though children need to know that parents are in charge, such parents will often capitulate to their child's defiance. Often it is the mother's need for agreement that dominates the domestic sphere, with father joining in occasionally, often even capriciously, becoming one of the kids, supposedly agreeing with mother, but actually competing for his entitlements of mother. Conflict-avoiding parents practice pseudomutuality (Wynne, 1958) that looks like closeness (one observes only sameness and agreement) but that actually implies great distance and lack of recognition of each other.

This burdened, displaced balance of parenting may explain why contemporary childlessness seems to be more determined by wives than husbands. Now, more than ever in history, a woman is aware of her role as burdened by motherhood, a heavy and largely unacknowledged (socially unrewarded) role with the added vulnerability of an increasingly high risk of divorce. If she commits herself to exclusive parenting, she runs the risk of being abandoned, withdrawn from the marketplace competition and given increased domestic responsibilities. Our society has come out with seriously conflicting values on maternal care for children and sexual freedom for parents.

Assuming that the new parents and child have managed through the first three years, an ever more common option emerges: out-of-the-home child care. Junior is toilet trained and therefore eligible for enrollment in day-care or preschool, or some kind of child group situation in which people other than parents are directly responsible for the child for some regularly scheduled block of time one or more days a week (an exception is co-op nurseries where parents participate in child care). New vistas emerge in this situation, or old visions, clouded by the functional myopia of early parent-childhood, reemerge. In early infancy, some parents manage to develop in-the-home child care through the services of day or live-in help. Usually in the upper and middle classes this is more likely nonkin. In this instance, an infant born to poor parents may have one advantage over the "advantaged class": his care person is more likely to be family.

Usually the mother is the parent whose vistas have been obscured by child care. Her intention to get back into the nondomestic workworld becomes a critical point in the family process. She may be motivated by a desire to restitute her sense of self and rebalance her adult relationships and achieve social validation. Of course, greater role stresses are experienced by parents who attempt to coordinate two jobs with the responsibility for children. This is especially true if they cling to the concept that only mothers are parents or other household agents.

If another pregnancy follows soon, children define a new family equilibrium and the wife-woman fades away as "mother" becomes her social identity. When a second birth occurs, assuming the couple has accepted parenthood, they may accept the second child with greater equanimity perhaps because it is less disruptive to the established equilibrium than the initial transition to parenthood. After the first pregnancy, the threat of role change is minimized for the husband. However, both parents may feel themselves taken for granted by the other. Marriage seems less fulfilling, tedious. Sex is frequently equated with intimacy or closeness especially by husbands, but not so often by wives who are otherwise out of contact with their husbands. Extramarital liaisons for either parent become more likely as each recalibrates the feeling of closeness with or distance from the other. Clinically, it is not uncommon to learn that an affair has taken place close in time to pregnancy or to greater involvement in the nondomestic sphere by either spouse. Divorce is increasingly common during the generative years of the family life cycle, regardless of the ages of children.

OTHER CHILDREN

In *The Joy of the Only Child* (Peck, 1977) (also on the "How to Parent" library shelf), Ellen Peck argues that parents should stand pat with one child. She sees the world as crowded with too few distinguished and successful people, and compared with being a sibling, only children are "achieving people." According to her, people have trouble getting along with each other because there are too many people. Peck believes if fewer children were born, and those born were only children, there would be fewer problems, a better life, and the few born would naturally bring their achievements to bear on making a better world.

In fact, the birth rate has declined in recent years indicating a popular swing toward one- or two-child, or even no-child, families. Statistics once showed 2.1 children per family; currently statistics indicate slightly less than 2 children constitute the child membership of American families. (A rapidly growing census category is single dwellers.)

If Peck's views and statistics represent a trend, there is a resultant loss of experience of sharing, and cooperating, competing, and conflicting as peers in a sibship. The experiences of symmetrical negotiation, multiplicity, diversity, and similarity are lost. Parents with only children, rather than a number of children, gravitate toward more egalitarian (peer) nonhierarchial relationships with their young. It could be asked if only children come out with less familiarity with organizational hierarchy and less appropriate reciprocal peering.

Toman (1978) considers children with siblings born more than six years apart to be functionally only children. In Peck's view, siblings, regardless of age, means sibling rivalry and she thinks children should be protected from this trauma. Being an only child is her answer. To cut down on sibling rivalry and to avoid overtaxing parents, Dr. White encourages at least three years' spacing between children.

Optimum space between children is truly a matter of perspective. From the parents' standpoint, one child at a time is challenge enough, multiple births too close in time a disaster. From the child's standpoint, the perfect companion would be an identical twin, the optimum peer, a perfect mirror of oneself, an alter ego extraordinary. For parents, the birth of twins is far more stressful than single births, in large part because of the additional tasks involved. With the nuclear family generally isolated from the ongoing assistance from the extended family and in a culture where child care is often mainly mother's responsibility with little support or assistance from others, twins are a major challenge to her physical and emotional stamina as well as to the marriage relationship. Time is hard to find for rest, and even more difficult for romance.

That siblings inevitably create "a trauma" for one another seems more a function of availability of caring adults than of the inherent rivalry of children. The long standing family pattern of parenting being single-parenthood (mother) seems as much an explanation for sibling rivalry as the fact of close-in-age siblings. Cooperation can be as likely an outcome as competition, depending perhaps more on parents' availability and attitudes than on their children.

Competition is determined not only by the availability of parental adults, but by how parents relate to children. A parent who habitually tries to judge sibling squabbles encourages "sibling rivalry." A common error of parents is to hold one of their children accountable (to blame) rather than holding all children involved in a particular action accountable for working things out. Children are usually more cooperative with one another in the face of collective adversity, such as parents who expect all their children to cooperate. And paradoxically, one of the more poignant examples of cooperative interaction between siblings is among children who have been deprived of parents through death or other disruptions of the parent-child relationship, such as placement in an orphanage.

Children help each other to learn about the relationship world. Brother and sister may "play house," dramatizing their version of mother's and father's life together. This is possible when children have grown up with a clear sense of their status as children in the family, not as substitute adults for the vacuum in mother's or father's life.

As children mature, they become distinguished by their individual achievements at different stages. The concept of growing up helps children to accept disparities in ability and to acknowledge that others have different rights and needs at different times.

Having a brother or sister can increase the capacity to put oneself in the place of another and also to struggle to define one's own space (rather than only expecting that all space and priority belongs to self).

One whose life experience is organized to prevent frustration and sacrifice may be less able to cope with these in his or her own life, or appreciate the situations of others who do.

An egalitarian philosophy of family life encourages sibling rivalry. Egalitarianism—equal rights, privileges, and authority for parent or child—seems to some like the optimum state for family life. Just as it is important to learn to live cooperatively with peers (e.g., siblings), it is important to experience living with someone other than oneself in authority and to have responsibility for someone less able. In fact, childhood is a misnomer if a child has no parent in charge (see Boszormenyi-Nagy & Spark, 1973 on parentification). A child who already has adult privileges does not welcome another child as peer and potential companion. Almost inevitably, an only child is included in more adult activities than when there is more than one child. After the birth of a second child, the firstborn is often given messages to remember to set an example: "You're older." This may help firstborns to fit descriptions of firstborn children, but it may also undermine the potential of siblings to become cooperative peers. Some children, who should be peers, escape the close association, the opportunity of learning cooperation and of competing, by establishing territoriality. This is manifest by distinctly different and unrelated interests, friends, behaviors, attitudes. Earlier these siblings may have shared much in common. They may have competed for their parents' favor until one less often rewarded dropped out, to establish a separate (distinctly different) territory of interests and activities. Twins sometimes effect a split of interests that seems more determined by the developmental agenda of adolescence than by parental triangling.

Toman provides insights into the compatibility of parents with their children—for example, that a parent may identify with the same ranked child, e.g., firstborn fathers may be more identified with their firstborn child than with their youngest (1978). Other factors influence this, for example, children who symbolize certain overvalued or undervalued family members, not simply themselves. Alliances with or against particular children are often based on such intrafamilial transferences and encourage sibling rivalry.

Although circumstances, e.g., the physical presence and potential availability or absence of a parent, is an important factor, the sympathetic alignment of children with one parent more than the other is the outcome of a repetitive triangulation process that produces a sense of closeness with one parent and distance with the other. Sometimes the conflict (overt and/or covert) between parents is manifest in the interaction of siblings who fight over their parents' issues as if their own.

The greater the disparity in age between children, the greater the tendency to shift from a peer relationship to complementarity: a hierarchy, from the more authorative leader down through the chronologic rankings of children. Optimally this is growth-facilitating for all, just as teachers and students facilitate each other's growth.

Considerably older and younger siblings often have a different view of their nuclear family. Persons exploring extended family are surprised to learn of the different perceptions siblings have of the same family. For example, the financial circumstance of the family may be more constraining at one point than another. Father's or mother's career may have preempted their participation in the domestic sphere in the early or later phases of parenthood. The emotional climate and social network may have been quite different in one child's experience than in another's.

CHILDREN AND SOCIAL NETWORK

Children bring other people into the family. They are generally friendly, reaching out to other children and to adults. Children connect families with other families who can act as allies or opponents of parental values and expectations. Sometimes other adults besides parents and teachers become important adult models, for example, the recreation center director or the policeman at the intersection on the way to school.

Friends are often considered by parents to be their child's problem: either there aren't any or they are the wrong kind of children. Parents may say, "He gets in with the wrong crowd" and declare an embargo on the social commerce of their troubled child. I find it useful to review with parents and child who the friends are, and the structure of the nuclear families of these friends. Often the issues that concern children in their own family life are revealed in the lives of their friends. Children usually seek their own level, or wanting to feel one up, seek friends who seem to have it worse—already experiencing what a given child wishes or fears may be his or her fate. As children recover or discover more of their capabilities, their friendships shift and mirror their self-assessment.

Children without friends usually have parents who have few or no friends. As parents become more open to the world, their loner child may become more related to others.

THE EXTENDED FAMILY

The extended family is a resource to the nuclear family in calm and troubled times.

The decision to have a baby is the beginning of a shift away from the horizontal axis of marriage toward a realignment with the vertical thrust of the generations of the future and of the past. There are some families in which the majority of members consider the children of the family as their collective responsibility. This means initiatives for contact and relationship are mutual. Older, middle, and younger generations participate in sustaining the sense of membership and belonging. Geographic mobility of nuclear families may make it more difficult to draw from the extended family the support and help a new baby and new young parents need. Still, mothers and mothers-in-law, aunts, and uncles may mobilize to help the parents prepare for the baby and for the challenges of the immediate postpartum period. Less often than in generations past do expectant mothers go back home to their mothers and fathers to await the birth of a child. To whose family the new parents turn or from whom they receive help gives some indication of which extended family is more involved with and directly influential (nonrelating is influential too) to the nuclear family. The questions become: If there is a vertical realignment of the new family with extended, which family? Is this alignment supportive or detrimental to the (horizontal) relationship of marriage? How do the autonomous and interdependent directions of the family rebalance?

Although the urban American nuclear family is usually geographically isolated from extended family, what happens among the extended family has its impact on the nuclear family (C. Bradt, 1975). This fact is usually overlooked or dismissed by the troubled nuclear family. How this impact is transmitted remains an incompletely understood phenomenon. The concepts of fusion and differentiation offer partial explanations (see Figure 6.3). Whether extended family is close, distant, or cut-off gives evidence of reflexive responses—automatic reactions—to the nodal events of the extended family. Nodal events can disrupt stable relationships.

Sometimes one set of grandparents has difficulty accepting the other set as their peers. Sharing interest in the new grandchildren can facilitate this as well as reconcile a grandparent to this later stage of the life cycle. Becoming a grandparent brings to mind the finite reality of one's own life, as well as the possiblity of having to take a secondary place in relationship to both child and grandchild. Some parents overlook their child's marriage, and expect their child's loyalty to be greater to themselves than to their daughter-in-law or son-in-law. As one mother reminded her son: "I come first, then your children... then your wife." Other prospective grandparents, anxious about the style of their children's marriage, welcome the announcement of a grandchild, an answer to their wish that "they should have a child and settle down." So the child is seen as a stabilizer to the marriage rather than a person whose life course is to emerge with time. Some of these children end up in domestic and worldly careers as "peacemakers." Other children, far from peaceful, stabilize a marriage by their disturbing ways.

Some parents use being parents to justify reduced contact with extended family, as when they offer the excuse, "Our children need us at home." How often do adults with children have a contact with their own parent without the presence of (or subject of) their children? The focus of attention and activity around the grandchildren keeps them as hostages to reduce intergenerational tension. The avoidance and cut-off from grandparents keeps parents away from the depression or anxiety they experience when in contact with the older generation. Through their parents, children are vulnerable to the multigenerational family process. Children add their own reflexive behavior with their parents, short-circuiting the multigenerational process and containing it in the nuclear family until the birth of the next generation. This unipolar vertical process—an involvement with children, noninvolvement with one's parents—is circular: Avoidance of one's own parents creates a void or vacuum that can be filled by children, leaving less space for grandparents, etc. Locked in fusion relationships, intimacy is lacking. Misguided attempts are made to find it but cut-offs from the extended family and overintensity with children prohibit intimacy.

The extended family has a stabilizing influence on the unstable nuclear family, particularly if there has been avoidance or aloofness between the older and middle generations. A troublesome child may settle down considerably if cut-offs with extended family are bridged. And, on occasion, a less intense extended family member may be able to deal with a child more dispassionately, with more appropriate expectations of responsibility and accountability. Older members of the extended family may be called upon to provide the missing authority or leadership in a dysfunctioning family. An unmarried or childless aunt or uncle may assume leadership and parental functions in the place of a dysfunctional or absent parent. Children who relate to older family members as models will probably have more data, more identity, than those who are expected to be "like" someone with whom they have little or no personal relationship.

The family therapist usually sees the disconnected, fragmented, atrophied, or extincting branches of a family tree. In clinical practice, it seems that the larger the number of living extended family members, the better the prognosis, regardless of their state of closeness or distance. The most challenging, in my experience, is the truly small family. Friendships and the work world become much more important elements of the system than for larger families (Bradt, 1978).

To summarize the theory: Overbalancing toward the (present) horizontal (friends-spouse) axis, away from the vertical (past and future) parent-child axis, is to risk becoming neglectful of children and the elderly and to sacrifice the lessons and nourishment of continuity. Overbalancing toward the vertical axis away from the horizontal is to risk the decay of marriage in the void of difference seeking essential to growth, and this may lead to overly intense emotional bonding of parents with their children. Rebalancing distribution of time, energy, and psychosocial connections can activate powerful resources of a system to heal itself.

THE CHILD-FOCUSED FAMILY

At one extreme of unbalance, the nuclear family's overinvestment on the vertical axis precludes the involvement in relationships in the nondomestic sphere and erodes all horizontal processes. The child-focused family is representative of this extreme.

In 1971, Carolyn Moynihan and I wrote a study describing our experiences in working with fifty child-focused families (Bradt & Moynihan, 1971). Since then I have seen several hundred more such families and have further refined my views of that family process. The presence of a child with unusual problems does not constitute a child-focused family. The child focus is a process that seems to compartmentalize family tension by channeling it through a particular child. Thus it can be seen as a coping mechanism, which, like all mechanisms, has its limitations, its failure point. In this instance, the manifestation of breakdown is represented as a particular child. The child plays an active part in the process.

What I call the authentic child-focused family process is operative even before the child's birth and is only amplified by his or her presence and life course. The child's failure to advance successfully through the usual psychosocial developmental milestones intensifies the family process and encourages the label "problem" early in life. A history usually reveals multiple consultations with child health experts beginning early in life. Family therapists are not usually among the consultants who have been involved. The parents are highly invested in the child and express no other concerns. "It's a child problem, not a family problem."

There are payoffs for children caught in this process, although they and other family members are arrested in the development of a variety of relationships both in and outside the family. The child-focused process helps all to cope, and also to fail, in achieving a richness and diversity of human relationships.

Of the fifty child-focused families studied in 1971, some were representative of the authentic child-focused family:

The child was usually male, oldest or youngest in the family. Fathers were more often youngests, mothers more often firstborn in their families of origin. Perhaps reflecting their youngest position in their nuclear family, fathers had more than a twofold higher incidence of the loss of their mothers before the age of sixteen (24% as compared with 10% of mothers). By the time the family had begun family therapy (although the child was their concern), 54% of fathers and 52% of mothers had *lost their own fathers* through death, divorce and absolute cut off! Additionally, both fathers and mothers had a 14% incidence of loss of siblings.

The predominant styles of relationship in the nuclear family were peace-agree (74%) and nursing-caretaking (80%). In relationship to the extended family, 52% of husbands and 30% of wives were considered extremely distant from their extended family. Only 18% of fathers were considered closely involved with their extended families as compared with 38% of mothers, indicating a more active involvement with the maternal side of the extended family. (Bradt & Moynihan, 1971).

While families fitting this profile are considered authentic child-focused families, there are other forms of child focus including the so-called pseudo-child-focus, which is the opposite extreme of concern for a child.

We have concluded from this data that parent loss and resultant long-standing vertical and horizontal relational imbalance has a profound impact on the development of children. The significance of father loss has been particularly overlooked. A father in the home is important, even though many children with fathers in the home grow up with mother the only adult directly involved as a parent.

Some possible explanations of the authentic child-focused process as an outcome of loss of fathers in the childhood of parents are as follows:

A profound disturbance of the vertical axis encourages overcentering of meaning and investment of life energies in the child pole of the vertical axis. In terms of the process of loss and restitution, the loss of the parent-child relationship in one's early life has the potential to be restored again when the child who lost a parent becomes an adult who can have a child to parent. Marriage thus represents the means to become a parent. The relationship with one's spouse would be secondary at best in such cases (unless a spouse were placed in a child category). As a peer relationship, it would probably be of tertiary value, (maternal relationship with male child would be primary, relationship with maternal grandparents secondary, and the relationship with spouse tertiary). Often oldest daughters who lose fathers before age sixteen are recast in the role of surrogate mother for younger siblings, while the mother moves out into the world to try to earn a living. When the biologic mother is at home, she is more likely to spend her time mothering younger siblings, and tends to see the oldest daughter in the role vacated by the lost father. This makes for intensity between the oldest daughter and the mother, an intensity often driving daughters as young adults to marry to avoid their mother, and to try to be different in their relationship with their own children. This also means in parenthood over-balancing on the child pole of the vertical axis. Such oldest daughters who marry youngest sons who have also lost fathers are likely to be frustrated in their wish to find a comfortably authoritative, take-charge man who will be more father than peer or child looking for a parent replacement. Youngest males who expect to become the dominant adult in the marriage relationship may run afoul of the oldest daughter's automatic assumption of being in charge. Not only was she the oldest sibling, through the loss of her own father (and relatively, her own mother), she may also have been surrogate mother and stand-in father.

Profound and unresolved loss often seems to reduce affectual understanding and awareness. Peace-agree style is preferable to overt expression of affect, especially discordance and conflict. Distance and avoidance also help contain affectual expression and perception. Limit setting with children is more difficult. The acknowledgement of marital dissatisfaction is too threatening of loss. Conflict equals loss, and conflict is to be avoided. It is especially difficult to let go of a child who provides a vicarious restitution of relationship with a lost father and often fills the void of a distancing spouse.

The family therapist learns to balance the review of marriage and child issues, remembering that the child-focused process is a means of coping. Giving it up without something better to take its place is anxiety provoking. A fuller and more realistic comprehension of the lost parent through research and development of that person's "jack" (multidimensional reality) reduces the intense overinvestment in the child. Contact with and vitalization of extended family relationships facilitates exploration of the marriage relationship, which over time can be more fully reviewed without overwhelming anxiety.

BRIEF OVERVIEW: TECHNIQUE AND CLINICAL EXAMPLES

Parents with young children who seek *family* counseling are in the main concerned about a deterioration of the marriage, the threat of disruption, contemplation of separation or divorce, or the disturbed function of a spouse. Children are part of the consideration of the quality of family life, but are not usually the presenting problem. Because this book includes a chapter on divorce, this discussion on intervention is more about the family with a significant child focus.

In my clinical practice, the authentic child-focused family is on the decline. This may be because I am less often identified as a child psychiatrist and more identified as a family therapist, and in the child-focused family, there is nothing wrong with the family, only the child.

Preoccupation of parents with a child represents unipolar vertical axis intensity. Such intensity has two origins. 1.) The historic or current relationship of each parent with his or her mother and father. 2.) The relative weakness of horizontal relationships currently and/or historically. But family therapists do not rank high on the list of experts who might be consulted when parents are concerned about one of their children.

More often a child specialist—child psychiatrist, pediatrician, or schoolteacher—is consulted about a child, especially a younger child. Assuming that the child specialist is systemically oriented, the task will be to place the specific concerns in the context of the multigenerational family relationships; to rebalance the "domestic jack" from its unipolar emotional center on the youngest generation; to vitalize the horizontal relationships, especially marriage, siblingship, and friendship; and to rebalance the nondomestic and domestic spheres of the family.

To find solutions, one must ask the right questions. One must define the dysfunctions and resources of a system rather than of an individual. Equally important is the definition of power and motivation, who *can* and who *will* effect change? The process of shifting away from individual toward systemic considerations is begun in a concrete way through the construction of a family chart in the initial sessions (Bradt & Moynihan, 1971). Questions that have to do with the information recorded on the family chart refocus attention, energy, and investment about a multigenerational system including the living and the dead, rather than only discussion of various individuals and symptoms.

All reliably effective clinical techniques should be based on conceptual understanding of the family. For the family who presents a child as their concern it is important to:

1. Assess the parents' child concern as a coping process. What is the functional significance of the child focus? If the concerns are more representative of a family process to cope, what is the family coping with?
   a. Historically the loss experience of parents as children *or* the loss experience of grandparents, with whom parent(s) are (were) fused. (The authentic child focused-family.)
   b. Contemporary stresses (see Case Example 2 below).
   c. Covert or overt marital dysfunction—issues too threatening to address or patterns of long-standing avoidance that make open consideration of the marriage taboo.
2. Consider how much the child's symptoms are intensified by a stage in the psychosocial development of the child as well as the state of balance between the horizontal and vertical processes of the family.

One must judge whether the inclusion of the child in ongoing work is essential to engage the parents. If the child is seen separately, which is sometimes useful directly or indirectly (as a support to the family shift of focus), there *are* risks of reinforcing the child-focused process rather than bringing into awareness (1) problem redefinition, and (2) rebalancing tasks. The best outcomes when a child is seen are those in which the family receives relief of the total "child problem." As they become productive and hopeful about other concerns, the child is more free to move out of the "fixed position."

Shifting the process away from child concerns: Questions that use the child as a reference point allow entry into the extended family, e.g., "How would your mother deal with that kind of behavior from Rick?" "How much contact had you and Nelle had the week before Rick kicked over the lamp?" "How often do you notice that pattern?" etc.

Shifting the process toward the child: Parents who are anxious about a particular subject may shift away from the subject by making reference to the child, *or* the therapist may elect to refer back to the child if either parent is becoming too threatened or seems overly impatient with discussions about extended family. And the child may represent the only existent bridge between parents who have otherwise effected total distance in their marital relationship.

The following example is illustrative of a family experiencing multiple relationship difficulties, with a tendency to compartmentalize anxiety through a focus on their oldest child. The prognosis for this case would be favorable for greater intimacy between family members, an improved marital relationship, and the differentiation of the parents from their families of origin. (The parents are likely to emerge as the most differentiated members of their families of origin.)

Case Example 1

Bill, age thirty-five, an only child, and Nelle, age thirty-four, the older of two daughters, seemed constantly vexed by their older son, Rick, age eight. Their younger son caused them little concern. Although encouraged by a professional friend to see a family therapist rather than a child psychiatrist, many of the initial sessions with the family therapist were consumed by their descriptions of their child's behavior and problems.

Developing the family chart revealed that Nelle had grown up with a compliant and intense relationship with her mother who had married and divorced three times before Nelle was eighteen. Nelle had no contact with her biologic father and none with either stepfather. She did not want to be like her mother. Contact with her was taxing. She had always wanted children but had miscarried before each successful pregnancy. As an adult, Bill avoided his parents, feeling sorry for and disappointed by them. As a child, his father had worked shifts as long as Bill could remember, so he seldom saw his father except occasionally on weekends. Like Nelle, he had spent most of his childhood in the company of his mother, whom he considered the dominant parent. Bill spent exceptionally long hours working. His work system contained his "brother," a colleague with whom he had shared an office. This work friend proved to be the model for Bill's affair. His friend separated shortly after Rick's birth and confided in Bill about his relationships with other women. Later he introduced Bill to the woman with whom he became romantically involved.

A year after their first child, Rick, was born, Nelle started individual psychotherapy. When Bill's extramarital romance ended, he began individual psychotherapy about the same time Nelle terminated hers. Rick's infancy was filled with illness, so Nelle had little time to be out in the world and often felt lonely for Bill. Minor symptoms kept her visiting doctors for treatments. Except for health concerns, she and Bill talked very little. Each of them avoided arguments and tried to be pleasant in each other's presence. Since they saw little of each other, this was easy to manage.

Nelle welcomed her second successful pregnancy and enjoyed breastfeeding their second son through his first birthday. She was hurt when Bill seemed uninterested in her sexually, but found when she went back to school to obtain her degree that other men found her attractive. Four years after the birth of their second son, and with increasing difficulties in the management of Rick, they decided to seek counseling for the family. Bill was surprised by Nelle's recent complaints about the marriage, but believed that Rick's problems explained the marital tension.

Initially in marriage both parents had worked and both enjoyed their leisure together. Each was active in both domestic and nondomestic spheres. Eighteen months before Rick was born they bought a house. Four months before Rick's birth Nelle quit working. After that Bill invested even more heavily in his work career. Nelle was happy in their new home awaiting Rick's birth. After delivery, Rick's respiratory illnesses, her own illnesses, and general caretaking of the family increasingly occupied Nelle's time. She saw less and less of Bill, who was seemingly "on his way up" at work. He was more invested in the work sphere, she in the home. Nelle was frightened by the prospect of going back to school, but Bill assured her of his support—as long as she kept up with her responsibilities at home. This was the beginning of reequilibration of energy distribution between Bill and Nelle in the domestic and nondomestic spheres.

Therapy involved rebalancing the vertical axis of the family. Interventions were aimed at renewing contact with their parents, bridging cut-offs, and developing their horizontal relationships. Each developed contact and a one-to-one relationship with their distant parents (in both cases their fathers). This required learning more about the details of their fathers' nuclear families. Nelle also worked at their peer relationships, increasing her contact with her younger sister, who had been considered the frail child in their growing up years. Bill, an only child, was encouraged to contact cousins and male peers, and developed a number of close friendships with them. Where previously the avoidance patterns of the marriage were sustained by work and child focus, the expression of differences in the marriage were now reframed to mean vitality rather than potential abandonment.

Another brief case example may serve to illustrate a more authentically child-focused family. In this case, the most successful outcome hoped for would probably be a long remission of the child-focused process. Marital issues would probably remain unaddressed and unresolved until the grandparents were no longer living.

Case Example 2

By the end of kindergarten, Charles established a school reputation as hyperactive and abusive to other children. His mother and father had always had difficulty managing Charles, but had learned to live with his behavior. At the suggestion of the school, his mother consulted a child guidance center in May 1979. Charles and his three-year-younger brother were both wanted children. His brother had incurred birth injuries, cerebral palsy with a considerable neuromuscular handicap, and visual difficulties. He required extrordinary amounts of time for treatments and doctors' visits, and was slow developmentally. Nodal events included:

1970	Paternal grandfather died
1971	Charles's parents married
April 1973	Charles born
1974	Mother's unmarried brother died in auto accident
April 1976	Brother born
August 1978	Father, who had been adopted, quit job and borrowed money from his mother to start his own business

In the family interview, it was apparent that Charles was hyperactive and unused to limits and that his father was a stranger to the children. The mother was feeling overwhelmed and depressed about feeling responsible for her brother's death and her children's difficulties. She attributed none of her feelings to the marriage. The father was reluctant to participate because he "didn't want to be away from his new business." Both parents avoided talking about unpleasant subjects. Neither acknowledged concerns other than about the children.

In the domestic sphere, the mother was overfunctioning (under-limit-setting) as mother and wife, while the father was underfunctioning as father and husband. Both parents showed limited competence with peers, in addition to avoidance of discussion about the quality of their marriage. With a void in the marriage, the mother was overinvested in the children and in her own parents. She was isolated and avoided friends. She felt depressed "because of the children." Through work, the father avoided not only his wife whose need for him had increased since the birth of their children, but also his mother who had become increasingly dependent as a result of the loss of her husband and had not yet fully accepted her son's marriage.

It seemed clear that neither parent would participate in therapy unless the child was seen individually. Therapy involved encouraging both the child and parents to increase the child's involvement with other adults besides mother, i.e., father, grandparents, etc. The mother was instructed about limit setting for children. (This had implications for her relationship with her husband as well.) The intensity of mother's involvement with the child was reduced, and the grief about Charles and his "damaged" brother was dealt with. More contact was established between the parents, and the prevailing equilibrium was challenged. Mother was coached on her relationship with her husband and mother-in-law. Therepeutic intervention focused also on overcoming the imbalance of the parents' investment in the domestic and nondomestic spheres.

CONCLUSION

"Normal" families as well as disturbed families may be dysfunctional. The family therapist has contributed to the understanding of "normal" family process, but his case material is usually a family threatened by dysfunction. In this chapter, emphasis is on clinical intervention with the dysfunctional family more than the "normal" families never seen. The theoretical concepts presented apply to both the coping "normal" family and the family seeking help.

Becoming a parent is a major nodal event in the family life cycle. Nodal events, like all challenges, have the potential to stimulate growth and strengthen the family system or to stimulate dysfunction. Clinically, it seems that becoming parents is often associated with a deterioration of the marriage. Yet sustaining the intimacy of marriage is essential to the well-being of children. The author looks at the spectrum of married adult attitudes about children—potential parents who see children as a threat to their relationship, and other parents who feel marriage is coincidental to having children. Voluntarily childless couples have no room for children. Their attitude about marriage is often gauged by how the relationship feels. Are their "needs" being met? To have children means to risk, to invest with no guarantee of "return." How much of one's life is lived in the service of self and how much of one's life is lived in the service of others, determines whether children are born, thrive, and establish themselves as adults to become parents of children, themselves, and members of a multigenerational family.

Functionally, single parenthood has been common in intact nuclear families for generations. And whether through actual loss or the usual contemporary functional absence of fathers from the domestic sphere of life, the mother-child relationship is commonly overly intense.

But change is in the wind. In the domestic sphere, many couples are practicing collaborative parenting, maintaining continuity with parents and the past, and creating alternatives to overinvestment in the nondomestic sphere. Equally shared responsibility for the care of children and sustained interaction and involvement over the course of childhood seems the most promising route to sexual equality and the avoidance of fusion or distance in marriage. Intimacy, rather than overly intense relationships, not only between parents and children, but in all of one's "personal life," is evidence of a vital process of balance and creativity in peer and complementary relationships.

REFERENCES

Boszormenyi-Nagy, I., and Spark, G. *Invisible Loyalties,* Hagerstown, Md.: Harper & Row, 1973.

Bowen, M., "The Use of Family Theory in Clinical Practice," *Comprehensive Psychiatry* 7:345-74, 1966.

Bradt, C. J., The Nuclear Family—Life in a Vacuum. 245-49 Systems Thinking and the Quality of Life. Proceedings of 1975 Annual North American Meeting. Society for General Systems Research. Washington, D.C., 1975.

Bradt, J.O., Friendship, Kinship and the Work System, 1978 Synopsis of the First Annual Maryland (D.C.) Virginia Network Symposium. Family Therapy Practice Olney, Maryland. The Family Therapy Practice Network, Inc., 1978.

_____, and Moynihan, C. J., "Opening the Safe: A Study of the Child-Focused Families," 1-25, *Systems Therapy,* Bradt and Moynihan, ed., Washington, D.C.: Georgetown Family Center, 1971.

Bronfenbrenner, U., "Who Needs Parent Education," Sept. 29-30 1977, Working Conference on Parent Education, Flint, Michigan.

Calhoun, J., "The Human Family." Conference, Georgetown Family Center, Washington, D.C., September 1978.

Gorney, R., *The Human Agenda,* New York: Simon and Schuster, 1968.

Mahler, M.S., "On Childhood Psychosis and Schizophrenia: Autistic and Symbiotic Infantile Psychosis," in R.S. Eissler, et al., eds. *The Psychoanalytic Study of the Child,* Vol. VII, New York: International Universities Press, 1952.

Ooms, T., *Family Perspective on Mental Health* (Background paper for joint meeting of Family Impact Seminar and President's Commission on Mental Health staff, June 24, 1977), Washington, D.C.

Peck, Ellen, *The Joy of the Only Child,* New York: Delacorte Press, 1977.

Rebelsky, F., and Hanks, C., "Father's Verbal Interaction with Infants in the First Three months of Life," *Child Development* 42:63-68, 1971.

Rockefeller Illustrative. "The Decline in World Fertility: Bip or Dip? 4:2," New York: The Rockefeller Foundation, September 1978.

Spitz, R.A., "Hospitalism: An Inquiry into the Genesis of Psychiatric Conditions in Early Childhood," *The Psychoanalytic Study of the Child,* 1: International Books, 1945.

Toman, W., *Family Constellation,* 3d ed., New York: Springer, 1978.

White, B.L. *The First Three Years of Life,* Englewood Cliffs, N.J.: Prentice-Hall, 1975.

Wynne, L.C., et al, "Pseudomutuality in the Family Relations of Schizophrenics," *Psychiatry,* 21:205-20, 1958.

7
The Family with Adolescents

Norman J. Ackerman, M.D.

Albert Einstein College of Medicine

INTRODUCTION

Less than two decades ago, men like Ackerman (1) and Bell (2) were pleading with the psychotherapeutic community to look closely at the family in connection with the assessment of adolescent problems. Now, almost casually and without any fanfare, we take the quantum leap of giving primacy to the social unit of interaction, in this case the family, and ask what effects do individuals and events have upon it? It may be that the dramatic shift has not been noticed because our central interest, man, has not changed. It is simply that we finally see that man is not a solitary traveler moving through an environment; he is *part* of the environment and, perhaps, an "indispensable element of nature" at that, exhibiting "the fragility and vulnerability that always accompany high specialization in biology" (3). Looking at the family, the cradle and emotional headquarters of man, may therefore be part and parcel of some dull apperception of ours that man is an endangered species.

And no one can "hoist danger signals" (1) more loudly and dramatically than adolescents. On the international scene, storms of adolescent protest are surefire indicators that governments or societies are sleeping or headed into blind alleys. On the family level, it means, "Mom and Dad better get it together before I go out on my own for good." This is one end of the spectrum of ordinary development wherein a family muddles along, functioning passably with unresolved parental or extended family problems at the expense of one or more individual's growth. At the other end, well-lubricated family organizations can enjoy the antics of the adolescent and enrich

147

themselves with the torrent of information that is theirs for the listening. The adolescent challenges the family daily with new styles, new language, new mannerisms, and new values for behavior. More than any other family member, the adolescent is not only a conduit to the world at large, but a bridge between old and new. Functioning as "his majesty's loyal opposition," the teenager can be harshly critical and brutally frank, but rarely dull. At times, in the midst of pushing an adult to the wall with various provocations or testing of authority, a sudden exposure of vulnerability or total childlike trust and affection can melt the heart. It is just this mix of child and adult that confuses the family in its dealings with the adolescent member. Should this pronouncement or that bit of behavior be taken very seriously or just passed over lightly? Is this new interest a passing fancy, or a new trend that needs to be either nipped in the bud or incorporated into family life? Is this friend or that group just a chance meeting or must the relationship be evaluated for its possible impact on the family? Is it possible to assess all the teenager brings home? Is there time? How much can the family pry? When to set limits? When to let grow?

Truly it is impossible to raise teenagers. In the end they must use what they have and meet the world on their own as best they can. If the family can roll with the punches and learn something of the latest generation from their teen, they will remain a haven for the return of the adolescent from time to time when toes are stubbed and knees are bruised. In the long-term if the family can take care of itself, it will be doing the best thing for the adolescent. The saving grace is that with all the turbulence and instability characteristic of adolescent growth, the ordinary teenager retains a playfulness and sense of humor that is easily tapped. And the spurt of growth with its release of new yet ancient biological rhythms is exciting and potentially rewarding for those who will partake of it.

FAMILY ORGANIZATION

The ideal family is organized around balanced threesomes as I have described in detail elsewhere (4) (see Figure 7.1). Each relationship is a mutual give and take, each person taking responsibility for self *according to his or her natural capability* and neither overfunctioning nor underfunctioning. Note that this definition can be applied to infants or the handicapped and certainly to adolescents. The transactions of each relationship are open to all other relationships in the family and therefore affect, and are affected by, all other relationships. Moreover, the intensity of each relationship, measured by the rate of interaction, is the same ($a = b = c$) over a reasonable period of time.[1] This means that no one is shut out and no one is swal-

---

[1] Clearly, a large increase or decrease in interaction between any two members over a one-day period does not indicate an imbalance, whereas a lesser change among people living together over several weeks may be significant.

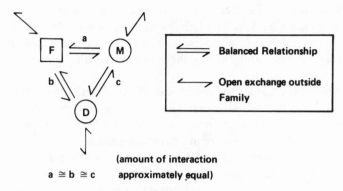

(amount of interaction
a ≅ b ≅ c   approximately equal)

Figure 7.1

lowed up. At the same time, each relationship is mobile; that is, each individual is free to increase interaction ("Let's make love" or "I have a bone to pick with you") or decrease interaction ("I want to be quiet" or "I'm interested in something else now") at any given moment. Finally, there is a free flow of communications outside the family; any member is free to relate to nonmembers and does so.

In any balanced threesome, the total amount of interaction remains approximately the same ($a + b + c = k$). This means that if one relationship becomes more intense, another one, or generally two, become less intense. Conversely, if one member of a threesome withdraws, the other two are drawn together (see Figure 7.2). It is an apparent paradox that a stable

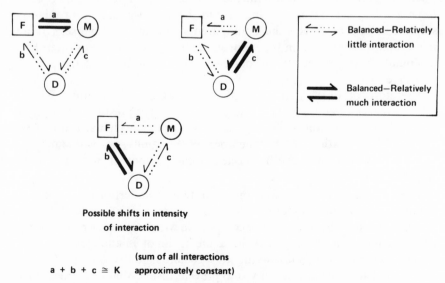

Possible shifts in intensity
of interaction

(sum of all interactions
a + b + c ≅ K   approximately constant)

Figure 7.2

family is one that is most fluid. To tolerate new arrivals, death, or illness, all relationships must be flexible. (The diagram becomes much more complex when other members are added; e.g., our old-fashioned family of six has fifteen relationships and twenty threesomes, but the principles are the same.)

One must also consider the reciprocal effects of extended family and nuclear family. An individual generally relates to members of his or her nuclear family in the same manner as he or she learned to relate to the original family. An overfunctioning parent, for example, is often simply repeating the early experience of having grown up with an underfunctioning parent. The parent may rationalize this behavior by saying that it is a deliberate attempt not to make the same mistakes as the grandparent, to spare the third generation the pain of the second, and to "prevent my children from having the same hangups as me". The result is that the third generation turns out to be like the first. The child of an underfunctioning parent rears an underfunctioning child. A mother, used to an intense relationship with her mother and little interaction with her father, may repeat this pattern with her daughter and husband. Moreover, the relationship between daughter and husband will tend to mimic the relationship between the grandparents in both quality and intensity. It is amazing how often the relationships in the nuclear family tend to be mirror images of both extended families. This means that the child, particularly the adolescent, may often become a special kind of peer of a grandparent, either competing for nurturing or control, or in a sympathetic alliance. The rules of intensity also apply here. When the adolescent either makes demands on the parent (increasing intensity) or rejects the parent (decreasing intensity), there tends to be a reciprocal decrease or increase in the parent-grandparent relationship. This, in turn, affects the grandparents' marriage. Conversely, retirement, illness, migration and, of course, death of a grandparent often have profound consequences for the parent-child relationship and the parents' marriage.

Therefore, of all the natural events which occur in the family life cycle, the emergence of adolescence is the one most likely to test the flexibility of the family organization. This is not due to the dramatic changes adolescents can exhibit in relation to other members of the family, nor is it simply because adolescents can move from one extreme to another in a trice, allowing little time for adaptation.

The adolescent overfunctions one minute and underfunctions the next. He or she wants total responsibility for self or none at all; indeed, being a "tweenager" may be inherently incompatible with balance of responsibility and the clinician is hardput to evaluate the health of an adolescent relationship in these terms. (It is fascinating to speculate here that a major function of so-called adolescent instability is to prevent fusion; that is, entrenchment of the underfunctioing or overfunctioning side vis-à-vis a significant other). In turn, each member of the family must bend if a working relationship is to be maintained with the adolescent. Big brothers must be able to become peers at times and even little brothers. Little sisters may suddenly find themselves confidantes. Parents may have to coddle at times and allow themselves to be looked after tenderly at others. Grandparents, after whom the teenager is modeled by his parents, may find themselves the target of sudden hostility or surprising endearments. Everyone's mettle is tested. Everyone has a chance to grow.

At the same time, the adolescent is rapidly changing the intensities of his or her relationships. The young girl who used to cuddle with her daddy, now becoming a woman and sensing her father's awkwardness, rebuffs him shyly. Father, somewhat confused and angry, may maintain contact with an endless cycle of condemnation against her rebellion, or may turn to mother with demands for which she is unprepared. Daughter, too, may now turn to mother for more nurturing or control. The beleaguered mother is now pulled away from *her* mother whom she has been parenting (see Figure 7.3). The ramifications are deep and the ripple effect is wide. I have seen grandparents' marriages of forty years suddenly become intolerable under such circumstances. A young man, intensely engrossed in his own pursuits for the time being, may so force the parents to look at each other that they must deal for the first time with such issues as lack of companionship, sexual difficulties or dominance. The results can be explosive (see Figure 7.4).

Finally, the adolescent is a peer grouper and explorer *par excellence,* forever sallying forth into the community and bringing back new ideas, experimenting with new modes of behavior and offering new values. More than that, he or she is forever bringing in new people (literally or figuratively, depending how receptive the family is), many of whom are more or less alien. This is always somewhat of a threat to the family. In the first place, it forecasts the eventual leaving of the individual, the natural demise of the family and the involution of the parents. This is an ordinary event that occurs to all, but can be looked upon with equanimity by only a few. Secondly, the new input forces the family to reevaluate itself, often painfully. The adolescent frequently becomes a critic, exposes hypocrisies and undermines longstanding prejudices. For example, a young man, finding himself newly interested in the arts, defies his father and refuses to go into the family business and compete for materialistic things to make up for his father's lack of success. The father must now face his own sense of failure and perhaps look at *his* father's overcompetitiveness with him as grandfather berates him for not controlling son (see Figure 7.5). Or a young woman, demanding that she be given a chance to carve out a career, eschews marriage and children while pointing to the unfulfilled drudgery of the mother and the emptiness of the parental relationship. The mother, in turn, may be stirred to remem-

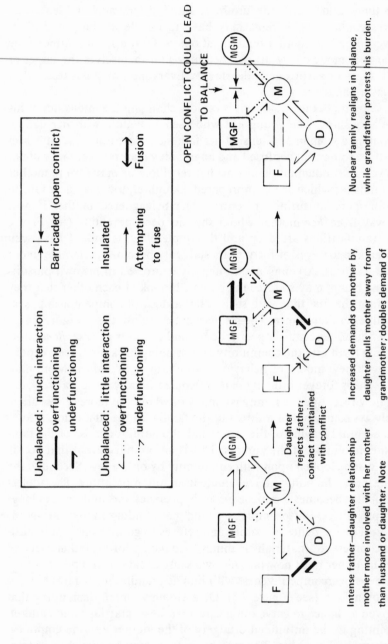

Unbalanced: much interaction

⟶ overfunctioning

↗ underfunctioning

⟶|⟶ Barricaded (open conflict)

Unbalanced: little interaction

⟋⋯ overfunctioning

⋯⋯⇢ underfunctioning

⋯⋯⋯ Insulated

⟶ Attempting to fuse

⇕ Fusion

Daughter rejects father; contact maintained with conflict

Intense father–daughter relationship mother more involved with her mother than husband or daughter. Note nuclear family and mother's original family are mirror images.

Increased demands on mother by daughter pulls mother away from grandmother; doubles demand of grandmother on grandfather.

OPEN CONFLICT COULD LEAD TO BALANCE

Nuclear family realigns in balance, while grandfather protests his burden.

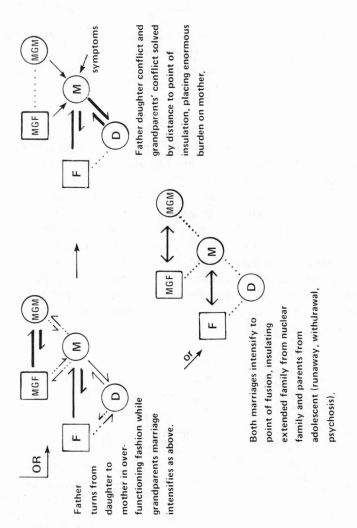

Father turns from daughter to mother in over-functioning fashion while grandparents marriage intensifies as above.

Both marriages intensify to point of fusion, insulating extended family from nuclear family and parents from adolescent (runaway, withdrawal, psychosis).

Father daughter conflict and grandparents' conflict solved by distance to point of insulation, placing enormous burden on mother.

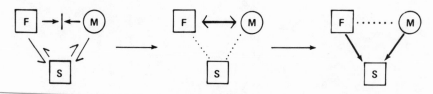

| Typical triangulation | Son distances to point of insulation forcing fusion of parents. | Marriage explodes (e.g., divorce). Each parent pursues son. |

Figure 7.4

ber the pooh-poohing of her childhood ambition to be a nurse and even take it up with *her* father (see Figure 7.6). Again, the effects of adolescent happenings may be far-reaching and soul-shaking.

To repeat three major aspects of family organization are regularly and simultaneously being shifted in families with ordinary adolescents. The balance of responsibility along the overfunctioning-underfunctioning axis in each relationship seesaws. There are marked shifts in intesity of interaction of some relationships with concomitant compensations in others. There is a great surge of exchange with the community at large, with input coming not only from the adolescent and friends, but from teachers, other parents, and officials, while the family must necessarily expose itself through the same process.

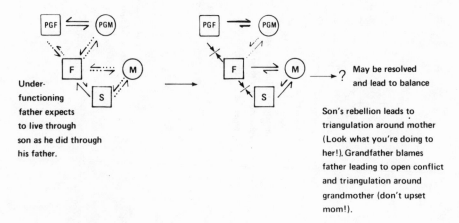

Underfunctioning father expects to live through son as he did through his father.

Son's rebellion leads to triangulation around mother (Look what you're doing to her!). Grandfather blames father leading to open conflict and triangulation around grandmother (don't upset mom!).

? May be resolved and lead to balance

Figure 7.5

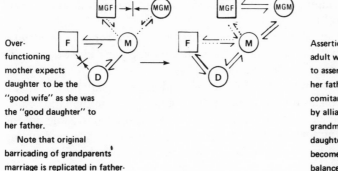

Over-functioning mother expects daughter to be the "good wife" as she was the "good daughter" to her father.

   Note that original barricading of grandparents' marriage is replicated in father-daughter relationship.

Assertion of daughter as adult with both parents leads to assertion of mother with her father and husband, con-comitant with or preceded by alliance of maternal grandmother and grand-daughter. All relationships become renegotiated and balanced.

Figure 7.6

TREATMENT OF THE FAMILY WITH ADOLESCENTS

It is no wonder, then, that so many families come to treatment with adolescents. Or maybe these families are simply more memorable (eight out of eleven well-known family therapists chose families with adolescents for their detailed presentations in Peggy Papp's book (5). As noted before, the average family seems to weather the storm, adapt to it, and grow. I only know this from retrospective studies done with families who have reared adolescents, escaped therapy, but then came later for other reasons. It has been my observation that all of these families realigned in some way and renegotiated relationships for the better. Those who do not make it come apart at the seams. I have not seen families simply muddle through, maintaining old patterns as they may in the case of other major events like birth and death. This finding again speaks for adolescence being a very special nodal point in family life.

It is well known that adolescence is a common time for the onset of major mental illness. This is apparently associated with the biologic fragility of the adolescent combined with the almost inevitable decreased involvement of adolescent with family. The adolescent may leave home or become deeply involved in outside affairs. The family may be unable to partake of adolescent happenings or comprehend adolescent ways. The loss of emotional headquarters can lead to breakdown. Once breakdown actually occurs, however, the family is dealing with many factors above and beyond those peculiar to adolescence. Catastrophic illness, acute or chronic, generally means involvement with outside authorities and the whole mental health care delivery apparatus. At this point, a family therapist, even in a hospital setting, frequently has little control over the situation. The most important thing one can do then is to help the family maintain contact with the adolescent in as meaningful a way as possible while focusing on other family relationships that need help.

I should like to offer now some remarks regarding some families who present themselves for help with adolescents, paying particular attention to the effect the adolescent has had on the family.

The four possible ways that families with adolescents may present themselves are the same as for any other family, namely, (a) symptomatic behavior of the adolescent (frequently a school referral); (b) trouble in the marriage; (c) symptomatic behavior of a sibling (usually a younger sibling noticed or picked upon more intensely since the adolescent has distanced or refused to be triangulated); and (d) symptomatic behavior of one of the parents (frequently with extended family problems). Regardless of the manner of presentation, all four of the above phenomena are involved to some degree and all three of the process parameters already described are always present. For clinical purposes, the manner of presentation is relatively unimportant except that one must always bear in mind that only the tip of the iceberg is offered. A marital problem is always much more than just that. Our evaluation of process, which is tantamount to family diagnosis, is much more important, for the predominant patterns discernable provide the best clues for effective intervention.

Symptomatic Behavior of the Adolescent

Symptomatic behavior of the adolescent is a commonplace. The adolescent is either increasing or decreasing intensity of involvement with family. Examples of the former are intense involvement with peers, general withdrawal into self, and "rebellious" running away. Examples of the latter are shifting from one parent to another and speaking for self vis-à-vis both parents who had been triangulating about the adolescent. The latter is also frequently labeled rebellion. In the first instance, the therapist must help the parents to keep in contact with the adolescent without chasing after him or her. They must be available and responsive when the adolescent moves toward them. Often this involves overcoming their own feelings of rejection and recognizing even hostile responses of the adolescent as signs of the bond between them. Always there is a resultant intensification of interaction in the marital relationship or with extended family, and it behooves the therapist to examine these shifts for dysfunction. Often a judgment must be made whether the adolescent should be given free rein since the behavior is a move toward health, or be taken in tow like a preadolescent since the behavior is too extreme. Guidelines here are twofold: (a) judging from the family pattern before complaints, is the adolescent moving toward more balance or less? If the parent-child relationship was extremely intense before, decreasing intensity can be useful and some overshooting of the mark can be expected; and (b) is the adolescent still in contact with the family or in danger of losing contact completely? The latter calls for retrieving action.

When the adolescent is increasing intensity, it is often done with anger and it is a great challenge for family members to see the positive aspects rather than reject all assertions out of hand. Again process judgments have to be made by the therapist. Is the adolescent detriangulating himself or shifting from an overintense parent relationship to the less intense parent relationship? If so, the move needs to be supported. If the adolescent is reverting to an old pattern after difficulty in the outside world, it must be discouraged.

Whether the adolescent is moving toward or away from family, parental authority and control is always an issue. Here an assessment must be made as to the adequacy of the nurturing function which is primary. If it is not adequate, it must be dealt with in reality terms. The most deprived children will accept control if they are sure that the parents are fairly distributing the family resources, and caring for them as well as they can under the circumstances. Among the rich, if the parents are delinquent runaways, there is no point in trying to help them control their teen until they can be more present. Once this occurs, it may be helpful to distinguish between obedience and assumption of responsibility. If a boy is to get to school on time above all, he must be awakened by someone regularly. If he is to learn to hear the alarm, he will probably have to be late or absent at times. Parents must judge which priorities take precedence at any given time. Therapists must judge whether parental priorities are consistent with the changes in process for which they are aiming. Both must learn not to attempt the impossible. As stated before, making judgments about teenage behavior may tax our wisdom strenuously. Being able to take a longitudinal view of family process, rather than relying upon symptoms alone or a mental status check, helps immeasurably here. Nonetheless, it is important that we be humble and are prepared to be wrong. A frequent mistake is to go along with the family's assessment of health (usually based on symptoms). Bear in mind that change is always stressful and viewed by people as a threat. In some instances, if the parents are told firmly that they have "a normal teenager" on their hands, nature takes care of the rest. Sometimes it is helpful to establish a "checkup" relationship with a family so that such judgments can be periodically reassessed.

Symptomatic Behavior of a Sibling

Symptomatic behavior of a younger sibling is frequently a moment in the life cycle of the family when a therapist has the opportunity to be truly preventive. The pattern is generally not yet entrenched. Most often, the younger sibling has become the focus of parental attention due to withdrawal of the eldest. The degree of withdrawal of the eldest should be evaluated. If it appears reasonable, as for example when an eldest goes to college while maintaining contact, leave it alone. If it is unsound with danger of loss of contact, an attempt to retrieve the eldest should be made. This is not only for the sake of the eldest, but also to reduce the intensity of the parent-younger sibling relationship, which may be all the intervention the younger sibling needs. If the eldest is left alone, then other strategies must be used. If the younger is triangulated by the parents, then one must either help the youngster talk for self vis-à-vis the parents or usurp the place of the youngster by dealing directly with the parents, which could result in the parents attempting to triangulate around the therapist. If the younger sibling is too intensely involved with one parent, increasing involvement with the other parent is the best strategy.

Symptoms in a Parent and a Marital Problem: A Case Example

I will now offer in some detail an account of a family that presented as a combination of symptoms in a parent and a marital problem and required effort with three generations for a successful conclusion. Although the mother labeled herself as the problem initially, she immediately pointed to her husband and marriage as a cause. Energetic exploration further revealed the difficulties to be initiated by adolescent shifting of a delicate three-generation balance. In my judgment, this situation is much more typical than hitherto supposed. We are so used to thinking of adolescence as a time of turmoil, and the families that complain about their adolescent members are such a commonplace, that even family therapists do not generally look for the adolescent effect if a family presents with symptoms in an adult or with marital problems. Moreover, many parents are reluctant to bring in their adolescents, particularly those who are well-functioning or striving toward a more healthy adaptation. From the point of view of preventive therapy, acceptance of a marital problem as simply that, is often a lost opportunity.

A woman in her late thirties called because she was "depressed." In tears she explained at the first session that she could no longer take her husband's anger. He shouted at her for minor transgressions like not making the tea right and gave her the "silent treatment" for a week at a time if she dared to fight back. The story this pretty but frightened woman told was that she had gone from an unhappy home into an unhappy marriage fifteen years before. Her husband, a hardworking professional, had always been demanding, cold, and insensitive to her needs. She had always catered to him and "made the best of it," taking solace in the material comforts she had and "not feeling strong enough to go it alone." When questioned about the courtship, our patient described it as a whirlwind romance during which her husband-to-be pursued her vigorously, worshipped her, and even kissed her feet. She did not bargain for the fact that after marriage her husband would consciously and deliberately demand the same behavior of her in return.

During the first two years of their marriage, the husband was in the armed forces and traveled frequently, establishing an early pattern of alternating extremes of intensity. This allowed the couple to sweep their conflicts under the rug and lessened the tension. In addition, pregnancy occurred before the end of the first year and the wife became preoccupied with herself and the child, a girl. Two years later, after the husband was discharged from service, a boy was born simultaneously with husband's intense preoccupation with his own career.

So far so good. All pointed to the necessity for keeping the intensity of the marital relationship optimal. But what went wrong? The woman could give no clues. She was very happy with her children and was sure they had no problems. The girl, now thirteen, was blinking a bit and somewhat irritable lately, but that did not seem important. The maternal grandmother, it was revealed upon inquiry, was always somewhat of a problem, but no different lately. She had been widowed when our initial patient first entered school, now lived alone and made constant demands upon the patient for services. Moreover, husband never liked his mother-in-law, clashed with her, and avoided her as much as possible. The patient felt caught between them and could not understand why her husband did not put himself out for her mother the way she did for his parents. She asked me if I agreed that that was selfish and unfair and I said I was more interested in finding solutions than in making judgments. I asked for an example, preferably in the future, of the kind of difficulty this situation might cause. It turned out that there was to be a family gathering in a week to which her mother wanted to be transported. This would mean considerable traveling out of the way for the patient and her husband, and she was certain he would object. On the other hand, she had already promised to take her mother, did not object to the traveling herself, and really wanted her mother to attend. The gathering was in honor of the patient's older brother who was visiting from out of town for a few days and was at the home of the eldest brother. These brothers, eight and ten years older than the patient, had been quite devoted to their little sister as youngsters, but were frequently at loggerheads with their mother, and now had little to do with her. The patient admitted to some resentment that her brothers did not offer to transport her mother (and her mother would not ask them), but she accepted her role of being in the middle here as inevitable, and viewed it as no longer important since it occurred so rarely now. Here, then, was the original triangulation process which was being repeated in the nuclear family (see Figure 7.7).

Still, there was no clue as to what rocked the boat. I contented myself with suggesting to the patient that she tell her husband that she wanted to take her mother to the party, and that it would be perfectly all right with her if he demurred and either went separately or did not attend. She agreed willingly, although she did not want to "make a habit" of doing things herself. I then told

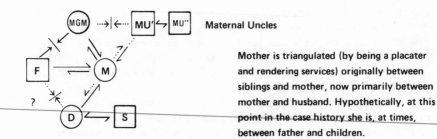

Maternal Uncles

Mother is triangulated (by being a placater and rendering services) originally between siblings and mother, now primarily between mother and husband. Hypothetically, at this point in the case history she is, at times, between father and children.

Figure 7.7

her I wanted to see her husband with her and, when she told me the usual "he won't come because he says there's nothing wrong with him," I instructed her to ask him to help with her treatment. She readily agreed, but expressed the opinion that it would make no difference.

The next day, the patient called, surprised and hesitant. She reported that her husband agreed to come in, but she thought it might not be worthwhile since he would be "on his best behavior in front of a psychiatrist." I congratulated her on her effectiveness and set a date for two weeks hence. In person, the husband was blandly intellectual and waxed expansive on "the reasoning" behind all the behavior to which his wife objected. He tended to hog the scene and, when his wife interjected occasionally, he would gesture in a brushing way with the side of his hand toward his wife's face and say, "That's not the issue." He would continue his monologue, and she would lapse into silence. He informed me that he was delighted that his wife elected to go into treatment, since he had advised her to do so ten years ago, but she had refused. He was also glad to give me any information I needed, reckoning it would take about one session and then I could continue with his wife until such time as I might need him again. He was a very reasonable man, he proclaimed, totally devoted to his family, but the way his wife was needling him and screaming lately was intolerable and he would chuck the marriage if it continued. He was launching into a convoluted theory of his wife's "neurosis" when I interrupted to ask how he had handled his wife's wanting to transport her mother to his brother-in-law's party. Both husband and wife were surprised at this, having attached no importance to it, and could barely remember what happened except that the husband did pick up mother-in-law and return her. To his comment, "I generally do," she retorted, "This is the first time without anger!" Next came a lively discussion about each other's mother, each other's personality, each other as parents, and finally the children, particularly the girl. I functioned as a switchboard, having each one talk to me in turn, insisting that the wife respond, and the husband not interrupt. Often I repeated the wife's statements when the husband would go off on a tangent.

It was clear that husband and wife tended to relate to me as if I were the maternal grandmother; that is to say, they behaved in their customary manner with significant others, in this instance someone in whom they invested authority. The husband tended to compete with me as the expert, and the wife tended to submit to both of us, while encouraging us to regard her as the patient and debate over what was best for her. This process replicated the wife's original family in that she often had elicited the aid of her big brother against her mother. It also replicated the husband's original family in that his mother often reprimanded him as a youngster for his condescending attitude toward his father. The husband would also engage his mother by defending his younger sister against her authority. In this session, I went along with the pattern to some extent, allowing the husband to speak his piece and responding to some of the wife's pleas for direction. As the session progressed, I tended more and more to assert my responsibility for the conduct of the therapy, declining to debate with the husband and insisting that the wife voice her objections more directly toward him (see Figure 7.8). The couple accommodated me, but were unable to maintain a more balanced interaction between themselves for more than a minute or two without my intervention. I therefore made the judgment that I needed more of a therapeutic handle and proceeded to explore further.

What had emerged was that the predominant pattern had been repeated early in the marriage when the couple lived with the husband's parents and the paternal grandmother tended to admonish the husband for not paying enough attention to his wife at times. After the couple moved into a home of their own, the maternal mother-in-law became more involved with the wife, and the husband would periodically fight with her or make demands on the wife when he deemed mother-in-law to be "taking over too much." In recent months, however, he had simply been withdrawing from the field, "tired of fighting," as he saw it. The wife saw it as abandonment and part of his "sickness," an increasing preoccupation with religion. In mentioning this during a heated exchange, the wife threw in for good measure that the husband was imposing his religious practices on their daughter and "turning daughter against mother." The husband retorted that he had imposed nothing; rather, it was the daughter that had challenged him to practice what he preached and it was "after finding her arguments sound" that he had embarked upon an intense study of his religion. I saw that this behavior mimicked the intensely studious days of this man's youth under

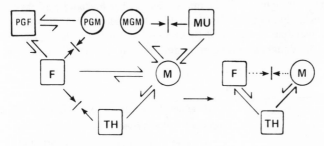

Initial engagement: Therapy system is mirror image of both parents' original system.

As therapist takes control intermittent open conflict develops between parents.

Figure 7.8

the guidance of his ambitious mother and, by insisting on details about the daughter, I was finally able to enlarge my understanding of what had transpired in this family.

In her preteen years, the daughter had been more involved with the wife than the husband, tending to be solicitous and directive toward the former and noncommunicative with the latter. She thus functioned similarly to the maternal grandmother and there was a reciprocal relationship between the intensity of the daughter-mother relationship and that of the mother-grandmother relationship. After daughter became a teenager, she became increasingly friendly with neighboring teenagers who attended a parochial school, spent time with their families, and developed an interest in their customs. This became the issue around which she began to communicate with her father. At first, she pointed to inconsistencies between father's proclaimed beliefs and actions. Next, they engaged in long discussions and eventually father became very active in the house of worship and both children entered parochial school. At the same time, daughter began to pull away from mother and rejected mother's pursuits. Occasionally, there were open clashes and mother accused father of enjoying daughter's "freshness." Father withdrew further from mother, and mother found herself appealing more and more to grandmother. Grandmother, in turn, inveighed against father and daughter and then proceeded to make more and more demands upon our unhappy mother (see Figure 7.9).

We were all able to agree that mother needed to learn how to handle her own mother and I told the father that we needed his help in this effort. He was to encourage his wife but not get involved with grandmother himself and, at all costs, he must not fight his wife's battles for her. I specifically requested that he return with three examples of how his mother-in-law interfered with his household or imposed upon his wife so that we could formulate tactics. The husband thought this "very reasonable." I was eager to bring in the children, but both parents could see "little purpose" in this idea, so I bided my time.

Sure enough, two weeks later mother reported that just the day before, daughter had "opened up a vile mouth" to her for the first time and she, mother, was overwhelmed and distraught. To make matters worse, her husband was present and seemed to laugh. "Shouldn't he, in a case like this, make his daughter apologize to me?" she pleaded. I responded by saying that I believed mother could learn how to handle daughter competently and, indeed, she had done well by

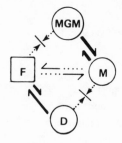

As daughter shifts from underfunctioning with mother to intense overfunctioning with father, marital relationship becomes less intense and mother falls back on her mother intensely.

Figure 7.9

condemning daughter's language and refusing to further discuss the minor issue involved. Moreover, I commended father for "refraining from interferring." Father denied laughing and pointed out that there wasn't much room for him since grandmother happened to be on the telephone with mother at the same time threatening to break granddaughter's arm if she spoke to mother like that again. One couldn't ask for a better example of child and grandparent relating as peers over an underfunctioning parent. Daughter also related to father as *his* mother, let us remember, and father confirmed this by blurting out that daughter told him not to let the psychiatrist get the idea that she was brainwashed by father. I quickly pointed out that this was a message that daughter had a few things to say and she ought to have the right to speak for herself. Both parents agreed somewhat reluctantly to bring in the children, and the rest of the time was devoted to husband's homework and giving guidelines to the wife on how she might assert herself with her mother in a useful way.

In the fourth session, two weeks later, both children appeared friendly and interested, the boy clearly allied with and supportive of his older sister. In response to my query, mother reported that daughter had come to her on her own the day after our last session to apologize. I praised the daughter and suggested that mother thank father for his wisdom in allowing mother and daughter to work things out for themselves. Mother did so and also complimented me for helping them, saying that her husband had been much "nicer." He refused this left-handed compliment, attributing his even-temperedness to less tension at work and hinting that in the future he might erupt again. I mildly observed that he had turned something positive into a negative and daughter chimed in that he was very critical. She recounted how she had looked up to him because he seemed so much stronger than her mother, and also stated that she couldn't stand her mother's intrusiveness. When she called her father a hypocrite regarding religion, he seemed to take it very well and actually did something about it, earning her respect and affection. Now, however, he had become the expert and was constantly criticizing her and demanding that she be ever more exact in her religious observances. She was beginning to think that father was just as bad as mother in his own way. She loved them both but there were problems with both. Here was a good point on the pendulum swing between mother and father from which to work. It turned out that daughter was very upset herself. She had a pronounced tic as she told of her despair at "getting mother to understand" her bid for more freedom. Turning to father had some merits but was no substitute. And grandmother was something else lately! Brother had similar gripes on a lesser scale. Mother had been "fussing" at him more lately since sister was with father, and grandma, too, had become much more concerned about his clothes and manners. Brother was slated to take sister's place were she to withdraw. Both parents were struck by this appeal from their children and listened attentively, their own cyclical debate forgotten. We were in business. From this point on, the therapy proceeded apace. I kept a watchful eye on the balance in the nuclear family by including the children from time to time and giving guidance to the parents, while both of them proceeded to renegotiate relationships with their respective parents.

My strategy, derived from my understanding of the total family organization, was to increase interaction between mother and daughter while maintaining contact with father and daughter. This tended to deintensify the mother-grandmother relationship so mother could learn to assert herself in a useful way with husband's cooperation. Eventually, husband would work on the relationship with *his* mother and the wife would cooperate in this venture. In order to achieve these ends, two types of dysfunctional processes had to be constantly monitored and corrected. One was the tendency of mother and father to underfunction and overfunction respectively vis-à-vis daughter, maternal grandmother, and each other. Such tendencies lead to too much or too little interaction and hence promote instability. The second was the tendency to triangulate. This family exhibited what I have called the pattern of shifting triangles (4): mother and father debated about their daughter and respective mothers; mother and daughter looked to father for judgments about their relationship; and father and daughter often communicated through mother (see Figure 7.10). It is necessary to detriangulate each relationship in order for it to be renegotiated.

Some therapists work on the marital relationship exclusively while others direct their attention to the extended family in the belief that this will decrease the tension in the nuclear family, and that the rest will take care of itself. My experience has convinced me that, especially in the case of the family with adolescents, active attention to both nuclear and extended families is more efficient, more widely applicable, and less dangerous. For me, it is also more fun.

In the above illustration, relieving some of mother's anxiety about husband and daughter increased her feeling of competence and lent impetus to her resolve to "learn how to be a whole person with her mother." More important, reinvolvement of mother with her husband and daughter was a fast way of deintensifying the mother-grandmother relationship. Had mother

Shifts in the Triangulation Pattern

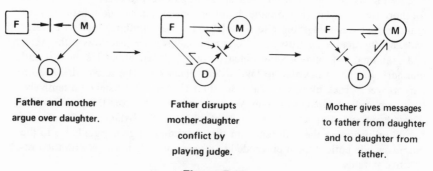

Father and mother argue over daughter.

Father disrupts mother-daughter conflict by playing judge.

Mother gives messages to father from daughter and to daughter from father.

Figure 7.10

been pushed to "become a self" with her mother too early, it might have resulted in useless confrontations requiring more difficult fresh starts or even in destructive explosions. True, this would be due to poor clinical judgment rather than a fault of the method, but I have seen major errors of this kind in the best hands. My point is that it is generally easier to make judgments when all parties are seen. (Grandmother was brought in "live" at one point during the course of treatment.) One of the best tactics for detriangulation is still to have all three parties present and to encourage all three to speak for themselves. This does not mean that the therapist is taking over family functions any more than a football coach is kicking and passing when watching a game; but he surely can spot the problems faster than when being told about the game.

The method I have described is more widely applicable because many families and individuals are not well enough put together to carry out tasks on their own, particularly when it comes to dealing with their family of origin. I firmly believe that the ultimate payload for each one of us comes from learning to conduct ourselves as adults after reviving childhood patterns with our original family. I am not willing, however, to consign those who are unable or unwilling to do it to the therapeutic ashheap. When much of the dysfunction remains with the extended family, the children may be better integrated than their parents and therefore a source of strength for the family. Not utilizing such strength is a waste. Adolescents frequently make good therapeutic allies.

Finally, to focus only on the marriage and/or the extended families, if successful, necessarily means decreasing the intensity of the parent-child relationship and increasing the anxiety of the child. Adolescents don't generally sit still under these conditions and I have, unfortunately, seen many destructive acts and suicide attempts on the part of adolescents when the therapist ignored them. It is not necessary and sometimes not humane to do so.

The opening phases of the above example demonstrate that, although the principles are simple, the nuances of language and the subtleties of behavior may confound understanding. For instance, the wife reported that the clashes with her husband were most disturbing, but it was my judgment that the overall decrease in interaction precipitated the clashes. Later, the woman admitted to feeling excluded by husband and daughter. Both parents tended to downplay the role of the daughter and this had to be energetically investigated. The decision to facilitate mother-daughter interaction was made not only to balance the intensity between both parents, but because it was deemed that, despite their difficulties, mother and daughter were the most well-functioning pair. Had father been as flexible as he claimed, I might have chosen to focus at first on the father-daughter relationship and father's extended family.

General Considerations of Treatment

In many instances, one parental-child relationship is so intense or "toxic" that deintensification is a must. Generally, the parent involved is only too willing to "take a vacation" (at least temporarily) and the other parent will agree to take over responsibility, having been critical of the other parent anyway and not really knowing firsthand what the water feels like. Here again, it is helpful to have the adolescent actively participate in the plan to shift parental responsibility.

The above considerations apply to those families where there has been some combination of shifting of the overfunctioning-underfunctioning axis of relationship with an adolescent and a shifting of intensity from one relationship to another. As already mentioned in connection with the symptomatic adolescent, the remaining possibility is that the adolescent has withdrawn from all family members. This can occur in a mild way, as in the instance of an adolescent becoming increasingly involved in a peer group yet maintaining reasonable contact with the family. This increases intensity in the parental relationship and/or parent-other sibling relationship, and may bring out some conflict or tendency toward imbalance of functioning, but generally the realignment becomes balanced within time (see Figure 7.11).

At the other extreme, the adolescent may insulate him- or herself from the family by running away (literally or figuratively) or becoming totally self-absorbed. I use the term insulation to describe the process reciprocal to fusion, the latter being the overfunctioning-underfunctioning process carried to extremes. Fusion and insulation are truly complementary and are al-

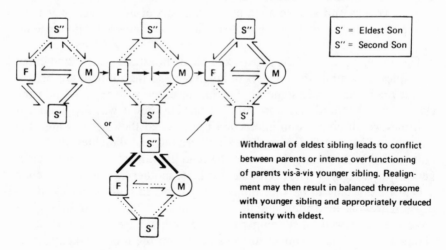

S' = Eldest Son
S'' = Second Son

or

Withdrawal of eldest sibling leads to conflict between parents or intense overfunctioning of parents vis-à-vis younger sibling. Realignment may then result in balanced threesome with younger sibling and appropriately reduced intensity with eldest.

Figure 7.11

ways, and only, present together in a family. An insulated adolescent is always avoiding either a severe triangulation process or a fusion, and the family has to compensate by fusing or triangulating elsewhere (see Figure 7.12). These families are often cut off from their extended families and the adolescent is only replicating behavior of the grandparents. A chronic situation easily develops and it is most difficult to treat. Such families can be treated but, in my experience, only by convening the whole family and coaching them directly how to reestablish contact, first with the adolescent and then with the extended family. Here especially, if the adolescent is ignored, he or she may be lost forever.

CONCLUSIONS

The various ways in which adolescent behavior may affect a family as well as the major implications for future health of the family have been out-

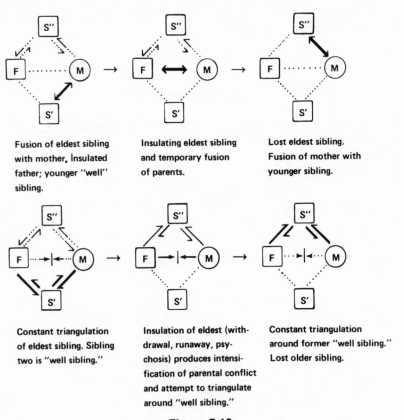

Fusion of eldest sibling with mother. Insulated father; younger "well" sibling.

Insulating eldest sibling and temporary fusion of parents.

Lost eldest sibling. Fusion of mother with younger sibling.

Constant triangulation of eldest sibling. Sibling two is "well sibling."

Insulation of eldest (withdrawal, runaway, psychosis) produces intensification of parental conflict and attempt to triangulate around "well sibling."

Constant triangulation around former "well sibling." Lost older sibling.

Figure 7.12

lined. The usual presentation of adolescent "with problems" has been underplayed. I hope to have given some sense of the diagnostic and therapeutic challenge that families with adolescents offer. I have implied that correct assessment of family process leads to correct therapeutic strategies, but I caution the reader to remember that diagnosis and intervention go hand-in-hand in family therapy. It is frequently only after false starts and unsuccessful interventions that a meaningful picture emerges. I have refrained from discussing specific tactics to be used by the therapist in pursuing the decided strategy. Tactics are, at least in part, a function of the idiosyncratic relationship between therapist and family. What works with one, may not work with another. Tactics are best learned, therefore, working with families under the tutelage of a flexible teacher who can allow the student therapist to be innovative within the framework of a consistent theory.

I think it fair to say that the attainment of adolescence by a family member always constitutes a profound landmark in the life cycle of the family with attendant pitfalls and opportunities. Treating such families is always a challenge and may try the acumen and fortitude of the most seasoned therapist. As with the families themselves, however, if the therapist can weather the storm, the rewards can be substantial.

REFERENCES

1. Ackerman, Nathan W. "Adolescent Problems: A Symptom of Family Disorder." *Family Process* (2), 1962.
2. Bell, John Elderkin. *Family Group Therapy in the Treatment of Juvenile and Adult Offenders.* Read at 36th Annual Conference of California Probation, Parole and Correctional Association, San Diego, California, May 26, 1966. In *Family Therapy.* New York: Jason Aronson, 1975.
3. Thomas, Lewis. *Natural Man. The Lives of a Cell.* New York: Viking Press, 1974.
4. Ackerman, Norman J. *The Canon of Family Systems.* New York: Gardner Press, In press.
5. Papp, Peggy, ed. *Family Therapy Full Length Case Studies.* New York: Gardner Press, 1977.

BIBLIOGRAPHY

General Correlates of Adolescent Behavior and Adolescence
Dentler, R. A., and Monroe, L. J. Social Correlates of Early Adolescent Theft. *American Sociological Review* 26 (1961).
Glueck, S., and Glueck, E. T. *Family Environment and Delinquency.* Boston: Houghton Mifflin Co. (1962).

Joffel, D. Delinquency Proneness and Family Anomie. *Journal of Criminal Law, Criminology and Political Science* 51 (1963).

Nye, F. I. *Family Relations and Delinquent Behavior.* New York: John Wiley & Sons, Inc. (1958).

Peterson, D. R. and Becker, W.C . Family Interaction and Delinquency. In Quay, H. C., ed., *Juvenile Delinquency, Theory and Research.* Princeton, N.J.: D. Van Nostrand (1965).

Middle-Age Crisis

Anderson, W. J. *Design for Family Living.* Minneapolis, Minn.: T. S. Dennison & Co., Inc. (1964).

Renne, K. S. Correlates of Dissatisfaction in Marriage. *Journal of Marriage and the Family* 32 (1970).

Scherz, F. H. Crisis of Adolescence in Family Life. *Social Casework* 48 (1967).

8
Launching Children and Moving On

Paulina McCullough, A.C.S.W.
University of Pittsburgh

This chapter will present the developmental issues, tasks, and certain of the clinical problems of families for the stage of life that begins with the launching of the children and continues until retirement or until approximately age sixty-five. In terms of the age of the parents, this stage usually extends from the mid-forties to the mid-sixties.

The quality of life for families in this stage has changed dramatically over the last several decades reflecting the demographic, social, economic, and health changes of society in general. The duration of this stage, as measured by the median time span in years between the marriage of the last child and the death of one parent, has increased since the first decade of the century from less than two to almost thirteen years. This reflects both greater life expectancy and the younger age of the mother when the last child leaves home. The average number of children has decreased from 3.9 in the first decade of this century to 2.5 for the 1970s. The smaller family and the greater employment of women, both before the launching period and continuing into the middle years, have importance in terms of activities and interests available. These changes, which will be discussed in more detail below, suggest that this stage of life deserves to be thought of more in terms of its own strengths and resources and less as an "empty nest syndrome."

Because of the newness of this phase and our limited language for describing systems, we have no adequate terminology to define this period.

We are aware that the title of this chapter refers only to the very first issue of this stage rather than to the tasks of the stage itself. Because "post-child-rearing" refers to the previous stage, "empty nest" is a rather negative definition, and "post-parental" inaccurate since parents always remain parents, we could not find a title that describes exactly what this phase *is* about. This lack reflects the very problem of the period: This time in life has not existed before for most couples and we need to find ways to help families experience it productively, rather than letting family members become isolated in the prime of life because their childrearing activities are over.

One important aspect of family dynamics in this phase is its ebb and flow. This state is particularly varied in that it is punctuated by numerous entries and exits of family members. It begins with a transitory ebb in the launching of the children. This is quickly followed by the creation of new states of relatedness when the offspring begin courting and subsequently marrying. The preparation for the addition of new members—spouses and of the extended in-law families—provides new momentum to the early part of this period. This proliferation of relationships is followed by the birth of new offspring leading to shifts in both nomenclature and roles: parents become grandparents and each generation takes one step up the family ladder. A parallel or later development is family attrition with the death of the older generation. The impact of deaths will depend on the previous state of family relatedness and on the importance that each dying member held in the functioning of the family.

For the purpose of this chapter, the focus will be on those families in which both parents were present through the childrearing stage and who are continuing together into the post-launching period. There is a fairly large population where divorce has occurred previously or during this period. The fact that one out of three marriages ends in divorce is significant, but more to the purpose of this chapter is the fact that almost two-thirds of all marriages remain intact. Moreover, most of the divorced parents remarry rather quickly, creating "reconstituted families." In these and in one-parent families, there are extra tasks for this stage that are dealt with elsewhere in this book (McGoldrick & Carter, Chapter 12).

The focus of this chapter will be on family rather than on individual dynamics. A three-generational perspective will be used with the view that this allows for both continuity and expansion. Knowledge and awareness of the way in which past generations have dealt with rites of passage and nodal events (Bradt, 1971) provide a general backdrop by which to gauge present happenings.

A broad theoretical model would postulate that families fall on a continuum of functioning. For the more functional families, rites of passage are dealt with as part and parcel of family life; the more dysfunctional families may find many of the nodal events to be either more disruptive or potentially conflictual. Many of these families have dealt with events during previous stages as "crises" of one kind or another. For still other families, previous stages have been completed with difficulty and some unresolved problems have been brought along to the present stage. To some degree, within each stage there is a "recapitulation" of previous issues. In more functional families, issues get dealt with and resolved as they occur. In less functional families, old unresolved issues crop up again and again, making the new ones harder to deal with.

For some families, reaching this stage may be seen as a time of fruition, completion, and as a second opportunity to consolidate or expand by exploring new avenues and new roles. For others, taking a second look may lead to disruption (divorce and other problems), a sense of overwhelming loss (empty nest syndrome), and general disintegration (illness and death).

The specifics of family dynamics for families with grown children will constitute the main body of the chapter with accompanying clinical examples. This material is offered to suggest the range of possibilities and limitations for clinical intervention in this stage of family development. The chapter will end with some therapeutic considerations of some of the most common problems.

DEMOGRAPHIC AND SOCIAL CHANGES

Over the last several decades, changes have occurred that affect the duration of the post-childrearing stage of family life (the middle years) and the quality of life—the opportunities and resources—for this stage. These changes reflect the general demographic, economic, and social changes that have occurred in our society. However, more research will be necessary before the significance of these changes can be interpreted fully for the benefit of the clinician. A few observations describing the extent of these trends will be noted here.

A remarkable analysis of certain demographic data reported by Paul C. Glick (1977) reveals the increased duration of the grown child stage and permits some speculation on its significance. His findings are reported in Table 8.1.

First, certain general observations from table 8.1: The median age of mothers at the time of first marriage has remained fairly constant over the eighty year period (although increasing in recent years); the age of the mother at the birth of the first child varied little, but the age of the mother at the birth of the last child has dropped appreciably. The age of the mother at marriage of the last child has also dropped. And finally, the age of the mother at the time of the death of one of the parents has *increased* greatly.

Table 8.1.

Median Age of Mothers at Selected Life Events

Life Event	80 year average	Approximate date of birth of mother				
		1880s	1900s	1920s	1940s	1950s
		Median age of mothers				
First marriage	20.9	21.4	21.0	20.7	20.5	21.2
Birth of first child	22.6	23.0	22.8	22.7	21.8	22.7
Birth of last child	31.3	32.9	31.0	31.5	30.1	29.6
Marriage of last child	53.5	55.4	53.0	53.2	52.7	52.3
Death of spouse	62.8	57.0	62.3	64.4	65.1	65.2

Source: Paul C. Glick, "Updating the Life Cycle of the Family," *Journal of Marriage and Family,* February 1977, p. 5.

Increased labor force participation by women generally, and specifically in the forty-five to sixty-four age range, represents another factor that is changing the situation of couples in the post-childrearing period. The fact is that 55% of all women forty-five to fifty-four and 41.1% of all women fifty-five to sixty-four were in the labor force in 1976 (Keyserling, 1977). Unfortunately, no analysis has been made of either the employment status or the general economic status of families at this stage that would help in the understanding of the effect of these factors on family well-being. One possible inference may be drawn, i.e., improved economic well-being of these families appears to influence their intergenerational activities. For example, many middle-aged parents are actively engaged in helping their retired parents and/or their adult children.

DEFINING THIS PHASE

As early as 1937, McIver (1937) referred to this period as "the empty nest" stage. As indicated, this appears to place undue emphasis on only one of the many characteristics of this cycle. Duvall (1971) divided the period into two stages: (1) families as launching centers (first child gone to last child leaving home), and (2) middle aged parents (empty nest to retirement).

Part of the reason for the many titles and the different divisions rests with the fact that the concept of the life cycle has not been commonly used to describe family functioning. Until recently, family dynamics have taken second place to individual dynamics, at least in the psychiatric literature. If one compares American culture to others, one finds much less emphasis on the continuity provided by transgenerational studies, perhaps because the focus tends to be on present or future. Another generalization may be that cultural emphasis has been more on achievement, highlighting a person's occupation, rather than family role. As compared to many other cultures (e.g., the Japanese), the roles of parents and grandparents in this country are more ambiguous and fraught with friction.

Nevertheless, the fact that technology and demographic changes have made this stage almost as lengthy as the childrearing stage lends new impetus to the need for research on this period to help families negotiate their many transitions productively.

Schram (1979), in discussing some of the gaps in our knowledge about life stages in general, and about this stage in particular, stated: "The emphasis of a developmental perspective is on the sequencing of the various stages. We need to know how the transition from one stage to the next is experienced. We need to identify constricted versus expanded roles." She was addressing problems of research in the area of marital adjustment, but these comments also apply to what clinicians need to utilize the theoretical framework of the life cycle in therapy.

Solomon (1973) writes cogently on the definition and tasks for this stage. He calls it the "actual departure of the children" and sees it extending until the death of one parent, initiating the final stage which he describes as "integration of loss." He adds that tasks for the middle (parents) and younger (children) generations overlap. The task for the family of origin involves "relinquishing the primary nature of the gratification involved in the role of parents.... This necessitates the existence of a stabilized marital relationship." He states that failure to accomplish this task may mobilize the family to hold onto the last child.

REVIEW OF THE LITERATURE

The variety of terms, the disparity in what are considered the length and natural division between stages, have led Schram (1979) to suggest that "the use of different criteria for the family life cycle stages make samples of post-parental families incomparable." (p. 8).

Schram concludes that research efforts in the area of families with grown children are partial, inconclusive, and at times contradictory in their premises and subsequent findings. The author, after reviewing literature on marital satisfaction for this stage, concludes there are three competing descriptions of what happens in the post–childrearing stage: (a) the "empty nest syndrome," which posits that there are problems for one or both of the parents; (b) the "curvilinear model," which claims increased freedom and independence for the couple; and (c) variations that are minor in nature. All these theoretical premises need further validation. At the general level of conceptualization, Solomon (1973) offers the theoretical assumption that the family cycle is comparable to the individual life cycle (Erikson, 1964) in that it "requires mastery of one stage before moving into the next."

There has been a variety of studies on this population. Results have depended on whether or not the sample concentrated on normal (asymptomatic individuals) or on symptomatic ones. Anderson et al. (1977) studied 100 asymptomatic families through self reports. One of the questions measured parents' expected reactions when their children, now in adolescence, would finally leave home. They found that "although 33 percent expected a loss of sense of family, 51 percent anticipated new opportunities and 21 percent even expected a sense of relief (p. 12)" at having completed this stage. For the last two groups, "the often cited empty nest syndrome did not appear to be a major problem (p. 12)." The authors provide bibliographic data on other studies confirming this view (Lowenthal, 1972).

In a recent study on the subject, Harkins (1978), reviewing a sample of 318 "normal" women she felt to be representative, determined that effects of "empty nest" are slight and disappear within two years. She found no effect of the transition on physical well-being and, in fact, a positive effect on psychological well-being.

This same study suggests one clue about what might be classified as the "intermediate" group, i.e., those having some difficulties with the transition. The variables she studied include: women's roles; employment status; job satisfaction; size of family; satisfaction with children; socioeconomic status; attitudes toward an "empty nest" transition; and whether or not a family was "off-schedule," that is, the child's leaving was delayed. Although the hypothesis would be that a number of life events have bearing on adjustment, the only variable showing a relationship to adjustment was what she termed "being off schedule." She concluded, "The only threat to well being may be in having a child who does not become successfully independent when expected" (p. 555).

Moving toward the more symptomatic individuals and families, Deyken et al. (1966) studied sixteen women in this stage of the life cycle who had been hospitalized with depression. She established that overt conflict with children was positively related to early age at the mother's marriage, holding onto European values, and, most importantly, to the death of the spouse. Solomon (1973) refers to another issue at this stage: "If the solidification of the marriage has not taken place and reinvestment is not possible, the family usually mobilizes itself to hold on to the last child. Prior to that, the family may avoid the conflict around separation by allowing one child to leave and subsequently focusing on the next in line" (p. 186). Clarification of how this process operates (shifting from child to child as opposed to concentrating on one child) is still needed. For example, a serious physical or psychological impairment may prevent parent-child separation (an instance of this will be presented later).

This stage has received a great deal of interest in recent years from both scientific and popular writers. Depending on the orientation of the author, the middle years are seen as constituting more or less a "crisis" (Sheehy, 1976; Levinson, 1978). A family orientation uses a different framework to assess the same phenomenon, using additional dimensions to understand this process. Some of these factors are reviewed in the next section.

A TRANSGENERATIONAL MODEL FOR THIS STAGE

One way to conceptualize the potential for successful coping in the middle years is to observe how the family has coped with previous nodal events. The assumption is that past unresolved issues are reactivated during this stage.

In taking a three-generational view of this stage, it is necessary to consider what issues exist between nuclear and extended families. The degree of success that the parents have demonstrated in dealing with issues of autonomy, responsibility, and connectedness with their respective families of origin will have definitive impact on their success in handling these issues with their grown children.

Underlying unresolved issues may be triggered in any of the three generations. Depending on the degree of anxiety generated, all three subsystems may respond with accompanying shifts or upsets of the family equilibrium. An example of this phenomenon might be a situation in which a twenty-year-old girl involved in overt sexual experimentation decides to live with her boyfriend. The mother's response might be acute anxiety, depression, anger, and some form of rejection. Underlying the above feelings might be the need to reexamine her own sense of competence or fulfillment in her marriage and the fact that her degree of autonomy at her daughter's age was seriously curtailed. She might also feel very reluctant to discuss this issue with her own mother. She might feel a mixture of anger and inadequacy both as daughter and as mother. Bowen (1977) has produced a videotape where he demonstrates how issues between a woman in her forties and her young adult daughter become resolved when the mother takes up the disquieting problem with her own mother.

The example also highlights another point: A transgenerational view is helpful in establishing which issues may be "difficult" for a family.

The following is a summary of the main tasks for the three generations during this phase. Tasks for the older and younger generations are summarily addressed since they will be discussed in detail in other chapters. There will be comparatively more detail regarding the tasks for the stage under discussion, i.e., the middle generation.

The Older Generation (Grandparents)

1. Impending retirement may precipitate different degrees of anxiety in older people about the use of more leisure time and possibly financial security.

2. There may be difficulties for the couple in having to spend more time together. If their interdependence has not been worked out in a sound way, being in closer touch tends to produce an increase in marital tension.

3. There can be a decrease in physical functioning and an increase of physical symptoms independent of or related to life stresses.

4. The state of intergenerational relatedness will have bearing on all of the above. Realistic interdependence with the rest of the family will be conducive to less stress and/or better stress management. By the same token, conflict in the middle or younger generation usually has a negative impact on older adults. Efforts to "keep grandparents in the dark" are often counterproductive. Reliance for support on others (friends, other relatives) will also be helpful.

5. Death of one spouse is one of the major tasks facing older adults. Neugarten (1976) has found that families' reaction and oldsters' response to death cover a wide range. She concludes that a considerable number show great acceptance and the death causes little disruption.

6. The degree of financial security will have considerable bearing on the capacity for autonomy and problem solving for the remaining spouse.

7. All of the above may result in decisions about autonomous living versus moving in with a son or daughter or selecting a nursing home.

Younger Generation (Offspring)

1. A key factor is younger people's ability and freedom to move toward independence and make decisions on future life goals.

2. Exploration and consolidation of friendships and choosing of possible mates are primary issues at this phase. This will lead to marriage and some state of connectedness with an in-law family plus an eventual new role as parent.

3. There is a need to address a new state of relatedness with parents and other family members, on the basis of mutual adulthood, rather than adult to child.

4. Prolongation of financial dependency, e.g., when pursuing a professional education, will delay the establishment of autonomy from parents and require their continued involvement.

5. The addition of a fourth generation leads to a new state of relatedness. Parents become grandparents, etc. Feikema (1978) has elaborated on the significance of this transition for the family system.

Middle Generation (Parents)

1. There is a decreased investment in the caretaking parental role. This calls for increased acceptance of independent pursuits in the children, culminating in physical separation and establishment by each young person of his or her own nuclear family or some comparable arrangement.

2. Separation from the children may not be smooth. Children may re-enter the parental family literally by returning home while starting a professional career, or figuratively by requesting extended financial help through studies. The degree of financial solvency will have an effect on how prolonged this period is.

3. Marriage of the children will create a new state of relatedness. The addition of the "in-law" subsystem may create some strain. Many times the need to "hold on" may be expressed by a rejection of the fiance, or, in any case, difficulty accepting a child's new spouse into the family.

4. Simultaneous with "letting go" is the need to invest more in individual pursuits. Women, in particular, may pursue work, a career, or return to school.

5. There is generally a pull to reinvest in the marriage or to change some of the basic tenets of the relationship. If "empty nest" coincides with the wife's increased autonomy through work or career, there may be a temporary increase in marital conflict.

6. At times, the imbalance created by the increased autonomy of wife and children may lead either spouse to respond to the vacuum left in the family by pursuing extramarital relationships. If it happens at the beginning of the phase, it is usually defined as part of the "midlife crisis." If it happens toward the end of the period, it may be defined as "the last fling." Generally, the system imbalance related to the affair is minimized or overtly denied.

7. Successful coping at this stage should lead to consolidating previous gains in terms of work stability, physical comfort, and attainment of mastery through experience.

8. The middle part of the phase will require a capacity to explore new avenues, make new choices—to expand horizons and deepen interests.

9. At some point in the phase, another shift in the state of relatedness will occur. Parents become grandparents with the addition of another generation. For many families, this role is steeped in tradition. Grandparents are authority figures who help the parents in the socialization of children by the articulation of expectations regarding them. For other families, however, especially in the case of younger grandparents, the role is more one of "funseeking" (Neugarten, 1976) where the adult joins the child for the specific purpose of having fun.

10. Generally toward the latter part of the phase another shift takes place: The middle generation has to deal with changing relationships with their own parents and having to face their retirement, physical disability, increased dependency, and death.

In analyzing the tasks outlined above, one should bear in mind that this phase often lasts approximately twenty years. At the beginning of the period separation from children takes center stage. There is a gradual refocusing on individual pursuits and on the marriage. It is a time for reevaluation with awareness of increased autonomy on the one hand, but a realization also of the finiteness of one's pursuits. With retirement approaching at the end of the cycle, there is yet another shift from "making a living" to "living out options." Somewhere during the middle or end of this period, relations with parents (grandparents) regain prominence through illness and/or death of one or both grandparents. In some cases, the middle generation must become caretakers for their parents, leading to still another major shift in the family balance.

Listing the above tasks as separate items tends to deprive them of their interactional dimensions. Viewing them in terms of their interrelatedness adds a different perspective to the problem solving process. In real life, these tasks all overlap and coexist.

A special word should perhaps be said about the important entry of the next generation during this phase. The potential for generational family conflict may either diminish or escalate with the birth of a grandchild. Often when extended families have been unwilling to accept a son's (or daughter's) new spouse, they may be reconciled with the entrance of a grandchild because adding a new generation binds the outsider and the family permanently and unalterably together. On some occasions new parents may use the birth of offspring to complete the drawing of boundaries around their nuclear family that were initiated with the marriage. It may also involve blocking out the third generation to the detriment of the whole family. Friction at this point tends to subside more easily if the grandparents are able to understand that their children's struggle represents a wish and need for increased autonomy as a subsystem, and if the new parents can recognize and appreciate the richness of the interplay of the extended family with their new children. It is common for the maternal grandparents to be incorporated more easily, especially when the relationship with the daughter has been largely worked out. Relations between the generations around a new baby vary greatly. Where the family is cohesive, grandparents seem to move in and out at will and not to wait for overtures or formal invitations from the new parents; in families where the young nuclear family has drawn more clear physical or psychological boundaries, grandparents visit and interact mostly following their children's cues. Grandparenthood can lead to triangling over which extended family is the favorite, who sends the best presents, which set of grandchildren is the favorite, and so on. As usual, such conflicts tend to reflect triangles flowing from one generation to the next, i.e., the favorite son usually produces the favorite grandson.

CLINICAL CONSIDERATIONS

The examples that follow do not convey the full range of possibilities but are suggestive rather of the scope and the interrelatedness for the family.

Family I. A Problem in the Marriage Interferes with the Launching of a Child (Figure 8.1)

The Doane family epitomizes unresolved marital issues that are manifested by problems in an offspring.

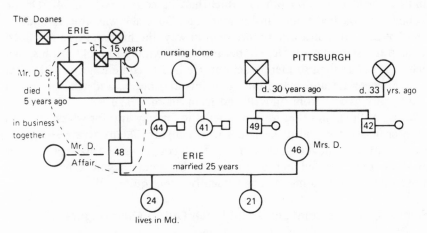

Figure 8.1 Family I—A Problem in the Marriage Interferes with the Launching of a Child

About three years ago, Mrs. Doane, a woman in her forties, consulted about problems with her daughter Lily, aged twenty-one. While the older daughter had graduated from college and was living away, Lily was floundering both about career and life. She had moved back home after starting two unsuccessful college ventures; she was currently unemployed and she was involved in a conflictual relationship with a young man. She was excessively dependent and demanding of Mrs. Doane, who was resentful of her daughter's intrusiveness and constant bids for attention. Mrs. Doane regarded Lily's move back home as "impulsive" and her unsuccessful college career as "immature." She did not see problems in herself, in her husband or in her marriage. She presented herself as so self-possessed that her strong feelings about her daughter seemed somewhat discrepant. The same pseudocontrolled attitude permeated her attitude in therapy. After three sessions she claimed that she knew what she had to do about Lily and promised to return if she needed to.

Six months later she returned to therapy announcing that her husband had suddenly left her after calmly stating that he needed a separation "for himself" without providing any further explanation. She seemed at a loss to understand this occurrence and was quite depressed to find herself emotionally alienated from her husband. She subsequently learned that the husband's departure followed a year-long affair with a woman in her twenties. Mr. Doane's actions were in sharp contrast with his previous behavior; throughout his life he had always done what was expected of him. He had been a "good" son following in his father's footsteps by working in the business he had created; he had been a "perfect" husband and father. Shortly after his father's death he plunged into an artistic venture that he enjoyed and where he met the new woman; he had a strong desire to "leave everything behind" and to start a new life. It was when he first started to "pull away" from his wife that Lily "moved back" into the family.

Therapy first addressed the issues of Mrs. Doane's apparent dominance and her need to control others, which had its counterpart in Mr. Doane feeling "encroached upon" in his marriage. Once she was able to address some of these responses in a more helpful way, the husband had less need to keep himself unavailable. He became more willing to look into his own behavior rather than to merely act out. He had to come to grips with what were appropriate and inappropriate wants and needs, and what he could realistically expect from himself and from his marriage.

Many of the issues that were problematic for Lily and for which she had been criticized were also the issues to which Mr. Doane was responding. Shortly after he moved back home and the couple agreed to explore their troubles, Lily stopped her unproductive behavior, began a new career, moved away from home, and is presently doing quite well.

Family II. Out of Sight Does Not Mean Out of Mind (Figure 8.2)

The following example shows a family's reaction to what was considered "unacceptable" behavior in an offspring; a son was ousted from the family

The Kostas

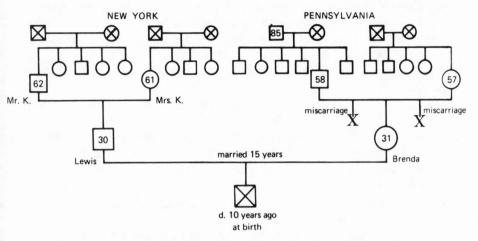

Figure 8.2. Family II—Out of Sight Does Not Mean Out of Mind

when he married into the "wrong" cultural and religious group. When he sought help it seemed as though the total cut-off from family had been accepted and surmounted. His reason for seeking therapy was supposedly "marital" in nature. Even though therapy involved only the younger generation, the problem stemming from the older generation changed, in spite of the fact that they were never seen in therapy.

Lewis and Brenda, a couple in their early thirties, came to the office complaining of marital upset. After a few discussions of their conflict over largely inconsequential matters, it became evident that they had excessive reliance on each other, excessive dependence, and an incapacity to establish other relationships. The overall sense was that all they had in the world was each other and this was obviously insufficient. Moreover, Lewis responded to conflict by withdrawing and feeling worthless, reactions which were also prominent in his responses to his own family of origin. It became increasingly clear that the cut-off from his own family had immediate relevance with what was occurring in the marriage. Further exploration of family history revealed some important clues. The mother was the one who had responded with the greatest disapproval to the marriage. Her position in her own family was pivotal in that she had been the caretaker of her own parents until their death and was now the head of the clan. Her directives were taken by the family as law and they all went along with her objections to the marriage and her total rejection of her son. However, in fact, Mrs. Kostas had been overly involved with Lewis throughout his life. The fact that he was an only child and that her husband was continuously absent from home probably contributed to the emotional fusion. Thus, Mrs. Kostas blamed the cultural and religious differences for what was in reality a deeply felt need to "hold on" to her son and a failure to accept his independence and autonomy.

The case also illustrates another important dynamic: The new spouse was rejected from the start and neither she nor her family ever became incorporated into the family. The process that needs to be set in motion by marriage, i.e., the joining of the two extended families, was permanently disrupted by an intense emotional process.

In this particular instance, the cut-off was dramatic and its relation to the problem did not go undetected for long. In many instances, individuals with cut-off fail to see the connection between unfinished business with family of origin and current life crises.

The above phenomenon exemplifies the continuities and discontinuities in the life cycle. Bowen (1978) has mentioned that some individuals deal with emotional fusion, i.e., inability to develop a strong sense of identity, by artificially separating from the family. But the underlying pull toward fusion is still there. Thus, individuals who use physical distance or total "cut-off" to become more comfortable with the parental fusion will often, through marriage, join a family that is cohesive and in which it will be possible to remain the outsider. However, all the unresolved issues with parents may either create depression after the parent's death or, as often happens, appear in a symptom in a child.

Another common mechanism is for the parent who cuts off (particularly when there was a violent "tearing away") to cling to one or several of the children. It is as though he or she were trying to redeem the breakup with the other parent by remaining overly attached to the child.

Furthermore, as the above example shows, a cut-off from the family of origin will tax the nuclear family. The original stress and anxiety will be transferred to the marriage.

Family III. The Bird That Stuck to the Nest (Figure 8.3)

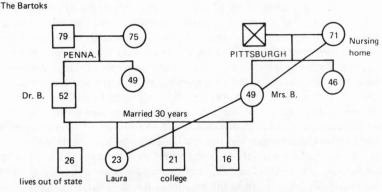

Figure 8.3. Family III—The Bird That Stuck to the Nest

Dr. and Mrs. Bartok came to the office upon referral by a psychiatrist who was treating their twenty-three-year-old daughter, Laura. She had returned to live at home after having failed in her second year of college. She remained largely nonfunctional and had few friends or outside interests.

A review of the various subsystems revealed that the father, a physician, held rather stilted, impersonal relations with both of his parents and his only sister. He maintained the same seemingly detached attitude toward his wife and children, but he was also dependent on his wife and he was overly responsive to her criticism. Mrs. Bartok, on her part, had a history of overattachment to her parents and to her children. She had become, after the death of her father, her "mother's keeper." The mother's intense dependency and demands triggered resentment and guilt in her. Laura was also clinging and dependent on her mother; in addition, she was openly hostile toward her. Mrs. Bartok evidenced some of the same reactions to her daughter that she did to her mother. Dr. Bartok's aloofness overtaxed the intense emotional fusion in the maternal axis and thus perpetuated the dysfunctional circularity. There had been previous signs of stress in the family. About ten years earlier, Dr. Bartok had been in therapy for approximately three years for depression and again both parents had been in counselling during a previous episode when Laura was in high school. Both of these efforts at therapy had left difficulties in the marital relationship largely untouched.

This family illustrates a variety of issues. The most striking is that of a pattern found often in families of impaired offspring: not only the failure to separate but the recurrence of that failure for at least three generations. In this case the fact that Laura was the only daughter probably contributed to making her the chosen one. Mrs. Bartok's emotions governed her actions; she was moved by fear, guilt, and resentment. She considered both her mother and daughter to be fragile and unable to cope. Her feeling of helplessness was displaced onto the marriage and she perceived herself as the victim of an uncaring, unhelpful husband from whom she felt estranged. The husband's inability to express or respond to feelings, and his traditional tendency to withdraw from conflict, perpetuated this state of affairs.

Therapeutic intervention had to address all the different subsystems starting with the lopsided marital relationship, but also requiring concurrent shifts in relationships with the younger and older generation. Dr. Bartok needed to become more involved in all the different sets, thus enabling Mrs. Bartok to become less involved and less taxed. The combined shifts resulted in the fact that, after approximately one year, Mrs. Bartok was capable of making a realistic assessment of her mother's failing condition and her own limited capacity to care for her. She was able to place her mother in a nursing home. Once she could make this decision she was ready to insist that her daughter move out on her own. This is not always the outcome in such cases. As was stated previously, it is important to establish what function the offspring is fulfilling by remaining at home, and how strong and prevalent the symbiotic patterns have been for the family. In many cases, a child's failure to fly forces upon the parents the function of prolonged babysitting. The parents may fall into this trap especially when they feel dissatisfied with their own marriage, when they have few outside interests, and when their level of self-confidence is low.

Family IV. Marriage Revisited (Figure 8.4)

Dr. and Mrs. Amato, a couple in their late forties, came to the office because of a six-month depressive episode in Mrs. Amato. The couple had three children, two of them in college. Dr. Amato had been employed in one of the teaching hospitals for at least fifteen years and Mrs. Amato was obtaining a degree in a health related profession. Mrs. Amato conceded that the "problem" was mainly in her but expressed a preference for being seen in conjunction with her husband. Dr. Amato was equally clear and defensive about not having any problem and not wanting any part of therapy even if it were for his wife. Mrs. Amato was given the option of "going at it alone." She called about a month later and stated that her depression had cleared and that she would momentarily forego therapy.

The couple returned about six months later and by this time Mrs. Amato had been transformed from the "adaptive," "depressed" partner into an angry and even verbally abusive person. It was clear that the sudden "transformation" had left her controlled and controlling husband at a loss about how to deal with her. The "precipitating" event was a "caring and loving,' relationship that Dr. Amato had developed with a much younger woman who worked for him in the hospi-

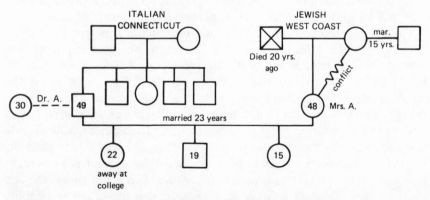

Figure 8.4. Family IV—Marriage Revisited

tal. Mrs. Amato, depending on the intensity of her emotions, fluctuated between considering it a very special bond and accusing her husband of having an outright sexual "affair." Dr. Amato vehemently denied all charges and only admitted to responding "in kind" to the consideration offered him by a conscientious, loyal, and thoughtful subordinate. What the "alleged affair" brought into bold relief were the unsatisfactory aspects of the marital bond for both spouses. Furthermore, it provided Mrs. Amato with a legitimate reason to insist on the discussion of what heretofore had been unacceptable subjects. In their married life, Mrs. Amato had been the Jewish "refugee" from a bad parental situation (the parents were divorced) who had been "taken" in by a cohesive and loving Italian family. These beginnings had set the tone for their relationship. In the past, Mrs. Amato had essentially accepted what she considered her husband's many shortcomings, particularly around affection, with the rationale that "he did not know any different." These thoughts were no longer tenable in the face of Dr. Amato's caring behavior with someone else.

Paramount is the need to take a "second look" at the marriage. All the dysfunctional aspects of the marriage plus the individual's proclivities that "make it so" need to be addressed in therapy. Some of the underlying myths also get called into question. In this instance, Dr. Amato's previous refusal to address any of the controversial aspects of their interaction was up for scrutiny. Equally important was a thrust to consider the missing aspects of their relationship and how both partners tended to perpetuate it. A pervasive myth for this couple was the notion that Dr. Amato was more important to Mrs. Amato than she was to him. In the course of therapy, Mrs. Amato's increased willingness to test out assumptions led to a short trial separation. Several misconceptions were corrected as a result of this move. When it was over, both partners were aware that the interdependence was quite reciprocal. Mrs. Amato also realized that she was more autonomous and resourceful than she had known. Dr. Amato emerged as a more pliable individual who was quite able to accept changes. Two additional insights revealed the systemic issues impinging on this family: One, Dr. Amato's infatuation coincided with personal and professional problems involving a rival colleague and the hospital administration which eventually resulted in his demotion; the second, Mrs. Amato's pervasive isolation from her own family of origin constituted a very serious loss for her. This was sharply brought to her awareness with the death of her father a couple of years earlier. Her almost "total transplantation" made her more entrenched and dependent on her husband and his family.

Four general areas of problems and concerns for this stage can be extrapolated from the above examples. These areas are problems with the older generation; problems with the younger generation; marital difficulties; and moves toward self-definition or differentiation.

Resolving Problems with the Older Generation

My experience and that of other practitioners seem to indicate that the older generation does not usually seek psychiatric treatment. Often results are obtained by helping individuals in the middle years to deal with problems with their parents.

In the bulk of my work with adults in the middle years, there seems to be "unfinished business" of all gradations with their parents. In some cases, the unfinished business may take a new form upon the death of a parent. In the Bartok family, Mrs. Bartok's father died and the surviving mother shifted her dependency to the daughter, intensifying an already over-dependent relationship.

Death of the older person need not be a crisis for the family. In support of this notion, Neugarten (1976) describes the attitudes of functional families toward these deaths as more of a natural happening. Problems arise when relationship difficulties in the family have not been resolved. For some families, the overriding reaction to the death of the parent is guilt, signaling unresolved issues. In the above families, this was prominent in the cases of Mrs. Doane and Mrs. Amato. Frequently, guilt is not necessarily related to having been distant or in conflict with a parent. In the case of Mrs. Bartok, she had been overresponsible and overinvolved with her parents for the greater portion of her life. The underlying dynamic, which is always the significant variable, is a failure to successfully separate self from parents. This is operative in varying degrees with all families. In the Bartok case, despite the intensity of the symbiosis, Mrs. Bartok could finally make some decisions based on thought rather than emotion. Another issue—common for most caretakers—was Mrs. Bartok's resentment of her younger sister, who had been minimally involved and lacking in anxiety regarding her mother's care. When approached with this imbalance, Mrs. Bartok replied like a true caretaker. She offered countless reasons to show how she was the only one who could get the job done. Recently, she has asked for and received more help from her sister.

News of critical illness and approaching death may be met with strong emotions. Individuals sometimes need help in discussing the situation and the feelings with an ailing parent. Fears of making the situation worse, not knowing the "right way" or the "right" words or taking away "hope" from the ill member are some of the forms in which individuals couch their anxieties and hesitations. The unresolved parts of the relationship are brought out in bold relief. Some are painfully cognizant that discussing personal matters was not part of the relationship; for others the realization is one of too much existing emotion with the accompanying fears of being overwhelmed, of crying, or of totally losing control. The therapeutic effort is to help the individual obtain a better grasp of the situation, and his or her role in it, and to encourage personal contact and communication with members of the extended family.

In many instances, malaise regarding parents stems from not being able to respond to what older people view as problematic areas. Too often the tendency on the part of the adult is to minimize the oldster's concern, to become impatient or in other ways deny the aged person's perceptions. Efforts on the part of the clinician can be geared to concentrating on what triggers the evasive or angry responses to older family members. In most cases, it relates to an inability on the part of the son or daughter to accept the parent on the parent's own terms, feeling enveloped by the parent's negativity. It is my belief that aging parents are often aware of feelings of rejection and their own responses about their lives may be strongly determined by this perception. When the son or daughter can become less critical, the parents can often take a less negativistic view of their own lives.

A related point is that the person in the middle years has the opportunity to learn something for himself or herself and be helpful to oldsters by supporting them in their life review. This entails encouraging older people to ponder out loud what their lives have meant, what their successes and failures have been, and who the significant people involved were. The important point is that what the oldsters mostly want and appreciate is a friendly and accepting person, rather than somebody who will attempt to reassure or convince them that things were really better or different.

Individuals in the middle generation may also have trouble with what they consider the parents' uninvolved, uncaring, or somewhat rejecting attitudes. Many times these feelings are prompted by the grandparents' responses to the growing grandchildren. The unspoken or perceived criticism from grandparents that parents have been too lax or incompetent will cause strife in the relationship. The same general principles are used to help give the parents a more objective view of their own involvement in the "family dance." Being able to hear the grandparents' criticism as a measure of their interest and an expression of their own anxiety will usually help parents to respond less defensively. The critical element for the parents is to become more connected with their families of origin.

Two final statements need to be made about clinical work with older people. The first one is that it is not essential to have the older generation in the room to resolve unfinished business. It suffices to coach the motivated adult to engage in different behavior. The second is that motivation to modify patterns with the older generation varies considerably. Roughly half of the individuals discussed above worked on their extended families. Death of the parents (as in the cases of Mrs. Doane and Mrs. Amato) seems to compound the difficulties. This finding is consistent with my experience

with other families, and with the literature, that the probability of successfully resolving past problems seems to diminish with the death of both parents (Bowen, 1978).

Resolving Problems with Grown Children

Families in which the problem seems to center on a symptomatic or difficult young adult offspring are those in which the issues of separation and
autonomy have not been successfully worked out. In actuality, many families do not regard autonomy and independence as necessary or even worthwhile goals. Many prefer having married children living next door or in
close physical proximity. It is equally true that cohesiveness per se does not
necessarily breed symptomatic behavior; dysfunction seems to occur when
the degree and quality of the closeness becomes fixed between two people
or when two people triangle in a third one, such as in the examples cited
above. Even after a symptom appears in a young adult, he or she is not always the one to seek therapy, and in my practice, I am approached as often
by parents as by the symptomatic offspring.

Success in approaching the issue of a "problem" adult child depends to
some extent on the capacity to determine the function that the symptomatic
behavior serves for the family as well as the position that the "problematic"
one holds. In the case of the Doanes and Bartoks, the "triangled" child was
also the most dysfunctional member of the unit. Therapy involved only the
parents (although the offspring were seen a couple of times).

In many instances, the problematic young adult seems to be satisfied with
letting the parents be primary movers in therapy. In most cases involving a
young adult who is "stuck," the first move is to help the parents to let go of
the offspring. This may be quite difficult, as in the case of Mrs. Bartok.

Concurrent with loosening the mother-child tie, the therapeutic efforts
also center on the marital relationship. In all of the above families, redirecting efforts from the child to the marriage was fairly easy to accomplish. This
is not always true when there are symptomatic offspring and the capacity to
redirect the locus of the parents' concern seems to be partially related to the
time of appearance of the acute symptomatic behavior. Other factors that
seem to affect the length and degree of progress in therapy are the intensity
of the enmeshment, and how functional, motivated, and/or uncomfortable
the person seeking therapy is.

In many cases (as with the Kostas) conflict seems to originate with a new
marriage or in difficulties with in-laws; however, these are generally manifestations of unsuccessful separation between parent and offspring. Incorporation of in-laws will be more difficult when the offspring's choice of
mate is based on a "reactive" or challenging stand taken "against" parents
and where the action appears to be a rejection of values the family holds as

important. In other instances, the mate is chosen largely to help the young adult to "fend off" the family and the spouse is literally used as a "wedge" against the family. Very often this mate will embrace the negative views that the spouse has of the family and will regard the partner as "victimized" and the family as the "victimizer." In-laws will have more difficulty becoming a part of the new family if there has been previous strife between the parents of the new daughter- or son-in-law. It is rare that difficulties with in-laws are not displacements of more immediate unresolved family problems unrelated to the offspring. Conflicts may also be expressed by the young couple struggling in a "tug of war" over which set of in-laws will get them for the holidays, etc. Again, such struggles probably have most to do with lack of differentiation of each spouse with his or her family of origin.

Friedman (Chapter 17) elaborates on the notion that rites of passage such as engagement, marriage, birth, and death give people an opportunity to work out previous "unfinished business." I have found this to be true in my work with families, particularly in those cases where the person is motivated for an ongoing venture with the extended family. In some instances, the young adult will approach the grandparent as a way to resolve some pending business (Lepinson, 1978).

From the above discussion, it is evident that when the problem is between the middle generation and the younger generation, either segment of the family may engage in resolving the problems of separation and individuation.

Marital Difficulties

The marital relationship constitutes one main target for people in the middle years. The reworking of the marital bond was mentioned previously as one of the tasks for this stage. Many forces within the family system seem to accentuate the need to refocus, review, and often accomplish a different arrangement in the marriage. Letting go of childrearing leaves more time available for couples to devote to self-reflection. Often the marriage of the children may reawaken and activate in the parents (and grandparents) the impetus to think about their own marriages. Awareness of the growing frailties or the death of a parent further highlight the need to ensure a good quality to one's own life. Moreover, at this juncture the individual can better assess his or her priorities. For many individuals, the shift has been gradual or there does not seem to be a great urgency to change; for others, there seems to be a sudden awakening to some forgotten aspect of life or an impulse to undertake some very different direction.

By this time, the marriage has endured many shifts: from the more romantic, idealistic, and/or sexual emphasis through the more prosaic, childrearing, teammate era. These previous sequences might have culminated in a relationship that is seasoned, stable, and more satisfactory than at any other time. It might also be more conflictual, more tenuous, and more alienated. In the absence of children, the bond will gain prominence. By the same token, more reliance on it will make existing strains more obvious. The question of autonomy (which will be reviewed in the next section) becomes important when analyzing the conjugal bond. More often than not, the state of the marriage is a good gauge for individual functioning and autonomy. One obvious question is to what degree the marriage has accommodated the needs for intimacy and separateness. In other words, how well has the interdependency worked. Too much interdependence may stress the bond in at least one (the more adaptive) partner. Too much distance may make one partner feel "out of touch," "uncared for," leading to stress and dissatisfaction.

Schram (1979), in reviewing this phase, suggests that there are "constricted versus expanded roles." These differences may not only exist between but even within the same couple. Greater freedom from parental responsibilities may prompt the husband toward expansion and the wife toward "holding on" to the marriage and her husband. On the other hand, the wife might start a move in the direction of expansion by pursuing a separate venture or career. If the marriage was based on her being adaptive, essentially a caretaker, and responsible for fulfilling most of the husband's wants, the shift will create an imbalance that will be keenly felt by the husband, resulting in temporary or extended disruption.

The Doane family is a good case in point. One might hypothesize that had the couple been approached two years earlier regarding the quality of their marriage, both of them would have rated it as quite satisfactory. Had Mr. Doane been encouraged to be more introspective, he might have acknowledged a certain "malaise" related to his own mediocre and uninspiring working career; or his pervasive need to make others happy, even to his own detriment; or the fact that in his nuclear family he had allowed himself to become progressively more encroached upon and dissatisfied. In the absence of such external promptings, it was only after the death of his father, the one person who had influenced his responses to others, that he was finally catapulted into seeking new avenues, culminating with the "affair" and the mirage of a transformation into a totally different and more rewarding life. It is quite likely that the daughter's trials and tribulations with similar issues may have played a part in activating the father's actions. Another point that this and other cases suggest is that usually the adaptive member in the couple is the one who impulsively moves into an extramarital relationship as a way of "breaking out."

The Doanes also exemplify many of the therapeutic considerations in dealing with these issues. The assumption on the part of the therapist of the existence of a strong interdependence that is being taxed from different angles is helpful in gaining some settling down of the crisis and the concomitant negative responses to what one of the individuals perceives as a rejection. The rejected one should be helped to defocus on the affair and to view it as part of a larger process. Hopefully, if this partner becomes less critical and concentrates on improving his or her part in the relationship, then the spouse can realize that "acting out" sexually may be related to other system issues. In such cases, the chances to resolve both the separation and the affair are considerably enhanced.

Knowledge on the part of the therapist that temporary strain can result in newly gained autonomy and higher functioning for the family may act as an important adjunct in allaying anxiety, mistrust, and anger. The splitting process becomes more difficult to stop and reverse in those instances in which some version of an "emotional divorce" has been in operation for a protracted length of time, or in which one of the protagonists perceives divorce as the answer to all existing troubles.

Moves toward Differentiation

Throughout the case examples and the discussions of therapeutic interventions, there is an emerging notion of individual functioning and family dynamics. I am stressing this point because the "eye of the beholder" is important in the way present phenomena are analyzed and interpreted. If one uses an intergenerational approach to comprehend individual functioning, any one individual stands at the apex of multiple forces. Viewed in this manner, experiences with which individuals have to deal at any stage, and the outcome, will depend more on what that individual's position has been in the family than on the events themselves. If one takes a multigenerational view of phenomena, it is easy to discover antecedents for behavior. I can recall many families where men, for instance, seem to experience rather tumultuous changes at forty, whereas other families seem to make the transition more gradually. Even more often, it is possible to see how some individuals in one family are able to surmount the different stages where other individuals' pursuits seem problematic in previous stages and during this stage.

Regardless how individuals or therapists choose to label the presenting problems in therapy, most of the therapeutic locus will eventually involve efforts on the part of the individuals toward increased differentiation. When the framework is a three-generational one, differentiation will be accomplished by increased autonomy in relations with parents or other parental figures, spouse, and children. The details of this approach have been presented elsewhere (Bowen, 1978 Carter & Orfanidis, 1976). In my practice, the process is no different from that used with individuals at other stages, although the content of the complaints may vary.

Failure to accomplish the differentiating task may sometimes be blamed on age or on a previous life history of accomodation and adaptation. However, success at this stage of the life cycle seems much more related to the ability to identify how one is getting "stuck" and the capacity to do something about it, than age or having been the "adaptive" one prior to reaching this stage.

SUMMARY

The post-childrearing stage is often a time of consolidation; functioning, as expressed by experience, maturity, and financial solvency in the middle and upper classes, is generally at its peak. With the childrearing period behind them, parents can look forward to a realization of their full potential. Difficulties at this stage relate to reworking of previous bonds with their parents and their offspring, and adding the new roles of "in-laws" and "grandparents." Most individuals in the middle generation lose one or both parents at this juncture and they themselves become the older generation.

The major advantage of thinking about families within a life cycle framework is that it clarifies the predictable tasks to be accomplished at a given stage. The use of the transgenerational dimension offers a means for tracing familial patterns which indicate how the family has traditionally dealt with the rites of passage. My experience bears out the principle that in all instances in which there is a serious family problem at this stage—even when there had been no previous evidence of turmoil—there are always apparent and preexisting dysfunctional components in the family system.

REFERENCES

Anderson, Carol et al. "A computer analysis of marital coping styles in families of children of normal and atypical development," unpublished paper presented at the American Academy of Child Psychiatry Annual Meeting, Houston, Texas, October 1977.

Bowen, Murray. *Family Therapy in Clinical Practice,* New York: Jason Aronson, 1978.

Bradt, Jack O. & Moynihan, C. J. "Opening the Safe—The Child Focused Family," in *Systems Therapy,* Jack O. Bradt and C.J. Moynihan, eds., Groome Child Guidance Center, Washington, D.C., 1971.

Carter, E. & Orfanidis, M. "Family therapy with one person and the therapist's own family," in *Family Therapy,* Philip J. Guerin, ed., New York: Gardner Press, 1976.

Deyken, Eva et al. "The empty nest: psychosocial aspects of conflict between depressed women and their grown children," *American Journal of Psychiatry* 122, 1966.

Duvall, Evelyn. *Family Development,* Philadelphia. J. B. Lippincott Co., 1971.

Erikson, Erik. *Childhood and Society,* New York: W.W. Norton Co., 1964.

Feikema, Robert J. "Birth: the addition of a new generation and its impact on a family system," in *Second Pittsburgh Family Systems Symposium: A Collection of Papers,* P. McCullough et al. eds., University of Pittsburgh, 1979.

Glick, Paul. "Updating the life cycle of the family," *Journal of Marriage and Family* February 1977.

Harkins, Elizabeth. "Effects of the empty nest transition: a self report of psychological well being," *Journal of Marriage and the Family* August 1978.

Keyserling, Mary. "Women's stake in full employment," U.S. Congress, Joint Economic Committee, *American Women Workers in a Full Employment Economy,* Sept. 15, 1977, pp. 26–27.

Lepinson, Marie. "Researching death in my family: how it led to differentiation," in *First Family Systems Symposium; Collection of Papers,* McCullough et al., ed., Pittsburgh, 1978.

Levinson, Daniel J. *The Season's of a Man's Life,* New York: Alfred A. Knopf, 1978.

Lowenthal, M. & Chiriboga, D. "Transition to the empty nest," *Archives of General Psychiatry* 26, January 1972.

McIver, R.M. *Society: A Textbook of Sociology,* New York: Farrar and Reinhart 1937.

Neugarten, Bernice. "Adaptation and the life cycle," *The Counseling Psychologist,* 6/1, 1976.

Schram, Rosalyn. "Marital satisfaction over the family life cycle: a critique of proposal," *Journal of Marriage and the Family* February, 1979.

Sheehy, Gail. *Passages, Predictable Crises of Adult Life,* New York: E.P. Dutton, 1976.

Solomon, Michael. "A developmental conceptual premise for family therapy," *Family Process* 12/2, 1973.

9
The Family in Later Life

Froma Walsh, Ph.D.

The Center for Family Studies
The Family Institute of Chicago
Northwestern University Medical School

Old age. We dread becoming old almost as much as we dread not living long enough to reach old age. The elderly in our society have been stereotyped and dismissed as old-fashioned, rigid, senile, boring, useless, and burdensome.

In rebellious defiance of such negative cultural expectations and constraints have emerged such recent film heroines as Maude in *Harold and Maude* and Madame Berthe in *The Shameless Old Lady,* and heroes such as Dersu in *Dersu Uzala* and Harry in *Harry and Tonto.* Each film reflects and fosters a growing sensitivity to a *person* who is attempting, with courage and daring, to adapt to losses and challenges of later life in ways that fit needs for self-identity, satisfying companionship, and meaningful experience.

Yet, in none of these films are options seen for healthy later life adjustment within family and social context. Each hero(ine) is seen to be marginal to the social community and each finds solutions only by choosing to become more deviant, by breaking with society altogether, and even by flaunting legal, moral, or sexual codes. Notably, each is widowed and either *has no family* or *takes flight from family.* Mme. Berthe, in fact, to the horror of her adult children, prefers the company of a barmaid of questionable repute and an anarchistic shoemaker.

Pessimistic views of the family in later life prevail. Myths hold that most elderly either have no families or, at best, have infrequent, obligatory contact; that adult children don't care about their aged parents and abandon them or dump them in institutions; and that families in later life are too set in their ways to change long-standing interactional patterns. Through such misconceptions the family in later life, like the older individual, has been stereotyped and dismissed.

In fact, family relationships continue to be important throughout later life for most adults in our society. Nine out of ten persons over sixty-five do not live alone. Most live with spouses or other relatives, including siblings and aged parents. While only one in four lives with adult children, over 80% live within an hour's distance of at least one child. Despite the preference to maintain separate households, most elders and their children sustain frequent contact, reciprocal emotional ties, and mutual support bonds in a pattern that has been aptly termed "intimacy at a distance."[1]

The family as a system, along with its elder members, confronts major adaptational challenges in later life. Stresses of retirement, widowhood, grandparenthood, and illness require family support, adjustment to loss, reorientation, and reorganization. Past and current family relationships play a critical role in the resolution of the major psychosocial task of later life, the achievement of integrity versus despair regarding the acceptance of one's own life and death (Erikson, 1950). The salient transitions and tasks of later life hold potential for loss and dysfunction, but also for transformation and growth.

The mental health field, unfortunately, has not given sufficient attention to the later phases of individual and family life, despite the fact that adults over sixty-five are the group most susceptible to mental illness (Butler, 1975). The incidence of psychopathology increases with age, particularly organic brain disease and functional disorders such as depression, anxiety, and paranoid states. Suicide also rises with age, with the highest rate among elderly white men. While older adults comprise 11% of our population, they account for 25% of all suicides. Many disturbances are associated with difficulties in family adaptation to the transitions and tasks of later life.

LATER LIFE TRANSITIONS AND TASKS

Launching: Setting the Stage

Each family's response to later life challenges evolves from earlier family patterns developed for stability and integration. How the family and its

---

[1]The reader is referred to excellent review articles by Bengston and Black, 1973; Butler & Lewis, 1977; Rosenmayr, 1965; Spark and Brody, 1970; Streib, 1972; Sussman, 1976; Sussman & Burchinal, 1968; and Troll, 1971.

members cope depends largely on the type of system they have created over the years and the ability and modes of the system to adjust to losses and to new demands. Certain established patterns, once functional, may become dysfunctional with the changing life cycle needs of members (Howells, 1975).

Launching of the last child from home sets the stage for family relations in the second half of life (Deutscher, 1964; Solomon, 1973). The structural contraction of the family from a two-generational household to the marital dyad presents tasks of parent-child separation and a shift for the parents from investment in their children to refocusing on their marriage. The loss in maternal role functioning makes this transition especially crucial for women.

While most adjust well to this "empty nest" transition (Neugarten, 1970), the ability to do so may depend, in part, on how empty the nest feels (Walsh, 1978). The transition may be impeded by an unsatisfying marital relationship and overattachment to a child. In some families, a young adult child who is locked into such a triangle may become symptomatic at that time (Haley, 1967; Walsh, 1979). In other cases, a failure to negotiate this transition can have a delayed impact, interfering with the family's subsequent ability to deal with later life transitions. The following clinical case[2] illustrates such a time bomb effect:

Stanley, age sixty-seven, was hospitalized at his wife's insistence for serious alcohol abuse of onset following retirement. Living in the home were Stanley, his wife, and their forty-two-year-old son who had never left home. Long-standing overinvolvement between mother and son had served to stabilize a chronically conflictual marriage over the years as long as Stanley had been involved in his work outside the home. Retirement shifted the homeostatic balance as Stanley, now home all day, felt himself to be an unwanted intruder. Lacking his work source of self-esteem, he felt himself to be an unworthy competitor to his son for his wife's affection, at a time in his life when he was longing for more companionship with her. The rivalry between father and son erupted into angry confrontations when Stanley was drunk, with his wife siding with the son and threatening divorce. (Figure 9.1)

In this family the tasks of the launching stage were never mastered and a post-parental marital relationship was never established. The family's de-

---

[2]This case and several others that follow were adapted from a clinical research sample gathered by the author and colleagues in a joint Northwestern University-University of Chicago Clinical Training Program in Later Life. Acknowledgement is given to David Gutmann, Ph.D., and Morton Lieberman, Ph.D., co-directors; Joanna Gutmann, M.S.W., older-adult clinical coordinator; Jerome Grunes, M.D., consultant; and Leslie Groves, research assistant.

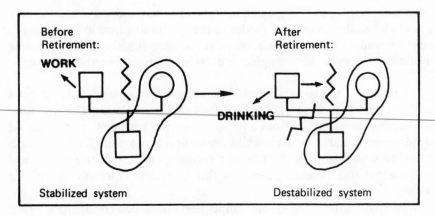

Figure 9.1.
Failure To Resolve Earlier Family Developmental Task Complicates Later Life Transition

fensive mode of adaptation served to avoid conflict and intimacy in the marriage for many years, but it broke down when retirement demanded new adjustments and reorganization of the system.

Retirement

Following an ebb in marital satisfaction when children are in adolescence, most couples experience increased marital satisfaction after adjustment to the launching of children and throughout their later years together (Rollins and Feldman, 1970; Lowenthal, Thurner, and Chiriboga, 1975). Companionship and mutual caring and caretaking become highly valued in the marital relationship, as well as in sexual intimacy, which continues for many into advanced years (Masters & Johnson, 1968; Lowenthal et al., 1975).

Retirement represents a significant milestone and adjustment for the marital pair (Medley, 1977). For the individual who retires, particularly for men in our society, there is a loss of meaningful job roles, productivity, and relationships that have been central throughout adult life. Whether retirement was desired or forced will affect adjustment. Loss of the role as family provider and a likely income reduction may bring additional stress. Working women may experience less difficulty with their own retirement if they maintain role continuity as homemakers. They often have greater difficulty with their husbands' retirement (Heyman, 1970), which may bring loss of job related status and social network. The trend of residential change at retirement adds further dislocation and loss of connectedness with family, neighbors, and community. The transition involves a reorientation of values and goals and a redirection of energies.

The major task facing the couple with the husband's retirement is his incorporation inside the home, with a change in age-role expectations and the quality of interaction (Hill, 1968). Most couples work out this reintegration well. Some couples, however, experience difficulty, as the following case illustrates:

> Mrs. Barnett sought treatment for depression a year after her husband's retirement from a business management position. Mr. Barnett seemed to be adjusting well to his retirement. In place of his job investment he had taken up and excelled at gourmet cooking. In doing so, he virtually took over the kitchen, formerly his wife's domain. Also, he found ready application of his business expertise in assuming management of the household budget, another former responsibility of Mrs. Barnett. He expressed satisfaction with his new activities and was proud that he could continue to be a good husband by sharing the household work load and relieving his wife of burdensome chores she had carried alone over the years. Mrs. Barnett, thinking she ought to feel grateful for her husband's consideration, was puzzled as to why she was so depressed in her new leisure. She began phoning her married daughter several times a day, becoming increasingly concerned about her daughter's marriage. The more mother and daughter talked, the worse the daughter's marital discord became. Finally, the daughter, exasperated with her mother's intrusion and feeling helpless to alleviate her mother's depression, arranged psychiatric consultation for her. (Figure 9.2)

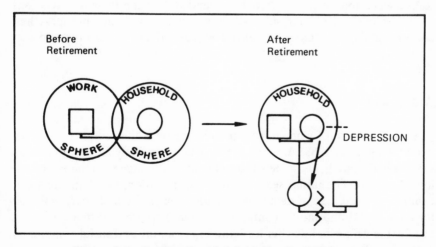

Figure 9.2. Dysfunctional Adaptation to Retirement

Couples therapy brought out the main issues straining the family system. Before retirement, each partner had maintained separate fields or spheres of influence and activity from which they each derived satisfaction, meaning, and self-esteem. Clear boundaries maintained differentiation. With retirement Mr. Barnett invaded his wife's turf, taking over her major activities. The outlets he found for himself were precisely those responsibilities that had given her life meaning and structure over the years, especially since their children had grown up. Mrs. Barnett's field seemed to shrink, her boundaries became confused, and her sense of worth and competence were diminished by her husband's dominance and success in her sphere. She felt useless and helpless. The more depressed she became, the more her husband took over to "unburden" her. In despair, Mrs. Barnett began to focus on her daughter, projecting her own dissatisfaction and resentment onto her daughter's marriage. The daughter's own anxiety about her adequacy in her marriage was triggered and minor problems escalated.

The couples treatment revealed further issues. As Mr. Barnett cut back on household activity, he became depressed. His immediate substitution of home activity for job involvement had served to keep him from recognition of the losses he felt in giving up his job. He also worried about the future and how he would manage to provide financially for his wife and himself on a limited, fixed pension in inflationary times. Mrs. Barnett acknowledged that she too had those concerns, but had kept them from her husband to protect him, out of a greater fear that he might suffer the same fate as her father, who had become despondent at retirement and had died within a year. She dreaded losing her husband and being left to a lonely widowhood as her mother had.

With feelings and concerns shared and communication more open, the couple were able to grieve their losses and to reshape their role relations. They explored new interests and activities that not only brought them deeper mutual satisfaction, but also strengthened and better prepared each for whatever the future might bring.

Widowhood

A chief concern of women from middle age on is the prospect of widowhood (Neugarten, 1968). Women are four times as likely as men to become widows and more likely to be widowed at an earlier age with many years of life yet ahead. The initial sense of loss, disorientation, and loneliness contribute to an increase in death and suicide rates in the first year, especially for men. Social and family contacts are often disrupted for men, since it is usually the wife who links her husband to the family and social community, especially after retirement.

The psychosocial task of this transition is to grieve over the loss and then to reinvest in future functioning. Three phases in this adjustment process for women have been identified by Lopata (1973, 1975). The primary task in the first phase is to loosen bonds to the spouse and take in the fact that he is dead, transforming shared experiences into memories. The encouragement of overt expression of grief and loss were found to be important. In the second phase, typically within a year, attention turns to the reality demands of daily functioning, of self-support, and of household management. The adjustment to being physically alone may, in itself, be difficult. Within one to two years, adjustment in the third phase shifts to new activities and interest in others.

Lopata notes that the label of "widow" can be harsh, stating, "I am a woman who has lost a husband." This identity can interfere with the process of reentry, particularly when family and friends have not faced their loss nor come to terms with their own mortality or possibility of widowhood. Distancing and cut-offs may happen in such cases.

Further dislocation may occur if in widowhood one's home is given up or if financial problems or illness impede independent functioning. In such events, widows are likely to move in with adult children, siblings, and even very aged parents. One woman prepared for the possible loss of her husband by reassuring herself that she could always go home to her mother. Her mother's death, followed in a year by the death of her husband, was devastating.

Remarriage is becoming an option for many elderly (Cleveland & Gianturco, 1976), especially men, who may find more women available (McCain, 1972). Economic and legal constraints are contributing to a recent trend of elderly couples living together without marriage, despite the social stigma that this entails for their generation.

A critical variable in the success of remarriage is the relationship with children and the children's approval of the remarriage. A difficulty can arise when a child views remarriage as disloyalty to the deceased parent. Concerns about a will may arise, particularly if children view inheritance as compensation for earlier disappointments or as evidence that they will still come before the new marriage.

Grandparenthood

Seventy percent of persons over sixty-five have grandchildren and one-third are great-grandparents (Townsend, 1968). The experience can be of great significance for older adults. Margaret Mead has commented on her own response to becoming a grandparent:

I had never thought how strange it was to be involved at a distance in the birth of a biological descendant... the extraordinary sense of having been transformed not by any act of one's own but by the act of one's child (1972, p. 302).

Grandparenthood can offer a "new lease on life" (Benedek, 1970) in numerous ways. First, it fulfills the wish to survive, thereby assisting in the acceptance of one's own mortality. As Mead experienced, "In the presence of grandparent and grandchild, past and future merge in the present" (1972, p. 311). This is true as well in the sense that grandparenthood stimulates the reliving of one's own earlier childrearing experiences. Such reminiscence and new perspective can be valuable in reviewing and coming to accept one's life, and, in particular, one's parenting satisfactions and achievements as well as any disappointments or failures.

Grandparenthood offers a variety of role possibilities (Neugarten & Weinstein, 1968) and opportunities for meaningful interaction.[3] In fact, cgrandparents and grandchildren may enjoy a special bond that is not complicated by the responsibilities, obligations, and conflicts inherent in the parent-child relationship. Not surprisingly, it is commonly said that grandparents and grandchildren get along so well because they have a common enemy. Actually, such an alliance can become problematic if a grandchild is triangulated in a conflict between parent and grandparent, as in the following case:

> After the death of her father and her divorce, Joan, age thirty-six, and her son Billy, age ten, moved in with Joan's mother to consolidate limited resources. The family was seen in conjoint therapy when Joan complained that Billy was behaving badly, was disrespectful to her, and out of her control. When the family arrived for the first therapy session, Billy went to grandmother for help in taking off his boots. Grandmother quickly attempted to take over the session while Joan appeared passive and helpless. Billy, sitting between them, glanced frequently to grandmother for cues. Each time the therapist uncovered conflict between Joan and her mother, Billy drew attention to himself by misbehaving. Joan's attempts to quiet him were ineffectual, while Billy responded immediately to a word from grandmother.

> Grandmother complained that she was overburdened by having to take care of both "children." Yet she undercut Joan's efforts to assume more responsibility at home by criticizing everything she did as "not right," meaning not the way she would have done things. Grandmother's need to be in control stemmed largely from underlying depression and anxiety about her own well-being since the

---

[3]Foster grandparenting also holds great potential for the enrichment of later life, as a resource for single and working parents, and for connectedness among the generations (Saltz, 1977).

death of her husband. The objectives of therapy centered on working out more balanced and generationally appropriate family role relations, so that Joan could be a more effective mother to her son while grandmother's role as head of the household was redefined from position of control to honored elder status.

In other cases, overinvolved grandparents can be drawn into marital conflicts, particularly regarding parenting issues, with grandchildren again triangulated. At such times, the grandparents may present themselves as safety valves or outlets for conflict in the nuclear family (Bell, 1962; Cohn & Talmadge, 1976).

While most grandparents may be relieved not to have primary caretaking demands, the expectation to be a resource and yet not an interference can be as burdensome. Mead asserts:

> I think we do not allow sufficiently for the obligation we lay on grandparents to keep themselves out of the picture—not to interfere, not to spoil, not to insist, not to intrude (1972, p. 303).

It was in just such an uncomfortable situation that Mme. Berthe, cinema's "Shameless Old Lady," found herself after her husband's death, as she visited her married children, attempting to fit in but only feeling in the way. The tension was unbearable. The audience cheered as she packed her bags and ran off with the family savings for an adventurous holiday with her new found friend.

And yet, Mme. Berthe died cut off from her family. Given the potentially destructive impact of cut-offs (Bowen, 1971), the likelihood of emotional fallout throughout the family is great: that hurt, disappointment, misunderstanding, anger, alienation, and sense of failure and guilt may have accompanied Mme. Berthe on her last journey, and accompanied her children and grandchildren into their future relationships, only to have the painful scenario reinacted in their later lives.

Such cut-offs are understandable, given the confusing reorientation of widowhood complicated by the unclarity and complicated feelings generally present in parent-grandparent role relations. Yet hopefully, cut-offs can be prevented and repaired before the end of life. Helping multiple family generations to redefine and reintegrate their role relations late in life are important challenges to the family therapist. One can only speculate that Mme. Berthe's trip could have been even more meaningful if shared with family, or at least, if a loving farewell had been possible.

Illness and Dependency

Illness is a prominent concern to most older adults. Fears of loss of physical and mental functioning, of chronic painful ailment, and of progressively degenerating condition are common preoccupations even though most elderly do maintain good health. Physical and mental deterioration may be exacerbated by depression, helplessness, hopelessness, and fears of loss of control. Such concerns reverberate with anxiety of other family members as the family responds to an illness.

A disequilibrium in the marital relationship may ensue with the illness of one spouse. The capacities of the partner can be drained if caretaking has little outside financial and emotional support. In some cases, the partner may use the caretaking role and focus on the spouse's illness in avoidance of his or her own vulnerability, anxiety, or longings to be dependent and taken care of. Need for the spouse to be underfunctioning in relation to the overfunctioning caretaker can impede recovery of maximum potential.

The issue of dependency comes to the fore in intergenerational relations as aging parents experience—or fear—a decline in their capacities, as in illness. In a normal family, handling increasing needs for dependency of aging parents does not involve a "role reversal" as some imply (Goldfarb, 1966). Even when instrumental and emotional support is given by adult children to aging parents, the child remains in the relationship of child to parent and does not become a parent to his or her parent. It should be kept in mind that despite childlike appearances, the aged parent has had over fifty years of adult life and experience (Spark & Brody, 1970).

The resolution of dependency issues requires a realistic acceptance of strengths and limitations by the older adult, and the ability to allow oneself to be dependent when need be. It also requires the adult child's ability to accept a *filial* role (Blenkner, 1965), taking responsibility for what he or she can appropriately do for aging parents, as well as recognition of what he or she can not or should not do. This capacity may be constrained by the child's own physical, emotional, and social situation. If, for example, adult children are confronting their own aging demands that require major adaptation of functioning, the expectation of meeting their parents' dependency needs may not be realistic (Brody, 1974).

In other cases, an aging parent may become overly dependent on adult children. If the children, through their own anxiety, become overly responsible, a vicious cycle may ensue, whereby the more they do for the parent, the more helpless or incompetent the parent becomes, with escalating neediness, burden, and resentment. Ambivalent overattachment and dependence are common (Kahana, 1971). Siblings may go to opposite extremes in regard to filial responsibilities, as in the following case:

Mrs. Z., a seventy-four-year-old widow, was hospitalized with multiple somatic problems exacerbated by symptoms of senility including disorientation, recent memory loss, and confusion. She reported that she had two sons, Tim, age forty-six, and Roger, age forty-three, but complained that they didn't care whether she lived or died. The sons reluctantly agreed to come in for a family interview. On the phone Roger stated that, in his opinion, the hospitalization was merely a ploy for sympathy on his mother's part, an attempt to make him feel guilty for not being at her beck and call as Tim was. He said he had learned years ago that the best relationship with her was no relationship at all. In contrast, Tim had become increasingly responsible for his mother, particularly since she had been widowed. Yet, the more "helpful" he became, the more dependent and helpless she became in managing her own life. At the point of hospitalization he felt drained by his mother's growing neediness.

Two stages of therapeutic work were undertaken. First, the overresponsible son was coached to be more "helpful" by challenging his mother to function maximally rather than doing for her. The under-involved son was asked to join with his brother and to relieve him of some limited, specific burdens. Both sons were encouraged to communicate their feelings and concerns directly with their mother and to be patient in listening to her. They were advised not to be alarmed if their mother was initially resistent to the changes. With anxiety in the system reduced and the family working together, Mrs. Z.'s thought disorder cleared and her functioning improved markedly.

The second phase of treatment involved a "family life review," in which mother and sons shared reminiscences of their family life history. Members were assisted in exploring developmental periods of particular emotional import, evoking crucial memories, responses, and understanding. The brothers' long-standing rivalry was explored and put in perspective. Roger's cut-off became better understood as originating in a late adolescent conflict over dependency that he handled by leaving home in anger, severing contact, and vowing to remain self-sufficient. His relationship with his parents had become frozen at that point, but now could be brought up to the present. Finally, mother and sons mourned, for the first time together, the death of the father, and each revealed a secret fear they had overburdened him with their own concerns and had hastened his death. Most importantly, the therapy accomplished a reconciliation and new understanding and caring among the surviving family members.

The application of life review therapy (Lewis & Butler, 1974) to whole families has been found by the present author to be of potentially great benefit to many families in later life. It extends the process of reminiscence, which facilitates resolution of the tasks of acceptance of one's life and death, to include the perceptions and direct involvement of significant family members who are central to such resolution. Family albums, scrapbooks, geneologies, reunions, and pilgrimages can assist this work. The resolution of later life issues rests on the foundation of all earlier life stages. Conflicts or disappointments in earlier stages that may have resulted in cut-offs or frozen images and expectations can be reconsidered from a new vantage point at a later life stage and from perspectives of other family members. Successive life phases can be reviewed so that relationships can be brought up to date. The transmission of family history to younger generations can be an additional bonus to such work.

The importance of supporting maximal functioning and competence in elderly family members, as seen above, is underscored in the next case, where clinical staff became overly responsible caretakers and underestimated potential functioning and assets of an elderly patient:

Rita, a seventy-eight-year-old widow, was admitted to the psychiatric inpatient unit with a diagnosis of confusional state and acute paranoia, following an incident in which Rita accused her landlord of plotting to get rid of her. When asked what brought her to the hospital, Rita replied that the only problem she had was her failing vision. When asked if she lived alone, she responded, "I live with my books."

Rita's increasing blindness was making independent living more difficult and hazardous. The landlord reported that her apartment was in constant disarray and that she seemed unable to manage simple living tasks like grocery shopping. She angrily refused any assistance from neighbors and maintained social isolation. Her only surviving family was a married sister, living in another state. Rita's deteriorating eye condition and lack of supportive network led the hospital staff to predict that she would be unable to continue to function independently. A nursing home placement was recommended. Rita vehemently objected, insisting that she wanted only to return to her own apartment. Hospitalization was extended to "deal with her resistance" to the treatment plan worked out *for* her. Fortunately, a sensitive interview with Rita led to a new appreciation of her and to a very different discharge plan arrived at *with* her.

Rita had been happily married, without children, until her husband's sudden death sixteen years earlier. In response to that painful and unexpected loss, she withdrew from family and friends, never to become dependent on anyone else again. She centered her life on her work and on her books. A job colleague remembered Rita as a "tough cookie," who was respected for her high functioning and perseverance through difficult assignments, until her forced retirement at seventy. Since then, Rita immersed herself in her books, which served many vital functions. They were a source of knowledge, giving her a sense of competence and mastery. The novels, biographies, and atlases offered pleasurable contact with the world, with other people, places, and times. Most importantly, the books had special meaning because she had inherited them from her father, a scholar, who died shortly after her husband's death. The books linked her to her father, reviving her close childhood relationship with him. Now Rita's failing eyesight was cutting her off from these contacts she valued most.

In Rita's strong identification with her father was an intense pride in his part-Indian heritage, carrying a sense of constitutional superiority that showed itself in a perseverance in adversity, a toughness, and a will to survive and adapt. This fierce determination was revealed in a visit to Rita's apartment. At first glance, all appeared chaotic: piles of books everywhere; clothing and food containers out on every counter, table, and chair. However, a closer inspection revealed that Rita had carefully ordered her environment in a system that made sense to her need to adapt to visual impairment. With a magic marker she had color coded all food; clothes were arranged according to function; books were stacked by their subject and meaning to her. Almost blindly, she could easily locate everything she needed.

Rita's denial of dependency needs could be regarded as pathological, yet self-reliance served Rita well for many years. It was the breakdown of her mode of adaptation—her vision—that brought confusion and anxiety. Still, realistically, Rita would require some assistance to maintain independent living. Her reluctance to become dependent on any caretaker made her reject any aid with one exception: she herself had contacted a religious organization that sent someone to read to her whenever she called to request the service. She could allow help when she maintained control over the circumstances: when she initiated the request, when they came to her, and when she herself determined the limits and boundaries of the dependent relationship.

A new treatment plan was worked out supporting Rita's objective of independent living and incorporating her values. Her natural ability to take responsibility for herself and her determination to function as autonomously as possible were reinforced. To help her feel less out of control and cut off by her sight limitation, a network therapy approach was employed. She was encouraged to select, and initiate contact with, a few neighbors and shopkeepers who could provide occasional backup service. In exchange, she would teach them about American Indian culture and relate Indian lore that had been passed on to her by her father.

The point at which failing health requires consideration of institutionalization, or nursing home placement, is a crisis for the family (Kramer & Kramer, 1976; Tobin & Lieberman, 1976). Contrary to myth, adult children generally do not dump their elderly in institutions. Only 4% of all elderly live in institutions (Streib, 1972), almost half may have organic brain disease, and the average age at admission is eighty (Butler, 1975). Institutions tend to be turned to only as the last resort, usually when family resources are strained to the limit (Townsend, 1975). Nevertheless, feelings of guilt and abandonment can make the decision for institutionalization highly stressful for families, and particularly for adult daughters, on whom the caretaking responsibility is typically concentrated, as the following case illustrates:

Mrs. Arletti called the psychiatric facility for help, stating that she feared that her teenage son needed to be institutionalized. Mrs. Arletti was seen with her son, who admitted to truancy and behavior problems that the mother felt helpless to control. A full assessment of the family system revealed that the problems had developed over the past eight months, since Mrs. Arletti's aged mother had been taken into their home. The son acknowledged that he frequently cut school and spent all day in his room, which was next to his grandmother's room. Mrs. Arletti burst into tears as she described her mother's Parkinson's condition, and her difficulty in taking care of her mother who required round-the-clock attention when she herself, a single parent, had to keep a full-time job. She was alarmed by her mother's occasional loss of balance and falling, feeling helpless and out of control to assist her if it should occur while she was at work. Her concern about institutionalization was really in regard to her mother.

This case underscores the importance of a full family assessment and inquiry about elderly members even when presenting problems appear elsewhere in the system and may function in the service of the family in crisis.

When institutionalization is being considered, or when a family is realistically overburdened but fearful of raising the possibility, family sessions including the elder member can be useful in weighing advantages and costs of the various options, taking into account the strengths and limitations of the elder member and the family, and sharing feelings and concerns before arriving at a decision together. Often through discussion new solutions emerge that can support the elder's remaining in the community without undue burden on any member. Organizations such as the Visiting Nurses Association can be helpful in providing homebound services and informing families of community backup.

Dealing with terminal illness is perhaps the most difficult task for a family, which, like the individual, has its characteristic adaptive response to issues of death and dying (Kubler-Ross, 1969). Similar mechanisms operate for the family in denial, anger, guilt, aware acceptance, and adjustment. Denial, silence, and secret-keeping tend to be ultimately dysfunctional. When patient and family hide knowledge of terminal illness, and try to protect their own and each other's feelings, communication barriers create distance and misunderstanding and prevent preparatory grief. The therapist can be helpful in encouraging family members to share feelings of helplessness, anger, loss of control, or guilt that they didn't do more. It may be easier for younger family members to accept the loss of elders, whose time has come, than for elders to accept the loss—and their own survival—of peers or of their own children who die first. The death of the last member of the oldest generation is a milestone for a family, signifying that the next generation is now the oldest and the next to face death. It is important, also, not to ignore the impact of an elder's death on grandchildren, for whom the loss of a grandparent may be their first experience with death.

Crossgenerational Interplay of Life Cycle Issues

Within every family the later life tasks of the elderly interact with the particular concerns prominent for child and grandchild generations at their own life phases, as has been seen in cases above. The intergenerational conflicts that can arise may vary depending on the relative ages and concurrent stages of family members, as illustrated in Figure 9.3. The issues that come

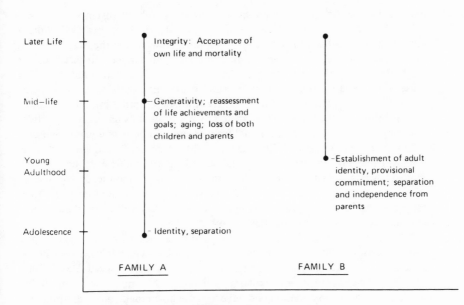

Figure 9.3.
Family Response to Later Life Issues Dependent on Family Generational Composition and Interaction of Life Stage Concerns of All Generations

to the fore in one family (Family B) between an older adult and young adult child may be different, and more complicated, than those that arise in another family (Family A) between older adult, middle-aged child, and adolescent grandchild.

A lack of complementarity or fit may occur when diverse developmental strivings are incompatible (Hill, 1968). In the case of Family B, the needs and concerns of an aging mother, confronting painful deterioration and death, collided with separation, identity, and commitment issues of her young adult daughter:

Julia was in her mid-twenties, beginning a social work career and engaged to be married when her sixty-nine-year-old mother, two thousand miles away, developed cardiovascular disease and began a long and painful physical decline. Julia had always been close to her mother and felt torn in response to her mother's strong, but indirect, pleas to return home. She felt an inner pull to go to her mother, but an even stronger resistance to giving up her new job and postponing marriage plans indefinitely.

The situation was complicated by Julia's recently emerging separation and identity issues. She had always been her mother's daughter, a "good girl" who never opposed her mother's wishes or values. Only after leaving home had she begun to differentiate. In attempting to do so, she accentuated differences between herself and her mother and disagreed openly about issues that mattered most to her mother, especially religion. The geographical distance she established from home helped to bolster efforts to test herself on her own without relying on her mother for direction and support. Now, just at the time Julia was needing to pull away, to function autonomously, and to be self-directed, her mother was needing to be close and dependent on Julia. Julia feared losing her sense of self and having her own priorities submerged by her mother's needs.

Weekly phone calls became increasingly strained, erupting into open conflict. Julia's failure to return home was labeled by her mother as uncaring and selfish. She snapped, "What kind of a social worker can you be if you can't even care about your own mother?" Julia made a brief visit home, feeling guilty and yet resentful that no matter how long she stayed, it wouldn't be enough for her mother. Anxious just before leaving, Julia defiantly announced that she no longer believed in God and did not intend to bring her children up in any religion. Her mother was stung, taking this as a total rejection of her and her values, and feeling that she had failed as a mother.

Julia sent her mother gifts. One was picked with special care and affection: a leather bound book, inscribed "For your memoirs." On her next visit home, Julia discovered all her gifts stacked away on a closet shelf, unused. Deeply hurt, she screamed at her mother to explain, particularly, the empty book. Her mother replied, "If I wrote my memoirs I'd have to write how much you've disappointed me." Julia cut her visit short. Returning to her own home, conflict erupted with her fiancé and the wedding plans were soon cancelled. Julia, deeply upset by the breakup, phoned her parents for consolation. Her mother replied coldly, "Well now that you aren't going to be married, I have nothing left to live for." A few hours later she had a stroke. Julia, furious at her mother's self-centeredness and apparent manipulation, did not return home again before the long-anticipated call came one night from her father informing her, "Mom is dead."

Julia scarcely grieved. She married within weeks to someone she had only recently met. It was not until the breakup of that marriage that feelings of loss of her mother surfaced, with guilt and regrets at the final alienation and the fact that it was too late to change things. She determined that she would repair her strained relationship with her father—whom she had not visited since her mother's death—before that was too late, with coaching by a family therapist. She established new relationships with her mother's family, learning about her mother's life from various perspectives, and coming to appreciate her fully as a person. She also learned that her mother had lost her own mother shortly after making a life choice that had greatly disappointed the elder woman and had not seen her to repair the cut-off before her mother's death. Julia's own process of differentiation was catalyzed by her work. Finally, using gestalt techniques with her therapist, Julia had an important conversation "with her mother," expressing what she wished she had been able to share with her.

This case illustrates that the timing of events can be critical in adjustment (Neugarten, 1970). The mother's developmental needs to come to terms with her life and her impending death occurred "off-time" from the perspective of the daughter's developmental readiness. The aging mother was needing to draw her family close at the end of her life, to reaffirm her life values, and to feel she had successfully fulfilled her role as a mother.[4] The young adult daughter was threatened by the surge of longings for closeness and dependency at a time of impending loss when she was not yet secure in her own individuation.

Further study of parent loss in young adulthood is needed. As Erikson (1950, 1959) has noted, the young adult is emerging from the search for identity into issues of commitment. The fear of ego loss in situations calling for self-abandon may lead to isolation and self-absorption. As Levinson has observed in young men (1978), this may accentuate the normal pre-occupation with making the first choices and commitments, especially marriage, occupation, and residence, that define one's place in the adult world. Responding to the needs and threatened loss of aging parents at this life stage may be frought with complications.

ROLE FLEXIBILITY AND SUCCESSFUL AGING

Studies of normal adult development indicate that a variety of adaptive responses, rather than one single pattern, may be associated with successful later life adjustment. This diversity reflects differences in individual personality styles (Maas & Kuyper, 1977), sex-roles (Troll, 1971; Gutmann, 1977), and sociocultural context (Jackson, 1971, 1972; Cohler, 1979).

Traditional sex-role distinctions of earlier adulthood tend to shift. Older men show increasing passivity and accommodation in response to environmental challenges, and greater needs for nurturance and affiliation, while older women become more assertive and active in the service of meeting their own needs (Gutmann, 1977). The development of more androgenous modes of response, of aspects of the personality that were earlier denied, can enable a greater role flexibility that may be related to longevity and greater life satisfaction in old age (Sinott, 1977).

Likewise, the successful functioning of families in later life requires a flexibility in structure, roles, and responses to new developmental needs and challenges. Patterns that may have been functional in earlier stages may no longer fit and new options must be explored. The loss of functioning and death of significant family members require that others be called upon to assume new roles and responsibilities.

---

[4]Crossgenerational anniversary reactions complicated the picture as issues from the mother's relationship with her own mother at life's end were revived and replicated with disappointment projected onto the daughter and cut-off ending the relationship before death.

The diversity, complexity, and importance of family relations in later life can be expected to become even greater in the future. By 1990, the number of persons sixty-five and over will jump from the present twenty million to twenty-eight million. When today's young adults reach old age, they will comprise at least 20% of the population. As social institutions take over more instrumental aspects of life, such as income maintenance and health care, the family may become even more important in providing lasting emotional ties, a sense of identity, and a sense of self-worth (Neugarten, 1974).

With the lengthening life span, couples may have thirty to forty years ahead after the children leave home. Four-and five-generation families will become common. More "young old" couples at retirement age with diminishing resources will be involved in caring for their "old old" parents. The growing number of blended families through divorce and remarriage will enlarge and complicate the extended family network. On the other hand is the trend toward having fewer or no children. The implications of nonparenthood for later life adjustment are unknown and warrant study given the significant role of children and grandchildren in the resolution of later life tasks. Of note is the large proportion of older adult psychiatric inpatients, in the experience of the author and colleagues, who are childless.

Because people are living longer than their elders did in the past, we lack role models for later life family relations just as we lack appropriate labels and role definitions. The term "post-parental" is unfortunate, for parents never cease to be parents. Instead, it is the *nature* of parent-child relationships that changes in later life. We are only beginning to explore the possibilities in that transformation. Maggie Kuhn, the vibrant seventy-three-year-old cofounder of the Grey Panthers, sees the responsibility of elders to be innovative and to explore new role options, as society's futurists. She believes that the wisdom and experience of old people, linked with the energy and new knowledge of the young, can be the basis for rich interchange and planning for the future (Kuhn, 1979). Important is a sense of pride in age, in one's history, life experience, and capacity to cope with change. Maggie Kuhn boasts, "I enjoy my wrinkles and regard them as badges of distinction—I've worked hard for them!"

Clinical services must be flexible to fit the diversity of family constellations and to support optimal functioning and independent living in the community. New treatment options need to be developed to fit new demands and needs.

CLINICAL ASSESSMENT AND TREATMENT ISSUES

The mental health profession has been largely unaware of and unresponsive to the service needs of older adults and their families. Several factors, including the invisibility of the elderly and professional "ageism," have contributed to this neglect.

Invisibility

Functional problems involving family relations with elderly members are often "hidden." First, older adults are much more likely to present somatic problems to medical services than to present emotional problems to psychiatric facilities. In a medical assessment such functional problems as depression, confusion, and anxiety may not be detected, or may be assumed to be merely an irreversible accompaniment to organic disease. The possible role of family stress precipitants may not be considered.

Even when organic brain disease or other serious physical disorders are present, the family may play an important part in maintaining or exacerbating the condition and can be crucial determinants in the course and outcome. As noted above, the vicious cycle of family overfunctioning/patient underfunctioning can hasten and perpetuate symptoms labeled as "senility." It is important for clinicians to assess the family component in any medical dysfunction and to involve family members directly in relating to the patient and encouraging maximal functioning.

A second problem of visibility occurs when clinicians mistakenly assume or accept an older adult's initial claim—that there is no family or that the family is not important in later life. Given the prevalent pattern of "intimacy at a distance," the clinician must look beyond the sharing of a household to identify significant relationships. Emotionally meaningful bonds may transcend geographic distance or apparent biological distance, as with a daughter-in-law, a nephew, or a "distant cousin." With the loss of one's spouse, not only descendents but also family of origin—and spouse's family of origin—may hold more importance. The very statement that one "has no family left" may indicate continuing emotional significance and unresolved mourning issues regarding multiple family members who may have died within a short period of time. Other long-standing cut-offs may hold potential for repair. The complexity and diversity of family networks require careful clinical assessment. Drawing a genogram with an elder can be particularly useful in identifying significant others and potential supportive linkages.

A third problem of visibility occurs when younger generations present themselves or their children for treatment. Problems involving elderly family members may be hidden behind complaints or symptoms elsewhere in the system. It is not uncommon in a "complete" diagnostic evaluation of an adult requesting treatment to include a detailed assessment of early childhood family history with little or no mention of current ongoing relationships or recent changes that may have precipitated presenting symptoms.

Whatever the age or problem of the symptom bearer, it is important to inquire about elder members in the family system.

Clinicians are trained and accustomed to evaluate families from a model based on early developmental stages when structure, roles, and functioning are geared to childrearing imperatives and integration of a two generational household (Lidz, 1968). We must be careful not to transfer assumptions unquestioningly to family functioning in later life. Clearly the later life challenges and the diversity and changes in family networks require that we develop new and more flexible conceptualizations for understanding family functioning and dysfunction as they bear on the accomplishment of later life tasks. Family assessments should determine how a family, given its particular composition, modes of adaptation, and needs of its members, has responded to later life imperatives. Where it has broken down in adaptation to challenges, we need to consider the variety of options possible for reorganization of the family and transformation of relationships to meet changing needs and requirements.

Ageism

Negative stereotyping of older people and their families by mental health systems and professionals has led to assumptions that they are a poor investment for therapy, too resistent to change, or simply untreatable. Functional problems may be discounted as merely a natural and irreversible part of aging and organic deterioration. The label of senility is indiscriminately applied to elders presenting a range of symptoms of impaired intellectual functioning or responsiveness to others (Nowakowski, 1978). Clinical training programs emphasize early developmental stages and offer limited exposure to elders and their families. Outpatient and inpatient psychiatric settings tend to be organized around the treatment needs of younger patients deemed more interesting and treatable. Elders are too often treated custodially or expected to fit into programs geared to the younger patients (Walsh, 1978).

Butler (1975) views professional ageism as stemming from an attempt to avoid the personal reality of aging and death. It is important for clinicians to develop awareness of our own apprehensions, a perspective on the whole life span, and an appreciation of what it is like to be old.

Clinicians' interfacing of issues with our own families—particularly with our own aging or deceased parents—may contribute to anxiety, avoidance, overresponsibility, or empathic difficulties with elders (Simon, Chapter 14). As we reach out to become better acquainted with the elders in our own families, as we strive to resolve our own losses and grievances, and as we explore new relational possibilities for ourselves, therapeutic work with families in later life will take on new meaning and options.

ACKNOWLEDGMENT

This chapter is dedicated to Dr. Roy R. Grinker, a pioneer in the field of psychiatry, in his recognition of the psychosomatic aspects of illness and stress response, and in his systems orientation to the understanding of psychopathology. Throughout his later life Dr. Grinker has continued to make major contributions to the mental health field. I have been privileged to work with him and to learn from him during this full season of his life.

REFERENCES

Bell, N.W. Extended Family Relations of Disturbed and Well Families. *Family Process* 1:175-192, 1962.

Benedek, T. Parenthood During the Life Cycle. In E.J. Anthony and T. Benedek (eds.), *Parenthood: Its Psychology and Psychopathology.* Boston:Little, Brown and Company, 1970.

Bengston, V.L. and Black, K.D. Intergenerational Relations and Continuities in Socialization. In P. Baltes and W. Schaie (eds.), *Personality and Socialization.* New York:Academic Press, 1973.

Bowen, M. Use of Family Theory in Clinical Practice. In J. Haley (ed.), *Changing Families.* New York:Grune & Stratton, 1971.

Brody, E.M. Aging and Family Personality: A Developmental View. *Family Process* 13:23-37, 1974.

Butler, R.N. Psychiatry and the Elderly: An Overview. *American Journal of Psychiatry* 132:893-900, 1975.

————, and Lewis, M.I. *Aging and Mental Health: Positive Psychosocial Approaches.* 2nd ed. St. Louis:C.V. Mosby Company, 1977.

Cleveland, W.P. and Gianturco, D.T. Remarriage Possibilities After Widowhood: A Retrospective Method. *Journal of Gerontology* 31:99-103, 1976.

Cohler, B. and Lieberman, M. Personality Change Across the Second-Half of Life: Findings From a Study of Irish, Italian, and Polish-American Men and Women. In D. Gelfand and A. Kutzik (eds.), *Ethnicity and Aging.* New York:Springer Publishing Company. in press.

Cohn, C.K. and Talmadge, J.M. Extended Family Presents. *Family Therapy,* 3:235-44, 1976.

Deutscher, I. The Quality of Post-parental Life. *Journal of Marriage and Family* 26:52-60, 1964.

Erikson, E.H. Identity and the Life Cycle. *Psychol. Issues,* Vol. 1, No. 1, Monograph 1. New York:International Universities Press, 1959.

————, *Childhood and Society.* New York:W. W. Norton, 1950.

Goldfarb, A. Psychodynamics of the Three-generation Family. In E. Shanas and G. Streib (eds.), *Social Structure and the Family: Generational Relations.* Englewood Cliffs, N.J.:Prentice-Hall, Inc., 1965.

Gutmann, D. Notes Toward a Comparative Psychology of Aging. In J. Birren and K. Schaie (eds.), *Handbook of the Psychology of Aging.* New York:Van Nostrand Reinhold, 1977.

Haley, J. Toward a Theory of Pathological Systems. In G. Zuk and I. Boszormenyi-Nagy (eds.), *Family Therapy and Disturbed Families.* Palto Alto:Science and Behavior Books, 1967.

Heyman, D. Does a Wife Retire? *Gerontologist* 10:54–56, 1970.

Hill, R. Decision Making and the Family Life Cycle. In B. Neugarten (ed.), *Middle Age and Aging*. Chicago:University of Chicago Press, 1968.

Howells, J.G. Family Psychopathology. In J. G. Howells (ed.), *Modern Perspectives in the Psychiatry of Old Age*. New York:Brunner/Mazel, 1975.

Jackson, J.J. Sex and Social Class Variations in Black Aged Parent-Adult Child Relationships. *Aging and Human Development* 2:96–107, 1971.

—————, Marital Life Among Aging Blacks. *Family Coordinator* 21:21–27, 1972.

Kahana, R. and Levin, S. Aging and the Conflict of Generations. *Journal of Geriatric Psychiatry* 4:115–35, 1971.

Kramer, C. and Kramer, J. *Basic Principles of Long-Term Patient Care*. Springfield, Ill.:Charles C. Thomas, Publisher, 1976.

Kubler-Ross, E. *On Death and Dying*. New York:Macmillan Company, 1969.

Kuhn, M. Liberating Aging, An Interview by Ken Dychtwald. *New Age Magazine* February, 1979.

Levinson, D. *The Seasons of a Man's Life*. New York:Alfred A. Knopf, 1978.

Lewis, M.I. and Butler, R.N. Life Review Therapy. *Geriatrics* 29:165–73, 1974.

Lidz, T. *The Person*. New York:Basic Books, 1968.

Lopata, H. *Widowhood in an American City*. Cambridge, Mass.:Schenkman Publishing Company, 1973.

—————, Couple Companionate Relationships in Marriage and Widowhood. In N. G. Malbin (ed.), *Old Family/New Family*. New York:Van Nostrand, 1975.

Lowenthal, M., Thurner, M., and Chiriboga, D. *Four Stages of Life*. San Francisco:Jossey-Bass, Inc., 1975.

Maas, H., & J. Kuypers, *From Thirty to Seventy*, San Francisco: Jossey-Bass, 1977.

McCain, W.C. A New Look at Older Marriages. *The Family Coordinator* 21:61–69, 1972.

Masters, W.H. and Johnson, V.E. Human Sexual Response: The Aging Female and the Aging Male, in B. Neugarten (ed.), *Middle Age and Aging*. Chicago:University of Chicago Press, 1968.

Mead, M., *Blackberry Winter*, New York: William Morrow & Company, 1972.

Medley, M. Marital Adjustment in the Post-Retirement Years. *Family Coordinator* 26:5–11, 1977.

Neugarten, B. Dynamics of Transition of Middle Age to Old Age: Adaptation and the Life Cycle. *Journal of Geriatric Psychiatry* 4:71–87, 1970.

—————, Successful Aging in 1970 and 1990. In E. Pfeiffer (ed.), *Successful Aging: A Conference Report*. Duke University, 1974.

—————, and Weinstein, K. The Changing American Grandparent. In B. Neugarten (ed.), *Middle Age and Aging*. Chicago: University of Chicago Press, 1968.

Nowakowski, L. *Utilization of Knowledge of Aging in Clinical Practice*. Paper presented at 15th Annual Georgetown Symposium, Washington, D.C. October 1978.

Rollins, B. and Feldman, H. Marital Satisfaction over the Family Life Cycle. *Journal of Marriage and Family* 32:20–28, 1970.

Rosenmayr, L. The Family—A Source of Hope for the Elderly? In E. Shanas and G. Streib (eds.), *Social Structure and the Family: Generational Relations*. Englewood Cliffs, N.J.:Prentice-Hall, Inc., 1965.

Saltz, R. Fostergrandparenting: A Unique Child-care Service. In L. Troll, J. Israel, and K. Israel (eds.), *Looking Ahead: A Woman's Guide to the Problems and Joys of Growing Older*. Englewood Cliffs, N.J.:Prentice-Hall, Inc. 1977.

Sinott, J.D. Sex-role Inconstancy, Biology, and Successful Aging: A Dialectical Model. *Gerontologist* 17:459-63, 1977.

Solomon, M.A. A Developmental, Conceptual Premise for Family Therapy. *Family Process* 12:179-88, 1973.

Spark, G. and Brody, E.M. The Aged are Family Members. *Family Process* 9:195-210, 1970.

Streib, G. Older Families and their Troubles: Familial and Social Responses. *The Family Coordinator* 21:5-19, 1972.

Sussman, M. The Family Life of Old People. In R. Binstock and E. Shanas (eds.), *Handbook of Aging and the Social Sciences.* New York:Van Nostrand Reinhold Co., 1976.

_____, and Burchinal, L. Kin Family Network: Unheralded Structure in Current Conceptualizations of Family Functioning. In B. Neugarten (ed.) *Middle Age and Aging.* Chicago: University of Chicago Press, 1968.

Tobin, S.S. and Lieberman, M.A. *Last Home for the Aged: Critical Implications of Institutionalization.* San Francisco:Jossey-Bass, Inc., 1976.

Townsend, P. The Emergence of the Four-generation Family in Industrial Society. In B. Neugarten, (ed.), *Middle Age and Aging.* Chicago:University of Chicago Press, 1968.

_____, The Effects of Family Structure on the Likelihood of Admission to an Institution in Old Age: The Application of a Gereral Theory. In E. Shanas and G. Streib (eds.), *Social Structure and the Family.* Englewood Cliffs, N.J.:Prentice-Hall, Inc., 1965.

Troll, L. The Family of Later Life: A Decade Review. *Journal of Marriage and the Family* 33:263-90, 1971.

Walsh, F. Breaching of Generational Boundaries in Families of Schizophrenics, Disturbed Non-Schizophrenics, and Normals. *International Journal of Family Therapy* 1:3. Fall, 1979.

_____, *Pre-Internship and Internship Training: Problems and Issues in Establishing Training Programs.* Paper presented at Symposium on Clinical Training in Aging, Annual Meeting, American Psychological Association, Toronto, 1978.

_____, and Gutmann, D. *The Post-Parental Family.* Paper presented at Northwestern University Medical School Community Lecture Series, March 1978.

ADDITIONAL READINGS

Blenkner, M. Social Work and Family Relationships in Later Life with Some Thoughts on Filial Maturity. In E. Shanas & G. Streib (eds.), *Social Structure and the Family: Generational Relations.* Englewood Cliffs, N.J.:Prentice-Hall, Inc., 1965.

Boszormenyi-Nagy, I. and Spark, G. *Invisible Loyalties: Reciprocity in Intergenerational Family Therapy.* Hagerstown, Md.:Harper & Row, Publishers, 1973.

Cumming, E. and Henry, W.E. *Growing Old.* New York:Basic Books, 1961.

Curtin, Sharon R. *Nobody Ever Died of Old Age.* Atlanta:Little, Brown and Company, 1973.

Finkle, A.L. Sexual Aspects of Aging. In L. Bellak and T. Karasu (eds.), *Geriatric Psychiatry.* New York:Grune & Stratton, 1976.

Framo, J. Family of Origin as a Therapeutic Resource for Adults in Marital and Family Therapy: You Can and Should Go Home Again. *Family Process* 15:193-210, 1976.

Glick, P. Updating the Life Cycle of the Family. *Journal of Marriage and The Family* 39:5-13, 1977.

Hadley, T.R. et al. The Relationship Between Family Developmental Crisis and the Appearance of Symptoms in a Family Member. *Family Process* 13:207-14, 1974.

Haley, J. The Family Life Cycle. *Uncommon Therapy.* New York: W. W. Norton, 1973.

Headley, L. *Adults and Their Parents in Family Therapy.* New York:Plenum Press, 1977.

Hill, R., Foote, N., Aldous, J., Carlson, R. and MacDonald, R. *Family Development in Three Generations.* Cambridge:Schenkman, 1970.

Horowitz, L. Treatment of the Family with a Dying Member. *Family Process* 14:95-106, 1975.

Kerckhoff, A. Family and Retirement. In I. Simpson and J. McKinney (eds.), *Social Aspects of Aging.* Durham, N.C.: Duke University Press, 1966.

Neugarten, B. Personality Change in Later Life: A Developmental Perspective. In C. Eisdorfer and M.P. Lawton (eds.), *The Psychology of Adult Development and Aging.* Washington, D.C.,:American Psychological Association, 1973.

Newman, B. and Newman P. *Development Through Life: A Psychosocial Approach.* Homewood, Ill.:The Dorsey Press, 1975.

Sorensen, E.M. Family Interaction with the Elderly. In P. Watzlawick and J. Weakland (eds.), *The Interactional View: Studies at the Mental Research Institute, Palto Alto, 1965-1974.* New York:W.W. Norton & Company, 1977.

Spark, G. Grandparents and Intergenerational Family Therapy. *Family Process* 13:225-38, 1974.

Part 3

Special Issues in Families and in Family Therapy

10

The Impact of Death and Serious Illness on the Family Life Cycle

Fredda Herz, R.N., Ph.D.

Herbert H. Lehman College
Family Institute of Westchester

One thing we are certain of in our lifetime is that we will die. In fact, it can be said that from the moment we are born, we are dying. There is probably no subject to which families react with more emotion than death, and its effects a family's emotional functioning can be both widespread and prolonged.

Although families are greatly affected by the death or anticipated death of a member, a great number of people die emotionally alone, isolated from those with whom they have been most intimately involved throughout their life cycle. Societal, familial, and intrapsychic processes all operate to promote the isolation of the dying. Our society, in keeping with its massive denial of death, has created "death specialists" for dealing with all aspects of the dying: hospitals to house the critically ill, morticians to handle the preparation of the body for burial, and funeral directors to deal with the details of burial. With all of these individuals handling death, the family has gotten increasingly distant from the dying person.

Families operate generally to keep the emotional tension down and the equilibrium stabilized. Since anticipated or actual death disrupts the family equilibrium, family members react automatically in a fashion that will be least disruptive and upsetting to themselves and to each other. Such handling of stress is an emotional reflex. Thus, it is not unusual for families to distance from the reality of death and to allow the death specialists to take over. The dying person, like his or her family, operates partly in a denial of death and partly to prevent upset in others. Tolstoy gave a great example of this in "The Death of Ivan Ilych" (1960). Thus, at a time when open relationships can be most beneficial to the resolution of a life crisis and to the emotional functioning of the family, the effects of these joint forces often render the family incapable of dealing openly with the stress of death.

My interest in family reactions to actual or anticipated death began years ago in work as a nurse with families of chronically and/or seriously ill children. This interest was rekindled by work with families dealing with unresolved grief and by involvement in an innovative clinical project for cancer patients and their families. My efforts to understand family reactions and adjustment to serious illness and death, and my attempts to develop appropriate interventions have evolved jointly. However, for the sake of clarity, each of these areas will be discussed separately.

FAMILY REACTION TO DEATH AND SERIOUS ILLNESS

The death or serious illness of any family member leads to disruption in the family equilibrium. The degree of disruption to the family system is affected by a number of factors, the most significant of which are (1) the timing of the death or serious illness in the life cycle; (2) the nature of the death or serious illness; (3) the openness of the family system; and (4) the family position of the seriously ill, dying, or dead family member.

Timing of Death and Serious Illness in the Life Cycle

According to the census data, Americans now live longer than they did several decades ago (Glick, 1977). Most people now live until the seventh or eighth decade of life. Generally, the farther along in the life cycle, the less the degree of family stress associated with death and serious illness. Death in older age is viewed as a natural process. In fact, Lieberman's (1973) study of the elderly indicated that "coming to grips" with death is a developmental task of the aged. It is when a grandparent or greatgrandparent dies that most people first become personally aware of death (Schneidman, 1971). Schneidman reported that in a death awareness study conducted for *Psychology Today,* most people interviewed expressed the belief that they would die in old age, and preferred that their death be sudden, nonviolent, quiet, and dignified. Unfortunately, census statistics suggest that the longer we live, the more likely we are to die of a debilitating disease, the most common of which are cardiovascular disease and cancer—certainly not sudden or quiet and most likely not dignified.

Although death of the elderly is viewed as an expected part of the family life cycle, it is certainly not without its stresses. Part of the stress evolves from the effects of the debilitating illness itself. For instance, what happens when the elderly are unable to care for themselves? The family must decide who will care for them. If the family decides to take the responsibility, not only must they cope with the stresses of an additional household member, but also of continuous care. The expense of outside care is often great, and since the elderly are often also poor, the family must deal with the financial burden of their decision. However, a major portion of the family stress arises because the death of an elderly generation brings each succeeding generation closer to its own death. I have personally experienced this fact during the last several years as a whole generation of my family has died. With each death I was brought closer to the reality that my parents were now next in line. In talking with my parents and others of their generation whose parents have recently died, I realized how much this was a factor in their own grieving—they were partially grieving for their own impending deaths.

Whereas an elderly family member is viewed as having completed his or her life and has few remaining tasks and/or responsibilities, serious illness or death at another life cycle phase is considered to be an incomplete life. Death or serious illness in other life cycle phases does not follow the normative course of life—the timing is off; it is out of sync. In my experience, those deaths or serious illnesses in which an individual is in the prime of life are the most disruptive to the family. This can be partly understood by the fact that it is at this phase of the life cycle that an individual has the greatest family responsibilities. The death or serious illness of an individual at this point in the life cycle leaves the family with a gap in functioning that is difficult if not impossible to fill, and may therefore prevent the family from completing its life cycle tasks. In both earlier and later phases of the life cycle, the individual has fewer essential family responsibilities. So there appears to be a critical period of approximately twenty years in which, all things being equal, death and serious illness have the greatest impact. However, let us go backward in the life cycle from the elderly generation and consider the family stresses engendered first, by the death and/or serious illness of an adult family member, and then, by the death or serious illness of a child or adolescent.

Recently a couple with a grown son and daughter sought treatment. The wife was dying a slow, painful death from cancer of the bone that had metastasized from a breast cancer six years before. The woman had become bedridden, and the husband continued therapy. He had expressed some concern about his twenty-eight-year-old son's reaction to the mother's death. When the father and son met jointly, the son attempted to explain to his father the concerns he had about his mother's death. First, the son said, "I think it is harder for you to lose your wife than for me to lose my mother. I know that now since I've been married—the relationship with a wife is different! Also, Dad, you and Mom have been looking forward to this time when you could be alone again—have time again for each other with no children around—just the two of you. I'll miss Mom; I love her a lot. I feel the most upset when I think that she will not ever get to see her grandchildren. I also worry about what will happen to you."

The son expressed beautifully the issues and unfinished tasks for the family with grown children in which a spouse/mother dies. Death ends a time in their lives when most couples are beginning to experience fewer family responsibilities and are looking forward to time alone together to enjoy themselves, their children, and their grandchildren. When a marriage lasts until this time, death's greatest impact is on the spouse who must consider spending the later years of his or her life alone or beginning again with someone else.

This family's experience would be very different if the son were an adolescent or young adult still in the parental home at the time of his mother's illness. Serious illness or death of a parent with children still at home may result in the family's not resolving the tasks of these stages of the life cycle. In the family with adolescents or young adults, the major life cycle task is the mutual weaning of parents and children. The serious illness (or death) of a parent may impede the completion of this process. The following is an example:

> The family of a sixteen-year-old girl sought treatment when the young woman's grades in school dropped from "A" or "B" work to "barely passing." In doing an overview of recent stresses on the family, I was told by the mother that she had multiple sclerosis and had been hospitalized several times during the past two years (just when the girl's school work had gone down). Mother continued by saying, "I don't know what to do—I want my daughter to be able to be with her friends and do things like other kids her age do—*but* I also need her to help me with things around the house—I just can't do many things anymore. I tire easily—she needs to make dinner, put the kids (three other children) to bed very often. Maybe she's just too tired to do any school work." The daughter was quick to add, "But I don't mind."

Not only does the serious illness of a parent at this life cycle phase interfere with the adolescent's achieving independence through the usual rebellion and focus outside of the family, but it may set the adolescent up as a parental surrogate with siblings and thus hold him or her tightly within the family.

For the other spouse, the financial, domestic, and emotional responsibilities are more than doubled, for he or she must not only care for the spouse, but also do the spouse's share. Death after a prolonged illness may be a relief from caring for and trying to fill in for mother (or father) and "acting as if" you don't mind, or maybe even like, doing so.

A couple I saw recently depicts the issues for a family with young children coping with the dying of an adult. The husband was twenty-eight years of age and dying of leukemia. He often stated in the course of treatment: "Day in and day out, I am confronted with the reality of never seeing my kids grow up. It's hard to even look at them, much less plan for their future." At a time when life should be in its prime, in terms of hoped for plans and dreams, it was coming to an end for him. The death of a mother or a father in a family at this phase of the life cycle leaves many childrearing tasks and family responsibilities for the remaining parent. The reactions of a child to a parental death are varied and appear to be influenced mainly by the child's age, level of emotional and cognitive development, and emotional closeness to the dead parent (Bowen, 1976; Schiff, 1977; Kubler-Ross, 1976). However, the most influential factor in the child's reaction to the loss of a parent appears to be the ability of the remaining parent to not allow his or her own emotions to create distance from the child. (Bowen, 1976; Schiff, 1977).

The death of a child is viewed by most people as life's greatest tragedy. This view derives from the fact that a child's death appears so egregiously out of place in the life cycle. However, in terms of the instrumental functioning of the family system, the young child is a family member with few responsibilities and, emotional factors aside, such a death does not leave an unfillable gap in the responsibilities of the family.

How then does one account for the drastic and lasting impact of a child's death or serious illness? I believe that a major portion of the emotionality can be accounted for by the family projection process through which children become important to the emotional functioning of a family. Although in actuality a child may have few family or personal responsibilities, most parents, to a greater or lesser extent, view their children as extensions of their own hopes and dreams in life. As extensions of the parent, a child takes on an important emotional position in the family and functions as a part of the parent's emotional self. In any one family, some or all children can take on this emotional significance. (Bowen, 1976). The more emotionally incomplete the parents experience themselves, the more likely they are to view their children as extensions of themselves. In my experience, the degree of emotional fusion between a parent and child is a good predictor of the degree of family disruption at the death or illness of the child. That is, the more the child is viewed as an emotional extension of self, the more disruptive his or her serious illness or death will be to the family. The literature on childhood death suggests that family disruption is a common aftereffect. The effects of a child's death on the spouses is profound, with separation or divorce occuring in an estimated seventy to ninety percent of all cases (Schiff, 1977; Tietz et al., 1977). In any case, the appearance of marital conflict after a filial death is significant. Clinical studies of the impact of death and/or serious illness of a young child report a range of symptoms in the siblings from behavioral and school difficulties to physical illness and suicide especially for the child next in line (Schiff, 1977; Tietz, et al., 1977, Hare-Mustin, 1979). In some families, a child is conceived to take the place of a dead child or the dead child is idealized by the family (Teitz, et al., 1977) to the detriment of the other children.

For most families, adolescence is a time of great turmoil. There are probably few other times in the family life cycle in which such turmoil is viewed as normative. Most of the turmoil of this stage centers on the difficulties of accomplishing the life cycle task of the mutual weaning of parents and children. Difficulties usually arise because although the adolescents are "vascillating into" adulthood, they must still live in a family in which they experience being alternately treated as adults (when there is a job to do) and as children (when they want to do something else). Thus the particular dilemma of family life at this time is one in which the family cast doesn't change, but the weaning process begins. The serious illness or death of an adolescent can be viewed as the addition of a great deal more stress to an already stressful life phase. The fact that most adolescents who die do so suddenly from accidents or willfully by suicide (U.S. Bureau of Vital Statistics, 1976) further compounds the degree of family disruption. The symptoms of this family disruption are often enduring and range from the dissolution of a family through separation and/or divorce to emotional symptomatology such as depression or physical illness, often in another adolescent child.

Several years ago, a young woman submitted to me a clinical paper on adolescent suicide as part of a family therapy course requirement. The major focus of her paper was a family systems analysis of the disruptive effects of adolescent suicide and therapeutic strategies for assisting families to deal with the disruption. I discovered as I read the paper that the author had more than a professional interest in the topic. She had personally experienced the effects of suicide at the death of her adolescent brother eleven years before. She began the paper by stating that its writing was another step (for her) in understanding the suicide and the part it played in her family's life. She then went on to describe her own and other families' experiences and the ways in which a family therapist might have assisted them. First she described the family shame in admitting that the death was suicidal and the promotion of this by religious and societal norms. Associated with the shame (and perhaps at its roots) is the assignment of blame in an attempt to understand the suicide: if their child and/or sibling killed himself, they must be to blame and they "should" feel ashamed. She described her parents' anger at their son's irresponsible behavior and her own and her siblings' sense of being affronted by his behavior. She concluded the paper with a description of her efforts to understand the breakup of her parents' marriage, her mother's severe depressions, and her own siblings' continued sense of guilt for the brother's death and their life.

For this family and others like it, the weaning process is at the same time both abruptly and never terminated. That is, they are often left in a permanent state of suspended animation—never truly able to complete their life cycle task of weaning from that adolescent child.

In contrast to this type of suspended animation of the family life cycle are those instances in which the adolescent is chronically or seriously ill. In such circumstances, the adolescent and the family often are engaged in a prolonged weaning process. The family, fearful and concerned about their child's health, often act to protect the child by keeping the adolescent within the family fold. The parents' need to keep the adolescent within the family confines is extreme when extrafamilial contacts or activities may pose a real or imagined threat to the adolescent's health. Furthermore, there are some types of chronic or serious illnesses that will realistically impede the adolescent's leaving the family, such as adolescents with arthritis, mental retardation, or cancer. The seriously ill adolescent may rebel against the curtailments of the disease and/or of the family by doing such things as refusing to take medication and eating prohibited foods, or may accept the curtailments and become the family patient. The family, especially the parents, may alternate between overt power struggles, anger, and helpless confusion. Siblings often resent the attention shown the ill one. The manifestations of this prolonged weaning process can be varied, but the process remains essentially the same.

I have presented here only a brief overview regarding the timing of death in the family life cycle. However, it should be clear that understanding the life cycle tasks and issues for the family are crucial to understanding the effects of death on that family.

The Nature of Death

Death can be expected or unexpected and may or may not involve long periods of caretaking. Death can even take place before birth as is the case with stillbirths, miscarriages, and abortions. Each type of death has implications for the family's reaction and adjustment. Sudden deaths give the individual and/or the family little warning. The family reacts with shock. There is no time for goodbyes or the resolution of relationship issues. There is no anticipatory mourning.

In addition to this lack of psychological preparation for the death, there may also be a lack of preparation for the realities of death such as a will, insurance, or other financial arrangements. After the initial intense reaction to these deaths, the loss is often covered over and becomes a "taboo" subject, as described by Solomon and Hersch (1979). These families tend to begin a long course of family difficulties usually viewed as unrelated to the death. Although the person most directly affected by the death may develop symptoms, it is not uncommon for another family member, sensitive to family anxiety, to develop symptoms. The following is an example:

> The client, a thirty-six-year-old divorced mother of three children, began treatment for "depression" that she related to marital separation of three years. In the course of obtaining a family history and genogram, I noted that the client's father had died suddenly of a heart attack four years ago. The woman described her relationship to her father as intense and close—"In fact, this may sound dumb—I'm really embarrassed, but I keep a box of candy he gave me before he died—I know it's silly, but I can't seem to throw it away." This woman then described a life course since the death that involved many physical illnesses and a lack of concentration. She described similar difficulties in her third and favorite child, her only son. A major part of the treatment was focused on the resolution of the father's death. After a year, the box of candy found its final resting place—the garbage.

While the major disadvantage of sudden death is related to difficulty resolving the loss, an advantage of this type of death (if there can be one) is that it is not preceeded by a long period of stress. This period of long-term stress is the major difficulty associated with expected deaths resulting from debilitating illnesses. Families in which a member has a long illness, such as cancer, suffer from the stresses of permanent uncertainty. They are never sure of the course of the illness. Every remission brings the hope of life; every exacerbation, the fear of death. This constant uncertainty wears the family out emotionally. Watching a family member dying in pain is very draining on all the family. The emotional strain is intensified by the financial drain of a long-term illness. Toward the end of such a long process, it is not unusual for the dying individual and family to wish for death. The intense stress of a long-term illness is difficult for any family to deal with on a continuing basis. It is difficult to achieve a balance between living and dying. Often the family and the dying individual, acting to protect each other from the intensity of the anxiety, close down communications and relationships. The resulting inability to deal with the tension creates distance and further tension manifested in a variety of symptoms. However, if they are willing to work at it, terminal illness of a family member (unlike sudden death) does allow the family, if the system remains open, to resolve relationship issues, reality issues, and to say the final goodbye before death.

The following is an example of a family in which these goals were not achieved:

> A father in his early thirties was dying of leukemia. Numerous times through-out the course of the man's illness, he had attempted to talk with his wife about his feelings and his plans. When she distanced because of her own anxiety, he gave up. A fixed distance developed between them. Shortly, the wife became involved in an affair. Their six-year-old boy began experiencing difficulties in school, and their nine-year-old daughter began thinking and speaking about dying.

A special category of family reactions to the nature of death belongs to those deaths which occur before birth. I do not here mean to enter into a discussion of whether life exists with conception or with birth. That is a point of discussion that will be keeping the Right to Life-Right and pro-abortion organizations busy for years. I also do not mean to make little of the discussion. However, I do believe that family reactions to these types of "death" are different enough from other types to warrant a separate consideration.

Stillbirths, abortions, and miscarriages all occur before a mutual relationship system is established between the child and the family. However, this very fact is what makes these types of situations different. In contrast to other expected or unexpected deaths in which the dying or dead individual has formed a relationship with the family, the dead or dying fetus has not formed an emotional connection with the family, whether that be a single person or a group of people. The family, however, has formed an emotional connection to (and has feelings about) the unborn child. The following is an example that illustrates the issues for a family with this type of death:

> Recently, a midwife asked for consultation regarding a family—mother, thirty-two, father, thirty-four, and two children—that had just experienced a stillbirth. The five therapy sessions took place three months after the experience. The midwife was concerned about the mother's depression and inability to relate to her children, who were anxiously asking about their baby sister. During the second session with the husband and wife, the wife described her repetitive dreams of losing the baby and her other children. A great deal of her thinking time was being spent in wondering what the child looked like, why it died, and what she had done to "make" it die. Although she wanted to see the baby after birth, the hospital staff and physician had said it was better that she didn't. Their refusal only solidified her belief that the child was defective and that she was too weak (or inadequate) to handle the situation. When she told her husband of her request, he could not understand her need to see the child. She went on to describe her ambivalence about the conception of the child and her pregnancy. When she attempted to discuss these feelings with her husband, he would say it was no use discussing it. A fixed distance developed in which the wife became

increasingly involved in her thoughts about the child and less involved with the family.

All family members develop certain expectations, wishes, fantasies, etc., during the course of pregnancy. The possibility of a mutual relationship is abruptly terminated with the death of a child at or before birth. Furthermore, the expectations, fantasies, etc., tend to continue after the death unless the process is terminated in some way such as by seeing the baby and doing some grief work. In this respect, the reactions to a stillbirth are often similar to the reactions in those instances in which the family elects not to have the child (abortion) or in which the mother is unable to carry through to term (miscarriage). In general, the differences in reaction are often ones of intensity. The more the mother wants the child (for whatever reasons); or the greater ambivalence there is in either parent, or disagreement between the parents regarding the pregnancy or birth and the longer the duration of the pregnancy, the more severe the family stress and disruption.

The Openness of the Family System

Many family emotional reactions and long-term adjustment difficulties arising from death originate in the lack of openness in the system. By openness, I mean the ability of each family member to stay nonreactive to the emotional intensity in the system and to communicate his or her thoughts and feelings to the others without expecting the others to act on them. According to Bowen's theory (1976), two interrelated continua determine the degree to which a family system is open. The first continuum defines a family system according to the level of differentiation (roughly equivalent to level of emotional maturity). Differentiation defines people according to the degree of distinction between emotional and intellectual functioning. Briefly, this concept suggests that those individuals whose lives are more or less dominated by emotional reactions are those in which the emotional and intellectual functioning are fused. The actions of these individuals are based on what "feels" right or comfortable and/or upon the reactions of others. A more differentiated individual can remain nonreactive to the emotionality of others. This person is able to define his position on the basis of thought or principle and can hear the other's thoughts without overreacting. The individual's level of differentiation is determined by the degree to which he or she is caught in the emotional process in the family of origin. Siblings come out of families with different levels of differentiation and opposite emotional "styles." The lower the level of differentiation of spouses the less able they are to directly express to each other divergent or anxiety-provoking thoughts and feelings without becoming angry or upset.

The more undifferentiated, the more likely it is that when stress is high, marital conflict, fusion, and dysfunction in a spouse or child will develop.

The level of family stress, the second continuum, is the crucial element in the evolution of family symptomatology. A family can be relatively undifferentiated, have little stress, and be free of symptoms. On the other hand, a well-differentiated family can develop symptoms when stress is high. In several studies of the effects of family stress on the development of illness, Holmes and his associates (1973) have found that death of a spouse is the life event associated with the greatest degree of stress. Furthermore, they have found a high degree of association between reported health changes and family life cycle events, one of which is death of a spouse.

In families dealing with death or terminal illness, I have found that there is a greater likelihood of emotional and/or physical symptom development when family members are unable to deal openly with one another about the death. However, no matter how well-differentiated the family, the ability to remain open, to express one's thoughts and feelings and to remain nonreactive to the other's anxiety, is related to the intensity and duration of the stress. The longer and more intense the family stress, the more difficult it is for the family relationships to remain open and the more likely it is that dysfunction will develop. In addition, the very nature of death and terminal illness often isolates the family from external networks such as friends and work. This isolation further closes the system. I am becoming more firmly convinced that exacerbations in the illness in the terminally ill correlate in part with the degree of openness of a particular system.

> For example, a couple came to a cancer group because the wife was finding it difficult to cope with the impending loss of her husband, who at fifty was dying of pancreatic cancer. Her life had been spent in total devotion (fusion) to her husband. As his death began to appear imminent, she became increasingly anxious about living without him. As she became more anxious and more verbose, her husband began to distance from her. His distance further increased her anxiety and the process continued to escalate. Their two sons, sixteen and twenty, also did not communicate their thoughts and feelings directly to their father, but rather to their mother. The end result was a system in which each member was isolated from the other and in which anxiety continued to escalate. Physical symptoms began to develop in each of the family members leading to frequent hospitalizations.

The Family Position of the Dying or Dead Family Member

Not all deaths have equal importance to the family system. In general, the more emotionally significant the dying or dead family member is to the family, the more likely it is that his or her death will be followed by an emotional shock wave or ripple effect up and down the generations. The reason for this effect is twofold: the disruption in the family equilibrium and the family tendency to deny emotional dependence when that dependence is great.

An individual's significance to the family can be understood in terms of the functional role in the family and the degree of emotional dependence of the family on the individual. For instance, the loss of either parent when the children are young removes the functional and emotional positions of breadwinner and/or parent when the family is most dependent upon these functions. The death of a grandparent who functions as the head of the clan is another example of a serious functional loss in the family. In general, the more central the dying or dead individual's position, the greater the family's emotional reaction.

It can also be observed that the more the family depends emotionally on the dying or dead family member, the greater the reaction. For instance, in couples with extreme marital fusion or dependence, the loss of the spouse usually represents an emotional loss of self to the other spouse. The same is true of families in which there is emotional dependence on a child. Any family member who functions in an emotionally overresponsible position is likely to have others in the family who are emotionally dependent on him or her, and who will thus react strongly to the death.

The impact of a functional and/or emotional loss is expressed in the phenomenon of an emotional shockwave, first described in the literature by Bowen. This can be described as a series of underground aftershocks to the emotional/functional system. They are most likely to occur in families in which emotional dependence is denied and therefore not dealt with directly. The symptoms in a shockwave can be any problem, (emotional, social, or physical), in multiple family members. The family often views these events as unrelated and denies the significance and impact of the death that preceded them.

FAMILY TREATMENT INTERVENTIONS

Of the four factors affecting the family reaction and adjustment to death discussed previously, the only one on which the family or the family therapist has a handle is the openness of the system. There is no way for the family (or the therapist) to change the timing or the nature of death, or the position of the dying or dead individual in the family system. Therefore, most family interventions before, at the time of, or after death, are directed toward opening up the family emotional system.

Interventions Before or at the Time of Death

The major purpose of family interventions in these situations is the prevention of family symptomatology and dysfunction during the illness and after death. This can be accomplished by assisting the family in dealing with the stress of serious illness or death. There are six interventions that are important in this regard: (1) using open and factual terminology and information; (2) establishing at least one open relationship in the family; (3) respecting the hope of life and living; (4) remaining unreactive; (5) checking on the progress of relationships; and (6) utilizing the family rituals, customs, and styles.

Using open and factual terminology and information. It is important that the family therapist avoid using terms or expressions that are indirect such as "deceased," "passed away," or "passed on." These terms imply that the therapist is unable to speak directly about death and therefore the family shouldn't either. Using direct words such as death and dying suggests to the family that the therapist is able to be open and relatively comfortable with such a discussion. The same principle is true of the presentation of information. Families with a seriously ill individual are often confronted with health professionals controlling the relevant information about the illness. The health professionals, doctors, or nurses decide what and how much to tell the patient. Furthermore, families often themselves decide to withhold information from the patient. It is important for the therapist to be a model by presenting information in a factual way to the family, including the patient, and letting them make the decisions regarding the use of information. In this way, the therapist encourages the family, including the dying person, to take maximum responsibility for life decisions.

Establishing at least one open relationship in the family system. The reader will notice that the focus of this intervention is on a relationship *within* the family system. An open discussion of death between the therapist and any one family member in isolation from the others is not opening up the family relationships. It may lower the anxiety enough to prevent the family from dealing with each other. In fact, it often invites dysfunction because the therapist becomes involved in a triangle with the family. In order for individuals to gain from an open discussion of death, it must occur in the context of the intimate family relationships. Since one of the major difficulties all families have is being able to communicate directly about a toxic or taboo issue, it is not surprising that the discussion of death often provokes much tension in the family members. It is not uncommon that as the tension increases between any two of the family members around the death issue, the most uncomfortable individual will draw in a third to relieve his tension. Another variant of the same process is that the twosome will collude in avoiding a discussion of the impending death.

The family therapist is often confronted with either one of these variations of a triangle (a dysfunctional relationship in which the relationship of any two depends on the relationship with a third). The task is to help at least one of the three to detriangle. One can accomplish this task in several ways. One way is to "look" for the most uncomfortable person, who may be the most motivated to change his or her role in the process. By coaching this person to control his or her emotions and to plan a method to broach the death issue, the family therapist is often successful in opening the system to deal with the death. Other times, the utilization of displacement material may open up the death issue. For instance, I have played Bowen's taped lecture on death (Georgetown University Medical Center videotape) for a family as a way of helping them start to talk about the death issue. I have also found that giving the family reading material can be most helpful. Families respond positively to material such as the work of Anderson (1974), and Schiff (1977), popular films such as "I Never Sang for My Father," (Columbia Pictures), and the T.V. movie "Death Be Not Proud." The use of multiple family and self-help group settings has also been helpful in the process. It always amazes me how much these groups normalize the family's experience of death and dying.

Respecting the hope for life and living. Very frequently I am confronted by the following statement by a family therapy trainee: "But that parent only has three months to live and the family is still discussing the son." No one knows exactly when someone will die, except perhaps the dying person, who often senses the time of death. Often patients outlast the predicted survival time; often they live a shorter length of time. Since families are constantly living on an emotional seesaw of uncertainty, it is very difficult for them to deal continuously with death. I have found that clients will not deal with some death related issues during a remission, but will deal with this same issue during exacerbations. Each family develops a timing and style of accomplishing their work. Although mental health professionals may want the family to deal with the death issue at all times, they need to develop a respect for the family's timing and need for hope.

> One client, a widowed mother of four children, began treatment four years after her lung cancer was diagnosed. This woman would attend sessions irregularly—only when she had some difficulty with the children. I kept asking about her plans for the children and herself. Each time, she would say that there were too many other problems to deal with and that she would deal with her death when that was imminent. After a two-year course of irregular sessions, this woman announced that she would die shortly and that she had a number of issues to deal with for herself and with her kids. She died six months later when her plans for the children were complete. The children, three years later, are doing very well emotionally.

This illustrates the necessity to balance issues relating to dying with those related to living, and to understand that tasks have their sequence in the life cycle. Although we are all eager and impatient to assist families with dying, we must respect their hopes to continue living and to deal with their life issues.

Remaining calm or unreactive. In order to be of assistance to families dealing with death and dying, the therapist must be able to remain calm and to think clearly. Families who are dealing with anticipated or actual death are not only coping with the normal life cycle stresses but also have the additional stress of living with dying. Families often seek treatment when the stress is high and they are unable to decrease it. A family therapist who is unable to remain calm increases the family stress even further. I do not mean that the therapist cannot experience emotions, but only that his or her actions should not be guided by emotions. If death is a toxic issue for the therapist, then he or she will often be reactive and reflexively cut off discussion, collude with the family in not discussing the issue, or, conversely, insist that the family deal with the death, or even present the family with his or her own tears or upset emotions to deal with. The therapist who begins behaving in one of these ways must examine his or her own feelings about and experiences with death. Families will teach one about death, and will grow from such an experience, if the therapist can remain clear thinking and calm.

Checking on the progress of relationships and issues. With the stress level so high in these families, it is not unusual for the therapist to be presented with numerous "sideshows." Sideshows are what I call symptoms developing in some part of the system because tension is not being dealt with in another area. For instance, a young wife whose husband has terminal cancer begins to have an affair, or a child begins to develop symptoms. The sideshows are not to be ignored; they are an indication of stress. However, the family therapist should be wary of getting sidetracked into spending too much time on the symptom. It is important to check on the family's progress in dealing with the major stress in the relationships. One family that I was seeing over a three-year period would present a new "symptom" every month or two. Each time, I would spend a brief amount of time questioning them about the new symptom and their plans for dealing with it. Then I would check on how they were doing in dealing with a previous issue. After a short period of time, the family began making the connection themselves and used the symptom or dysfunction as a signal of some stress to be dealt with more directly.

Utilizing the family rituals, customs, and styles. All families have personal and/or religious rituals or customs for dealing with death. In obtaining a family genogram, it is always useful to ask families about the ways in which deaths have been handled in the extended families. Not only does one obtain a picture of the rituals, but one also gains information regarding the way families deal emotionally with death, whether it be angry fights over money, cut-offs, or depression. Another area that should always be discussed with families is the client's plan for his or her death, funeral, and burial. That is, where does the client want to die, who does he or she want present, where will he or she be buried, and what will the funeral be like? I am always interested in having these plans discussed in the family. In this discussion process, I am given the opportunity to observe the family's reactiveness to the plans and begin coaching them. I never take a position on the "right" way or the "best" way since what is right or best is what they want and agree to. I do have some general guidelines I use in terms of coaching the family on the funeral ritual.

First, rituals are important because they mark an event. Second, the ritual should be in keeping with their religious and philosophical beliefs. Third, it should be as personalized as possible. Fourth, family members should see the individual after death in order to make death more real. Fifth, children need to be told of the death and given the opportunity to attend the funeral, see the dead family member, and say goodbye. (Most children want to go when given the choice.) Lastly, the family should talk frequently of the dead individual. When given the options, most families can carry these guidelines through to completion.

After Death

Families do not generally seek treatment for issues relating to a recent or past death. Treatment is often sought for a problem or dysfunction in a family member or relationship. Although the symptoms are part of the emotional shockwave following a death, the family does not view the death as the important issue in their current problem so they will usually not mention it. Unless the therapist routinely does a genogram and a chronology of important life events, he or she may not suspect or know that a death has occurred in the family. If the therapist mentions the relationship between the symptom development and the death, the family will deny it or say it is a matter of coincidence. Pushing the issues will only bring more denial and possibly treatment withdrawal. The family therapist must remain relevant to the problem presented by the family, coaching the family in that area and beginning to ask questions about the dead family member's relationships. Frequently after the initial problem has been relieved to some extent, the focus of the sessions begins to shift. The goal of treatment becomes the resolution of the past relationship. In this regard, several common factors about these situations are important.

First, the dead family member tends to be either idealized or bastardized, but is not seen as a person with both strengths and weaknesses. Second, there are some issues that were not resolved in the relationship with the dead family member and this lack of resolution interferes with other relationships. Third, the facts surrounding the death are often confused, uncertain, or unreal. Fourth, the client either never speaks of dead family members or overfocuses on them, often as though they were still alive. The following example will illustrate how the knowledge of these factors can be used in treatment.

A forty-two-year-old mother of two children, thirteen and sixteen years of age, began treatment for a depression she viewed as related to her husband's sudden death three years previously. After much effort, this woman was able to reestablish contact with her dead husband's family and friends, to view him as a human being, not as an idol, and to visit his grave to say goodbye. She refused to bring the children in for a session throughout this time, and discontinued treatment after a year. One year later, she became seriously interested in a man and they began to plan their marriage. At this point, her daughter, then almost eighteen years of age, began to be argumentative with her mother and refused to leave her mother and her fiancé alone. Mother and daughter sought treatment. During the first session, the daughter began to cry. She expressed her wish that her father were still alive and described how she would fantasize him holding her when things got bad at school or with her mother's boyfriend. She said that the boyfriend was okay, but he didn't compare with her father and that as far as she was concerned, her father would always be there when she needed him. I suggested that unless she put her father in his grave, she would not be able to get on with her life.

I outlined a plan that necessitated contact with her father's old friends, business associates, and family; a visit to the grave with and without her mother; and a discussion with mother of the events the night of her father's death. I also suggested that she seek out occasions to mention her father several times a day. She came back for two more sessions, two weeks apart, to report on her progress in following through with this plan. She was not only pleased with herself, but was pleased with her new relationship to both mother and soon-to-be stepfather. She began the last session by saying, "I put my father to rest—I don't need him to be here to rescue me anymore."

One might say that this young woman was exceptional, and she probably was in her youth and motivation. However, I have seen many other individuals who are able to accept the challenge and carry out such a plan. The benefits can be enormous.

REFERENCES

Anderson, R. "Notes of A Survivor," in *The Patient, Death and The Family.* ed. by Troop, S. & Green, C. New York: Scribner's, 1974.

Anonymous. "A Family Therapist's Own Family," *The Family* 1/1, Nov. 1973, pp. 26-32.

Anonymous. "Taking A Giant Step. First Moves Back Into My Family," *Georgetown Family Symposia, Collected Papers,* Vol. II. Ed. by Loria, J. E., and McClenathan, L. Washington D.C.: Family Center, 1977.

Bowen, M. "Theory in the Practice of Psychotherapy," in *Family Therapy: Theory and Practice.* Ed. by Guerin, P. New York: Gardner Press, 1976.

Bowen, M. "Family Reaction to Death" in *Family Therapy: Theory and Practice.* Ed. by Guerin, P. New York: Gardner Press, 1976.

Glick, P. Current Population Report, U.S. Dept. of Commerce, Bureau of Census, Series P.-20, No. 297, 1975.

Hare-Mustin, Rachel T. "Family Therapy Following the Death of a Child," *Journal of Marital and Family Therapy* 5/2, April 1979, p. 51.

Holmes, T. and Masuda, M. "Life Change and Illness Susceptibility," in *Separation and Depression Clinical & Research Aspects (Pub. 94).* Washington, D.C.: American Association for the Advancement of Science, 1973.

Kubler-Ross, E. *Death and Dying.* Interview on Public Broadcasting Systems, January 8, 1976.

Lieberman, M.D. "New Insights into the Crises of Aging," *University of Chicago Magazine,* 66/1, 1973, pp. 11-14.

Schiff, H. S. *The Bereaved Parent,* New York: Crown Publishers, 1977.

Schneidman, E. S. "You and Death," *Psychology Today,* 5/11, 1971, p. 44.

Solomon, M. and Hersch, L.B. "Death in the Family, Implications for Family Development," *Journal of Marital and Family Therapy* 5/2, April 1979, p. 43.

Teitz, W., McSherry, L., and Britt, B. "Family Sequelae After a Child's Death due to Cancer," *American Journal of Psychotherapy* 31/3, 1977, pp. 417-25.

Tolstoy, L.N. *The Death of Ivan Ilych and Other Stories.* Ed. by Almer, M. New York: Signature Classics, 1960.

Vital Statistics, U.S. Dept. of Health Education & Welfare, 1976.

11

Separation, Divorce, and Single-Parent Families

Edward W. Beal, M.D.

Georgetown University School of Medicine
Private Practice of Psychiatry, Bethesda, Maryland

Divorce is a nodal event in the life cycle of the family, which has been occurring with increasing frequency in recent years in the United States. If the divorce rate were to stabilize in the future at its current rate, approximately 40% of all people now marrying would end their marriages in divorce (Glick, 1977). With the number of families now experiencing divorce, it is important for our society to develop better means of negotiating this difficult transition. Unlike all other major shifts in family composition, there exist virtually no rituals or rites of passage to assist families with the difficulties inherent in the process of divorce. Absence of rituals reflects absence of resolution of emotional attachment. In fact it can be said that divorce adds a whole stage to the family life cycle for those who must go through it.

Many studies focus on divorce as an event in time that affects individuals. This chapter will focus on divorce as a process that occurs in a family over a period of time and that has far-reaching effects throughout the nuclear and extended family systems.

The primary focus of the chapter is on the demography and process of divorce, the impact and clinical implications of divorce at different stages of the family life cycle, and suggestions for clinical interventions directed at divorce as a major process of family life cycle disruption. In addition, the chapter will consider the special problems of single-parent families at different family life cycle stages.

DEMOGRAPHY OF DIVORCE

Critical events in the life cycle of divorcing families include age at time of marriage, length of marriage, age at time of divorce, and the interval between marriages. General demographic data reflect not only that the divorce rate in the United States has been rising, but also that it has always been consistently higher than that of any other country. Figure 11.1 illustrates the median age at marital events for American men and women born 1900–1959. Table 11.1 presents the changes in the median number of years between marital events for American men and women in 1967 and 1975. These two charts indicate a change in the nature of the family life cycle. Young adults are not only entering first marriages later and getting divorced sooner, but are also remarrying and redivorcing sooner than ever before. These statistics indicate that those who divorce, remarry, and/or redivorce, are moving through these transitions in a shorter span of years than before. For those who divorce, one-half of those who remarry do so within three years. Second divorces after remarriage occur one and a half to two years sooner than first divorces. Two-thirds of all women who divorce do so before age thirty, and seven-eigths of all women who divorce do so before age forty. Thus, of couples who divorce, almost all do so before middle age. Of those who remarry, childless couples under age thirty tend to remarry sooner than divorcees with children; and divorced women with children are more likely to remain single than those without children.

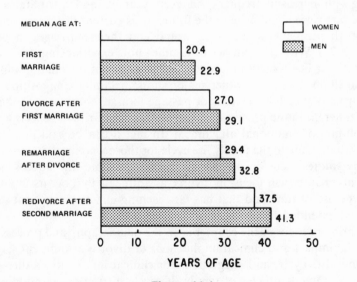

Figure 11.1
Median Age at Marital Events for Men and Women Born between 1900 and 1959: June 1975

Table 11.1

Median Number of	Men		Women	
Years Between–	1967	1975	1967	1975
First marriage and divorce	7.7	6.7	7.9	7.3
Divorce and remarriage	3.1	3.1	3.4	3.2
Remarriage and redivorce	6.2	5.0	7.6	5.5

Source: U.S. Bureau of Census Current Population Reports, Series P-20, No. 297. "Number, Timing, and Duration of Marriages and Divorces in the United States: June 1975."

Divorce occurring at different stages in the family life cycle has different impact on family structure and functioning. Examining the family life cycle of married women who have had at least one child in the past two decades reveals that the current median age at first marriage for women is twenty-one years, and the current median age of mothers at the birth of their last child is thirty years. Two-thirds of women who divorce do so before age thirty; thus, most children of divorce are under age seven at the time of physical separation and/or legal divorce.

The functioning of spouses during the time they live together without children reflects the stability of the marital dyad. In general, the couple who plans marriage can expect to live together for two years before the birth of the first child. Nowadays, marriages extend on the average eleven years beyond the marriage of their last child. The typical couple not divorcing can expect a marriage of approximately forty-four years, thirteen of which will be lived as a two-person system without dependent children. In 1880 the marriage of the last child and the death of one of the spouses in the family occurred on the average at nearly the same time. At least one-half of the parental marriages did not endure beyond the marriage of the last child. The fact that there is an increase currently in the divorce rate among those married longer than thirty years, may reflect the difficulty in managing this longer joint survival period (Glick, 1977). Research is needed on divorce in marriages lasting more than thirty years.

There are certain demographic characteristics that appear to coincide with the predicted stability of a marriage. Divorce is more likely in couples who marry before the age of twenty or after the age of thirty. Marriages associated with premarital pregnancy or downward social mobility of the husband tend to be less stable. Having less education than either parent increases a man's chances of marital instability to a greater extent than having more education than either parent. Women who have completed college have a much lower rate of divorce than women with incomplete college educations. Therefore, some combination of personal, social, and economic circumstances associated with reaching a terminal educational point is associated with a more stable marriage. However, women with post-college education have a greater chance of divorcing than women who have a four-year college degree (Glick, 1977).

Because the statistics on divorce are changing so rapidly in our time, it is difficult to compare divorce rates at different ages in order to clarify to what extent life cycle pressures influence the rate of divorce. Three-fifths of all divorces occur in the twenty-five to thirty-nine age group, which may reflect this complex and burdensome period in family life; however, those now over thirty-nine were raised in an era when the societal and family attitudes toward divorce were different.

Between 1968 and 1975, the divorce rate increased 50% for those under twenty-five and those forty to sixty-four years of age. It did not rise as rapidly as the 70% increase for those twenty-five to thirty-nine years of age (Glick, 1979).

THE MARITAL RELATIONSHIP

The study of divorce necessarily focuses on the relationship patterns established in the marital dyad. Family systems theory describes the range of marital dyad patterns in the following ways (Bowen, 1978). One spouse may assume a dominant position in relation to emotionally based issues and the other spouse assumes a more adaptive role. This pattern of interaction may function well unless a high level of anxiety affects this relationship to the point that the efforts of the adaptive spouse become sufficiently ineffective and he or she becomes symptomatic. The dominant spouse may then respond to the symptomatic adaptive spouse by physical or emotional distance leading to divorce. An example of this pattern might include the goal-directed, professionally-oriented individual whose spouse becomes anxious and depressed. The symptomatic spouse may be referred to a mental health professional, allowing the nonsymptomatic spouse to leave the marriage with less guilt knowing that the spouse is "in good hands." It is a moot point as to whether the adaptive spouse forces the other to be dominant or the dominant spouse forces the other to be adaptive.

A second major relationship pattern in the marital dyad involves both spouses primarily assuming dominant positions in relation to emotionally based issues. During the introduction of anxiety, this relationship pattern is most likely to appear as marital conflict. If each spouse is unable to reduce his or her own anxiety or reactiveness, this pattern is most likely to lead to physical separation.

A third major relationship pattern in the spouse dyad involves both spouses primarily assuming adaptive positions in relation to emotionally based issues between them. This type of interaction may lead to mutual action paralysis or symptoms in both spouses. These marriages may be characterized by long-term or chronic symptoms in both spouses or a long-term, highly conflictual marriage with no effective resolution.

A fourth major relationship pattern in the marital dyad is characterized by significant emotional distance between spouses and emotional over-involvement of one spouse with the children. Theoretically, this pattern has the greatest potential of undermining the emotional autonomy of a child. Classic examples of this pattern might include parent-child "role reversals" in which a child takes on an adultlike caretaking posture toward the parent.

The phenomenon of divorce clearly illustrates the concept of intense emotional fusion in the marital dyad. This intensity can be experienced to such a degree that individuals believe that their autonomy or ability to function cannot be maintained with frequent contact with their spouse. Many of these individuals hold similar beliefs about their relationship with their parents. Among the interactional patterns in divorcing families, the pattern of physical distance or emotional cutoff between spouses develops and may predominate. Nevertheless, the family life cycle continues and family developmental issues preferably performed by a well-functioning parental pair now must fall more to one parent than the other.

The same number of tasks are being performed by one-half of the parents under conditions of changed family structure. Task overload can occur and outsiders are sought for assistance. Long-term family integrity and functioning are presumably best preserved when the responsibility for these tasks is kept within the family, assuming this can be done without high anxiety and/or loss of functioning. If sources outside the family intervene in a way that undermines family functioning, it is detrimental to the resolution of the emotional fusion in the divorce process. Outside intervention by mental health professionals is best focused on maintenance of individual functioning and resolution of emotional fusion within the family structure. Precipitous or premature emotional support to individual family members may promote the divorce process rather than decrease family anxiety and resolve emotional fusion.

THE DIVORCE PROCESS

The resolution of emotional attachment through divorce is an extremely complex process. Resolution occurs to some degree in many divorcing families. Complete resolution occurs in very few divorcing families. The divorce process has its origins in and is influenced by multigenerational family patterns.

Pope (1976) and Mueller (1977) explain the mechanism by which the intergenerational transmission of marital instability from parent to child occurs. In these studies they propose that marital instability is transmitted by inappropriate role models—either parental, sexual or marital. Other studies by Pope and Mueller and their review of the literature find the role model concept an insufficient explanation.

Their further studies show a stronger explanation to be that the intergenerational transmission of marital instability occurs through the mechanisms of mate selection outcomes such as age and education at marriage, occupation of male at time of marriage, and premarital pregnancy. They imply support for the idea that parental marital instability leads to high-risk mate selection outcomes for children, which in turn leads to their higher marital dissolution rates. These factors seemed more accurate for women with siblings and a limited education, who married early to a man with a limited education. The age of the husband and his prior marital history could not be shown to be a mediator of the intergenerational transmission of parental marital instability.

The complexity of divorce is indicated by the research of Kressel and Deutsch (1977), who considered the therapeutic role exercised by authoritative mental health professionals toward divorcing couples. The approach of these professionals includes 1) helping clients decide whether to divorce, and 2) assisting in the negotiation of a final divorce settlement. Their concept of the divorce process is largely a dyadic one and did not address itself to the concept of emotional triads, so basic to the divorce process.

Families present for therapy around the decision to separate or divorce in a variety of ways. Some of the typical presentations include one "good spouse" and one "bad spouse," or one functional spouse and the other dysfunctional (socially, physically, emotionally, or with serious debilitating problems such as alcoholism). Another common presentation is the spouse who is complaining about the affair of the other, or the spouse who is guilt-ridden about having an affair. Many people in a highly conflictual marriage are also concerned about whether the parental conflict "harms" the children or whether the marriage should be preserved "for the sake of the children." It has been well established that children in highly conflictual marriages tend to do less well academically than children who live without significant conflict in single-parent families (Nye, 1957; McCord, 1961). The decline in functioning can be measured by I.Q. scores and most commonly appears in problem solving abilities and tasks that require maintenance of a good concentration span.

It is important for a therapist to be aware of the concept of emotional triangles, in order to avoid making a decision for a marital pair or inadvertently aligning with one of the pair (Vigyikan, 1978). One spouse or the other will frequently present the relationship in such a manner that one is considered to be the victim and the other the victimizer. The therapist, by training or by the role in which he or she is cast by the marital pair, can easily be trapped in the role of rescuer. Although anxiety and symptoms may be temporarily decreased, no basic or fundamental change occurs in the marital dyad when the mental health professional serves as the rescuer in a "persecutor-persecuted" dyad.

Clearly, in order for a divorce to occur, emotional triangles will develop. If a spouse wanting to disengage from the marital relationship is feeling guilty about leaving, it is not uncommon for him or her to seek help for the symptomatic spouse. Less conflict over the decision to divorce may occur when the less functional spouse experiences support from the therapist. If an important emotional relationship is established between the therapist and the apparently dysfunctional spouse, the issue of guilt over abandonment is often "resolved" so that the apparently more functional spouse can leave the marriage.

While the establishment of the above triangle may allow a couple to divorce more easily, it does not necessarily change the future relationship patterns of the individuals in the marriage. In order to keep the conflictual issues and the decision to divorce between the marital pair, the therapist's emotional nonalignment is essential. Overfocus on the divorce decision can contribute to a couple's belief that making this decision is the only real problematic issue in their relationship. The process of the emotional dissolution of a long-term intimate relationship never occurs with a simple decision. The therapist can use numerous emotional issues in an attempt to decrease the intensity of the marital conflict. Whether reconciliation or divorce is the outcome, individuals can enhance their own functioning, learn a great deal about themselves, and improve the quality of their relationship by working through the process of marital conflict.

Many factors influence the likelihood of divorce in a conflictual marriage. Demographic characteristics of divorcing individuals have been discussed. The length of the courtship and the decision making process regarding marriage are good indicators of expectations of marriage. Exploring an individual's premarital fantasy about a future partner is a useful indicator of the course of a marriage. Some people marry for peer companship. Others marry in order to have children. Fixed differing expectations between individuals predictably lead to marital conflict.

Marriages established in the context of significant losses such as the death of a parent or after a disappointing love affair or marriage are more likely to be unstable. Prior unresolved losses make subsequent separations more difficult to manage. Such individuals may find it more difficult to deal with normal life cycle events such as children leaving home to establish their own families.

Two critical factors in the assessment of a marital conflict are the emotional attachment of each spouse to his or her own parents and the evolution of the emotional attachment within the marital relationship. Some spouses grow away from their family of origin while still remaining emotionally close. Other spouses separate from their family of origin by running away, especially into their own marriage. This emotional cut-off can be managed externally by geographical distance and decreased relationship activity, or internally by maintaining superficial contact devoid of meaningful emotional interaction.

Intense emotional attachments are more vulnerable to deterioration under stress. Intense emotional cut-offs between a spouse and his or her parent will predictably influence the development of problems in the marriage and/or new family. Although they assert that the mechanism is unclear, Mueller and Pope (1977) have established that marital instability is transmitted from one generation to another. The evaluation of the emotional attachment between spouses must always be conceptualized in the context of each spouse's relationship with his or her parents. The evolution of conflict or closeness and distance in the marital dyad may only reflect an intergenerational imbalance in the spouse-parent relationship.

A critical factor for each person considering divorce is whether the dysfunction manifesting itself as marital conflict can in some way be resolved through the divorce process. If an individual presents the following guidelines for decision making, it generally means that the emotional loss in the divorce process will be greater, and less will be resolved by a decision to divorce:

1. A belief that the problem lies in the current relationship and is not likely to be found in subsequent relationships.
2. A belief that a divorce will produce a long-term rather than short-term serious loss in the sense of self or sense of identity.
3. A high level of denial about the possibility of loss in the divorce process.
4. A belief that the only important thing is to get away from the other.
5. Making a decision solely on the basis of what "feels" right or what is legally possible for the purpose of revenge.

Other factors associated with greater loss in the divorce process include marital relationship activity defined primarily as "doing something for the other," or somatic symptoms associated with marital interaction.

On the other hand, decisions that: (1) place emphasis on flexibility; (2) focus on consequences; and (3) work toward resolving emotional interdependencies and maintaining one's own functioning, are generally associated with less intense experiences of loss in the divorce process (Cristofori, 1977).

In spite of the potentially extreme emotional upheaval of the divorce process, a couple who can work toward maintaining a friendship during and after the divorce probably will have a less intense experience of loss. Flexibility and adaptability in this type of relationship will more likely allow a dissolution of the marital relationship while maintaining the relationship between each parent and the children. The survival of an intact, functioning parent-child relationship following a marital dissolution is critical to the functioning of the post-divorce family.

> An example of a reactive divorce was Evelyn M., aged thirty-three, who married while pregnant at age nineteen largely to get away from her parents, whom she considered the source of her problems. After fourteen years of marriage, during which she dedicated herself to taking care of her husband and children, she felt progressively oppressed "by their making it impossible" for her to live. In her haste to get away from the "source of the problem" she believed that her adolescent children would do well without her. Only after the divorce and the development of significant reactions in her children did she realize the similarity in her reactivity to this family and her family of origin.

Clinically, it is important to evaluate an individual's "blaming all of life's problems on the family" as a function of his or her anxiety and reactivity. In the case of Evelyn M., clinical intervention designed to calm the reactive running away and to enlarge the relationship context to extended as well as nuclear family, might have preserved the integrity of the family and reduced her feelings of oppression. The major factor in the success of a divorce decision is the degree to which individuals involved can work toward a resolution of the emotional attachment and assume responsibility for their part in the marital problems.

DIVORCE AT DIFFERENT STAGES OF THE FAMILY LIFE CYCLE

The probability of divorce for any couple is related to the intensity and balance of their emotional attachment. Stages of the family life cycle influence the balance of this attachment. The specific form in which the divorce process occurs varies with the stage of the life cycle.

The influence of divorce on children is related to two broad issues: (1) the intensity of the emotional attachment and conflict between parents, and (2) the degree to which the child is the focus of family emotional processes. The child's specific developmental stage shapes the nature of his or her response to the divorce process but the family projection process determines the long-term intensity of the child's response.

In general, all siblings in a family are not equal recipients of parental anxieties or conflicts. One child is often sensitive to or the recipient of parental anxieties. To the extent that a child becomes the focus of parental anxieties, he or she becomes a more relationship-oriented child. Some of the parental anxiety becomes shared with the child. As anxiety increases, the parent-child relationship is defined around mutual concern and worry within the child. In this type of relationship, a child retains less energy for goal-directed behavior. If anxiety remains high for lengthy periods, a child becomes more influenced by others than by himself or herself. Eventually, these children become more influenced by the relationships with others and less by goals set by themselves. In general, a more relationship-oriented child has greater difficulty dealing with parental divorce.

Families without Children

Couples who divorce within the first few years of marriage before producing children either have highly intense emotional attachments to one another or to their families of origin, or have not found a way to regulate or stabilize this intensity. These couples often report that their early marriage was either a highly pleasurable or highly conflictual, but rather labile, relationship. Many of these individuals choose marriage as a way of leaving a highly intense relationship with their family of origin. Using physical distance as a major mechanism for regulating relationships with the family of origin makes these couples more prone to using divorce as a way of dealing with their marital problems.

These couples may be younger in age, more emotionally cut off from their families of origin, or become involved in extramarital affairs that temporarily stabilize the relationship while promoting subsequent repercussions. Divorce at this stage of the life cycle may have fewer immediate consequences. Individuals do not have to concern themselves with the effects of the divorce on children and they frequently believe they have a lifetime remaining for another marriage.

Divorce at this time may be treated either as a youthful mistake and never discussed by the individuals, or it can foster an emotional cut-off with one's family of origin related to feelings of guilt, shame, or blame. Failure to resolve the emotional attachment to parents and former spouse has long-term consequences that will surface over the course of the life cycle in future relationships and subsequent marriage.

Joan T., greatly attracted to a man of whom her parents strongly disapproved, married at age eighteen. Her husband's father had disappeared years previously, leaving her husband as an only child. The husband's mother died of cancer shortly before he met Joan. Within a year, the intensity of the attachment and the isolation of this marital dyad from extended family influenced her husband to return to a life pattern of gambling and involvement with other women. Confirmed in their opinion that the marriage would never work, her parents accepted Joan's return home without comment. The dissolution and abandonment in her first marriage were never discussed. After her youngest child by her second marriage began school, Joan became acutely depressed. Therapy revealed the lack of resolution of attachments that led to Joan's feelings of abandonment and depression. Clinical intervention at the time of the first marriage or divorce could have focused on the closed system of relationships in which emotionally intense issues were not directly dealt with by family members. Such a closed system of relationships can be identified in part by the fact that the individuals involved do not discuss emotionally important issues with one another.

Families with Young Children

The highest incidence of divorce occurs with families at this stage of the life cycle, and these families have been the focus of the best research on the effects of divorce on parents and children. This section will not only discuss the specific response of family members to a divorce at this stage, but will also give a longitudinal perspective for families with young children who experience divorce along with their other developmental tasks.

Younger children under five years of age appear to have greater difficulty adjusting to parental divorce than children over five (Wallerstein, 1975). Latency-age and adolescent children experience fewer developmental deviations than do the youngest children (Wallerstein, 1974, 1976).

Normal children aged two-and-a-half to three-and-a-half experience intense regressions in cognition, behavior, and self-control at the time of divorce. Age-appropriate developmental progress can be restored with continuity of care by any competent caretaker. Normal children aged three-and-three-quarters to four-and-three-quarters tend to experience self-blame, poor self-esteem, and disruptions in sense of order and dependability at time of divorce. Developmental progress is usually restored within one year as long as there is continuity of care.

Normal children who are the focus of family emotional process such as marital conflict tend to experience depression and developmental delays at time of divorce. A post-divorce decline in the quality of the mother-child relationship is strongly associated with deterioration in the child's emotional functioning. Improvement in the father-child dyad does not offset deterioration in the child's functioning if the custodial mother's functioning remains impaired. Continued post-divorce parental conflict correlates with impaired functioning in children in this age group.

Children of five years and older have the capability to respond to parental divorce without developmental delays. Although normal children of this age usually respond with anxiety and sadness as well as temper tantrums, whining, and irritability, their contacts outside the family usually allow them sufficient emotional distance to stabilize their reactiveness. Normal children who are the focus of the family projection process experience delays in development and learning, phobias, depression, and encapsulated and prolonged fantasies regarding oedipal resolutions (Wallerstein, 1975).

School-age children focus more of their emotional energy on learning, peers, and nonfamily adults than do younger children. The degree to which divorce and parental dysfunction prevents a child from keeping a major focus outside the family is related to the degree of impaired functioning in the child. Those latency-age children who are not sufficiently disengaged from post-divorce parental problems experience depression, peer problems, and school performance difficulties.

Hetherington (1977) performed a longitudinal evaluation of divorce in families with young children, examining economic stress, individual functioning, relations between divorced partners, and parent-child relationships. If a father in a family had been involved in conventional roles prior to the onset of divorce, he was more likely to experience increased dysfunctioning as a single parent in the areas of routine management of the household. If he functioned well in these areas before the divorce, he usually functions better afterward in the areas of practical management of his home. Many couples report increased economic stress after a divorce, and they are likely to seek second jobs. However, in middle-class families no statistically significant correlations have been made between level of income or feeling financially distressed, and specific parent-child interaction patterns or developmental deviations in the child. It is possible that in a lower financial income group where families may be deprived of necessities, economic stress may correlate with specific parent-child interaction patterns or developmental deviation in the children of divorce.

Usually, the greatest initial decrease in self-concept is experienced by fathers, reported as anxiety, depression, anger, rejection, or incompetence. It has been assumed that these symptoms relate to the lack of structure and to leaving one's home and children. Fathers who are very emotionally involved with their children tend to cope with this situation by seeing their children often initially; but after about two years, they see them less frequently. Some fathers who enjoy the contact with their children report that periodic contact is too painful to be maintained. Rather than experience the reactivation of the loss with each visit, they choose to have no contact.

Where there has been a high degree of marital conflict, fathers often report an initial sense of elation and freedom from the relationship. This temporary relief is likely to be followed by a sense of depression after about a year, and a more level affective state after two years. In general, fathers who have had a high degree of conflict with their wives report an increasingly positive relationship with their children initially after the divorce, which may be a function of seeing the children away from their wives.

In the area of interpersonal problems, fathers report feeling shut out of their family secondary to decreased contact. One response to decreased family contact is a strong increase in their social activities and a pervasive sense of loneliness. Both spouses tend to associate happiness and a better self-concept with finding intense emotional involvement with another person.

Both spouses report a continued preoccupation with the relationship between the children and the ex-spouse. In spite of the fact that most spouses report that they would call on their ex-spouses in a time of crisis, they continue to have frequent conflicts over finances, support, visitation, child-rearing, and intimate relationships with others.

As the first year following the divorce evolves, there tends to be a decrease in both frequency of conflicts and the intensity of the emotional attachment. Establishing other intimate relationships and/or remarriage decreases the intensity of the emotional attachment between divorced spouses. However, shifting the emotional attachment from an ex-spouse to a new spouse does not necessarily imply resolution of the attachment.

Hetherington's (1977) studies have shown that the first year after the divorce is most stressful for both partners. One year after divorce, two-thirds of the fathers and three-fourths of the mothers report that the divorce may have been a mistake, that they should have tried harder, and that they find alternative life-styles less satisfying. Nevertheless, at the end of the second year post-divorce, only about one-fourth of the partners report divorce as a possible mistake. Remarriage helps the marrying spouse make a post-divorce adjustment, but tends to reactivate the old conflicts of the nonmarried spouse, especially the mother, regarding finances, split loyalties of the children, and above all, jealousy toward the new wife.

The relationship between parents and children in post-divorce families is one of the most emotional aspects of divorce. At the end of two months, Hetherington's studies have shown that fathers have almost as much contact with families as fathers from intact families (Hetherington, 1977). After two months, one-fourth of the fathers have more contact than they had when their family was together. Some fathers report more contact because of a deep attachment to the child and wife or out of a sense of duty, guilt, or trying to maintain some sense of continuity of life. But others are motivated by a wish to annoy, compete, or retaliate against the spouse. After two years, one-fourth of the fathers and one-half of the mothers report a better relationship with their children than in the period before the divorce. But the other fathers usually have less contact with their children and ex-spouses after two years than they did when the family was together or immediately after the divorce.

Divorcing parents report different patterns of interaction in social and employment contacts. Fathers are active in self-improvement courses and social contact with other couples, and complain less about being caught in a child's world than do mothers. Mothers tend to report more disorganization in the post-divorce period, reflecting their task overload around household maintenance, child care, and employment. Mothers experience decreased frequency of social contact with other couples as compared with fathers, but a short-term increase in contact between themselves and other divorcées is evident. Nonworking mothers complain more than working mothers about being caught in a child's world. Almost all ex-spouses believe that one of the most important factors in improving their view of themselves is the establishment of intimate post-divorce heterosexual relationships (Hetherington, 1977).

Families with Adolescents

Divorce in families with adolescents necessarily means the breakup of at least a fifteen- to twenty-year marital relationship. The longer a couple has been married, the more self-concept and sense of identity may be affected by a divorce (Hetherington, 1977).

If divorce occurs, there are advantages and disadvantages for adolescents over younger children. Normal adolescents have a capacity to establish more emotional distance from parent conflicts. This adaptive capacity is critical to maintenance of generational boundaries and developmental tasks (Wallerstein, 1974). Adolescents can have a choice in custody decisions and in retaining independent contact with both sides of the extended family. These two options allow a greater opportunity for mastery of the crisis and for maintaining balanced, open relationships with all family members involved.

Adolescents whose parents are divorcing experience a rapid telescoping of normal adolescent tasks. There is a diminished ability to exercise control over sexual development and identity formation. Within one year after divorce, those adolescents who have maintained sufficient emotional distance from parental problems develop a more measured mastery of these tasks and return to prior levels of functioning (Wallerstein, 1974).

Adolescents who have been the focus of family problems in the past experience significant intensifications of their problems reflected in a decreased adaptiveness to adolescent developmental tasks. Parental regressions across generational boundaries are particularly difficult for them. Emotionally isolated fathers may become inappropriately dependent for emotional support on adolescent daughters. Adolescent sons of divorced parents may find themselves propelled into a spouselike or peer relationship with their mother. These circumstances can lead to greater manipulation of loyalty ties so frequently seen by all members of divorcing families.

The inability to modify the blurring of generational boundaries may lead to emotional bonds between parent and adolescent that effectively prevent age-appropriate separation from the family. The failure to resolve emotional attachments at this stage of the life cycle may hinder the subsequent establishment by adolescents of their own nuclear family.

Families with Adult Children

The increased incidence of divorce after thirty years of marriage reflects the longer joint survival of the marital dyad after children leave home (Glick, 1977). Those marriages stabilized from within, with little dysfunction, are more likely to remain intact when the children grow away. Those marriages characterized by emotional distance with a strong emotional attachment of one spouse to the children, are more likely to become unstable when the children depart.

Post-divorce adjustment following a lengthy marriage may be especially difficult, and not only because of the length of time the couple have been together. Whereas the death of a parent may draw the surviving parent and adult children together, the divorce of parents has a tendency to polarize the relationships of parents and their adult children.

The greatest problems will be faced by those spouses who are emotionally cut off from their extended families. The divorce may even precipitate emotional cut offs from both family and friends, leaving older divorcing adults without resources at a difficult time in their lives. Dating, after a thirty or forty year relationship with one person, may be particularly hard to resume.

Although Mildred and Dan R. had been married for thirty years, their relationship faltered after the marriage of their youngest child. Mildred became increasingly depressed and demanding of time and attention from Dan. Dan's increasing emotional distance from this marital conflict lead him to "fall in love" with his younger secretary. Mildred's functioning in the marriage had always been stabilized by her heavy investment in the lives of her husband and children, and she became progressively bitter and depressed about the divorce. She viewed her husband betraying her "after all I've done for him." She greatly feared making social contacts on her own and became quite rigidly focused on how her husband was ruining her life.

Therapeutic intervention aimed at expanding her view of her relationship system and the part she played in it. Although her eighty-year-old mother resided in a nursing home, she remained lucid and supportive to her daughter, once Mildred began honestly reporting what was happening in her life. Her older brother, the favored sibling, responded warmly to Mildred's efforts for a more personal relationship. When she stopped blaming her husband for the divorce, the couple began for the first time to speak openly about issues in the relationship painful to each of them.

SINGLE-PARENT FAMILIES

The Census Bureau defines a family as two or more persons related to each other by blood, marriage, or adoption who live together. In 1975, approximately 84% of all families were headed by a marital couple, 13% were mother-headed, and 2–3% were father-headed. In mother-headed families, approximately 44% were separated and/or divorced, 35% were widowed, 13% were never married, and 4% had husbands living in institutions or in other geographic areas.

Although there are multiple reasons for single-parent homes, the increasing divorce rate in the United States is probably the most significant and largest contributor. There are currently over 11.3 million children living in single-parent homes. The number of children living in father-headed homes is increasing, yet only about 10% of children living with a divorced parent live with their father. The incidence of children being raised in single-parent families is increasing so that at the current rate almost one-half of the children born in the United States in 1977 can expect to spend several months of their lives as members of a single-parent family (Glick, 1977).

Much of the vast literature on mother-headed, single-parent families has focused on father absence as a significant factor. This section of the chapter will focus on the differences between single-parent and intact families as reflected in family functioning, use and availability of support systems, and reactivity to stress. The assumption is that the alteration in family structure leads to an alteration or intensification of family emotional processes. Increases in anxiety in family relationships affects family functioning and task performance depending on the frequency of contact, the quality of the relationships, and the maturity of the individuals involved.

Every family must establish an income, maintain a household, develop social and emotional relationships in the neighborhood and at work, and relate to children in a way that makes them productive members of society. The differences between an intact family and a single-parent family are reflected in the quality of relationships maintained between parent and child and between spouses. The reasons for being a single parent (death of a spouse, separation, divorce, illness, or institutionalization) have different impacts on the functioning of the family. The length of the separation, age of the child at the onset of separation, plus socioeconomic status and birth order of children, are also important factors (Hetherington, 1977).

A major problem for single-parent families is task overload. Task overload probably is most evident in the life cycle stage of single-motherhood with young children. If these families with young children have a high level of family organization and/or appropriate support systems, task performance can be maintained. If these families have a lower level of organization, economic problems and/or high levels of anxiety, there is a deterioration of task performance that parallels family disorganization.

Intact families have an average income that is twice as high as single-parent families. A single-parent mother with young children finding herself in a situation of economic hardship may frequently seek employment. If adequate child care and supervision can be provided, there is some evidence that maternal functioning and family organization can be maintained. Nevertheless, if adequate child care cannot be provided, or if a mother begins working at the same time as the separation and divorce and the child experiences the loss of both mother and father, an increased rate of behavior problems in children has been seen (Hetherington, 1977). The research of Wallerstein and Kelly (1975) implies that when a mother divorces and seeks employment at the same time, the impact is greater on young children rather than on adolescents.

Although one of the functions of a family is to maintain social and family relationships with members outside the nuclear family, single parents frequently find themselves emotionally cut off from extended family relationships and social networks. Many recently separated single-parent women state that contacts with parents and siblings do not appear to improve their loneliness and depression. Women who become single parents secondary to a divorce, as opposed to those who become single parents after a spouse's death, are significantly more emotionally cut off from their husband's extended family system. Additionally, women who are divorced tend to have fewer friends and belong to fewer organizations than do married women (Stack, 1972; Pearlin, 1975; Spicer, 1975). The social isolation experienced by single-parent mothers tends to intensify the parent-child relationship in such a manner that these women frequently complain of being trapped in a world of children. Since preschool children are far less capable than adolescents of maintaining their own social contacts, social isolation of parents tends to affect the functioning of young children more so than the functioning of adolescents.

The major task of raising children is now primarily performed by one parent where previously there were two. Social isolation, increased anxiety, depression, and loneliness may serve to foster decreased functioning in a single parent. The two-against-one paradigm of the intact nuclear family that may serve to make children more compliant with parental wishes is less likely to exist in a single-parent family. Dysfunctional parent-child relationships can no longer be compensated for by a sympathetic other parent. With preschool children, improvement in the father-child dyad does not offset deterioration in the child's functioning if the custodial mother's functioning remains impaired (Wallerstein, 1975).

Children in single-parent families exhibit more noncompliant and deviant behavior than children in intact families. Nevertheless, research findings clearly indicate that children reared in conflict-laden intact families may be more poorly adjusted than children in well functioning single-parent homes (Nye, 1957; McCord, 1962). Rutter (1971) has shown that as the quality of the marital relationship decreases, there is a parallel increase in acting-out behavior in children in intact families. Many clinicians have observed that in legally intact families, an emotional divorce may have already occurred. A very common pattern in these families is an emotionally distant or absent father with a dyad of intense emotional attachment between mother and children.

The major point is that the single parent (usually the mother) is the focus especially for younger children, around which all task performance occurs and through which all anxiety and stress must be processed. Although the family relationship processes in an intact family may be very similar to those of a single-parent family, the likelihood of decreased functioning in single-parent families is increased because of the added stress and modification of family structure. One specific way of comparing single-parent and intact families is the development of intellectual performance and the pattern of intellectual abilities in children raised in the two types of families. Shinn (1977) reported that the differences in cognitive performance between children from intact families and single-parent families is considerable. Recent studies have concluded that the children in single-parent families show decreased functioning on cognitive performance as measured by I. Q. tests, achievement tests, and school performance (Biller, 1974; Shinn, 1977).

Deutsch and Brown (1964) stated that the differences in intellectual performance of children emerged and increased only over the course of development in school years and are rarely seen in preschool children. Since most children of divorce are seven years of age or younger at the time of divorce or separation, these decreased cognitive skills may not appear until years following the transition to a single-parent family. Hetherington (1977) has reported that early loss of the father is more harmful than later separation and that effects may be cumulative.

Studies of intact families in which the father is measured as an infrequent or poor participator in family activities indicate that the children show decreased intellectual achievement similar to those in single-parent families. A number of investigators have shown that children with stepfathers have performed the same or better on cognitive abilities tests than children in intact families (Lessing, 1970; Santrock, 1972; Solomon, 1972). One conclusion that can be drawn is that the presence or absence of a father in a family is not nearly as critical as the quantity and quality of the marital relationship. Clinical research in the area of family functioning also supports the idea that the quantity and quality of the husband-wife relationship affects the intellectual and emotional adjustment of children.

Underscoring all these studies is that Glick reports from his census studies that in 1977 nearly one-half of the children in single-parent families live with a parent who has never completed high school. This proportion is about twice as large as that for two-parent families. Therefore, children in single-parent families more so than children from intact families live in an environment where education has been less available or less attainable for their parents. By virtue of their educational background, employment for single parents will generally be at a less economically rewarding level than employment for parents who are married.

Several explanations have been offered regarding the differences in intellectual functioning of children from intact and single-parent families. Hetherington offers three possible explanations (Nelson, 1966). A major thesis is that stress is more likely to interfere with problem solving skills than verbal skills. Stress in a family can be a function of the loss of either mother or father, or of high conflict in intact families, or of living in a single-parent family. However, divorce and separation have been shown to have more effect on overall cognitive performance than do other types of separation. A second major thesis is that children in single-parent homes have lower quantity or a different quality of interaction with parents, which may be a crucial factor in intellectual development. A third explanation was that in divorced families there is a marked decrease in consistent parental control over children, fewer demands for mature, independent behavior, and less rational and explanatory communication with children. She proposed that poor parental control may lead to poorer self-control in children, higher levels of distractability, and lack of persistence in children that could influence problem solving performance. In general it can be said that the quality as well as the quantity of maternal interaction in single-parent families may very well be a factor in the intellectual development and the discrepancies observed between children seen in intact families versus mother-headed families (Hetherington, 1977).

Adolescents in single-parent families can be distinguished from adolescents in intact families by several criteria: male-female relationships, marital instability, and juvenile delinquency. The dissolution of the marriage leaves parents and adolescents with similar life cycle tasks such as the establishment of heterosexual relationships. This similarity can be mutually anxiety-provoking or mutually rewarding. If parents and adolescents can maintain sufficient emotional distance from one another so as to master their own heterosexual relationships, parental regressions across generational boundaries are less likely to occur. If sufficient emotional distance cannot be maintained, then mutual support may become inappropriate mutual dependency, preventing age appropriate departure of the adolescent from his or her family.

Although any explanation of the relationship between maternal behavior and an adolescent's heterosexual behavior is speculative, it is accurate that daughters of divorcées have more problematic heterosexual relations than do daughters of widows (Hetherington, 1972). Adolescents from mother-headed families have a higher incidence of delinquency than adolescents from intact families. Since deviant adolescent behavior can be viewed as a function of increased stress in the parent-adolescent relationship, the higher incidence of delinquency in mother-headed families may be related to the increased stress and conflict reported by single-parent mothers (Lynn, 1974; Biller, 1976).

The incidence of divorce is higher in children from single-parent families. However, the incidence varies as to what life cycle event created single parenthood and how the parents dealt with the event. Divorce is more likely to occur in children of single-parent families if the child lives with the mother rather than the father, or if the separation is secondary to divorce rather than death of one parent (Pope, 1976; Mueller, 1977). Since the incidence of marital instability among children of single-parent families varies according to the type and reason for single parenthood, the instability is not just a function of having a single parent. One can only speculate whether the above differences reflect that single-parent mothers experience more distress and decreased functioning than do single-parent fathers. Some observers note that women in the social network are more likely to move in supportively toward a single-parent male raising children than to a single-parent woman. Judged by their parenting, single-parent widows appear to function better than single-parent divorcées. This observation also reflects differing responses of families and society to death and divorce. Single-parent divorcées are generally younger, have smaller children, and get less support from extended family and social systems at the time of separation than do single-parent widows (Hetherington, 1972). It could be that divorce is one specific life cycle event to which nonparticipants have a greater difficulty relating.

CLINICAL IMPLICATIONS

While there are no simple solutions to the complex and far-reaching issues in the divorce process, a few clinical principles based on knowledge of the family and its life cycle are indicated. Divorce is basically a family problem and as such a systematic family approach is indicated (Bowen, 1978). Exclusive therapeutic focus on vested individual interests or a single relationship avoids important aspects of the extended family system.

Therapeutic focus on the resolution of the emotional attachment in the marital dyad is necessary to preserve balanced intergenerational continuity to family relationships. Although the marital relationship ceases, the child, parent, and grandparent relationships continue. Distortions in the resolution of the marital dyad can lead to far-reaching distortions in the continuity of these intergenerational bonds. A spouse who "wins" the children and cuts off this segment of the family from the other spouse may find the same imbalance being repeated in the marriages of his or her children.

Clinical intervention must focus on reducing the intensity of the divorcing process so that parenting functions can be maintained while marital relationships are resolving. Identification of patterns of attachment and the part each individual plays is critical. Resolution of personal loss and grief without projection of responsibility to others is of utmost importance.

Patterns of resolving attachments from past generations almost always appear in the divorce process. Enlarging the therapeutic perspective through a three-generational examination of these patterns can reduce marital stress and focus on parental responsibilities. Enlarging the focus of attachment to extended family members can reduce marital conflict and promote intergenerational contact. The more supportive and nonpolarized the involvement of the extended family, the better the resolution in the marital dyad.

Mental health professionals should be aware that lawyers can intervene in divorce proceedings in many different ways. The most basic method of intervention for lawyers is based on the adversary system. However, other methods of legal intervention such as that of negotiator, arbitrator, financial manager, or psychological counselor may at times be equally important. If the attorney's method of intervention is designed to match the client's expectation of him, then a conflictual marital dissolution is likely to evoke the lawyer's adversarial capabilities.

Although from a legal standpoint it may be preferable that a lawyer intervene in a manner consistent with a client's expectations, knowledge of family emotional systems indicates that what is best for one member of a divorcing family may not be best for the family as a whole. Continuing the marital conflict in the courtroom may only further impair parent-child relationships.

Interdisciplinary cooperation between lawyers and mental health professional is critical. Lawyers should be aware that spouses can be their own best negotiators. Mental health professionals should be aware that a thorough understanding of legal options can enhance an individual's emotional functioning. If one spouse has sought legal advice, it is appropriate to refer the other spouse for advice on his or her legal options provided the referral can be made without enhancing adversarial possibilities. The greater the resolution of the emotional attachment between spouses, the more likely the legal intervention can be oriented toward the long-term impact of the marital dissolution. Both legal and mental health professionals in their efforts to assist dissolving marriages must focus the energy of each spouse on establishing a legal, financial, and emotional climate that fosters the autonomy of all individuals within the family. In general, legal representation prior to emotional resolution of the attachment tends to enhance advocacy and retard resolution.

Custody disputes precipitate and resurrect marital conflicts not easily modified by therapeutic intervention. Each spouse vies for loyalty and alignment from the therapist just as he or she does from the child. Custody decisions raise great anxiety among most participants in a divorce and lead to highly emotional interactions that may continue for years beyond the actual decision. Although custody disputes may be legally resolved, the lack of emotional resolution in the marriage will manifest itself around visitation. Frequent visitation by the noncustodial spouse is associated with better adjustment and self-control in the child under the following conditions: parental agreement regarding childrearing, low level of conflict in the parental dyad, and emotional stability of the noncustodial spouse. Frequent visitation by the noncustodial parent is associated with poor adjustment in the custodial parent-child dyad under the following conditions: parental disagreement regarding childrearing, high level of conflict in the parental dyad, and emotional instability of the noncustodial parent (Hetherington, 1977).

Although there is evidence that the increasing divorce rate may be leveling off, there is little doubt that divorce will continue at a higher rate in this generation and in future ones than occurred in the past and will effect a greater percentage of the total population in future generations. The impact and the intensity of the divorce process clearly modifies the shape and structure of those families as well as the shape of their subsequent family life cycle. Custody determinations, parental visitation, remarriage, and single-parent status will increasingly influence the emotional attachments in existing family life. The multigenerational impact of these modifications may be enormous.

It is the task of the mental health profession, the legal profession, and all those in contact with divorcing families to understand and assist families in resolving these emotional attachments. Problems occurring in nuclear families can be resolved within, passed on to children, or externalized into society. Society's willingness to accept responsibility for resolving family problems influences a family's ability to resolve the problem from within. The less resolution within families, the more instability within society. Those of us in the helping professions have the opportunity to become a part of the problem or a part of the solution.

REFERENCES

Biller, HG: *Parental Deprivation: Family, School, Sexuality, and Society,* Lexington, MA: D.C. Heath and Company, 1974.

Biller HB: The father and personality development: paternal deprivation and sex-role development, in *The Role of The Family in Child Development,* edited by Lamb ME, New York: Wiley, 1976, 89–156.

Bowen, M: *Family Therapy in Clinical Practice,* New York: Jason Aronson, 1978.

Cristofori, RH: Modification of loss in divorce: a report from clinical practice, in *The Family* 5/1:25–30, 1977.

Deutsch M, Brown B: Social influences in negro-white intelligence differences, in *Journal of Social Issues* 20:24–35, 1964.

Glick PC, Norton AJ: Marrying, divorcing and living together in the U.S. today, in *Population Bulletin,* 1977, 32/5 (Population Reference Bureau, Inc., Washington, D.C.).

_____, The future of the American family in current population reports, in *Special Studies Series* P-23, No. 78, 1979 (U.S. Government Printing Office, Washington, D.C.).

Hetherington EM: Effects of paternal absence on personality development in adolescent daughters, in *Developmental Psychology* 7:313–26, 1972.

_____, Cox M, Cox R: The aftermath of divorce, in *Mother-Child, Father- Child Relations,* edited by Stevens JH Jr., Matthews M, Washington D.C.: National Association for the Education of Young Children, 1978.

Kelly J, Wallerstein J: The effects of parental divorce: experiences of the child in early latency, in *American Journal of Orthopsychiatry* 46/1:20–32, 1976.

Kressel K, Deutsch M: Divorce therapy: an in-depth survey of therapists' views, *Family Process* 16/4:413–43, 1977.

Lessing EE, Zagorin SW, Nelson D: WISC subtest and I.Q. score correlates of father absence, in *Journal of Genetic Psychology* 117:181–95, 1970.

Lynn DB: *The Father: His Role in Child Development,* Belmont, California: Brooks/Cole, 1974.

McCord J, McCord W, Thurber E: Some effects of parental absence on male children, in *Journal of Abnormal and Social Psychology* 64:361–69, 1962.

Mueller CW, Pope H: Marital instability: a study of its transmission between generations, in *Journal of Marriage and the Family,* February, 1/39:89–94, 1977.

Nelson EA, Maccoby EE: The relationship between social development and differential abilities on the Scholastic Aptitude Test, in *Merrill-Palmer Quarterly* 12:269–89, 1966.

Nye FI: Child adjustment in broken and in unhappy unbroken homes, in *Marriage and Family Living,* 19:356–60, 1957.

Pearlin LI, Johnson JS: *Marital status, life-strains, and depression,* Unpublished manuscript, 1975.

Pope H, Meuller CW: The intergenerational transmission of marital instability: comparisons by race and sex, in *Journal of Social Issues* 321:149–66, 1976.

Rutter M: Parent-child separation: psychological effects on the children, in *Journal of Child Psychology and Psychiatry* 12:233–60, 1971.

Santrock JW: Relation of type and onset of father-absence of cognitive development, in *Child Development* 43:455-69, 1972.

Shinn M: Father absence and children's cognitive development, in *Psychology Bulletin,* Vol. 85/2:295-324, March, 1978.

Solomon D, Hirsch JG, Scheinfeld DR, Jackson JC: Family characteristics and elementary school achievement in an urban ghetto, in *Journal of Consulting and Clinical Psychology,* 39:462-66, 1972.

Spicer JW, Hampe GD: Kinship interaction after divorce, in *Journal of Marriage and the Family* 37:113-19, 1975.

Stack CB: Black kindreds: parenthood and personal kindreds among urban blacks, in *Journal of Comparative Family Studies* 194-206, 1972.

The Group for the Advancement of Psychiatry: Committee on the Family, *Child Custody Litigation in Divorce* New York: GAP, in press 1980.

Wallerstein J, Kelly J: The effects of parental divorce: the adolescent experience, in *The Child in his Family—Children at a Psychiatric Risk* 3:479-505, edited by Koupernik A, New York: Wiley, 1974.

_____, _____, The effects of parental divorce: experiences of the preschool child, in *Journal of the American Academy of Child Psychiatry* 14/4:600-616, 1975.

_____, _____, The effects of parental divorce: experiences of the child in later latency, in *American Journal of Orthopsychiatry* 46/2:256-69, 1976.

_____, _____, Divorce counseling, a community service for families in the midst of divorce, in *American Journal of Orthopsychiatry* 47/1:4-22, 1977.

_____, _____, Brief interventions with children in divorcing families, in *American Journal of Orthopsychiatry* 47/1:23-29, 1977.

Vigyikan PD: *Triangles,* Philadelphia: Dorrance and Company, 1978.

12

FORMING A REMARRIED FAMILY

Monica McGoldrick, A.C.S.W.

C.M.D.N.J.–Rutgers Medical School and
Community Mental Health Center

Family Institute of Westchester

Elizabeth A. Carter, A.C.S.W.

Family Institute of Westchester

INTRODUCTION

As a first marriage signifies the joining of two families, so a second marriage involves the interweaving of three, four, or more families, whose previous family life cycle course has been disrupted by death or divorce. So complex is the process whereby the remarried family system stabilizes and regains its forward developmental thrust that we have come to think of this process as adding a whole additional phase to the family life cycle for those involved. By 1975, there were 15 million children under age eighteen living in stepfamilies, and about 25 million stepparents in this country, with a million more being added yearly (Roosevelt & Lofas, 1976; Visher & Visher, 1978). According to the demographer Paul Glick, 38% of first marriages are likely to end in divorce, and of those who divorce, 75% are likely to remarry. Add to this the number of people who remarry after the death of a spouse, and it is evident that this process involves a great many families. And since the rate of redivorce is 44% (Glick & Norton, 1976), we can infer that the process is often poorly understood or dealt with.

Most family research has focused on intact first families. There have as yet been no longitudinal studies of remarried families in formation, and thus the "normal" process of reconstituting a family has not really been defined. The built-in ambiguity of boundaries and membership defies simple definition, and our culture lacks any established patterns or rituals to help families with this transition. We provide no guidelines or traditions for the complex relationships of acquired family members. Such kinship terms as our culture provides have negative connotations (e.g., stepmother), which increase the difficulties for families trying to work out these relationships.

Our society abounds in romantic myths about the joys of family life that seem to require second families to bend themselves into the shape of the mythological "happy intact family," whose structure, in any case, is almost irrelevant to the shifting boundaries and membership of remarried families. If they are not pressured to be like intact families, remarried families are offered two opposing myths of stepfamily life: the cruel picture of the fairy tales (Cinderella, Snow White, and the like) for which the only solution is escape, or the dream of becoming the Brady Bunch, the big jolly family that works it all out comfortably with no dangling ends or unresolvable feelings.

It is easy to understand the wish for clear and quick resolution when one has been through the pain of a first family ending, but, unfortunately, the "instant intimacy" that remarried families expect of themselves is impossible to achieve and the new relationships are all the harder to negotiate because they do not develop slowly, as intact families do, but must begin midstream, after another family's life cycle has been dislocated. Naturally, second families carry the scars of first families. Neither parents, nor children, nor grandparents can forget the relationships that went before. Children never give up their attachment to their first parent, no matter how negative the relationship with that parent was or is. Having the patience to tolerate the ambiguity of the situation and allowing each other the space and time for feelings about past relationships is crucial to the process of forming a remarried family. However, the "battle fatigue" of family members quite naturally leads to a tendency to seek comfort, often resulting in the characteristic pseudomutuality (Goldstein, 1974) that denies difficulties and thus prevents their resolution.

This chapter will review efforts to study and outline the process of remarriage, discuss the implications of its occurrence at different stages of the family life cycle, and suggest clinical interventions for families who become stuck in this process. It is our experience that this is one of the most difficult transitions for families to negotiate. This is because of the wish for premature closure to end the ambiguity and pain, and because of the likelihood that the previous stage (mourning a death or working out the emotional complexities of a divorce) has been inadequately dealt with, and will, in any case, be emotionally reactivated. Much therapeutic effort must be directed toward educating families about the built-in complexities of the process, so that they can work toward establishing a viable, open system that will permit restoration of the developmental processes for future life cycle phases.

STUDIES OF REMARRIAGE: CLINICALLY USEFUL FINDINGS

As previously stated, there is no scientifically satisfactory research available on the process of remarriage or the adjustment to it. However, the tentative findings of several studies are suggestive of directions that, it is hoped, will be explored and tested clinically in the future. For thorough coverage of this topic, readers are referred to Visher and Visher's excellent book, *Stepfamilies: A Guide to Working with Stepparents and Stepchildren* (1979), and to the "An Annotated Bibliography of the Remarried, the Living Together, and Their Children," by Walker et al. (1979).

E. Mavis Hetherington, studying forty-eight intact and forty-eight divorced couples (1977), found the following:

1. In 70% of divorced couples studied, one of the divorcing spouses was involved in an affair, but only 15% of them later married this person.

2. Remarriage of a former spouse was accompanied by a reactivation of feelings of depression, helplessness, anger, and anxiety, particularly for women. Men, possibly for financial reasons, and because they are usually less central to the emotional system, tended to be less upset at the remarriage of an ex-wife.

3. Upset feelings of ex-wives were likely to contribute to a renewal of financial and/or visitation and custody difficulties. New wives frequently precipitated or reacted to the first wives' upset by entering hostile, competitive struggles around the children and childrearing practices.

In another study by Estelle Duberman (1975), eighty-eight remarried couples were interviewed to determine their level of "family integration." Duberman found that:

1. Family integration was better if the previous spouse had died rather than divorced.

2. Family integration was better if the new spouse had divorced rather than been a bachelor.

3. The longer the new family had been together as a unit, the higher the level of family integration.

4. All parent-child relationships were better when the remarried couple had children of their own.

5. All parent-child relationships were better when the wife's children from her first marriage were with her.

6. Men who had left children behind with an ex-wife did not relate to their stepchildren as well as bachelors did.

7. All stepmothers related better to younger children than to teenagers.

8. Widows related to their stepchildren better than did divorcées.

9. The stepmother-stepdaughter relationship was the most problematic of all stepfamily relationships.

10. Remarried relationships were best when extended family approved or accepted the marriage, second best when extended family disapproved and were negative, and worst when extended family were cut off or indifferent.

Another study by Stern (1978) of discipline and stepfather integration in thirty stepfather families found that it took stepfathers almost two years to become comanagers of their stepchildren with their wives. They had first to become friends of the children, and only gradually could they move into the role of active parenting.

Of special relevance to our view is the finding of Nolan (1977) that children of divorce function best if they are able to maintain satisfactory contact with both parents.

PREDICTABLE EMOTIONAL ISSUES IN REMARRIAGE

The basic premise of family systems theory is that we all carry into our new relationships the emotional baggage of unresolved issues from important past relationships. This baggage makes us emotionally sensitive in the new relationships, and we tend to react in one of two ways: either we become self-protective, closed off, and afraid to make ourselves vulnerable to further hurt—i.e., we put up barriers to intimacy—or we become intensely expectant and demanding that the new relationships make up for or erase past hurts.

Either of these stances complicates the new relationships. In first marriages, the baggage we bring is from our families of origin: our unresolved feelings about parents and siblings. In remarriage, there are usually at least three sets of emotional baggage:

1. from the family of origin;
2. from the first marriage;
3. from the process of separation, divorce, and the period between marriages.

To the extent that either or both remarried partners expect the other to relieve them of this baggage, the new relationship will become problematic. On the other hand, to the extent that each spouse can work to resolve his or her own emotional issues with significant people from the past, the new relationship can proceed on its own merits.

There are a number of major predictable emotional issues in remarriage that will be briefly summarized here. They have been dealt with in greater depth elsewhere (Visher & Visher, 1978; Schulman, 1972; and Goldstein, 1974).

Complex, Conflicting, and Ambiguous New Roles and Relationships

Instead of a step-by-step progression from courtship to marriage to parenthood, remarried families must plunge into instant multiple roles, as a bachelor becomes overnight a husband and stepfather, or a single mother of two becomes a wife and stepmother of four. In such situations, the parent-child relationship predates the couple relationship, with the obvious complications this entails.

The complexity of remarried families would probably not present quite so many problems for its members if our society provided guidelines for the roles and relationships, but we do not even have language or kinship labels to help orient the members of remarried families positively toward their newly acquired kin. These problems are by no means trivial, and they immediately invade every aspect of family life and contact with outsiders. How do children explain that their brother has a different last name and their mother yet another? How do they address their new stepgrandparents? And how do they learn to be middle children, when they have for years been the oldest?

Our cultural forms, rituals, and assumptions still relate chiefly to the intact, first marriage family, and the most ordinary event, such as filling out a form or celebrating a holiday, can become a source of acute embarrassment or discomfort for members of remarried families.

Complex and Ambiguous Boundaries of the System

Boundary difficulties include issues of:

1. Membership (Who are the "real" members of the family?)
2. Space (What space is mine? Where do I really belong?)
3. Authority (Who is really in charge? Of discipline? money? decisions? etc.)

4. Time (Who gets how much of my time and how much do I get of theirs?)

This cluster of issues is central and must be negotiated by remarried families, since one simple boundary cannot be drawn around the members of the household as in most first families. Great flexibility is called for to enable the new family to constantly expand and contract its boundaries, to include visiting children and then let them go, while also establishing its own stable life-style. An additional boundary problem arises when "instant incest taboos" are called for, as when several previously unrelated teenagers are suddenly supposed to view each other as siblings, or a new stepfather isn't supposed to have sexual feelings toward his attractive stepdaughter.

Affective Problems: Wishing for the Resolution of Ambiguity

Intense conflictual feelings, or their denial, are predictable problems in remarried families.

Guilt is an especially difficult issue. For example, if a father has left the children of his first marriage with his ex-wife, he may be moved by guilt to be a "better" father in the new family, bringing a special intensity to his relationships with his stepchildren. Or a wife may not really like her husband's children, may find them ill-mannered or intrusive, but at the same time feel that they are "part of the bargain," that they need her because of their previous losses, or that her husband is relying on her to do a good job with them. One of the most harmful injunctions afloat in remarried families is that a person must love another's children as much as his or her own, and that anything less is heartless. "Overtrying" by the new parent is a major problem in such families, often related to guilt about unresolved or unresolvable aspects of the system.

Another major source of difficulty is loyalty conflicts. Children will always feel loyalty to their natural parents, no matter what. One of the greatest strains on parents is to let their children have and express the full range of negative and positive feelings toward their parents and stepparents. A parent may prohibit a child from expressing negative feelings about a dead parent, or positive feelings about a parent who has divorced and left them. Often parents want the child's whole allegiance, and most children fear that if they love one parent they will somehow hurt the other. If they don't love a new stepparent, they fear they will hurt and anger one parent; if they do love the stepparent, they fear disloyalty to the other.

The Tendency toward Pseudomutuality or Fusion

Remarried families are formed against a background of hurt and failure. The sense of vulnerability, fear, and mistrust is very difficult to deal with. As a result, families often tend to cover over conflicts, fearing that their expression will lead to more hurt and separation. There is often a sense of, "Let's not rock the boat this time."

THE PROCESS OF REMARRIAGE

As a stormy adolescent phase in a family's life cycle must be viewed as part of a process going back to the child's birth (and before), so remarriage must be viewed as part of an emotional process going back at least to the disintegration of the first marriage. The intensity of emotion unleashed by the life cycle disruption of divorce must be dealt with over and over again before the dislocated systems are restabilized (Beal, Chapter 11). One-quarter of divorced women restabilize permanently in single-parent or nonmarital households; for three-quarters of them, however, there is the additional phase of remarriage. The emotions connected with the break up of the first marriage can be visualized as a "roller coaster" graph with peaks of intensity at the point of:

1. decision to separate;
2. actual separation;
3. legal divorce;
4. remarriage of either spouse;
5. death of either ex-spouse.
6. life cycle transitions of children (graduations, marriage, illness etc.)

Seen in this way, it should be clear that no amount of "dealing with" the emotional difficulties of divorce will finish off the process once and for all before remarriage, although it appears clinically that the more emotional work done at each step, the less intense and disruptive the subsequent reactivations will be. Failure to deal sufficiently with the process at each peak may jam it enough to prevent remarried family stabilization from ever occurring.

We are including an outline (Table 12.1) of the developmental steps required for remarried family formation, similar in many respects to that described by Ransom, Schlesinger, and Derdeyn (1979). Their outline is particularly fortuitous in addressing the need to conceptualize and plan for the new marriage. Although it is certainly true that more advance planning

TABLE 12.1

REMARRIED FAMILY FORMATION: A DEVELOPMENTAL OUTLINE *

Steps	Prerequisite Attitude	Developmental Issues
1. Entering the new Relationship	Recovery from loss of first marriage (adequate "emotional divorce")	Recommitment to marriage and to forming a family with readiness to deal with the complexity and ambiguity
2. Conceptualizing and planning new marriage and family	Accepting one's own fears and those of new spouse and children about remarriage and forming a stepfamily	a. Work on openness in the new relationships to avoid pseudomutuality.
	Accepting need for time and patience for adjustment to complexity and ambiguity of:	b. Plan for maintenance of cooperative co—parental relationships with ex—spouses.
	1. Multiple new roles	c. Plan to help children deal with fears, loyalty conflicts and membership in two systems.
	2. Boundaries: space, time, membership and authority.	d. Realignment of relationships with extended family to include new spouse and children.
	3. Affective Issues: guilt, loyalty conflicts, desire for mutuality, unresolvable past hurts	e. Plan maintenance of connections for children with extended family of ex—spouses(s).
3. Remarriage and Reconsitution of Family	Final resolution of attachment to previous spouse and ideal of "intact" family;	a. Restructuring family boundaries to allow for inclusion of new spouse—stepparent.
	Acceptance of a different model of family with permeable boundaries	b. Realignment of relationships throughout subsystems to permit interweaving of several systems.
		c. Making room for relationships of all children with biological (non—custodial) parents, grandparents, and other extended family.
		d. Sharing memories and histories to enhance stepfamily integration.

* Variation on a developmental schema presented by Ransom *et al.* (1979)

would also be helpful in first marriages, it is an essential ingredient for successful remarriage, because of the different conceptual model required, and because of the number of family relationships that must be renegotiated at the same time as the new marriage. We have expanded Ransom's outline to include conceptualizing and planning for the new family as well as for the marriage. This is because, as they themselves have observed, "The presence of children at the earliest stages prevents the establishment of an exclusive spouse-to-spouse relationship which predates the undertaking of parenthood" (p. 37). We have also added to Ransom's framework extended family relationships, which we consider vital to stabilization of the system.

It is our opinion that the emotional tasks listed in column II of our table are key attitudes in the transitions that permit the family to work on the tasks in column III. If, as clinicians, we find ourselves struggling with the family over column III issues before column II has been accomplished, we are probably wasting our efforts. In addition to the emotional work, time is an essential ingredient in this process. Hetherington (1977) found that an average time of two years was required for restabilization of the family after divorce. Other studies have suggested (Stern, 1978), and we have observed clinically, that it takes about two years for stabilization to occur in remarried families. Research on nonclinical families going through this process would be extremely valuable, since clinical populations are special samples.

From our clinical experience we have outlined a number of predictors of difficulty in making the transition to remarriage:

1. A wide discrepancy between the family life cycle stages of the families.

2. Denial of prior loss and/or a short interval between marriages.

3. Failure to resolve the intense relationship issues of the first family, for example if family members still feel intense anger or bitterness about the divorced spouse.

4. Expectations that remarriage will be easily accepted by the children and a lack of awareness of the emotional difficulties of remarriage for them.

5. The inability to give up the ideal of the intact first family and move to a new conceptual model of family.

6. Efforts to draw firm boundaries around the new household membership and push for primary loyalty and cohesiveness in the new family.

7. Exclusion of natural parents or grandparents or combatting their influence.

8. Denial of differences and difficulties and acting "as if" this is just an ordinary household.

9. Shift in custody of children near the time of remarriage.

THE IMPACT OF REMARRIAGE AT VARIOUS PHASES
OF THE FAMILY LIFE CYCLE

Spouses at Different Life Cycle Phases

To be useful to clinicians, a family life cycle view of human development must provide for the variations in structure of remarried families. The same complexity that does not always provide a simple answer to questions such as "Who are your parents?" or "Where do you live?" applies equally to the clinicians's attempt to locate the remarried family at a particular phase of the family life cycle. In fact, the two subsystems now joined in remarriage may come from quite different phases, and this difference in experience and approach to current responsibilities may cause considerable difficulty if not explicitly addressed by the new spouses.

In general, the wider the discrepancy in family life cycle experience between the new spouses, the greater the difficulty of transition and the longer it will take to integrate a workable new family. A father of late adolescent and/or young adult children with a new young wife never previously married should expect a rather strenuous and lengthy period of adjustment during which he will have to juggle his emotional and financial responsibilities toward the new marriage and toward his (probably upset) children. His wife, looking forward to the romantic aspects of a first marriage, will meanwhile encounter instead the many stresses of dealing with adolescents who probably don't take too kindly to her. This is so whether the children live with the couple or not. If either spouse tries to pull the other exclusively into a life-style or attitude that denies or restricts the other spouse's family life cycle tasks, difficulties will expand into serious problems. Thus, if the husband expects his new wife to undertake immediately a major successful role in his children's lives, or to be the one who always backs down gracefully when her interests and preferences clash with those of the children, there will be serious trouble in the new marriage, as the formation of the new couple bond is continuously given second priority. On the other hand, if the new wife tries overtly or covertly to cut off or drastically loosen the tie between father and children, or if she insists that her claims always have his prior attention, forcing her husband to choose between them, there will also be serious trouble. Variations in which the new wife claims to support her husband but embarks on a battle with his ex-wife as the source of the difficulties are equally dysfunctional.

Since it is not possible emotionally either to erase or acquire experience overnight, it is useful to conceptualize the joining of partners at two discrepant life cycle phases as a process in which both spouses have to learn to function in several different life cycle phases simultaneously and out of their usual sequence. The new wife will have to struggle with the role of stepmother to teenagers before becoming an experienced wife or a mother herself. The husband will have to retraverse with her several phases that he has passed through before: the honeymoon, the new marriage with its emphasis on romance and social activities, and the birth and rearing of any new children of their own. Both need to be aware that a second passage through these phases automatically reactivates some of the intensity over issues that were problematic the first time around. Attempts to "make up for" past mistakes or grievances may overload the new relationship. The focus needs to be on having the experiences again, not on undoing, redoing, or denying the past. With open discussion, mutual support, understanding, and a lot of thoughtful planning, this straddling of several phases simultaneously can provide rejuvenation for the older and experience for the younger spouse that can enrich their lives. If the difficulties are not understood and dealt with, they will surface as conflict or emotional distance at each life cycle transition in any subsystem of the remarried family.

Spouses at Same Life Cycle Phase

When the remarried spouses come together at the same phase of the family life cycle, they have the advantage of bringing the same life cycle tasks and the same general previous experience to the new family. Their greatest difficulties will tend to be related to whether they are at a childrearing phase or not. Obviously, spouses with no children from previous marriages bring the least complexity to the new situation. Families with grown children and grandchildren on both sides are complex systems with long histories and will require some careful thought to negotiate successfully. Neither of these circumstances, however, is likely to provide anything like the degree of strain involved at phases including either young or adolescent children, where the roles of active parenting and stepparenting must be included in the new family. Unfortunately, the advantage of having similar tasks, responsiblities, and experiences is frequently swamped in a competitive struggle that stems from the overload of these tasks and concerns (six children are not as easy to raise or support as three); the intense emotional investment in good parenting ("My methods are better than your methods"); and the need to include both ex-spouses in the many arrangements regarding the children ("Why do you let him or her dictate our lives?").

Reactions of Children to Remarriage

The most complex remarried families, and they are in the majority, are those in which one or both spouses have children under eighteen. Recent estimates (Maddox, 1975) are that one million children per year become stepchildren in the United States through divorce or death of parents, or out-of-wedlock birth. Visher and Visher (1979) estimate that one out of every six American children under eighteen is a stepchild.

In evaluating the probable issues involved in remarried families with children, it is necessary to consider several important factors: the degree of recognition of previous profound loss (whether by death or divorce); the length of time that was available between marriages for dealing with the previous loss; the extent to which previous family loss and/or conflict has actually been resolved; and recognition and acceptance of the emotional issues important to children at the time of remarriage, and their age-related methods of handling these issues.

Clinically, we find that denial of the importance of prior loss, little time between marriages, failure to resolve intense relationship issues in the first family (including extended family), and expectations that the remarriage will be quickly or easily accepted by the children are all associated with poor adjustment of children in the stepfamily.

Visher and Visher (1979) have devoted several chapters of their book to the crucial issues for children of various ages. Their summary is based on their clinical work with this problem over many years and the small but important body of research on the subject, notably the work of Wallerstein and Kelley (1974, 1975, 1976). The Vishers identify the major issues concerning children at the time of remarriage, as follows:

1. Dealing with loss.
2. Divided loyalties.
3. Where do I belong? (Shift in sibling position, role in family structure, family traditions.)
4. Membership in two households.
5. Unreasonable expectations.
6. Fantasies of natural parents reuniting.
7. Guilt over causing the divorce.
8. For adolescents, additional problems with identity and sexuality.

The children's struggles with these issues surface as school and/or behavior problems, withdrawal from family and peers, or "acting out" behavior, any of which complicates, or may completely obstruct, the process of stepfamily reorganization. There are indications that preschool children, if given some time and help in mourning their previous loss, adjust most easily to a new stepfamily, and that the adjustment is most difficult for stepfamilies with teenagers (Visher & Visher, 1979). Children of latency age seem to have the most difficulty resolving their feelings of divided loyalty (Wallerstein & Kelley, 1976), and benefit from careful attention to their need for contact with both parents. Clearly, children of all ages suffer when there is intense conflict between their natural parents and benefit when their parents maintain a civil, cooperative, coparental relationship (Nolan, 1970).

Stepfamilies with Adolescents

Since the difficulties of most American families with adolescents are legendary, it is not surprising that the additional complications of this phase in stepfamilies can push the stress level out of manageable bounds. Our clinical observations indicate that the following are the most common issues in stepfamilies at this phase:

1. The stepfamily push for cohesiveness at a time when the adolescent is concentrating on separation.
2. The lack of agreement on all sides as to how much active stepparenting or discipline an adolescent needs or will accept.
3. The adolescent's tendency to resolve divided loyalties by taking sides (Wallerstein & Kelley, 1974) or actively playing one side against the other.
4. The adolescent's resentment of major shifts in his or her customary family role and frequent overt resistance to learning new roles or engaging in new family relationships at a stage when he or she is concerned with growing away from the family.
5. The stress of sexual issues: dealing with sexual attraction to stepparent or stepsiblings; accepting the natural parent's sexuality.

Impact of Remarriage in Later Life Cycle Phases

Although there is not the daily strain of living with stepchildren and stepparents, remarriage at a post-childrearing phase of the family life cycle requires significant readjustment of relationships throughout both family systems, which may now include in-laws and grandchildren. Whereas there is some evidence (Bowerman & Irish, 1962) that it is initially harder for children to replace a parent lost through death than through divorce, it is probable that grown children and grandchildren will accept a remarriage after death of a parent more easily than after a divorce in middle or later years. There will often be great relief throughout the family if a widowed older parent finds a new spouse and a new lease on life, whereas a later-life divorce usually arouses concern and dismay throughout the family. One grown man spoke of feeling that all of his childhood memories had been challenged and required rearranging when his parents divorced in their sixties. He said he felt angry at both of them when they remarried for requiring him to try to figure out two new "foreign" relationships, and for depriving his children of "normal" grandparents. A grown daughter complained of the stress of sorting out the guest list for birthdays, graduations, and holidays, and was particularly upset when her father and his new wife remained in her old childhood home, "changing and redecorating my past." A frequent problem for older remarried couples is negotiating with each other how much financial assistance should be given to either set of adult children and how their wills should be made. The latter is likely to be even more of a problem where financial resources are large.

Clinically, we find that the major factor in three-generational family adjustment to remarriage in late middle or older age is the amount of acrimony or cooperation between the ex-spouses. Where the relationship is cooperative enough to permit joint attendance at important family functions of children and grandchildren, and where holiday arrangements can be jointly agreed upon, family acceptance of a new marriage tends to follow.

FAMILY THERAPY WITH REMARRIED FAMILIES: CLINICAL PROCEDURES AND ILLUSTRATIONS

Several years ago, finding ourselves faced with increasing numbers of remarried families in our own clinical work and in the caseloads of our trainees, we embarked on an informal project, discussing cases and developing clinical procedures for working with these families. The following is a summary of our work.

As indicated in column II of our developmental outline (Table 12.1), there are at least three key emotional attitudes that permit transition through the developmental steps involved in the formation and stabilization process for remarried families: resolution of the emotional attachment to the ex-spouse(s); giving up attachment to the ideal of first-family structure and accepting a different conceptual model of family; and accepting the time, space, ambivalence, and difficulty of all family members in moving toward stepfamily organization. Failure to achieve sufficient emotional grasp of these "enabling attitudes" will seriously hamper, delay, or prevent the reorganization and future development of the family.

Endless difficulties arise from well-intentioned, but misguided, efforts to draw firm boundaries around new household memberships; to push for primary loyalty and cohesiveness similar to first-marriage families; to exclude or combat the influence of natural parents and grandparents on their children; to deny differences and difficulties, or to try to act "as if" this family is just an ordinary household of parents and kids like the one next door. While it is true that the presenting problems frequently sound the same as the intact family next door, if the clinician fails to appreciate the structural differences and complexities, the family will receive little help.

Family therapists typically look back one or two generations to understand the presenting family problem. Thus, difficulty with a child will involve an evaluation of the parental marriage and of the parents' relationships with the grandparent generation. Whatever the presenting problem in a remarried family, it is essential to look laterally as well as back and to evaluate current and past relationships with previous spouses to determine the degree to which the family needs help in working out the patterns required by their new structure. Generally, we take the position that the more open the lines are to all family members, and the clearer the roles, the more functional the new structure. Ongoing conflict or cut-offs with ex-spouses, natural parents, and grandparents will tend to overload the relationships in the remarried family and make them problematic.

In first-marriage families, the major problematic triangles involve the parents with any or all of the children, and each parent with his or her own parents. In the more complex structures of remarried families, we have identified six of the most common triangles, and interlocking triangles. For the purposes of this chapter, we have limited our clinical illustrations to those commonly presenting in the households and nuclear subsystems of remarried families. In no way do we mean to suggest by this focus that the triangles with the extended family and grandparental generations are unimportant to the understanding and the therapy of remarried families. However, this process has been fully explicated elsewhere (Guerin, 1976; Bowen, 1978). In our clinical work with remarried families, coaching of the adults on further differentiation in relation to their families of origin proceeds in tandem with work on nuclear family problems for those clients motivated to do so. This aspect of the family therapy has been mostly deleted from the examples below because of the focus of this chapter.

One final caveat: the brief case stories are meant to illustrate possible clinical moves. What they fail to convey is the enormous intensity aroused by attempts to shift these relationships, the extreme anger and fear that block change, the many, many slips back, and the recycling of old conflicts that accompany each move forward. Our experience indicates that families willing to include work in their families of origin do better than those who do not.

Key Presenting Triangles in Remarried Families

1. The husband, the second wife, and the ex-wife. Or—the wife, the second husband, and the ex-husband.

Clinically, the variations of this triangle will usually be presented directly as the main problem only when the remarried couple acknowledge their own marital difficulties and come to therapy for that reason. (Actually, either or both variations of this are usually present, though perhaps not acknowledged, in problems with children and stepchildren.) When this triangle is presented as the main difficulty, usually around financial issues or sexual jealousy, it is likely that an emotional divorce has not been accomplished by the ex-spouses. There may be conflict among all three in the triangle, or a spouse may defend or excuse an ex-spouse's intrusions, while claiming to have no emotional attachment to the ex-spouse. In either case, therapy would need to focus on the completion of the emotional divorce between the ex-spouses. The first step in this most tricky clinical work is for the therapist to establish a working alliance with the new spouse, who will otherwise sabotage efforts to focus on the first marriage. Efforts to work on the resolution of the divorce by having either the ex-spouses alone or all three in sessions together will probably create more anxiety than the system can handle, and we have found that such work goes most smoothly when a spouse is coached in the presence of the new spouse to undertake steps outside of the therapy sessions that will change the relationship he or she currently maintains with the ex-spouse. This may require a lessening of contact, if the divorced spouses are still emotionally dependent on each other, or it may require becoming civil and friendly, if they have maintained their emotional attachment through intense conflict. Along the way, the new spouse will have to learn to acknowledge the past importance of that bond to his or her spouse and to accept the fact that some degree of caring will probably always remain in the relationship, depending on the length of time the first marriage lasted and whether or not there were children.

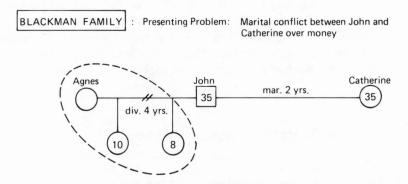

Figure 12.1.
KEY TRIANGLES IN REMARRIED FAMILIES
1. Triangle of Husband—Second Wife—Ex-wife

Blackman Family. Catherine and John Blackman, both in their mid-thirties, came for marital therapy after two years of marriage. He had been married before; she had not. John's first marriage had ended in divorce two years prior to their marriage, and his two daughters, ages eight and ten, lived with their mother, Agnes. Catherine and John described their problem as "endless conflict over money," which was caused, Catherine said, because John put the needs of his ex-wife over hers and gave in to her every demand for extra money. John defended his ex-wife's need for money and her refusal to work on the grounds that the children needed her. He said he felt guilty for leaving his first marriage, even though it had been unhappy, and that Catherine refused to understand his financial obligations to his previous family. Agnes had been drinking since their divorce, found the care of the children a burden, had no social life, and he could not kick her while she was down. John said that Catherine's claims that he cared more about Agnes than about her were untrue, as he barely responded to his first wife's frequent phone calls and never saw her alone.

After several sessions, Catherine agreed that John could not be free to plan a life with her until he had resolved the guilty attachment to his first wife, and that this would not be resolved, but exacerbated, by urging him to fight her or cut off all contact with her. Thereafter, with Catherine's somewhat ambivalent support, John arranged several meetings with Agnes during which he explained the limitations of his future financial support and offered to keep the children temporarily while she reorganized her life.

Since Agnes's angry accusations about the divorce had been predicted in a therapy session, John was able to hear them out fairly well without counterattacking. In joint sessions with Catherine alternating with John's outside meetings with Agnes and his children, he slowly rode out her angry tirades about the past, responded to the children's questions about the divorce, took responsibility for his part in their marital problems and his decision to divorce, and became firmer in his insistence that Agnes either work out a plan with him for the financial and emotional care of the children, or give custody of the children to him. Eventually, when her attacks on him provoked neither counterattacks nor guilty withdrawal, Agnes accepted the reality of the divorce and turned her attention to improving her life and the children's. With continued effort on John's part, their contact became both more friendly and less frequent. By the time they left therapy, Agnes phoned John only when necessary and had ceased criticizing Catherine to the children, who were now less hostile to her. During their joint sessions, and in sessions with John's children, Catherine had heard John express his sorrow at the failure of his first marriage and had learned to accept that part of his past without reacting personally. She moved very cautiously with the children, leaving all disciplinary decisions to John and Agnes.

2. The "pseudomutual" remarried couple; an ex-spouse; and a child or children.

In this triangle, the presenting problem is usually acting out or school problems with one or more children, or perhaps a child's request to have custody shifted from one parent to another. The remarried couple present themselves as having no disagreements whatsoever, and blame either the child or ex-spouse (or both) for the trouble. Although the request in therapy will be for help for the child, or for managing the child's behavior, the background story will usually show intense conflict between the ex-spouses, with the new spouse totally supportive of the battle against the former one, and the natural parent supportive of his or her spouse in conflicts with the stepchild. The first move in sorting out this triangle is to put the management of the child's behavior temporarily in the hands of the natural parent and get the new spouse to take a neutral position, rather than siding against the child. This move will probably calm things down, but they will usually not stay calm unless the pseudomutuality of the remarried couple is worked on, permitting differences and disagreements to be aired and resolved, and permitting the child to have a relationship with his or her natural parent that does not automatically include the new spouse every step of the way. Finally, work will need to be done to end the battle with the ex-spouse and complete the emotional divorce, the lack of which is perpetuated by the intense conflict over the child or children.

Bergman Family. Dr. and Mrs. Bergman came to therapy for help in dealing with Dr. Bergman's son, Larry, age fourteen. They had been married for one year, during which Larry lived with his mother, and visited on weekends. Nora Bergman's daughter, from her first marriage, Louise, age nine, lived with the couple. Nora's first husband had died of cancer when Louise was five. The Bergmans reported that their marriage was extremely harmonious, and that Louise was bright, cheerful, and pleasant, and had an excellent relationship with both

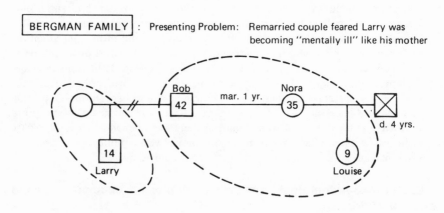

Figure 12.1.
KEY TRIANGLES IN REMARRIED FAMILIES
2. Triangle of Pseudomutual Couple—Ex-spouse—Child(ren)

her mother and stepfather. They were worried that Larry was becoming "seriously disturbed" in that his school grades had suddenly dropped dramatically and he was becoming increasingly truculent and withdrawn during weekend visits, provoking endless fights with Louise and refusing simple requests from Nora to pick up his belongings. Since Larry's mother was "an unbalanced person" who used every opportunity to "harrass" them, the Bergmans wondered if Larry were "also becoming mentally ill."

Bob Bergman worked long hours and left the management of the household and children to his wife, who, he reported, dealt pleasantly and "impartially" with both children. Mrs. Bergman agreed, saying that she loved Larry "as if he were my own son," and devoted herself entirely to the welfare of her "new family of four." She tried her best to be polite to the ex-Mrs. Bergman, but found her rude and almost impossible to deal with. She also felt the ex-Mrs. Bergman was a "harmful influence" on Larry, treating him inconsistently and occasionally leaving him alone when she went on dates. Larry reported that both of the Bergmans "hated" his mother, and he could not stand to hear them talk about her. He said his mother only phoned to check on his welfare because she knew that his father "left everything to that woman."

Therapy proceeded as outlined above. Bob Bergman agreed to be the liason to his son's school and was put in total charge of his behavior. He was also encouraged to take Larry on occasional trips alone. He admitted, after a lot of encouragement, that he and his wife had some different ideas on raising boys, but that he had not wanted to argue with her, since she was doing such a great job generally. Nora, when given permission to do so, finally admitted that it was difficult to be a part-time mother to a stranger, and was encouraged to rethink her role, since Larry already had a mother. When she backed off, Larry's behavior improved and the couple agreed to work on their relations with Larry's mother, although warning the therapist that she was "quite crazy." As the Bergmans stopped their end of the battle, the "crazy" behavior of Larry's mother diminished, although Bob was not willing to go very far toward resolving the old issues between himself and his ex-wife. The new Mrs. Bergman, however, did considerable work on resolving the mourning for her first husband, which had been incomplete, and was able for the first time to start telling her daughter about him and sharing old picture albums with her. This work, she said, made it easier for her to enjoy her second family and not try so hard to make everyone happy.

3. The remarried couple in conflict over the child or children of one of them: A. The husband, the second wife, and the husband's children.

This triangle, although not the most common household composition, is the most problematic, because of the central role of the stepmother in the lives of live-in stepchildren. If the stepmother has never been married before and if the children's mother is alive and has a less than ideal relationship with her ex-husband, it may be an almost impossible situation. Even the procedure of giving temporary complete management of the child or children to the natural parent is quite difficult if the father works long hours and the stepmother is the one who is at home. Nevertheless, some version of this is recommended, with the stepmother pulling back long enough to renegotiate with both her husband and the children what her role should realistically be. She is in the very difficult position of being expected to be the primary caretaker although she cannot replace the children's mother. No woman can successfully function in this situation while being overtly or covertly criticized by the children's father. She will have to be less fastidious and accommodate probably to fewer rules and restrictions; but he will have to actively participate in making and enforcing such rules as are agreed upon. When their immediate household is in order, the husband will have to work on establishing a cooperative coparental relationship with his ex-wife, or the conflict with her will set the children off again and inevitably reinvolve his new wife.

If the husband's first wife is dead, he may need to complete his mourning for her and help his children to do so, in order to let the past go and not see his second wife as a poor replacement of his first.

Burns Family. Sandy and Jim Burns came for marital therapy on the verge of divorce. Jim's first wife, Susie, had died of cancer when Jim's daughters were ages three and four. He had married Sandy a year later, and she had moved into their house, which Susie had decorated with exquisite taste. Although uncomfortable to be so thoroughly surrounded by signs of Susie, Sandy rationalized that it would be "wasteful" to redecorate the house and settled into it. She listened carefully while Jim explained all about the girls' routines, likes and dislikes, and tried to keep their lives exactly as they had been. As the years went by, with Jim criticizing every departure from "the way Susie did it," Sandy's nerves began to

BURNS FAMILY: Presenting Problem: Marital conflict over the children

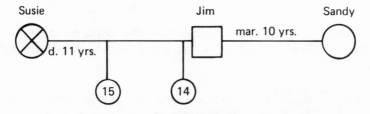

Figure 12.3A.
KEY TRIANGLES IN REMARRIED FAMILIES
3. Triangle of Remarried Couple in Conflict over Child(ren)
A. Husband—Second Wife—Husband's Children

fray and she became, in her own words, "a wicked stepmother." She screamed at the girls and at Jim and they exchanged glances and whispered about her. Once she threatened to redecorate the house, but backed down under Jim's anger. Now, with both girls teenagers and increasingly rude to her, and Jim withdrawn and sullen much of the time, she thought perhaps she should admit to failure and leave the marriage.

The first turning point in therapy came when Jim realized that in his grief for his first wife and his concern for his children's welfare, he had never really "made a place" for Sandy in the tightly knit bereaved system of himself and his daughters. He had never supported her authority with them and had continued to join them in their rebellion against her. He then willingly took charge of the girls' behavior and started supporting Sandy's authority with them. The next corner was rounded when the girls tested the shift with a great to-do about something, and Jim sided with Sandy against them. When Jim and Sandy's relationship was in better shape and the girls' behavior had improved, the therapy focused on the incomplete griefwork of Jim and the girls, who visited Susie's grave several times together. On their third visit, Jim invited Sandy to join them. After that, Sandy redecorated the house and hung a picture of Susie with their other family pictures. Throughout this period, Sandy worked on relationships in her family of origin, particularly with her mother, who had spent most of her life resisting Sandy's father's attempts to "tell her what to do."

B. The wife, the second husband, and the wife's children.

Numerically, this is the most common triangle in remarried households. As in the above example, the new spouse is seen as both rescuer and intruder. He is supposed to help his wife with the burden of raising her children, but may be given no point of entry into their system, which has had a long history before his time, perhaps drawing closer in the interval between the mother's marriages.

Cooper Family. Harold and Nancy Cooper sought treatment for Nancy's seventeen-year-old daughter, Susan, who had been arrested for shoplifting. Harold and Nancy had been married for three years, a second marriage for both. Harold's two daughters had remained in their mother's custody out of state, and Harold saw them infrequently. Not wanting to "fail at fatherhood twice," he had invested himself in making a good home for Nancy and her two children, Susan, fourteen at the time of the remarriage, and Kevin, twelve. Nancy's first marriage had ended in a bitter divorce and custody fight when the children were ages nine and seven, and they had spent the five years between the marriages as a tightly knit, beleaguered household of three, isolated from Nancy's parents, who didn't approve of divorce, and wracked by continuing legal battles between Nancy and her ex-husband. Harold complained that they had been in a state of turmoil since their marriage, in spite of great efforts to "become a 'real' family."

Harold blamed Nancy's "unruly" children, who did not know how to appreciate a good father, and Nancy alternately blamed Harold's "inconsistent han-

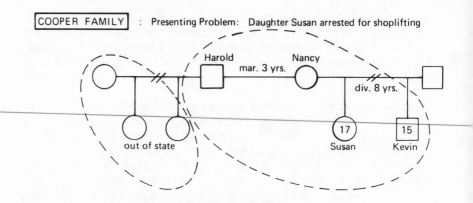

Figure 12.3B.
KEY TRIANGLES IN REMARRIED FAMILIES
3. Triangle of Remarried Couple in Conflict over Child(ren)
B. Wife—Second Husband—Wife's Children

dling" of her children, and her ex-husband's harrassment of them. She was desperately afraid that the trouble with the police would enable her ex-husband to succeed in his periodic attempts to gain custody of the children.

In an attempt to calm down the household before going into the triangles involving both ex-spouses, the therapist used the usual crisis technique of putting the natural parent completely in charge of the symptomatic child or children. However, because of Nancy's feelings of helplessness with her children and because of Harold's overinvestment in being a father to them, this "simple" shift was not accomplished for a very long time. Nancy and Harold agreed to try it, but Nancy consistently complained about Susan to Harold, who then intervened, sometimes criticizing Nancy, sometimes lecturing Susan, and was then strongly criticized by Nancy for his "poor handling" of the situation. The therapist, in a separate session, coached Harold to remain neutral in the conflicts between Nancy and Susan, with comments such as, "Why don't you two let me know how this comes out?" or "You're so perfectly matched, I don't know whom to bet on." For months and months, Harold tried to hold this position—sometimes succeeding—sometimes failing.

While the attempt to shift the presenting triangle went on in the background, the therapist addressed the interlocking triangles with both ex-spouses. When Nancy admitted that she invested more emotional energy in fighting her ex-spouse than she did in getting along with her present spouse, Harold was congratulated by the therapist, with paradoxical intention, for the support he gave to Nancy's "inspiring" dedication of her life to vengeance against her ex-husband. Both reacted strongly to this twist, and several weeks later Nancy announced that, if necessary, her ex-husband could have custody; she would fight him no longer. Throughout these events, the therapist discussed with Harold the history of his relationship with his natural children, bringing to the surface his agony at leaving them and his attempt to replace them with Nancy's children.

With the therapist's encouragement, and over frantic objections from Nancy, Harold began to write, phone, and visit his own children. At this point, he was finally able to detach from the conflict between Nancy and Susan, and that conflict subsided. Finally, Nancy was helped to let Harold deal with her children in his own way and not to call him into conflicts she had with them. In many concrete ways, Nancy "moved over" and let Harold into the system. Harold, having reinstated himself as father to his own natural children, now ceased demanding an intense relationship with Nancy's children and is working on defining for himself and with the children what a "stepfather" is. Nancy is contemplating what it would take to "bury the hatchet" with her ex-husband and develop a cooperative relationship with him.

4. The "pseudomutual" remarried couple; his children; and her children.

This triangle presents as a happily remarried couple with "no difficulties" except that their two sets of children fight constantly with each other. The children are usually fighting out the conflicts denied by the remarried couple either in their own marriage or in the relationship with either or both ex-spouses. Since direct confrontation of the pseudomutuality stiffens resistance, and since the presenting request is made for the children, it is wise to begin with an exploration of the triangles involving the children and ex-spouses, focusing on the welfare of the children.

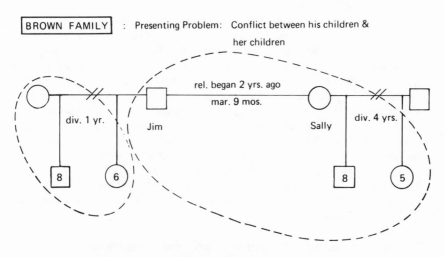

BROWN FAMILY : Presenting Problem: Conflict between his children & her children

rel. began 2 yrs. ago
mar. 9 mos.

div. 1 yr.   Jim   Sally   div. 4 yrs.

8   6   8   5

Figure 12.4.
KEY TRIANGELS IN REMARRIED FAMILIES
4. Triangle of Pseudomutual Couple—His Children—Her Children

Brown Family. Jim and Sally Brown requested family therapy because of the endless fighting between their children whenever Jim's children visited. Jim and Sally were in their thirties and had been married for less than a year. Their relationship had begun as an affair while Jim was still married, a fact that they believed was not known by Jim's ex-wife or children, two boys ages eight and six. Sally had been divorced two years prior to the affair with Jim and had custody of her two children, a boy of eight and a girl of five. The couple reported that they supported each other on all issues related to their ex-spouses; in fact, Jim frequently arranged the visits for Sally's children to their natural father, since it "upset Sally to argue with him." Jim's wife was a "disturbed person," whom he could hardly deal with, but, again, they worked together not to let her cause trouble for them. Sally had assured Jim that if his ex-wife's "irrationality" became too disturbing for his children, she would support him in attempts to gain custody of them and raise them with her own children.

Since none of this struck Jim or Sally as having anything to do with their children's battles with each other, the therapist spent several sessions educating them on children's loyalty conflicts and reactions to divorce and remarriage; their need, particularly at their ages, for support in the maintenance of relationships with both natural parents; and the time required for them to accept stepparenting. When this registered on Jim and he considered steps to improve his relationship with his ex-wife, their pseudomutual cover was blown as Sally collapsed in tears, threatening separation, termination of therapy, or whatever else she thought would deter Jim. In subsequent sessions, she confessed strong feelings of guilt and insecurity because of the affair, fearing that she had "taken him away from his wife, who would therefore be justified in trying to take him back." Very much later in treatment, Sally also recognized that the hidden agenda in her offer to raise Jim's children was the wish to eliminate contact between Jim and his ex-wife.

With the issues now out on the table where they could be dealt with, Jim and Sally were responsive to the therapist's suggestions that each take on, without the "help" of the other, the jobs of dealing with their respective ex-spouses, and managing their own children. Sally backed away from Jim's kids, they went on special outings with Jim alone, and the conflict between the two sets of children abated. The work of each of them in relationship to their ex-spouses was long and intense and they threatened to give it up, or divorce each other, many times during the process. The lack of time between Jim's marriages made his struggles with his guilty attachment to his ex-wife particularly intense, which then ticked off Sally's guilt and insecurity. Only after some period of work in their families of origin was each of them able to understand and take responsibility for his and her own contribution to the failure of their first marriages. Feeling less like "victims," they were able to reduce their tendency to huddle together helplessly against the "outside."

5. A parent, the natural children, and the stepchildren

As in the above case, this triangle may present as "simple" household conflict with the parent caught in the middle between his or her natural children and stepchildren. It is, in fact, quite complex, always interlocking with the triangle involving the remarried couple (who may have either a pseudomutual or a conflictual relationship), and the triangles with both ex-spouses.

Green Family. Florence Green sought a consultation to help her resolve a battle she was involved in with her eighteen-year-old son, Donald, who was threatening not to go to college at all if he couldn't go to the expensive school of his choice rather than the moderately priced college Florence preferred for him. Florence said she wanted to clarify her own position on this issue, which, she said, kept shifting. When she argued with Donald, she pointed out the sensible choices and good work habits of her stepson, Jimmy, also eighteen; yet, in the frequent and bitter battles with her husband, she accused him of always favoring "his" son over "hers." Florence reported that in their fifteen years of marriage, they had not yet become a family. The main reason she stayed in the marriage, she implied, was that she and her second husband had a mutual son who was only thirteen.

The Green family is an example of a remarried family that has not achieved integration and restabilization even after the passage of many years. They had married within a year of the termination in divorce of their first marriages. Florence had cut off her ex-husband, who, she said, only disappointed and neglected their son, Donald. Dr. Green, a wealthy physician, had engaged in a series of bitter custody battles with his ex-wife, which continued to the present day. A history of the attempts to integrate as a remarried family revealed that Florence, heavily invested in obtaining a "good father" for Donald, both pushed her husband toward her son, and then criticized his handling of the boy. In an attempt to make things work out, she made extra efforts to get along with her husband's son, Jimmy, which then aroused Donald's resentment. On his side, her hus-

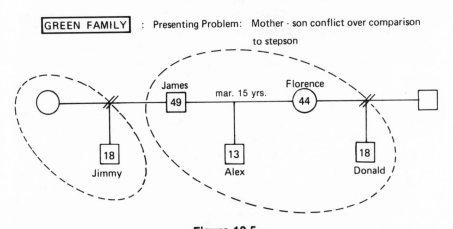

Figure 12.5.
KEY TRIANGLES IN REMARRIED FAMILIES
5. Triangle of Parent—Natural Children—Stepchildren

band's emotional energies went into the custody battles with his ex-wife and his professional practice, which was extremely demanding. He could not understand his wife's failure to appreciate the security he gave her and her son and became increasingly resentful of Donald's antagonism toward him and his son, Jimmy. The family alliances were prefectly reflected in James Green's recently drawn will, which left the major share of his estate to his son, Jimmy, a secondary legacy to the couple's mutual son, Alex, a smaller amount to Florence, and nothing to Donald. Florence worried that the uneven inheritances would continue the family feud in subsequent generations, pitting her own two natural sons, Donald and Alex, against each other, as well as destroying any relationship between Donald and Jimmy.

Family therapy in this complex situation required motivation on Florence's part to go back to the unresolved tasks of fifteen years ago and pull herself out of the triangles involving her husband and Donald on the one hand, and Donald and Jimmy on the other. Better progress would have been made initially if her husband could have been involved in the treatment and been persuaded to give up the battles with his ex-wife. Eventually Donald requested help in extricating himself from the scapegoat position and reconnecting with his natural father. Since the marital bond was in question, Florence had to find the motivation to initiate these changes for the sake of herself and her children. Once she could change her own part in the problems, and work on reducing her angry blaming of her ex-husband and present husband, she was able to decide that it was worth working toward stabilizing her second marriage.

6. The remarried spouses and the parents of either.

This triangle features the in-laws as part of the presenting problem, but it should be remembered that relationships with the grandparental generation are as crucial in remarried families as they are in all other families, and their exploration should be a part of a routine evaluation. The presentation of the older generation as part of the current problem is most likely to occur if they have disapproved of the divorce and remarriage, and/or been actively involved in caring for their grandchildren before or during the remarriage.

Hendrix Family. Mr. and Mrs. Hendrix had been married for two years when they appeared for marital therapy. John was a businessman in his middle forties and had been previously married. His ex-wife had custody of his three sons, the oldest of whom now lived with John's parents "because of the excellent high school in their town." Joan Hendrix was fifteen years younger than her husband and had not been married before. John said that their major problem was that Joan constantly fought with his mother and put him "in the middle." Joan stated that John's mother had never accepted John's divorce or their marriage, and that she talked and acted as if John were still married to his ex-wife, Ethel, with whom the older Mrs. Hendrix retained a very close relationship. Further, Joan complained, she had not yet had a honeymoon trip and every weekend was devoted to "entertaining" John's children in either their small New York apartment, or, worse, at John's parents' home in the suburbs. On the latter occasions, Joan said, her mother-in-law was cold and hostile toward her, interfered with every move she made toward John's children, and spoke constantly of Ethel's loneliness and financial difficulties. When they stayed overnight, John's mother insisted that the younger children room with them rather than "mess up" the living room. John never called his mother to task for any of this, but expected Joan to "understand that she meant well."

Since both John and Joan wanted their marriage to work out, they agreed to a bargain whereby Joan would stop criticizing and arguing with her mother-in-law, and John would clarify the boundary of his new marriage with his parents, his children, and his ex-wife. For openers, John and Joan took a belated honeymoon trip over the objections of his mother that he should not leave his children for so long a period. Thereafter, however, John's part of the bargain was easier said than done. During the extended period that John spent renegotiating his visitation arrangements, resolving his guilty attachment to his first wife, and reworking his relationships with his parents, there were many eruptions throughout the system. One of his children started failing in school, the older boy returned to live with his ex-wife, his father had a heart attack, and his ex-wife was hospitalized briefly for depression. With each upsurge of tension, Joan was pulled back into conflicts with her mother-in-law. These occasions lessened considerably when she started serious work in her own family of origin, from whom she had been estranged since her marriage. Although very pleased with the outcome after several years of intensive work, Joan said that she had "aged ten years trying to work out a marriage to a whole family instead of just to a person."

During the course of treatment, the therapist involved all of the family subsystems in sessions: the remarried couple alone, with John's children, and with

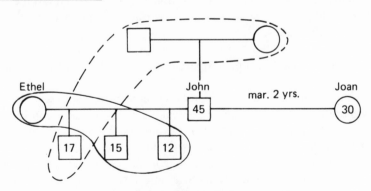

HENDRIX FAMILY : Presenting Problem: Marital conflict over husband's mother

Ethel   John   Joan
mar. 2 yrs.
45   30
17   15   12

Figure 12.6.
KEY TRIANGLES IN REMARRIED FAMILIES
6. Triangle of Remarried Spouses—Parents of Either

John's parents; Joan and her parents; Ethel and the children; Ethel alone; Ethel and her parents; and once, Ethel, John, Joan, John's mother, and the oldest son.

A few comments are in order here about our practice of involving ex-spouses in remarried family therapy. We include ex-spouses in joint sessions only when we have to deal with specific, relatively serious, child-focused agendas. Even in such situations, the level of tension and the lack of personal bonding between the first and second spouse often creates a climate of high anxiety and offers the therapist precious little leverage in his search for constructive resolution of family difficulties. Such a meeting may have primarily diagnostic value or be useful to underscore the seriousness of the child's situation. For some families only the passage of time helps them accept the inevitability of having to deal with each other.

However, we routinely contact an ex-spouse and invite him or her to meet alone or with the children to hear a report on our opinion concerning the children's problems that have been brought to our attention by the remarried family. When we inform the family of our intention to do this, we are frequently warned that the ex-spouse in question doesn't care, won't respond, or is "crazy." Nevertheless, such a phone call frequently locates a concerned parent who is perfectly willing to come in (although warning us that our client is "crazy"). These ex-spouses can frequently be engaged in subsequent sessions alone or with the children.

CONCLUDING REMARKS

With the repeated warning that no list of do's and don'ts can take the place of a clear theoretical framework and experienced clinical judgment, we would like to conclude with an outline of some attitudes and procedures that have helped us get a handle on the complexity of remarried families.

Our general goals involve establishing an open system with workable boundaries. This includes:

1. Developing a working, open coparental relationship between former spouses.

2. Working out the emotional divorce between former spouses. We assume this is not resolved if they are not speaking or if they have continuous conflicts. Anger is, of course, a very strong bond. As Truman Capote put it: "You can lose a lot of good friends, but it's hard to lose a good enemy."

3. Children should never have the power to decide on remarriage, custody, or visitation. The parental boundaries and responsibilities need to be clear, although children's input into decisions obviously increases with age.

4. Parents need to help children have the full range of feelings for all parents—accepting the divided loyalties.

As more specific rules of thumb, we have outlined the following:

1. (Obviously) Get a three-generational genogram and an outline of the previous marriages before plunging into the current household problems.

2. Keep in mind particular difficulties related to: (a) families being at different life cycle stages; (b) the emotionally central role of women in families and the special difficulties for them in moving into a new system; and (c) trying to maintain the myth of the perfect family.

3. Beware of families struggling with developmental tasks before they have adopted the prerequisite attitudes for remarriage (for example, parent pushing child and stepparent to be close without accepting that their relationship will take time to develop).

4. Related to #3—Help the family gain the patience to tolerate the ambiguity and not "overtry" to make things work out. This includes accepting that family ties do not develop overnight. Encourage stepparents to understand that a child's negative reactions are not to be taken personally, and help them to tolerate guilt, conflicted feelings, ambivalence, divided loyalties, and the like.

5. Include the new spouse in sessions in which you coach a spouse to resolve his or her relationship with an ex-spouse, at least in the beginning.

6. Take the frequent characterization of an ex-spouse as "crazy" with a large grain of salt. The list of the ex-spouse's outrageous behavior interdigitates with a list of your client's provocations and/or retaliations—it takes both to maintain and escalate the battle.

7. Where the remarriage ends a close single-parent/child relationship, the feelings of loss, especially for the child, have to be dealt with and the shift to a new system will take time.

8. If the child is presented as the problem, try to involve all parents and stepparents as early as possible in therapy. If joint sessions are held, the discussion should be directed toward cooperative work to resolve the child's difficulties (we do not permit discussion of marital issues at these meetings).

9. In problems involving child-focused uproar, help the stepparent back off and put the natural parent in charge of the child (more difficult with stepmothers). When the uproar subsides, coach the natural parent on ways to "move over" and include his or her spouse in the system—first, as spouse only. Warn the family that the shift to active stepparenting may take several years and will require the active support of the natural parent. In the case of older adolescents, it may not be appropriate to expect the shift to occur to any great degree at all.

10. Look at the "hidden agenda" in sudden proposals to rearrange custody, visitation, or financial arrangements.

11. Include work on the spouse's families of origin as early in treatment as possible.

REFERENCES

Bowen, M. *Family Therapy in Clinical Practice,* New York: Jason Aronson, 1978.

Bowerman, C. E., & D. P. Irish, "Some Relationships of Stepchildren to their Parents," *Marriage and Family Living,* May 1972.

Duberman, L., *The Reconstituted Family: A Study of Remarried Couples and Their Children,* Chicago: Nelson-Hall, 1975.

Glick, P.C., & A.J. Norton, "Number, Timing and Duration of Marriages and Divorces in the U.S.: June 1975," *Current Population Reports,* Washington, D.C., October 1976.

Goldstein, H.S., "Reconstituted Families: The Second Marriage and Its Children," *The Psychiatric Quarterly,* 48:3, 433–41, 1974.

Guerin, P.J., ed., *Family Therapy,* New York: Gardner Press, 1976.

Hetherington, E.M., M. Cox, & R. Cox, "The Aftermath of Divorce," in J.J. Stevens, & M. Matthews, eds., *Mother-Child, Father-Child Relations,* Washington, D.C.: NAEYC, 1977.

Kelley, J., & J. Wallerstein, "The Effects of Parental Divorce: Experiences of the Child in Early Latency," *American Journal of Orthopsychiatry,* 46/1, 20-32 January 1976.

Maddox, B., *The Half Parent: Living with Other People's Children,* New York: Evans, 1975.

Nolan, J.F., "The Impact of Divorce on Children," *Conciliation Courts Review,* 15/2, 25–29, 1977.

Ransom, J.W., S. Schlesinger, & A. Derdeyn, "A Stepfamily in Formation," *American Journal of Orthopsychiatry,* 49/1, January 1979.

Roosevelt, R., & J. Lofas, *Living in Step,* New York: Stein & Day, 1976.

Schulman, G., "Myths That Intrude on the Adaptation of the Step Family," *Social Casework,* March 1972.

Stern, P.N., "Stepfather Families: Integration Around Child Discipline," *Issues in Mental Health Nursing,* 1978.

Visher, E.B., & J.S. Visher, "Common Problems of Stepparents and Their Spouses," *American Journal of Orthopsychiatry,* 48:252–62, 1978.

———, *Stepfamilies: A Guide to Working with Stepparents and Stepchildren,* New York: Brunner/Mazel, 1979.

Walker, L., H. Brown, H. Crohn, E. Rodstein, E. Zeisel, & C. Sager, "An Annotated Bibliography of the Remarried, The Living Together, and Their Children," *Family Process,* 18/2, June 1979.

Wallerstein, J. & J. Kelley, "The Effects of Parental Divorce: The Adolescent Experience," *The Child in His Family,* Vol. 3, Anthony & Koupernik, eds., New York: Wiley, 1974.

———, "The Effects of Parental Divorce: Experiences of the Preschool Child," *Journal of the American Academy of Child Psychiatry,* 14/4, 1975.

13
Women in Families

Nora Reiner Gluck, A.C.S.W

Family Institute of Westchester

Yale University School of Medicine

Elaine Dannefer, A.C.S.W.

Family Therapist and Consultant in private practice,
Rochester, New York

Kathryn Milea

College of Medicine and Dentistry of New Jersey–
Rutgers Medical School

Women have always been central to the functioning of the family and their
identity defined in terms of their role as wives and mothers. The profound
changes in the lives of women over the last fifteen years created by the
Women's Liberation movement as well as social and economic forces have
brought a majority of women out of the home and into the workplace, yet
they still remain pivotal figures in the family. While new options and opportunities exist for women because of these changes, the complex choices
facing women today create new problems and pressures often stemming
from the conflict between their needs as individuals and their continued
role as primary caretaker of the family. In this chapter, we will examine
some of these changes, how they are affecting women as they move through
the family life cycle, and how they are changing the face of the family life
cycle itself.

Women are the barometers of family tensions and anxieties, and it should surprise no one that it is women, rather than men, who most often seek therapy for themselves, their marriages, and their children. In their role as physical and emotional caretakers of the family, their daily experiences are directly affected by the changes in each member within the family system, as they move together through the family life cycle.

From early childhood, girls are geared to see themselves in terms of their relationships to and connectedness with others. According to Russo (1979), the traditional female:

> . . . is expected to structure her life around many contingencies (Angrist, 1969): the need to fit the expectancies of an unknown spouse; the uncertainty about whether she will marry, and the necessity to provide a backup education and training "just in case" she does not; the possibility of childlessness, with the concomitant need to develop alternative activities; the disruption of routine when the children leave home, with the concomitant need to develop other options; and the possibility of divorce or widowhood; with the resulting necessity to prepare for some sort of occupation, again "just in case." (Russo, 1978, p. 114)

In contrast, men have traditionally had the responsibility for the family's economic welfare, and being the breadwinner generally precluded caring for the children. This split between the domestic and public spheres resulted in a father's becoming somewhat of a stranger in his own home, and often denied him the rewards of a close relationship with his children. However, it has also enabled men to use work to distance themselves from the stresses of family life while women have been left to provide the emotional haven for their families.

In the male experience, chronological age is seen as the key variable in adult developmental theories, and the common assumption is of a linear experience of stages and stage-related tasks, only some of which are directly related to the context of the family (Levinson, 1978; Gould, 1978; Vaillant, 1977). For women, on the other hand, the main determinants of life experience have been related to their functions in the family as wives and mothers.

Today's women are moving through the life cycle more rapidly than their grandmothers, and while they may put off the need to develop personal goals beyond the realm of the family, they can no longer ignore it. In addition, modern household appliances, processed foods, and factory-made clothing have reduced the historically varied functions of a housewife to that of consumer. In the last century, the home has evolved into little more than a human personality factory, with mother as chief engineer. Yet even those women who have children and choose to stay home with them face an "empty nest" stage that now equals in length the years primarily devoted to childcare. It would appear that the modern feminist movement was inevitable.

More than ever before, women are struggling to make room for their own personal growth in addition to their role as caretakers. They are changing the conditions of the traditional family life cycle by marrying later, having fewer children, divorcing and remarrying in unprecedented numbers, and simply living longer. Affirmative action programs have started to give some women equal pay for equal work, and helped some women choose careers and personal achievement for their own sake. But while the women's movement has opened up new vistas for women, it has also created unforeseen problems for them, as well as for their families.

Most women who enter therapy, regardless of the nature of the presenting problem, need help primarily in balancing their own personal needs with those of other family members. Many of these women have never truly experienced the phase of the unattached young adult, where one formulates personal goals and establishes a separate identity. Others may be the first in their families to attempt to do so, and are feeling anxious about exploring previously uncharted territory.

It is important for the therapist to be aware of the social, economic and psychological dilemmas that women bring with them to therapy. However, the premise that women are victims—of men, of society, of tradition, or whatever—implies total powerlessness and the inability to effect change. While we do not wish to deny that there are women who are physically and emotionally abused by their husbands and that following the traditional feminine path may make it extremely difficult for some women to initiate change, we wish to emphasize that each of us participates in maintaining the status quo, and has the responsibility to bring about change in our lives.

As family therapists, our focus must be to help the individual woman confront the origins and options of her situation, identify the part she plays in maintaining an undesirable set of circumstances, and work to change that part, while preparing to deal with the consequences of that change. In doing so, the therapist needs to be aware of the interrelated biological, sociocultural, psychological, and economic realties facing women, which increase the complexities of all their choices.

That there is an optimum time for childbearing is indisputable, and those women who delay marriage or having children to concentrate on careers must eventually come to terms with their own biological timeclock. In our society, both men and women have been committed to the idea that women should be the primary caretakers of children. At the same time, however, post-industrial society has devalued the role of wife and mother, and placed its emphasis on achievement in the workplace. Although women have more options than ever before, the structure of the workplace has not yet adapted to the needs of the family.

Men have never viewed career and family as mutually exclusive, because they have usually been blessed with the time-saving device of a wife. In fact, husbands whose wives have worked generally report less satisfaction in their marriages than those whose wives do not work outside the home. Since successfully combining career and family is somewhat of a super-human feat, women often feel caught between the two. The fact that women in their twenties and thirties are now experiencing greater psychological stress than women of comparable ages twenty years ago may be an indicator of the cost of that choice to some women (Friedan, 1980).

What is still more unfortunate is that most of the mothers who do work outside the home are working because they have no choice. They are either single parents or they have found that one income is no longer sufficient to manage a household. These women are doubly burdened, for the majority have also maintained primary responsibility for the children and the household chores.

The amount of stress a woman will experience at any particular phase of the family life cycle is, of course, dependent on her individual multigenerational history. While it is obvious that many women are now making choices without precedent in their families of origin, the infinite variety of cultural influences and individual family patterns makes it difficult to generalize about women's problems. For example, one could hardly expect the granddaughter of a suffragette to share the same problems with the daughter of a Mexican immigrant, and, in fact, Gump (1978) reported that black women do not seem to experience the same conflict about working that white women do.

Nevertheless, since women have been the keystone in the family structure, it is critical to our understanding of family problems to explore some of the particular dilemmas they face as they move through the family life cycle.

THE UNATTACHED YOUNG ADULT

Until recently, the major goal of most unattached young women was to find an unattached young man, and adolescent feminine self-esteem was usually based on male admiration. Of course, many upper- and middle-class women experienced the pseudoindependence of the college campus, but with their parents generally picking up the tab, it was hardly a substitute for knowing that one could take care of oneself. And, rather than plan their own careers or develop their own identities, most went to make themselves more marriageable and to find a husband of the appropriate social class.

For those who did not go to college, getting married was the only acceptable way for a daughter to move out of her parents' home; those with the highest degree of conflict with their parents often married the earliest, and the least successfully. Many of these early marriages were precipitated by premarital pregnancies, with nearly one-third of all first births in the early 1970s conceived before marriage (Glick & Norton, 1977).

For girls of any class, the peer group was of secondary importance, while boys seemed to value male companionship for its own sake. It was a rare adolescent boy who was left home on a Friday night because his steady was "out with the girls." On the other hand, girls had an "understanding"—a date automatically took first priority over plans with a girlfriend.

Aside from the anxiety generated by the need to be popular, and the fear of not having a date for the big dance, this stage may have been significantly less problematic for past generations of women. It was young men who were faced with the critical life choice, "What will I be when I grow up?" For women, there were fewer choices and less pressure for personal achievement.

When women did work, their occupational choices were representative of traditional feminine values, as well as of the status of women in the culture. They nurtured children as teachers, comforted the sick as nurses, helped the disadvantaged as social workers, and assisted male executives as secretaries. Employment was viewed as filling a present need, something to do until a husband was found or a child born. The most future-oriented women saw teaching or nursing as something they could "go back to," a career that would fit the needs of a family.

This lack of future orientation is also reflected in the promotional patterns in predominantly female occupations. Teaching is an end in itself, and other than yearly pay increments there are very limited possibilities for promotion within school systems. The fact that most principals are men narrows those possibilities somewhat further. Nursing and social work offer similar lack of advancement, and a secretary's status within an organization rests not on her own title, but on that of her boss. Considering that these occupations represent some of the better choices open to women in the past, it is not difficult to see why marriage and family seemed like a preferable option to most women.

Then why have some women always been able to succeed in a man's world? Margaret Hennig's study (1973) of the family dynamics of twenty-five high-achieving women suggests that their relationships with both parents were good, with both mother and father valuing femininity and achievement. What is even more interesting is that each of these women was either an only child or the eldest in a family of two or three girls. It seems that these women received parental support for achievement that might ordinarily have been diverted to a brother. Each of these women also postponed marriage until her career was settled, and none of them had children.

In a similar study, Lozoff (1973) noted that high-achieving women generally had mothers who were the admiring wives of brilliant men. Perhaps because of their strong positive identification with their fathers, and because they found something lacking in their mother's role, they chose a less traditionally feminine path for themselves.

Radical societal changes over the last decade have opened up a variety of options to women, and today more young women are likely to be ambivalent about traditional feminine goals. While the average age for women at first marriage in 1978 was 21.8, in that same year almost 50% of the women aged 20 to 24 were still single (an increase of one-half since 1960), and 18% of those between 25 and 29 were unmarried (Census Bureau, 1978). This dramatic increase in the number of women in the unattached young adult stage suggests that more and more young women feel there is an alternative to early marriage, but it may also reflect the growing caution among young adults in the wake of the soaring divorce rate.

Many who seek clinical help are either overly close to or cut-off from their parents. They may suffer from loneliness because their inability to form comfortable and stable intimate relationships with peers has led them to hang on to unsatisfactory and even destructive relationships, or to avoid emotional attachments. Others exhibit difficulties with work or career plans due to underlying role conflict.

However, other single young women who come for therapy may be basically healthy, have good relationships with their families of origin and with peers, but are struggling with some of the pressures of being a woman in our society. In trying to get priorities for the development of a self, a process that young men usually take for granted, women have few role models. So, a young women finds herself caught between the desire to have a permanent relationship with a man and her own needs for self-exploration and personal growth.

The following example illustrates some of the problems of a young woman who is struggling with these issues. Although the forms that these problems take are somewhat extreme, the underlying themes are fairly typical.

> Carol, a twenty-five-year-old teacher and Ph.D. candidate, had been cut-off from her family for several years since her mother's death. Feeling lonely and isolated, she became involved with a young man who was very ambivalent about their relationship and critical of her because she was sexually experienced. Not only was he hostile to her, as her father had been when she was growing up, but he threatened to break up with her because he thought she was flirting with his friend. This led her to seek psychiatric help. She was unable to do any work on her thesis, and was finding it difficult to make friends. Despite the destructiveness of the relationship with the young man, she continued to fantasize about marrying him, and feared losing him because she felt she had nothing else in her life.

Carol's mother had been single until her late twenties and lived with her parents on a farm until Carol's father appeared. Her mother was so desperate to marry that she literally married the first man who came along. She remained passive in an unhappy marriage and developed uterine cancer in her late forties, which caused her premature death.

Carol despised her father for the control he excercised over his wife, but she was also contemptuous of her mother's passivity and was determined not to end up in the same position. She had derived most of her self-esteem as a teenager from scholastic achievement, which was valued by her mother who encouraged her to apply to graduate school. Her father, however, thought higher education was a waste of time and money for women and he constantly reminded her that the most important thing in life for a woman was marriage and children. Despite her father's negative attitude, she managed to obtain a fellowship for graduate study and completed her course work for a Ph.D. However, after her mother's death during graduate school she began to feel an overwhelming need for a man to "save my life and solve my problems." Through therapy she began to reconnect with her father and deal with him in a different way, particularly around the issue of her decision to pursue educational and career goals. She then decided to leave her boyfriend, work on her thesis, and find a job. While she still felt quite anxious about getting married, she came to realize that unless she could find her own identity in work and her family of origin, she would end up completely dependent on a man, just as her mother had been.

A woman's view of her mother's life choices and the quality of her parents relationship are of critical importance at this stage, for she has learned about marriage and family relationships from observing how her own mother has handled them. For example, if she feels her mother has sacrificed too much of herself for husband and children, she may postpone marriage and pursue a career. If a woman is having difficulty separating from her family of origin, she will have a hard time defining who she is and making choices for herself. If she has been able to separate, her choices are more apt to be guided by her own inner needs and desires and not by her parent's program for her. The issue of how to divide life between marriage, family, and career is crucial to women throughout the life cycle, but it is at this stage that the question is of special concern (Stewart, 1976).

Actually, it is no wonder that "liberated" young women are having difficulty with their pioneer trek through this phase today. One of their chief problems is lack of role models. Studies of successful men have illustrated the pivotal role a mentor often plays in a man's career (Levinson, 1978; Roche, 1979). A mentor serves the function of a substitute father in a man's professional life, offering encouragement and special guidance to his protégé. The twenty-five women in the Hennig study also had mentors, relationships we could assume found their antecedents in their positive relationships with their fathers.

Perhaps for many other competent women, relationships with potential male mentors developed in more traditional ways, such as the office romance or trysts between professors and students. If a young woman should seek therapy at this stage of her life, a female therapist may serve this mentor function by being an effective female adult who has a career (Hare-Mustin, 1978). This role model function will be particularly important to the woman who has received mixed messages about the value of being a wife and mother (Stewart, 1976). Hopefully, the next generation of young women will have more female role models to help them through this transition.

What of a woman who remains single until her late twenties or early thirties? She may successfully have separated from her family of origin, found a positive and rewarding work identity, and be able to have intimate peer relationships. Her ambivalence about making a commitment to marriage may spring from her negative view of her parents' marriage and her fear of repeating their pattern. Even if she is able to work this out, she may find it difficult to find an appropriate mate due to the diminishing availability of eligible men as she gets older. At this point, she may come to terms with the fact that she may never marry, and reevaluate her career plans. She might decide to go back to school for a higher degree or to work toward job advancement in her chosen career.

If a woman remains single after completing the tasks of this stage, she does not stop developing. Her personal growth continues, although her commitment may be to a career, a social cause, or a small group of friends instead of to a husband and children. She may experience relating to children through nephews and nieces, or the children of close friends. While feelings about having remained unmarried and childless may come up for her at a later stage—as for example when most of her contemporaries are having grandchildren—it is probably sometime in her thirties that she will have to do the most work with herself and her family around her decision.

THE NEWLY FORMED FAMILY

Even with many women choosing to remain single until their mid-twenties, the average age for women at first marriage is still relatively young. Most women want to and do get married before the age of thirty.

The majority of women find the early years of marriage before the birth of children among the most satisfying, but they have also seen it as merely a stepping stone to the next stage. The average couple moves into the next phase within two or three years of marriage, and the purpose of this stage is usually seen as taking some time to adjust to each other first, thereby becoming more fit for parenting.

However, it would appear that marriages at this stage may come the closest to being the egalitarian ideal of modern marriage. Almost all wives work until the birth of their first child, and roles of husbands and wives are far less polarized than at later stages, which may account for the wife's greater happiness relative to other stages of the family life cycle. In recent years, the increasing numbers of men attending graduate and professional schools have resulted in many young wives becoming the sole provider at this stage. This arrangement may give a woman a position of relative power in her marriage never to be enjoyed again. In fact, the woman who alters her own career plans and/or place of residence, and either quits school or takes a dead-end job, reduces her future bargaining power. Her short-term happiness may be high, but in the long-run her adaptive response consolidates her dependent position, making her more likely to develop symptoms at a later time, as for example when her children are adolescents.

Such a pattern was almost universal in marriage cohorts before the 1970s. Younger men seem to find it easier than older men to accept a woman's quest for an independent life, but it appears that most men still expect women to fit their lives into a more traditional pattern (Lynn, 1974). Even men who are sincerely concerned about sexism find it difficult to change the subtle forms of sexist assumptions in their own behavior, and when both husband and wife work or have equal careers, the woman is still likely to take most of the responsibility for running the household and for the emotional relationships in the family.

More young wives are now demanding that their husbands share housework, and fewer husbands are daring to refuse. However, while the tacit agreement may be that they will share the housework, this is probably much easier said than done. A woman who learned to be a housewife at her mother's knee is likely to see household chores much differently from her husband who learned they were someone else's problem.

Even though the woman's movement has raised the expectations women have for marriage, few couples seek therapy at this stage of the family life cycle. It would appear that most wives are able to satisfactorily manage a job and household chores, and this stage is not nearly as stressful as the one precipitated by the birth of the first child.

Before the advent of children, there may also be less incentive to negotiate issues that are causing problems in the marriage. As more of the basic assumptions of the marriages of their parents and grandparents become subject for conflict, many women are leaving relationships they feel will hinder their growth as individuals.

The reality is that marriage today is a pretty risky proposition—one out of three marriages ends in divorce—and that married women are more likely than unmarried ones to seek psychiatric help, report stress-related symptoms, and attempt suicide (Seiden, 1976). Research indicates that marriage seems to lower the incidence of depression in men, but increases it in women (Weissman, 1977).

At this stage of the life cycle, as at others, women characteristically make a bigger ego investment in their relationships with others, while their husbands concentrate their energies on personal achievement. Goodrich, et al. (1968) found that young wives with a history of conflict within their families of origin felt less happily married, were having trouble getting along with friends and their husband's family, and also had frequent disagreements over housekeeping. These findings were to be expected, since childhood or adolescent unhappiness is thought to be positively correlated with marital dissatisfaction.

However, at the same time, they found that men from similar family of origin backgrounds did not report the same high levels of marital dissatisfaction their female counterparts did. Instead, they tended to find wives who were more traditional—substitute mothers, perhaps—and then concerned themselves with their own occupational issues. One could argue that this is a defense against intimacy, but it is a defense that is certainly supported by the larger society.

By far the most difficult choice many couples make today is whether or not to have children. As opportunities for women have increased, the option of remaining childless and pursuing a career has become more attractive to some women. In 1967, only 1.7% of wives between the ages of twenty-two and twenty-four expected to remain childless, while in 1976 women in the same age group reported that 5.3% expected not to have children (Blake, 1979). Although we are still talking about a relatively small percentage of the population, there has been a substantial rise in the incidence of voluntary childlessness. As more women are giving serious consideration to the question of whether or when to have children, more couples are coming into therapy over this issue, as in the following example.

Diane, a twenty-seven-year-old graduate student, began to feel depressed about her marriage to Jerry, became attracted to another man, and decided to separate from her husband. She felt this was her last chance to find out if she wanted to make a lifetime commitment to Jerry, who was finishing graduate school and starting to talk about his desire for children. She feared that since he was extremely involved in his own work, the responsiblities of children would fall primarily to her.

As we explored Diane's family of origin, it became clear that she felt very close to her father, whom she admired and with whom she identified. She was afraid she would eventually feel trapped, as her mother had, in an unsatisfying marriage. Her mother's dissatisfaction was becoming more apparent since her youngest brother had left home to attend college, and Diane sensed this, even though her mother was 3,000 miles away.

When she spoke to her mother about her own marital dissatisfaction and trial separation, her mother said she was also seriously considering divorce from her husband after almost thirty years of marriage. She said she felt she could do this now that all her children were leaving. In view of her mother's life, Diane perceived the decision to have children as having great significance for her future. It became clear to her that she was not ready to make such a commitment since she did not feel certain about her marriage to Jerry. Jerry was pressuring Diane to return to their apartment, but she felt a compelling need to be by herself at this time.

The therapist's job was a difficult one, for each was pushing for a fast and painless solution—Jerry for immediate reconciliation and Diane for instant freedom to experiment with other relationships.

A woman in conflict about whether or not to have a child often has not resolved her feelings about her parents. Family of origin coaching can be very useful in helping her establish an adult relationship with each of her parents and open up important issues in all of their lives. Of particular significance in the decision about having a child will be those issues relating to her mother's feelings about her life as a wife and mother. By becoming more objective about her own mother, the young woman is better able to make choices based on her own inner needs.

The decision to have a child is usually a conflictual one for a woman with a serious career commitment. It is crucial for her to have a marital relationship that is flexible enough to accommodate her desires regarding career and family. Since she is likely to be primarily reponsible for child care, she must also work out a number of issues with her employers.

Women who ultimately decide not to have children may need help in dealing with all the familial, societal, and peer pressures to bear children. Of course, as more women opt not to have children, the stigma of childlessness in marriage will undoubtedly lessen, and Rossi (1975) predicts that in the next decade, as many as 10% of married women may choose this path.

On the other side of the coin are the couples who are unable to conceive. Among the increasing ranks of women who marry later and postpone pregnancy until after their most fertile years, there may be reduced fertility. While the use of birth control pills and the availability of abortion have allowed women more control over when and under what circumstances to have children, they have also contributed to fertility problems. Regardless of the individual circumstances, the stress on the marriage caused by the discovery of infertility should not be minimized, since most people who marry expect to have children. Whether it draws the couple together or creates distance between them will depend on the individuals involved, but many women may need help in reevaluating their marital relationship at this time. If her life has been based on traditional feminine goals, a wife will have a much bigger personal adjustment to make than her husband.

Until recently women were generally blamed and stigmatized for the inability to have children. This failure was attributed to deep inner conflicts about their femininity and ambivalence toward motherhood (Mazor, 1979; Kleiman, 1979). Therapists should be aware of what a devastating blow it can be for a woman to realize that she may not be able to have a child, and help her go through the mourning process for the children she will never have.

THE FAMILY WITH YOUNG CHILDREN

Pregnancy offers nine months to get ready for motherhood, but there is very little in a woman's previous life experience to prepare her for the reality of being totally responsible for the welfare of an infant. Although motherhood is deeply satisfying for most women, a child's need for round-the-clock nurturance stretches beyond the capacity of any one person. The frequency of postpartum depression, particularly after the birth of the first child, is often thought to be triggered by a hormonal imbalance. However, it may also reflect the woman's sense of the loss of her former freedom and the overwhelming nature of her new responsibilities. Her sense of losing her connectedness to the outside world may be especially strong if she has left her job to devote her energies to full-time motherhood. In addition, the birth of a child requires that a woman rework many of the important relationships in her life. The amount of difficulty she will have in doing this will depend on how successful she has been in accomplishing the tasks of the previous stages. She will have less time for her husband, her family, her friends, and herself. Her husband, in particular, may resent that his wife's reduced energy level interferes with their sex life, or that they are not able to socialize as much. Since his wife is no longer working, he may now assume that household chores are her sole responsibility, even if he had been more helpful before. His difficulty in accepting second place in his wife's affections may cause him to distance into work at this time (see Bradt, Chapter 6).

Unresolved conflicts with parents, especially the woman's mother, are also likely to surface at this time. Even if the couple were successful in setting boundaries for their parents, the birth of a grandchild will usually signal their active reentry into the system. If a young woman is either cut-off from or fused with her mother, she is apt to be much more uncertain and anxious about her new role, and may need help to reconnect with her mother in a more adult way.

Mothers often report that the births of subsequent children are easier than the first, probably because they are more sure of their capacity to mother. However, each additional child multiplies the problems of routine and the complexity of family relationships.

Although much has been written about the effect of parents on children, little research has been done on the impact of a child's development on his or her parents. This stage of the family life cycle is not only characterized by the intense demands of small children, but their extremely rapid development requires an almost constant process of readjustment for their parents. Within one year, a child progresses from a suckling infant who needs to be fed every three to four hours and held almost constantly, to a toddler who, though he or she may sleep through the night, is capable of climbing on furniture, crawling upstairs, and generally destroying anything in his or her path. A mother must not only rearrange her daily activities to accommodate her child's growth, she must also gradually move from almost complete absorption with her newborn infant to allowing the child ever-increasing autonomy as it becomes appropriate.

A mother's success in this may have something to do with the tempermental "fit" between herself and her child. For instance, if a mother has a rather low energy level, and her child a high-energy level, she may perceive the child as difficult. A child's resemblance (real or imagined) to a person with whom the mother or father has unresolved conflicts—spouse, parent, sibling, or even self—can also interfere with the relationship between parents and child. A child who is perceived as "special" by the mother or father (or both) because of birth order, sex, adoption, or being handicapped or physically ill, is at greater risk for becoming the focus of the nuclear family projection process. Child abuse illustrates an extreme example of the projection process, as most abusive parents were themselves abused as children, and abusive mothers are generally isolated young women cut-off from family and unable to form close friendships.

The reason that we are emphasizing the mother's relationship with the child is because of her position of centrality in the family. Thus, while the father also has emotional issues with his children, it is usually the mother who must deal directly with them on a daily basis. A father may distance to work during the day and be protected from his wife's problems with the children when he is home, making it likely that the mother will become overinvolved with them. Not only does she react to her own emotional issues with her children, but she may also be acting on her husband's behalf as well. While this is done under the guise of protecting him from becoming emotionally upset, it is likely to lead to more tensions for her, thereby creating the almost classic triangle of overinvolved mother, distant "daddy," and conflictual or distant spouses.

Isolation from family support systems and friendship networks adds further stress to the lives of many young mothers. With the average American family moving at least once every seven years, many more nuclear families are hundreds or even thousands of miles away from their extended families, who might be able to help a mother with her childcare responsibilities. In their study of the effects of moving on families, Weissman and Paykel (1972) found that depressive symptoms were often the result of a move, and that women were more subject to the stresses created by moving than were men. This is because the mother is usually left to her own devices while her husband is pursuing his advancement up the career ladder at work. The following clinical example illustrates the case of a woman who became severely depressed following a move.

> Susan, a twenty-six-year-old married woman with a two-year-old son, came to the clinic because she had been depressed for several months and began feeling suicidal.
>
> Susan's pregnancy had been unplanned and the birth of her son was stressful. After the delivery, she not only had primary responsibility for child care, but she also had to keep the house immaculate to meet the demands of her husband, Don. In addition, she worked as a nurse to help support the family while Don completed his education. Her depression had not become apparent until she and her husband moved in the hope that he could find a permanent job. He had not yet been able to do so, and Susan was furious at him. Her feelings of emotional isolation and entrapment led to resentment toward her husband and thoughts of suicide.
>
> In addition to helping Susan separate from her family of origin, a task she had never completed, therapy focused on teaching her to communicate some of her anxiety to her husband, who then became more receptive to her needs and less demanding of her. They began to go out more as a couple and make friends with other couples. But more to the point, Susan came to define her life more for herself and rearranged her housekeeping and childcare schedule to include a variety of her own social and educational pursuits.

Even a move from a city neighborhood to a nearby suburb can be an isolating experience for a mother of young children. She may find it increasingly difficult to make friends since women are delaying childbearing and having fewer children, and half of all women with children (including one-third of all women whose children are under three) are now in the labor force. Mothers who choose to stay at home now sometimes feel they have to explain being "just a housewife."

However, employment is not the answer for all women. For some this means increased personal options, but for others it means additional burdens and even less time or energy to think of their own needs. A job may seem particularly oppressive to the young woman who returns to work sooner than she might ordinarily have done in order to contribute to the family income. Families appear to do best when mothers who prefer to be housewives stay home, and those who prefer employment can find work (Seiden, 1976).

Lack of adequate day-care facilities and the persistence of traditional male attitudes make returning to work difficult for any mother. In addition, every mother has to face her own guilt at leaving her young child in the care of someone else. Society, especially the childrearing experts, still define a good mother as one who is home with her children. Mothers have been assigned the responsibility for their child's mental health, and husbands and grandmothers often collaborate in this, adding to the young mother's burden of guilt.

Sheehy (1976) noted that a woman may find it impossible to "do it all" in her twenties, while a mother in her thirties may have a better chance. With more women pursuing careers prior to marriage and childbirth, there is currently a marked increase in older mothers of young children. However, since a woman's most fertile years are in her twenties, a woman who tries to become pregnant after thirty or thirty-five faces increased risks in conceiving, carrying and giving birth to a child. Amniocentesis can detect certain chromosomal defects, such as Down's Syndrome, more likely to occur in older women, and provide the option to abort; but there are other birth defects and risks to both mother and child that cannot be predicted or prevented.

Yet many older mothers feel that the rewards of late motherhood outweigh the difficulties. Unlike her younger counterparts, she is more likely to have a supportive husband who has accepted her commitment to a career, and is willing to share in the childrearing, as well as help to provide money for child-care arrangements. The older mother may also have the advantage of having a career that is sufficiently well developed as to enable her to cut down on her work commitments in order to spend more time with a new baby.

Nonetheless, the stresses of trying to balance marriage, motherhood and career should not be minimized; and they can be compounded by the reduced physical energy of a woman in her thirties, who often finds herself out of step with friends who may already have adolescent children. No matter how independent and mature, few women are completely free of guilt and concern about not staying home with their young children. In most situations, there is not enough flexibility in the career woman's work schedule to allow her as much time at home as she might like, and even in dual-career marriages, the woman is probably going to feel overburdened (Bird, 1979). Bird found that egalitarian arrangements occurred most often in marriages where the wife's income was equal to or more than her husband's, a circumstance not common to most marriages.

Although the birth of the first child and the years of caring for young children are considered to be stressful, many women are able to move through these transitions with relative ease. In fact, married women with young children do not usually seek treatment for themselves for several reasons. It may be that the societal myth that motherhood is the fulfillment of her purpose in life inhibits any expression of unhappiness that would mark a woman as lacking in the area where she is supposed to be most competent. It could also be that she lacks the time and energy to be concerned enough about her own needs to seek therapy. If her husband is opposed to her seeking treatment she may not have the financial resources to do so on her own, or she may doubt whether her personal happiness is worth the investment. Mothers of preschoolers might benefit most from concrete services such as day-care and homemaker services, as well as the opportunity to discuss common concerns with other young mothers (while someone else watches the children).

Sometimes it is when the child begins school that symptoms are noticed that bring the family into treatment (Haley, 1973). Many mothers of children who are referred to child guidance clinics or family service agencies are depressed themselves (Weissman, et al., 1972). Often these are child-focused families in which the parents deny their own problems and concentrate on their symptomatic child; as therapy progresses, work on the marriage, and then on each individual can be introduced. The mother should be encouraged to look at her own life and to begin to explore issues of her personal identity, and perhaps expand her life to include activities outside of the family.

This is sometimes a difficult adjustment for a husband who expects his wife to devote all her energies to home and family. For many women it is just as difficult to relinquish control of the home and children. A wife may complain about her husband's lack of involvement and then criticize his every move toward more participation in family life. If he is to take a more active role, she must first learn to pull back and leave some space. For a husband to fully participate, he must do it *his* way (paper plates, uncertain bedtimes, whatever), and the wife must resign as "expert" if she wants more balance in the family.

Sometimes resistance to change may take the form of active opposition to women's rights, as if progress and equality were a threat to women's continued importance in family life. It is important that the therapist be sensitive to a woman's fears of being discarded or displaced by moves away from her family. If the therapist is a woman, a female client may view the therapist as trying to force "liberation" on her and this may mobilize her resistance to change. In these cases, the therapist should be careful not to impose her own solution on her clients, and in particular not to oversell work outside the home as an answer. As Hare-Mustin (1978) points out, jobs for women are frequently boring and underpaid, and "the encouragement of women to go out and work without reduction in their work load at home may be but a thinly disguised punitive act." Also, some women genuinely enjoy being housewives and have no desire for paid employment. These women may feel subtly "put down" for choosing to remain at home. A therapist can help alleviate a client's feeling that she "should" work and this may free her to choose a direction that is genuinely rewarding to her, such as community involvement, learning a craft, or taking a course.

In any case, if the issue of expanding her activities outside the home does not come up during this phase of the family life cycle, it is likely to come up in the next phase as her children begin to separate from the family.

THE FAMILY WITH ADOLESCENT CHILDREN

At this stage in the family life cycle, both parent and child are undergoing major interlocking transitions in their development. Adolescence signifies a shift in allegiance to the peer group that coincides with their parents' mid-life crisis.

As adolescents begin the process of separating from their families, conformity to the peer group is valued above all else. They are prone to adopt distinctive styles of dress and often develop an affinity for blaring rock music on their stereos. These, of course, are among the mildest forms of teenage rebellion. Other forms of acting out behavior—drinking, drug abuse, vandalizing public property, and sexual experimentation—are much more distressing, particularly to the mother whose identity is tied up in parenting. What makes this stage even more confusing to parents is that it is never clear when an adolescent is making a genuine move towards independence or when he or she is really looking for a parent to set limits. The child's behavior may lead a mother to feel useless and ineffective. These feelings of rejection can make it more difficult for her to be there when her child does need her.

Concern with adolescent children is a common theme for women at this stage. Since mothers are generally more in tune with the emotional ups and downs of family members than fathers, they are apt to respond more to the many mood swings of their adolescents. A woman who has based her self-esteem on how well her child is doing is likely to be more affected by her child's struggle to separate (Spence & Loner, 1971). Lowenthal, et al. (1977) found significant stress among those women whose children show signs of not adopting parental values or life-style, and for many of these women the issue of control may lead to parent-child conflict. Adolescent children also evoke memories of a parent's own adolescent turmoil, and if a mother's adolescence was especially stressful, she may become less sure of her parenting. For example, if a woman had difficulty handling sexual issues as an adolescent, her adolescent child's budding sexuality may become a tense issue between them. (Of course, this is equally true for fathers and their adolescent children.)

These developmental issues require shifts in the family system, not only to allow children to move in and out, but also for reassessment of the marital relationship. Idealistic adolescent children, by virtue of their tendency to find fault with all their parents' values, and their increased ability to verbalize such criticisms, may even be the catalyst for marital problems. Some research suggests that marital dissatisfaction tends to peak toward the end of this phase of the family life cycle. Rollins and Feldman (1970), Burr (1970), and Lowenthal, et al. (1977) all found women whose youngest child was a senior in high school more negative than their husbands about their marriage and more affected by conflict over children. While the men reported being stressed by work-related problems, the women, including those women who worked outside the home, focused on children and spouse-related problems. This may account for the fact that it is generally the woman who initiates therapy for adolescent children or marital problems. The following clinical example is a good illustration of a woman with adolescent children who is faced with problems in her marriage.

> Sheryl was a severely depressed thirty-seven-year-old woman whose husband refused to acknowledge the need for marital therapy. Her marriage was a very traditional one in which she was the primary nurturer and caretaker, and he the provider who worked two jobs. Realizing that he had many women friends, kept late hours, and had increased his use of alcohol, she was left with a sense of panic because she feared being rejected by him.
>
> The first step was to work on her family of origin, going back to issues not adequately dealt with when she was a separating young adult. Her relationship with her parents had always been fairly distant. During her childhood, her father had exhibited outbursts of temper, and she readily related that when her husband became angry he looked like her father. She had repeated her mother's pattern of stepping in to protect the children and had dealt with her own fear of her husband's anger by lying about things that would lead to conflict, or by avoiding contact.
>
> As Sheryl began to establish a relationship with her parents, especially her father, she began to lessen her pursuit of her husband and became less reactive to her husband's anger. She also began to stay out of the go-between position with her husband and children. These steps enabled her to begin dealing with her sense of emptiness and fear of being alone, and the need to create a more satisfactory life for herself.

It is common for women in this stage to refocus on the tasks left uncompleted in the unattached young adult stage, particularly on those issues concerned with their identity. They may alternately find themselves blaming "men" and the societal "trap" of marriage and children as they question how they will spend the rest of their life now that the childrearing phase is coming to an end. Women at this stage frequently express the desire to break out of the family and pursue personal growth (Lowenthal, et al.,

1977). The signs of aging in their own bodies add a sense of urgency to their search for a new identity.

A woman may also shift her attention back to unresolved conflicts with her own parents. Perhaps a daughter's intention to establish a career may bring a mother back to her own decision to marry and have children. If her parents pushed her toward a more traditional choice she may feel resentful toward them, since her earlier life choices will now limit her current options.

A woman who has not worked outside the home for many years is understandably apprehensive about looking for a job. Her years of absence from the job market usually result in a total loss of seniority, and a woman may find she has to learn new skills to adapt to the needs of today's employers. Some men, especially more successful ones, may oppose a wife's return to work, suggesting that it will only "cost" them money. A woman might also feel her teenagers need her more than ever before, and point to working mothers as the cause of the increase in juvenile delinquency. Aging parents may begin to turn to her for nurturing, and present another obstacle to exploring personal interests.

Despite these obstacles, many women do finally begin to struggle for the changes they want in their lives, sometimes through therapy. They may need guidance in determining where their interests lie, in establishing new activities, and, perhaps in vocational planning. However, just as at previous stages, it is dangerous for a therapist to assume that work or a career is the answer to every woman's problems. Women often need help in rebalancing their lives while learning to cope with the effects this may have on their marriage.

LAUNCHING CHILDREN AND MOVING ON

The period of disengagement from active parenting is marked by a "now I need you, now I don't," kind of phenomenon, as the family contracts and expands in response to departures, returns, and marriages of young adult offspring. Hill's (1970) study found that 40% of young married adults still saw parents at least weekly, and received substantial forms of support from them. This is also a time when the parents of the middle-aged may require more attention because of aging and illness.

However, there is strong evidence that much of the accepted wisdom about the nature of women's lives during this phase is based on mistaken or outdated assumptions. Recent research has disspelled several myths about the psychological problems women typically encounter in middle age. For example, the cessation of menstruation has generally been viewed as a negative change, or even illness. While it is true that some women do attribute severe anxiety and depression to menopause, Neugarten (1970) found that a majority of women saw menopause not as pathological, but rather as a normal, temporary, physical process. In fact, Brown (1976) found that most of those who display psychiatric symptoms at menopause had a history of psychological difficulties, which simply intensify or reemerge at this time.

A second negative image is embodied in the "empty nest" label. Women relieved of direct childrearing activities have many opportunities to expand their social life, explore new leisure-time activities, and to relate to their husbands. Many marriages that last this long may return to a balance missing since the birth of the first child. Other research shows that women are less likely to be distraught by the departure of children than to welcome the relief from parenting (Neugarten, 1970; Lowenthal, et al., 1977). Women also report a greater sense of well-being and less depression than do women in the earlier stages of the family life cycle (Harkins, 1978; Lowenthal, et al., 1977; Deutscher, 1968). There are indications that during this phase of the family life cycle many women actually become more assertive and independent, while their husbands seek more closeness in the relationship.

Nevertheless, a great number of women still experience some degree of ambivalence and need a period of readjustment to cope with the many relationship shifts that occur in this phase. The mother's average age when the last child leaves home is forty-eight (Glick, 1977), but the obviously wide variation in the age of parents at the time children depart is an important factor in defining the situation women face at this stage. For example, the woman whose children leave as she enters her forties may have already begun to think about a new career or the expansion of an existing one by further education or training. Her situation is quite different from that of the woman whose children leave when she is in her fifties, who is more likely to be concerned with health problems, retirement, and the use of leisure time than she is with career issues.

Regardless of when it occurs, the departure of grown children produces a void that must be filled. Women whose lives have been devoted almost solely to reproduction and nurturing may react to these changes as major crises. In a study of "newly alcoholic" women between forty-five and sixty-five, Curlee (1969) found that her subjects had been unusually dependent on husband and/or children for a sense of identity and purpose, and had experienced a loss of those relationships. Women who have remained single and have been designated the caretaker of parents may suffer a similar loss of identity when the parents die. Clinical data show that women who have based their sense of self-worth on others' responses have an especially hard time in letting their children disengage or in dealing with the loss of a husband or parent through divorce or death.

Other transgenerational conflicts may also be activated at this particular stage. For instance, a mother whose unmarried daughter decided to move into her own apartment might find this way of leaving the family unacceptable, perceiving it as rejection. She may, in fact, be reacting to her own mother's disapproval of her departure from home before marriage, and to the ensuing conflict and rejection.

Marital problems that were previously ignored or buffered by the presence of children will require attention at this stage. Due to decreasing family size and increasing life expectancy, the average length of time a couple spends together after the marriage of the last child has expanded to an average of thirteen years (Glick, 1977). The phase is actually more likely to span twenty years, since it begins when the oldest child leaves for college.

Of course, there is considerable variation in the problems that may surround this marital refocus. For example, women who are moving to explore the world outside the family may find their husbands looking to them for increased intimacy and companionship (Levinson, 1978). Or women who have been overinvolved with children and now become interested in renewing the marital relationship may find that their husbands have distanced from the family long ago.

The failure in early marriage to establish a separate identity within the marital relationship can have serious consequences at this stage. Birnbaum (1975) found professional women in midlife higher in self-esteem and satisfaction than women who had remained homemakers. Another study of college-educated women in their late fifties found those employed full-time had significantly fewer psychiatric symptoms than women not employed outside the home, with women employed part-time occupying an intermediate position (Powell, 1977). However, while 55% of all women forty-five to fifty-four and 41% of those fifty-five to sixty-four were in the labor force in 1976, most held routine, low-level jobs with no hope of advancement. These women are very likely to continue to see their jobs as secondary to their family involvement (Lowenthal, et al., 1977).

For poorly differentiated women, the underlying terror of not knowing who they are or how to assert themselves may be masked by blaming the spouse, thus further delaying the search for identity. The following clinical example concerns a woman who is attempting to renegotiate her marital relationship to accommodate individual growth and the launching of young adult offspring, at the same time as she confronts an unresolved conflict with her mother.

> Shirley, a forty-eight-year-old mother of two college children, called the clinic complaining of severe depression, anxiety attacks, and constant rage towards her husband. She asked that he not be told because she was afraid he would become abusive, but finally agreed to his involvement.
>
> A highly intelligent and creative woman, she had hopes of returning to a career in art that had been laid aside during her childrearing years. Her husband had recently left his job with the hopes of starting his own business and she

feared this would place constraints on her own options. She was furious at him for this but was unable to express her feelings directly because she feared his angry outbursts. Instead, she would ask his advice or approval about her plans for herself. He would say, "Do whatever will make you happy," but would then add that he would like her to work with him in starting his own business.

She was afraid that if she pursued what she wanted for herself, the marriage would dissolve. On the other hand, she feared that if she continued on in her caretaking and adaptive role, she would end up like her mother, severely depressed and isolated in a nursing home until her death. Thoughts of her mother's last years preoccupied her. She felt both guilty and angry, as well as fearful that she was just like her.

As therapy helped her husband to pull back, Shirley began to pursue her painting. The marital relationship improved and the couple began to enjoy spending time together and planning for the future. Shirley no longer felt angry at her mother, but had a tremendous sense of sadness that she had not been closer to her.

Things went smoothly until their daughter returned home after graduating from college. Once again, Shirley felt overwhelmed by the demands to be a caretaker and to adjust her schedule around her daughter's needs. Her lifelong position as an adaptive female still makes it hard for her to assert her own interests. Interestingly, her daughter is seriously trying to pursue a career in art. While Shirley states that she would like this, she also seems somewhat threatened by her. Feelings of competition and envy may be adding to her current difficulty with her daughter's reentry into the home.

A child who does not exit on cue can be one of the major problems a woman can face at this stage of the life cycle (Harkins, 1978); but the difficulty of many couples to adjust to the departure of children by renegotiating their marriage can lead a mother to actively hold on to one of her children. Sometimes the stress is expressed by physical or emotional illness in a child who is in the process of leaving the family. Such cases do not usually come to the attention of the therapeutic community unless such a child has a psychotic break, but may sometimes come to light through the efforts of a sensitive young adult who is actively struggling to formulate his or her own identity.

A woman's plans for a new life can also be curtailed by the sickness or disability of an aging parent. Arranging for someone to care for an older person may be even more difficult than finding a babysitter for a child and a woman may continue to feel the pressure to minister to the needs of others. Sometimes, the woman is expected to take care of her husband's parents, especially if they have no daughters. This may cause a great deal of resentment and lead to marital stress, particularly if the wife is at a point in her life where she is ready to do something for herself, as in the following example:

Evelyn, a fifty-eight-year-old wife and mother of two grown sons, had returned to school after the departure of her children and began enjoying a rewarding new career. She was extremely competent and was offered a promotion at work that would involve a full-time commitment to her job. When she discussed it with her husband, he informed her that his eighty-five-year-old mother could no longer live by herself, and he felt obligated to ask her to live with them. He admitted that this would mean his wife could not accept the promotion at work and might even have to cut down her hours. In addition, they would have to hire someone to be with her while they were at work, unless she wished to quit her job. Evelyn became depressed and requested therapy for herself. Although initially her husband Al refused to come, he eventually came when the therapist coached the wife to return the responsibility for his mother to her husband and his brother, with whom he had not been on speaking terms since their father's death ten years before. Within a short time, Al agreed to talk to his brother, so that they could discuss arrangements for their mother. Evelyn accepted the promotion at work and her depression lifted.

By far the most pleasant intergenerational occurrences of this stage will be the births of her grandchildren. This offers a second chance to enjoy the pleasures of small children without having to be fully responsible for them. Women who wish to may be of great assistance to a daughter or daughter-in-law who is trying to combine marriage and career. However, as many young couples postpone or permanently forego having children, or live a great distance from their parents, a woman can no longer count on being able to find total fulfillment in her role as grandmother.

Therapists do not generally see women at this stage unless they have severe problems. This is partly because family life may be somewhat less stressful than at previous stages of the life cycle, but also because at this point in the game many women may feel "stuck" with their choices and not see the possibility for change.

Sometimes women in this stage may come into therapy after the death of a husband. Half of all widowed women are under the age of seventy (Troll, 1975), and their adjustment tends to be especially difficult because their husband's deaths were unexpected. At a time when the support of friends is most important, the continuation of friendships with couples or with women who still have their husbands is often not possible. Since much of social life is couple-oriented, the younger widow occupies a kind of marginal status, and if she is perceived to be attractive, she may be considered a threat to the marriages of her friends. Because there are so many more women than men at this stage of the life cycle, the widow is often considered a social liability, while the widower may be deluged by invitations and opportunities to socialize with the opposite sex. Not only does the widow have to deal with others viewing her as an "extra," she must also deal with her own feelings of vulnerability in social situations. One widow, describing the experience of not having a man at her side when she went out, compared it to being "naked." In addition to her emotional and social problems, the widow may also be financially burdened, especially if the couple has not made adequate financial arrangements.

THE FAMILY IN OLDER AGE

This phase often starts with the retirement of the husband, and this event, just as many others in the family life cycle, will require a rebalancing of the marital relationship. Sometimes the wife of a newly retired man will feel like her personal space has literally been invaded when after forty years of marriage, he begins to follow her around the house as she performs her daily chores. Or she may feel overwhelmed by the whirlwind of activities he plans to replace his work commitments. She might argue with him about moving to Florida if she feels seeing her grandchildren regularly is more important than being able to play golf everyday. In fact, women who have never worked outside the home, since they experience greater role continuity, may find this stage easier to accept than their husbands.

Of course, the reality is that women who have devoted their lives to being wives and mothers often go through the final stage of the family life cycle without husbands. Women can be said to have a whole stage of the family life cycle beyond that of men, since the majority of women, but only a minority of men, can expect to live this long. Only 21% of women have husbands at ages seventy-five to seventy-nine, 14% at ages eighty to eighty-four, and 6% over eighty-five. In contrast, 61% of men at ages seventy-five to seventy-nine have wives, 49% at eighty to eighty-four, and 84% over age eighty-five (Glick & Norton, 1977).

Women tend to maintain close emotional ties to the next generation, and at this stage they tend to increase their dependency on their children. Troll (1975) found that most women lived within extended family networks, usually involving a daughter, and that 89% of women over eighty live either with a child or within ten minutes of one. These ties are obviously important sources of support, but the evidence indicates that the elderly also contribute support to their children, so that the relationship is, more than we have previously assumed, one of mutual aid (Riley, 1968; Troll, 1971).

Problems of ill-health can shift the balance to complete physical dependence on the younger generation, and this is often compounded by financial dependence. Feelings of duty, love, and guilt govern the solutions that are worked out by families for the older generation. The prevailing myth that old people are supposed to be sickly and dependent may lead the family to tolerate illness and disability that might be treatable (Troll, 1975;

Herr & Weakland, 1979), or the failure to communicate about painful steps such as hospitalization or institutionalization may delay taking actions that would be best for all involved.

For the most part, family therapists come in contact with women in old age through the middle-aged generation. Elsie, aged seventy-five, provides an example of a woman at this stage who came to our attention through her adult daughter:

> Florence, aged fifty, came for therapy for herself with complaints of feeling depressed for no apparent reason. Her two children were both in college and doing well and she denied any marital problems. "It's not my husband—our marriage is good—there's something wrong with me and I just don't understand what it is or why I'm so depressed." In the course of the interview, she related that her mother, Elsie, aged seventy-five, had been living with the family since she was widowed at age fifty. She had been a useful and valuable member of the household, helping Florence with cooking and childrearing, and was close to her grandchildren. Recently, however, she was becoming argumentative and senile and in Florence's words, "impossible to live with." Her husband suggested that she should "simply put the old lady in a nursing home," which Florence felt she could not do. The therapist made a contract to see Florence alone, and assured her that she had a real problem for which she deserved some help. As therapy progressed, the therapist was able to get Florence to involve her two brothers, who lived in another state and had been relatively distant from the problem, to share in the responsibility of caring for their mother. In addition, the therapist began to coach Florence to resolve some of her own issues with her mother. Despite her initial protests that her mother was too senile to carry on a conversation, she was able to become objective enough to notice when her mother might be more receptive to her and to learn how to bring up sensitive issues, such as her feelings about having her mother move into her home in the early years of her marriage.

This case underscores the importance of involving all family generations, including the aging adult, in handling this family situation. It is unfortunate that reciprocal affection and material assistance among elderly widows often makes these relationships more satisfying than family ties with their formalized obligations (Arling, 1976). However, while a friendship network may take the place of family ties for those who are cut-off from family, it is certainly not preferable. The importance of family relationships for the older person should not be minimized and, as is true at all stages of the life cycle, those who are in good contact with extended family are likely to function better than those who are emotionally cut-off (Kerr, 1979).

The problems of the elderly are most frequently encountered by health care professionals and social workers in nursing homes or senior citizen centers. Raising the consciousness of these professionals to family systems theory could be of help to many women in coping with the tasks of this phase: defining themselves beyond their family caretaking functions, maintaining their interests as long as possible, and coming to terms with the life they have led and its impending closure. They could also be instrumental in helping other family members resolve underlying conflicts before the older person's death makes these issues extremely difficult ever to resolve.

WOMEN AND DIVORCE

The soaring divorce rate means that an ever-increasing proportion of women will have to face the breakup of a marriage, an experience that requires the renegotiation of a number of important relationships as well as, in most cases, the taking on of more financial responsibility for self and family.

Divorce can be either an option or a threat to a woman at any stage of the family life cycle. Although it can be an alternative to living with an abusive spouse, many women fail to initiate changes in their marital relationships because they fear their husbands will leave them. The higher a woman's income, the more likely she is to see divorce as a "liberating" experience, and women with postgraduate education are more apt to divorce than either women with less education, or men with postgraduate education (Glick & Norton, 1977).

Reentry into the single world is relatively easy for the childless woman under thirty who decides to get a divorce; 80% of these women remarry in two or three years (Glick & Norton, 1977). For many of them, this move represents a second chance to experience the unattached young adult phase, although the emotional scars from an unhappy marriage distinguish them from their never-married peers.

The unfortunate reality is that the majority of divorces occur in families with young children. Women are the custodial parent in the overwhelming majority of these divorces. Separation and divorce for women with young children are never easy solutions. A large majority of men pay no alimony and inadequate child support, so that the problems of raising children without a husband are compounded by some harsh economic realities. Even those women whose ex-husbands are willing to support them and their children adequately must keep in mind that it is almost impossible to be emotionally independent when one is financially dependent.

All women with young children who are divorced face the task of coping with their children's hurt and angry reactions to parental separation, which can be very difficult because it occurs at a time when they themselves are under great personal stress. A recent study by Wallerstein and Kelly (1979) showed that it took women who were divorced an average of three and one-half years to reestablish a sense of stability in their lives (the average time required by men was two and one-half years), and for many of their children, this meant a period of turmoil and relative instability (Wallerstein & Kelly, 1979). Yet several studies suggest that children do as well in divorced households as in unhappy two-parent families (Zill, 1978). This is more likely to be the case if a woman has good contact with her family of origin and adequate financial resources. If she has rewarding work or is able to go to school to work toward economic independence, she may even experience the divorce as a growth-producing experience (Tcheng-Laroche & Prince, 1979).

Divorced mothers of adolescents may find themselves in competition with their teenagers around dating, and often worry about the appropriate way to handle the fact of their own sexual activity with their children. Some divorced women become overinvolved with their adolescent children and look to them for support and companionship. Others may be so caught up in their new freedom and pursuit of personal growth that they neglect their children's needs. Clearly, finding a balance between their own needs and those of adolescent children, and maintaining clear boundaries between the generations are critical issues for divorced women at this stage of the life cycle.

Some women seek therapy for divorce-related issues and usually need help in negotiating the unfamiliar and complicated issues surrounding the dissolution of a marriage (See McGoldrick and Carter, Chapter 12).

Maryann, a forty-five-year-old woman, after years of marital conflict, decided to leave her husband. With two children in late adolescence and her youngest approaching adolescence, she felt a need to expand her activities outside the home, but her husband had actively opposed this.

Her children were very angry about the separation. She had to deal with their emotional outbursts along with her own depression about the failure of her marriage and anxiety about reentry into the job market and a new social world. Although feminist ideas gave her some sense of support, they were not able to eliminate the difficulties inherent in her choice.

When she was growing up, Maryann's mother had always appeared threatened by her desire to pursue a career. Her mother, who had been unhappily married herself, conveyed to Maryann a distrust of men, yet had pushed her into a traditional feminine role.

Sessions involved all members of the family in differing combinations. Initially, husband and wife were seen together to discuss the decision to separate. Once the wife had made a definite decision to separate, the children were included to discuss their feelings. When tensions between the couple escalated to a point where they could not be in the room together, a one-way mirror was used to allow each spouse an opportunity to observe the session with the other spouse and children. Also, each spouse was seen once with extended family. After the separation, Maryann continued to be seen, usually by herself but with one or all of her children when needed. Therapy focused on helping her to achieve an emotional divorce from her husband by letting go of stored-up anger toward him and working toward economic independence. In addition, she needed help in dealing with her guilt feelings toward her children, particularly her youngest who had been used to constant companionship from her older brother and sister, now in college, and from her "supermom" who was no longer always available. As therapy progressed, Maryann needed support and encouragement around reestablishing a social network. She joined some singles social groups and began to date. Currently, she is trying to rework her relationship with her own mother, realizing that "I'll never have a decent relationship with a man until I can deal better with my mother."

It is likely that more women at this stage will experience these difficulties in the future. The proportion of divorced women between thirty-five and fifty-four increased by one-third between 1970 and 1975, and there are indications that the trend will probably continue upward (Glick & Norton, 1977).

The increased incidence of divorce after the departure of grown children may be a reflection of the greater length of time couples will spend together without children. Women who choose to leave a dysfunctional relationship at this stage may do so because they see no other way to end their own adaptive, undifferentiated role in the marriage. The euphoria of freedom may soon be replaced by many of the problems facing those women who enter divorce unwillingly. Finding a new social network and intimate relationships, overcoming financial hardships, and sharing the adult child's loyalty to the former spouse are some of the tasks faced by these women. Herman (1977) suggests that middle-aged women who have devoted themselves primarily to the family may find regaining autonomy especially painful, leading to such symptoms as depression, feelings of helplessness, anger, and repeated suicide attempts.

Three-quarters of all women who divorce eventually remarry and many will become stepmothers to another woman's children. The role of stepmother is probably the most difficult of roles in the remarried family. The situation will be most problematic if the new husband's children are living with the couple on a full-time basis, and particularly so if the children's mother is still alive. The stepmother is likely to do better if the children's mother is dead, and will do better with young children than with teenagers. Because she is often expected to be the primary caretaker in the new family, her position is more difficult than that of a stepfather, whose role is more peripheral (McGoldrick & Carter, Chapter 12). If the husband is critical of his new wife's efforts to mother his children, her situation is almost impossible, and serious problems are likely to erupt in the family.

To understand why the stepmother role is fraught with so many dangers, it is important to realize that she is expected to take on a central position in the new family before she has had a chance to adjust to a new marriage or work out a relationship with her stepchildren.

A twenty-four-year-old, never-married woman married a widower with two children, aged four and six. He had been quite overwhelmed by his wife's death and having to care for two young children by himself. When Margie, a schoolteacher, agreed to marry him, he felt a tremendous sense of relief. She, not being experienced as a wife or a mother, was expected to take on the responsibility for the care of two children who regarded her as an intruder. Her fastidiousness and perfectionism, which served her well as a teacher, had the effect of upsetting the children and turning her husband against her. His criticisms made her job extremely difficult. She hoped that having her own child would ease the tensions in the family, but the birth of her son only added to them. When it was suggested that she pull back and let her husband take over with his kids, it became clear how totally he had expected her to function as a replacement for his deceased wife. This expectation, while not expressed directly, made Margie feel devalued and unappreciated by her husband as well as by his children, and led to an intense overinvolvement with her natural son. When her husband's unresolved mourning for his first wife could be openly discussed, Margie was better able to understand the impact that her death had had on him and his children and could then loosen up with the kids. As she became more accepting of their feelings of attachment to their mother, she took their sometimes provocative behavior toward her less personally. Despite her efforts, her relationship with her stepdaughter remained tense and conflictual.

It is not unusual to find the relationship between a stepmother and stepdaughter to be the most problematic (see McGoldrick & Carter, Chapter 12). In addition to loyalty conflicts experienced by all children in a stepfamily situation, the daughter's reaction to her stepmother is likely to be intensified by feelings of competitiveness that are normally present toward the same-sex parent but that are even more pronounced toward the woman her father has brought in as a replacement for her mother. If she has had a particularly close relationship with her father, the new woman in his life may be perceived as an unwelcome intruder. While the same holds true for boys and their mothers, a stepfather usually is not in as central a position in regard to childrearing, so there is far less contact and involvement than with a stepmother.

CONCLUSION

The emergence of women's issues during the past few decades has left its mark on all of us. While problems of establishing long-term relationships and achieving career goals may become more central in the future, at present most women are confronted with the complex and conflicting challenges of balancing caretaking with needs for personal development. Although the conflict assumes different forms at each stage of the life cycle, the task of resolving it becomes increasingly significant in the light of recent social and economic changes that have propelled more and more women into working outside the home.

Caretaking can be a rewarding activity, but many women feel oppressed and limited when their sense of self is defined exclusively in terms of other's needs or expectations (Miller, 1976; Rubin, 1976). Anxiety, depression, and phobias are characteristic symptoms of women who have not sufficiently individuated from the people whose needs they serve (Franks & Burtle, 1974; Gornick & Moran, 1971; Rogers, 1978). Therapists must view women who present with such symptoms in the context of both the role they play in their family system and their particular stage of the family life cycle. This view needs to be further modified by keeping in mind the current social milieu. Women are now asking themselves some serious questions about the meaning of their lives. They are looking for answers that therapy alone cannot give them.

Indeed, the great majority of family therapists are women. Every female therapist brings her own intergenerational issues with her into the therapeutic situation. Although her experiences may make her more sympathetic to the problems of her female client, she must be careful not to push her own solutions on a woman in treatment.

However, a therapist who comes in contact with any woman at any stage of the life cycle can help her to see her life as a series of stages, and to help her formulate her life goals in this context. For example, even if she chooses to be a full-time homemaker while she raises her family, a young woman might be much better prepared for subsequent stages of the life cycle if she has given serious thought to what interests she might develop and commitments she might make in the future.

It is our view that both men and women need more balance between emotional involvement in the family and the pursuit of personal interests outside the family. As Betty Friedan said recently,

> The great challenge we face in the 1980's is to frame a new agenda that makes it possible for women to be able to work and love—in equality with men—and to choose, if they desire, to have children. For the choices we have sought in the '70's are not as simple as they once seemed. Indeed, some of the choices women are supposed to have won are not real choices at all. And even the measure of equality we have achieved is not secure until we face these unanticipated conflicts between the demands of the workplace and professional success on the one hand, and the demands of the family on the other. These conflicts seem insoluble because of the way the family and the workplace have been structured in America. The second feminist agenda for the '80's must call for the restructuring of the institutions of home and work. (Friedan, 1979, p. 49)

REFERENCES

Arling, G., "The Elderly Widow and Her Family, Neighbors and Friends," *Journal of Marriage and the Family* 38/4, Nov. 1976.

Bird, C., *The Two Paycheck Marriage,* New York: Rawson, Wade, 1979.

Birnbaum, J. A., "Life Patterns and Self-Esteem in Gifted Family-Oriented and Career-Committed Women," *Woman and Achievement: Social and Motivational Analysis,* Mednick, S. Tangri, & L. Hoffman, eds., New York: Wiley, 1975.

Blake, J., "Is Zero Preferred? American Attitudes Towards Childlessness in the 1970s," *Journal of Marriage and the Family* 41/2, May 1979.

Brown, J. R. W., & M. E. C. Brown, "Psychiatric Disorders Associated with the Menopause," *The Menopause,* R. J. Beard, ed., Lancaster, England: MTP Press Ltd., 1976.

Burr, W., "Satisfaction with Various Aspects of Marriage Over the Life Cycle: A Random Middle-Class Sample," *Journal of Marriage and the Family* 32/1, February 1970.

Census Bureau, March 1978, as quoted in *The New York Times* June 26, 1979.

Curlee, J., "Alcoholism and the Empty Nest," *Bulletin of the Menninger Clinic* 33, 1969.

Deutscher, I., "The Quality of Postparental life," *Middle Age and Aging,* B. L. Neugarten, ed., Chicago: University of Chicago Press, 1968.

Franks, V. & U. Burtle, *Women in Therapy: New Psychotherapies in a Changing Society,* New York: Brunner/Mazel, 1974.

Friedan, B., "Feminism Takes a New Turn," *The New York Times Magazine,* November 18, 1979.

———, "The Second Stage: An Urgent New Challenge," *Redbook* 154/3, January 1980.

Glick, P. C. & A. J. Norton, "Marrying, Divorcing and Living Together in the United States Today," *Population Bulletin,* 1977.

Goodrich, W., et al., "Patterns of Newlywed Marriage," *Journal of Marriage and the Family* 30/3, August 1968.

Gornick, V. & B. K. Moran, eds., *Women in a Sexist Society; Studies in Power and Powerlessness,* New York: Basic Books, 1971.

Gould, R. I., *Transformations,* New York: Simon and Schuster, 1978.

Gump, J. P., "Reality and Myth: Employment and Sex Role Ideology in Black Women," *The Psychology of Women: Future Directions in Research,* J. A. Sherman & F. L. Denmark, eds., New York: Psychological Dimensions, 1978.

Haley, J., *Uncommon Therapy,* New York: W. W. Norton, 1973.

Hare-Mustin, R. T., "A Feminist Approach to Family Therapy," *Family Process* 17, June 1978.

Harkins, E., "Effects of the Empty Nest Transition: A Self Report of Psychological Well Being," *Journal of Marriage and the Family* 40/3, August 1978.

Hennig, M. M., "Family Dynamics for Developing Positive Achievement Motivation in Women: The Successful Woman Executive," *Annals of the New York Academy of Sciences* 208, March 15, 1973.

Herman, S. J., "Women, Divorce and Suicide," *Journal of Divorce* 1/2, Winter 1977.

Herr, J. J., & J. H. Weakland, *Counseling Elders and Their Families*, New York: Springer 1979.

Hill, R., et al., *Family Development in Three Generations*, Cambridge: Schenkman, 1970.

Kerr, K. B., "Issues in Aging From a Family Theory Perspective," *The Family* 7/1, 1979.

Kleiman, D., "Anguished Search to Cure Infertility," *The New York Times Magazine*, December 16, 1979.

Levinson, D. J., *The Seasons of A Man's Life*, New York: Alfred A. Knopf, 1978.

Lowenthal, M. F., et al., *Four Stages of Life*, San Francisco: Jossey-Bass 1977.

Lozoff, M. U., "Father and Autonomy in Women," *Annals of the New York Academy of Sciences* 208, March 15, 1973.

Lynn, D. B., *The Father: His Role in Child Development*, Monterey, California: Brooks/Cole Publishing Company, 1974.

Mazor, M., "Barren Couples," *Psychology Today*, May 1979.

Miller, J. B., *Toward a New Psychology of Women*, Boston: Beacon Press, 1976.

Neugarten, B. L., "Dynamics of Transition of Middle Age to Old Age," *Journal of Geriatric Psychiatry* 4, 1970.

Powell, B., "The Empty Nest, Employment and Psychiatric Symptoms in College-Educated Women," *Psychology of Women Quarterly* 2/1, Fall 1977.

Riley, M. W., Anne Foner and Associates, *Aging and Society, Vol. 1 An Inventory of Research Findings*, New York: Russell Sage Foundation, 1968.

Roche, G. R., "Much Ado About Mentors," *Harvard Business Review*, January/February 1979.

Rogers, M., "Fascinating Womanhood as a Regression in the Emotional Maturation of Women," *Psychology of Women Quarterly* 2, Spring 1978.

Rollins, B. C. & H. Feldman, "Marital Satisfaction Over the Family Life Cycle," *Journal of Marriage and the Family* 32/1, February 1970.

Rossi, A. S., "Intimacy and Autonomy: The Pleasures and Pains of Sex Role Change," Lecture presented at Smith College Centennial, February 25, 1975, Northampton, Massachusetts.

Rubin, L. B., *Worlds of Pain/Life in the Working Class Family*, New York: Basic Books, 1976.

Russo, N. F., "Beyond Adolescence: Some Suggested New Directions For Study of Female Development in the Middle and Later Years," *The Psychology of Women: Future Directions in Research*, J. A. Sherman and F. L. Denmark, eds., New York: Psychological Dimensions, Inc. 1978.

Seiden, A., "Overview: Research of the Psychology of Women II: Women in Families, Work, and Psychotherapy," *American Journal of Psychiatry* 133, October 1976.

Sheehy, G., *Passages, Predictable Crisis of Adult Life*, New York: Dutton, 1976.

Spence, D. & T. Lonner, "The 'Empty Nest': A Transition within Motherhood," *The Family Coordinator*, October 1971.

Stewart, W. A., "The Formation of the Early Adult Life Structure in Women," doctoral dissertation in clinical psychology, Teachers College, Columbia University, 1976.

Tcheng-Laroche, F. & R. H. Prince, "Middle Income Divorced Female Heads of Families: Their Lifesytle, Health and Stress Levels," *Canadian Journal of Psychiatry* 24/7, 1979.

Troll, L. E., "The Family of Later Life: A Decade of Review," *Journal of Marriage and the Family* 33/2, May 1971.

――――, *Early and Middle Adulthood,* Belmont, California: Wadsworth 1975.

Vaillant, G. E., *Adaptation to Life,* Boston: Little, Brown, 1977.

Wallerstein, J. S. & J. B. Kelly, "Children and Divorce: A Review," *Social Work* 24/6, November 1979.

Weissman, M. et al., "The Depressed Woman as Mother," *Social Psychiatry* 7, 1972.

Weissman, M. & G. Klerman, "Sex Differences and the Epidemiology of Depression," *Archives of General Psychiatry* 34, January 1977.

Weissman, M. M. & E. S. Paykel, "Moving," *Yale Alumni Magazine,* October 1972.

Zill, N., "Divorce, Marital Happiness and the Mental Health of Children: Findings from the FDC National Survey of Children," Prepared for NIMH Workshop on Divorce and Children, Bethesda, Maryland, February 7–8, 1978.

14

Family Life Cycle Issues in the Therapy System

Robert M. Simon, M.D.
Ackerman Institute for Family Therapy

One of psychotherapy's unique qualities is its juxtaposition of two variable systems: the therapist and the patient. Psychotherapy differs from medicine in that the physician, at least in theory, remains constant in relation to the patient's fluctuating health. The correct dose of penicillin is the same whether the doctor is a beginning intern or a Nobel Prize winner, whether he or she is fulfilled, depressed, anxious, or whatever. Personal qualities are relegated to "bedside manner." In psychotherapy, however, variation in the therapist is more relevant to outcome.

Variations in the family therapist may be evanescent, like an upset stomach that interferes with attentive listening. Others are phasic, such as fluctuations in the therapist's relationship with his[1] spouse. Still others are cyclic, having to do with the personal development of the therapist through adult life. How he deals with a family, and what impact he has on them, may differ markedly when he is twenty-five, when he is forty-five, and when he is sixty. These developments are independent of the acquisition of new technical knowledge, although that will (we hope) increase with age. This chapter examines the therapist/family interface from two points of view: (1) How should life cycle issues be evaluated in the understanding of a given family? (2) What are the consequences for therapy when the life cycle events of the family do or do not match with those of the therapist?

[1]To be accurate, feminine pronouns should be used in referring to family therapists, because most of them are women. However, so much of this paper is based on the author's personal experience that it would be absurd not to use the masculine form. The choice is therefore expressive, not traditional.

It would be beyond our scope here to consider those situations where the therapist and the family exist, as it were, in two different worlds. Race, gender, ethnicity, religion, social class, and so on, can sometimes constitute challenges in the conduct of therapy that require a discourse all their own. I imagine that a continuum extends from one extreme in which there is no way for therapist and patient to understand each other, to another extreme where their life situations are as identical as people can have. The encounter of family and therapist falls somewhere on that continuum: it requires a commonality of human experience, but recognizes that no two people ever tread exactly the same path through life.

FAMILY LIFE CYCLE AS A DIAGNOSTIC ISSUE

There are many questions therapists must ask themselves in relation to a family's life cycle. The first is to identify where the family is in this sequence, all of whose phases have been described in the foregoing chapters of this book. Included in this concept are situations that are not phases of a cycle *per se*, but that nevertheless have a profound influence upon family life. I refer to divorce, remarriage, and bereavement. They can occur at any time and, although not necessarily psychopathological, can set off profound disturbances. In any case, they rank with predictable life cycle events as worthy of the therapist's consideration when orienting himself to a particular family.

A second question is: How does the life cycle create disturbance for a particular family? To answer this question properly, the therapist needs to be familiar with the normative emotional process involved in making the transition from each phase of the life cycle to the next, as well as with the predictable issues the family can be expected to be dealing with at each phase. With this knowledge, the therapist can ask questions that are pertinent to their situation whether the family recognizes them or not. Thus, a family that presents around school adjustment of a three- to six-year-old should routinely be asked how they handled the adjustments in the family required by the birth of the child, or an "empty nest" couple complaining about a late adolescent's behavior would be questioned about the marital adjustments and renegotiations they are making or planning to make as their children leave home, and, of course, about the health and circumstances of their elderly parents. A routine procedure of this kind in the evaluation process will immediately highlight major life cycle issues related to the presenting problem, and how the family is or is not dealing with them. Other factors that will influence the prognosis and the treatment plan are whether the difficulties originated in the transition to or course of the family's current life cycle phase, or whether the problems have piled up through several phases, or perhaps over several generations, due to an earlier transition point not adequately negotiated.

A further diagnostic consideration for the therapist is to locate the life cycle event on a "map" of the total family system. In other words, "where" is the key issue that has precipitated or contributes to the presenting problem? We should not assume that the nuclear family presenting itself for treatment is necessarily the locus of the decisive events. This point warrants further elaboration.

Old habits die hard, and for family therapists many old habits have to do with a dyadic conception of the therapist vis-à-vis an individual client. This is exemplified by the psychoanalytic model that is basic training for so many therapists. A beginner's model of family therapy is frequently to try to translate "patient" into "family," meaning a marital pair or a nuclear household. However, terminology and concepts cannot effectively be transplanted onto phenomena they were never meant to explain, and clinical experience eventually requires further elaboration of thinking to a systems level. One dimension of the family system is that which spreads laterally in space (extended family) and backwards in time (triangles and family themes). Embodied in each nuclear family are issues that have been inherited through several generations. Unconscious loyalty to family themes and the need for an ethical existential relationship with one's family of origin have been described in detail by Boszormenyi-Nagy and Spark (1). Thus, the nuclear family actually represents a confluence of four families, two for each of the parents. The therapist, it may be added, comes to the performance of his duties with preexisting loyalties to his own two sets of families. Even in the simplest situations, therefore—husband and wife sitting down with a therapist—the room contains the issues of no fewer than six families!

Viewed in this way, the life cycle—whether of therapist or family—has a less specific meaning. If we set our perspectives high enough, what is anyone's life cycle? If we choose to study skin, what is the life of the cell? A cell grows old, dies, is replaced by a new generation, but skin endures. A cell thinks it has an important life cycle; skin smiles, knows what really is important. This dermatological fancy is meant to illustrate that every stage of what we call the life cycle is complemented and in a sense neutralized, somewhere else in the extended family. If we speak of "the empty nest," for instance, we imply a stage of life wherein middle-aged parents gradually bid farewell to their children. If we observe from a "higher altitude," however, we can see the extended family: alongside the "empty nest" is the adolescent stage of the youngest child; the emergence into adulthood of the older children; problems of old age experienced by the parents of our "empty nest" couple. To which aspects should the therapist address himself and in what order? The family sometimes establishes the priority by calling attention clearly to one aspect or the other. In many cases, however, only the manifest disturbance surfaces. The therapist must seek the pertinent life cycle issues through questioning based on his sensitivity to the ghostly presence of the extended family, and his knowledge of the relevant issues involved at all stages of the life cycle.

> Ed and Sheila Warren were in their mid-forties with four children ranging in age from fifteen- to twenty-two years old. The original request for help came because of increasing tension between Ed and Phillip, the seventeen-year-old son. Initial contact with the family disclosed tension between all of the children and their father, tension subtly abetted by Sheila. Further questioning revealed that the oldest daughter, Nancy, was supposed to be married soon, but kept postponing the date. In spite of their protests that extended family information was irrelevant, I discovered that Sheila's elderly parents were doing poorly in their retirement home in Arizona and that she secretly planned to invite them to move in with them as soon as Nancy's departure made room. After this disclosure, the resulting explosion in the office left little doubt in anyone's mind as to the most problematic issue in the family as it headed into the "empty nest" phase of the life cycle.

A final consideration in the evaluation stage of therapy is whether current life cycle issues are primary or secondary in the presenting problem. The therapist should determine whether the current life cycle transition basically *is* the problem (as in the Warren family), or whether it has merely triggered more serious problems based upon existing weaknesses in family structure, perhaps going back to previous generations. At the risk of oversimplifying, in the Warren case the main task for the therapist was to enable the family to work on several central life cycle issues in such a way that conflict over any one of them did not obscure or impede progress on the others: shifting the long-standing mother-children coalition with father on the outside, freeing Nancy from the family entanglements so she could decide whether to marry or not, addressing the marital relationship and the requirement for open negotiation, and addressing the issue of Sheila's concerns for her unhappy elderly parents. In such a situation, the therapist should recognize that this is basically a *normal* time of trouble. Otherwise, the family may become "pathologized" by the therapy experience itself—a tacit agreement between therapist and family that they are really sick or subfunctional. Specific tactics in such situations include opening and clarifying communication, calming down overheated affect, detriangling, and an overall effort toward encouraging family members to differentiate as adults. These principles are set forth in rich detail by Bandler, Grinder, and Satir (2); Bowen (3); and Hoffman (4).

Now let us look at a situation in which the basic problem relates not to the current life cycle phase of the nuclear family but to unresolved issues with the family of origin that have contributed to a logjam of difficulties for several generations through several phases of the life cycle:

Connie and Mark Green, each twenty-nine years old, were referred for treatment because of a "sex problem." They had previously enjoyed an exciting and mutually gratifying sex life, but since the birth of their first child, six-and-a-half years prior to treatment, the frequency of intercourse had decreased to once every four to six weeks. Fatigue, preoccupation with work, and the care of their children were the explanations they had given each other.

Shortly before therapy began, however, Mark had lost twenty-five pounds and had begun to be more interested in sex. He was also in the process of switching to a more challenging job and was feeling more generally assertive. Connie labeled this as "demanding," and further contrasted his exciting new job prospects with her own boring routine of housework and child care. Further exploration revealed that, although she loved her children and had no particular complaints about their behavior or development, she had had a sinking feeling since the first child's birth that she was making a mistake in having her children before completing graduate school educaton in psychology, a field in which she had planned a career. Her own mother had temporarily given up her career when she was born, had regretted it, and had urged Connie not to make the same mistake. However, Connie said, Mark strongly objected to career women (including Connie's mother) and had convinced her that young children need their mothers home full time, as his had been. She had not argued this out with Mark either before or after their daughter's birth and, indeed, had not really recognized her strong conflicted feelings on this issue and others relating to marriage, careers, and motherhood.

In the above situation, it was clear that extensive work in their respective families of origin would have to be undertaken before either of them could obtain clarity of their own ideas on marriage, work, and family life. This example also points up the fact that myths about the supposedly "normal" family life cycle can limit options at transition points.

THE FAMILY LIFE CYCLE AS A THERAPY ISSUE

Having reviewed diagnostic considerations of the family life cycle that the therapist must make, let us now look at the interaction of his own life cycle with that of the treatment family.

There are three possible situations at the interface with the therapist's family life cycle: (a) the therapist has not yet experienced the family's stage; (b) the therapist has already been through that stage of the life cycle; (c) the therapist is going through the same stage of the life cycle as the family. There are unique assets and liabilities in each of the situations, and in order to describe them I must first comment on the role of the therapist.

This role, in my view, is essentially that of introducing change that mobilizes the family's resources in a different way than had previously been the case. In order to accomplish this, the therapist must (a) join with the family, (b) make an accurate diagnosis of the family's structure and dynamics, and

(c) have the skills to introduce change in a way that realigns the family's relationship system (5). That a certain amount of good feeling may develop between therapist and family members is expectable and, when it occurs, is a pleasant bonus for each. It is not, however, the therapist's primary task, nor is it a measure of his skill or of the family's responsiveness.

It seems to be "understanding" that patients particularly prize in their therapists. It can be experienced more on the emotional side of the spectrum ("so warm and human!") or more as an intellectual quality ("a genius!"). It is central in the therapeutic relationship, but it is not synonymous with sentimental attachment. Whether we are congruent or discrepant with our treatment families' life cycles, the Greek ideal, "Know Thyself" is always applicable. Daniel Levinson has written, "I can truly understand the suffering of others only if I can identify with them through an awareness of my own weakness and destructiveness. Without this self-awareness, I am capable only of the kind of sympathy, pity and altruism that reduces the other's hardship but leaves him still a victim" (6, p. 30).

Therapist Not Yet at the Family's Stage of the Life Cycle

From the technical point of view, this is the weakest spot in which a therapist can find himself. It is very hard, perhaps impossible, to be understanding (in its fullest sense) about people's lives if some similar personal experience is lacking. Book knowledge helps, of course, but there remains the possibility that family members perceive the therapist as not relating fully to their problems. A familiar example is the training clinic in which young therapists attempt to help families in which parents struggle with rebellious adolescents. The young therapist can easily identify with the children, whose life experience he has not long passed, but he is alien to the experience of the parents. It was in just such a situation that an irate mother yelled, "Why don't they have a law against *parent* abuse?" She was understandably piqued by the warmth I showed (and felt) towards her son. I confess that at that youthful stage of my career, my principal experience with provocative adolescents was with myself.

A young therapist's identification with adolescents or a middle-aged therapist's identification with parents is only one type of pitfall, and an obvious one at that. Actually, a therapist may emotionally side with *any* generation. Many subtle conditions can evoke such events. Taking as an example our familiar adolescent rebellion stage, we may postulate that a young therapist knows this phase from the point of view of the child, not of the parents. Suppose Therapist X experienced that stage as a personal struggle with mother's bossiness and has remained on guard with his mother ever since. That is, the issue was never fully resolved. We now have inexperience compounded by powerful affect. Therapist X now gets embroiled in putting the mother down. In this particular family, he should perhaps be helping the mother deal with the father's expert sabotage of her limit setting for the children.

Psychotherapy being the paradoxical business that it is, we should also consider what *assets* may accrue to the younger therapist. Primarily, the therapist's inexperience stimulates a family to rely on its own resources. There is little danger that a couple in their forties will look to a twenty-six-year-old therapist for "guidance." They may value him as a facilitator of communication, as a person with certain social/political power, and so on, but they are not likely to make him into a guru. Haley puts it succinctly: "When a therapist is young, he should not try to appear wiser than he is" (7, p. 165). Families are good supervisors in this respect, and it strengthens them. One other asset in this situation belongs to the therapist exclusively: working with an older family may stimulate some thinking about his own parents. If a young therapist has dealt with his own conflicts with his parents to the point where he has an emotional grasp of his parents' life experience and how these illuminate the parents' point of view, he will be able to use this as a reference in his work with treatment families.

Therapists whose present life cycle stage lies between that of the family members may at times be in a particularly advantageous position in dealing with warring generations. Adolescents, for example, may develop a positive alliance with a therapist in his twenties or thirties whom they see as having experience closer to their own than do their parents. The parents may likewise respond well to a younger therapist who is able to strike up an alliance with their adolescent children, but who has passed the rebellious stage.

From a systems perspective, it does not appear that it is the similarity of experience between the therapist and family that determines the effectiveness of treatment. The aim, rather, is to maximize the therapist's ability to help families solve their own problems and negotiate their developmental processes for themselves. To this end, the therapist will want to take advantage of his assets and beware of his liabilities in life cycle experience when responding to families in treatment. For example, some research (8) indicates that unmarried, attractive female therapists do poorly with intact families in which the wife is between the ages of forty-five and fifty-five. The life cycle implications of this are clear, and perhaps if therapists were more aware of the potential problems in certain family identifications they could circumvent them.

A colleague reported the following anecdote.

Supervising a twenty-eight-year-old psychologist, she watched a videotape of him conducting a family interview. The family consisted of a couple in their forties with two teenage daughters, the older of whom had been threatened with expulsion from school for cutting class repeatedly. The mother berated her daughter and the young therapist intervened several times to defend the daughter. As he finally made several attempts to get the focus of discussion off the daughter, the other girl made several thinly veiled suggestions that the father was seeing another woman. Ignoring the girl's comments, John, the therapist, returned to the problem of the older daughter's school behavior and gave the parents patronizing advice on dealing with their daughter and the school.

In the supervisory discussion, John recognized that he had sided with the daughter against her parents, particularly the mother, and readily traced this to his reactivity to his own mother. What astounded him, however, was that he had not heard nor understood the comments of the younger girl until the supervisor pointed them out and replayed them several times.

Asked whether this blind spot was related in some way to his own family, John reported that his parents had separated briefly when he was about fifteen. They had given him no specific explanation of that event or their subsequent reconciliation, but he had suspected his father was having an affair.

Shaken by the impact of this almost forgotten incident on his work, John was motivated to spend more time talking with each of his parents, clarifying family history and working on various personal issues in his relationship with them. With periodic coaching in the supervisory group, John identified and worked on many problems that had prevented his understanding his parents and how they came to be who they were. By the time he discovered that his father had, in fact, *not* had an affair, that issue was among the least important on his agenda. His work with older families improved appreciably throughout the year.

Therapist is Past the Family's Stage in the Life Cycle

Since this situation would generally be considered an asset, its positive aspects will be reviewed first. It is obvious that a therapist who has already passed through some of the trials of the family life cycle can be very understanding. Family members feel that this therapist immediately recognizes their problem; he is not fazed by it; he has a good fund of practical suggestions that worked in his personal life. The therapist catches the rich interconnections of life cycle and personal issues. He shows the family that their situation is normal, not pathological (wasn't his?). Thus, work with him is reassuring. He even knows enough not to play the mentor, having discarded mentors in his own life—Levinson points out that no man wants a mentor after age forty (6, p. 147). To the extent that clients seek a "mature wisdom," and that is to a considerable extent, this therapist has much to offer.

Now the paradox: In some circumstances, this very life experience may work to the detriment of the therapy. A therapist who had a difficult time in a past stage of the life cycle may find that working with a particular family opens doors on ghosts and ancient curses of his own. In self-defense he may become distant, cynical, or patronizing. He acts as though only *his* solutions can work for the family, or alternatively conveys the feeling that nothing much will work at all. This therapist needs to do some housecleaning.

Finally, there are therapists who are *too* knowledgeable and take an all-knowing, overresponsible stance with the family. The family abandons its own resources and falls back on trying to imitate the expert and follow his advice. Family members want to hang on to therapy because life presents new problems all the time. At some point the fount of infallibility runs dry. Bitterness waits in the wings: "What did we ever see in him?"

> In this example the therapist's being "ahead" of the family was mainly an asset. John and Terry Bannister, a couple in their early thirties, sought help after seven years of marriage. At that time they had two sons, ages three and one respectively (the children were not included in treatment). I was then forty-one and had a teenager and a ten-year-old.
>
> The initial complaint was one of severe marital discord that had only become worse during a period of individual psychotherapy for Terry. The couple was locked into a pattern of mutual blaming, especially over money. They had an elaborate duel of provocation and revenge, upon which the variations were endless and inventive. His chief weapon was to withold money; hers was to patronize him with psychological expertise, particularly regarding his relationship with the children.
>
> Naturally, in the first phase of treatment, each presented a "case" as though we were in a courtroom. The problem of therapeutic alliance was especially significant at this time because the difficulty of establishing it with the husband was exactly matched by the ease with which it could be established with the wife. Terry was always ready to accept my least opinion as Gospel and to lecture John on the wisdom of my statements. John did not relate easily to another man to begin with, and Terry's unquestioning acceptance of me would immediately provoke him to a jealous put-down. Therefore, a major effort was made to establish trust between John and me; at the same time, Terry was encouraged to develop her own ideas and to outdo me in understanding herself and her family. All of this was work for a midlife therapist. It required a certain age and professional status to engage John's interest in an alliance; he would have been merely contemptuous of a younger therapist. I also suspect that, at a younger age, I would have had considerably more difficulty playing dumb. This is not to say that a younger therapist could not have treated this couple, merely that this particular strategy was enhanced by middle age.

Therapist is in the Same Stage of the Life Cycle as the Family

This situation is the most treacherous one for the family therapist. Since any stage of life transition is bound to be full of pain and upheaval, the therapist can easily empathize with a family going through something that he is experiencing himself. He is not likely to pathologize the situation unnecessarily since he knows it from personal experience. On the other hand, there may simply be too many emotional triggers for the therapist to handle. How these are dealt with, of course, depends on the particular therapist. Some defend themselves with blind spots, so that important issues are overlooked. Some therapists may show reactive contempt for the family. This can betray itself in details such as not being on time for their appointments. Probably contempt speaks loudest when the case is discussed with colleagues.

It may even happen that a therapist becomes jealous of the family's attempted solution. Suppose that in working through the late-adolescent phase of the life cycle, a mother and son become much closer to each other. A therapist whose relationship with his own mother has been based on avoidance and whose own son is closer to his wife than to him, may define the mother-son closeness as unhealthy, "too oedipal," etc. The mother's value as a mentor and as a model for a later conjugal relationship is ignored. Another example of therapist jealousy might be seen when a midlife couple experiments with a sexually "open marriage." If this arrangement is attractive but untried for the therapist, he might denounce it as sick or avoid the issue altogether. In any case, therapist rage, boredom, or helplessness are pretty good indicators that a personal wound has been opened, and the therapist would be well advised to work on it in his own family, rather than reacting to it in his work.

Special issues in the therapist's life cycle may interfere with his work with certain families in therapy. If a therapist's parents divorced in their late forties and he himself is having marital difficulties as his children depart, he may have the sense that marital issues are not resolvable at this phase and may stay stuck with families who come to him in such situations. It seems that major disruption in the family life cycle patterns of the therapist (early deaths, prolonged illnesses, divorce, remarriage, etc.) may set him up for difficulty in responding to these processes in clinical families.

These issues are illustrated by the following vignette, contributed by a colleague.

A thirty-five-year-old social worker, Arlene, worked with a couple in their mid-thirties with two children, ages thirteen and twelve. The couple argued about whether or not the wife should go back to school and undertake a career in which she was interested. The husband was violently against the idea while the wife herself was highly ambivalent. The therapist subtly pushed the wife in the direction of the school-career decision.

In the discussion following the interview, the supervisory group pointed this out to Arlene, reminding her also of her own statements in prior meetings that her husband disapproved of her own new career on the grounds that teenagers needed their mother more, not less. Arlene was at first highly defensive and tried to provoke a "women's lib" argument. Eventually the group, which consisted mostly of women, was able to help her see that she was defensively pushing her own solution onto the treatment family and would be better advised to go home and resolve the issue with her husband.

It would be nice to conclude this chapter with specific advice to family therapists that, if followed carefully, could lead them to overcome totally problems of discrepancy or congruence between their life cycles and those of the family. Alas, this is not to be—or it is to be only partially. We must accept the fact that human consciousness cannot be manipulated, nor should it be, to suit the demands of a profession. There is no way that a thirty-year-old can have the same view as a fifty-year-old. The two people may feel for each other, share ideals, and ideas; nevertheless, their consciousness cannot be the same. That this is more obvious to fifty than to thirty in itself exemplifies the consciousness gap.

If these differences are to be adequately resolved, we must consider both the "inside" of the therapist and also the context in which family therapy is practiced. The first of these considerations could be a paper in itself; here I will highlight three central issues: The first is an *attitude of receptivity*. This is the therapist's willingness to experience the family openly, objectively, nonjudgmentally, and with appropriate reservations about his own omnipotence. Second is a *theoretical framework* that allows the therapist to translate observed phenomena into effective action. There are many competing theories of family at present, and my point is not to endorse one of them but to suggest that the therapist have a known and preferred model of working. The clinical-theoretical model is what sustains us not only through life cycle problems but through the many clinical difficulties we face.

The third necessary quality of the therapist's "insides" is his *sense of self in relation to his family of origin*. No matter where the therapist is in the life cycle, he is part of a family system in which all aspects of the life cycle have been experienced. When he was small his parents were getting established and his grandparents faced an empty nest. When he established his career, his parents were in midlife transition, and so on. He has been through this terrain many times, but each time occupying a different seat on the bus. The more the therapist learns about the experience of the past two generations vis-à-vis his own, the more he is equipped to deal with the life cycle of his client family. The more work he has done to resolve his own emotional issues within his family, the less likely he will be to get caught when these issues arise in his treatment families.

As for the context in which family therapy is practiced, it seems to me that therapists in solo practice have the greatest struggle with life cycle issues, because they have only their own resources to use. Therapists who practice in groups or in agencies attending to staff development may grapple better with life cycle issues. Their colleagues are apt to be from all adult age groups, and if the professional program includes sharing experiences in a colleagual atmosphere, then the input of younger and older peers becomes an important personal resource.

The question of supervision and training is relevant here. An older supervisor brings not only more clinical experience but also more life experience to the struggles of a younger colleague. But when treatment gets really stuck, sage advice alone may not suffice. Unfortunately, crisis time is not the best time to get into the trainee's family background; it may then sound like an elegant form of blaming. The proverbial ounce of prevention here is an exploration of the trainee's family of origin—especially its metamorphosis through the life cycle—as early as possible in supervision. What is theoretical at first may become indispensable when least expected.

The therapist's family of procreation is another part of this context. The spouse in particular enhances not only a therapist's general development, but specifically his ability to deal with life cycle issues. This is because the life cycle is so powerfully colored by role expectations of male and female in our society. A male therapist, for instance, should learn from his wife about the experience of femininity, the frustrations of women in our society, the conflicts a woman may face in moving between motherhood and careerhood, and so on. In the light of this knowledge, his own definitions of masculinity and self-expectations must change. In this intimacy, the career of therapist becomes a context for his life as much as his life is a context for his career.

Ars longa, vita brevis. There are no perfect families, no perfectly negotiated life cycles, and above all, no perfect therapists. The fascination of a career in this field is that our imperfections are constantly changing. As we travel this road, we become different therapists and engage new issues with our families. Any career that thus reflects reality is indeed a moveable feast.

REFERENCES

1. Boszormenyi-Nagy, I., and Spark, G., *Invisible Loyalties,* New York: Harper & Row, 1973.
2. Bandler, R., Grinder, J., and Satir, V., *Changing with Families,* Palo Alto, California: Science and Behavior Books, 1976.
3. Bowen, M., "Theory in the Practice of Psychotherapy," in Guerin, P. (ed.), *Family Therapy,* New York: Gardner, 1976.
4. Hoffman, L., "Breaking the Homeostatic Cycle," in Guerin, *Op. cit.*
5. Minuchin, S., *Families and Family Therapy,* Cambridge, Massachusetts: Harvard University Press, 1974.
6. Levinson, D., *The Seasons of a Man's Life,* New York: Knopf, 1978.
7. Haley, J., *Problem-Solving Therapy,* San Francisco: Jossey-Bass, 1976.
8. Woodward, J., et al., "Client and Therapist Characteristics as Related to Family Training Outcome: Closure and Follow Up Evaluation." Submitted for Publication, McMaster U., Ontario, Canada.

Part 4

Major Variations
in the Family Life Cycle

15
The Family Life Cycle of the Multiproblem Poor Family

Fernando Colón, Ph.D.

Catholic Social Services, Ann Arbor, Michigan

INTRODUCTION

The multiproblem poor family has attracted the attention of many people. Concerned persons are acutely aware that the multiproblem poor family is not merely a family in one or another kind of trouble; it is a family whose many problems will challenge the capacities of any agent or agencies to help it. Because our methods for working with other populations fail miserably with these families, it is easy to become overwhelmed by the demands they can put upon us. Even so, personal involvement with them convinces us that these families are not in a category apart from us.

The assumption pervading this chapter is that the multiproblem poor family, like all others, is best understood within the context of the three-generational family system structure that reproduces itself across the family life cycle. The three-generational family system structure is defined as all members of the family both living and dead who are biologically related to one another. This definition includes all members of the immediate nuclear family (father, mother, and children), all members of the extended family on both the father's and the mother's side (grandparents, siblings, cousins, nieces and nephews), as well as the membership of stepfamilies, foster families and adoptive families who are in contact with the biological families.

The three-generational family system defined in this way suggests that the family system structure has the potential for becoming a rich reservoir of human resources for its members. This family system structure is the *ground* from which all forms of the *figure* of the family emerges—whatever the culture, race, social class, ethnic heritage, or time and place in human history. Every family system structure in every class and in every culture has to cope with the succession of its generations and their progression through its repeating family life cycle.

Moreover, when working with poor families we cannot disregard the political, social, and economic ecosystems within which the family lives out its generational and life cycle vicissitudes. The starkness of that *contextual* reality has to be reckoned with, and has to become an integral part of our approach.

In this chapter I have chosen to focus on the multiproblem poor family in particular—on the family with no sense of a stable economic base beneath it. These are nonworking families, members of the *underclass*. For them there is no shred of hope for anything but sporadic, menial work. Thus they are long-standing clients of public agencies such as housing, public health, welfare, and the courts. They are as well a continuous source of concern for the schools and the communities in which they live. Life in these families is often blighted by separation, divorce, child abuse and neglect, drug use, delinquent behavior, and criminal and violent behavior. They often seem to be in a state of disorganization, disintegration, and chaos. Indeed, their life cycle constitutes a virtually endless series of crises.

All members of such families share a profoundly hopeless set of assumptions—that they are not needed, that they have no right to exist, that society is saying there is nothing they can do, and that they are being destroyed by society itself. The self-esteem of the adult members of the multiproblem poor family is especially assaulted by the pervasive absence of adequate jobs.

In earlier eras, many unskilled jobs were available. Higher education was not as critical, fewer technological skills were required, and life was simpler. More recently, life has become more complex. Because the needed skills are more technologically complex, education has become critical. Because they have neither education nor the chance of acquiring it, the members of the multiproblem poor family are locked into poverty with no way out.

The result is that the jobless poor adults have the conviction, not contradicted by reality, that no matter what they do to get or keep a job, they will get nowhere. Often the only options for economic gain are illegal ones. For such reasons the multiproblem poor family develops a pervasive sense of impotence, rage, and despair. The only struggle is for survival; in the rural as well as the urban underclass, rage is directed at society, at members of one's family, at one's self, The work of Robert Coles (1964, 1967, 1970, 1978) has documented the lives of those families who live in rural poverty. The inevitable outcome is personal and familial disintegration.

In this chapter I will proceed as follows. First, I will briefly survey the literature on the sociology of the poor; second, I will review models of the family and methods of assessing and intervening with the multiproblem poor family; third, I will attempt to describe the family life cycle of the multiproblem poor family; fourth, I will discuss some hazards and pitfalls commonly encountered in therapeutic work with the poor family; fifth, I will present three case studies to illustrate therapeutic work with the poor family at its various life cycle stages; and finally, I will make some concluding remarks.

THE SOCIOLOGY OF THE POOR

The most recently published census report (Current Population Reports, 1979) indicates that in 1977 there were 25.8 million poor people in the United States. In this report, a nonfarm family of four is considered poor if its income is less than $6,191 annually. There are many kinds of poor families, varying as a function of race, color, language, ethnicity, and ability to cope. They also vary enormously as to whether their ongoing familial interconnectedness is active, infrequent, or nonexistent. In these regards they are not different from their middle-class and upper-class counterparts. Gans (1968) concludes from his reading of all available studies that there is as much variety among the poor as there is among the affluent.

> Some have been poor for generations, others are poor periodically, some are downwardly mobile, others are upwardly mobile. Many share middle-class values; others embrace working class values; some because of chronic deprivation have difficulty in adapting to new opportunities; and some are subject to physical and emotional illness which makes them unable to adapt to nonpathological situations. The research has not been done to tell us what percent of poor people fit into each of these categories. (1968, pp. 205–206)

Although the actual number of multiproblem poor families is not known, it is generally agreed that the farther one goes down the scale of economic deprivation, the more likely one is to encounter such families. It is important to note, however, that the disorganized and disintegrating family system is *not* unique to the underclass. Any family of any class may be subjected to such chronic, unremitting stress that it, too, will collapse.

Sociologists have tried hard to determine whether or not there is a distinct "culture of the poor." The cultural view emphasizes cross-generational family socialization processes that create and perpetuate the features of the poor. The situational view stresses the structural features of society that create and perpetuate those features of the occupational system that prevent the poor from ever improving their families' economic position.

Rossi and Blum (1968) doubt the existence of a "culture of the poor":

> The empirical evidence from our review of the literature does not support the idea of a culture of poverty in which the poor are distinctly different from other layers of society. Nor does the evidence from intergenerational mobility studies support the idea of a culture of poverty in the sense of the poor being composed largely of persons themselves coming from families living in poverty. (1968, pp. 43–44)

The underclass, however, do share more unemployment, family instability, high school dropouts, mental disorder, delinquency, mortality, and incidence of physical disorders, and a greater sense of alienation from the predominant middle class than is true of those immediately above them in socioeconomic status. However, these are quantitative, not qualitative, differences.

The dubious note sounded by Rossi and Blum, who question the validity of the concept of a distinct culture of poverty, is sounded as well by Gans. He believes that:

> The only proper research perspective is to look at the poor as an economically and politically deprived population whose behavior, values, and pathologies are adaptations to their existential situations, just as the behaviors, values and pathologies of the affluent are adaptations to their existential situation. In both instances, adaptation results in a mixture of moral and immoral, legal and illegal practices, but the nature of the mix is a function of the external situation. (1968, p. 216)

In addition, Gans also points to those "persisting cultural (and behavioral) patterns among the affluent that, deliberately or not, keep their fellow citizens poor" (p. 216).

Gans concludes his review of the status of the poor by stating, "Insofar as poverty research should focus on the poor at all it should deal with behavior patterns, norms and aspirations on an individual basis, relate them to their situational origin, and determine how much the behavioral norms related to poverty would persist under changing conditions" (p. 219). Thus Gans makes a plea for placing less emphasis on the study of the existing conditions of the poor and more emphasis on the field studies of the poor in experimentally improved situational conditions. I would only add that such studies should focus not on individuals, but rather on families and their capacity to change over time in an improved environment.

Sociological data on the working class, such as Komarovsky's (1962), are rich and potentially useful to family therapists who would understand their client families. So too is the literature on ethnicity (Spiegel & Papajohn, 1975; Giordano and Pineiro-Giordano, 1977; which describes the values and contexts of various groups. On such groups there is a growing body of literature including, for example, material on blacks (Clark, 1962; Billingsley, 1968; Hill, 1972, 1977; Foley, 1975; Stack, 1975; Boyd, 1977, 1980; McAdoo, 1977); Puerto Ricans (Cayo-Sexton, 1966; Montalvo, 1974; Mizio, 1979); Chinese-Americans (Nee and Nee, 1974); Irish (McGoldrick & Pearce, in press); Jews (Zborowshi and Herzog, 1976; Zuk, 1978); Mexican-Americans (Falicov and Karrer, Chapter 16); and Slovak-Americans (Stein, 1978).

For family therapists ethnicity is a major topic in itself, one that merits serious consideration if we would truly understand the variety of family systems that we encounter in our work. Giordano and Pineiro-Giordano (1977) state the case well when they write, "Significant gaps in theory, knowledge and methods of dealing with ethnicity remain. There is an obvious need to develop an overall conceptual and ideological approach that integrates the ethnocultural factor into all aspects of mental health practice" (p. 17).

Without knowledge of this kind, our interventions may be more destructive than constructive. In Spanish Harlem, for example, there is the need to recognize the importance of the role of the "spiritualist." A married woman was caught in infidelity to her husband. They both went to consult with the spiritualist. He and they attributed the wife's behavior to her being possessed by the spirit of a prostitute. He then assigned the couple the task of going on a vacation together. While on the vacation they were to take a chicken leg and nail it on a tree and thereby exorcise the evil spirit. When these instructions were followed, they enabled the husband to forgive his wife and to trust her again. Unfortunately, it is often all too easy for those of us who are unfamiliar with such folkways to dismiss them as primitive and superstitious beliefs when, in fact, they can be viable interventions (Minuchin et al., 1967).

With these necessarily brief comments on the sociology of the poor, let us now turn our attention to the efforts of the mental health community to understand, assess, and help the underclass family.

MODELS, ASSESSMENT, AND INTERVENTIONS

Models

In their classic study, *Families of the Slums* (1967), Minuchin, Montalvo, and their coworkers have attempted to observe, assess, intervene, and document both their successes and their failures in working with the poor ghetto family. They decided to study a sample of "those disadvantaged hard core families that produced more than one acting out child juvenile delinquent" (p. 368). Their sample consisted of twelve delinquent-producing families and twelve comparable control families that were without delinquents. Although their work focused largely on a limited number of nuclear families, they nevertheless were able to map out a beginning description of the disorganized poor ghetto family. They saw each of the delinquent-producing families for thirty ninety-minute sessions over an eight-month period. From this work they were able to delineate the organization of two kinds of families: the "disengaged" and the "enmeshed."

The "disengaged" family is characterized by a sense of anomie. The family appears to be in an atomistic field within which the members move in isolated orbits unrelated to each other. Their responses to each other are delayed and they appear to make no vital contact with each other. The mother is unresponsive, apathetic, overwhelmed, and depressed. She is unable to control the children. A parental child often tries to fill this parental vacuum. There is little interest on the part of one family member toward another. This family's social contact is extremely limited or nonexistent. The mother is often completely isolated, with a history of poor continuity in relationships either with men or with a stable work structure. If this family has any contact with social agencies, it is usually characterized by extreme passivity and dependency on the part of the mother.

The "enmeshed" family is a tightly interlocked system. Attempts of one member to change are quickly and complementarily resisted by other family members. Immediate reactivity is the dominant characteristic of the "enmeshed" family. When the children act up, the mother controls immediately. Mother and children seem caught in a circle of rebellious and counterreactive control responses. In this system, power conflicts are continuous. Escalation and counterescalation are typical. If the mother loses control of the kids, she gets anxious and fears she will become helpless. She has an overwhelming need to have a continual hold on the children.

The "enmeshed" family's tendency toward immediate reactivity and toward power struggles appears to generalize to the mother's interaction with therapists and other agencies. It leads the families to a greater sense of alienation, anonymity, and powerlessness. In spite of this, they do appear to be open to extrafamily resources. However, they tend to view agencies that help as "suckers" and do not hesitate to manipulate and exploit them if it suits their survival needs. They see the courts and the police as tough authorities, to be avoided if at all possible.

Oscar Lewis has described families living in the "culture of poverty" as suffering from feelings of marginality and helplessness. They have a minimum of organization beyond the level of the household and have very little sense of local community structure (Lewis, 1968). Minuchin and Montalvo (1967) were among the first to develop effective ways of working with such family systems. In their book, *Families of the Slums,* which was a landmark work in this area both theoretically and clinically, they described such families as disorganized, lacking in clear generational boundaries and differentiated communication patterns. They described the disorganized family as follows:

> The stereotyped interaction in our families can be expressed as a result of paucity and rigidity of interpersonal transactional patterns and also on a higher level of abstraction, as frozen development of the family as a total system. The system is "at rest" as a relatively simple social "organism" with a concomitant lack of specialization and differentiation in the component functions of its members. (1967, p. 368)

Aponte (1974, 1976), who has devoted himself to working with such families, has noted that while they have often been referred to as "disorganized," he prefers to use the term "underorganized,"

> to suggest not so much an improper kind of organization as a deficiency in the degree of constancy, differentiation, and flexibility of the structural organization of the family system. This kind of internal underorganization is accompanied by a lack of organizational continuity of the family with the structure of its societal context . . . its ecology. (1976, p. 433)

Aponte has distinguished three structural underpinnings of operational patterns in social systems: alignment, force, and boundary. He describes underorganized families as lacking in these underpinnings:

> Alignment refers to the joining or opposition of one member of a system to another in carrying out an operation. Force defines the relative influence of each member on the outcome of an activity. Boundary tells who is included and excluded from the activity. . . . Individuals or groups who are not effectively integrated within their ecological set lack alignments with other units in their society to help them achieve their social goals. They are short on the force to exert their portion of control over the actions taken in their social context that affect them. They also find themselves outside many of the operations of their society that are meant to enrich the units within the system. These structural conditions are descriptive of the poor in our society. (1976, p. 434)

Although Bowen (1978) has not specifically focused his attention on the multiproblem poor family, he has created a useful model of family functioning that is applicable to such families. In his model he has developed a differentiation of self scale to describe a person's level or differentiation of himself or herself from his or her family of origin. At the lower levels of the scale a person's sense of self is confused, disorganized, and chaotic. Persons at this end of the continuum are either cut off or highly isolated from their families or they are hoplessly enmeshed in conflict laden fusions and symbiotic attachments to their families. Persons higher on the scale of differentiation of self are freer of these problems.

It is a natural step to think of families as also being distributed along such a continuum. Beavers (1976) has developed a schema that describes three basic levels of family functioning: the severely disturbed family, the midrange family, and the healthy family. Within Beaver's schema, it is possible to construct a grid that compares low, middle, and high functioning families on a number of variables. Which family characteristics fall where is highly consistent with Bowen's schema of different levels of differentiation and with Minuchin's description of the poor ghetto family. In Table 15.1, I have attempted to pull these ideas together so that the reader can get a sense of some of the differences between families that might be placed at different points of the continuum. Entries 1 through 8 reflect Lewis's, Bowen's and Minuchin's work, while entries 9 through 11 reflect my additions.

Lewis et al. (1976) studied twenty-three high-income and middle- to upper-middle-class white Protestant families. Twelve of the families had a member who was one of a series of consecutive admissions to an inpatient adolescent service. Eleven families who were demographically comparable were obtained on a volunteer basis from a large local Protestant church. For these families to qualify for the study, no member of the family could be in psychiatric treatment or in difficulty with the legal authorities. Based on the schema described above, Lewis was able to differentiate these high-income families across the three different levels of the family functioning continuum.

The striking feature of the work of Minuchin, Bowen, Lewis, and their colleagues is that their work appears to converge around a model of family functioning that is consistent with the notion that families can be described on the basis of a rough typology. This seems to be the case even though Minuchin studied families at the low end of the economic scale and Lewis studied families at the high end of the scale.

However, two caveats are in order. First, these models did not systematically take into account the powerful effect of the context on the functioning of the family. It is for this reason that I have added the ninth through eleventh entries to the table. Contextual factors and their impact upon the family need to be researched so that a full field description of the family in different contexts will become possible. As yet, we have hardly begun to do this. The other caveat is that all the models described above do have a middle-class conception of family roles built into them. For example, other cultures do not stress competition and individual achievement but rather cooperation and a primary concern for what is best for the family and for the community.

TABLE 15.1

CHARACTERISTICS OF FAMILIES AS A FUNCTION OF LEVEL OF FAMILY ORGANIZATION

Level of Family Organization	LOW Severely Disturbed	MIDDLE Moderately Disturbed	HIGH No Disturbance
(1) View of Reality	· sameness · no differentiation	· black/white · good/bad	· shades of grey · differentiated
(2) Nuclear and Extended Family Organization	· fusions · cut-offs · fluidity · overt breakdown · overt cross-generational collusions	· limited extended family contact · not enough to absorb stress · rigidity · covert cross-generational collusions	· active extended family contact · enough to absorb N.F. stress · spouse unit dominant · sib sub-unit different from spouse unit
(3) Sense of Time	· sense of timelessness · time does not seem to pass · things don't change	· distorted · passage of time not fully accepted	· passage of time is accepted · time changes are celebrated
(4) Vulnerability to Stress	· very high · multi-problems	· are subject to stress · there are unresolved problem areas	· less subject to stress · can resolve problems
(5) Parental Control	· intrusive · tell kids what to think and feel · pervasive denial of responsibility	· criticism is frequent · attempt to control what kids think and feel · rigid rules	· accept kids thoughts and feelings · try to shape kids behavior · clear, flexible rules
(6) Communication	· unable to complete communication sequences · reactive response to one another · unable to resolve conflict	· able to complete some communication sequence · able to achieve partial resolutions · rules more rigid	· able to complete communication sequences · able to achieve full resolutions · all are to be listened to and responded to
(7) Affect	· negative · chaotic · without variety	· negative · some variety · competitive	· O.K. to express both positive and negative · cooperative
(8) Reaction to Separation, Loss, Death	· very disorganized · refuse to accept or to mourn · denial of death	· frozen reaction · limited acceptance · partial mourning	· do accept loss · do let go · do mourn
(9) Physical Context	· impoverished · sub-standard housing · inadequate food and clothing	· more options · adequate food, clothing and housing	· many options · abundance of food, clothing and housing
(10) Employment Context	· none or very limited · no sense of the future being better	· usually employed on regular basis · jobs tend to be routine · limited opportunity to advance	· regularly employed · interesting jobs · opportunities to advance
(11) Social Context	· isolated · alienated · fragmented	· less alienation · some connection and cohesiveness	· not alienated · active, viable social contact · many options

Assessment

Adequate assessment of the multiproblem poor family, as of all families, requires the gathering of information for a genogram (Bowen, 1978; Guerin, 1976). This is a three-generational assessment of the family system over the course of the family life cycle. As suggested by the work of Glick (1964), a complete genogram will include family demographic data. This would include such life events as births, entry into school, entry into work, marriages, separations, divorces, household formation and dissolution, moves to a different home, illnesses, handicaps, and deaths. These demographic data and their accompanying details nicely parallel and factually describe the family as it moves through its life cycle stages.

As Hoffman (1969, 1974), Aponte (1974, 1976), and Montalvo (1974) have emphasized, the therapist also needs to pay particular attention to the social network and ecosystem of the family. This can include neighbors, friends, grocery store owners, police, the schools, the fire department, and the church. The interface between the family and its ecosystem may be strong or weak. For the multiproblem poor family the problem is not only whether it can viably connect with the sources of support and continuity that lie outside the family, but also whether such supports external to the family do in fact exist.

Interventions

Interventions with poor families appear to fall into four general categories. First, there are those therapies that take place in the clinic described by Minuchin (1967, 1974), Haley (1976), and Boszormeniyi-Nagy and Spark (1973). Second, there are those that involve therapy in the family's home. Of this category Klein (1964) describes an excellent example. Third is the approach of Speck (1973) who, although he works in the home, directly involves the social network of the family as well as the family itself. His work is very promising if, in fact, one can identify a viable social network for the family.

Finally, there are the rehabilitative approaches designed to help the family connect with and revitalize their participation in their social milieu. Bush (1977) describes this kind of approach as one taken by the Lower East Side Family Union of New York City. The Family Union coordinates the efforts of agencies such as the school, the court, the health department, and the social services department by arranging specific service contracts between the agencies and the family. Moreover, the Union puts much effort into building and reestablishing the informal neighborhood social networks that can also provide for self-help. In these ways they are able to help high-risk families to reconnect in viable ways with their social environments, thus reducing the chronic stress experienced by these families.

When we attempt to intervene with the multiproblem poor family, we need to begin by rebuilding the family's social network. Interventions that fail to take into account the social context of the family are not likely to succeed. After the family's basic structure within the social-economic milieu has been stabilized (Aponte, 1974, 1976), the structural-therapeutic approaches developed by Minuchin (1967, 1974) and Haley (1976) can then be applied. The structural approach will enable the family to begin to reestablish itself as a functioning unit in the interface between itself and its social context.

Minuchin and his colleagues have provided the most useful model of short-term family therapy with multiproblem poor families (the structural model). Aponte, a prominent exponent of this model, has made work with this population his specialty; through workshops and articles (1974, 1976), he has promulgated techniques directly applicable to the poor family in crisis. With concrete and other social services as backup, the practitioners of the structural method move in rapidly to shore up the family's sagging hierarchy (usually reliant on only mother or grandmother) and define the generational boundaries. Their method of "joining" the family in style and language permits them rapid access to a position of influence in the system, and it requires minimal adaptation on the family's part to the arcane rituals of middle-class professional practice. While working on crisis issues, it is necessary for the therapist to move with the ebb and flow of broken and missed appointments, to reach out through check-up or reminder phone calls, and in other ways accommodate to the family's different sense and use of time—to a poor family time does not mean money or opportunity.

However, useful this short-term crisis model of family therapy is in the majority of cases, it is also worthwhile to be on the alert for the occasional family, or individual family member, who is willing or able to respond to more than crisis intervention. For this reason it is useful to routinely construct a three-generational genogram, and, in addition to focusing on the current crisis in the household, to probe the family's involvement with distant or absent family members. When it happens that a person or persons from an underclass family shows a willingness to work in therapy beyond the crisis, this base line data can be very useful.

One of the most innovative approaches for working with poor families was the project developed by Minuchin, Haley, Weiner, Walters, Ford, and Montalvo at the Philadelphia Child Guidance Clinic (Haley, 1972). They instituted a special training program to train poor people to work with poor black families. The idea was to determine whether such persons, without prior therapeutic experience or academic credentials, who were competently managing their own lives and who were judged to be helpful persons, could be trained to be effective family therapists with poor families. The training program consisted of simulating family interviews, live supervision, and some lecture material—but no reading assignments. The teaching was done primarily through the active treatment of families, was very successful as a means of providing treatment for underclass families.

If a poor family is to be enabled to use itself as a resource, then it will need ongoing family therapy to restore the basis of mutual trust among its members. Recent elaborations of the "contextual family therapy" approach is an especially promising model in this regard (Boszormeniyi-Nagy, 1980; Boszormeniyi-Nagy and Krasner, 1979). Boszormeniyi-Nagy and his co-workers seek to establish the ethical basis of all family relationships. They are concerned with rebuilding mutual trust among broken and dysfunctional family relationships. Their model emphasizes the need to rework and to redefine the legacy of accumulated loyalties, obligations, debts, and hurts that are a part of the history in the three-generational family system. Their work merits the attention of the serious student of family theory, therapy, and technique.

THE FAMILY LIFE CYCLE OF THE MULTIPROBLEM POOR FAMILY

My effort to describe the family life cycle of the poor will use as its point of departure the work of Minuchin and his colleagues (1967). This effort is an initial attempt to describe the nature and quality of the family life cycle of the multiproblem poor family. As such, it is highly speculative and tentative, intended to provoke thought rather than to set down conclusions. My description must be seen as a "variation" from the middle-class, culture bound view of the family life cycle that predominates in the United States. I want to highlight the aspects of the multiproblem poor family that are a function of its context rather than of its so-called "deviant" qualities. (I am very indebted to P. Friedman [1979] for his thoughts on this section of the chapter. Mr. Friedman has spent many years working with the poor.)

We in the profession have developed a view of the family life cycle of the middle class as one in which there is typically an intact nuclear family with ongoing, mutually satisfying contact with the extended family across several generations. In fact, we need to modify this view, for this prototypical family system itself is increasingly at risk. Given the mobility of modern life and the high rate of divorce, middle-class families also experience considerable dislocation; in this respect they are not far removed from poor families. These facts, coupled with the obsession with individual achievement so characteristic of our culture, are enough to raise serious questions about how intact the three-generational middle-class family system really is.

Nevertheless, in some quarters the three-generational family system is alive and well, as among the Mormons, for example, and other religious or ethnic groups within both urban and rural settings. Whether we look at the middle-class or at the poor family, the prototype of the three-generational family system can be a useful model. By comparing the family life cycle of the poor to that of the middle-class norm, we can pinpoint more accurately the stresses and strains that poor families encounter as they go through life.

Viewed across the usual three-generational time frame, the life cycle of poor families seems more truncated than that of middle-class families. The multiproblem poor person leaves home, marries, has children, gets divorced, becomes a grandparent, gets old, and dies earlier than the middle-class counterpart. Poor families are subject to more abrupt loss of membership through cut-offs, deaths, imprisonment, and drug addiction. This requires remaining family members to assume new roles and responsibilities, often before they are developmentally capable of doing so. Multiproblem poor families seem to have less calendar time for the unfolding of various developmental stages throughout their shortened life cycle. Thus there is less distinctness and more blurring of the boundaries of the life stages of this family. The shortened duration of the family life cycle means that there is often inadequate time to resolve the developmental tasks of each life stage. Subsequent stages are necessarily more difficult to traverse because the solid underpinnings of previously resolved tasks are not available.

All of these factors result in the development of a family system that is less complex, less adequately organized to cope with its needs, and less well-differentiated than its middle-class counterpart (Aponte 1974, 1976). Indeed, in the proposed three-stage family life cycle of the poor that follows, it will be seen that these families appear to lump themselves into Stage 2. This is the stage where a female is the head of the household. The household consists of the mother, her children, and often her daughters' children without their respective roles clearly delineated.

The phenomenon of females being the head of a household is not an isolated one. The current Population Reports (1979) state that between 1969 and 1977 the number of poor families with a female head, with no husband present, rose from 1.8 million to 2.6 million. In 1977, the poverty rate for families with a female head was 32% compared with only 6% for all other families. Thus the multiproblem poor family does not tend to change, adapt, and develop into a three-generational set of subsystems. At each stage of its life cycle there is difficulty in letting go of old roles and assuming new ones. There is a blurring of the shift from child and adolescent roles to marital, parental, and grandparental roles, without clear transitional demarcations or rites of passage. If it is to survive in such contexts, the family system must develop a variant adaptive form of family structure. However, the poor family exists in a context that presents formidable barriers to the unfolding of normative developmental processes.

Although this chapter focuses on the family structure of the multiproblem poor family, and what follows is a description of a truncated family system that turns out to be dysfunctional, certainly not all families with female heads are dysfunctional. Of those that are functional, most have access to adequate contextual resources and retain rich, viable ties with their extended families and with their communities (Hill, 1977; Klausner, 1978). In the material that follows it must be kept in mind that I am describing a family system response and adaptation to a *pernicious* negative context.

Bowen's (1978) work on the differentiation of the self is highly useful when this concept is applied to the evolution and differentiation of a family system. However, it is easy to make the mistake of assuming that the highly differentiated person or family is an autonomous individual or unit. In fact, no person or family system functions in the absence of supportive ecosystems. Not taking this reality into account is like forgetting that a fish needs water. In this sense, lack of differentiation and fusion is seen as the beginning phase of a developmental process. At high levels of differentiation there is rich emotional, intellectual, and social intercourse, both within the family structure and within the family's social-community context.

Terkelsen, in Chapter 2 of this book, has given us an excellent beginning framework for a theory of the family life cycle. However, he, too, makes an assumption about an autonomous family that belies the reality of every family's need for ongoing mutual interdependence and support. At the end of his chapter he speaks about the goals of enabling families to be sufficient by means of restoration, supplementation, and replacement. In supplementation, the treatment plan includes the creation of a more or less permanent attachment between the family and some external support such as Al-Anon, and the like. But all functional families have permanent external supports. However, for those of the middle class we use different names, such as the country club, the church, the Lion's Club, and so forth.

When Terkelsen speaks of replacement, he refers to families with such limited resources that without extensive supplementation they can't provide the elements needed for growth. This leads to the use of foster care, group living situations, halfway houses, and so on. Again, I would caution against the use of the notion of "replacement" because even the most limited family structures are *not* replaceable. Continued connection to the family structure is a vital human resource. Alternate living situations, such as foster care, can be seen as links in a process of continued connection between the family and the person in foster care or other placement settings. These ideas, fully detailed in my previous papers (Colón; 1973; 1978), point to the sense that whatever a person's family of origin situation, it always remains a vital part of the person's context and a very central aspect of his or her existence.

Stage 1—The Unattached Young Adult

The developmental tasks for the young adult are to fashion an identity and to commit himself or herself to work and marriage. Adolescents from multiproblem poor families are often either thrown out of the home to fend for themselves, or clung to desperately by the one-parent family because they represent a potential source of income in a context with very limited resources. Inevitably, most adolescents find the pressure of staying home unbearable. The pull of their peers is powerful, and they draw away from the burden of the family, hoping to make their own way.

Because they tear away and do not grow away from their families, they are ill-equipped with the skills that it takes to do well in society. Typically, they are high school dropouts and they have no job options except menial ones. Occasionally, they may be so lucky as to obtain a civil service job. What is open to them is illegal activity and because it promises to put a quick end to the pain of poverty, its appeal is powerful.

Most critical of all stages is that of the unattached young adult. There is an all-or-nothing, do-or-die, make-it-or-break-it quality to the adolescent experience. What is truly frightening is that adolescents among the poor are confronted with this stark reality at increasingly younger ages. What used to occur at sixteen to seventeen years of age is now occurring at ten to eleven years of age. The impact of the adolescent peer group is critical in determining which way the young adult will go. The press for a self-destructive solution is enormous. It is not difficult to see why these young people, with no hope for adequate employment, so often resort to such criminal activity as prostitution and drug traffic, and thus come to addiction and alcoholism.

Many adolescents simply go under at this point. Others, far too few, are lucky. They happen to meet the right people at the right time, are able to get a glimpse of other possibilities, and with the support of concerned people within committed relationships, they are able to move up and out. If adolescents can garner enough time and avoid the minefields that are all around them, they might have a chance. The odds are not good that they will. Although a few adolescents make it, they are usually exceptional people in terms of brains, genes, and luck. They make it out of underclass poverty only by dint of extraordinary energy, fortitude, and courage. They also have to cope with deep feelings of guilt for leaving their families and their peers behind. In light of these obstacles, it is very difficult indeed for poor young adults to develop a keen sense of themselves and to commit themselves to the world of work and marriage. Without viable work options, commitment to anything other than survival is not possible.

For the adolescent female, the situation is equally bleak. However, being female makes her less likely to wind up in jail and more likely to be on the streets, securing income via prostitution and living a harsh, brutal, violent, and manipulated life. Her only identity option is to be a mother; it is as a mother that she will probably live out her life. The adolescent male, because of limited job options, is a transient and peripheral figure in his heterosexual relationships. He serves a procreative function but frequently cannot go beyond that. Consequently, his identity often remains fragmentary and incomplete. In his life, he may rarely have seen adult men functioning in the parental capacity with legitimate, stable job roles.

Stage 2—The Family with Children

When a young man and woman do get together in either an unmarried or married state, the relationship is inherently unstable. They have had precious few models for stable married life, except those they see on television, which are difficult to identify with because the resources of the television families are so much more abundant than theirs. The pull of the old, more exciting single life is powerful when compared to their present circumstances of drudgery with no sense of a future that would include a steady job, a home, and children. Because of their limited resources, and because they live in a context where people are concerned for themselves only, it is extremely difficult for a couple to sustain itself as a viable unit in the context of chronic stress and difficulty.

The advent of children, with no jobs, spells trouble for the new family. What then evolves is a family pattern in which the mother obtains Aid to Dependent Children (ADC) and the father becomes the peripheral male. In this situation, another pattern that can develop is that the parents remain juvenile and do not become parental. That is, they remain primarily identified with their adolescent peer groups and avoid the adult parenting roles. Thus the functions of adult mutuality and shared responsibility for the children do not develop, and the children can be left to fend for themselves (Minuchin et al., 1967).

As this system evolves, the male becomes more peripheral and the female more central and dominant. The mother becomes the organizing force within the family. She may continue to receive ADC support by having a series of additional children both within or outside of wedlock. Therapeutic goals aimed at bolstering the self-esteem of the peripheral father miss the mark. In his adult role in society he is treated like a child so that he is hardpressed to maintain a consistent sense of himself as an adult. The press to procreate may be bolstered by the need to insure some sense of continuity. Procreation is about the only source of continuity available to the underclass couple.

Marital instability marked by infidelity, desertion, illegitimacy, and divorce is very common and widespread among the poor. Meyer, in Chapter

4 of this book, rightly asks whether repeated marriages, postponement of marriages, living alone, or being divorced are signs of serious family and social problems or rather signs of progress and greater flexibility. Within the underclass these signs are often defined by the dominant middle class as symptoms of family dysfunction and disintegration.

When a family evolves without a husband and father consistently in the picture, the members of the family can lose rich sources of identification with the marital subsystem and the role of the father. There are data that suggest that the father may be the most important parent in the psychosexual development of the children of either sex (Hetherington, 1973). However, even if the husband/father does stay in the picture, the spouse subsystem may remain vaguely delineated or undefined (Minuchin, 1967). This is because in a context of scarcity the father's role as breadwinner will supercede any other role he might have, including that of spouse.

Husband/wife transactions are typically unfinished, vague, and unresolved. Conflictual issues that involve use of time, and money are so fluid that the couples are unable to explore, negotiate, and modify those areas of their lives. Only their parenting role seems to offer stable channels for them to focus upon. Spouse conflict appears to arise from a host of unfinished role definitions. Unfinished role definitions are roles that have not fully evolved, so that the person has *not* had the opportunity to be a child or be an adolescent prior to entering adulthood. There are gaps, inconsistencies, confusion, and uncertainty as to how these roles are carried out. This is a function of their own parents' impoverished interpersonal, social, and emotional histories. The failure to adequately define themselves in their previous roles can lead them to have an intense need to overemploy the role of the parent. The parental role becomes the role for experiencing some kind of reflected identity. Their organization around the role of being parents does offer some justification for their existence. But, in time, the children accept the idea of the male's role as useless, if not unknown. Male children are handicapped by this derogated concept of maleness and the related inability to visualize their future role in the family. The pimp, the numbers man, the dope pusher become their sources of identification and further confuse male children by equating irresponsibility and violence with masculinity. Because of the ADC economic setup, the mother soon runs the show and the father inevitably becomes highly peripheral to the family or completely disengaged.

So the mother is left with the children and soon she is overburdened. Within the context of scarcity, survival is the name of the game. Conflict, tension, and anxiety are high; cooperation is low or nonexistent. In time, the "parental child" may emerge who attempts to fill the parental vacuum that the overburdened mother has understandably abdicated. But the parental child is in an impossible situation. With inadequate skills or power, this child can become the object of his or her siblings' rage. They may be jealous of his or her special favor with the mother and/or enraged at the mother for failing to be an adequate parent (Minuchin et al., 1967).

For the school-age children of multiproblem poor families, life is grim. The mother, who is chronically overburdened and often depressed, may be unable to respond to her children on an individual basis. She responds to their needs collectively, and the children, without individual attention from their mother or absent father, fail to develop the cognitive, affective, and communicational skills that will enable them to benefit from a middle-class oriented school system. When the child enters school, the teacher often expects him or her to fail, and given both the reality from which the child comes and the teacher's negative expectation, he or she does fail. If the child goes to a ghetto school, the prospects are even worse, as Kozol (1972) so passionately describes in his book about a ghetto school in which he taught. Aponte (1976) addresses this issue in his paper that describes working at the interface of the school and the family system. In an excellent paper, Hoffman (1974) has given a poignant description of the negative labelling process that occurred to a child in a school system, along with some thoughts about how one might counteract the school's "amplification of deviance" process.

The childrearing stage of the multiproblem poor family tends to be protracted as more children are born over an extended period of time. In time, the mother is unable to control the older children and releases them to their peer group. Thus she loses any effective capacity to influence them, even if she had the motivation to do so. In the latency age, children look to their older siblings for guidance, control, and direction, but they too are soon absorbed by the peer culture.

Stage 3—The Family in Later Life

When the parental child described in Stage 2 is a daughter, the press to escape from her impossible role is a powerful factor in pushing her into the role of unwed mother. However, when the baby is born, the daughter may be unable to make the shift from being a "parental" daughter to being a mother; and her own mother may be unable either to allow her daughter to become a mother or to shift into the role of being a grandmother. Both shifts are necessary in order for the generational process to maintain its forward momentum, which would further differentiate the family system.

The forward thrust of the generational process becomes stalled, if not derailed. Instead, the daughter's mother makes the grandchild another one of her children; daughter remains a daughter; and the new child experiences its mother as an older sister. This leads to a family system that is devoted to survival and homeostasis, not change and growth. Roles are not clearly delineated, except for that of the mother/grandmother whose role is strenuous indeed, but who has much greater power and importance than her middle-class counterpart.

The extended family of the multiproblem poor family can become totally fragmented, or it can live together with very few resources in a single, distressingly crowded, inadequate dwelling. As such, the extended family is unable to provide any tangible supports for the mother. If the extended family is living together, it often is a further drain upon the mother's already very meager resources.

The next major event in the family life cycle of these families is the death of the mother/grandmother. This can have a devastating effect upon the family. At this point the system can go into total collapse and disintegrate. However, the oldest daughter, who was unable to become a mother, now may be able to step into the role played by her mother and thereby begin to repeat the life cycle of the family.

If the nonevolved grandmother does not die at a relatively early age, which is in itself quite remarkable because her problems have been so immense every step of the way, she may have the misfortune to find herself in a nursing home. Often these women are great sources of strength and human wisdom because they did, indeed, survive and that fact makes them extraordinary people.

HAZARDS COMMONLY ENCOUNTERED IN THERAPEUTIC WORK WITH THE MULTIPROBLEM POOR FAMILY

There are many pitfalls for those of us who would work with the multi-problem poor family. There are problems with public agencies, with the allocation of scarce resources, with politics, with graft, and with the delivery of services. Descriptions by Hoffman (1969, 1974) aptly review the frustrating complexity of these problems and how they can work against therapeutic efforts to encourage family and individual functioning. The multiproblem poor family relies upon societal support systems, and a therapist cannot help the family unless he or she is willing to get involved with social services, the health department, the schools, and the courts.

The poor family's mistrust of the professional is usually based on previous bad experience with various agencies. It is important for the therapist to understand this negative attitude, not to take it personally; to clarify expectations both negative and positive; and to be prepared to state clearly what kind of help the family can realistically expect to receive from him or her. It is important to get an idea of the family's previous experience with the helping professions and to listen sympathetically to their complaints without defending the agencies or promising what cannot be delivered. Patronizing poor families or treating them like children who cannot be expected to assume any responsibility is the most glaring pitfall of all.

Another common error with the poor is to get so quickly caught up in their presenting crisis that we neglect to take the same careful three-generational information that we routinely get on middle- and upper-class families. For most families there is an extended family (Klausner, 1978; Hill, 1977), whether in Puerto Rico, the South, Appalachia, Mexico, or even further away. No matter how remote, their existence and state of relatedness to the family is important, and no complete assessment can be made without such information. The attempt to restore these intergenerational connections and continuities when possible is vital. Krasner (1979) states that "the poor are disconnected from the past and future and so... reconstructing the familial context is the major task of therapy."

A middle-class therapist who remains ignorant of the culture and structural adaptations of the poor family and attempts to push them toward middle-class family structure and values will not help the family. This means retaining a flexible view of family (and therapy) membership; transient members of the household should be included, even if unrelated; absent fathers (there may be several) should be inquired about and possibly invited. The family should not be urged to separate physically, but rather be helped to define generational boundaries within their common household. This would be especially true of the process of role shifts for the mother, oldest daughter, and daughter's child, with the goal of effecting delineation and differentiation of role function, so that the forward thrust of the generational process can be reinstituted.

The personal experience of therapists with multiproblem poor families, and their emotional reactions to such cases, also bear scrutiny. Negative stereotypes of the poor as being lazy, inadequate, and pathological tend to obscure the existence of many strengths. The clinician's own personal experience or lack of experience with poor families can lead to feelings of anxiety, avoidance, and/or guilt, or to overresponsible reactions. Therapists at times experience stagnation because they cannot justify their own affluence in the face of their client's poverty. Or poorly paid community workers may overidentify with their poor clients, thereby rendering themselves equally ineffective. Attempts to operate on the basis of guilt or a "bleeding heart" will inevitably fail. A useful goal is to stay personally connected with the poor, but also to stay connected with one's own viable contextual base, which can make it possible for therapists to bridge the distance between themselves and the poor family. This means staying in regular, active contact with one's own extended family, which provides a continuing base for the therapist's own hope and vitality.

Perhaps the place where we are most vulnerable in our work with poor families is in our reactions to abuse and neglect of children. When we encounter a situation where the life of a child is at stake, it is not unusual to find therapists taking over, threatening and coercing the family to change its ways. This is understandable, and at times it may even be necessary. But perhaps we tend to do this more than it is really necessary for due to the high anxiety engendered in most of us when we encounter violence. If we cannot control our own anxiety, we tend to override, if not crush, the family's capacity to be responsible for, and to help, itself. We thus keep the family in a state of powerlessness. This is a critical issue and calls for a continuous effort to work *with* and not *on* the poor family.

Kapelle, Scott, and Western (1976) report that it is possible to effectively help families who abuse their children through the use of volunteer parent aids: "The aide plays the role of loving friend to the parents, visiting and being available by telephone on a twenty-four-hour basis. The aide becomes the resource always available when the loneliness, the stress, and the crisis is about to overwhelm" (p. 21). These families are invariably demanding, exhausting and difficult. It is impressive to see how these parents are enabled to change their behavior within the context of a deeply committed human relationship. Few professionals can engage in this kind of effort, and yet this kind of effort is precisely what is needed.

Finally, it is not uncommon for the therapist who deals with poor families to "burn out." One would do well to heed the advice of Beels (1976), who comments on the phenomenon of "burn out" when dealing with families who have a schizophrenic member.

> The intensity of this work, the constant facing of defeat without becoming personally defeated, the finding of some way to redefine a situation to include the possibility of hope and constructive action is an exhausting personal encounter. One must be able to retreat sometimes. No one can do this work all week long or every year of his life. The working life of the staff must include times of retreat and reflection. Otherwise they get burned out—permanently turned off from too much coping." (1976, p. 281)

His remarks can be readily applied to the family therapist working with the multiproblem poor family. Staff doing this kind of work need greater flexibility and administrative support in order to function effectively.

CASE ILLUSTRATIONS

The case illustrations that follow reflect attempts to work with the multiproblem poor family. I have selected three cases to represent the three stages of the family life cycle of the multiproblem poor family discussed in this chapter. Neither definitive nor complete, these presentations are not meant to be sterling examples of how to do effective work with poor families, but rather to illustrate the present state of the art. Each case is actually a composite in order to protect the confidentiality of the persons involved and in order to more fully illustrate some of the ideas suggested in this chapter.

Case 1. The Unattached Young Adult: Susan (See Figure 15.1)

Presenting Problems. Susan, a single twenty-eight-year-old Asian-American graduate student, was born and raised within the context of a multiproblem poor family. At the time Susan began therapy, she had been cut off from her family for over two years because all contact with them had been consistently negative and painful. The forward motion of her life had reached a standstill. The central therapeutic consideration was to see whether or not Susan could be helped to come to terms with her life experience by reconnecting herself to her family in spite of their prevailing rejecting attitude towards her. It was clear that

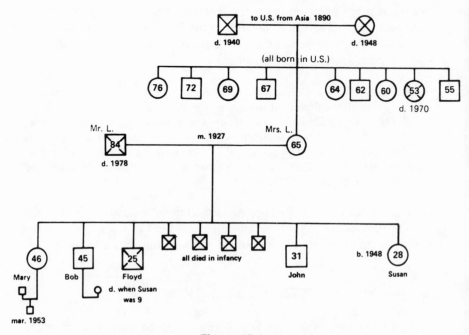

Figure 15.1.
The Unattached Young Adult: Susan

her continual lack of connection to them was further deepening her sense of despair, hoplessness, and futility.

Sue's initial concern was that she felt she could no longer compete academically. The pressures of competition and lack of support were getting to her. She became emotionally immobilized in class and no longer felt that she belonged in graduate school. When she had left the area where her family lived to go to school, they had been very upset with her. They labelled her as useless, self-indulgent, living the easy life, and going to school to avoid working. Thus, she attended graduate school with no emotional, social, or material support from her family. In fact, she was breaking the family's Asian tradition by not enhancing her value to the family through marriage. She was, indeed, seeking something different for her own life. After she left for school, her family did not communicate with her.

After we had established a good working relationship, I encouraged Susan to make a visit home. She was not warmly received. Her family still did not understand her academic aspirations and believed that she wanted nothing to do with them and thought of her as trying to be "different" from them. During this trip she learned that her oldest brother, Bob, whom she had not seen for five years, had moved to within 200 miles of her but had not contacted her. This increased her sense of alienation and isolation from her family. Indeed, she felt, "If I go on and get more education, I'll lose my family and my identity." But she nevertheless felt powerfully driven to continue with her education. One month after this trip home, she learned belatedly that her father was critically ill. She was upset, hurt, and furious that her family had put forth no effort to inform her. This incident reaffirmed her feeling that her family's attitude toward her had not changed in spite of her visit home.

Family Background. Sue's family lived in the poor section of town. When she was a child she lived in substandard, inadequately heated housing. Fights, stabbings, and drunks in the streets were not unusual where she lived. Her father, Mr. L., had immigrated from Asia to the United States to escape starvation in the 1920s. Sue knew nothing about his extended family except that he came from a rural farming village. He was approximately twenty years older than her mother.

Susan's mother, Mrs. L., came from a large extended family. Mrs. L's parents had married in the 1890s in Asia before immigrating to the United States. Mrs. L. was the fifth child of eleven siblings, all of whom were born in the United States. Only Mrs. L had a traditionally arranged marriage. Although Susan's aunts all married Oriental men, they took an active part in selecting their mates. Eight of Mrs. L's sibs married, two did not. Five of them had children; as a result, Susan had fifteen first cousins. Susan's parents had nine children: two girls and seven boys. Four of the sons died in infancy. Another son, Floyd, died at age twenty-five. This left four survivors: an oldest daughter, Mary; two older sons, Bob and John; and Sue, the youngest.

When Mr. and Mrs. L married in 1927, the United States was in the Depression and times for them were very hard. Mere survival became the overriding issue. Susan's mother never developed her own sense of what she wanted out of life. Unlike her sibs, who did quite well in school, she was a slow learner, disliked school, and was only able to complete the sixth grade by the time she was sixteen. When she was seventeen she married Mr. L. and apparently accepted her arranged marriage as her lot in life.

Mrs. L. was unprepared for motherhood. Floyd, her third child, was unwell at birth. He became quite ill at the time he completed first grade, and Mr. and Mrs. L. failed to secure adequate medical help for him even though Mrs. L's sisters urged them to do so. This led Mr. L. to cut off contact between himself and his wife's extended family. The family then went through a very difficult period, from 1933 to 1937, during which the next four sons all died in infancy.

As this period came to an end, Mrs. L's sisters, responding to Mrs. L.'s dire circumstances, often had her children Mary and Bob over for weekends and summers. This helped to offset their experience of deprivation and helped the family to get going again. Mary subsequently married in 1955 and left the state. Bob left home and joined the Air Force where he stayed until he retired. In 1945 John was born. Both he and Bob were valued by Mr. L. because they were male and he hoped, as is the Asian tradition, that someday they would support him. However, this never happened, probably because of the great gulf between them due to age and clash of cultural values. Floyd, who was sick with TB most of his life, was viewed as a burden to the family. Mary and Susan, as daughters, were expected to marry in the traditional way and bring a compensating dowry into the family.

Born in 1945, after the family had lost four sons, John became the recipient of overwhelming expectations to make up to his depressed parents for the loss of his four older brothers. Susan was born in 1948. Because her mother was overwhelmed, Susan's older sister Mary often cared for her. Mary was Susan's primary caretaker until Susan was six years old; at that time Mary left home. As a child Sue experienced a lot of abuse and neglect. Her barely functioning mother often witnessed John's physical and psychological abuse of Susan, but she did nothing to intervene. John often threatened to kill Susan and was often physically abusive to his father as well.

As long as Floyd was in the picture, Susan had some degree of protections. Floyd had attended first grade after a very bleak childhood. School opened a whole new, exiciting world for him. He was extremely intelligent. After first grade he became ill, but the school sent teaching tutors to the home, thereby adding a critical outside resource to the family. His teachers liked him, and Floyd felt teaching was one of the most important professions one could have. Learning made his life worth living. Floyd earned his General Educational Development Certificate and although chronically ill, succeeded in getting through two years of college.

Floyd took a vital interest in Susan and taught her to read and write before she entered the first grade. Without ever verbalizing it, he taught her that education was her salvation. He held a vision for her of a different life if she made the right choices and got an education. When Susan started first grade, she was with a teacher who discriminated against her. However, another teacher, who had been Floyd's first grade teacher, had Susan placed in her class. This was a marker event, because thereafter through the eighth grade Susan was almost always at the top 10% of her class.

When Susan was nine years old, Floyd finally died of TB. Without Floyd to protect her, Sue was at the mercy of her disintegrating family. The tension escalated continuously from the time she was nine until she was fourteen. She experienced some relief when she spent weekends and some time during the summers at her maternal aunts. However, since there were several aunts involved, she could never meet their demands, and some thought her inadequate like her mother. When she was at home, her life was in a constant state of threat so that she became convinced that her family did not want her to live. On occasion, she would go to her room and totally destroy it, giving vent to her rage. Then she was told by her family that she was crazy. She had to learn to display no emotion to the family, because if she did, she was abused until she stopped crying.

At age fourteen, the family problems culminated in Susan's bringing her parents to court for abuse and neglect. They all appeared in court and testified against one another. The mother's extended family regarded Susan's family with disdain because of their poverty, fighting, violence, and general instability. The outcome of the court hearing was that her parents were declared unfit, and Susan was placed in foster care. From then until she was eighteen she lived in three foster homes, none of which was a positive experience. During this period she still managed to maintain a B average in high school. She graduated from high school and went to work as a receptionist-secretary. Her boss was supportive, advising her against an early marriage, and encouraging her to attend college. She followed his advice and worked her way through undergraduate school, where she excelled academically. During this period she had occasional contact with her family, but it was never a positive, supportive experience.

Interventions. During the initial phase of treatment, Susan began to face her past, which she had suppressed for so long. This confrontation with her history was frightening because she felt "disjointed" from it. Indeed, she felt that she had been fleeing from her past by pursuing her education. As she reexperienced it, she felt out of place, disrupted, and lost. She recollected many painful events and realized that the only point of stability that she could fall back upon was her relationship to her brother Floyd. She felt nothing else of value existed for her in her nuclear family. Within her family it appeared to be everyone for himself or herself, that individual survival was central even at the expense of other family members' lives via neglect and abuse. Along with these feelings was the dread that if she failed academically there would be no place for her to go, and yet she was finding it increasingly difficult to function in that area.

As we continued, Susan began to more fully recover her one positive family tie: Floyd. After his death, the family acted as if he had never existed, especially when Susan spoke about him. When she did, they would attack her for it. She experienced much despair, had deep feelings that she had no foundation to stand on, that she was sinking, and that suicide might be the best way out. As we continued to focus on Floyd, it became clear that his investment in her gave her the right to live and no one could take that away from her. This tie was indeed *her* base.

Then Susan became close friends with two other graduate students and found this to be very supportive. She was also involved with a student group and received some support there as well. But she felt intimidated in her graduate studies because she felt that she did not have the verbal fluency of her peers, which was not true.

During the next phase of therapy, we continued to work through her past. I encouraged her to write a chronology to reconstruct her history. This was useful, and over time it enabled her to recover aspects of herself by validating that these things had happened to her and that she was perceiving reality accurately. This led to a greater sense of continuity and wholeness. However, it was also a very difficult time because she often felt overwhelmed, overextended, and in danger of losing her grip. At times she would cry for hours, thus releasing the tears that until then had been blocked. She would sleep for twelve to fourteen hours many days. For several months, she went through this period of "recovery." She worked through her terror again and again. She recollected her attempts to kill herself by lying in the street when she was eight and her brother Floyd was dying.

After this period of intense work, she began to socialize again. She dressed attractively and actively took care of herself. She then decided to take a leave of absence from school for emotional and financial reasons. During the next period of "recuperation," Susan was on unemployment for eight months. We focused on completing her mourning process for Floyd. Not having done this made it difficult for her to attach herself to a love relationship. The funeral of an Asian-American male friend was the trigger event that enabled those unresolved feelings to emerge.

I suggested that Sue visit home again, even though we knew it would be a negative experience. She did visit, and it was negative; but it helped her to recover still more old unresolved feelings. She also had the support of an excellent, mature woman friend and colleague during this period who remained loyal to her through the difficult times. While home, she visited Floyd's grave and realized that it was unrealistic to expect her brother, Bob, to replace him. She saw her father, mother, brother, a cousin, and two aunts. This event represented a major shift from her previous status of being cut off from them for the previous two years. After this trip, she began to sleep better. She realized that her memories and perceptions were accurate. She knew that her family was disturbed; but her sense of the context of this previously inexplicable behavior was getting much clearer, and she was experiencing a sense of connection with her family, even though it was still negative.

She then took a job where she worked for one and a half years. During this time she discontinued therapy and reestablished her financial base. During this period her father died and again she found out about it belatedly. However, she did find out in time to prevent her father from being buried by the state. She took time off from work and made arrangements for a funeral, which was attended by several members of her mother's extended family. This experience, although unsettling, had a powerfully positive impact upon her. She discovered, acknowledged, and could accept some of these people into her life.

Currently Susan is back as a full-time student in graduate school to complete her work for an advanced degree. She has regained a positive sense of herself and is receiving emotional support from one of her uncles. In short, she is reconnected in a viable way to her extended family.

This case represents a situation in which a young woman from a multiproblem poor family was able to commit herself to long-term therapeutic work on the many problems she faced regarding her family background. Her life was not able to move forward until this work had been done. Susan had unusual strength and motivation to resist the destructive forces in her family and to come to terms with many painful experiences. Her story is illustrative of the many issues that emerge as one works within a family life cycle perspective with the unattached young adult from a multiproblem poor family. It shows the kind of effort that is called for to reclaim a life that otherwise might have been lost.

Case 2. The Family with Young Children: the Jones Family (See Figure 15.2)

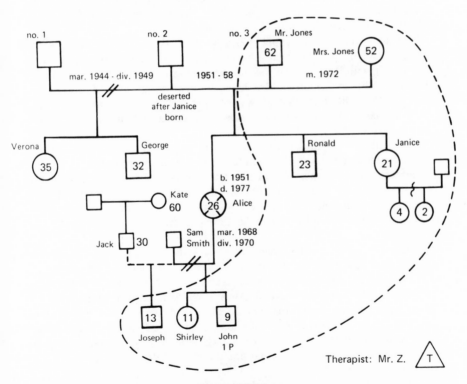

Figure 15.2.
The Family with Young Children: The Jones-Smith Family

Presenting Problems. Mrs. Jones was referred to the clinic by the school because John, her nine-year-old grandson, was a behavior problem. He was hyperactive, did not do his school work, and disrupted his classmates. Mrs. Jones was asked to bring everyone living in the home to the first interview. However, only she and her three grandchildren, Joseph, thirteen, Shirley, eleven, and John, nine, appeared. During the initial interview the children appeared quiet and rather depressed. Joseph played the role of the typical parental child, answering for his brother and sister and reprimanding them if they moved. They seemed to turn to him for permission or cues about the situation.

Mrs. Jones appeared depressed and overburdened. She stated that Joseph, Shirley, and John were the children of her daughter Alice, who had died two years ago of a drug overdose. Since then the children had been living with her and her husband. Mr. Jones did not come to the interview because his health was poor and he didn't believe in going to clinics. Mrs. Jones handled most of the family's responsibilities. She worked in a factory and also had her two youngest children living with her. Ronald, aged twenty-three, was unemployed and had recently been released from jail after being convicted for breaking and entering. Her youngest child, Janice, twenty-one, had just left her boyfriend because he was drinking and abusing her. Janice moved home with her two daughters. She did not attend the session because she had gone to visit Mrs. Jones's oldest daughter Verona, thirty-five, who lived nearby.

Mrs. Jones felt that the school referral with regard to John's behavior was yet another burden for her to bear. This only added more stress to the trouble she was having with Ronald, who was not yet supporting himself, and the return of Janice with her two children. Mrs. Jones did not see her husband as a resource. When pushed, she stated that she was not sure she wanted him included even if he would come, because the marriage was not going well and she was thinking about separating.

She went on to say that she was tired of raising children. While she felt sorry for her grandchildren, she also had much unresolved anger toward her deceased daughter, Alice. The therapist, Mr. Z., felt that these feelings merited attention but as yet had not been dealt with. Mrs. Jones tended to rely upon her oldest grandson, Joseph, who acted in a psuedomature manner. The burden this placed upon him was reflected by the fact that he had no friends or activities of his own.

Family Background. Mrs. Jones, who is fifty-two, was first married in 1944. She had two children from this marriage: Verona and George. She and her first husband were divorced in 1949 after five years of marriage. She remarried in 1954 and had three more children: Alice, Ronald, and Janice. Her second husband deserted after Janice was born. Mrs. Jones remarried fourteen years later, in 1972, when Janice was entering adolescence. Mrs. Jones's grandson Joseph was Alice's firstborn by her boyfriend, Jack. After Joseph was born, his father left the area but Joseph's paternal grandmother, Kate, maintained occasional contact with him.

Alice married Sam in 1968, and from this union Shirley, eleven, and John, nine, were born. Sam and Alice were divorced in 1970, shortly after John's birth. Since the divorce the children have had only occasional contact with their father. Alice died of a drug overdose in 1977; and it was quite apparent that this issue had not been dealt with by the children at all.

Given this configuration it was not surprising that John, who was essentially cut off from his father and his father's family, who had lost his mother and whose grandmother was overburdened by her many responsibilities, showed the family's stress in his poor school behavior.

Interventions. The first goal in treatment was to ally with Mrs. Jones and to help her to cope with her overwhelming situation. It was very clear that it would be very difficult to mobilize any family resources immediately on John's behalf. The initial plan focused upon trying to form an alliance with the school to get special help for John. The therapist, Mr. Z., explained that he was very interested in helping Mrs. Jones and did not want to add to her burden.

Negotiating for the needed inputs from the other systems was no easy matter. Mr. Z. learned that John's school was located in a poor urban setting. It was full of frustrated teachers, an overwhelmed administration, and children who were not learning. Initially, the administration felt the clinic was trying to "dump" the problem back onto the school. Strong efforts had to be made to get the opportunity to work directly with John's teacher. Mr. Z. hoped that if he could support John's teacher, she might be able to help John. Once the administrative anxieties were dealt with, the teacher turned out to be quite willing to accept help in dealing with John. This was especially true after Mr. Z. explained to her how concerned he was to help her with John, since the family situation just did not seem capable of giving John the special help he needed. A special evaluation was made of John's learning problems, which resulted in his being assigned a teacher's aide for attention on a regular basis. This attention was directly related to an improvement in his school performance.

Mr. Z. then turned his attention to Joseph, who in his role as the parental child was unable to develop his own friendships. Mr. Z. expressed concern about Joseph's social isolation and suggested a "big brother" for him. Mrs. Jones liked the idea. These efforts failed to materialize. However, six months later a young male staff member was hired by the clinic to work with adolescents, so that Joseph was then seen by him for individual therapy, and later he participated in a group. In addition, a session was held with Joseph's grandmother, his father's mother, Kate. She was quite interested in Joseph and his education. Subsequently, her contacts with Joseph were encouraged and supported by Mrs. Jones.

After the initial session, Mr. Z. asked Mrs. Jones to bring in her other children in order to secure a fuller evaluation of the family. The second session included Mrs. Jones, her son Ronald, her daughter Janice, and Janice's two children, as well as the three grandchildren. Ronald seemed quite interested in his deceased sister's three children. However, he kept missing subsequent sessions; so the work with him did not continue.

Janice seemed unconcerned about managing her children during the interview. Instead, Mrs. Jones took over and did not seem to expect Janice to handle them. Mr. Z. addressed Janice directly about her plans for herself and her two children, connecting this topic to his concern about Mrs. Jones's health. Janice did not seem to see much need to take more responsibility for herself and her children, but the discussion did lead to the topic of Alice's death.

The family reviewed the period before and after Alice's death. The children talked a little about memories they had of her. The last part of the session was spent with Mrs. Jones, alone, to continue to build an alliance with her. In this segment of the interview she was much more openly expressive about her conflicting feelings toward her deceased daughter. She stated that she did not like to talk about Alice in front of the children. It upset her to think about what Alice had put her children through, because she was always drinking or taking drugs. Mrs. Jones feared that their experiences with Alice might have given the children emotional problems. She was especially concerned about John, who found his mother after she died and apparently had never been able to cry about his mother's death.

In the next session, all the children seemed somewhat brighter, although the family could find no explanation for this. Mrs. Jones noted that John for the first time had asked a question about his mother. This session was followed by additional family sessions over many months, interrupted by missed appointments. John's behavior improved in school; and Shirley, who had been stealing from Mrs. Jones, and lying, stopped both activities. Attempts to deal with Janice's responsibilities for her life and for her children were unsuccessful.

A followup contact one year later revealed that Janice had moved out of Mrs. Jones's home to live with a new boyfriend. Mrs. Jones had several additional sessions for herself. In them she talked about her various problems and her ambivalence about staying married. She decided to stay in the marriage and appeared to have come to terms with it although it was not satisfying. Her son Ronald was in jail again for breaking and entering, but the three grandchildren were doing relatively well.

This case illustrates that when a family therapist works with a multiproblem poor family, he or she must seek to activate both external and internal sources of familial support. When there are not enough resources within the family to enable them to deal with all their developmental needs, mobilizing outside support is important. In this case the school, Joseph's paternal grandmother, and, finally, Joseph's therapist, provided the extra supports the family really needed. As John and Shirley continue to develop, it would be useful to make attempts to enable them to reconnect with their father, Sam, and his extended family. This would give them additional familial connections and hopefully additional permanent sources of emotional support.

It is also important to note that when the family has limited resources, they cannot make the changes that are available to their middle-class counterparts. For example, it turned out that a major reason Mrs. Jones decided to stay with her husband even though she was dissatisfied was because he was able to provide some financial assistance by means of his disability income. Again, because of Janice's limited resources, Mrs. Jones did not feel she could ask Janice and her children to leave after they moved into her home. It was also apparent that the negative life course Ronald was on was something Mrs. Jones felt powerless to influence. Dealing fully with both Janice's and Ronald's situations would have required commitment by the family as well as a substantial additional effort on the part of the therapist and the clinic's staff. Nevertheless, the flexible contract that Mr. Z. worked out with the family, along with the time he spent in negotiating other outside supports for the family, was probably crucial to the successes that were achieved in this case.

Three of Mrs. Jones's children (Alice, Ronald, and Janice) were unable to work out ways to function adequately by the time they had reached their twenties. This fact only compounded Mrs. Jones's difficulties as she attempted to cope not only with them but with her grandchildren as well. The three generations were unable to separate themselves from each other adequately enough so that each generation could assume its proper role and role responsibilities. Hopefully, as time goes on other interventions with this family may become possible. Stress lies ahead as the grandchildren are now approaching adolescence and the separating and launching stage of their own lives. When this occurs, further linkages for Joseph with his father's family of origin and further linkages for Shirley and John with their father's family of origin could provide them with critical ongoing support and help them to make the transition more successfully than their mother, aunt, and uncle.

Case 3. The Family in Later Life: The Arnold Family (See Figure 15.3)

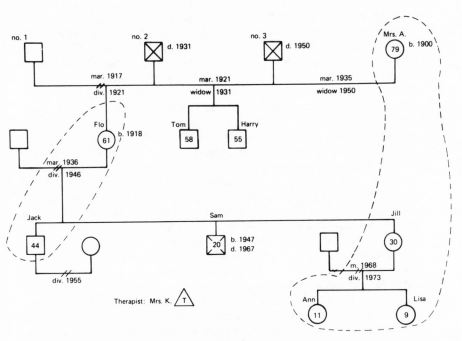

Figure 15.3.
The Family in Older Age: The Arnold Family

Presenting Problems. Mrs. Arnold, seventy-nine, once divorced and twice widowed great-grandmother, was referred to the family service agency by her public health nurse. Since she was confined to a wheelchair after having had a stroke, it was necessary for the therapist to work with her at home. During her convalescence, Mrs. Arnold was visited by the public health nurse and a nurse's aide. They helped her to recover from the stroke, and also to quit drinking. However, it was apparent that she was having family problems with her great-granddaughters, Ann and Lisa, both of whom lived in her household.

Mrs. Arnold owns her own one-bedroom home, which is constantly crowded. The house requires a lot of fuel to keep it warm in the winter. Mrs. Arnold marginally supports herself by means of social security and some disability income. Although she manages quite well, any unexpected expense can put the family in financial stress. By arrangement with Jill, her granddaughter, Mrs. Arnold takes care of Ann and Lisa while Jill works. Jill works full-time for the minimum wage, and is supposed to contribute financially but usually doesn't. This leads to conflict between Mrs. Arnold and Jill, with Mrs. Arnold threatening to stop caring for the children and Jill spending most of her free time drinking with her friends at the bar. This leaves Mrs. Arnold feeling overburdened and enraged because Jill won't assume more responsibility.

Family Background. During the initial interviews with Mrs. Arnold, the family therapist, Mrs. Kaye, learned that Mrs. Arnold had been married three times. She was first married in 1917 when she was seventeen years old. Her only child, Flo, was born in 1918. In 1921, she divorced her first husband after four years of marriage, stating that they were just too immature. The next year she married her second husband. This union lasted nine years, until he died in 1931. Her second husband was a stable figure who worked on a regular basis. During the time when Flo was between the ages of four and nine she was raised with her two stepbrothers, Tom and Harry, who were three and six years younger than she. In 1935 when Flo was seventeen years old, Mrs. Arnold married her third and last husband.

About one year later Flo married Don. They had three children, Jack, Sam, and Jill, who now live with their grandmother, Mrs. Arnold. Flo and Don divorced after ten years of marriage, in 1946. Sam died of heart failure when he was twenty. Jack divorced after ten years of marriage, and now lives with his mother, who has a drinking problem. Jill married when she was nineteen, had the two great granddaughters, Ann and Lisa, and then divorced in 1971 after six years of marriage. For awhile, she lived on ADC as a single parent, but was unable to manage the children and a job. For a while, the children were placed in foster care until they were subsequently placed with Mrs. Arnold, where they have remained for the past four and a half years.

Mrs. Arnold and Flo, her only child, have never gotten along well together. The same is true of Flo's relationship to Jill, her daughter. This pattern has carried into the fourth generation in that Jill has relatively little to do with her own girls, Ann and Lisa. As Mrs. Kaye reviewed the family history, it became apparent that because of Mrs. Arnold's three marriages, Flo had been intermittently close to Mrs. Arnold when Mrs. Arnold was divorced or widowed, only to be excluded each time she remarried. It seemed that Flo attempted to cope with this by marrying at about the same age her mother did, shortly after her mother's third marriage. Flo's marriage finally did not work, but she developed an intense attachment to her son, Jack, which appeared to have been a central factor in his own marriage ending in divorce. Since Jack was his mother's favorite, Jill always felt that she got a "raw deal" from her mother because her mother always "did" for Jack but not for her.

Interventions. As Mrs. Kaye reviewed this material it was apparent that this family was having difficulty in being able to effect adequate parent-child relationships and adult-to-adult relationships across the generations. Since Mrs. Arnold would soon be eighty years old and was confined to a wheelchair, she was less and less able to cope adequately with her granddaughter Jill and her children. The almost total absence of any active male in this family was striking. In this sense, the family was shrinking, and the women were unable to differentiate their respective generational roles with each other. The central parenting figure had always been Mrs. Arnold while Flo, aged sixty-one, and Jill, aged thirty, had assumed relatively little of the parental responsibility. Since Mrs. Arnold's ability to cope was decreasing, it seemed strategic to try to activate the involvement of both Flo and Jill to do more and to help Mrs. Arnold do less.

The initial step in this process was to form a strong alliance with Mrs. Arnold, who was clearly the dominant force in the family. Mrs. Kaye accomplished this by getting a ramp built for Mrs. Arnold at her home. The next step was to involve Flo in the meetings with Mrs. Arnold so as to try to redefine that primary relationship. This step, forty years late, was very difficult to achieve. Initially, all efforts on the part of Mrs. Arnold and Mrs. Kaye to reach Flo failed. After repeated efforts, however, they succeeded in meeting with Flo at Mrs. Arnold's home on a fairly regular basis. These initial meetings were rather tense, as Mrs. Arnold and Flo began to relate to each other very hesitantly after such a long absence of any contact between them. They spent a great deal of time reviewing their history, focusing on the three men who had been husbands and fathers, the loss of these men through divorce or death, and its effect upon them both.

After this process was under way and it became apparent that Mrs. Arnold and Flo were having a positive experience with each other, Mrs. Kaye encouraged Flo to move toward her daughter, Jill. This, too, was a difficult long-term project. However, this effort was aided by the success of Flo's work with her mother, Mrs. Arnold. It gave her a sense of the possibilities that could exist in a relationship for her and Jill. Understandably, Jill was guarded and suspicious and initially unresponsive. But in time she responded and began to address her relationship to her mother in sessions that included Jill, Flo, and Mrs. Kaye at Mrs. Arnold's house.

The last step was for Mrs. Kaye to bring all three women together to help Mrs. Arnold, Flo, and Jill to further differentiate their respective roles with respect to each other and to further solidify and integrate the gains they had made. These sessions were not without difficulty. Again, it was a slow process but a very worthwhile process: as Flo and Jill worked out their issues with their mothers, they were more able to be effective mothers to their daughters. When this happened, Mrs. Arnold began to let go of some of her responsibility for Ann and Lisa. Flo, who was not working, picked up more responsibilities for grand-parenting Jill's children. Meanwhile, Jill began to take a more active interest in her children. As these intergenerational changes began to affect the family system, growth in all the relationships was seen.

Currently, Mrs. Kaye meets on a monthly basis with Mrs. Arnold, Flo, and Jill. These meetings continue to be useful and productive. On occasion, Ann and Lisa are included in this process. All of them are now functioning at an adequate level. Mrs. Kaye plans to taper off her involvement with the family, but plans to be available when needed.

This case illustrates the problems, challenges, and dilemmas of the family therapist facing a family crisis brought about by the disability of a nonevolved grandmother. The issues of blurred generational boundaries and the need to address them before the mothers and daughters can assume effective responsibility for their own children is apparent. If this can be done, the momentum of the crossgenerational process can be reactivated as the parenting role is once again handed on from one generation to another.

CONCLUDING REMARKS

My goals in this chapter were to briefly survey the literature on the sociology of the poor; to review models of the family and methods of assessing and intervening with the multiproblem poor family; to describe the family life cycle of the underclass poor family; to discuss the hazards commonly encountered in therapeutic work with these families; and to present case studies that illustrated therapeutic work at each stage of the poor family's life cycle.

Three stages of the multiproblem poor family's life were described: the unattached young adult, the family with children, and the family in later life. In the development of these ideas and their applications, four factors emerged repeatedly which bear on this work: the three generational family system structure as a resource model; the process of reconnecting with that resource; the universality of the unresolved family relationship issues that play themselves out in all families whether they are affluent or poor; and the critical need to consider the contextual factors of the poor family.

Margaret Mead (1978) states that "It is true that the continuity of all cultures depends upon the living presence of at least three generations" (p. 14). Minuchin and his coworkers (1967) also noted that those families who arrive in a new context with an intact three-generational family system function well, whereas those that do not arrive with an intact three-generational family system often function poorly. These findings suggest that where there is an absence of an intact three-generational family system structure, that family's organization and function are at risk. For the multiproblem poor family described in this chapter, that risk is fully realized.

The fundamental importance of enabling families to reestablish and to reactivate their family ties to each other cannot be overemphasized. This process is vital in helping a family restore its growth and use its own resources. We are beginning to learn how to do this, but there is yet much to be developed in this area. Although this process of reconnection and revitalization of family ties may be most clear in the case of Susan, the other two cases illustrate that reconnection is a constant issue that has to be addressed diligently. Persistent focus upon reconnection does yield handsome returns in actualizing latent and untapped family resources.

This chapter and the case studies suggest that multiproblem poor families have to contend with unresolved family relationship issues as well as with many external reality problems. The relationship issues include legacies of crossgenerational injury, hurt, destruction of mutual trust, and split family loyalties. These issues must be addressed within a context of fairness and multilateral relational dialogues between family members.

The importance of considering the nature of the particular context in which the poor family lives has, I hope, been adequately documented and illustrated. It is in this area that we need to learn much more in order to fully understand and effectively help the multiproblem poor family. The powerful impact of the context made an indelible impression upon me when I was a foster child. I shall never forget the incredible transformation that occurred in one of my foster brothers after he lived with us for several months. He was about eight years old when he came to our house. In his previous foster home setting, he had been kept locked in the basement and given only food on a regular basis. He had been severely neglected. When the foster care agency discovered his status, he was sent to a summer camp. When he arrived at our foster home he was still quite retarded socially, intellectually, and emotionally. But as the weeks went by, he responded to our efforts to reach, teach, and train him. At the end of three months, he had learned to laugh, to eat with utensils, to ride a bike, to box, and to talk much more effectively. He was by no means fully caught up developmentally, but the changed context of our foster home certainly had a tremendously positive impact upon him.

If this can be the case for persons, it can also be true for families. This is not to say that the problems of the multiproblem poor family can be solved by uprooting them and putting them in better housing. If such moves are made, particular attention must be paid to the specificities of the families' social community network. Here the work of Speck (1973) with familial and social community networks is especially relevant and helpful. In an earlier book, Speck (1972) emphasizes the fact that we are in an increasingly pluralistic society and rather than attempting to get all families to conform to the middle-class form of the family, we have to be able to accept and tolerate a range of family structures, rather than label differences as deviant. His point is well taken.

Ramirez (1978) in his review of the factors that affect the utilization of mental health services, notes that:

> Knowledge of how people actually deal with personal and family crises and collective problems outside the purview of professional agencies is vital. There is the probability that our present strategies of professionalizing and institutionalizing every problem may cause damage to those natural systems and in the long run exacerbate rather than better our situation. The professionalization and institutionalizaton of problems which remove people from the natural setting may provide for temporary relief, but it also depletes a community of experience and resources for dealing with this and similar problems in the future. My argument is that in bypassing existing helping structures (or failing to create them with the people) we may systematically lower the adaptive capacity of many human populations and weaken those indigenous resources which in times of crisis may be the only ones available and operative. (1978, pp. 58–59)

Cayo-Sexton (1966) points to the need for large numbers of volunteers who are willing to personally involve themselves in the lives of the poor. She calls for individual initiatve, group initiative, and political initiative. She recognizes that ultimately no basic, enduring contextual changes will occur unless there is major change in federal economic policy that would include planned economic growth, the creation of skilled and unskilled jobs, and the "redistribution of wealth so that the poor may get their just share of the nation's resources" (p. 193). She also asserts that the poor must be given a sense that they "can, through their own initiative (and political action), affect the world around them," and "that they can, through solidarity with others, organize to alter successfully their environment" (p. 195).

Finally, we have to acknowledge that the poor have been unjustly treated historically, and that the affluent have isolated themselves from the lives of the poor. It is clear that for the poor to have the experience of solidarity with others, both they and the affluent must be committed to the values of justice, fairness, and compassion. This would take time to develop because the poor have been so unjustly treated and the affluent have so cut themselves off from the lives of the poor. However, the poor and the affluent need to work with each other in mutually cooperative ways in order to realize their human potential. Their mutual effort must be grounded in a base of mutual trust that can only emerge within the context of long-term commitments. I can think of no greater challenge to those of us who continue to be concerned about the multiproblem poor family.

BIBLIOGRAPHY

Aponte, H.J. "The Family School Interview: An Eco-Structural Approach," *Family Process* 15/3 1976, pp. 303–312.

————, "Psychotherapy for the Poor: An Eco-Structural Approach to Treatment," *Delaware Medical Journal* March 1974, pp. 1–7.

————, "Underorganization in the Poor Family," in *Family Therapy: Theory and Practice*, ed. P.J. Guerin, Jr., New York: Gardner, 1976, pp. 433–434.

Beavers, W.R. "A Theoretical Basis For Family Functioning," in *No Single Thread, Psychological Health in Family Systems*, New York: Brunner-Mazel, 1976, pp. 46–82.

Beels, C.C. "Family and Social Management of Schizophrenia," *Family Therapy: Theory and Practice*, ed. P.J. Guerin, Jr., New York: Gardner, 1976, pp. 249–83.

Billingsley, A. *Black Families in America*, Englewood Cliffs, N.J.: Prentice-Hall, 1968.

Boszormenyi-Nagy. "Contextual Therapy: Therapeutic Leverages in Mobilizing Trust," unpublished manuscript, 1980.

Boszormenyi-Nagy and B. Krasner. "Trust Based Therapy: Contextual Approach," unpublished manuscript 1980.

Boszormeniyi-Nagy, I. and Spark, G. *Invisible Loyalties: Reciprocity in Intergenerational Family Therapy*, New York: Harper & Row, 1973.

Bowen, M. *Family Therapy in Clinical Practice*, New York: Jason Aronson, 1978.

Boyd, Nancy. "Black Families in Therapy: A Study of Clinicians' Perceptions," Unpublished Doctoral Dissertation, Teachers College, Columbia University, New York, 1977.

————, "Family Therapy with Black Families," *Minority Mental Health*, eds. S. Corchin & E. Jones, New York: Holt, Rinehart & Winston, 1980.

Bush, S. "A Family Program That Really Works," *Psychology Today* 10/12, 1977, pp. 48–50.

Cayo-Sexton, P. *Spanish Harlem*, New York: Harper Colophon, 1966, pp. 193–95.

Clark, K.B. *Dark Ghetto*, New York: Vintage Books, 1962.

Coles, R. *Uprooted Children*, Pittsburgh: University of Pittsburgh Press, 1970.

————, *Migrants, Sharecroppers, Mountaineers*, Boston: Little, Brown, 1967.

————, *Children of Crisis: A Study of Courage and Fear*, Boston: Little, Brown, 1964.

————, and Coles, J. Hallowell. *Women of Crisis*, New York: Delacorte, 1978.

Colón, F. "Family Ties and Child Placement," *Family Process* 17/3, Sept. 1978, pp. 289–312.

————, "In Search of One's Past: An Identity Trip," *Family Process* 12/4, Dec. 1973, pp. 429–38.

Current Population Reports—Consumer Income, Characteristics of the Population Below the Poverty Level: 1977, U.S. Department of Commerce, Bureau of the Census, March 1979, Series P-60, No. 119, p. 3.

Foley, V. "Family Therapy with Black Disadvantaged Families: Some Observations on Roles, Communication, and Techniques," *Journal of Marriage and Family Counseling* 1, 1975, pp. 29–38.

Friedman, P. Personal communication, June 29, 1979.

Gans, H.J. "Culture and Class in the Study of Poverty: An Approach to Anti-Poverty Research," in *On Understanding Poverty*, ed. D.P. Moynihan, New York: Basic Books, 1968, pp. 205–206, 216, and 219.

Giordano, J. and Pineiro-Giordano, G. "The Ethno-Cultural Factor in Mental Health," literature review and bibliography, New York: Institute on Pluralism and Group Identity of the American Jewish Committee, 1977, p. 17.

Glick, P.G. "Demographic Analysis of Family Data," *Handbook of Marriage and*

The Family, ed. H.T. Christensen, Chicago: Rand McNally, 1964, p. 313, Figure 1.

Guerin, Jr., P.J. and Pendagast, E.G. "Evaluation of Family System and Genogram," *Family Therapy, Theory and Practice,* ed. P.J. Guerin, Jr., New York: Gardner, 1976.

Haley, J. "We Became Family Therapists," *Book of Family Therapy,* ed. A. Ferber, M. Mendelsohn, and A. Napier, Science House, 1972, pp. 118–20.

————, *Problem Solving Therapy,* San Francisco: Jossey-Bass, 1976.

Hetherington, E.M. and Park, R. *Child Psychology: A Contemporary Viewpoint,* New York: McGraw-Hill, 1973, p. 373.

Hill, Robert B., *Informal Adoption Among Black Families,* Washington, D.C. National Urban League, 1977.

————, *The Strengths of Black Families,* A National Urban League Research Study, Washington, D.C. 1972.

Hoffman, L. and Long, L. "A Systems Dilemma," *Family Process* 8/3, Sept. 1969.

————, "An Escalating Spiral: The Case of David B.," unpublished paper, 1974.

Kapelle, B., Scott, V., and Western, S., "Model Design and Training Manual For A Parent Aide Program," Michigan State Department of Social Services, Division of Protective Services, July 2, 1976, p. 21.

Klausner, Samuel Z. *Six Years in the Lives of the Impoverished: An Examination of the WIN Thesis,* Center for Research on the Acts of Man, Philadelphia, 1978.

Klein, R.A. "Treatment in the Home: An Experiment with Low-Income Multiproblem Families," *Mental Health of the Poor,* ed. F. Reissman, J. Cohen, and A. Pearl, New York: Free Press, 1964, pp. 329–35.

Komarovsky, M. *Blue Collar Marriage,* New York: Vintage, 1962.

Kozol, J. *Free Schools,* Boston: Houghton Mifflin, 1972.

Krasner, B. Personal communication, June 22, 1979.

Lewis, J.M., Beavers, R.W., Gossett, J.T., and Phillips, V.A. *No Single Thread: Psychological Health in Family Systems,* New York: Brunner-Mazel, 1976.

Lewis, O. *La Vida,* New York: Vintage, 1968.

McAdoo, Harriet. "Family Therapy in the Black Community," *American Journal of Orthopsychiatry* 47/1, Jan. 1977.

McGoldrick, M., & J.K. Pearce, "Family Therapy with Irish Americans," paper submitted for publication, 1980.

Mead, M. *Culture and Commitment,* New York: Columbia University Press, 1978, p. 14.

Minuchin, S, Montalvo, B., Rosman, B.L., and Schumer, R. *Families of the Slums,* New York: Basic Books, 1967, p. 368.

————, and ————, "Techniques for Working with Disorganized Low Socioeconomic Families," *American Journal of Orthopsychiatry* 37/5, October 1967.

————, *Families and Family Therapy,* Cambridge, Mass.: Harvard University Press, 1974.

Mizio, E., ed. *Puerto Rican Task Force Report—Project on Ethnicity,* New York: Family Service Association of America, 1979.

Montalvo, B. "Home-School Conflict and the Puerto Rican Child," *Social Casework* Feb. 1974.

Nee, V.G. and Nee, B.D. *Longtime Californ: A Documentary Study of an American Chinatown,* 2nd ed., Boston: Houghton Mifflin Co., 1974.

Ramirez, O. "Chicano Mental Health Status and Implications for Services," Preliminary Examination Paper, Dept. Of Psychology, U. of Michigan, Ann Arbor, Michigan, April 1978, pp. 58–59.

Rossi, P.H. and Blum, Z.D. "Class, Status and Poverty," in *On Understanding*

Poverty, ed. D.P. Moynihan, New York: Basic Books, 1968, pp. 43-44.

Spiegel, J. and Papajohn, J. *Transactions in Families,* San Farancisco: Jossey-Bass, 1975.

Stack, C. *All Our Kin: Strategies for Survival in a Black Community,"* New York: Harper & Row, 1975.

Speck, R.V. and Attneave, C.L. *Family Networks,* New York: Pantheon, 1973.

———, Barr, J., Eisenman, R., Foulks, E., Goldman, A., and Lincoln, J. *The New Families,* New York: Basic Books, 1972.

Stein, H.F. "The Slovak-American 'Swaddling Ethos': Homeostat for Family Dynamics and Cultural Persistence," *Family Process March 1978, pp. 31-45.*

Zborowski, M. and Herzog, E. *Life is with People: The Culture of the Shtetl,* New York; Schocken, 1976.

Zuk, G., "A Therapist's Perspective on Jewish American Values," *Journal of Marriage and Family Counseling* 4/1, January 1978.

16
Cultural Variations
In the Family Life Cycle:
The Mexican-American Family

Celia J. Falicov, Ph.D.
Institute for Juvenile Research, Chicago
San Diego Family Institute

Betty M. Karrer, M.A.
Institute for Juvenile Research, Chicago

The concept of the family life cycle as a framework for thinking about expectable events in a family's life span should always consider the family in its sociocultural context. Every culture marks off stages of living, each with its appropriate experiences. What it means to be a man or woman, to be young, to grow up and leave home, to get married and have children, to grow old and die depends on socially approved definitions.

The timing, the tasks, the rituals for transition, the themes, coping mechanisms, and meaning attached to the different stages of the family life cycle vary from culture to culture and from subculture to subculture. Age norms, for example, get internalized and translated into psychological expectations for self and others, lending a sense of being on time or off time, of being early or late while undergoing life events (Neugarten, 1964). Remaining single until her late twenties would not lend an Irish woman a sense of being late nor earn her the label of "spinster" as it would in Latin American cultures. Reaching age thirteen for an American Jewish boy provides a ritual demarcation for the family of his entrance into manhood, while the same age has no particular meaning for his black classmate's family. Ending one's life through suicide may have a dramatically opposed meaning in Japanese and in Arab young males. Divorce in a middle-aged Italian couple requires a more difficult shift in extended family loyalties than for an English couple.

Studies of the family life cycle have not taken into consideration effects of such cultural variables as social class, ethnicity, and religion. It would be more accurate to talk about several typical life cycles (Schultz, 1976), but most recent work has concentrated in describing the life cycle of middle-class America. Not only do the content and themes of the different stages vary with race, class, religion, and ethnicity, but also the original family structures, the developmental tasks, and the mechanisms by which changes take place may differ.

Awareness by the clinician of cultural variations in the family life cycle has applications relevant and even crucial to the treatment process, such as recognizing family crisis points, differentiating functional from dysfunctional behavior, and selecting treatment goals and interventions that are culturally appropriate.

This chapter describes the life cycle of the Mexican-American family, focusing on issues relevant to the practitioner of family therapy. The attitudes and behaviors described for families of Mexican descent affect all immigrant groups. Common features are shared with immigrants from other Latin American countries such as Puerto Rico, Cuba, Guatemala, Colombia, and other parts of Central and South America. The similarities can be attributed to the Roman Catholic religion and other Hispanic influences mixed with the Indian heritage, the rural and semirural backgrounds, lower socioeconomic level, and language. Traditional family values and the extended family context account for much of the similarity among these societies. Important differences exist, however, which can be traced to each country's geographical, historical, economical, political, and cultural influences.

The model presented reflects extensive work with a large Mexican-American population in a midwestern setting. Mexican-American populations living in Texas and the Southwest may require variations in the model.

The families are, as a rule, large, consisting of the parents and several children, usually five or more. They have immigrated to the United States within the last two decades to better their economic situation and in some cases for personal or familial reasons. In another paper (Karrer & Falicov, 1980), we have used the term "Mexican-American" to define an intermediate stage of acculturation that ranges from cultural alienation to integration. A large proportion are nondocumented immigrants who underutilize medical and mental health services and are uncertain about whether they can remain in this country.

The pattern of immigration usually involves separation from extended family. It may also involve separation from nuclear family members. Most families tend to come at the earlier stages of family formation. The husband usually comes first and later brings his wife and children. Immigration may also separate parents from children; for example, both parents bring some of the children, leaving others with extended family. Gradually all members of the nuclear, and many of the extended family, will join them in the new country.

Initially isolated, especially the wife, they experience considerable stress due to relocation and loss of family and friends. The men are employed in factories where they associate primarily with other Mexican-American co-workers. The children's school and the local church represent the value orientations of the dominant society. However, a social network is generally established in the ethnic neighborhood after approximately five years.

As soon as some stability is achieved, they may sponsor the immigration of extended family members such as a maternal or paternal sister or mother who provides child care and enables the mother to go to work. In some cases the older generation remains behind and join their grown children during old age. The accessibility of Mexico facilitates visits to and from the native village for vacations or at a time of crisis, such as an adolescent runaway.

Three stages of acculturation often exist within the family. Mother and the grandparents may be at the beginning stage with the father at an intermediate level while the children may be at an advanced stage of acculturation. The discrepancies between stages give rise to conflicting expectations and norms within the family. Intrafamilial dissonance is usually expressed through heightened conflict between the generations or between the sexes and will affect developmental transitions. In all these families the Spanish language is maintained. In fact, all the therapy sessions reported in this chapter were conducted in Spanish. Occasionally English was used by some of the most acculturated members of the family.

SOCIETY AND FAMILY STRUCTURE

In order to understand the adaptational and developmental tasks faced by the Mexican-American family at each life stage, it is essential to consider the family structures and the social context in which development takes place.

In Mexican society, the nuclear family is typically embedded in an extended family network. In this extended family, work needed for survival is distributed within the group. Men and youths work in the outside world, while wives are in charge of childbearing, housekeeping, and supportive roles. Older women and adolescent girls engage in child care; the aged have knowledge based on experience and oral tradition that can be passed on. Each member is responsible to others and this creates group inter-dependence and a strong sense of family identity. Control of social behavior is exercised mainly through the family rather than relying on societal institutions.

Within this framework opportunities for individual expression, autonomy, self-sufficiency, and a differentiated identity are reduced. The family protects the individual while it demands allegiance to itself. Family loyalties stand in the way of individual choices, such as marrying outside the ethnic or religious group. Extended families expect a lineal hierarchial arrangement, where age is the important determinant of power, authority and control.

CULTURE CHANGE AND FAMILY STRUCTURE

Migration and the process of relocation change the family's structure and disrupt the patterns of intrafamilial help and control. Yet, there is a tendency among Mexicans in the United States to reconstitute, whenever possible, the original extended family group (Moore, 1970; Carlos & Sellers, 1972). Mutual financial support, child care, and other forms of practical and emotional reliance on relatives are widespread.

This persistence of the extended family and traditional values is adaptive to situations of poverty, environmental stress, and the sociocultural isolation of the ethnic neighborhood. The presence of extended family members in the community exerts supervisory pressures upon children and adolescents. When these community influences are missing they are supplied by the parents through restrictions on children's activities, selection of friends, and increased discipline. Values of family cohesiveness and interdependency may provide inner controls even when the extended family is absent. And, some Mexican-American parents manage to utilize friends as extensions of the family. They act as buffers against the stress of acculturation. However, intergenerational value conflict surfaces as the length of time lived in the United States increases and erodes the internal foundation of the immigrant family. Additionally, when situations of poverty exist, the environmental supports may not be strong enough to prevent symptoms of social stress, such as drug abuse and delinquency (Heller, 1966).

The presence of the extended family at times interferes with the process of acculturation and can contribute additional stresses. Contacts with neighbors, reliance on institutions, or searching for friendships with Americans may be reduced, while intrafamilial problems, such as interference of the grandparental generation in the marital or parental subsystem, may be increased.

FAMILY STRUCTURE AND THE FAMILY LIFE CYCLE

Family configuration involves functional patterns of transaction and relationship rules or norms.[1] Nonetheless, each type of configuration or structure has inherent vulnerabilities that manifest themselves at different points in the family life cycle. Responses to developmental requirements also differ in the various family configurations. The habitual transactions in an extended family, for example, facilitate immediate incorporation of lonely or bereaved extended kin without considering the future consequences for the family's organization. In contrast, today's nuclear households tend to lack other family supports and will experience greater hesitation about the permanent inclusion of relatives.

In the modern nuclear family, democratic and egalitarian norms facilitate self-expression and creativity, but ambivalence in exerting parental control leaves the adolescent alone to decide important issues concerning self-identity. Extended families have more authoritarian controls that impede self-expression and autonomy. This gives the adolescent a sense of security and connectedness, but conflict with parents arises around individuation efforts. Family size is also an important modifier of family development. Small families experience more stress around separation while large families tend to induce parentification of older children; transactions among spouses and among siblings are also affected by family size.

As clinicians are aware, interactions among the different individual life stages occur simultaneously for the various generations, but the impact is more strongly felt when living in an extended family. Pressures to be "on time" in achieving certain developmental transitions may be felt intensely, as in the case of a twenty-seven-year-old married woman whose parents and parents-in-law began to label her as "barren" when her twenty-two-year-old sister had a baby. A similar pressure could have been operating on a young man who made a hasty decision to get married immediately following the baptism of his brother's first son. A wedding, a birth, an ill relative, or a death, has reverberations upon a whole network of nuclear families who are in close practical and emotional interdependence.

[1]Norms as herein used describe rules that govern interpersonal behavior. Culture is an important determinant of norms since "we assume that a given set of norms or relationship rules is more common in one culture than another" (Jackson, 1965). Similarly, a given set of norms is more common in one type of family structure than in another.

At each life stage, Mexican-American norms reflect and are consonant with extended family arrangements. In contrast, American norms tend to support the autonomous nuclear family. Thus, the Mexican family life cycle is more clearly three-generational than the Anglo-American family life cycle.

CULTURE CHANGE, FAMILY ADAPTATION, AND THE FAMILY LIFE CYCLE

Each society conditions the family to transmit rules that are adaptive to societal requirements. In turn, each family prepares its members to live in their own society. When the family faces adaptation to developmental changes, it is aided by a cultural backdrop that shares similar developmental expectations.

If the family moves to a different country, they face the possibility of incongruence with the new society. A lack of reciprocity or lack of "fit" is frequently found between the dominant society and the immigrant family (Minuchin, et al., 1967). Patterns that are adaptive for individuals and families in a Mexican rural village do not function effectively in a Chicago urban ghetto. The values, norms, and role behaviors learned in the home country become a source of stress when the family comes in contact with the new culture.

When the immigrant family faces inevitable developmental changes, it lacks consonant society structures. The immigrant parents' model of child-rearing is "out of phase" with the dominant culture's model, as represented in the school or peer group. However, it may continue to be reinforced by similar cultural attitudes held by Mexican-American adults living in the ethnic neighborhood. The discrepancy between the two models of child-rearing will become evident at significant points in the family life cycle, such as the time of each child's school entry.

Normal developmental stresses are thus intensified by cultural dissonance. In addition, the family needs to cope with developmental crucibles that require shifts in boundaries, role functions, and family rules at a time when it is already taxed by its efforts to adapt to a new environment.[2] For example, at the time of school entry, all families are faced with the developmental task of opening up their boundaries to share with the school the education of the child. For the immigrant family the loneliness of the

[2]For a comprehensive model of the progressive stages that unfold during the process of migration and acculturation, and their implication for treatment, see Sluzki (1978).

mother will increase her reluctance to allow the separation from the child. In addition, the lack of fit in cultural values with the school will further hamper this process. Some of the stresses experienced are not solely due to lack of familiarity or the clash of cultural values. The dissonance may be felt also at the social level, particularly in relation to the issue of minority status. Migration transforms a family into the disadvantaged position of being a member of a racial and socioeconomic minority. This stress strongly influences the process of adaptation. Being a minority member is deleterious to intellectual performance, overall behavior, and family stability.[3]

Thus at each developmental stage, the internal reorganization and response of the family system is a product of the combined effects of expectable developmental events occuring under the impact of relocation and of culture and social status change. Consequently, the necessary changes to pass from one developmental stage to another may become more difficult. The successful adaptation to these multiple stresses will depend on favorable external circumstances and the family's flexibility.

ACCULTURATION AND THE FAMILY LIFE CYCLE

Repeated contact with the new values over a prolonged period of time changes the family's outlook on issues such as childrearing, sex roles, and philosophy of life. Studies on the impact of acculturation on immigrant groups (Schulz, 1974) report that the integration of native and traditional values with the dominant culture's current values is a conflictual process that takes at least three generations. In spite of gradual change in which the family developmental or organizational norms incorporate many elements and begin to approximate the American culture, it should be stressed that families of Mexican descent residing in the United States for several generations preserve identifiable threads of the original culture in many aspects of their life. Even families who are upwardly mobile become acculturated

[3] De Vos (1969) elucidated the effect of minority status on the behavior of a Japanese population. The group studied was racially and culturally consonant with the prevailing Japanese culture, but was assigned the role of "outcast" on the basis of social factors. Once this label was solidified and integrated into the culture, it became increasingly difficult for the group defined as "outcasts" to perform at an acceptable level in consonance with the rest of society. Predictably, their performance on achievement and intelligence tests consistently came out below the average level. Their ability to secure and maintain jobs was also reduced and their overall adaptation level was considered below Japanese standards. Attitudes of alienation, bitterness, and peripherality were observed and proved difficult to ameliorate. This study points out the fact that being a minority is deleterious even in situations where cultural and racial similarities exist.

but not assimilated and many retain their language and ethnic identity (Gordon, 1964; Teske & Nelson, 1976).

STAGES OF DEVELOPMENT IN THE MEXICAN-AMERICAN FAMILY LIFE CYCLE

The following model offers a description of how the different stages of the life cycle are generally experienced by Mexican-American families. The descriptions are general and provide a broad picture of transmitted traditions, age and sex role expectations, and value orientations of Mexican-Americans. It is intended as a model that clinicians can utilize in formulating and testing hypotheses, while exercising sensitivity to idiosyncratic differences. The picture illustrates cultural values and norms about Mexican family life, i.e., the public reality shared by all family members. Idiosyncratic patterns of interactions also exist in all families; they constitute the private reality of the family, not necessarily related to their cultural background. Both sets of norms govern many aspects of family relationships; they both affect transitions during the life cycle and need to be evaluated in the therapeutic situation. The therapeutic implications relevant to each stage of the Mexican-American life cycle are interwoven with the descriptions.

The diagram shown in figure 16.1 graphically illustrates the differences in length of stage, and the timing of entrances and exits of family members in the Mexican-American family (inner circle) relative to the dominant Anglo-American family life cycle (outer ring).

Courtship

In many Mexican-American families the courtship and marriage of the parents takes place in Mexico before migration. The expectation is that the children will follow similar patterns of courtship and marriage in the new country.

Courtship tends to be longer for Mexican families (see figure 16.1). This is due to the predominant view that marriage is a very serious decision, a commitment for a lifetime. In addition to traditional views about family life, Catholicism exerts an important influence on attitudes toward courtship, marriage, and divorce. In Mexican-American families, parents often "check out" potential candidates for steady dating whenever the daughter appears to be seeing a young man with some frequency. Good manners, financial capability, seriousness, and education all enter into consideration in this covert assessment process. Once an opinion has been formed, parents

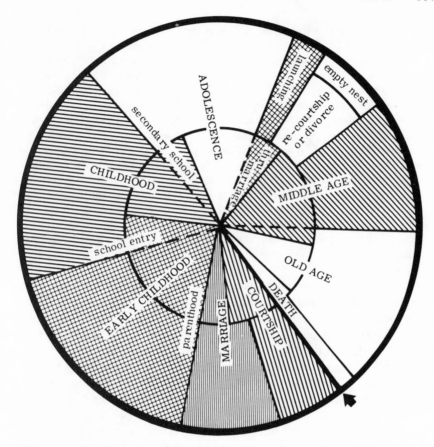

INNER CIRCLE: Mexican-American
OUTER RING: Anglo-American

Figure 16.1.
The Mexican-American and the Anglo-American Family Life Cycle.

will try to influence the daughter's involvement with the young man. Thus, the immediate family exerts considerable pressure in favor of, or against, the selection of a particular mate. A similar "self-appointed" parental involvement in the decision making process is common when sons choose a bride. In urban America, parents of Mexican descent attempting to preserve their ethnic identity will disapprove of their children dating people of other ethnic backgrounds. Parents will also judge their own children's qualities as potential mates for desirable candidates and will use these evaluations to control deviations, as in the following example:

A seventeen-year-old Mexican-American girl, Lupe, in her junior year of high school developed bouts of crying and a persistent refusal to talk and to attend school. The parents were concerned that the girl might be hiding a pregnancy, but found it difficult to discuss this possibility openly. After many interrogations, Lupe finally said she wanted to be transferred to another school but would not explain why. Only in the privacy of an individual interview, Lupe "confessed" that she was infatuated with a Puerto Rican boy in her school and feared her family would disown her forever. When the therapist suggested alternative ways that would allow her to remain in the same school and test out the reality of her feelings, she related that Teresa, her older sister, had fallen in love with a Puerto Rican gang member. When her father discovered a token of love that the young man had given to Teresa, he broke her lip with a slap and told her in no uncertain terms that she had tarnished her family's name. Furthermore, he would be the first to warn other respectable interested young men about her past. Teresa was in this way paradoxically condemned to be only worthy of the Puerto Rican boy. Lupe's refuge into total silence could then be seen as the response of a person in a double bind situation where she was damned if she defied parental authority or damned if she obeyed it.

Most parents expect casual dating for girls to begin around age sixteen and for boys somewhat later. Steady courtship is usually legitimized by a *compromiso,* or engagement, which involves a public announcement, festivity, and formal giving of engagement rings, and it may take place even when the wedding date has been set. As a custom it was also prevalent in America of yesteryear but has gradually lost popularity. Besides symbolizing a couple's commitment to marriage, it allows for the coming together of both extended families who will begin including each other in their get-togethers. As a ritual, it also begins to delineate a boundary around the couple and the separation from each family of origin. Although premarital sex is not allowed and young people have very limited access to private places, the engagement ceremony may act as a covert signal for condoning premarital sex.

Dating patterns are clearly influenced by how the launching stage of the family life cycle is regulated. Launching from the family of origin is generally accomplished through marriage, since other avenues for leaving home—such as going to college, getting a job, and living independently or with a roommate—are not encouraged. Financial limitations play a definite role but the value placed on family interdependence versus individual autonomy are equally compelling. Thus, a young man and woman will tend to remain in the parental household until the time of marriage.

Since steady dating is the only sanctioned manner of separating from parents and siblings, courtship is a functional equivalent of launching. The tasks of separating from one's parents, achieving a more differentiated identity, and beginning to strengthen ties with a prospective mate occur simultaneously and are accomplished slowly. Many deep loyalties to one's parents and siblings are active during this period. The young man, for example, may experience conflicting demands between his mother and his fiancée. The young woman may feel confused or resentful that her "ownership" has been transferred from her family to her husband-to-be. Lack of resolution of these intergenerational issues may reappear at later points in the family life cycle.

In extended families, if courtship never takes place or fails, the unmarried adult man or woman tends never to move out of the parental household. If both parents die, the bachelor or "spinster" often goes to live with a married sibling, since this is more acceptable than living on one's own. The presence of a maternal or paternal aunt in our client population households is a pattern that we have observed so frequently that we have come to label it *la tia* (the aunt). In some cases, the aunt serves useful affective and instrumental functions while subsystem boundaries are maintained. In other cases, depending on the age and role relationships within the family, the aunt may form a crossgenerational coalition with a parent or a child or attempt to act as intermediary between the two, producing complications at various points in the life cycle, as in the following example:

> Charito, age thirty-three, moved in with her brother, his wife, and their children. She quickly became triangulated into a family conflict. Maria, her fourteen-year-old niece, formed a coalition with Charito against Maria's father on the basis that Charito understood young people much better in areas such as fashion, curfew, or friends. There was reality to this, in that the aunt had recently arrived from Mexico with "more advanced" ideas than Maria's father, who had migrated fifteen years before. The aunt's role as mediator was functional at times, but at other times her protecting stance prevented the parents from negotiating and reaching agreements directly with their daughter. In addition, this coalition also inflamed the covert conflict between Charito and Maria's father, who had always exerted his authority as older brother rather sternly.

The inclusion of a single extended family member in the nuclear Mexican-American family should always be explored.

Marriage

Socially acceptable ages for marriage are the early twenties for both men and women, but there is greater tolerance for a later marriage in a man. Marriage is likely to be the first time in which young people establish an intimate relationship outside of the family and learn instrumental and financial responsibilities for setting up a separate household. The families of origin need to reorganize and adapt to the departure of the young adult and facilitate the formation of a new marital unit.

If the marriage takes place in Mexico or in the beginning stages of acculturation in the United States, each prospective spouse undergoes with the respective families the preparation of the wedding, or *casamiento*. Like all

Mexican *fiestas* are a colorful and joyous celebration. It is usually an elaborate church and dinner affair with very formal attire and hundreds of guests. These ritualized preparations probably pave the way for the family to accept the separation of the young adult children and their parents. In most cases, this is a period of family turmoil. It may become further complicated by the young couple's rebelliousness against the traditional wedding ceremony, when the family is in the intermediate acculturation stage.

In contrast to Anglo-American values, identity seeking or "finding oneself" is not a primary concern of Mexican-American young adults. The impetus for individuation is expressed or submerged in the dyadic context of forming a marital system with a common goal and negotiation of values, priorities, and everyday routines. This can make of early marriage a complicated stage, but most couples cope with it.

Financial limitations and family interdependence often slows down the process of setting up separate households, since the newly constituted family may come to America and live with or nearby the husband's family and receive temporary economic support. Occasionally, couples go to live with the wife's family, but this may be perceived socially as lack of masculinity on the husband's part. Physical proximity and emotional involvement with families of origin perpetuate interdependence, and may hamper the shift in loyalties. It often prevents the couple from exploring and establishing their separate identities as the husband and wife of a new family, particularly if one of the spouses performed valuable functions in his or her family. An example of one couple's difficulties that escalated into a dysfunctional pattern at this stage illustrates several of these points:

> Mrs. Olivia P., a twenty-three-year-old Mexican woman, was referred for individual treatment. She had been married for six months when she developed intense fluctuations in mood, from depression to "paranoid ideations," which involved being "persecuted" by other people, including her twenty-six-year-old husband. For example, she accused him of intentionally ruining her plants by putting a fan in front of them for prolonged periods. During an interview with the couple the following information was obtained.
>
> Mr. P. had been in the United States for ten years when he decided to find a wife for himself. Since he could not find a suitable Mexican young woman, he began exploring possibilities of finding a wife in Mexico and came across a Mexican magazine containing ads for pen pals. He began a letter relationship with Olivia, who corresponded with him for several months. The relationship was highly romanticized and idealized by the distance, both feeling "madly in love."
>
> After some time, Mr. P. went to Mexico to marry Mrs. P. and then brought her to the United States with him. Assuming that she would not object, he neglected to mention that they would be living in his parents' home. In addition to Mr. P's parents, there were four sisters in the household, with Mr. P. having as-

sumed for many years the masculine role in the family since his father had suffered a stroke.

Olivia felt initially shocked. Not only had she not been told about the plans, she also perceived veiled intense hostility from the other women in the household towards her. However, every time she attempted to discuss her feelings with her husband, he would forcefully defend his family, never agreeing with her observations. On the other hand, he was often approached by his mother and sisters with complaints about his wife's mood and attitudes; they even hinted at a "possible drinking problem." He would only feebly defend his wife and began hearing their advice on how to deal with her, including taking her to a psychiatrist.

The long-established organization of this family of origin was not adjusting to the separation of a key member, thereby producing a conflict of loyalties in the son. In this type of organization, the newly arrived daughter-in-law felt, that "as a daughter in her parents-in-law's home she could never become a wife, especially of a favorite son, and felt she was the lowest in the hierarchy." Since generational and territorial hierarchy did not allow her to express her resentment directly to her in-laws, she turned it towards herself or her husband.

In order to decrease the degree of resentment and delineate an area of private communication that had proven successful to them in the past, the therapist suggested that the couple not talk to each other. Instead, they were to correspond three times a week. The letters were to date from the time just before the wedding and then continue. The husband was to explain in great detail exactly what to expect in his familial household and encourage her to ask for clarifications. This exercise created a temporary truce while it clarified many issues for the husband, who began to change his attitude towards his wife. Seeing this, Olivia became more willing to help him create a boundary around himself as a husband, rather than as a son to his parents, or a brother to his sisters.

Even if they do not live in the parental household, soon after the marital ceremony the young couple begin frequent social contact with their families of origin and their kinship network. They often live in the same or nearby buildings or neighborhoods. Young wives may talk on the phone to their mothers everyday. Many young husbands visit their parents once or twice a week. Perhaps the involvement is more frequent now than during their steady courtship, where the young couple is usually left alone to explore their relationship. After marriage and even more so after having a baby, the couple can legitimately enter what up to now has been the impenetrable world of adults, although generational hierarchies are still maintained.

As in many traditional families, complementarity of marital roles is stressed. Although this is changing through women's emergent role in society, the dominant position of men relative to women is still part of the acceptable public norms. When one moves from the public, social level to the private level of transactions between individuals, many discrepancies between role norms and actual role behaviors are found.

Much has been written about the patriarchal power structure of the family of Mexican descent. "Machismo" has been said to be a typical pattern of behavior among males of Mexican descent: they dominate their wives, carry their family obligations as they see fit, are sexually assertive, and may even maintain a concubine (*casa chica* or second household). Complimenting the husband's position, the wife is supposed to be submissive and chaste and place the husband's needs, desires, and decisions before her own. The stereotypical pattern is not as prevalent as it is made to be, as evidenced for example by a recent study that found a very high proportion of migrant Mexican-American families to have an egalitarian pattern of decision making and action taking (Hawkes & Taylor, 1975). Even in situations where the man appears to be dominant and the wife submissive, underneath this public complementarity very symmetrical patterns may exist where the wife exerts her influence in other areas of life. *Hembrismo*, or *marianismo*, i.e., the dominance of the self-sacrificing mother over the family, may be equally significant in families of Mexican descent (Stevens, 1973).

In helping correct structural imbalances, the therapist who has achieved a good understanding of the value orientations of a family can utilize cultural values as "cultural strategies"[4] for restructuring purposes. In this type of intervention, the therapist has to address the public reality that the family has professed. For example, if the therapist thinks a Mexican husband should assume a more ascendant role and be regarded as more influential by his family, it is useful to phrase this intervention in the context of what "ought to be" according to the culture, and not what "it is." Whenever a question was asked from one Mexican husband, he appeared nervous and reluctant to answer, glancing around the room. His seemingly domineering wife would typically begin answering for him at great length. His hesitancy was reframed as his subtle, calm way of giving her permission to talk, as a well-educated, traditional Mexican male should. A similar intervention when dealing with an acculturated couple where the wife is an ardent advocate of women's liberation would be strategically incorrect.

One area in which the traditional view of male-female relationships influences the couple is that of sexual relationships. Finding a mutually satisfactory sexual relationship may prove difficult since Roman Catholic upbringing limits the exploration of sexuality, particularly for the woman, even within the confines of the marriage (Rainwater, 1975; Stevens, 1973).

---

[4]Don Jackson (1965) lucidly discussed the use of cultural values as homeostatic devices within the family. He said, "Because values represent an extrafamilial coalition (with religion, society, culture, etc.) they exert leverage on relationships within the family. Thus, from our perspective inside the family looking out, so to speak, values are used as interpersonal tactics which affirm or enforce a norm." To paraphrase from a therapist's perspective, outside the family looking in, values can be used as therapeutic strategies.

Mexican-Americans seldom stress happiness in marriage as a goal to be attained—although they are, of course, distressed about marital unhappiness. Satisfaction in marriage is the result of good fortune and wise choices and cannot be corrected by working towards "marital improvement." Therefore, very seldom will Mexican-American couples seek marital counseling, unless they are middle class and/or acculturated. Searching for compensatory factors or resignation are common solutions. Separation or divorce are uncommon. The majority of Mexican-American families are two-parent families throughout their lifetime.

Since not much investment is placed on reaching marital or sexual satisfaction per se, a couple stage tends to be much shorter than in America (see figure 16.1). The love and romanticism of the courtship period shift quickly towards a parental basis for the formation of a family, since the primary purpose of marriage is procreation. In family therapy this should be taken into account.

Mexican-American families mostly come for assistance when they have a problem with a child. If it appears necessary to discuss issues of marital harmony directly, at any point in the family's life cycle, more therapeutic leverage could be obtained by utilizing the family or children's well-being rather than discussing the values of a good marital relationship. Likewise, Mexican-American women feel much more challenged by shortcomings in the performance of their maternal role than by any failure to be a good companion or sexual partner to their husbands.

If migration from Mexico occurs in the early stages of marriage, the stresses of adaptation may bring couples to therapy. The relationship may be complicated by sex differences in rates of acculturation related to the different social circumstances of men and women in the adoptive country. Processes of grief and mourning for the separation from parents, relatives, friends, and familiar sights and objects are experienced by both spouses, often paralleled by optimism and excitement about a better future. Sometimes one spouse expresses one side, the loss and grief and the wish to go back, while the other only focuses on the optimism and the determination to "make it." Husband and wife may homeostatically divide these roles; their seemingly different acculturation levels may be utilized by the immediate or extended family in the formation of alliances and splits and become further rigidified. Or the conflict may threaten to escalate, as in the following example:

> Juanita and Nemesio had been married for three years when the husband's small business suffered a serious setback and he decided to immigrate "temporarily" to improve their economic situation. As many of his countrymen, he came alone first to explore the situation before bringing Juanita and their two young children. When they arrived, Juanita took an instant dislike to Chicago, refused to learn English, because as she put it, she wanted to "create a barrier" to this country and was afraid that if she learned the language or got used to liv-

ing here, they would never go back. She waited anxiously for daily letters from her mother and sisters. The more she disliked it, the more he tried to make her see that she was exaggerating the differences between the two countries and the happiness she could have back home. Money matters became another focus of conflict, where they blamed each other for not making enough or spending too much. Juanita went back to Mexico once and stayed for three months. The therapist faced a dilemma. It was clear that in this symmetrical escalation the couple could not cooperate or reach any decisions, because any course of action could be construed by one or the other as proof of commitment or lack of commitment to acculturation. Since the therapist did not conceive her role as an acculturation agent, she could not side with one or the other in this matter either. To overcome this impasse, a truce and trial period of one year was agreed upon, during which all the behaviors engaged by husband or wife would be cooperatively negotiated on the basis of their potential benefit for "human adaptation and enrichment" in any country. For example, if the wife were to learn English or take on a part-time job, these could be regarded as useful skills (or money earned) in any country, all important experiences for a young woman to have. If the husband was to spend more time with his isolated wife, it could be construed as having the experience of acting as a "modern" husband. A parallel can be seen with therapeutic impasses in dealing with couples contemplating divorce who will immobilize themselves in marital therapy, for fear things will get better and they will have to forego divorce.

For other couples, a movement from a traditional to a more egalitarian structure may evolve over time as a result of migration (Tharp, et al., 1968).

The Family with Young Children (Birth to Five Years of Age)

The arrival of a first child establishes the marital couple as a family. The developmental tasks of this period involve the revision of established dyadic transactions between husband and wife to make room for the baby. The couple must learn to be parents together and enable each other to assume appropriate and satisfying functions with the child, while maintaining their identity and transactions as spouses (Falicov, 1971). The families of origin need to accept the new family unit and provide help and support to the new parents without excessive interference.

The ritual baptism or *bautismo* that initiates the infant into membership of the Roman Catholic church is important for Mexican-American families. It crowns the final acceptance of the new family and it serves as an extended family reunion even in situations where the marriage was accepted reluctantly by the elders. The infant is sponsored by a godfather and a godmother, who are selected from among the social network of relatives, friends and important acquaintances of the family. Godparents or *padrinos* become coparents to the children and *compadres* or peers to the parents.

This relationship among extended kin has a certain saliency from which special mutual favors can be expected.

The existence of godparents as part of the family's natural network can be a valuable aid in family treatment. Godparents can have many auxiliary functions as advocates for the child, temporary relief for parents, or intermediaries between the two, since they have formal kinship legitimacy outside the biological family. Given their relative emotional distance from the family, they may be more effective in those roles than grandparents.

Entrance into parenthood is not experienced as a major crisis. Since not much emphasis is placed on the romantic, sexual ties of the couple, the perception of loss of time and activities together alone at this point is not as keenly felt as it is in Anglo-American couples. Complementary expectations in the new roles of mother and father also facilitate this transition for the couple, which moves the wife towards a group of supportive women and allows the husband to be concerned primarily with economic pursuits. When the extended family is present, mother or mother-in-law will help out with many caretaking tasks so that early parenthood may not be as energy-consuming a stage as it is for the isolated nuclear family.

Anglo-American women regard motherhood as a symbol of emancipation from their families of origin and a passage from being a daughter (or a girl) to being "coequals" with their parents, particularly their mothers (Falicov, 1971). In contrast, Mexican-American women will not conceptualize this transition as a change of status in relation to their parents. To prove their self-sufficiency, Anglo-American women often limit their mother's visit at postpartum to an average of one per week. Aware of rapid ideological and technical changes, they will derive their models from other young mothers and their information about child care from pediatricians, books, and magazines. In contrast, Mexican-American women will rely on the wisdom of their mother and other older women.

The first years of a child's life are typified by a nurturant, tolerant relationship with parents and extended family. The baby is especially close to the mother and other women in the family. Since the world is a given, not an object for change or mastery as it is for those raised in accordance with the Protestant work ethic, Mexican-American parents across socioeconomic groups adopt a relaxed attitude towards the achievement of developmental milestones, or the attainment of skills related to self-reliance. They appear to be less pressured than Anglo-American parents to achieve developmental goals or to correct minor deviances from the norm. Weaning from breast to bottle, for example, is normally achieved at approximately the same prescribed times as they are in the American family. However, an intermediate stage between breastfeeding and cup almost always occurs where the child is allowed to drink from a bottle or use a pacifier for a long time before being encouraged to drink from a cup. Occasionally a child becomes so attached to the bottle or pacifier that drastic methods are used, such as putting some bitter substance on the nipple. Variations in weaning and toilet training are dependent on family customs rather than prescribed social norms. As long as they are achieved within a "reasonable" length of time, there is no pride or shame attached to them.

To the Anglo-American therapist, Mexican-American children may appear to be infantilized, but in general there is no reason to be alarmed by a three-year-old sucking a pacifier, or by a four-year-old sitting on mother's lap, or by a young child not being encouraged to use a fork at the table because mother will cut up the meat and feed him. Mother conceptualizes her role of good mother as gratifying the child's needs rather than stimulating independence.

The role of the mother in relation to her children is idealized in the Mexican culture as being close to the Hispanic images of the Virgin Mary. It entails quiet self-sacrifice and abnegation. The burdens of child care are either not experienced or not openly expressed. To try to convince a Mexican-American mother that she needs time for herself, a vacation or relief from her children, usually meets with disbelief and denial since it goes against a cultural norm.

The father may or may not be involved in caretaking activities during the early upbringing of the children. We have seen fathers communicate very closely with babies and young children, but this affectionate indulgence may slowly wane as the child gets older. The role of the father with older children is to enforce discipline and to expect respect and obedience. Both parents may challenge the children to behave better through shaming or ridicule, which are culturally accepted childrearing practices.

The baby and young child continue to enjoy a close relationship with mother and a special position in the family until a new child is born or he or she enters nursery school or kindergarten. It is the external event, such as the arrival of a new child or school entry, that defines the child's passage to a new stage rather than concepts of internal readiness that prompt parents to begin expecting or demanding more from their children. Thus, children may be unprepared and experience abrupt discontinuities during developmental transitions.

Compensation for some of these discontinuites may be provided by the extended family. Often, more attention is given by grandparents, uncles, and aunts to a child who just had a sibling, in order to free mother, but also to gratify the older child's needs. In the absence of extended family, age differentiations that do not occur, or that occur only by default, may give rise to developmental impasses, as in the following example:

> The family consisted of father (thirty), mother (twenty-five), Rodolfo (five) and Marcia (five months). Rodolfo was referred to the clinic by the kinder-

garten teacher because of frequent absenteeism, crying, and fearfulness while in school. The first interview revealed a very isolated family. Mr. P. had been in this country for ten years and had finally brought his wife and child a year ago, after spending many years commuting between Chicago and Torreon, a town in northern Mexico. Both parents came from large families and were reluctant to leave the support of relatives and friends. After a long time and considerable pull from her husband, who found commuting expensive and tiresome, Mrs. P. had finally agreed to come and live in Chicago.

Mr. P. had adjusted to life in Chicago well. He had a stable job and worked long hours. On weekends, he spent some time with male friends. Other than the lack of relatives, his life had not changed significantly from the one he had experienced in Mexico. Mrs. P. however, felt depressed and isolated. Father could not understand his wife's complaints, since finally they were economically stable and together. He felt that his wife had enough activities with the house and the children to keep her occupied. He had no insight as to her loss, confusion or aloneness. Rodolfo's school entry increased the vacuum in his mother's life. His absence left her with the baby, who could not be, as Rodolfo, company for her. It soon became clear that she was giving ambivalent messages to the boy about school attendance, while father—who valued education—had no tolerance for Rodolfo's absenteeism. Mother was reluctant to send Rodolfo to school on cold days and responded easily to somatic concerns that would assure his staying at home.

Marcia was the first baby whom both parents raised together and without help. Mother's fears of bringing up a baby on her own without the assistance of relatives propelled her to overprotect the baby, to distance herself from her husband, and to give Rodolfo less attention. Rodolfo had been an only child until recently, and a favorite of mother and relatives in Mexico. He was disconcerted by the absence of the relatives and by the birth of Marcia, who was taking so much attention from mother away from him.

The recent immigration, the birth of a new child, and school entry had all contributed to this family's difficulties. If they had remained in their native village, the sibling rivalry and father's feeling of exclusion would have been present, but Rodolfo and his mother (and father) would have had many available adult figures to compensate for the stresses of this period .

The treatment initially focused on establishing a supportive network for Mrs. P. She was referred to the school community representative, who recommended her to attend a women's social group that met twice a week to learn English and discuss problems created by their immigration and acculturation. The women brought young children with them and frequently compared notes on their development. Considerable work had to be done to allow Mr. P to sanction these activities. He did not consider it necessary for his wife to leave the home twice a week just to "talk with a bunch of women."

Both parents were given support for their parenting skills and their wish to improve the family's economic stability and education. Within this context, mother was assigned the task of rewarding Rodolfo for growing up, which included school attendance. This fitted the father's conceptions of preparing him for a successful life. Mother and Rodolfo's attachment and the sibling rivalry were dealt with through a story-telling intervention. Mrs. P. and Rodolfo were instructed to spend thirty minutes twice a week after school, when Marcia was taking a nap, looking at baby photographs of Rodolfo. Mother would tell him a story surrounding the time of that photograph. The photographs were organized to begin with Rodolfo's birth and progressively moved to subsequent years. The emphasis was on showing Rodolfo his own growth. Father, who happened to be interested in photography, was assigned the complementary task of regularly taking photographs of the children and occasionally participated in the story-telling task.

Rodolfo's reluctance to attend school disappeared in two weeks. He was happy with the idea that his "mother was also attending school." The teacher reported no crying or fearfulness once attendance regularized. Mother found her meetings with the women in the group very supportive and she established some friendships among them. Father was particularly happy since his wife stopped looking depressed, began to support his plans for the education of the children and to share in his hopes to buy a home in Chicago. At the end of six months, Rodolfo and Marcia had established a clear sibling hierarchy, mother was proud of Rodolfo's school functioning and of Marcia's growing up. She focused much more on the positive accomplishments of both children and was ready to allow father and Rodolfo to participate in Marcia's caretaking.

In most families, the marital couple during these early stages of the family cycle enjoys little autonomy from parental functions. When away from the extended family—as in the case of the immigrant—the intense polarization of roles lacks a supportive social structure. The natural closeness of mother and children may become intensified by the isolation, thereby encouraging the father to become even more of a peripheral figure. Nevertheless, most families successfully master the transition to kindergarten where the child brings the family in closer contact with the dominant society's value orientations.

The Family with Elementary School Children (Ages Six to Twelve)

This stage of development requires that families facilitate and accommodate to their children's school entry and academic adjustment, their increasing involvement with external systems, and their psychosexual growth. As the children reach school age, the family embarks on a new phase. The family must be willing to expose children to influences outside the home and expose one of its products for scrutiny and evaluation.

School entry presents a first structured opportunity for interaction with nonfamilial adults and peers. For the family of Mexican descent, the school may be the first direct sustained and structured contact with the value orientations of the dominant society. As a transitional stage it requires flexibility at a time when the family may still be weakened by the losses of migration. Contemporary models of adaptation to separation from children and for dealing with secondary systems such as the school may be lacking. Although children of Mexican descent enter primary school at the same age as American children, there are differences in social and emotional readiness of the Mexican-American family to move into the more autonomous stage that is normative in the American culture at this point.

For Mexican-Americans, school entry does not necessarily signal the end of early childhood (see Figure 16.1). The relaxed, accepting attitude towards children's achievements that characterized the earlier stage of development also prevails during the first years of this stage. Stresses of adaptation may also contribute to the prolongation of this stage by immigrant parents who tend to hold on to their preschool children with great protectiveness. Releasing their first school-age child to an unknown system such as the American school is likely to create anxiety. There is no familiarity with the overall educational system, the teachers are strangers, their expectations as to discipline and acceptable behavior unknown.

For mothers, their reluctance to separate is aggravated by their isolation. As long as they have young children at home, their role is clear and their activities continue in a similar fashion as in their native town. If this is their youngest child, they may be reluctant to relinquish the last person within the family circle whom the parents can influence without interference from the new culture.

Sociocultural dissonances between the school and the family adversely affect the functioning of either or both. The Mexican-American family frequently reports being misunderstood, misinterpreted, or not listened to by school personnel. Similarly, school staff report frustration and inability to communicate problems or expectations to Mexican-American parents. In addition to genuine lack of understanding, the anxieties surrounding their nondocumented alien status probably contribute to the guardedness of many parents.

Scholastic achievement problems are frequently attributed by the school to obvious difficulties such as language problems (Moore, 1970), while little attention is paid to the sociocultural dislocation of the child and his or her family. For example, the family may prepare the young child to expect help from adults in the form of tying shoes and taking off coats, while the teacher may see this expectation on the child's part as dependency and lack of self-reliance. Other attitudinal differences may also result in dissonance. For example, the child who has been taught respect towards authority figures and shows it by lowering his or her eyes when talking to teachers will be out of phase with the teacher's expectations of directness and openness, and may be perceived as shy, or "sneaky." In addition, Mexican-American children may be out of phase with the American educational system, which uses competitive motives to promote and reward academic achievement, while the family emphasizes cooperation and affiliation (Kagan & Madsen, 1971). One study, for example (Minturn & Lambert, 1964), found that Mexican mothers discourage peer aggression while American mothers encourage it. Acceptance and affiliation are highly valued in interpersonal relationships (Diaz-Guerrero, 1975), in contrast to the individualism and achievement orientation which characterizes the Protestant ethnic. It would be a mistake, however, to conclude that Mexican-Americans are passive, cooperative, and compliant. They may be fiercely competitive in a soccer game where the rules of the game require it.

While some of these cultural differences in childrearing may account for Mexican-American children appearing infantilized or overprotected in Anglo-American eyes, occasionally what appears to be a cultural difference is in fact the product of a pattern of family adaptation to migration. Migrating families may leave some of their children in Mexico for practical or emotional reasons, such as their interdependence with or loyalty to their own family of origin. Often the parents will send for them to come to the United States around the time of school entry. The mother may quickly begin a campaign of overcompensation for the lost years of affection. She may compete with the images of her mother and/or her mother-in-law to be acknowledged as the real mother, and may "baby" the child more than she otherwise would. Thus, some Mexican-Americans may have been raised by several loving mothers before school entry.

Developmental difficulties that may arise in this kind of situation are illustrated in the following example:

> Juan, a seven-year-old boy of Mexican parents, had suffered a "mild" problem of encopresis from a very young age. In the past six months, however, the frequency of soiling had increased from one to two times a day, to five to six times daily, and his postural tension about elimination had also increased. His two- and one-half-year-old sister, Jazmin, was fully toilet trained.
>
> Father, Mr. S., appeared stern and distant from the boy, while mother, Mrs. S., was overprotective and very affectionate. She regularly tied his shoes, cut his meat, helped him with homework, and lay down in bed with him to help him fall asleep.
>
> Mrs. S's overprotection of Juan appeared to be a covert accusation towards her husband, who did not oppose his own mother's insistent request that Juan remain in San Antonio, Texas (where she had lived for the past eighteen years) when he was three years old because "she loved him so much." At that time, Mrs. S. did not want to leave Juan in Texas and come to Chicago with her husband alone, but she could not oppose her husband's family. Mr. S. was himself complying with cultural norms that constrain against challenging one's mother's desires.
>
> About two years later, when they brought him back to Chicago, Juan did not recognize his mother and instead called his grandmother "mama." To gain back her son, Mrs. S. became a "super mama." As a result, an alliance developed be-

tween mother and son. Whenever father tried to discipline the boy or suggested that mother should punish him for soiling his pants, the boy would ask the mother if his father did not love him and preferred Jazmin. This prompted Mrs. S. to reassure him and criticize the father. Cultural norms that conceptualize the role of a good mother as self-sacrificing and protecting condoned the mother's behavior in her eyes and in her husband's perception. The father's own father had been very strict and his mother often acted as mediator between father and children.

During the second session, the family informed the therapist that for a few months previous to therapy they had been planning a Christmas visit to the paternal grandmother. The recent increase in symptoms could now be seen as related to this situational threat. Treatment was geared to establish mother and father as the primary parental unit and help them create a boundary with the father's family in regard to Juan's development.

Parents expect children to assume responsibilities at this stage for errands, babysitting, or other forms of help to the mother, while father may continue to be uninvolved with household tasks. Greater individual responsibility for handling an allowance or small jobs outside the family, such as a newspaper route, are not customary for children. Although their help is expected within the household during middle childhood, the world of the child is relatively segregated from adults. Children interact with siblings while adults meet among themselves close by or in the same room. Curiosity about sexual issues that appears at this age is expressed with games and exploration, but this curiosity is very seldom expressed directly to adults.

The boundary between home and the extrafamilial world is clear and rather rigidly defined. Most Mexican-American children in the preadolescent years have a very limited peer group. The perceived dangers of the urban neighborhood restrict their activities to indoors, outside of school hours they tend to not see playmates. Siblings and cousins constitute the only friendships even if they are far apart in age. According to Maslow and Diaz-Guerrero (1960), Mexican children, compared to American children, live far more in the family and less in the peer group.

As a result, a family therapist may see a need for greater age differentiations or individuations. Suggesting greater responsibilities outside the home or increased contacts with peers, however, may be regarded by the family as attempts to socialize the child into the American ways. It is usually better to delineate increased responsibilities or privileges within the home or to help find individual differences among children while preserving the notion of responsibility to the family, particularly if the family is large.

As in previous stages, Mexican-American, (in contrast to Anglo-American) families may "extend" some aspects of childhood beyond the early pubescent years. (see Figure 16.1) For girls particularly, there is no clear demarcation between childhood and puberty. In spite of definite biological signs, a twelve-year-old girl may be considered a child even after menarche. Puberty, however, may reorganize the family at a more subtle level. Same-sex siblings may become closer and divide into masculine and feminine types of activities. Father-son and mother-daughter alliances may also be strengthened at a more covert level. Developing girls raised in traditional Mexican-American families living in an urban metropolis, where much more liberal behaviors prevail at this stage, may experience extreme tension and inability to disagree with the parents on any issue. In one such case, epilepsy precipitated with first menses. In two others, the girls started pulling their own hair and eyebrows. All were described by their families and others as extremely "good" girls.

Issues of school or work achievement may surface in the latter part of this stage, particularly for boys of families with middle-class aspirations. In the following example, a school achievement problem in a twelve-year-old boy appeared to be a symptom of marital dysfunction, which in turn hinged on issues of work success that had become poignant due to the father's midlife crisis:

Mr. S. (forty) and Mrs. S. (thirty-six) and their two children, Juan, twelve, and Jaime, thirteen, had been residing in the United States for the past ten years in a predominantly middle-income Mexican neighborhood. The initial interview took place in the school, where the teacher related to the parents and the therapist her numerous attempts to help Juan concentrate on his school work. Both parents reacted defensively, denying the academic difficulties. The only problems they acknowledged were Juan's nervous tics, which consistently disappeared during the summer time and reappeared with the academic year. The teacher wondered what effect Jaime's outstanding school performance had on Juan and why the two boys were never seen together. All the family members were visibly uncomfortable and presented a united front, maintaining that the family had no problems. The boys spoke with a very soft voice, constantly checking their words against their parents' glances. At the teacher's insistence they agreed to engage in family therapy.

A central theme of this family was marked preoccupation with professional and financial success. In contrast to his brother, who is an executive in Mexico City, Mr. S. was never a good student, but led a rather dissipated and happy youth, never obtaining his degree as a dental doctor and becoming instead, a dental technician. At present, Mr. S. appeared to be undergoing a rather painful midlife reevaluation of his life goals and spending after-work hours in sports.

In contrast to her husband, Mrs. S. had been an excellent student. Not only did she appear to be more competent verbally, she also corrected and typed letters for her husband and administered the finances. Mrs. S. together with her eldest, Jaime, formed a pair, a coalition based on being "the brains" of the family; they both spoke softly and had good manners. The younger son, Juan, and his father constituted the nonintellectual pair, their manners being clumsier, and their voices louder. They were more limited academically than mother or Jaime, but they had excellent skills for sports.

Many of the parents' communications about the two boys appeared to be metaphors for their unresolved conflicts around Mr. S.'s career aspirations. Indeed, the parents had decided in advance that Jaime "will become an architect and Juan will be the physician." In the event of the latter plan failing (a question raised only by the therapist), they hoped Juan would become an international air pilot. Both children seemed to accept these expectations. Negative elements in the marital relationship, particularly Mrs. S.'s dissatisfaction with Mr. S.'s overinvolvement in sports, seemed to be detoured onto Juan.

This degree of tension and maladaptive functioning in the family was attenuated and possibly perpetuated at a homeostatic level by the presence of Carmen, twenty-seven, Mrs. S.'s younger sister, in the household for the last two years. Mrs. S. had formed another coalition with her sister against her husband. This sister filled out many of the evening hours when Mr. S. was not home. The two women worked for the same agency, they ate and dieted together, went shopping, and carried on like intimate friends. Thus, there was great tension behind the apparent united front, a family system in which each individual was emotionally unsupported, experiencing a low level of self-esteem and exclusion or rejection in the family subsystems to which they belonged.

A remedial educational program to which Juan had to go alone was prescribed. This provided greater independence for Juan while it helped to form a rapid therapeutic alliance with the parents by attending to their values and concerns. However, it appeared that as long as father's self-esteem and wife's appreciation of him were dependent upon Juan's academic success, Juan would continue to respond to these unrealistic expectations with a cognitive and affective inhibition towards school work and with excessive nervous tension. Both parents needed to accept and value their accomplishments in life to successfully cope with their middle-life crisis.

Considerable effort had to be invested during family therapy to validate differences between Juan and Jaime and uncover disagreements between husband and wife. Once conflicts began to emerge, Mrs. S.'s disparaging remarks about her husband surfaced rapidly. To balance the marital relationship, the therapist reframed father's past career decisions as reflecting an honorable courage to be authentic. His search for authenticity was seen as providing the necessary spontaneity to complement and limit his wife's calculated strivings towards social conformity for their family, for which of course she also deserved praise. (This complementarity could be further supported as a form of integration of opposing cultural values).

In order to assess the role played by Mrs. S.'s sister in the relationship she formed with the couple, it was necessary to include her at this point. In the presence of her sister, Mrs. S. attacked Mr. S. in a virulent manner, criticizing him for his lack of consideration towards her and the children, his devotion to his football, and his lack of time to take her out to a movie or to a restaurant. She complained about this "stinginess," and threatened to leave him after the kids "grow up" to settle back in Mexico with her family. The therapist pointed out that she had in many ways already left her husband for her family of origin and added that it might actually be very hard for Mr. S. to "divorce" his football as long as she stayed "married" to her sister.

Therapeutic interventions were designed to debilitate the wife-sister coalition and strengthen the husband-wife relationship. A number of strategies were utilized for this purpose, ranging from direct ones, such as planning an evening out for husband and wife, to more indirect interventions such as finding common interests between the husband and his sister-in-law, making them a potential pair that would isolate the wife and spur her to seduce her husband back to her.

Gradually, Mr. S. began expressing resentment toward his sister-in-law who came to visit them for two weeks after the breakup of her engagement in Mexico and stayed for over two years. Around this time, the family went to Mexico on vacation as a unit, excluding Mrs. S.'s sister. Upon their return, everybody appeared to be more relaxed. Mr. and Mrs. S. had a more genuinely supportive and tolerant relationship. Mr. S. had definitely left the periphery of the family and entered the family circle, displacing his wife's sister from a privileged position. Both parents seemed to be more willing to ease up on the pressures and encourage a more individual evolution on Juan's part. The two boys were expressing themselves more openly and honestly towards both parents and seemed to have a more egalitarian relationship with greater flexibility to shift the roles of "dummy" and "smart" between the two, possibly reflecting a similar change in their parent's relationship. A few months after completion of therapy, the therapist was invited to a minigraduation for Juan since he had passed to eighth grade.

Successfully completing elementary school is a matter of great pride for Mexican-American families, often accompanied by a happy celebration. Members of the extended family may attend this graduation (graduación) at the school and as a ritual it can be used to facilitate family change during the transition to adolescence.

The Family with Adolescent Children (Ages Thirteen to Nineteen)

Adolescence confronts families with changes in sexuality, consideration of career or work choices, and issues of separation between children and parents. Changes in hierarchy are inevitable due to the adolescent's physical, sexual, and intellectual maturation. In addition to these universal stresses, the immigrant family suffers two additional stresses. First, when the family needs to allow their children increased interaction with the outside world, parents are frightened by the inner-city dangers unknown in their home town. And secondly, the adolescents have incorporated new values that enter into conflict with their parents' beliefs in family cohesiveness and respect for everlasting parental authority. The family is divided with both cultures and languages represented within, and these need to be reconciled or at least negotiated.

The axiom "be good to your parents" is a traditional norm in many cultures. However, different interpretations about transgressions of this rule result in different consequences. For Mexican-Americans, if adolescents answer back or deviate from obligations to their parents or other societal norms, it is not considered to be the parents' fault; it is their "bad luck" in having a bad son or daughter. For Anglo-Americans, if their children deviate from society's norms, it represents an indictment of the parents' ability to raise good or healthy citizens. The Mexican-American adolescent is guilty for misbehavior, while the American adolescent can always blame his parents.

Anglo-American parents accept that in certain periods of life young people may rebel against authority. Mexican-American parents expect obedience throughout life. An example:

> A Mexican woman expressed great admiration for her sister-in-law's (Mrs. R.) family, which she regarded as ideal. Mrs. R. had, on a certain occasion slapped her son's face for talking disrespectfully to her, i.e., he blamed her for a family problem. Her son (a thirty-year-old married engineer) dutifully lowered his head. The story was intended as instruction for her fifteen-year-old son who complained about her strictness.

Like adolescents everywhere, Mexican-American adolescents want to participate less in the parents' and extended family network and more in their own peer group. Parents do not easily approve, question how the adolescent can elect to be with friends, and may make many attempts to recover the adolescent. Some adolescents passively rebel against this, others openly assert themselves, but most come to accept the parents' position.[5]

Although defiance of authority is not allowed, other avenues for individuation and growth are open to the Mexican-American adolescent. There are sharper age differentiations within the family in terms of responsibilities, and indirect (humorous but respectful) expressions of value disagreements between parents and adolescents are permitted. In addition, rituals that demarcate sexual maturation and graduation from high school facilitate developmental transitions.[6]

[5]In situations of rapid culture change where a veritable "experiential chasm" between one generation and the next exists, the peer group often assumes a crucial and controversial socializing role. However, a crossnational study (Thomas & Weigert, 1971) found that compliance with peers was not consistently related to urbanization among Mexican-American adolescents, suggesting that parents continue to be influential during this period.

[6]Graduation from high school is celebrated with great pride and joy by Mexican Americans. Most families are aware that their children encounter many difficulties in inner-city schools that fail to meet their educational and social needs. In fact, the dropout rate of Mexican-Americans is considerably higher than that of blacks and almost double that of Anglo-Americans. Only 5% of Mexican-Americans have some college education (Grebler, 1970).

A ritual that often accompanies a girl's entrance into the romantic, pre-marital field is the *cotillion* or *quianceañera*. This is a party given for a girl by her parents and relatives on her fifteenth birthday. It involves a religious ceremony, a dinner, and a dance for 100–200 people. Protocol demands for-mal dress for the girl, her escort and fourteen other couples. This tradition has begun to wane in Mexico but tends to be preserved among Mexican-Americans (Horowitz & Schwartz, 1974).

As an initiation rite, the cotillion is similar to the American tradition of the debutante ball. However, the degree of social segregation between boys and girls up to the time of this ritual is much less marked for American than for Mexican-American adolescents, making the transition to dating more difficult for the latter. For the girl of Mexican descent this ritual demarcates early from later adolescence. It is an event by which she acquires a clearer status as a young woman. A girl's virginity, reputation, and potential ability for formal dating are affirmed through this ritual. In spite of this ritual, the Mexican-American parent may maintain that daughters should not begin dating until age sixteen or seventeen, should be home by nightfall, and should not engage in premarital sex. Norms regulating boys' dating behav-ior are more flexible. Casual dating without marriage as a goal has become more common for both sexes after age fifteen or sixteen, but the close pres-ence of the extended family often acts as a control on the number of differ-ent dating partners and the extent of physical involvement.[7]

Much more is expected from children after puberty in terms of respect, care of parents and household, and in responsibility toward younger sib-lings. Sharp age differentiations are made within the sibling group at this stage. Older sisters, in particular, have many responsibilities towards younger siblings. While this is a natural occurence in large families, struc-tural changes stemming from immigration and culture change complicate this situation. Parents who might otherwise work out a gradual separation find it impossible to do so because of their long-standing dependency on their older child to mediate with the larger culture in terms of language and institutional rules. The younger children in the family may also cling to the older sibling who appears to be much less old-fashioned and more under-standing than the parents. Having internalized the two languages and the two cultures, the child may find herself in the confusing but influential posi-

---

[7]In the past ten to fifteen years, premarital sex has become more prevalent in Mexico across different socioeconomic levels, although restrictions on premarital sex are imposed by the limitations of living in the parental household. Mexican-Americans have not "caught up" with this attitudinal change or may lack the envi-ronmental controls that will monitor the adolescent's degree of sexual involvement. Occasionally, an adolescent becomes aware during trips to Mexico about this dis-parity in "strictness" and may—"paradoxically"—prefer to spend summers in Mex-ico.

tion of "parent to her parents" and "parent to her siblings."[8] This position can pave the way for independence for self and other children, or it may result in an instrumental and emotional entrapment as in the following illustration:

Mary, a twenty-three-year-old Mexican-American woman, the oldest of a sibship of six (three of which were already married), called for an appointment to bring her parents and her thirteen-year-old sister Elsa to help resolve an ongoing daily conflict that centered around Elsa's disobedience of the 8:00 o'clock curfew time set by the parents. Initially, Mary explained the situation to the therapist. Continuing to speak in perfect English, she tried to convince Elsa that she had to collaborate with her parents and pay attention to her mother who had many health problems to contend with. She then abruptly turned to her parents and speaking fluent Spanish bitterly criticized them for their strictness, pouring out resentment for the many restrictions she herself suffered during her early adolescence. Mary was thirteen-years-old when her parents moved from Texas (where they had lived for eight years after migrating from Mexico) to Chicago. This move demanded a higher acculturation level and rapid urbanization of the family, resulting in more dependency upon and higher controls on their oldest daughter. Particularly painful for Mary were the memories about a failed courtship with a young man who, in her estimation, she could not have married because of her parents' excessive interference and disapproval of the relationship— although according to the parents it was Mary who broke off the engagement.

Witnessing her parents' difficulties in creating a more open and viable family system, she promised herself "to change" her parents and vindicate her past through "saving" her younger sister, thus perpetuating her position as parental child. This "solution" further prevented not only Mary's, but also her sister's transacting new family rules that could lead them towards greater individuation.

Mexican-American parents' ability to maintain their power and control over their children is accomplished by the maintenance of a clearly defined boundary between home and society, which contributes to a relatively closed system.[9] Most meaningful interpersonal transactions occur within the

[8]At a more sociological level, the influence and authority of the oldest child upon the family may represent an intermediate step between the authoritarian, tradition oriented family and the democratic family, where the status of the child and the distance between parent and child are reduced. Through this step, which has been called "primogeniture" (Slater, 1977), the oldest child inherits the tradition—and possibly the material possessions—while the younger one, who has no vested interests in the "status quo," and has not fully internalized the traditions, further transforms the family towards the contemporary conditions.

[9]The maintenance of generational boundaries and executive functions appears to be more problematic in third and fourth generation families of Mexican descent than in first and second generation immigrant families. A similar phenomenon has been observed in other tradition oriented families such as Japanese-Americans (Kitano, 1969).

nuclear and the extended family, partly as a result of isolation and limited acculturation. However, closeness with and loyalty to in-groups over out-groups is consistent with cultural values. Grandparents and other extended family members act as agents of social control in the neighborhood, forming an effective "grapevine." When absent, parents lack this supportive network and may become either more rigid or more relaxed in their controls. Visiting between households in the neighborhood is uncommon among adults, and not encouraged for adolescents. Occasionally neighbors may act as a supportive network or as agents of social control informing on adolescent's or husband's deviations; invidiousness among neighbors may also appear as a theme.

The traditional pattern of father in the role of disciplinarian and mother as mediator between father and children becomes more evident at this stage, but stresses of acculturation may contribute to a weakening of the father's authority. The father who remains a disciplinarian in a culturally isolated situation is less acceptable to the children because he no longer represents a community of adults who uphold the same views. He may become defensively rigid and end up virtually powerless, a mere "paper tiger." The aloofness of the father in this role may be increased if father migrated first while mother remained with the children during their early childhood. The spouses may have never totally recovered from the separation, or the father's promise of a better future never materializes, decreasing permanently his prestige and influence. This situation may lead to mother scapegoating father by a combination of public endorsement and private subversion of his authority. Mother may signal to the children that father is the source of all discomfort and she the source of all good. The children may see her as victimized and begin to protect her, or they may feel bound by gratitude to her. This type of family structure may present special difficulties during adolescence, as in the following example:

   Elena, a fifteen-year-old girl was referred to the clinic after a suicidal gesture. The family consisted of the two parents, Mr. M. (thirty-eight) and Mrs. M. (thirty-five), an older brother Tonio (seventeen), a younger sister Monica (thirteen), and three youngsters. The father had left Monterrey, Mexico, when Monica was born and stayed in the United States for five years before he was able to bring his wife and children. The younger children were born in Chicago. It was readily apparent that Mrs. M. and the older children formed an "enmeshed" subsystem ("her children") that isolated the father, who in turn was close and playful with the three younger children ("his children"). When the father talked, the adolescents quietly mocked him or muttered disparaging comments.

Mr. M. worked as a bus driver many hours of the day or night, both during the week and on weekends. At home he was tired but constantly asked the older children to do more to help the overworked mother. The children passively opposed him by delaying tactics, relying on the mother's tolerance, although she often complained to father about the amount of work she faced daily.

The precipitating event for Elena's suicidal gesture was her father's refusal to allow her to take the bus to visit a friend who had moved to another neighborhood. The father argued that: 1) the bus stop was in front of a tavern, not a place for a girl (an uncle had seen Elena around the tavern on several occasions); 2) he was upset by the loud and wild behavior he witnessed every day in the black and white adolescents who rode the buses in the inner-city and was trying to delay exposing his daughter to these bad examples; and 3) as a concerned father, he checked on all of his children's activities.

At some point the therapist wondered if what the adolescents labeled as control and intrusiveness were in fact ways in which father tried to be included in the family. A congenial, feisty man, Mr. M. rapidly responded that "he who appeared to have military manners had in fact suffered a civilian 'coup d'état' years ago and had never been able to regain the presidency." This metaphor became a central theme for the ousted father in the therapy. He explained that he felt guilty towards his wife because in spite of great effort he could not offer to the family the financial stability he had originally envisioned. He recollected that because of complications after his wife had their fourth child, the lack of medical insurance burdened the family with medical bills that took many years to pay. To compensate for all of this, he tried to enlist the older children's cooperation to make mother's life easier. The more he insisted, the more they resisted his demands, rendering him ineffective. Now he could see that some of his attempted solutions had become part of the problem. Mrs. M. was very surprised to see that Mr. M. recalled particularly painful incidents that she had occasionally mentioned to the children, particularly to Elena, because she was convinced they had not meant very much to him. Many years of distance between husband and wife could now be seen in a different light and positively connotated as protecting each other.

In the therapy situation, Mexican-American families are likely to resist suggestions that teenagers look for an attentive and sympathetic friend in their parents to whom they can confide or honestly speak up; or the suggestion that adolescents need the freedom to experiment and learn from their own experience. For the therapist to tell the parents that their over-possessiveness is squelching their children's search for independance and a separate identity, is the equivalent of requiring them to abdicate their cultural beliefs.

Existing rituals such as the cotillion or the graduation can be used as effective therapeutic tools in helping to separate parents from adolescent children. The therapist may at times effectively act as a "cultural mediator" or "family matchmaker"[10] in situations where the developmental time clock is out of phase between the generations and this conflict appears to be relevant to the identified problems.

If the therapist turns to the parents' marital relationship, it is better to approach it through the parental functions of the couple, but seldom to pursue greater marital satisfaction as a goal. If the family has developed a very trusting relationship with the therapist, an indirect, humorous approach to the marital difficulties can be very effective.

Living in large nuclear and extended families may naturally facilitate the resolution of this stage through the appearance of other developmental transitions: a younger child's entrance into school, an older married child's entrance into parenthood, the need for attention for aging parents. Therapists can direct attention to these new events and relieve pressure from the adolescent.

The Family with Middle-Aged Parents

Mexican-American middle-aged parents are confronted with the universal tasks of facilitating the separation of their children, negotiating a renewed marital relationship, and assuming the role of grandparents. Resolution of this developmental stage will depend on the ability of the parents to redefine their relationship with their grown children and to find a new meaning to their marital bond.

Because of cultural values that stress family interdependence, the separation of the grown children is accomplished with varying degrees of conflict, but in most cases the generations maintain considerable closeness and connectedness. The empty nest phenomenon described for upwardly mobile, nuclear Anglo-American families is not as visible in the Mexican-American working-class family (see figure 16.1). Leaving home is easier for sons than for daughters since cultural expectations facilitate this process for young men. Moving out of the home is approached gradually; sons frequently stay out of the home for increasingly longer hours, coming home only at night to sleep. Parents may occasionally complain about not seeing the son often enough but this peripheral role is acceptable. Eventually the young adult son smoothly moves out through work, marriage, or educational opportunities.

[10]The term "social matchmaker" has been used by Minuchin (1974) to denote the role of the therapist as a link between the isolated family and external systems. A similar role of mediator between different cultural norms existing within the family can be performed by the bicultural therapist.

The young adult daughter presents a more difficult task. She is perceived as far more vulnerable to external influence and in need of protection. The most acceptable manner for an adult daughter to leave home is through marriage. Within the last decade, an increasing number of young adult women of Mexican descent are leaving home to further their education. This is still a highly stressful event for the whole family and one that may bring them into the mental health clinic.

The role of older and younger siblings may get even more sharply differentiated during this stage than during adolescence. The older siblings pioneer the road to emancipation. When this is successful, as it is in most families, the road is partially paved for the younger ones to follow. But in other instances, as an older child leaves, parental alliances shift to the next in line, who may be unprepared to assume the roles vacated by the older one. Other children may then be "recruited" or "elected" for these roles with various degrees of success.

When young adults marry and leave home, the relationship between parents and young adults changes, but the availability to each other continues. The acceptance of the son- or daughter-in-law may become problematic if the parents continue to cling to their married children, or vice versa. With the advent of grandchildren, the grandparents assume an important role in childrearing. Their influence is felt and usually accepted by the new parents, and they do not experience the sense of peripherality and fear of intrusion that their middle-class American counterparts often feel. The sense of usefulness and involvement with the two younger generations also contributes to a prolongation of middle age relative to old age (see figure 16.1).

In the family of Mexican descent, it is common to find unmarried, widowed, separated, or divorced adults living at home with their parents and younger siblings. If the returning adult has children, child rearing is shared with the grandparents.

Three-generational imbalance may occur as the parents experience the death of their own parents and the incorporation of the survivor into their family unit. Incorporation of widowed parents also increases, the family unit while the children are being launched, and considerable accomodations must take place to cope with the combined stresses of launching and marriage of children, illnesses or death of parents, and a new relationship with in-law family members.

As children leave home the parents begin to face their future as a couple. This is particularly difficult since value orientations have prepared the couple for parenting while deemphasizing their marital role. Marital renewal in stable families is at best taken for granted, without necessarily deepening intimacy. The marital relationship is maintained by finding an acceptable, more disengaged manner of parenting their married children, focusing to a large extent on the children and grandchildren, and perhaps an increase in contact with relatives, in-laws, and significant kin. In dysfunctional systems this transitional stage often creates an impasse that will bring the families into treatment. A frequently observed pattern is distance between spouses and a type of emotional separation, with both spouses continuing to live together, carrying on their family duties but hardly relating to each other directly. Alliances coalesce along sex lines, or mother may ally with oldest son against her daughter-in-law, who in turn forms an alliance with her young son. In this manner the peripherality in both father and/or new husband and the mother-son overinvolvement may be family themes repeated in every generation, and never openly discussed.

The different acculturation levels found in Mexican-American families exacerbate the transitional problems of this stage by polarizing both parents and young adults. The young generation often find it difficult to accept their parents' life-style, question their marital arrangement, and rebel against the parental value orientations.

The following example illustrates a family with many of these conflicts present:

> Mrs. C., (forty-six), a resident of the United States for twenty-three years, was referred to our clinic with her family. She presented numerous psychosomatic complaints and talked about divorcing her husband (forty-eight) of twenty-five years. The couple had six children, Araceli (twenty-three), Marta (twenty-one), Rebeca (twenty), Michael (seventeen), Elizabeth (sixteen), and Gloria (fifteen). All were living at home. Araceli was finishing school in social work at a city college, Marta was working as a postal employee, Rebeca had plans to enter medical school, Michael had dropped out of high school and was erratically employed. Elizabeth and Gloria were both attending a neighborhood high school.
>
> The initial interview revealed a long-standing feud between the parents. They had settled their marital impasse by aligning with some of the children. Mother and Araceli had a stable coalition that maintained the status quo between the struggling spouses, blocked open conflict, and kept her at home. Her proposed separation to attend graduate school created an imbalance and precipitated a family crises. Marta, was feeling pressured but unwilling to assume the marital mediator role. Becky was openly defiant, clearly stating to the family that her plans to attend medical school were a priority for her; she openly challenged the parents marital arrangement and supported mother's talk of divorce. Elizabeth and Gloria had elected the passive observer role as the family's drama unfolded before them.
>
> Within this family the son appeared to be the most vulnerable. Father, greatly disappointed, had disengaged from Michael when he dropped out of school. Initially he had attempted to guide his son but did it in an ineffectual, lecturing manner, which Michael adeptly turned off. Michael avoided open conflict by being absent from most family activities, arriving home late at night and getting up late when other family members were not around.

The sibling subsystem was organized around two main themes: achievement and marriage. Araceli, Rebeca, and the two youngest girls together with father represented the achievement orientation in the family. Michael and Marta, on the other hand, expressed the wish to marry and settle down. Marta was particularly critical of her parents' marriage expressing her wish to establish a meaningful relationship where communication could be open. Michael could not state his preferences clearly but he felt marriage was the only way for him to leave his family.

The parents, totally unprepared for their children's separation and tenuously allied by their attack, could only defend themselves and speak of filial ingratitude. Both attempted to entrap Marta as the new mediator between them, but Marta did not accept this role as readily as Araceli had. Father, who worked as a laborer and at present was keenly aware of his own unfulfilled achievement aspirations, identified with his daughters' desire for education. Although a traditional man, he was able to defend his daughters' education as a way to get ahead in the world, but using models he incorporated when he was a young man in Mexico, he could not understand why the daughters had to move away in order to continue their studies. He was a bright and sensitive individual who wrote poetry and spoke in a preacherlike manner but he appeared to be frozen in time and unable to update his opinions.

Mrs. C. had recently begun to work as a seamstress and this experience had awakened in her some wishes for independence. She presented a good facade for making it on her own, but upon exploration she began to express considerable fears of aloneness, and concern about how she would manage to raise her younger daughters as a single parent. In a more subtle manner, she expressed ambivalence about losing her husband.

Negotiation around appropriate ways for the daughters to separate lasted for six months. Enactment and new resolutions of conflict situations in family therapy sessions were the primary modes of intervention. Sibling issues were resolved by sessions where the parents sat behind the one-way mirror to observe their children at work. This setting provided a new closeness for the spouses and distance from the children that facilitated their ability to negotiate when the family rejoined.

The parents remained married, but different working shifts minimized their involvement and made the relationship tolerable. Araceli left for college. Marta continued living at home and holding a job. Becky was accepted at medical school in Chicago. The younger girls continued attending high school, relieved to have the option to go away to school open to them. Michael got married and brought his wife, a sixteen-year-old girl, to live with his parents. The young couple was seen in treatment a year later because of marital difficulties.

The Family in Later Life

The developmental tasks of this period include adjustment to the physical and psychosocial concomitants of old age, such as grandparenthood, retirement, illnesses, and death. Marital, intergenerational, and peer relationships need to change and adapt. Acculturation stresses appear in two forms. The older person may have migrated forty to forty-five years ago and have incorporated traditional cultural patterns of aging that do not fit the changing norms of his or her children and grandchildren and have not been updated for an urban-egalitarian setting. Or the older person may be a new immigrant.

The parents of the first generation of young adult immigrants may have remained behind in rural Mexico. When they become too old or isolated they often move to America to be near their offspring, either living in the same house or close by their children. The older person arrives to an unknown urban setting, without knowledge of the language or any skills necessary for an independent living situation. Under these circumstances, the older person may or may not find a useful role. The older woman can be easily integrated into the parental and younger generation through housekeeping and babysitting. The functions of the older man may now be limited to babysitting and reporting on the children's performance, and running small errands if the ethnic neighborhood is close by. He may sit long hours on the porch or watch Spanish programs on television all day, deprived of the close lifelong associations that composed his previous social environment.

In spite of these losses, in the Mexican-American extended family the elderly retain other important roles. The presence of the aged helps reduce anxiety at times of stress for the nuclear family, such as illness of children, overtime work for the husband, and the like. Wisdom and sorcery are attributions given only to the old. Their usefulness and wisdom coupled with the younger generation's respect for authority allow older people to continue to exert considerable influence on their married or single children through criticism and reminders about appropriate behavior, including screening of suitors for grownup daughters.

The ability to become a "tough old bird"—energetic, involved, and self-confident—and perceive old age as "shorter" (see Figure 16.1) seems to be preserved among the Mexican-American elderly, as reported in investigations conducted at the Langley Porter Institute (Clark & Mendelson, 1975). This finding may be accounted for by the fact that Mexican culture values collectivism, conservation, cooperation, and continuity and therefore does not require the dramatic shifts in life orientation required for Anglo-Americans in later life.

Retirement from their usual occupation does not represent a significant turning point for older Mexican males, or their families. Productive work in one's occupation is not a central life task as it is for those raised in the Protestant ethic. In Mexico, there is a cultural tradition that values leisure. Furthermore, retirement does not entail a status loss since money and material possessions do not add up to self-worth. Various anchorage points that provide identification outside of work are found in male groups and extended family relationships. Few people retire in a prescribed compulsory manner. The only exceptions are bureaucratic employees who retire between sixty and sixty-five and receive pensions. A retirement date as an initiation rite is not necessary since older men continue to work while still possible. They gradually reduce their output and begin to move closer to the family orbit. There, the man joins a houseful of people rather than a wife who has learned to live alone for the past twenty years. In fact, retirement does not demand significant shifts for the wife or adjustment for the couple since they are still able to maintain separate spheres of social contact or common interests in grown children and grandchildren.

In Mexican-American culture, being old does not place people in an experiential island; it allows them to remain in the mainstream of life. The need to appear young or to pretend to be younger than one's age, to deceive oneself and others about aging and fearing the inevitable, decreases when the culture does not idealize youth. Self-sufficiency is not expected from a sick person and therefore the expectation is that the young will take care of the old until the end and not place parents in nursing homes. The entire family tends to respect at this point cultural values that emphasize the importance of interpersonal relationships and filial love, or at least obligation over efficiency and practicality. In Anglo-American culture, a sense of justice may indicate that older people get what is coming to them according to how they lived their lives. Those who worked hard, saved, planned ahead, raised a good family deserve more comfortable aging than the old derelict or alcoholic, who never provided adequately for his family, or perhaps even abused them. In Mexican culture, children are obligated to care for and respect their parents whether the older person rightfully deserves it or not.

Openness about fear of illness, physical complaints, or the prospect of death may appear more frequently under circumstances where old people do not need to apologize or "play games" with younger people about what is happening and what is to come (Webber, 1963). Sometimes nervousness, illnesses, and ailments are called upon to remind adult children about their obligations to their parents. One should not assume pathology, overpossessiveness, or egocentrism, since it is culturally acceptable for older parents to behave in this manner. "Coaching" the individual or couple on how to proceed in these cases to achieve greater differentiation while protecting the old can be useful, particularly when the generational differences in acculturation are marked.

Occasionally the old person becomes the center of attention and activity of a large Mexican-American extended family through numerous psychosomatic complaints, "sinking spells," and agitated calls to the family. The weary but enduring grown children and grandchildren may come to see these as "attention-getting" manipulations. However, the elderly "identified patient" may fulfill important functions for the organization of the family, as in the following example:

Mr. and Mrs. J., both in their late sixties, came from Jalisco, Mexico, after their ten adult children had immigrated over a period of twenty years. They went to live with their youngest son, when his wife went back to work after the birth of their first child. In the same apartment building lived a widowed daughter (forty-six) and her six children. In a third apartment lived a divorced daughter (thirty-nine) and her two children and two of her single brothers.

There were people in and out of the house constantly, with considerable conflict and accusations about responsibilities. Many of the grown children went to dance and drink on the weekends. Initially the parents disliked what they saw and attempted to control the outings and visitors through questions and criticisms. They were particularly critical of the two daughters, who they saw as "too old" to go out at night. Later they installed themselves at the porch or by the window and scrutinized anybody who walked in or out. Nothing changed. Now on weekends, Mrs J. gets dizzy spells and palpitations and gets frantically afraid of cancer or death. Her children need to cooperate, to decide what to do, and to call the ambulance during her faintings and attacks. Consistantly the doctors tell her the symptoms are due to "nerves." Mrs. J. or her husband always respond that the "nerves" will not get calmer until their children cooperate with each other as a family or at least behave.

Economic hardships, problems of isolation, and adaptation to an unknown environment are often involved in many difficulties presented by older Mexican-American people. Simple rather than complex interpretations should always be considered first, as in the following example:

A seventy-year-old emaciated Mexican-American lady who complained of numerous eating difficulties was referred to a mental health clinic by a priest, who after talking with her several times, thought she was anxious and depressed. After a few sessions a simple answer emerged—her teeth badly needed repair but she had not been able to find free dental care. Language difficulties and ignorance of resources prevented her and her forty-five-year-old daughter from resolving this problem.

Intergenerational conflicts or conflicts of loyalty between obligations to one's aging parents and to one's own family may create considerable stress at this point, and surface in any family member. These issues should be addressed and an attempt be made to resolve stress without insisting on a direct approach to dealing with the older generation, since most Mexican-Americans are likely to resist the idea of leveling hierarchies at this point. The adult son or daughter may feel indebted towards his parents for the practical help they still provide, but above all they are constrained by internalized respect for the older generation. If, for example, an older mother still controls many affective areas of her married son's life, a more effective strategy would be to enlist the cooperation of the wife—perhaps privately—to help him disengage from his mother (and block the wife's usual attempts to gain him through criticism of her mother-in-law), rather than insisting on an intergenerational resolution through direct clarification or confrontation.

Differences in developmental expectations, in attitudes towards sickness and death, and in intergenerational relationships result in different cultural perceptions about this life stage. Errors of clinical assessment emerge when these cultural differences are not taken into account, as in the following example:

> Toni was a seven-year-old Mexican-American boy who underwent heart surgery at a large metropolitan hospital for correction of a congenital anomaly. Following surgery, he recovered slowly but not completely. He appeared weak, ate very little, slept poorly, and had exaggerated breathing. The cardiology staff maintained that the operation had been successful. Emotional reasons began to be advanced as explanations for Toni's failure to recover. The hospital staff turned to Toni's home situation to seek the answers. The following observations were made.
>
> Toni's great-aunt, Mrs. R., a sixty-four-year-old woman who spoke little English, was the child's legal guardian and only visitor. Toni's mother had left him under the care of the great-aunt since infancy and her whereabouts were unknown.
>
> The nurses disliked Toni's great-aunt because she usually hovered around the child and attempted to feed and dress him rather than encourage him to do these tasks himself. She was seen as "spoiling" and overprotective of Toni. She appeared to be very anxious about his health in spite of repeated assurances by the doctors about his well-being. Mrs. R. was often seen praying with a rosary and a small cross near Toni's bed.
>
> Drawing on this information, the consulting psychiatrist concluded, "Toni has been unwanted and abandoned by his mother. He was raised by an older woman who probably resented such a burden and harbored unconscious death wishes which she defended against by a reaction formation, i.e., overprotecting him. Toni's failure to thrive could be seen as resulting from his own regressive wish to die and his aunt's not allowing him to resume normal activities." His respiratory problem was diagnosed as psychologically induced.
>
> This diagnosis intensified the hospital staff's scapegoating of the great-aunt. She began to perceive the blame implicit in statements made to her and felt confused and debilitated by it. Until the child entered congestive heart failure and died, the seriousness of his medical condition was underestimated, while the psychosocial component was overestimated because of the social and cultural differences between the family and the hospital staff.
>
> Mrs. R. was very upset about Toni's death but she also said at this point that for many months she had been trying to accept this possibility. Her talks with her priest and his encouragement were perceived by her as true sources of com-

fort and some hope that God may help where doctors can't. Indeed, all along she had seen Toni's lack of recovery as ominous.

The application of white American norms—which value independence and self-sufficiency—as standards of what is developmentally appropriate or socially acceptable led to erroneously judging as pathogenic and deviant, behaviors which were, in fact, consonant or adaptive within the Mexican-American culture.

Much suffering for family and hospital staff would have been spared if the so-called "abandonment" by the mother and the fact of being raised by an older relative would have been understood as a widespread phenomenon adaptive to the circumstances of the culture of poverty. Furthermore, what was labeled as "spoiling" and "overprotecting" in American terms is considered to be good nurturing in the Mexican culture. It is "inhuman" and "unkind" in Mexican terms to demand independence and self-sufficiency from a child or a sick person. Where the old are seen as functional active members of the family, no stigma is attached to their full participation in child care. Where old age is seen as equivalent with freedom from responsibility, as in Anglo-American culture, taking care of a sick child can be interpreted as a burden that produces intense hostility. Mrs. R.'s determination to rely on God and not "trust" the doctors completely by insisting that the child was still not well, appears antithetical to the behavior of Anglo-American patients that accept the doctors' expertise and generally try to cooperate by being as unobtrusive and self-sufficient as possible. By contrast, Mexican-American attitudes may cause irritations in a medical staff not accustomed to them.

Finally, important cultural differences in the experience of death should be mentioned. Perhaps the most striking difference is the fact that Mexicans do not ignore death as a constant fact of life. "The Day of the Dead" is a "fiesta" publicly held once a year in Mexico where folklore, religious litanies, sugar candy skulls, and tissue paper skeletons imitate and ridicule death. The presentations of devils and death, jokes and sayings about astute maneuverings that confuse and defeat death are common occurences, which have been interpreted as a counterphobic approach to death.[11]

[11]Octavio Paz (1961) eloquently describes the Mexican attitude toward death: "The word death is not pronounced in New York, in Paris, in London, because it burns the lips. The Mexican, in contrast, is familiar with death, jokes about it, caresses it, sleeps with it, celebrates it; it is one of his favorite toys and his most steadfast love. True, there is perhaps as much fear in his attitude as in that of others, but at least death is not hidden away: he looks at it face to face, with impatience, disdain or irony. As in a popular folk song, "if they are going to kill me tomorrow, let them kill me right away" (Paz, 1961).

Mexican-American society appears to be a relatively more open system relative to the Anglo-American society in matters related to death. An impending or recent death can be more openly discussed among relatives and friends. The physical and emotional support of the extended family and community provide resources and nurturance for the bereaved. Anger, guilt, blame, and sorrow are vented, perhaps because they are better tolerated and contained within a large closely knit group. In fact, cultural norms dictate how and when one must publicly display the depths of one's sentiments. The unexpressive son or daughter may raise suspicions and end up labeled as having a stone heart or *corazón de piedra*.

The boundaries between the nuclear and the extended family become more sharply delineated at the time of mourning. Who can mourn and how much is partly dictated by the degree of family connectedness. If someone is a distant relative but cries profusely, he or she may be criticized as not having sufficient *velas en este entierro* (candles in the wake).

Religion may resurface with impending loss, and as a guidance and consolation for the ill, elderly, or bereaved person. Two types of religious rituals provide a sense of involvement and encourage resignation to accept the inevitable. One of these rituals is to ask a priest for a small private mass to pray for the recovery of a seriously ill person. Relatives and friends can also organize a *velada* or community mass to pray for the recovery of the loved one or for the salvation of the person's soul. Both act as anticipatory mourning rituals. The belief in the immortality of the soul probably ameliorates some of the most frightening aspects of death.

When a person dies, the presence of the body in the home, the open casket, the quiet atmosphere, and the whispering voices during the wake encourage emotional expression among family members and friends. Events of the life and the death of the deceased are openly shared; sensitivities are high. Traditionally the wake is conducted at home, but the use of funeral parlors is increasing among Mexican-Americans. Aside from being excessively expensive, burials in a foreign land are emotionally very difficult for immigrants. The family often decides to send the deceased to be buried in Mexico as a final symbol of "belonging."

The custom of the oldest son being responsible for the funeral arrangements tends to be maintained. An additional stress caused by immigration may increase the difficulties for those in charge of decisions during this period. Mexican-Americans who immigrate as young adults have not been exposed, through observing their contemporaries, to the appropriate mechanisms and conduct expected in this situation. They may have to learn it alone and frequently feel confused. The presence of the extended family may be once more the best source and guidance for the preservation of healing traditions during the family's life cycle.

SUMMARY

This chapter considers the family life cycle in its sociocultural context and describes expectable life cycle events, from courtship to later life, for Mexican-American families. The descriptions provide a picture of age and sex role expectations, value orientations, and cultural traditions and rituals. The effects of immigration and culture change upon the family life cycle are extensively discussed. At each developmental stage, the internal reorganization and response of the family system is conceptualized as a product of the combined effects of expectable life cycle events occuring under the impact of relocation and acculturation.

Clinical examples illustrate developmental impasses encountered by Mexican-American families and suggest therapeutic approaches that take into account the family's original cultural values and the present cultural context.

REFERENCES

Carlos, M. L. and Sellers, L. "Family, kinship structure and modernization in Latin America." *Latin America Research Review* 7(2):95–124, 1972.

Clark, M. and Mendelson, M., "Mexican-American Aged in San Francisco." in Sze, W.C. (ed.) *Human Life Cycle*. New York: Jason Aronson, 1975.

De Vos, G.A. "Minority Group Identity." In Finney, J. C. (Ed.), *Culture Change, Mental Health and Poverty*. Lexington,.: University of Kentucky Press, 1969.

Diaz-Guerrero, R. *Psychology of the Mexican: Culture and Personality*. Austin, Tex. University of Texas Press, 1975.

Falicov, C. *Interpersonal Reorganizations during Pregnancy and Early Parenthood*. Doctoral dissertation, Committee on Human Development, The University of Chicago, January, 1971.

Gordon, M. *Assimilation in American Life: The Role of Race, Religion, and National Origins*. New York: Oxford , 1964.

Grebler, L. et al. *The Mexican-American People: The Nation's Second Largest Minority*. New York: Free Press, 1970.

Hawkes, G. and Taylor, M. "Power Structure in Mexican and Mexican-American Farm Labor Families." *Journal of Marriage and The Family* 37:807–811, 1975.

Heller, C. *Mexican-American Youth: Forgotten Youth at the Crossroads*. New York: Random House, 1966.

Horowitz, R. and Schwartz, G. "Honor, Normative Ambiguity and Gang Violence." *American Sociological Review* 39:238–51, 1974.

Jackson, D. "The Study of the Family." *Family Process* 4:1–20, 1965. Also in Watzlawick, P. and Weakland, J. (Eds.), *The Interactional View*. New York: Norton, 1977.

Kagan, S. and Madsen, M. "Cooperation and Competition of Mexican, Mexican-American and Anglo-American Children of Two Ages Under Four Instructional Sets." *Developmental Psychology* 5(1):32–39, 1971.

Karrer, B. and Falicov, C. "The Acculturation of the Mexican American Family: A Perspective" (submitted for publication, 1980).

Kitano, H. *Japanese-Americans: The Evaluation of a Subculture.* Englewood Cliffs, N. J.: Prentice-Hall, 1969.

Maslow, A., and Diaz-Guerrero, R. "Delinquency as a Value Disturbance," In Peatman, J., and Hartley. E. (eds), *Festschrift for Gardner Murphy,* New York: Harper, 1960.

Minuchin, S. et al., *Families of the Slums: An Exploration of Their Structure and Treatment.* New York: Basic Books, 1967.

Minuchin, S. *Families and Family Therapy.* Cambridge, Mass.: Harvard University Press, 1974.

Minturn, L. and Lambert, W. *Mothers of Six Cultures. Antecedents of Child-Rearing.* New York: Wiley, 1964.

Moore, Joan W. *Mexican-Americans.* Englewood Cliffs, N. J.: Prentice-Hall, 1970.

Neugarten, B. et al., *Personality in Middle and Late Life.* New York: Atherton, 1964.

Paz, O. The *Labyrinth of Solitude: Life and Thought in Mexico.* New York: Evergreen, 1961.

Rainwater, L. "Marital Sexuality in Four Cultures of Poverty." In Sze, W.C. (Ed.), *Human Life Cycle.* New York: Jason Aronson, 1975.

Schulz, D. *The Changing Family: Its Function and Future,* 2d Edition. Englewood Cliffs, N. J.: Prentice-Hall, 1976.

Slater, P. *Footholds: Understanding the Shifting Sexual and Family Tensions in Our Culture.* New York: Dutton, 1977.

Sluzki, C. "Migration and Family Conflict," Family Process, 18/4, 379-90, 1979.

Stevens, E. "Marianismo: The Other Face of Machismo." In Ann Pescatello (Ed.), *Female and Male in Latin America.* Pittsburgh: University of Pittsburgh Press, 1973.

Teske, R. H. and Nelson, B. H. "An Analysis of Differential Assimilation Rates Among Middle-Class Mexican-Americans." *The Sociological Quarterly* 17:218-35, Spring 1976.

Tharp, R. et al. "Changes in Marriage Roles Accompanying the Acculturation of the Mexican-American Wife." *Journal of Marriage and the Family.* 24:404-412, 1968.

Thomas, D. L. and Weigert, A.J. "Socialization and Adolescent Conformity to Significant Others: A Cross-National Analysis." *American Sociological Review* 36:835-47, 1971.

Webber, H. "Games." *The New Yorker,* March 30, 1963.

Part 5

Celebration of
the Family Life Cycle

17
SYSTEMS AND CEREMONIES: A FAMILY VIEW OF RITES OF PASSAGE

Edwin H. Friedman, M.A.

Consultant, Family Therapy, Saint Elizabeth's Hospital, Washington, D.C.

Rites of passage are usually associated with emotionally critical moments of life. Yet most studies of these ceremonies have tended to ignore the crucial role of the family at such events. The convention in the social sciences has been to place primary focus on the culture that provides the rites, or the individuals who are being passed through to a new stage in their life cycle. The role of the family at such occasions has tended to be seen as secondary, as occupying more of an intermediary position between the individual members to be passed and society. From this perspective, the family participates in the customs provided by a culture as a way of helping its members take their new position in that culture.

Twenty years experience as a clergyman and family therapist has given me an almost totally different perception of the role of families in rites of passage. I have found that the family, far from being an intermediary, is the primary force operating at such moments—primary not only in that it, and not the culture, determines the emotional quality of such occasions (and therefore the success of the passage), but also in that it is the family more than the culture that ultimately determines which rites are to be used. For families are far less determined by their culture's customs and ways of doing things than they are selective, according to their own characteristics and pathology, of their culture's ceremonial repertoire. Though, of course, the family will always say, "That's just the way we (Jews, Catholics, Fijis, Aborigines) have always done things (at our weddings, funerals, baptisms, bar mitzvas)."

Indeed, so central is the role of family process in rites of passage that it is probably correct to say it is really the family which is making the transition to a new stage of life at such a time rather than any "identified member" focused upon during the occasion.

What may be most significant, however, in switching one's primary focus to the family is that it enables one to see the enormous therapeutic potential inherent in natural family crisis. The one phenomenon which has stood out in my experience with families of all cultures is that the periods surrounding rites of passage function as "hinges of time."

All family relationship systems seem to unlock during the months before and after such events, and it is often possible to open doors (or close them) between various family members with less effort during these intensive periods than could ordinarily be achieved with years of agonizing efforts.

I believe this is true because with respect to timing, life cycle events are not as random as they appear. Rather they are usually the coming to fruition or culmination of family processes that have been moving toward those ends for some time. Life cycle events are always part and parcel of "other things going on." They always indicate movement, and it is simply easier to steer a ship when it is afloat, even if it is drifting in the wrong direction, than when it is still aground.

It will be the purpose of this chapter to strip away the cultural camouflage of rites of passage and to show how family process operates at emotionally significant moments of life cycle change. I will try to show how the time periods surrounding such moments are particularly useful for observing family process in the raw. I will give examples from my own experience to show how members of the helping professions may use a family understanding of rites of passage to turn the crisis always inherent in those events into an opportunity for beneficial change.

The ideas and examples that will be illustrated below come out of twenty years continuous experience in one community (the Washington metropolitan area) as both rabbi and family therapist. Over these two decades, my dual role enabled me to pass perceptions back and forth between positions as in each role I was able to gain a vantage point not usually available to individuals functioning in only one role. For example, my continuous experience in one community often gave me the opportunity to observe the same family throughout an entire generation. As their clergyman, I often gained intimate knowledge of that family, not only at important nodal points and rites of passage themselves, but also as I observed the changes that took place between those events. And, of course, all of these observations were informed by what I was learning about family process from my general family therapy experience. Similarly, since my therapy experience has always been ecumenical, and since Washington is a "Mecca" nationally and internationally, I was given an opportunity to observe families of many different cultures and backgrounds intimately. The latter experience enabled me to realize that what I had been observing among Jewish families had universal application. Eventually, I found I could quite successfully extrapolate the insights I had obtained from the rabbinic experience with the life cycle to families I was counseling about other problems, no matter what their cultural background.

The framework of this chapter will be to explore three natural life cycle events (death, marriage, pubescence), and then to comment on three nodal events that are less a natural part of the life cycle and more a creation of the times in which we live (divorce, retirement, geographical uprooting).

Before beginning that process, however, I would like to note briefly three myths that inhibit forming a family process view of rites of passage and four principles about the relationship of family process to rites of passage that are basic to my conceptualization.

THREE MYTHS THAT INHIBIT FORMING A FAMILY PROCESS VIEW

Three myths about life that inhibit the development of a family process view of rites of passage are as follows: (1) the family is breaking down; (2) culture determines family process in fundamental ways; and (3) the rite of passage is the same as the ceremony that celebrates it.

The Breakdown of the Family

The notion that the family is "breaking" down is supported by the higher divorce rates and by the greater physical distance between relatives which is produced by our highly mobile society. However, nodal events in family life have an absolutely transporting quality, able to transcend great distances or gulfs, as can be seen by the attendance of distant family members at funerals, weddings, or bar mitzvas. Sometimes it is only one or two individuals from another part of the country, but they are there to represent that part of the clan. Sometimes it works the other way of course, and individuals whom everybody expected would come, don't, allowing the physical distance or the climate to be their defense. Whichever the case, it seems important to point out that no necessary correlation exists between the

degree of physical distance or frequency of previous communication between family members and whether or not they appear at a given family
ritual. One member will have trouble getting a car out of the garage to
drive twenty miles, and another will, on finding the local airport snowed
in, drive 150 miles through a blizzard to another town, from which he or
she can take off. Nor can one always predict, based on previous relationships, who will do what. There is also no correlation between the distance
family members have to travel and their punctuality at the ceremony. If
anything, there is sometimes an inverse ratio.

It is possible, of course, to say that all this is proof of the breakdown of
the family and the underlying need for family relationships. It may not be
all that accidental, however, who appears at which event. In any case, the
therapeutic potential inherent in bringing family members together at life
cycle events should not be discounted because of distance. A better metaphor for the present state of family life than a "breakdown" might be to say
that the family has gone "underground," and nothing will coax various
parts of it to surface like a rite of passage. The umbilical cord is infinitely
elastic.

I have involved clients in overseas travel and overnight communication
that involved three continents, and found that even after decades, the
buried system is very much alive.

There is another reason for not confusing physical distance with emotional potential. One cannot assume that the members of a family who are
most distant from home base are those who are necessarily most independent, or least reactive, emotionally. On the contrary, often they are the members of the family who most needed physical distance in order to relate with
any independence at all to the family members back home.

For example, a woman has been maintaining an adaptive mode of relating to her critical husband in order to keep peace. She is visited by a sister
whose presence makes her feel less alone, or, the opposite, a mother whose
dependency requires a lot of thought and emotional energy. In either case,
the homeostasis of her marriage will be upset and the husband, feeling the
withdrawal of emotional energy, now perceiving his wife to be less cooperative or less attentive, becomes more critical than ever. Actually, I have
found it a general rule of thumb that when one marriage partner is visited
by relatives, the other often becomes more reactive during the stay. It is
particularly those relationships held together by distance, so to speak,
which will surface with all their original intensity at family get-togethers. In
addition, what often had been enabling such relationships to maintain great
distance was each family member correspondingly compensating by invest-
ing more emotion into their nearby relationships, e.g., with a spouse, while

cutting off the extended family. When the originally intense relationship comes alive, the energy now drawn away from the spouse is sensed immediately, thus creating problems "at home."

Such phenomena can occur at any family get-together, and probably help explain much of the increased anxiety around Christmas. (See below the comparison in family process terms between Christmas and bar mitzva around the issues of drinking, gift giving, and suicide rates.) But at family rituals which are associated with nodal events in the life cycle, the whole emotional energy system is higher to begin with; thus they are prime times for the confluence and the redirection of intensity. It may be more correct to say, therefore, that the major breakdown which occurs during rites of passage is not the family but the family's defense of physical distance.

Culture Determines Family Process

In 1970 I delivered a paper at the Georgetown Family Therapy Symposium entitled "Culture and Family Process." It was the thesis of this work that rather than determining family life in any significant way, culture was more the projection of family process on a societal level. I proposed that to try to understand family life through its customs and ceremonies was, therefore, circular reasoning. The new metaphor I suggested was that "culture is the *medium* through which family process works its art."

I tried to show that while a strict Catholic family, a rigid Methodist family, or an orthodox Jewish family might claim they are only following their religion when they operate in a given way, the fact of the matter is there are very few families that observe all the customs of their background in the proper way. In fact, what culture has general agreement among its leaders as to what is right? Obviously one can often find other families from the same culture, if not members of the same family, who do it differently.

What seems to happen in family life is that individuals and families adhere most closely to those values which coincide with their own life style. Every religious tradition and cultural background has its own neurotic usefulness.[1]

[1]In ethnic families it is almost impossible for a child growing up to distinguish a feeling about his or her family from a feeling about his or her ethnic background. I have tried to show elsewhere that commitment to tradition has nothing to do with marrying outside that tradition. In any ethnic family, the child marrying out is the child most important to the balance of the parents' relationship. See "Ethnic Identity as Extended Family in Jewish-Christian Marriage," delivered at the Fifth Georgetown Family Therapy Symposium, November 1968, published in *Systems Therapy*, ed. Bradt and Moynihan, 1971.

There are some crucially important ramifications of this reversal in conceptualizing how family and culture influence one another. The first is that it gets the therapist out of the middle—between the client and the client's background—when issues come up about rituals or ceremonies, and the client says, "I can't do that because it's against my tradition." Questions like, "Do all the members of your faith do it that way?" or "Do all the ministers of your religion agree with yours on that issue?" can open the door. Sometimes one can go the other way and ask, "How does it happen that you are so strict (orthodox or observant) about this particular religious or cultural matter when you do not follow so many other basic tenets of your faith?" For example, to a woman contemplating divorce: "Well, I can understand your decision never to marry again, as a good Catholic, but how did you decide to go against the Church on birth control?" It is not important whether or not they can make fine theological distinctions, but that they take responsibility for their decisions and thus in either case make themselves the final judge of who is to be judge.

It might be objected: "That won't be true on all issues; no orthodox Jew would ever sanction a mixed marriage, nor would a strict Catholic sanction marriage to a divorced person." First of all, that is not my experience. Again, as with physical distance correlations, so loyalty to tradition correlations do not seem to hold true when dealing with the complexities of family emotional systems at life cycle events. Beyond that, however, what is important is not the position individuals take at such times, but *how they function with that position.* Even if it were true that an orthodox Jew is more likely to object to a mixed marriage, or an observant Catholic to marriage to a divorcée, the intensity with which they react is another matter and that tells much about the family or their position in it. For example, an objection simply stated as such, or even a refusal to go to an event because it is against one's principles, can be understood as a definition of position. On the other hand, cutting off, disinheriting, constant harrassment, or heavy interference have nothing to do with cultural values and traditions, even though the family members acting that way may claim they are defending the faith. The roots of that kind of fanaticism will always be found in that family member's unworked-out relationships with his own family of origin. (See discussion below on weddings.)

It is just not possible to keep this kind of focus on family process clear as long as one assumes that family members' behavior is determined by, rather than selective of, cultural background. Actually, to the extent one can keep this focus clear, two other benefits accrue. First, it probably means that every time family members give a cultural explanation for why they do or can't do something, that cultural explanation at precisely that moment, far from being the enlightening comment it appears, is probably a denial of family process. Therefore, rather than dutifully writing it down as one more significant datum, the therapist should recognize such an explanation as a warning light—an indication of where those persons are stuck in their own family.

The second benefit that comes with keeping one's focus on family process is that culture and custom can then be used as a tracer element for getting a better reading on family member's relationships with one another. Take, for example, five grown siblings in their fifties or later, only one of whom keeps kosher, or only one of whom is still a pillar of the local parish. You may safely hypothesize that he or she was the child stuck with responsibility for Momma's memory.

Noting such clues can often be helpful in understanding why certain family members are functioning the way they are during any rite of passage.

Ceremony is the Rite of Passage

The third myth which inhibits a family view of rites of passage is the assumption that the ceremony is the rite of passage. After all, some individuals are married long before the ceremony, and some never do leave home. Some family members are buried long before they expire and some remain around to haunt for years, if not generations. This myth has a corollary, which is that the members of the family who are the focus of the ceremony are the only ones who are going through the passage. The whole family goes through the passage at nodal events in the life cycle, and the passage often begins months before and ends months after the ceremony.

Ceremonies celebrate. From an emotional systems point of view, they are not in themselves efficacious. Rather, their effect is determined by what has already been developing within the emotional system of the family. Ceremonies do focalize the events, however, in that they bring family members into conscious contact with one another and in that they bring processes to a head.

On the one hand, therefore, the celebration event itself can be a very useful occasion for meeting people, for putting people together, for reestablishing relationships, for learning about the family (both by observation and the hearing of tales), for creating transitions, for example in leadership, or for the opportunity to function outside or against one's normal role, e.g., getting "looped" when one has always been expected to be the sober one.

On the other hand, my experience with rites of passage suggests that the more important time for becoming involved with one's family is in the months before and after the celebration, using the event more as an excuse for reentry. Though, naturally, the more one prepares the soil before the celebration, the richer the harvest will be at the event itself.

For example, it would be nice to use the state of flux in a family system usually present at a funeral, to bring a brother and sister into verbal communication again. But this is more likely to happen at the funeral if one initiates communication with each of them while the family member to be buried is dying.

Perhaps the most important point to be made about distinguishing the ceremony from the passage is that the potential for change which I have found near nodal family events could not be that great if the event were just the event.

The notion feeds back into itself. For if one can get things going right before any given ceremony, then all the natural healing processes which age-old traditions have captured in their rites of passage will take over and, at the celebration, do much of your work for you. Elsewhere I have been developing this theme for clergy of all faiths, suggesting that an awareness of family process can enable a minister to draw on the natural strengths in families to enrich religious experience. The idea is not to psychologize religion. Rather the thesis is that when clergymen facilitate the meaningful involvement of family members at life cycle ceremonies, they are in fact allowing natural healing processes to flow, and doing what religion had always intuited, but what in modern times has come to be called therapy.[2]

As I often put it to couples worried about relatives' opinions: if the family relationship is not operating pathologically, and this marriage is no more than routinely upsetting to the balance of your family system, then you could even include a ritual murder as part of the wedding and everyone would still probably walk out commenting, "Wasn't that a lovely wedding?" If, on the other hand, there are severe rifts in the family, or if the marriage is particularly disturbing to the balance of the parents' marriage, then it is a different matter. For then no amount of precaution about following customs and ceremonies properly will shield the couple from the infinite capacity that intensity harbors for the manufacture of criticism.

The logical conclusion to be drawn from this is, if you're worried about the length of your gown or the shape of the baptismal fount, go to work on the triangles with your parents. In fact, you may never have a better opportunity.

Giving up these myths leads to some very useful principles, which in turn lead to the observation of confirming patterns. For the other side of the notion that the rite of passage is more than the ceremony, and the individuals going through the passage are more than those identified with the ceremony, is the idea that rites of passage always indicate significant movement

[2]I have expanded on the notion that mature traditions already are in touch with family process in "Enriching the Lifecycle Through Creative Family Participation," Draft 40 pp., 1977. Paper written for the Committee on Family Life of the Central Conference of American Rabbis. Presented to the full Conference, Toronto, June, 1978. See also section on Pubescence—bar mitzva.

in a family system. Therefore, not only can a family approach to rites of passage make them smoother journeys, but the crises these events precipitate become golden opportunities for inducing change in otherwise stable dysfunctional relationship patterns. As mentioned earlier, family systems seem to unlock during these periods.

On the basis of my experience with families of many cultures, I would venture to assert the following principles regarding rites of passage for families regardless of cultural background.

1. Rites of passage are family events coming at the time they do because of emotional processes that have been at work in the nuclear and extended family of the member(s) who is (are) the focus of the ceremony.

2. The ceremony or the event itself reflects the fact that processes in the family have been undergoing change and are in a state of flux.

3. The ceremony and the time before and after it are therefore opportune periods for inducing change in the family system.

4. There seem to be certain "normal" time periods for the change and working through of emotional processes at times of life cycle transition, and *attempts to hasten or shorten those periods unduly are always indications that there are important unresolved issues in the family relationship system.*

This last principle leads to the observation of certain patterns. The incredible similarity in the way the first three principles appeared, no matter what the culture, made me realize I was observing something natural and organic to the human phenomenon. Then it became clear that a key to understanding not only families in the midst of a rite of passage, but at any time, was to note in the family history how they functioned at past rites of passage as indications of the major issues in the family. While it is not possible to pinpoint the exact range of "normality," and here culture will affect the norms, enough of a range may be established to create a benchmark for judging the extremes.

In Table 17.1 are seven continua describing time periods around the rites of passage of marriage, birth, and divorce. The center column represents a range that I have found most people fall within when they are objectively going about the decision to make a change. This is the benchmark period. It is not meant to be all-inclusive, and could perhaps be seen as a slide rule that might expand or contract between the extremes, depending on the culture. What is important is not how exact this column is, but rather what it points to in each direction. On the basis of my experience, I would say that to the extent members of a family come near those extremes, they are making decisions more with their guts than with their heads and there are important unworked-out issues still to be resolved with the family of origin.

TABLE 17.1

EXTREME	BENCHMARK PERIOD	EXTREME

1. Age when married

teenage elopement	21 – 27	no marriage or mid·forties

←——————————————————————————————————————→

2. Length of courtship

love at first sight – 10 days	6 months to 1 year	five years of going steady or living together

←——————————————————————————————————————→

3. Length of engagement

eloping right after decision	3 – 6 months	many years of putting it off

←——————————————————————————————————————→

4. Time to birth of first child

pregnancy before marriage	2 – 3 years	childless for whatever reason

←——————————————————————————————————————→

5. Time between separation and divorce

attempt to hasten legal limits	1 – 2 years after legal limits	till death do us part

←——————————————————————————————————————→

6. Time between separation from one mate and going steady with future mate

affair with future mate	2 – 4 years	withdrawal, promiscuity

←——————————————————————————————————————→

7. Time between divorce and remarriage

same as examples 5 and 6	2 – 5 years	same as examples 5 and 6

←——————————————————————————————————————→

---

from The Curvature of Emotional Space

The table also suggests that the opposite extremes say something similar. I emphasize this because these opposite extremes may show up in different generations or different siblings, but reflect similar patterns.[3]

I am in no way saying, however, that families with members who fall on the extremes in one scale will necessarily fall on the extremes in the other scales. It is important to realize also that these continua should not be taken too literally. They are designed primarily to create a tool for gaining perspective and will be less specifically accurate at any given point along the line, though more generally accurate as one moves toward the extremes. (Warning: anyone caught trying to rate himself by means of these "scales" will be considered to have fallen off the ends completely.) While the scales still need refinement, I think the model may hold, even if it makes it appear that some families have members going through life holding one end of their umbilical cord in their hand, looking for someone else to plug it into, or the reverse, as when family members are unable to commit themselves to anyone.

What can be said about individuals who tend to operate near the extremes is that they come from families that have trouble elasticizing their relationships, by which I mean they have difficulty maintaining different distances with a person over time. They tend to control their feelings with an on/off switch. It is all or nothing. Other clues have tended to show this also. For example, when either no one or everyone is invited to an event it may say something similar. And with regard to funerals, cremation hints the same sort of difficulty in allowing the pain of the emotional processes to operate naturally. Generally speaking, anything that shows a rush to replace loss or an inability to fill the gap indicates a lack of flexibility in the system.

But the most important ramification of these findings for a family approach to rites of passage is, I believe, that in their universality they support the notion that the human species has developed rites of passage out of its own nature. Traditions, no matter what the culture, reflect or capture this, and ultimately that is why in the emotional life of any family, the rites of passage through the life cycle are ideal times for learning about the family as well as helping it heal itself.

THREE NATURAL RITES OF PASSAGE

I will now discuss three natural rites of passage: funerals, weddings, and puberty rites, and give some examples of how a family approach can make the passage less fraught with anxiety and even turn it into an opportunity for helping the family in broader terms. Then I will comment briefly on

---

[3]In emotional life any situation can produce exactly opposite effects and any effect can come from totally opposite situations. An awareness of this is important in observing patterns that may superficially appear different. I tried to develop this theme more fully in "The Curvature of Emotional Space," delivered at the 14th Georgetown University Family Therapy Symposium, 1977, unpublished.

three nodal points in the modern life cycle which are not as natural, but which are becoming so widespread as to approach traditional rites of passage in emotional significance: divorce, retirement, and geographical uprooting.

Funerals

I begin with an event which is usually considered to mark the end of the life cycle because death is undoubtedly the single most important event in family life. Over the years I have seen more change in families—marriage, divorce, pregnancy, geographical moves, other deaths—occur within a year after the death of a family member than after any other nodal point in the life cycle. Another reason for beginning with the end is that this event, especially if it is associated with a particularly important member of the family, can influence the celebration of other nodal events which follow. For example, at the first wedding, baptism, bar mitzva, etc., following the death of a person important to the system, there is likely to be a larger turnout than one might have been otherwise led to expect. When that occurs, the phenomenon itself may give an indication of who is going to replace the deceased member of the family. On the contrary, the turnout for a funeral appears less likely to be influenced by the nodal events which preceded it.

Death creates a vacuum, and emotional systems, as physical systems, will rush to fill it. In the process, cut-offs between family members will begin and end, freedom and getting stuck will be the fate of others. Shifts in responsibility are normal, and replacement becomes a goal for many. The fluidity of a system around the time of death is thus also greater, though not necessarily for an indefinite period. In other words, if one is going to take advantage of that period, the funeral, its preparations, and its "celebration" can be a crystalizing experience. And while there may be more anxiety and pain for the family when a death is expected, such cases offer more opportunity for change. Six major kinds of opportunity become available during this rite of passage:

1. The chance to take or shift responsibility;
2. The opportunity to reestablish contact with distant relatives (or close relatives that are distant);
3. The opportunity to learn family history;
4. The chance to learn how to deal with the most anxious forces that formed one's emotional being;
5. Though this may subsume the previous, the opportunity to shift energy directions in the family triangles, all of which seem to resurrect themselves at such moments;
6. The opportunity to reduce the debilitating effects of grief.

This latter has the character of a time warp, since it involves affecting what usually comes after death by what one does in the family before death. But it may be the most crucial one of all, and better than any other notion encapsulates the idea that a rite of passage is more than a ceremony. The basic notion is: *grief is the residue of the unworked-out part of a relationship.*[4]

Several of these are exemplified by the following story in which I was contacted in my role as clergyman, but where I was able to use my knowledge of family process to let flow the natural healing forces released by rites of passage.

A woman who was very involved in community mental health called and asked if I would be willing to do a "nonreligious" funeral for her husband, a renowned scientist, aged forty-six, who was terminal and might die any day. The rub was, she didn't want him to know about it. He was very areligious, but she wanted to do this for her sons, nineteen and twelve. I replied that I couldn't agree to do a funeral for a man while he was still alive unless I could meet him. (There were additional reasons for my taking this position, having to do with my general ideas that secrecy almost always stabilizes dysfunction, and increases anxiety in a system. I concluded this after observing numerous clients in therapy where the impending death of a loved one was handled in a hush-hush way.[5])

The woman said that meeting her husband was out of the question, and I just said, "Think it over." She called back later that day and said she had indeed spoken to her husband and he had agreed to meet with me. I told her that I did not want to meet with him alone, but together with her and her two sons. She agreed, but warned me that she did not want any therapy. I agreed, and said I would only ask questions.

The husband had just come back from the hospital to die at home. When I arrived he was lying in bed, and while physically weak, was perfectly lucid. He was an only child, and kept a phone next to his bed so that when his aged parents called from the midwest, they would not realize how bad things really were.

The older son was there, but I was informed that the younger son, who had asthma, had been sent to mother's mother. I began by telling the dying man (in front of his wife and son) that I had never met anyone who knew he was going to die, and wondered what he thought about it. He responded in a self-denying way, seemingly trying to convey that he was approaching his end with perfect equanimity. I pushed the point by saying that his wife had said he was a very nonreligious man, and I wondered if he was now hedging his bet before he met his maker. He again responded lucidly and with a great sense of character,

[4] I am indebted to Dr. Murray Bowen for this insight reported at a Georgetown clinical monthly meeting after the death of his father.

[5] The full expansion of this view of the pernicious effects of secrets in families is in "Secrets and Systems," delivered at the 10th Georgetown University Family Therapy Symposium, 1973. Published in Volume II, *Selected Papers,* ed. Lorio and McClenathan, 1977.

"No." He knew this was really going to be final. I then asked him what he wanted said at his funeral. (I had already told him that I had found some passages from Albert Einstein that I thought would be appropriate, but I was now speaking in terms of a eulogy.) He again replied with amazing humility that there was nothing particular about himself that he wanted emphasized.

As far as I was concerned, to this point all the questions were just "probing the line." I now turned to the son and asked him in front of his father what he wanted said at his father's funeral. At this point, by the way, a fortuitous ring of the phone took mother out of the room; she never came back in. I proceeded to catalyze a conversation of the most personal kind between father and son over the issue of what was to be said at father's funeral. The man died the next day. The son, at my urging, wrote and delivered the eulogy, and the mother, several days later, sent me a long thank you note and a copy of Kübler-Ross's On Death and Dying.[6]

As a clergyman I had an unusual opportunity in this situation, but I think that what happened there could only have occurred in that family during such a rite of passage. Such experiences clarified for me that there are ways of encouraging such a process if you are "lucky" enough to be seeing a client around the time of a death in the family.

My own experience with the dying, the dead, and their survivors, is that it is not an individual that is dying as much as a member of a family, that is, part of an organism is dying. When this focus is maintained, as impersonal and cold as it may sound at first, many new ways of seeing things unfold. For example, using the principle of extremes mentioned before, I believe that where extraordinary efforts are made, either to end the person's life, "to reduce suffering," or to prolong a person's life when he or she is biologically alive but existentially dead, the family is either desirous of rushing through the passage or fearful of entering it. In either case it will say something about the family and the importance of the dying person to it at that moment. Such an approach also refocuses the so-called ethical issues around the "right to die."

There is another important way in which the focus on the dying person, rather than the family, misguides this rite of passage; it requires that the dying be compis mentis. In many cases, they are psychotically senile, unconscious, in a coma, obstreperously denying, or just plain hopelessly confused. In those situations, from the point of view of that individual person's existence, "he might as well be dead." But that is in no way true from the point

[6]Another experience I had with the shifting emotional forces that take place at funerals, a woman trying to kidnap her mother after her father's death because the distance from her husband makes her feel she will mourn alone, can be found in "Family Systems Thinking and a New View of Man," CCAR Journal, Volume 18, No.1, January 1971.

of view of the family. As long as the dying person is above ground, he or she is a live part of the organism. (Compare the extraordinary efforts to keep political leaders alive even though they are no longer capable of ruling.) Systems know the extraordinary significance of burial.

Recently I had the opportunity to put into practice much of what I have been preaching, when my own mother, who had been deteriorating for several years with advanced artereosclerosis, went into her final decline. I present here in outline how I functioned during that period, since I believe the recounting of my own experience will capsulize much of what I have been trying to convey about funerals.

In August of 1977, my mother, aged seventy-nine, whose mental and physical condition had been deteriorating for several years, and who, throughout this period, had to live with a home attendant, fell and broke a small bone in her leg. Because she had almost no pulse below her waist, the cast almost immediately created a pressure sore which would have become gangrenous without constant attention. She was put in the hospital in an attempt to debris the wound and save her leg.

Since my mother had all but stopped walking anyway, the surgeon wanted to amputate. The decision would have to be mine since I was her only child and my father had died twenty-five years previously. She seemed no longer capable of really understanding what was happening. Remembering my mother as a person who did not give up easily, I stayed on the side of trying to save the leg, but I was already thinking of her funeral. What complicated my own ability to think clearly during this period was the incredible anxiety of her sister who lived next door to my mother. My aunt had made it to her eighties by using her anxiety to get others to take responsibility. Throughout those last four months she would constantly criticize the home attendant to me, and me to everyone else. In an effort to defuse the intensity of the triangle between my mother, my aunt, and myself, I began to contact other members of the extended family whom I perceived to be in interlocking triangles with me and my mother or me and my aunt. I started a process in which I tried to establish or reestablish as many relationships as possible with other members of the family and close friends of my mother's all over the United States. I kept informing them of what I was doing and what was happening. I found great support in doing this; the process of involving family members at a distance also seemed to redistribute the guilt and the responsibility, spread the risk and make me more objective about what was happening nearby.[7]

For six weeks the situation stayed the same, and then, just as we were all about to give up, I made one last attempt to break through to my mother,

[7]For more background on my family system, and a glimpse of my anxious aunt ten years earlier (she is the one who goes through the glass sliding door), see "The Birthday Party: An Experiment in Obtaining Change in One's Own Extended Family," *Family Process,* Volume 10, No.3, September 1971.

directly telling her I was giving up. To our surprise the leg began to heal and my mother was able to return home. However, shortly afterward the visiting nurse tied the bandage too tight and my mother developed gangrene. At this point positions switched, the surgeon now saying that my mother was so close to death that amputation would be a "heroic" act. Since I had done a lot of thinking about how unresolved attachment makes it difficult to let someone die, I had difficulty with this one. My aunt, who had from the beginning been against amputation, was still against it. I, however, made the decision for the amputation on the ground that I could not let my mother's body poison itself when that was preventable; she would have to die "naturally." After the amputation, she actually seemed to perk up for a while. Again, throughout this period, I stayed in constant touch with the family and friends, informing them of what was happening, but in each case, only after I made the decision, so that I could keep my decisions clear of family anxiety. Throughout this period my aunt and those closest to her kept attacking me for my failure to put her in a nursing home much earlier where "she" would have been more comfortable (meaning *they* would have been more comfortable).

Shortly after my mother came home from the hospital, it became clear to me that her body had gone beyond all thresholds and I began to prepare for her death and funeral. Then the same visiting nurse, severely chastened by the doctors for her previous mistake and feeling anxious about her condition, wanted to put her back in the hospital. Luckily, I was called first. For three years I had fought against much family pressure to keep her out of institutions. It was now clear that she had less time left than it would take to reverse the process of her illness. With great difficulty I made the decision not to let her go back in the hospital and die in the institution, but to let ill-nature take its course. I stopped interfering. Within five days she was dead.

I had prepared a list of family telephone numbers and when I received word of her death I began to follow out a plan I had thought out while my mother was dying. I called each relative to tell them my mother had died and took advantage of the natural reminiscing we went through to make notes of what each person said about my mother. At the funeral I read a "family eulogy" which included my own remarks and those of the other family members. Then I asked those present to add anything they wished.

My remarks about my mother were as straightforward and honest as I could make them. I talked about how I thought her qualities had influenced (or spoiled) me and made reference back to how she had taken care of her mother for the family. As for me, after the funeral I felt a greatly strengthened sense of my ability to deal with acutely anxious crises.

Here are some things which happened during this rite of passage in my personal life and in my work with families.

1. Three years previously, I was cut off for one reason or another from everyone who eventually came to the funeral. Now things had swung so far the other way that one cousin even invited my whole family to stay for a visit. I felt I was a member of the family again.

2. My anxious aunt's grandson, who had recently gotten married, unbeknownst to the family to a woman he had been living with for years, came and introduced his wife to the family for the first time.

3. Knowing how money channels are emotional channels and having seen so many families split up over inheritance, I tried to use that phenomenon in reverse by giving the newlyweds my mother's furniture, which they appreciated greatly.

4. I found myself able to go back to work immediately and with enthusiasm, with no depression, and I found if anything an increased sense of creativity and competence in my work.

5. There were ramifications for my work systems also. Regarding my family therapy clients, several families went into crisis around this time. As I saw it, when I learned to deal with the forming forces of anxiety that had made me "me," I inadvertently pulled out some of the supports with which I had been previously buttressing these clients in my anxiety over their anxiety. They almost all made leaps of growth, however, as it seems that I did not respond anxiously to these "inviting" crises either.

6. There was also an interesting analagous reaction within the small congregation I served and that I had helped to establish fourteen years previously. Annually at contract time I had come to expect some attack from the "loyal opposition." In the past I usually became quite engaged with these members, often going to great lengths to refute the content of their charges, motivated I believe by anxiety over my own security or anxiety over continuation of the congregation's philosophy. This time, however, the content of their charges, though not different in nature, seemed almost silly if not boring, and I did not take the initial complaints very seriously. (Not surprisingly the reactions to my disengagement escalated.)[8]

One last point: twenty-five years previously I had for several months helplessly watched my father slowly die in a hospital. I had not dared to take the opportunity to tell him what he meant to me, to discuss with him his impending death or to function in any way that might have proved helpful to my survivorship or my mother's eventual widowhood. The atmosphere had been overcast with anxiety and denial. His wake left me with a sense of relief that it was all over, but it was a relief wrapped in confusion, guilt, and a pervasive feeling of something left incomplete. He had made one statement to me when it seemed he knew he was going to die, something enigmatic like, "Eddie, do what you want to do." Totally out of the context of a more intimate surrounding experience, it became over the years like some mysterious pearl of advice one carries away from an audience with an oracle, which one is bound to plumb and ponder for a life-

[8]I have not discussed here the effects of rites of passage on work systems, simply because of space. I have developed the theme somewhat in "Leadership and Self in a Congregational Family," *CCAR Journal,* Winter 1978.

time. On the other hand, after my mother's death, it was an entirely different story. Though she had been anything but concerned about my future, in fact she had been often bitter, complaining, contrary, and sometimes in the confusion of her senile psychosis a name-calling witch, I had a sense of completeness, fulfillment and peace. Finally, I would say that treating a funeral as a family rite of passage and making the most out of that opportunity for one's own differentiation is the only way I know to get out of that horrible, forever-after haunting dilemma of wishing it would all be over soon.

Weddings

If death is the most portentious event in family life, marriage may be the most symptomatic, in two senses. First, my experience with over 2,000 couples before marriage has led me to the conclusion that the timing of weddings is far from random. I have found, for example, that many couples either meet their spouse or decide to marry within six months of a major change in the family of origin of one of the partners. It is not that romance doesn't count, but simply that it isn't enough to move a relationship to marriage. Weddings can also be symptomatic of family process in that stresses surrounding the engagement and wedding preparation period seem to really make the seams show. This can be true with funerals also, but there are some major differences. More likely than not, death will have an implosive effect on a family, in which all the members pull together, even if after the funeral they fight forever over the inheritance. With weddings one must decide whether to invite those one doesn't want to be with and the burden of choice can become almost overbearing, depending on how many sides one is trying to please. Whereas with a funeral the need for comfort makes the closest relatives willing to be with one another, with a wedding the desire to be joyous makes some of those same relatives anathema. Another major difference between weddings and funerals is that in death one is dealing with the loss of an insider; with marriage the problem is the inclusion of an outsider, despite the old saw, "I am not losing a daughter but gaining a son."

There can be, of course, a light side to weddings: the obsessive concern with etiquette, the inappropriateness of some gifts, even the jealousy of who gets seated with whom, though, once again, when viewed in family process terms, these little things sometimes carry more significance than we might think. Sometimes it is blatant, like the mother who during the wedding whispered to the bride as she partook of the ceremonial wine, "Not too much now, dear." Similarly a humerous but often significant warning signal comes when the mother or father makes the first contact with the clergyman, either because their son "works," or because their daughter lives in Alaska and "it would be a long distance call."

On the other hand, some families handle such situations with amazing perceptiveness. One man who was marrying a woman with a five-year-old daughter turned to the little girl immediately after the pronouncement and also gave the child a ring. He knew what he was doing; under those conditions he really did marry *them* and not only his bride.

One of the aspects of family ceremonies that has always appalled me, yet also proved to me that the unseen family process has more power than the ceremony, is the loss of critical taste at family events. I have performed very sloppy weddings in the most uncomfortable settings (bees literally in my bonnet) and had everyone come up afterward congratulating me on the warmest wedding they have ever seen. But I have also been part of such anxious systems that even in the most elaborately arranged settings the most eloquent homilies were ignored and I had all I could do to keep from inadvertantly stepping on the bridal gown and tripping the bride.

As an opportunity for inducing change, I have found that the rite of passage surrounding a wedding is the most propitious for redirecting focus. The opportunities for learning about the family and reworking triangles described with regard to funerals are there also, but the time around weddings stands out primarily as the time to redirect a parent's focus, and once again crisis is opportunity.

Though this is clearly the case, most couples experiencing difficulties with their parents over a wedding see this period as just something to be gotten through until they can get married and get away; this avoidance of the experience might be similar to cremation after death. Of course the real getting away only occurs if they use that period to develop more differentiation of self in the relationships with their parents. And again, couples who are experiencing pain at such moments (as with terminal deaths) may be more fortunate. Where problems arise in the family of origin during wedding preparations, the opportunities for redirection of focus are plentiful.[9]

To begin with, I can say categorically that I have never seen a religious, social, or other issue worked out regarding a marital choice, where the ef-

[9]I have developed the general notion of the interrelationship between marriage and family of origin in two papers: "The Nature of the Marital Bond," delivered at the 11th Georgetown University Family Therapy Symposium, 1974, published in Volume II, *Collection of Selected Papers,* ed. Lorio and McClenathan, 1977; and "Engagement and Disengagement—Family Therapy with Couples During Courtship," delivered at the 8th Georgetown University Family Therapy Symposium, 1971, published in *Collection of Symposium Papers,* Volume 1, ed. Andres and Lorio, 1977.

forts have been made directly on the content of the issue. For example, if parents are critical of the marital choice on the ground of different religious or social backgrounds, efforts to change the parents' minds by saying things like, "But Mom, you were always so liberal yourself," or, "Dad, you always taught me to treat everyone equally," are doomed to failure. Over and over I have seen a bride or groom spend an entire weekend with critical parents showing them the illogic of their ways, return thinking that they have changed their parent's minds, and then receive a letter later in the week showing that they are back at ground zero. These efforts to deal with the content of the parent's complaint are ineffective because one is dealing with symptom, not cause. The cause of almost all severe parental reactions to marital choice is the failure of the reacting parent to have worked out something important in other relationships. The focus has been misplaced. On the other hand, I have found almost one hundred percent success in reducing the significance of such issues, if not eliminating them altogether, when the bride or groom is able to refocus the reacting parent on their own parents.

There are three major factors always present in the reacting relative's position in the family: (1) he or she is having great difficulty differentiating from the child getting married; (2) and not necessarily distinct from one, the child getting married is very important to the balance of the parents' marriage; and (3) that parent or relative is caught in some emotionally responsible position in his or her own family of origin.

There is little question that the third is most important, but it is also often the most difficult to get to. Some starting moves for refocus that I have found helpful in factors one and two are: "Well, Dad, it's all your fault, you should have sent me to Hebrew school (church on Sundays) more often." If the response is, "We tried, but you wouldn't go," the point is carried further. "Well, you were the parent, why didn't you try harder?" "It's a good thing your mother isn't here to see this." Or, for interfering mother telling daughter what to do at the wedding: "Mom, here is a list of 100 aspects of the wedding; I know how important it is to you to please your sister (mother, mother-in-law, friends); would you look it over at your leisure and give me as full answers as possible? I am particularly interested in knowing whether you want the traditional approach to putting the knives next to the spoons, or the newer idea that the knife should be in front of the plate." These won't bring complete change, but they are sure to bring breathing room. One refocusing effort, however, has worked without fail. While to some readers it may seem merely an effort to lighten a toxic issue and to others a sarcastic or nasty remark, I have yet to find a better way for a bride to refocus her mother's attention. It goes something like this.

"Mother, I know you are opposed to John, and you have a right to your position, but you are still my mother and I believe you owe me one more thing before John and I marry. We have never had a frank talk about sex. What has been the secret to your marital success? How many times a week would you say a man likes it? And when you don't want it, how do you keep a man away?" I have yet to find a better way to refocus a parent on her own marriage (parents satisfied in their own marriage just do not put that much energy into their children). But not every daughter can make that little speech. So, from the other side, maybe the one hundred percent success I have seen with this one is that any daughter who can say that to her mother is well on her way to disengagement anyway.[10]

Sometimes a wedding gives one the opportunity to go to work in the primary triangle with mother and father. The key to any triangle is not to get caught in the middle as the focus of an unresolved issue between the other two. If one family member is caught, not only does he or she have less maneuverability, but the other two wind up with a pseudostabilization of their relationship. One of the best ways to get "detriangled" is to put the other two members of the triangle together. This is true whether the triangle is classic as with an extramarital affair or where the third member is a symptom (physical or emotional) of one's partner, parent, or child. By seeming to encourage a togetherness that really has more appearance than substance, it is often possible to make the hidden issue surface where it belongs. (Anyone who doubts this should try the opposite, namely, separating the other two persons, or the other person and his or her symptom and watch them respond by absolutely falling in love with each other.) When a person getting married can avoid the content of the objecting parent's remark and concentrate instead on the emotional processes of the triangle, that bride or groom will become defocused as a natural part of any new process, which now focuses the parents on one another.

For example, usually it is mother who tends to be more reactive about a marital choice or over wedding preparations. If this turns out to be the case and Dad starts to react also, then one has a wonderful opportunity to tell Dad how terrific it is to see the way he stands up for her even when it goes against his principles. If it is Dad who is the primary reactor and mother won't stand up to him, similar statements can be made about how true she is to the old-world standards of the adaptive wife. The key is to keep pushing them together and praising their togetherness as one goes along.

There is also an obverse side to this triangle. This occurs when the parents agree to come to the wedding but very reluctantly, conveying that they are only coming out of a sense of duty. This is a trap. Here they have again put the bride or groom in the middle by making their child responsible for

---

[10]For a description of the kind of family emotional system that I believe most objects to "outsiders" see "Conversion, Love and Togetherness," *Reconstructionist*, Volume 39, May 1973.

their behavior. Under such circumstances they will come with a vow not to enjoy themselves (which can be infectious.) They will stay to themselves in a corner, perhaps with a sibling, standing like gaunt, midwest farmers from a Grant Wood painting, adamant against a smile. The detriangling here involves making them come for themselves by giving them permission not to come: "Dear folks, I know you are only coming to please me, and I don't want to see you give up your principles just because I am your favorite; I would like you to be there, but I'll understand if you can't make it."

A typical pattern that often needs addressing is the parents' reference to their own extended families. In my experience, when the parent says, "My parents are upset," that has always been a projection; likewise, when they say, "This will kill them." I have never seen the grandparent react more than the parent, even when their old-worldliness would lead one to expect more reaction. This is more evidence that the issues have to do with the closeness of the relationship, not the subject of the issue. In all events, the following type of letter has excellent success in my experience:

Dear Grandma or Aunt, or Uncle:
As you may have heard (they probably haven't) I am going to marry a Jew (a Catholic, a black, a Martian). I would like to invite you to the wedding even though I know this probably goes so much against your principles that you may feel you cannot attend. I did want you to know, however. Also, I wondered if you could give me some advice. Your daughter, or "kid sister," (not: "my mother") is absolutely off the wall about this. She keeps telling me this will be the end of our relationship, calls me every night, says if you found out you would drop dead, etc. I wondered if you could give me any information that would explain why she is behaving this way, or any advice on how to deal with her.

My own experience has been that whenever that type of letter has been sent, no reply is received, but within weeks the issue has calmed down.[11] Sometimes the unresolved issue behind parents' reactivity near the rite of passage of a wedding has to do with a relationship between parents and a relative who is dead, e.g., their own parent, a spouse or another child. When this is true, a visit to the graveside with that parent can offer an opportunity for unlocking fixed attitudes and enabling refocus. The key, however, no matter which way of refocusing one chooses, is that an impending wedding is already a sign of a relationship system in flux. Some members are going to feel the pull of the forces of change more than others. Who is going to re-

[11]It can work in the opposite direction also. I have seen parents who were never really motivated to work on their relationships with a child, induced to begin when they originally came in concerned over the child's marital choice, and stay, literally for years after the ceremony, as they continue to bring change to the entire family.

act most depends on who stabilized his or her own life through some kind of emotional dependence on the person getting married. For example, some parents use a child as an anchor to keep from getting drawn back into the vortex of the parent's parent's pull. Or they invest in a child to compensate for the absence of affection in a marriage. The road to no change at such moments is to elope, cut off, or try to placate the parents as much as possible until one gets married and can start one's own family. Those latter approaches guarantee a transference of emotional intensity into the new family being formed. But where individuals can be taught to seize the opportunity at the rite of passage of a wedding, they leave a lot of unnecessary baggage at home.

Here is a clinical experience and a short case history that illustrates the extent to which a wedding as a rite of passage is a family event.

> A divorced man came in to get married, mentioning in the premarital interview that he was not going to keep up with his young child from his previous marriage, since it would "complicate things for the child." I gingerly mentioned that by doing this he might create ghosts. He didn't buy it and I didn't pursue it. I did, by the way, have the impression that it all somehow had to do with his mother, who was not coming to the wedding. In all events, after the wedding he refused to give me my fee, saying that he had only come in to get married, not for counseling. It was the only time that had ever occurred, and I made a mental note that I had touched something very deep.

Several years later a groom came in with the identical situation. Remembering the first experience and being a fool rather than an angel, I told this man what had happened the previous time I raised such an issue and added, "I know this must be a touchy subject, but have you thought about the possibility that for all your good will, your child might grow up wondering why her natural father rejected her by cutting off in such an absolute manner?" And I mentioned how often I had done family histories with adults who reported similar situations about their fathers or grandfathers who became ghosts in the system and how the residue of guilt those cut-offs had left continued to haunt the family. He laughed about the first groom, but said he simply didn't see it my way. Two days later he called to say he had decided to get married by someone else. Again I had the impression that it had something to do with his mother.

Several years after that a man came in to get married who happened to mention that after several years of cut-off he had just reestablished relationships with his children. I said, "Oh, then you must have made some major changes with your mother." This time the groom looked at me as if he had seen a ghost and responded, "How the hell did you know that?" I am still not sure how I knew, other than to say that whenever a relationship changes suddenly near the rite of passage of a wedding, whether it is a cut-off or the reestablishing of a dormant relationship, my experience has taught me there is usually a third member of the family who is part of the triangle. The wedding as a rite of passage is like the movement of an iceberg with most of what is in motion unseen by the human eye.

The second case example is about a family of five children in which the eldest came in at age forty for her second marriage. While well educated, she was the black sheep of the family. Her father, a very successful tyrant, had died several years previously. The family, that is, mother (and one unmarried brother in particular) were in a fury about her marital choice, threatening to disinherit her. In a session with mother and daughter, father's constant beatings of this daughter came out.

Though she had had a lot of therapy through her childhood, she found the subject very painful. I asked her at this point if she had ever seen father's beatings as symptomatic of mother's closeness with her. Her chains disintegrated before my eyes. She became motivated to lead the family instead of fighting it. And for two months before and six months after the wedding, she went to work on the triangles with her siblings, her mother, and every relative she could find. Mother, who was being shown great attention by a man for the first time since her husband's death, was told not to marry this man, that he was not good enough, etc., and what would *her* mother (now in her eighties) say? The brother who had inherited the father's superresponsible position (and who had not come to the wedding) was repeatedly complimented for being willing to give up his own personal happiness in order to keep the family together.

Both relationships almost immediately began to shift. It was as though they were now seeing this woman for the first time. It turned out that the other brother, a wandering Ph. D. in his late twenties, was between jobs or hobbies, and the youngest sister was an absolute slave to her rigid husband, with physical symptoms beginning to show up in her child.

Every one of these dysfunctional symptoms, which had been helped to operate covertly through the perpetual focus of the family on "poor sister," became approachable again, as if for the first time, around her wedding. Putting to service all the energy and intelligence characteristic of the family, which had been allowed previously to intensify pathology or to become sopped up by rebellion, the black sheep used the opportunity made possible by the family being in the midst of a rite of passage to defocus her scapegoat position, and everywhere the family began to change.

Pubescence

The third most universal rite of passage is that of puberty, the onset of adulthood. Of the three, this one has lost much of its family significance in modern culture, becoming associated often with cultural phenomena, graduations, dating, and so on. My own religious tradition, of course, has maintained it with the celebration of the bar (boy) or bat (girl) mitzva. I would like to shift gears in this section and talk within my own tradition's meta-phor about this rite of passage.[12]

The major reason I wish to stay within my own tradition on this one is that I have experimented with changes in the tradition based on what I have learned about family process and the results so far have been both as-tounding and enlightening. What I wish to show is first, how something as obviously individual, no less child-focused, is really very much a family rite; and second, how making everyone aware of that fact actually increases the effectiveness of the passage. There are other lessons that come forth also. First, that the message of the emotional system is a more powerful me-dium than the cultural tradition, establishing it or perverting it; second, old traditions, even without articulation of family process, have recognized it all the time.

The Jewish tradition of *bar mitzva* (literally, son of, or worthy of, the commandments) is 1,500 years old, at least. On a day close to the child's thirteenth birthday, he is called up to bless the scripture reading or read a portion. From the point of veiw of traditional Jewish law, he is now an adult able to give witness in court, be responsible for his own wrongdoing, and be counted as one of the ten men needed for a public service (*minyon*). In the 1920s (around the time of the nineteenth amendment, giving women the right to vote), progressive branches of Judiasm introduced bat mitzva for a girl, though the ceremony has only become widespread one-half cen-tury later, since the renaissance of the women's movement.

Today, from the religious point of view, depending on the branch of Judaism, the ceremony can be just the scripture blessing, a reading of the portion in Hebrew, where the child may have just memorized the Hebrew, or a rite with more emphasis on the meaning of the portion, with the child giving more than a stereotyped thank-you speech, adding instead a talk that interprets his portion.

In terms of contemporary sociology, the bar mitzva, especially for the Jews of middle-class suburbia, often appears to be an event of great social importance. In some places it has been joked, "The bar has become more important than the mitzva." And it might be added, "The caterer more im-portant than the rabbi."

But in either case, from the family process point of view, the ceremony al-ways appears to be *child-focused.*

The first time I began to think of bar mitzva in family terms was actually before I had trained to do family therapy. I was doing some work as a com-munity relations specialist for the White House. For the first time in my life

[12]An improvisional approach to the whole life cycle that tries to show how tradi-tion can actually be preserved through the insights of family process can be found in "Enriching The Life Cycle Through Creative Family Participation," Op. Cit.

I began to sense the pressures non-Jews feel around Christmas time. Colleagues I had worked with all year began to become extremely anxious; they began to shop compulsively for gifts beyond their means; drinking became more frequent. Then one Friday evening, as I was leaving a staff Christmas party, on my way to a weekend that was to include a bar mitzva, things seemed strangely familiar. The anxiety, the gift giving, the drinking— there was something the two had in common. Years later when I had the conceptual framework I began to understand.

It was the forces of family togetherness: All the family intensity, the problems with relatives, the unspoken feelings, the pressure to relate that many individuals spend much of a year trying to avoid, become unavoidable for a Christian near Christmas; for Jewish families, something similar occurs around bar mitzva. As I began to explore this notion, other events and findings propelled me further in that direction of observing family force fields. First, a father of a bar mitzva boy (unbeknownst to me, in line for a transplant) went into heart failure during his son's service, and died. He was an only child, sitting next to his widowed, terribly dependent mother at the time. This experience in turn led me to an extraordinary amount of additional information. For, as I related what had happened to others, I began to hear an incredible number of reports about parents going into dysfunction near the time of their son's bar mitzva, including suicides, breakdowns, and other forms of physical Illness. (It is, of course, well known that the suicide rate goes up nationally in late December.)

I began to put things together. No wonder I had never been really successful in calming a bar mitzva child's anxiety no matter how well prepared he was. It was not his anxiety I was dealing with. No wonder mothers whom I had previously perceived to be models of efficiency and astute reasonableness approached me almost on the verge of hysteria in seeking bar mitzva dates. No wonder fathers running top government agencies and used to living with daily crises seemed to go limp at this period. I was dealing with phenomena of far-ranging effects.

Since I knew that a most effective means of dealing with panic was to offer an alternative mode of behavior, I immediately hit upon involving the family members more in the ceremony and the preparation. I soon found to my surprise and delight that these efforts had more reward than I expected.

The first change I made was in the method of choosing the portion. Traditionally there is no choice; one goes by the calendar cycle. I began to meet with the child, learn a little about him and his family, add what I already knew, and then make several suggestions based on interest and style, leaving it to the child and parents to make final selections. Then I had a study session with the entire family; parents, siblings, grandparents if they were in town, in which discussion (even argument) was promoted about interpretation. At the end of the discussion, the child was given the charge that he would be the teacher for the day. He was told to divide his talk into three parts: a synopsis in his own words of the portion, his interpretation of what the Biblical author was trying to say, and any interpretation he wished to make for today.

After the family meetings I continued to meet with the bar or bat mitzva child several times to help with the writing of his talk, but I began to assume less responsibility. Whereas in former days I used to become terribly concerned about the articulation, coherence, and overall conceptualization of the talk, I was now primarily concerned to ask questions (which I wanted taken back to the family) that helped with the development of the ideas.

Soon I realized that my role had changed significantly. Instead of bearing the burden of helping this child through his rite of passage, I had a team, a team to which I was more a coach than the star player. With that in mind, I also began to make changes in the ceremony. First, I stopped giving any sermon myself other than an introduction, which described the development of bar mitzva in Jewish tradition and its further shaping by our congregation. The child was called "our teacher for today," and the father (or in some cases both parents) was asked to bless the child publicly, or privately. Since the congregation had a tradition of creative services from the beginning, families started creating their own services. Continuing with my role as coach, I would make available source books, ask for about six to ten passages, and then take responsibility for fitting them into the prayer order. Families, of course, differed in the extent to which they got into this aspect, some wanting to use standard material which I could select, some becoming so involved that they printed, at their own expense, a supplement which even contained the scripture portion itself in Hebrew and English, and artistic members of the family (sometimes the child himself) began to create designs for the cover. Sometimes a sibing wrote a poem for a frontispiece. One family had a coat of arms that went back for generations and decorated the cover with that.

All families were given the option of having the bar mitzva at home if they chose. Sometimes musical members of the family played an overture or background during the silent prayer. Sometimes a musical child played on a guitar or trumpet a tune he or she created for the service. The parents also gave out portions of the service to incoming relatives who read them to the congregation. Blessings over the meal were distributed also, each family being encouraged to give out these responsibilities as seemed natural.

The results have been beyond what I could have foreseen. Family anxiety seems greatly reduced, there is much less focus on materialistic expression, and, despite less direct involvement by me with the child, he or she generally does a better overall performance. In other words, though I have been trying less to "teach" the child myself, whatever process has been released by the transfer of my functioning to the family is also producing more thoughtful, deeper intellectual efforts on the part of the child. Finally, though I am less "out front," I seem to get more thanks than before from visiting relatives. The systems seem to know.

THREE NODAL LIFE CYCLE EVENTS

Funerals, weddings, and the onset of puberty have been universal rites of passage as long as the human species has had culture. Our modern culture seems to be producing three other nodal points of great consequence for the life cycle: divorce, retirement, and geographical uprooting. I should like to devote some words to these changes as family events also. However, I wish to make clear that I think there is an important difference between these three and the former three. The former are all connected to the life cycle biologically. They are part and parcel of being human. It is not as clear to me that in themselves the latter have the same power for change, unless perhaps they are, as is often the case, residuals of the former events, e.g., where the divorce or at least the separation came within a year after an important death; or the geographical move soon after the marriage. And of course both could be symptomatic of even larger forces flowing through the family arteries. These latter also differ in that they are not complete passages, but more the openings to a passage. With marriage, death, and pubescense, an individual is not simply leaving one state, but going to another that is well defined. Somehow, the beginning and the end are all subsumed as part of the complete passage of six months to a year; the new state toward which the family is headed is in some ways teleologically pulling the family through the crisis. Similarly, while the biological rites of passage all deal with loss and healing, these latter tend only to deal with loss. They are thus more open-ended. All of this is not to say they are not ripe times for bringing change to a family or in some cases symptomatic of changes already going on in the family, but they may not be in themselves natural family phenomena with all the power for healing that those experiences contain.

Divorce

The rate of divorce today is becoming so high as to suggest it is reaching the level of a biological imperative. And of these latter nonbiological nodal points in life, divorce would seem to portend more family change. Several religious groups sensing this have experimented with the creation of a divorce ceremony. (Jewish tradition has had one for 1,500 years in which the man hands the bill of divorce to his wife personally, if possible, and says, "I divorce you.") Since the thrust of this paper has been that rites of passage are family events, it may be that in many cases only the second marriage or a funeral really completes that passage. I do know of one person who sent out divorce announcements with an invitation to a party: "Mrs. _____ announces the divorce of her daughter from Mr. _____ on the steps of the Court House of _____." She said that many of her cousins took one look at it and destroyed the card before their husbands could see it.

In order to bring the full power of a family rite of passage to divorce, perhaps the following perspective would be helpful: To the extent a divorce comes about because the rite of passage of marriage did not do its work, (that is, successfully bring about disengagement in family of origin) the divorce is not likely to bring real change if the original triangles are still stuck. To the extent, on the other hand, the divorce is a result of changes in that originally stuck situation with the family of origin, which in turn unbalanced the marriage, then the divorce is more likely to offer opportunity.

In either case, if clients who come in to work on their fears of loneliness, instability, adjustment of their children, loss of moorings, etc., (the focus of most of the self-help books on divorce) can be focused on relationships with family of origin instead—and they often are more motivated to do so during this period—one will have made divorce a rite of passage in the fullest sense of the term.

Retirement

Retirement may have more ramifications for family life than has been realized, though therapists near military bases don't have to be told this fact. The number of divorces that occur after early military retirement is quite high. The general rule would seem to be this: Where the marriage was balanced by mother being intensely involved in the children, and father with the service (which becomes a sort of extended family), his retirement often unbalances the relationship, particularly if he now tries to reenter the family and finds himself excluded, or seeks a replacement in the form of an extramarital relationship. This phenomenon is not limited to the military and can occur with any profession that involves the husband deeply in his work relationship system (lawyers, clergy, etc.). That it has far-reaching ramifications may be seen from the following tale.

A couple, both only children, both twenty-seven, came in to get married after going steady for five years. They had just made the decision and wanted the wedding in a month. Naturally I asked them what they thought moved it on to marriage. Though well educated, introspective, and in no way threatened by the question, they had no idea. Poking around the family history I could find none of the usual family changes such as death, marriage, births. Then innocently she remarked, "Well, the only thing I can say that changed is that both our fathers retired last year." Five years of going steady and they suddenly realized they were right for one another.

One possible explanation of this is that when the fathers retired, they got closer to their wives, who inadvertantly let go of their children. Or, maybe this was more true of one who was the real holdout. In any event, theoretically, it is the exact opposite of the former military situation where divorce results when the wife refuses to be drawn closer to the now more available spouse and still clings to the child.

It is thus clear that retirement can have significant family ramifications, and can also be induced by family events as when a parent, after a loss (through death, divorce, or marriage), begins to wonder, "What's the point of working so hard?" and begins to change his or her sights. The so-called "leaving the nest" syndrome may be similar. Another major family ramification of retirement is the onset of senile processes. If experience with my mother and aunt have more universal application, the following rule may be true: If, around the time any older person begins to reduce significantly his or her functioning (through retirement or an illness,) there is available an overfunctioning, anxious family member who, at that moment has no receptacle for his or her energy, the likely outcome is senility for the former.

Geographical Uprooting

Geographical uprooting can also have severe consequences, particularly to the extent that it means leaving an emotionally important house or community. What is also crucial is the extent to which it changes the balance of a marriage. For example, if it takes a wife further away from her mother, it can either free her up or lead her to become more dependent. In general, it might be said that such uprooting, to the extent it takes a couple further from one spouse's extended family and closer to the other's, will shift the balance, though not necessarily always in the same direction. I have seen situations where couples move towards an area in which both extended systems reside and almost blow apart in months, despite a previously content relationship.

From the other side I have seen more than one family in therapy stuck for months on a marital problem or a problem with a child become suddenly motivated to "resolve things already" as a deadline nears so that they can get on with their new life.

Here the principle given earlier is borne out again, that families in flux during a rite of passage sometimes can be more easily changed at such periods. It also suggests that the changes which accompany and often precede geographical uprooting or retirement may be much more powerful forces than we realize. And once again the visible change, that is, the actual retirement or the move, may be symptomatic of emotional changes in the family that had been growing toward a climax for some time.

Our culture, of course, has done little to prepare families for the emotional shock waves of moves or retirement. Interestingly, the United States government, sensing the life cycle importance of retirement in recent years, has instituted a program of trial retirement, where the person can change his or her mind during the first year. But even that program may be little more helpful than trial marriage. For it is the homeostatic forces of emotional balance that count, and it is very hard to get a true reading on changes in that balance until commitment is made.

What then about new ceremonies that might help such transition? It might be possible to create such, but they would have to be centered in the family rather than the work system or the larger community, though of course members of those systems could be included.

For here we come face to face with what ceremonies are all about. From an individual point of view a ceremony can help mark a feeling of change or renewal and perhaps make one conscious of a benchmark period in one's life cycle. But it is so much more than that. Ceremonies, even today, get at processes the most ancient tribes were trying to deal with in their most primitive rites. After all, it is only when we think of a person as a member of the family that the term life cycle makes any sense. Otherwise we should be talking in terms of lifelines.

CONCLUSION

I have tried to show that the notion that families are primarily passive vehicles during rites of life passage, with little influence on either the outcome of the passage or the selection of the particular rites and ceremonies, does not hold up. The traditional social science focus on different cultures' customs, aided by concentration on the individual to be passed, completely ignores the possibility that the very obvious cultural differences are really rather unimportant themselves. They may be fun to compare, but are no where near as crucial as the unseen family process forces wearing those very cultural disguises. Indeed, all the cultures of mankind as they become more sophisticated may be participating in a great illusion—namely, that the medicine men for all their hocus-pocus have only succeeded in driving the spooks and spirits further from view, just making them, therefore, harder to exorcise or control. It is the demons that now wear the masks. There is a great irony here. For the function of ceremonies at rites of passage was originally to keep these very ghosts away from the passage. Now instead, the cultural disguises they have been enabled to assume allow them to go slipping through, right smack into the next generation.

An example is the parent who is having difficulty separating from a child. Instead of focusing on her difficulties in separating from her own parents, she attacks a culturally different child-in-law. For that matter, a child having difficulty separating from a parent who, instead of focusing on the emotional processes in the family which reared him, chooses a mate from a culture which doesn't operate as intensely, is participating in the same process.

But the *shiktza* (non-Jewish or generally nonethnic woman) to whose bosom the ethnic man runs always turns out to relate at least as intensely as the ethnic mother from whose bosom the man has fled. Indeed, further research will probably show that in-law problems existed in the previous generation even when everyone was of the "same faith."

On the other hand, there is a different ending where members of a family can see through the cultural camouflage and the diversion of the focused individual. When they can maintain their gaze on the family process which contributed to a rite of passage occurring at that particular time, as well as observing how these processes are at work during the rite of passage itself, that family is in a position to influence both the effectiveness of the passage and its own emotional system.

Author Index

461

Subject Index

Abortion, 129, 231, 232
Adolescents, 14, 65, 66, 147-169, 209, 210, 311, 312
  effects of parental illness on, 229
  in multiproblem poor families, 357
  mental illness and, 155, 156
  Mexican-American, 408-410
  suicide, 228
Adv H development, 3, 21
Ageism, 216

Boundaries
  grandparents and, 180, 181
  in multiproblem poor families, 349
  in remarried families, 269, 270
Bowen Systems Theory, 97, 105, 232, 233, 349, 350, 356
Burn-out, 363

Change, 9
  process of, 35-40, 81, 82, 85, 86
  theory of, 53-68
Child abuse, 307, 363
Child custody, 262
Child-focused family, 137-144
Childlessness, 95, 124, 145, 304, 305
Coaching, 84, 85
Cultural variations, 11, 12, 15, 346, 347, 383-425
Cybernetics, 54, 55, 59

Death, 15, 57, 178, 223-240, 440-446
  clinical interventions, 234-239
  depression, 239
  family position and, 233, 234
  funerals, 237-238
  fusion, 233, 234
  in Mexican-American families, 423
  of child, 227-229
  of parents, 227

  of spouse, 178, 202, 203, 227
  remarriage, 276, 277
  sudden, 229, 230
  terminal illness, 230, 231, 235-238
  timing of, 224-228
Depression, 201, 206, 239
  in women, 176, 308, 310, 314
Differentiation of self, 193, 194
Divorce, 15, 18, 72, 73, 228, 241-263, 456, 457
  clinical interventions, 245-247
  child custody, 262
  effects on children, 246, 249, 251, 257-259
  demography of, 242, 243
  family of origin and, 247-250, 255
  legal aspects, 261
  mate selection and, 245
  men and, 252, 253
  Mexican-American, 397
  premarital pregnancy and, 243
  process of, 245-249
  remarriage, 276, 277, 265-294
  women and, 243, 244, 253, 254, 257, 320-323
Double-bind, 62
Dual careers, 131, 309

Early childhood development, 129, 130
Emotional cutoffs, 182-185, 205, 211, 212, 244, 245, 248, 250, 255
Empty nest, 79, 171, 174, 176, 199
Extended family, 13, 14
  family with adolescents, 150-155, 158
  family with young children, 135, 136
  launching children, 178, 188-190
  Mexican-Americans, 385-388, 394, 395
  newlyweds, 102-108
  old age, 198, 204, 318
  unattached young adult, 80, 81

465